This book is dedicated to my Grandmother, Winifred 'Nin' Alice Roberts, my mother Joan, Tom, Charlotte and Grace

And to all the teachers who said I'd amount to nothing ...

MAN
With A
VAN

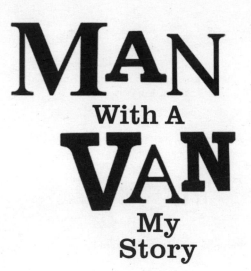

MAN
With A
VAN
My
Story

DREW
PRITCHARD

EBURY
PRESS

1

Ebury Press, an imprint of Ebury Publishing
20 Vauxhall Bridge Road
London SW1V 2SA

Ebury Press is part of the Penguin Random House group of companies
whose addresses can be found at global.penguinrandomhouse.com

Penguin
Random House
UK

First published by Ebury Press in 2021

www.penguin.co.uk

A CIP catalogue record for this book is available from the British Library

ISBN 9781529106732

Printed and bound in Great Britain by Clays Ltd, Elcograf S.p.A.

The authorised representative in the EEA is Penguin Random House
Ireland, Morrison Chambers, 32 Nassau Street, Dublin DO2 YH68

Penguin Random House is committed to a sustainable future
for our business, our readers and our planet. This book is
made from Forest Stewardship Council® certified paper.

CONTENTS

INTRODUCTION

About a year ago I was asked to write a book about who I am and how I got into the world of antiques, about some of my more memorable experiences and about my TV shows. I've been doing *Salvage Hunters* on Quest for the last ten years, and it's complemented by another series that shows how we restore the items I buy, as well as a third show about classic cars. Initially I wasn't sure, but in the end my desire to share this incredible business with as many people as possible outweighed any personal reservations.

This a business like no other. No two days are the same; it's exciting, diverse and gives an insight into not just when or how items of great beauty or value were made, but the lives of the people who made them. It's about specific artistic movements that echo periods in history when art and design mirrored what was going on in the world of politics, fashion and culture. That's the fascination, what I call the 'soul' of the trade, and I hope I can pass on some of what I've learned and something of my passion.

That passion began when I was eight years old in my hometown of Glan Conwy in North Wales, and I'm almost 50 now, but nothing has changed. I feel exactly the same as I did when my eyes were first opened to the possibilities offered by old, discarded junk that nobody wanted. I refer to those items as 'decorative salvage' (a phrase I think I coined, though I can't say for certain), and I'm on a never-ending search for inventory. This is a business that requires a revolving door when it comes to stock, not just for my Conwy showroom, but for a website with a customer base that spans the globe. The items I find on TV are bought with my own money. Nothing is done for show and if the TV cameras weren't rolling there would be no difference in the way I deal with the vendor. I'm always on the lookout for innovative stock and much of what we sell goes abroad. If I took my foot off the throttle for just a few days things would quickly go pear-shaped; it's a constant challenge to find quality antiques but without them there's no turnover and no profit.

I never buy anything I wouldn't be happy to have in my house and often that's where a piece resides until somebody wants to buy it. All my furniture is for sale, whether it's in the shop or at home; just the other day I got back from a trip looking forward to an evening on the sofa with Netflix, only to find there was no sofa.

Hunting down decorative salvage is a way of life I revere, and I encourage as many of you to get involved as possible. Since we've been doing the TV series, I've come across more and more people dabbling in buying and selling, and that's why I agreed to do the show in the first place. As far as I'm concerned, the greater the interest the better the trade will be, and I'm forever bumping into people looking for advice. To me it's simple: *if you have the passion follow it.* Don't copy anyone else (least of all me); create your own idea of what you want to achieve and get on with it. Don't be afraid of the setbacks. I spoke to a couple at a fair the other day who were just starting out, and were worried that one week they'd sold stacks of stuff and the next absolutely nothing. Welcome to the antiques business. It takes years to learn and, as you'll see, you have to roll with the punches.

CHAPTER 1

HUMBLE BEGINNINGS

By the time 55 alloy storage bins had been loaded into the van we were completely knackered. We weren't finished yet, though; before we left the Bradford linen mill, we'd added a couple of massive wicker baskets and an industrial trolley. We were satisfied; it had been a really good call (which is how the antiques trade refers to it when we're asked to show up and look at potential inventory) in one of those places you rarely see. There aren't many linen mills left but this one was thriving with over half a million metres of fabric sold every year, and I'd picked up some quality industrial furniture.

Back in the van I checked my phone, while T pulled out alongside a lorry that was hazing us with spray that might as well have come from a hosepipe. My long-term sidekick, I've known T since I was a boy in North Wales and he's an integral part of the TV show. It had been pissing with rain all week but that was nothing new. After so many years on the road we were used to torrential downpours and the motorway flooding.

'It's been a decent day, T,' I said.

'Van's full.' He was concentrating on the traffic. 'You'll make money on those bins, and I really like that trolley.'

It had been the best call we'd had in weeks and I was encouraged about another factory visit tomorrow. There wasn't much to do by way of restoration on the stuff we'd bought, just a bit of a clean-up really.

An hour later we left the motorway and found the hotel in Higher Bartle, near Preston. A beautiful old place and a far cry from my first few years on the road when a night away meant the back of the van and a burger from a kiosk in the lay-by. I checked in, dumped my bags and took a long, hot shower. After that I went down to have dinner with the rest of the crew. Tomorrow was Dan's last shoot as director on the show; he was still producing. The sound man Simon Jolly has been with me from the very first day of shooting, and for a long time it's been Sean or Steve wielding the camera.

After grabbing a pint, I sat down to update the website, already thinking about tomorrow. That's the buzz, the excitement, the sense of anticipation I have before we arrive at any call. It's the same today as it has been for as long as I can remember, an obsession that's shaped my entire life and something I love with a passion.

All this was on my mind because I had this book to write and didn't know where to begin. It was something I discussed with T when he came in from a precarious walk along the road with no pavement and no street lights. He's a year older than me; we're about the same build and cut from the same North Wales granite.

'We might need another van for tomorrow,' he stated. 'If so, I can sort it. So, tell me about this book then.'

I looked at him over my glasses. 'There's not much to tell yet. I really don't know how to get started.'

'Easy. Piccadilly Woods.'

'What?'

'Those old cars hanging in trees, remember? It must be forty years since we've been there.'

I remember how quiet the world was when T and I used to play football on the A470. Growing up in North Wales in the 1970s and 80s, there were no mobile phones or social media, and home computers were in their infancy. We made our own fun and, for me, that meant turning up what I thought were rusty treasures. From the age of eight, back in 1978, I was obsessed and had a way of finding beauty in things that others saw as worthless junk only fit for the skip. I was always turning up with old bits and pieces of bicycle or some piece of rusting military hardware. It started when we moved from Llandudno Junction to Glan Conwy and I had so much junk piling up my grandmother, 'Nin', referred to me as a 'shite-hawk'. A magnet for crap, I rarely came home without something someone else had thrown away.

CHAPTER 1

We started scouring the local tip to see what kind of stuff we could salvage. You don't see those tips any more, but back in the 1970s most towns and villages had a local dump where people would toss their old washing machines, bikes or whatever. There were a few of us lads who used to hang out, mostly it was me and T, Daz-Babs, a big lad who acted tough but was actually a bit of a baby, and another lad called Tyd. We roamed Glan Conwy like a pack of wolves, hunting junk all hours of the day. Daz-Babs and I were obsessed, and much of what we recovered came from the Second World War. North Wales is a military area, with RAF Valley on Anglesey and MOD buildings dotted all over. Most had become a dumping ground and we came up with all kinds of stuff: gas masks, ammunition cases, knives and bayonets. Daz-Babs amassed a huge collection of old bayonets and a lot of the older lads had guns from the period they would use to shoot ducks on the river. Glan Conwy is on an estuary and another source of junk was the sea. With constant tides there was always a good deal of debris washing up – oars, old water skis, bits of boat – and we'd comb the beach for anything interesting we could recover.

Going to the woods, though, that had been a dare not a salvage hunt. They were scary and particularly to an eight-year-old boy like me. It was already getting dark and we were supposed to be going home, but one of the lads suggested we check them out so off we went, Daz-Babs, Tyd, T and me. A developer had been building a new housing estate that wasn't finished yet, and we picked our way between piles of bricks and scaffolding. Beyond it the woodland was really thick and we had to forge a path until we came to a point where the hills grew up on either side of this massive V-shaped valley. Both sides were covered in trees that were so dense I could barely see. As I stared into the gloom, however, I began to make out something my eight-year-old brain could not get to grips with. Cars, loads of them, ancient rusty relics, seemed to be hanging in midair like ghosts of what they'd been.

It was the most amazing sight I'd ever seen. I didn't understand it at first but, as we got closer, I was able to figure it out. The cars weren't ghosts and they weren't hanging in the air, they were jammed between the edge of the V-shaped ravine and the trees. I got it: people had pushed their unwanted cars to the edge of the hill above and let them roll down into the V. Many had smashed into the trunks of trees and, as the years went by and the trees grew taller, so the cars grew with them until they were hoisted into the air. I was amazed. This was magical. There were cars from the 1930s and 40s, some going back as far as the Model T. A graveyard for old vehicles, they rested as if on burial scaffolds, smothered by the leaves of trees. What I saw wasn't a bunch of knackered old wrecks, though, it was beauty, history, money; as well as a sense of time and place that I'd never otherwise have seen.

It was exciting, exhilarating, the most incredible experience of my life so far. Not only that, I think that deep down I knew there was money to be made from the bits and pieces we might find there. We started rummaging around, but it was spooky, pretty dark and hard to see. The next day we were back, climbing into the trees to see what we could salvage. Most of the cars had been there for decades and were rusted to hell. It was lethal so we really had to take care (but didn't) and I set about prising badges from bonnets, ripping off old hub caps, gear knobs, anything I thought deserved to be saved and things I might be able to get a couple of quid for.

From then on, the passion really took hold. I would spend every waking moment thinking about what kind of stuff might be out there and I also started to read. My dad was an artist, a sign-writer by trade, and both he and Mum had an interest in antiques. They had a few Lyle books on antiques dotted around the house so I picked them up and began to read. Armed with a little bit of knowledge, I started finding old tins and boxes and they weren't just beautiful, they were useful. I could keep things in boxes but they had to be ones that really caught my eye. There was a scrapyard in Llandudno Junction that I used to hang around outside. As soon as it closed and everyone had gone, I'd jump over the fence and get lost in a wonderful world of my own. I wasn't there to nick anything, just to have a really good look around.

I have no idea why I became so obsessed, but I'm no different today. Doing what I do, travelling around the world locating things that otherwise might never be recovered, allows me a glimpse into the lives of the people that made them. The past comes to life in both time and place, and I get a sense of why someone decided to make something, paint something, build something that would outlive not only them, but me.

I was inspired by things that people just didn't appear to see. It was the same with the other lads. If one of us got word of an old bike in some shed in the middle of nowhere, or some derelict car somewhere, we would cycle for miles just to go and take a look at it. It was the only thing that interested me, aged stuff, things that had been made long ago. I always used to think about who had made them and why. I was fascinated by the history, the stories behind the stuff itself. It occupied my mind from the moment I woke to the moment I went to sleep. Nothing else seemed to matter. Certainly not school. I only studied if I was interested in the subject and that didn't include many of my lessons. I was there in body (most of the time) but never in spirit. I was learning nothing at all.

School did have its advantages though; from the age of ten or eleven, I started dealing in dinner tickets bought by our parents for 65p apiece. I'd buy them off other kids for 35p and sell them for 50p. Sometimes I'd swap them for cigarettes, which I'd sell on to buy air pistols and hunting knives, catapults, even pushbikes. Dr Marten boots were a favourite; pretty quickly I had quite the inventory and I realised I had a natural aptitude for buying and selling.

By this time, I had a shed in the garden my dad said I could use to keep all the stuff I was collecting. As a child I didn't go without, but a lot of the time the stuff I got was reworked and second-hand; a bike, for example, would never be new, as my parents were far from rolling in money. There was never quite enough to spread to the luxuries and that hung over the household like a cloud. It bothered me. I didn't want to be like that. I wanted to have more than 'enough' money and was determined to find a way to achieve that. I didn't know it then, but it would turn out to be from finding old bits and pieces of what looked like junk, but to me was opportunity. From a really early age, I would hunt down old bits and pieces of bicycle, fix them up and sell them from the side of the road.

Back then Dad was working from the house, sign-writing a lot of vans, and some of those vans belonged to antique dealers. Whenever they showed up, I noticed it was in top-of-the-line Range Rovers or Mercedes. I was already into cars, and by the time I was 15 I had 13 motors I was breaking up for spares. They took up all the garden and most of the wood next door. Our house was on the A470 with a large sloping wood out the back that drifted down the hill towards the estuary. People started to complain and, finally, someone from the council came to the house.

'Mrs Pritchard,' they said, when Mum opened the door, 'your son's running a scrapyard from your garden and that's not allowed.'

'Don't be so stupid.' She was vehement. 'Of course he's not, he's only a child.' She sent him off with a flea in his ear and slammed the door.

A little later I came in from school and she collared me in the kitchen. 'Drew, you're running a scrapyard and the council have been round. You have to get rid of the cars.'

There was nothing to be done so I enlisted the help of my mates and we literally pushed 13 cars onto trailers or down to the local scrapyard. All save one, that was reserved for the council. They'd put an end to a lucrative business, so one night we pushed it all the way to their offices and left it outside the main door.

With this fledgling business totally screwed, I was really pissed off and became even more disruptive at school, Ysgol Dyffryn Conwy in Llanrwst, which was a few miles from where we lived in Glan Conwy. It was a co-ed where the pupils were streamed into sets T, S, M, F and K depending on ability and application. They were just letters with no real significance, but we named them Top, Second, Middle, Fick and Kretins. I was in F for Fick. I wasn't thick, I just didn't try. I completely understood what the teachers were telling me, but I knew I'd never use any of it so what was the point of learning about oxbow lakes or the life cycle of an amoeba? I was bored shitless and I made that known to anyone and everyone. In the end I was so bad, so disruptive to the other kids and teachers, one of them sat me down.

'Pritchard,' he said, 'you've got to listen to what I tell you. That's the point of a lesson, you know.'

I looked at him with a derisive eye. 'Why should I listen to you, sir? You've got a shit job. I know exactly what I'm going to do when I leave and it's got nothing to do with anything you can teach me.'

That was my attitude; I had no interest at all and during the five years I was there I think I did my homework once. Of course, that wasn't acceptable, but they couldn't give me detention because we lived ten miles away and detention meant missing the bus. They had to do something though; and in those days there was still the cane so I took that and carried on just as before. I had absolutely no interest in academia; school just got in the way of what I wanted to do, which was to get out on my own. By the time the council took those cars off me, I'd already left school (mentally at least), but they made me stay another year. I knew what I wanted to do, I wanted to be an antique dealer, but I had no clue how to go about it. Those guys that showed up at home in their posh Range Rovers were always really interesting people. Loads of laughter and jokes; they seemed to really enjoy what they were doing and that's where I wanted to be.

Those memories seemed to resonate again as T and I went to join the rest of the crew at the table Dan had reserved so we could watch the latest episode of the show on TV. It was a good show, well put together, and I was happy with it, though I hate to see myself on screen; it's something I only do once for each show, when the episode first airs, so I can be around to answer any questions that might come up on social media. Ours is an interactive process: we have 19 million viewers covering 32 countries around the world, so it's important I'm on hand to reply to any comments or questions.

I slept pretty well and the following morning T and I set out for the day's filming in Chorley, an old Lancashire mill town between Wigan, Blackburn and Preston. Back in the day it would have been tall, brick chimneys raking the skyline as far as the eye could see. For generations the local factory was the centre of the community, with terraces of houses built all around it. Most are long gone now, with only a few dotted around, and one was the Droyt Soap Company, the factory we were going to visit.

It was established in Minsk, Belarus, in 1893, so I was keen to learn how the factory came to be in Chorley. It's not just the buying and selling that fascinates me, though I love that, of course; there's nothing better than spotting an item, making an offer and selling it at a profit. That's what we do but it's not the whole story. More than the money it's the soul of an item that gets me. Recently, I bought a lady's rocking chair from the 1840s. Many of these were normal four-legged chairs that were later modified with rockers, but this had been made specifically. I paid a lot of money for it, but with a little restorative care I'll sell it for a lot more. But that wasn't my motivation when I first saw it. I wondered who had made it, who sat in it, how many times it had been bought and sold. I thought about all the stories that chair could tell if only it could talk; almost two hundred years of history, including two world wars that it seemed to have survived unscathed. That's the real excitement of this business, and there was always the chance I'd come across that kind of gem today.

It was a little tight manoeuvring the van through the narrow streets, but we found the factory surrounded by houses. A true product of the Industrial Revolution with grilles over the windows, ancient brickwork that was so black and weather-beaten it looked like the place had been empty for years. But it wasn't; it was a thriving business selling to major retailers in the UK as well as far-flung places like Japan. After parking the van in the yard out back, we went around to the front and knocked on the panel door. A couple of minutes later it was opened by a tall, slim man who'd arranged the call.

'Alistair?' I said.

He nodded.

'I'm Drew. This is T. Nice to meet you.'

'Nice to meet you too,' he said. 'I'm the sales director. Welcome to the Droyt Soap Company.'

He led us into a pretty spectacular room with flagstone floor and cast-iron columns holding up a pitched ceiling made from old timber that reminded me of my first warehouse in Builder Street, Llandudno, which I bought in about 2005. This was a remnant of days long past, part of that Industrial Age you no longer see. As he pointed out the features, Alistair explained that the building started life in Victorian times as a cotton yarn mill while Droyt was being founded in Minsk. Before the company moved to Chorley, the original factory was relocated to the banks of the Volga River in Saratov. After the Russian Revolution it moved again, this time to Berlin. It seemed that war and social unrest was a big part of their history because they switched to Chorley a couple of years before the outbreak of the Second World War.

This was the only factory left round here, but there had been another across the road. That firm manufactured plastic tape, and between the two was an old lodge with foundations so rotten the place perpetually filled up with water. It got so bad that, finally, something was done and a firm of experts was brought in to drain the water away before the lodge could be demolished. When it was gone, they discovered a colony of two thousand frogs that had to be taken to a nearby nature reserve. Thinking of all those frogs lurking in the darkness, I was keen to take a look at what might be hiding here. That would have to wait a moment, though, because the first thing that struck me wasn't the original flags or pillars, it was the sound of a machine: *Bang, Bang – Bang. Bang, Bang – Bang. Bang, Bang – Bang.*

It bounced off the walls like an echo, mimicking the beat of the Queen anthem 'We Will Rock You'. In a far corner, three women in blue overalls and white mesh caps were gathered at a stamping machine. They explained that the soap had been dried and, cut and now they were stamping it into moulds. *Bang, Bang – Bang.*

Everywhere I looked there was soap, massive blocks of it, orange, blue and green; they had to be a metre and a half in length and at least half a metre thick. Alistair pointed out where the old weaving shed had been when this was a cotton mill. He explained that, when the factory was adapted from yarn to soap, the vats were fired by an old coal boiler that had to be lit by a specialist every day. The coal explained why the bricks outside were so black; this place had been coughing out columns of smoke for decades. Looking up at the ancient timber rafters I was reminded again of my first warehouse in Llandudno. I wish I hadn't sold it, but it was the usual story of an offer you can't refuse.

The place smelled of soap (of course it did, what else would it smell of? It was a soap factory) but it wasn't overpowering and not unpleasant. Alistair explained that the smell is supposed to fade when you wash, because soap is designed to do no more than leave you clean so you can splash on some cologne.

'They are scented, of course,' he said. 'The blocks. The orange one is mandarin, the green lime and basil.'

One of the crew piped up: 'What scent would a Drew Pritchard soap be?'

'Curry powder,' T said. 'Or lager.'

'Expensive lager,' I corrected.

Something had caught my eye, the first thing I'd seen here that I thought I might be able to buy. Just beyond the massive blocks of soap was an industrial cutting table. About the size of a small dining table, it was seriously over-engineered with legs made from folded steel. The surface was zinc plate mounted on timber planks, well used and worn with a nicely aged patina. It wouldn't need much doing to it other than a proper clean. I checked the legs and the welding really was 'belt and braces'. Alistair told me the table had been made by some ex-employees, and that's always a nice back story. I can sell tables like that all day long; this was something I wanted to buy.

'It really is over-engineered,' I said. 'But I love the look. I love the zinc top.' I tried to lift it. 'How much does it weigh?'

'A hundred and twenty kilos.'

About what I expected given the heavy-steel construction. 'Is it something you'd sell?'

'Yes,' Alistair said. 'I think so.'

'What d'you want for it?' I took another look at the zinc, working my thumb over the greasy surface. 'What's a new one going to cost you?'

CHAPTER 1

Alistair considered the table. 'I don't know,' he said. 'The last time we replaced one, it was a hundred and eighty pounds.'

The table had something going on and I was keen to have it. 'Alright,' I said. 'How much d'you want for it?' I was thinking about what I was prepared to pay and hoping we could come to an agreement. 'When I first started selling things like this thirty years ago, there was quite a lot of industrial stuff around but not so much now.' I stood back with a hand in my pocket. 'That makes a difference to the price. But I like it. What do you think?'

Alistair was quiet for a moment. 'All the others we have are stainless steel. This is zinc.'

'So, what're you telling me? If I buy it and start cleaning – it's going to bubble up?' We laughed, but it happens all the time. Alistair assured me it was cleaned every day with a special paraffin-based solution.

'I'll give you two-fifty,' I told him. 'Can't do any more. That's it.'

We shook on it. Deal done, the first of a few, I was hoping. A little back and forth on the price as usual, but I'd made him a decent offer and he took it. When I buy something, more often than not I'm taking a chance because I'm working off a gut feeling and not much more. Any research that might add value is done after. Even now, these deals are done on a handshake: old-school trust between two people who come to an

20

amicable arrangement; even extremely large deals are done that way.

I wasn't sure there would be big-ticket stuff here, and so far I'd only bought one item and was keen to find some more. I had a vanload of largish items from Bradford, so when Alistair brought out some old brass soap stamps, I was delighted. What we call smalls – less-expensive items that are vital to the business, keep the cashflow going and don't take up a lot of room. These stamps weren't that old but they had something about them. The engineering in particular, the way the stamp slotted so perfectly into the mould, really got me.

'I'd love to buy some of these,' I said. 'I'd like to buy them all, in fact. Are any for sale?'

They were made of bronze, which in itself isn't that expensive, but the casting, the artwork, clearly was. There was one for 'Lagerfeld', another for 'Heal's' and 'Liberty'; there was even one for 'Burger King'. Great ornamental pieces, I knew they'd walk out the door.

'Are any for sale?' I repeated.

Alistair wasn't sure. The stamps were part of the history of his company and I liked the fact he felt that was important. There was as much of a story in some of the stuff in this factory as there was in the rocking chair I mentioned before.

'You can't flog these ones, can you?' I indicated those with the moulds that seemed to slot together so perfectly.

'No, I can't. They're an important part of the company.'

21

'What about the others?' I pointed to the individual stamps without moulds. 'Which of these can you let go?' I had a couple between my fingers now, holding them like knuckle dusters. 'Obviously, you don't have to, but I'd like to buy them if you want to.'

He was prepared to sell some of those and after a little deliberation we settled on three, so I asked Alistair what he wanted.

'I suppose it depends on what it would cost to have a new one made.' He pointed out the 'Lagerfeld'. 'That one would be at least two hundred pounds.'

I shook my head. 'That's not going to happen; I can't give you two hundred pounds for all three. Best I can do is a hundred.'

'For all three?'

I nodded.

Alistair thought about that. 'Alright,' he said, and we shook on it.

This was good – a table and some smalls, and I hadn't paid too much. This kind of stuff is easy to sell and there was room for a decent profit. Alistair was needed by one of his staff, so I took the opportunity to check back with the showroom in Conwy, where someone was making an offer on a piece on the website I'd priced at just under £4,000. I had to look twice as the offer was so far off, I thought they must've typed in the wrong number. I asked one of the girls back in Conwy to check on that and make sure I got back to it later.

Having dealt with the request from his staff, Alistair took us up a very steep flight of stairs to another large production room, then into what he described as 'The Lab', a section full of chemicals and bottles of soap solution beyond a partition made from hand-made wooden boxes. A line about six metres long by two high, they had been nailed together like pigeon holes. The boxes originated in Argentina, where they had been lined with greaseproof paper and filled with liquid beef tallow which would cool and set before the lid was nailed on. Beef tallow had been an integral part of the soap-making process before BSE – mad cow disease – hit in the 1980s. In those days the three main components were the tallow, castor oil and coconut oil. Post-BSE, the beef tallow has been replaced with palm oil.

'Are they for sale?' I asked him. 'The boxes? I'd like to buy the lot.'

'No, they're part of the business, not to mention the wall.'

I hadn't been very hopeful, and shipping them without taking the boxes apart would have posed a few problems, but that was nothing we couldn't get over. No matter, already I'd spotted a couple of wooden boards with cast-iron hasps on the underside that had been used to stack blocks of soap. They would be great for someone's kitchen, food preparation or display. Alistair said he'd take 50 quid for the pair.

'No, that's undervaluing them,' I told him. 'I'll give you sixty.'

He seemed pleased with that and I took another look at the boxes. Ox-blood in colour, they would've made a great display somewhere and I knew there would be a market for them. But I had to be content with the soap stands and another bronze. From a metal cupboard Alistair brought out a whole stack of individual crafted moulds of various shapes and sizes. There were ducks, birds, cartoon characters – I'd have snapped them all up. That wasn't going to happen, though; these were pretty old, some dating back to the 1920s in Berlin and others that had been made when the factory moved to Chorley. I asked if they would let any go and Alistair offered me one mould of a sailor. His name was Jack and I could sell stuff like this easily enough, but I knew the retail price was only a couple of hundred quid. This was another bespoke piece and to replace it with something else that was hand-crafted would cost a couple of thousand. The only reason Alistair was prepared to sell at all was because the mould bore the 'Droyt' name and that was good marketing. I wanted it, but unless I spent money on the way it was displayed, I knew I couldn't get more than 200 quid. I had to think. I couldn't make him a ridiculous offer, but I had to take a chance. 'What about a hundred and forty?'

He was happy to take that, so Jack the Sailor was added to the inventory.

There were only a few items and we managed to squeeze them into the van, which saved the cost and bother of bringing down another. Job done we set off for Conwy in the driving rain. Today was Thursday, I'd been on the road all week, tomorrow I'd be in the shop then it was off again on Saturday.

'Remind me where we're going next week,' I said before we pulled out of the narrow gates.

T stopped the van and checked the call sheet before we continued. 'Sunday it's the flea market at Shepton Mallet. Then Dorset and Wiltshire.' We set off and he glanced across the cab as we came to the junction. 'On Saturday you said you were going to Bath, so I'll have to meet you after.'

The call to Bath Dec Fair wasn't for the TV show, it was purely business. There were dealers I needed to see. Right now, though, I'd have a breather, so I let T find our way back to the motorway. Before long, we were on the M6, with rain lashing the windscreen. 'Another pretty good day,' I said. 'I'm happy, T: we bought some good stuff today.'

'What're you going to do with the mould?'

'Jack the Sailor? Mount him, of course, what else would I do?'

Back home Gavin, my full-time restorer who's been with me for years, unloaded the van, and then I went to take Enzo for a walk. My beloved Jack Russell, he was getting pretty long in the tooth, but there's no better way of dusting off the cobwebs than taking your dog along the beach, regardless of the pouring rain. Unfortunately, he's gone now, having passed away while I was working on this book, and I miss him terribly. While he was sniffing around checking his wee-mails, I was thinking about tomorrow and Bath. I'd go by myself, take the 'posh van' (Range Rover) because that was big enough to load some stuff in the back, then I'd meet up with the TV crew in time for the shoot on Sunday. It struck me then that, despite all the setbacks, I'd achieved what I set out to do. The posh van was what the dealers who showed up at our house turned up in when I was a boy and now I had one as well.

It's things like that, and the other cars I've owned, that remind me how far I've come since that moment with the lads in Piccadilly Woods. It's not just the money, though, it's the business I'd set my heart on being a part of.

Only just done with school, I was a long way from being any kind of dealer and just as far from driving a Range Rover. I had the grand total of 12p in my pocket and no idea what I was going to do. I had a little bit of knowledge from reading catalogues and books, but the reality was the antiques business was like the Mafia. There was just no way in for a lad from Glan Conwy like me. Those guys didn't want anyone around with even half a brain cell; they wanted lads who could hump stuff, load it onto vans. There was no way I could get a job in the antiques trade and I was a bit scared to even ask. I had to do something, though, so, for some reason I'll never be able to explain, I decided to join the RAF. Luckily, I didn't get in. Given my record of attendance at school, it surprised no one (least of all me) when I missed an interview and that was the end of it, thank God.

Things changed when Dad finished a sign-writing job for Gordon Stewart, a local stained-glass restorer who operated out of an old farm above Abergele with another guy called Joe Sturges. By then my dad and I were no longer getting on, and our relationship was only going to get worse. For reasons I don't think I'll ever understand, things were pretty strained, and he didn't think I'd ever amount to anything. He wasn't going to let me sit around, though – not that I would – and when Gordon turned up at the house to pick up his van, they got talking about his business.

'You haven't got a job for my son, have you?' Dad said. 'He's fucking useless, doing nothing right now.'

'I might.' Gordon looked me up and down like I was some bull at a farm auction. Back then I was quite muscly. I used to play a lot of rugby, and rode a BMX bike everywhere. I was fit and strong.

'You look like you can lift a box of lead. Can you?'

'Yeah,' I said. 'Of course.'

'Alright, then. Monday morning.'

I was up for it, a job in the stained-glass window restoring business, it might just be a way into a world I never thought I'd have a chance to crack. I arrived early courtesy of a lift from Mum as I was only 16 and not yet driving. Gordon put me to work in what was called the 'Cementing Shed': a filthy little room, he pointed out a leaded window, the lead light cement etc., then told me to get the brush and use it to put the cement into the gap. When it was dry, I was to rub the top layer off so just the lead was left. It didn't seem too hard so I set about it and I was meticulous. I wasn't unhappy. I wasn't in school. I was on the YTS (Youth Training Scheme) getting £17.40 a week, which was a fortune to me, so I got stuck in.

A couple of days later a van showed up in the yard that had been sign-written 'Michael Maine Architectural Antiques' by my dad. This miserable-looking guy got out and called to me across the yard.

'Oi, boy! Come here and give us a hand.' He indicated the back doors.

I went to help unload and, when the doors were opened, I found myself staring at a load of different items that really caught my eye. I saw a wooden front door with butterflies painted into the stained glass. I saw old fireplaces, picture frames, bits of stone sill. Like someone had snapped their fingers or a light going on in my head, it was a Eureka moment, the first of a few I would have in my life. That's it, I thought. This is exactly where I want to be. I remember walking back into the cementing shed and closing the door. I remember looking at the piece I was working on, aware of all the knowledge I'd already amassed and thinking, Right, let's have this. This is what I'm going to do.

The very next day Gordon took me to a church that was being knocked down in Holyhead on Anglesey. The demolition contractor wanted all the stained-glass windows taken out as he planned to keep them. I learned how to take those windows out on the job, which was another great thing to do. When we were finished, we piled them into the guy's van and I thought no more about it as we drove back to Abergele.

CHAPTER 2

VOYAGE TO VINLAND

The day after I got home from Chorley, I was off early for the stop in Bath on my way to the flea market at Shepton Mallet. It was quite nice to be driving myself. I don't get to do it often, for years it's been me and T. The car is something of an office, though, and as I drove south, I had the phone plugged in, making call after call to keep the business rolling. When I got to the Bath Decorative Antiques Fair, I hooked up with the dealers I wanted to see and filled up the car with stock. After that it was a short hop to the Premier Inn at Frome where I met T and the rest of the TV crew.

By Sunday morning the rain that had plagued us all last week had finally packed in. It had been replaced by single-figure temperatures and a freezing wind that was buffeting across the country. The crew went ahead while T and I checked the van. When we were ready it was 12 miles through twisting country roads to the flea market at the Royal Bath Showground just outside Shepton Mallet. Even though it was bloody freezing, I was looking forward to the day. Flea markets can be hit and miss but this was usually a good one. For the last 20 years it's been run by Kate Ede, who was also behind the Decorative Fair in Bath where I'd been yesterday. Most of the stands are set up inside this massive, modern arena, something like 240 of them with another 200 outside. I make a point of visiting them all so we were going to be here all day.

No messing around, I walked the stalls with T, starting inside the arena and moving swiftly, the film crew following behind us. After so many years in the business my senses are pretty well tuned and I only stop if something really grabs my attention. It wasn't long before I spotted a hint of brass that appealed to me straightaway. A dealer from Odiham in Hampshire had a pair of three-tier Italian etag-eres, free-standing shelves for displaying books or orna-ments; these two looked to be from the late 1950s. Made of brass, the shelves themselves were what T and I decided to term 'Lino-flux'. They had a linoleum feel to them, but despite that I knew I could make good money. The dealer wanted £700 for the pair. I checked them over, no work to be done, the kind of thing I'd get a grand for, maybe 1,100.

'I'll give you six for the two.'

It was a good start, the first purchase of the day, I always like to get that out of the way. Outside we were in a biting wind that was so fierce half the items on the stalls seemed to be blowing away. I had to duck to avoid an old watering can that went flying as a gust sent it clattering across our path. We moved from stall to stall, though I stopped to speak to people on the way. Many of the people who attend these fairs also watch the show. It's funny, I was never some-one who wanted to be recognised (and still don't). It can go either way. Sometimes I walk into a room somewhere and every person knows who I am. At the same time, I can buy a cup of coffee in a crowded petrol station and nobody has a clue.

That stretch of stalls outside the main warehouse was heaving. There was some pretty good stuff around, some of it from dealers I knew. After stopping to chat to a few people who wanted selfies, I prised myself loose from one woman who left a big smacker on my cheek. T had spotted an articulated industrial lamp sitting on top of an ancient bar-football table, so I went over to take a look. I buy a lot of these lamps, they always sell well, but this wasn't in the best of condition and the price was more than I wanted to pay.

Switching from stall to stall, we paused at one where the dealer was selling everything from riding boots on shoe trees to ancient dustbins and books. Nothing there really caught my eye so we carried on. Up ahead I could see some metal chairs that looked interesting. They were being sold by a young guy from the back of a van but the wind was blowing so hard the path between the stalls was a mael-strom of flying bits and pieces. I liked the look of those chairs, though, so I took a closer look and asked the guy where he was from.

'Frome,' he said. 'Just up the road. My name's Chris.'

'I'm Drew,' I said. 'This is T. Are you a dealer?'

'No, I'm not a dealer. I sell coffee for a living. The chairs are from my shop.'

They were Tolix, designed by Xavier Pauchard, from Saint Leger in France, who died in 1948. Brand new these were 250 apiece and Chris wanted 120 for the pair.

'I'll take them,' I said.

Another quick and easy buy. No point messing around, I could double my money with nothing needed but a rudimentary clean.

This was going better than I'd thought. There was some nice stuff here; I picked up a confit pot for 15 quid and an old educational canvas poster for 60.

'Not a bad day so far,' T said as we headed for a dealer with a large steel potting table as well as a garden bench.

'Yeah, we've got some nice pieces, particularly those etageres.' I considered the potting table but there was a tag of 800 quid on it and the dealer was Elizabeth Lee. I knew she'd want that all day long and it was too rich for me.

'The bench, T: what do you think?'

'Nicely weathered,' he said.

'It's a Lutyens. He was an architect, but he designed a specific bench for a garden somewhere and this is a copy.'

'She's asking two-fifty,' T said.

I nodded. 'I've bought off her before and she's bought off me. No point pissing about, I can get four-fifty at least.' I took another good look at the bench. 'Ironic I should find this now. A year ago, Diane Keaton asked me for two Lutyens but I couldn't find one anywhere.'

'Diane Keaton the actress?'

'Yeah, she bought a lamp off me for her kitchen years ago. Now there's a woman with taste. You should see her houses; she's got the kind of eye most dealers would kill for.'

I shook hands on the deal with Elizabeth and told her we'd be back for the Lutyens later. As I said before, a hand-shake is the way this business is done and that was for 250 quid, but the antiques trade knows no boundaries and you can shake on tens of thousands.

An early experience of that was at my very first Newark Antiques Fair in 1993, which was mammoth compared to Shepton Mallet. By then I'd lost my job with Gordon Stewart, having spent seven years learning the restoration business. It was Christmas Eve in 1993 when he showed up unannounced at our house. I remember seeing him pull up outside and rubbing my hands, thinking, Christmas bonus, lovely. But that's not why he was there. He sat down looking drawn and pale, then told me that Michael Maine, his biggest customer, had gone bust on him and the knock-on effect meant Gordon had lost his house. He had lost everything, in fact. He couldn't pay me. I was 23 years old and no longer had a job.

After he'd gone, I remember sitting there wondering what I was going to do. All I had was 200 quid and an old VW Beetle with a roof rack. It was a bit of a shock. I didn't blame Gordon, I owe him a lot; under his tutelage I'd gone from the cement shed to being a highly skilled restorer, involved in major projects and design within the company. But, perhaps just as importantly, I'd encouraged him to start selling bits of stained glass, which he really couldn't be arsed to do. Now that came into play. Before he left, Gordon told me he couldn't pay me what was owed, but there was one last thing he could do. Back at the farm there was an old bull-pit where we used to store all the crap. Old doors, window frames, etc. that we'd dump after we'd salvaged the glass. Gordon said I could have whatever I wanted. It wasn't very inspiring. I knew what was there, a knackered old cupboard door with little art-nouveau windows, some door handles, bits of fireplaces, panelling; a whole load of shit, but it was my only option and I was sure there was something I could do with it.

Long ago I'd learned that what's shit to someone else is a thing of beauty to me, and I knew exactly what I was going to do. The very next day I set up 'Classical Glass', which was a rubbish name, but all I could think of at the time. My first proper business venture: seven years after unloading Michael Maine's van I had absolutely no clue how to do anything, but I'd have a go. What I did have was some knowledge and experience of antique dealers, having been working with them for the last few years. I suppose I was 'in the mix'. I knew one lad in particular from Manchester called Carl for whom I'd been doing a bit of restoration work. He had a door-stripping business and a barn where he sold stuff, which seemed like a really big deal to me. He was my first port of call, a phone call on a land line (no mobiles in those days), asking if he wanted any old stained glass. He said he'd take a look, so I piled all I could salvage from the bull-pit into my Beetle and drove to Manchester. And 450 quid later, I left his place with an empty Beetle, thinking, That's it, I'm off. I'm in.

Over a brew we'd had a long chat and Carl told me he was looking for 'top-light' windows, as many as I could find, and he'd give me a fiver apiece. They had just put the A55 road through North Wales, linking Colwyn Bay, Rhyl and Abergele, so I had a corridor to play with. A few days later I put a small advert in the *North Wales Weekly News*:

Wanted — Stained Glass & Architectural
Antiques. Cash Paid. Any Amount. Anywhere

I gave my parents' home number as the contact and the phone just rang off the hook. Back then, I was the only guy in North Wales buying glass and various other bits of salvage so every time a demolition came up the contractor would be on the phone. I had the whole of Anglesey and the Conwy Valley. Most of my mates from school were either builders or plumbers, and every Friday we'd meet up for a pint. Invariably, they'd tell me about a marble bath or sink they were stripping out of some old property somewhere.

Pretty quickly I found myself looking at a massive hoard of windows that had come off another old church. I had to buy this stuff and pay cash. The problem was, I'd bought a crappy Astra van and all I had to my name now was 300 quid. Somehow, I had to persuade these people to give me all that glass. Fortunately, I had some negotiation skills from my days bartering for dinner tickets and knocking on doors for old cars when I was a kid. That experience would come in handy now. I bought the broken pieces of glass for a pound each and the good ones for three quid.

For 18 months I worked with Carl, supplying not just the glass but old fireplaces and other bits and pieces I came across. I had a small restoration business. I was selling to other people here and there and all of it in cash. One day after I'd dropped off a load of top-lights, Carl asked if I knew about the Newark Antiques Fair.

'Sure,' I said. 'I've heard of it, but I've never been.'

'Go,' he said. 'Take everything you've got and charge triple what you charge me.'

He didn't need to tell me that. He just reiterated what I already knew, but in articulating it like that he did me a massive favour and I'll always thank him for that.

The fact was I had a lot of stuff; it was everywhere. I was renting garages, I had junk with friends all over the place. I'd moved out of my parents' house into a two-up, two-down in the middle of Conwy, and it was like a mini-warehouse. I had stuff in every room. I still had loads at my parents' place as well as my grandmother's and some of it was pretty good. There was some really nice eighteenth-century oak panelling I'd found on a farm above Abergele. I had a stack of arched church windows, tons of lead lights; far too much for the Astra, so I hired a 7.5 tonne truck.

Loaded to the gunwales, I drove across country to Newark, having never handled that kind of vehicle before. The fair was an eye-opener, amazing, with over five thousand stalls. It lasted three days and I couldn't afford anywhere to stay so I made some room in the back of the van, unrolled a sleeping bag and ate baked beans out of the can. I spent the night back there and by dawn I was raring to go. This was exciting, the anticipation incredible. I had no idea what to expect but I knew what I was going to do. Triple the prices, Carl had said, but there seemed to be so much money around I thought I could do better than that. Dragging all the stuff out of the van, I got set up and, by the 5:30am start, I was ready to go.

It was brutal, full-on; back then the antiques trade was still making massive money. That first morning it was trade only, and within a few minutes of my laying everything out an American dealer stopped and pointed to a window.

'How much?'

I looked it over, thinking I'd normally get 100 quid.

'Fifteen hundred,' I said.

'I'll take it. Have you got any more?'

'Four.'

'OK, I'll take them all.'

A little while later, Bob Mills (who used to run Robert Mills Antiques) rolled up and offered me eight grand for a bunch of other windows. He wrote a cheque, which I didn't want to take, having never had one before. But I spoke to another dealer and he told me a cheque from Bob was OK.

It just went on from there. In less than an hour I made more money than I'd earned in my entire life. A German guy came by and offered me £1,200 for the oak panelling, which I accepted. I had a pair of massive stained-glass windows that had come from a chapel that was demolished in Bangor, and they went as well.

That first day at Newark I started running out of stock and there were still two more days to go. So off I went to get some more with my pockets so full of cash I waddled from stall to stall. I started buying all sorts of stuff, working on the instinct I'd been developing every day since I was a kid, and it stood me in good stead when it came to trusting my eye. It really was the beginning of something, my first trade-fair experience, and I came away not just happy, but eager and hungry for more.

Things moved on, and a year or so after that first pitch at
Newark I was working from an inspection pit under my dad's
garage at the house where I grew up in Glan Conwy. It was
a tiny little space we'd partitioned with a single, head-height
window. By then I'd employed a lad called Darren who I was
teaching to restore in the same way Gordon Stewart and Joe
Sturges had taught me back when I was doing my apprenticeship. I'd spent seven years learning the stained-glass
business and I'd kept up on the reading: books, magazines,
catalogues from bygone auctions. They're stacked floor to
ceiling at home. Even now the last thing I do at night before
I go to sleep is read about antiques. The first thing I do
when I wake up in the morning is read about antiques. Back
then I'd done a lot of research into William Morris. He
and Edward Burne-Jones were artists and designers heavily
involved in re-energising the British stained-glass tradition
back in the nineteenth century. Both Pre-Raphaelites, and
born just a year apart, they worked closely together before
founding the decorative arts firm Morris, Marshall, Faulk-
ner and Co. in 1861. I loved Morris glass, though I'd not
come across that much. Actually, I had, and it was about to
bear fruit; I just didn't know it at the time.

I was in the workshop with Darren working on some
pieces when a call came in on my brand-new mobile phone
from a dealer who was making a fortune shipping stuff to
the United States. He told me he had a load of stained-glass
windows he'd come across and wanted to move them on.

I told him to bring them over so I could have a look. A couple of hours later he showed up, and when he opened the back of his van I just stood there trying not to gawp.

'Where did you get this?' I asked.

'Demolition contractor. He died recently and his wife called me to clear the house. Do you want it or not?'

For a moment I didn't speak. What I was looking at was the same stack of windows we'd removed from the Holyhead church on my second day working with Gordon Stewart. That was the day after I unloaded Michael Maine's van and knew this was exactly what I wanted to do. That was also the day I learned how to remove the glass without damaging it. The same batch of windows the contractor had wanted to keep, he'd done nothing with them, and now they were back with me.

It had been eight years since I'd seen them and a few pieces were in much better condition than the others. Taking my time, I turned back a couple to have a closer look and heard a sharp intake of breath. Glancing over my shoulder I could see Darren with his mouth hanging open.

'Don't say a word,' I whispered.

Three of the pieces were William Morris. When I'd painstakingly removed them from that old church, I knew nothing about him, but I did now. I could feel the hairs prickle on the back of my neck.

'What d'you want for it?' I said to the dealer, trying to sound as deadpan as I could.

'Four grand.'

I made a face. 'I've got three and a bit in cash.'

'Alright,' he said. 'That'll do.'

It was incredible, one of those moments that's unlikely ever to be repeated. Even now, when I think about it, I have to pinch myself. The dealer had no idea of their real worth and neither did I. But I had a hunch, and as soon as he'd gone I picked up the phone to a guy called Neil Phillips I'd met at Newark. In those days he was the biggest dealer of stained glass in the world; his family owned Hardman & Co., an incredibly successful manufacturer who started making Gothic stained-glass windows in the nineteenth century at the suggestion of Augustus Pugin, the architect who designed the Palace of Westminster.

I spoke to Neil and told him what I had and he said he wanted to see it. He wasn't going to drive all the way to Conwy, though, so I fetched my dad's knackered old Nikon and took photos of the three Morris windows, using the backdrop of my mum's kitchen window so you could see them properly. Film in hand, I trotted down to Boots, put it in to be developed and picked up the photos the next day. I sent them off and first thing the following morning Neil was on the phone.

'What d'you want for them?' he said.

I really didn't know, but one was called 'Voyage to Vinland the Good' and it was a belter.

'A lot,' I said. 'I know what I've got.'

'OK. Bring them down so I can see.'

'Can I come now?'

'Fine. I'll be waiting for you.'

After putting down the phone, I jumped in my van (by now a slightly less-shit Mercedes 208) and drove to Birmingham to show the windows to Neil. 'Voyage to Vinland' was actually by Morris & Co., which meant it was manufactured after William Morris's death, but it had been designed by him, Dante Gabriel Rossetti and Burne-Jones in period. I had done a bit more research and discovered that they'd only manufactured three. One had disappeared, one was in a museum in New York and the other belonged to me.

As soon as I got to Neil's place, I opened the back of the van and unwrapped the cloths. I could see his reaction, though, being a savvy guy, he did his best not to let it show.

I waited while he took a closer look.

'What do you think?' I said after he'd had a moment to evaluate what he was looking at.

He didn't reply and that's always a good sign. If something is crap people are very quick to let you know. I didn't press him. I knew what I had, so I waited.

'Alright,' he said. 'I'll give you fifty thousand for the three.'

I could feel the hairs again on the back of my neck. That kind of money was way more than I'd expected and it would have a radical impact on my business. I'd paid just over three grand for the whole lot and he was offering £50,000 for just a few. I should have taken that and shook his hand there and then, but for some reason I didn't.

'It's not enough,' I said, the words just coming out of their own accord; for the life of me I don't know why I said it.

Neil looked at me with a shake of his head and a sharp intake of breath. Then he was quiet for a moment. 'I'll give you fifty-five,' he said, 'but you have to leave them with me.'

I held out my hand and we shook on it.

'You can have them when the cheque clears,' I said.

That kind of find is something you never forget and it allowed me to pump money into stock so I could begin to expand the business. Looking back now it shows me how much I'd learned in a relatively short space of time and how ballsy I could be when it came to negotiation. Some 25 years later, both those skills were called for as the chilly spring of 2019 became a decent summer. At times it was absolutely blistering. Take 25 July, for example, not just the second hottest day of the year, it was close to the all-time record. Temperatures were supposed to hit more than 38°C and that was going to be painful. According to the news the roads would melt, power lines might sink and the train tracks were likely to buckle, so the trains would have to run at half-speed. It was hotter than it had been in Italy where I'd spent the last ten days trying to have a bit of a holiday while tracking down as much fresh stock as I could carry in my suitcase. I don't mind relaxing by the pool and it's important to recharge the batteries, but Italy is the country that brought us the Renaissance and there's always something that catches my eye. You don't have to go looking for it either, not with so many galleries and junkshops, not to mention stands selling stuff by the side of the road. Before my girlfriend Sam and I left for home, I'd bought 46 prints that I'd stripped from their frames and rolled up so I could get them in my suitcase. They weren't classic in terms of art, but they all had something about them. I've got an art-critic friend who jokingly likes to tell me that I have no taste, but he's not looking at the paintings the way I do. We don't buy for the same reason – to an art critic it's about the painting itself whereas to me it's the decorative quality. By that I mean how it speaks to me, how it's going to look hanging on the wall, so the subject matter or the artist, its place in the history of art, is less important.

Italy has to be my favourite country; I love the architecture and art, the food, the people and the relaxed way of living that's echoed in the quality of the wine. Many really good reds come from Italy, not least Valpolicella Ripasso, which I discovered on my third or fourth Decorative Fair at Battersea. That event holds huge importance for me and for all sorts of reasons. It's the most important date in the calendar and not just in terms of where an antique dealer is able to exhibit. It's only for dealers at the top of their game in terms of the quality of stock they deal in. You have to apply, and you're vetted before you're admitted.

On the day I discovered my love of Valpolicella Ripasso, I'd been at the fair for a couple of days and had arranged to deliver an Empire cellarette to a client on Cheyne Walk. A cellarette is a smallish wooden cabinet or box, which comes in a variety of different styles and designs, that was used to cool wine bottles at lavish parties. It was a piece I'd wanted to shift for a while and we'd been using it throughout the day to store open bottles of wine which we'd share with customers and other dealers. That's the nature of Battersea, it's not just about the quality of the antiques, it's about the people that get to display there: it's a very special place to be.

I remember being on my stand around lunchtime when this lairy, slightly scary-looking guy kept walking past and seemed to know everybody I did. At least six-foot-four, his name was Rob Black, a dealer I knew by reputation with an 'in-your-face' look about him. The third time he walked by, he spoke to me.

'Drew,' he said. 'I've been hearing good things about you. I like the cut of your jib. We should talk. How d'you fancy having dinner later?'

'Alright. I'll be finished around six.'

He showed up about quarter past and I was trying to work out how I was going to get the cellarette to Cheyne Walk.

'Alright, Drew,' he said, in an accent reminiscent of Del Boy in *Only Fools and Horses*. 'Are we set?'

'Pretty much, but I've sold this piece and I have to deliver it before we go.'

He recognised the cellarette as the one we'd used to store the bottles of wine we'd been drinking throughout the day. It was about 130cm long and 75cm tall, a bit of a beast with Empire feet, and I was glad to be rid of it. Empire is an early nineteenth-century design style that originated in France and was named after the Emperor Napoleon. An obvious example is the Arc de Triomphe that was commissioned after the Battle of Austerlitz during the Napoleonic Wars. Square, solid and functional, the cellarette echoed that style and would've been used at parties in rich people's houses. Packed with ice to keep the bottles cool, the residue drained from a plug in the base when the party was over.

'I tell you what,' he said. 'I'll give you a hand to carry it outside. We'll chuck it in a cab and drop it off then you can buy me dinner after.'

I seemed to remember him inviting me to dinner, but it really didn't matter who was paying, because I'd had a terrific day. Between us we manhandled the cellarette out to the street where we hailed a cab and drove to this fantastic townhouse on Cheyne Walk. Most of the adjoining properties had long since been turned into apartments but my client still owned his entire building. He told us he'd bought it in 1960 for pennies and now it was worth a fortune.

'What do you do again?' I asked him.

'I'm an estate agent. Land agent, actually, I do a lot of work for the Prince of Wales.'

We carried the cellarette inside and there was Empire furniture everywhere. Big stuff and lots of it; really over-the-top. To tell you the truth, Rob and I were a little tipsy so it was more of a chore than it should've been. The task was made harder when the guy said he wanted the cellarette on the top floor, but up we went with Rob cracking jokes about holding his end up and the agent joining in with the banter. Finally, we negotiated all four flights of stairs and, as we put the cellarette down, I glanced over my shoulder. I went very cold, suddenly completely sober. All the way down the stairs, and I'm talking all four flights, were splashes of red wine, made all the more obvious by the snow-white Axminster carpet.

'Oh shit,' I said, as the owner of the house looked where I did. We'd been stacking those open bottles all day and some of the wine must've spilled out into the bottom of the cellarette and seeped through the plug as we tilted it when we were climbing. I could not believe what I was seeing: instead of a profit, I was looking at a £20,000 bill for re-carpeting.

'God,' I said. 'I'm so sorry. I don't know what to say. I really am so sorry, believe me.'

Even Rob was aghast, but the owner just shook his head and reached in his pocket for his wallet. 'Don't worry about it,' he said. 'It's nothing that can't be fixed.' God bless him, he gave us a 50-quid tip.

I couldn't believe his reaction. He said the insurance would pay, it was one of those things and he genuinely wasn't concerned about it. Outside we hailed another cab and Rob gave the driver directions to take us to what turned out to be the best Italian restaurant I'd ever been to. He told me not to tell anyone because the place was the best-kept secret in London and he wanted it to remain that way. As we walked in the owner approached us with a welcoming smile. 'Boys,' he said, 'you look tired. Sit down and I will feed you like you've never been fed before.' We sat down at a table in the back and I took a look at the menu.

'Can I bring you a glass of wine?' the owner asked us.

'Thanks.' I needed a drink, having barely recovered from the episode with the carpet. 'That would be wonderful.'

A couple of minutes later he was back with two glasses of the best red wine I'd ever tasted. I knew about Valpolicella, of course, but I'd not drunk the Ripasso. It was really, really good; so good that, when the food came, I asked the waiter to bring us a bottle. Rob likes a drink. I mean he really

CHAPTER 2

likes a drink, and I've been known to sink a few myself, but back then I had no idea what kind of long-term effect that was going to have and how it would bite me later. By the time they brought the risotto we'd already drunk most of it, so I ordered another bottle. I'm a fan of risotto but this was like nothing I'd ever tasted. It arrived on a chunk of Parmesan cheese that had to be 45cm tall with a triangle cut out of the top. The risotto had been layered inside so, when the waiter served, he scooped out not only risotto but softened Parmesan cheese as well. It was the best Italian meal I've ever had and we quickly polished off the second bottle of Ripasso. I asked the waiter to bring another and we drank that, so I told him to keep it coming until we could barely raise our lips from the table. When the bill arrived, I found that the wine alone was £130 a throw. I didn't care. I'd avoided a £20,000 bill for four flights of Axminster stair carpet.

CHAPTER 3

FROM THE GROUND UP

So, 25 July 2019 was the second hottest day of the year, and I was only just back from the holiday/buying trip to Italy. It was Thursday and I was driving the short distance to the warehouse at Colwyn Bay to check on a batch of furniture the lads had brought back from Carmarthen in the early hours of the morning. Just a couple of miles from where I live in Conwy, the warehouse is small and compact, occupying one corner of a cul-de-sac of terraced houses. I rent it from Craig Hughes, who does all the reupholstery for me, and his place is on the other corner. The road in is pretty tight, always packed with cars, but there's just enough room to reverse a Luton up to the warehouse gates.

Before I left, I opened all the doors in my house then followed Enzo out to where the grass needed cutting badly. I like things a little wild, but this was ridiculous, and he'd need a snorkel if he was going to check out who'd been in his garden. As luck would have it, a lad was working on a

CHAPTER 3

neighbour's place across the road so I asked him if he could look at mine and he said he'd mow the lawn for me later.

I had to leave Enzo lying on the cool slate floor, which was his favourite spot, because it was too hot for him to be in the car. I left every window in the house open, which made it cool enough, and I gave him a chew (which is a slice of heaven to a Jack Russell) before leaving for the warehouse. More than a year had passed since I'd agreed to buy the furniture and I couldn't remember much of it. But I don't buy crap so, hopefully, the return would be worth the wait.

In one of those weird sets of circumstances that can happen in this trade, it began with a phone call from a guy who told me he was a property developer and antique dealer.

'Look,' he said. 'I've bought this old office in Carmarthen that's been used by at least four or five generations of solicitors and there's a whole stack of furniture.' That was odd because generally dealers don't ask for properties to be cleared, we're the ones doing the clearing.

'Do you want to come down?' he asked me.

'I don't know,' I said. 'Depends what's in there. Can you send me a couple of pictures?'

Carmarthen is a four-hour drive from Conwy and I didn't want to make the trip without some idea of what I'd be looking at. The market for 'Industrial Furniture' is generally good, though, and I've managed to do pretty well from it over the years. If this bloke wasn't bullshitting, it

52

might have something going on. Five generations meant the stuff should be at least a hundred years old, maybe a hundred and fifty.

Later that day the pictures came through and, from what I could see, the place looked as if it was worth a visit, but when I spoke to him again the developer told me that time was tight and he only had a couple of hours he could spare, so we had to make a firm arrangement. Once again, I wondered if this guy was telling the truth because, if he'd bought the place, then time shouldn't be such a problem. On the other hand, if the sale wasn't complete and all he had were the keys, he'd have to make sure he got them back to the agent pretty sharpish.

By the time I left I was more than a little suspicious but made the journey anyway. It took the full four hours before I arrived in a tiny Carmarthenshire village where the buildings slumped so much it looked as though the place had melted. It wasn't easy to access either; the roads were so narrow it was a struggle to get my four-by-four through without scratching the paintwork to pieces. A maze of tight little streets with nowhere to park; in the end I dumped the car, knowing I would come back to a parking ticket.

Finally, I found the building and it was a huge Georgian affair that towered over the street. I was beginning to think that, despite my suspicions, this call might have some potential. I was a bit late and the developer was looking at his watch, literally hopping from one foot to the other. He was agitated and certainly pressed for time and I knew then he hadn't bought the building. When it came to opening the door, he was fumbling around trying to find the right key and I realised I was here so he could use my expertise to find out what extra value there might be inside that he could weigh against the price he was paying.

It didn't matter; there might be a deal here so long as he was in a position to buy and not just a wannabe. Finally, he got the door open and it was worth the wait because I found myself walking into Ebenezer Scrooge's office. It was dark and cool, shadows in every corner, with four or five floors accessed by an ancient winding staircase. The steps were incredibly worn, broken in places and repaired with bits of old tin; I imagined Bob Cratchit going up and down by the light of a candle.

The first thing that caught my eye was a pair of tall oak bookcases. I didn't say anything and the guy showed me another two that were slightly smaller but, in many ways, just as impressive as the first. As we went deeper into the building, I came across another pair, the largest bookcases I'd ever seen in fact, and that really set the juices flowing. Fixed to both wall and floor, they towered all the way to the ceiling and I reckoned they'd be a bitch to get out but, hopefully, the lads would be able to do it.

'Impressive,' I said. 'So, what's for sale?'

'All of it.' He gestured. 'For the right price you can clear it.'

I moved from room to room and there were lots of bits and pieces, some of which I knew I could move pretty quickly. I picked out an old clerk's stool where the seat was worn at the front to the point it was sloping. The foot rail was bowed and worn, which indicated decades of use where some poor guy with a pen and parchment had worked away at his ledgers. I wondered how many clerks had sat on that stool. I thought about all the people who had worked in this place poring over contracts and documents.

There was something going on in every room and that included an attic full of solicitor's deed boxes. You know the kind of thing; large, made of metal, with the names of each estate written on them. The roof had been leaking, the place stank of damp and some of the boxes had popped open. Everywhere I looked there were papers; loads of them, literally tens of thousands of documents and all hand-written. The attic was split into two separate rooms, but I could barely get the door that separated them open. Weighing in with my shoulder, I managed to get it cracked far enough to stick my head around and saw it was crammed full of metal shelves and more deed boxes. Back when this was a working practice they would have been taken into court and various documents used as evidence. When the case was over, they'd be locked away and returned to the solicitor's office.

'Alright,' I said to the developer. 'I think we can do something. How much do you want for it?'

'Fifteen grand.'

That wasn't going to happen, 15 was way too steep. I had to bring this guy down to earth. 'I can't do that,' I said. 'I'll give you four thousand.'

He was shaking his head. 'I can't do four, not for all of it.'

'Alright,' I said. 'Let me look around some more and have a think.'

The guy was checking his watch, but he left me to have a wander so I totted up what it would cost to hire a couple of vans, pay for the diesel and wages of the boys that would come down here and collect it. There was a lot of work to be done and the tallest bookcases would be tough to get out and, on that second look, I decided half of the stuff wouldn't be worth the trouble anyway.

'I tell you what I'll do,' I said when I went back to him. 'I'll cherry-pick the bits I really want and leave you with the majority.'

'For four grand?'

'Five,' I said. 'That's the best I can do.'

He took a moment to think, then, begrudgingly, he shook hands with me.

I left him to contact me with a date when we could come down and headed back to my parking ticket. I was right about him not being a dealer and I was right about the state of play as regards the building. He was in the market for sure, but I soon discovered just how far he was from actually owning the place. We'd shaken hands on a deal for some of the contents but I didn't hear anything for over a year. I'd almost forgotten in fact when, finally, he called me.

'Right,' he said. 'The building is mine. Can you come and clear it right away?'

I had to think about that because we get calls about clearances on a daily basis and the diary is booked out for weeks.

'Can't do it for a month,' I said. 'We're pretty tied up and it's been a year since you talked to me.'

He wasn't happy but there was nothing I could do about that; if he wanted us, he had to accept our schedule. He'd kept me waiting a year so another month wouldn't hurt, though it was more like six weeks before the boys were able to make it.

It was 24 July when four guys drove down in two vans led by my full-time restorer Gavin and another good lad called Elwyn. They left Conwy at half-five in the morning and, around lunchtime, I'd had a phone call.

'Drew, it's Gav. We've got a problem.'

'What's up?'

'The two biggest bookcases, those massive ones attached to the wall – we can't get them free without tearing everything up and, even if we could, we'll never get them out the door.'

Shit, I thought. I'd been looking forward to getting those back. I knew they'd be a bitch but I hadn't known it would be this bad. Gavin's been with me for 20 years, though, and if he says he can't get something out of a building, it can't be done. When we met, he was about to start playing professional football in Florida but a snapped Achilles tendon put an end to his career before it ever began. He had to come back to Wales and, if you ask him where we met, he'll look you in the eye and tell you – deadpan – it was a gay bar, but really it was a farm shed. His mum and dad were cleaning the farmhouse I was living in at the time, and I needed someone to clear out a shed. They roped Gav in to help, and he and I got talking about the restoration business. He was keen to learn so I gave him a job and he's been with me ever since. I like to keep things local: most of the people I work with go back to the days when we kicked a ball about or climbed the scrapyard fence and tried to avoid the Alsatians.

Gavin can spot the value in a broken-down item and loves the fact he's on a constant learning curve. The job isn't without its risks; he still carries the scars from the time he nearly lost his arm to a stained-glass window. About 15 years ago, we were stripping out a local school with the same Gordon Stewart who gave me my apprenticeship. There was a lot to do and Gavin said he was going to climb a ladder and take out the upper window.

'Not on your own, mate,' I told him.

'It's fine. I'll be OK.'

'Gavin,' I said, 'there's no way you can take that window out by yourself, you need someone to foot the ladder.' I told him to wait for Gordon because the floor of the school hall had been polished to the point it was slick. But Gavin wasn't going to wait for anyone: he shimmied up the ladder and, of course, the feet slipped and he went straight through the window we were supposed to be removing. He hit the ground with blood spurting from a massive wound that all but sliced his arm off. We had to rush him to hospital, where a plastic surgeon had to reattach the blood vessels before they could stitch him up; he could barely move it for weeks after.

I had to suck up the loss of the big bookcases, but I wasn't going to part with five grand if it didn't include the two best pieces. There was some renegotiating to do, so I spoke to the developer and we did a little bit of back and forth before I ended up knocking 1,500 quid off the total. We were down to £3,500 now, but I spoke to Gavin again and he told me about another bookcase he'd spotted that he thought was worth a punt. He's got a good eye and I trust him so I bought that for £400. With a final tally of £3,900, they loaded up the vans and set out on the long drive home.

As I pulled up outside the warehouse, they were already unloading. After finding somewhere to park, I squeezed past the van and found Gavin in the yard with sweat rolling off him in rivers. It was baking in the yard, way hotter than it had been in Italy.

'You found the place then?' I said.

He muttered something about narrow fucking streets in the middle of fucking nowhere then rolled a cigarette. 'Pity about those bookcases. There's some good stuff here, but those were the jewels, weren't they?'

'You really couldn't get them out?'

'Not without taking out a bay window, and the building's listed.'

'So what? You can take the window out and put it back after. What is it – four screws and a bit of cement?'

'Tell that to the developer.'

Gav disappeared inside the warehouse as the other lads manhandled the larger bookcase over. Moments later the front doors opened, exposing the upper floor where Gav had the hoist ready. As they hauled the bookcase up, I could see it needed a little work on a cornice, so I made a mental note to phone Kevin, or 'Mr Measures', the guy I turn to for really intricate woodwork. The other bookcases were in good order, just a case of putting the shelves back and rubbing down with a cloth. By the end of the day they'd be photographed and on display in the showroom.

I followed Gav inside and he drew my attention to a chest of drawers I'd bought from Sir James Shuckburgh of Shuckburgh Hall in Northamptonshire. It had been in a hell of a state when we found it, but Kevin had been working on it and he'd done a shit-hot job as always. Precise, meticulous: 'Measures' by name and measures by nature; we couldn't have come up with a better nickname. Up here everyone has one: there's T, of course, and Daz-Babs. There's a lad we call Johnny-Five because, if you tell him something, five minutes later he's forgotten. I've got a mate called 'Phil the Box' who's a funeral director and the best of all is Dave Tuesday. Me and T were sitting in the pub one night having a pint when this really big bloke walked in and the whole room seemed to part like a wave before him.

'Who's that?' I asked as he strode past our table.

'Dave Tuesday,' T said.

'Why'd they call him that?'

'Because if he says it's Tuesday – it's fucking Tuesday.'

I called Mr Measures and told him I loved what he'd done with the chest; the only thing he still had to do was a bit of 'cock-beading'. That's a narrow, semi-circular bead which is slightly pronounced and quite often appears as decoration on drawers and doors of this age. Even Gav was impressed with the quality: the chest had been derelict when we dragged it out, but now it looked fantastic. The best restoration is when a piece is brought back to the condition it should be in given its age, without looking like it had been anywhere near an expert. With this piece, two of the handles had been missing, the legs were rotten and the sides bashed in. Looking at it now, I couldn't tell which were the old handles and which were the ones Kevin had made to replace them. The chest had been made by a provincial country manufacturer around 1825 and it was painted with faux-marbling. That was a common practice back then and

I like that sort of naivety. It's attractive and it makes an item look much more expensive than it was back then. I think I paid about 250 quid for this one and had another 250 in it. Now it was restored we should see 850 and someone would be very happy to pay it. It's not a massive profit, what we call a 'turn', and most of the time that's all there is. The big-ticket stuff is sporadic but it's out there and when you come across it there's money to be made, as I found out with those William Morris panels.

Satisfied we'd see a decent enough return, I took a look around the workshop to check on a few other items we'd yet to get to. Against the far wall was a pair of large desks I'd bought in Belgium, an old nineteenth-century haberdashery cabinet that needed a new side, and some stuff Gav clearly didn't want to be bothered with because he'd hidden it right at the back of the workshop. One thing caught my eye, the industrial table I'd bought in Chorley. It hadn't been photographed yet because Gav was using it as his workbench.

With photographs in mind, I took another look at the larger bookcases. They were really very handsome, with a plaque on each that confirmed they'd been presented to a vicar in Swansea in 1909. That was important, no guesswork here, we had provenance, the year they were made, and that added to the value. They were high quality, constructed from oak (though the backboards were pine, which lessened the value fractionally). Solid oak brings the most money, but these had adjustable shelving and the original dust-falls (removable leather flaps) that fit between the underside of the shelf and the top of the books to keep the dust off.

'What do you reckon we should ask for them?' I said to Gav.

'Twenty-eight hundred.'

'I was thinking two-seven so we're not far apart. Alright, two-eight.' I asked him to get them to Eleri (our brilliant photographer) as soon as possible.

Gavin showed me the bookcase he'd told me about on the phone that was complete with a set of solicitor's deed boxes. The lads lifted it out of the van and I took a look at the labelling: SEQUESTRATION OR DEBT ENFORCEMENT.

'You don't want to be on the end of that,' I said to nobody in particular.

Gav was standing next to me. 'My name'll be in there somewhere. CCJ behind it.'

The bookcase itself wasn't in the best of condition. At one time it had a set of doors but they'd been ripped off and that had caused the wood to crack down one side. It's the kind of thing that really grates on me.

'Why would anyone do that?' I said. 'Three screws; all you have to do is take them out. Why rip the bloody doors off?'

It was a shame because it was so unnecessary, but we weren't going to make another set – it wouldn't be cost-effective. Instead, Gav would splice some wood into the groove where the hinges had been and bead over the top. He'd match the colour with wax and it would go straight onto the website as a set of open pigeonholes.

For me this is the most exciting aspect of the job. Buying is great, but restoration is where I started, and I never get tired of breathing new life into something that's been left to rot. The lads were already on it and, this afternoon, we'd have the bookcases with Eleri, who would take the photos. They'd be on display in the showroom and this evening I would put them on the website. That's how quick we can work without cutting any corners in the restoration process. We make money, sometimes lots of it, and we get the odd derogatory tweet ... but there's a cost nobody sees. It's not just the difference between what we pay for something and what we sell it for; it's four lads, two vans, warehousing, the shop and website, as well as the cost of the restoration before it gets anywhere near a professional photographer.

Adding stuff we've bought and restored to the website is a huge part of what we do. It's a job only I do, and I'm meticulous about freshening the inventory. We sell a lot through the shop, it's important to have a physical presence, but the sales are nothing compared to the website.

When I first realised its potential, it was another 'Eureka' moment, probably the most important discovery I've ever made. Even now, not all dealers have a decent web presence, but when I realised there was a way of reaching the entire planet, 20 years ago, I jumped right on it. I went to see a mate called Rob Wilding from Ruthin, when I was working every second of every day but there were only so many deals to be made by physical contact or a phone call. I was frustrated, thinking that there had to be more to the business than grinding myself into the dust trying to see as many customers as possible. I knew Rob was making a small fortune selling car parts online, but had no idea what that was. He was into old cars and had discovered a niche bringing old VWs in from California to break down and sell as spares. I called by his place to get some parts for my Beetle and discovered he'd made enough money to buy a house, garage and storage shed.

I was like, 'Mate, how're you doing this?'

'Internet.'

'What's the internet?' (Yes, I really did say that. I hadn't got a clue.)

'The worldwide web.'

'What?'

'I've got a website.' He told me how he was using his computer to sell the parts he'd broken to customers all over the country. He showed me the website, and I could feel a tremendous sense of excitement. That's it, I thought, that's how I'm going to do it. That's how I can bring what I do to everyone and not just in this country. The antiques trade knows no boundaries. If I did this right, I could sell all over the world.

I spoke to a couple of people and within four weeks I had a computer, a website and a database. From that moment on I started selling stuff and in the next six weeks I'd turned over more than I'd done the entire previous year. It was like being back at Newark only tenfold and the whole world was my oyster. I sold to one of the Spice Girls. I sold to Diane Keaton and Marco Pierre White. I was all over the salvage news; the website had changed my world completely.

Gav was making a start on the clerk's stool where a few dots of white paint mottled one leg. He'd leave that; if the whole thing was coated, he'd rub it down, but those dots were part of the stool's story. By the end of the day the work would be done and it would join the bookcases in the photo studio. Sometimes it's that simple and with others it's complicated, like the chest of drawers from Shuckburgh. Either way, we're particular about how we restore things. Everything Gav was doing right now he'd learned from me and I'd learned it from Gordon Stewart and Joe Sturges during my apprenticeship in Abergele. It's a tradition that demands a lot of hard work and commitment, not to mention knowledge that can only be gained from experience. Gordon passed on what he knew to me, like a father figure; he helped me become the restorer I am today.

Since then I've been involved in replacing windows at Conwy Castle, and recreating Hogwarts School for a

Japanese businessman. I've done work for Disney and, a few years ago, I rebuilt the oldest stained-glass window in Wales at a church in Holt near Wrexham. I remember the first day on the job we were working on what's called a 'medley window'. During the Reformation, when Henry VIII was raiding the monasteries, a lot of windows were taken out and buried to stop them being destroyed. Much of it got smashed, though, and had to be pieced together in medley windows after it had been dug up again. The one we worked on had been inscribed by the man who put it back together in the eighteenth century; a lovely find that set the tone for the rest of the project.

I love old churches, they're a massive part of my life but not for religious reasons, as I'm a committed atheist. Ever since I can remember, I've wanted to own one, and I got my chance at 24 when I was still working out of those two rooms under my dad's workshop. It was ridiculous really, the ceiling was so low I scraped the top of my head, and I'm not the tallest guy in the world. But it didn't cost much and the money I was making was going back into the business.

I'm told I have an artistic eye and I probably get it from my father. I mentioned before that we have a shit relationship now, but when I first started to show an interest in antiques, he was actually pretty supportive. When I was only about eight or nine, I remember going shopping with my mum to help her pick out the clothes she wanted to buy. I would tell her what colours and style suited her, and my dad must've picked up on it because initially he tried to help me develop that eye. He's an incredibly talented artist, not just with paint, but sculpture and music. In the early 1950s he contracted tuberculosis and was sent to an isolation hospital where he had a lot of time to paint. TB was a killer back then; he told me that the closer your bed was to the door the sicker you knew you were, because there would be less disturbance to the other patients if you died in the night. When he got better, he went to work for a sign-writer in Llandudno, a lovely man called Mr Traversie, who helped bring on his talent.

Aware I had a similar appreciation for form and colour, he'd show me different paintings and ask what I thought was wrong with them. Invariably, I would pick up on something: a horse for example; the way a hoof was set, I'd want it at a slightly different angle. I was still only eight or nine, but he'd take me to stand in front of a building somewhere and ask me to tell him what I could see. Again, I would pick up on details: a window or beam, the thickness of a wall mounting or windowsill. Buildings, cars, art: I had a critical eye, one that could see beauty and potential where others couldn't.

Art was really important to my dad and, whenever he managed to scrape a little bit of money together, he would take me and my younger brother Guy to a museum. He would sit us in front of masterpieces and ask what we thought of them. Guy wasn't quite as interested as I was. We were pretty close as kids, but he chose a completely different career path to me. I loved being in those museums and still do. I didn't know anything about art. I didn't know the names of any of the artists, but I didn't care; there was beauty here and I appreciated it.

Ever since Dad first stood me in front of those old buildings, I've had a thing for Georgian architecture, particularly the British Regency period. In 1811 the mad King George III had been deemed unfit to rule and his son was named Prince Regent. There was a particular style about the buildings they built between then and 1820 that I don't think has been bettered. John Nash was one of the leading architects of the time and did some amazing things up and down the country. Regency is about proportion and space, ceiling height and window arrangement, or 'fenestration' as it's referred to. Most of the Georgian buildings had windows that graduated in size, which gave the façades a fantastic aesthetic. Bath is probably the best example, along with sections of Edinburgh, and there are large swathes, of course, in London.

Anyway, I was in the workshop one day when a friend of mine called on my mobile phone. 'Drew, it's Andy. I was wondering if I could borrow your van?'

'Of course. What d'you want it for?'

'Andrea has to move out of her house and I said I'd give her a hand.'

CHAPTER 3

Andrea was Andy's sister so I told him I'd help with the move and asked where she lived.

'A knackered old church house,' he said, 'in the Conwy Valley.'

I picked him up and he directed me through Eglwysbach to a beautifully tranquil spot made all the more so by a Regency Methodist chapel. It was the most amazing location and, as we drove up the overgrown lane, the hairs started to climb on the back of my neck. There were three buildings, including a two-storey stable block, a church house and the chapel itself, which was pretty much derelict. Andrea came out to meet us and I asked her why she was moving.

'I have to,' she said. 'They've sold the place.'

I took a closer look at the chapel and it was exactly the sort of building I'd dreamed of owning. The windows were wonderful, there was space and light, and the location was pure magic. As we started loading her gear into the van, I asked if she had any idea how much the seller had been asking, but all she could tell me was that someone had bought it and she had to vacate. I was intrigued now and wondered what the exact position was, because something is only ever 'sold' (and therefore out of reach) if money has changed hands. Right then I didn't know if that was the case or not, so I decided to do some digging.

Before we left, I wandered through a forest of two-metre-tall bracken that surrounded the chapel and could see where the roof had fallen in completely. There was no running water or inside toilet. Peeking through a window, I could tell that the floors were slate laid straight onto dirt – this place was totally virgin. The roof of the two-storey stable block was on the floor and the church house was very basic. Nothing had been touched since the place had been abandoned by the Methodists and I was determined to buy it.

Back in Conwy I rang the estate agent and asked him what was going on.

'Oh yeah, that place. It's sold,' he said. 'There's no point looking at it.'

'OK, I understand. Can I talk to the person who sold it?'

'No, you can't. The deal's already done, it's all taken care of.'

'Has money changed hands, contracts exchanged? When's completion?'

He couldn't tell me; he was mumbling, fumbling, and that aroused my suspicions. I was sure no deal had been completed, but when I pressed him, he refused to give me any details. I didn't leave it there. I made a right old noise, calling every council in North Wales, trying to find out who the seller was and who was planning to buy it. Word got back to the estate agent and we had another conversation.

'Look,' he said. 'The fact is, it isn't "sold" sold yet, but …'

'Well, if it's not sold, I want to buy it.'

CHAPTER 3

'You can't, somebody else is. It's not available.'

Bullshit. If something's for sale and no money's changed hands then it's still available. I put down the phone, then rang the Royal Commission for Wales who note the cultural importance for all such buildings.

'Oh,' they said. 'That one. It's been going on for a very long time and, as far as we know, nothing has been completed.' They told me a sale had been agreed for £17,000 but no contracts had been exchanged. I did some more digging and it turned out the place had never been on the open market. We're talking about an acre of land, a chapel and house, as well as a two-storey stable block, and the price was just £17,000.

I got back on the phone to the agent and told him I knew the chapel had never reached the open market. Legally, an agent has to put a property on the open market and it seemed he'd been keeping this place back so a mate of his could buy it. Now he had no choice and it would go to sealed bids. I was determined to get it, so I called Richard, another estate agent I knew.

'How much do you think this place is going to cost me if I want to secure it?' I asked.

'I'll find out.' He hung up and ten minutes later he phoned back. 'Go in at £31,500,' he said.

I did that, wrote my bid and sealed the envelope, then drove to the estate agent and stuffed it through the letterbox. Nine o'clock the next morning I called to ask if my bid

72

had won and they said they'd phone back in an hour and let me know. That hour came and went and nobody phoned. The day dragged on and still the phone didn't ring. I was beginning to wonder if the figure Richard had given me was too low, then, right at the end of the day, the agents finally rang me. 'It's yours,' they said. 'You won the bid.'

I could not believe it. I was the owner of a Regency building, something I'd dreamed about since I was a kid. I was absolutely euphoric, but I hadn't paid for it yet. I had to get a mortgage, but the place was so bad the agents didn't think anyone would lend on it. I had the deposit, however, and I knew what I was going to do with the place; it was a question of persuasion. When I sat down with the mortgage advisor, I told her a load of old cobblers about how much money I had and how I was going to spend it. What I wanted from her was the means to complete the purchase, but she didn't think it was worth lending on. I didn't let go. I kept on and on, basically chatting her up (which you couldn't do now), and I did have the full deposit. Although she had been pretty sceptical to begin with, it was old-school banking and in the end she agreed, so I got the rest of the money to buy it.

The deal completed on my 25th birthday and I took the day off to celebrate. It was the best present I could've had. I went to pick up the key for the church from the agents but they told me they didn't have one, only for the church house.

'What do you mean, you don't have a key?' I asked them.

'We've never had one. I'm not sure there's ever been one.'

No key then, so what? I'd just have to go up there and break in.

I drove back to the valley and got the door open with a crowbar, having bought the church without ever setting foot inside. Once I was in, I could see just how bad the place really was … we're talking falling to pieces. I didn't give a shit, I knew what I was going to do and, the next day, I took my parents to see it.

'This is it,' I said as I parked in a spot where the bracken didn't swamp everything. 'This is why I needed the mortgage.'

My mum just sat there, staring through the windscreen. 'You borrowed money to buy this? What on earth are you going to do with it?'

'Restore it, look at the position it's in.'

Even she had to agree it was perfect.

'I can build something incredibly special here,' I said. 'The bones of the building are solid; it's all about the location.'

So far, my dad had kept quiet. 'What do you think, Dad?' I asked.

'Fantastic,' he said. 'Brilliant buy. Fantastic.'

Hearing any kind of praise from my father had been rare for a long time, so when he opened his mouth and confirmed what I could see, that was good enough for me. Being an artist, he could see exactly what I did. It wasn't what we were looking at now, it was how it would look when it was finished. But that was a long way off, and for the next four years I immersed myself in the project. During the day I would restore glass, strip doors or sell what I'd bought to the trade at Newark, Manchester and Liverpool. After work I'd drive to the chapel and start tearing the place apart so I could build it backup again. Every scrap of cash I had I'd spend on wages for mates who'd come over to work with me at the weekends. I was pushing ahead with the salvage side of my business, so I was using materials I'd reclaimed to put into the restoration. First it was the chapel house that Andrea had rented, after that the stable block, before I finally got to the chapel itself. I ripped what was left of the house apart, rebuilt from the ground up and, six months after completing the deal, I moved in. I had no back door, just a piece of plywood, and there was no flooring upstairs, only the beams, where I fitted a toilet that rested in full view of everyone on the ground floor. It didn't bother me, but it did bother my girlfriend. She moved in thinking she could help with the restoration only to move out again six days later, and that wouldn't have happened if I'd taken more care of the relationship. But I was obsessed with the work, and it was easier to do that without any distractions, though there were plenty I couldn't have conceived back then that were only just around the corner.

CHAPTER 4

FRIENDS, FURNITURE AND FOUR-WHEELED THINGS OF BEAUTY

With the Carmarthen restoration under way, I left the lads to finish the bookcases and went next door to speak to Craig about some chairs he was working on. He's been around a long time and what he doesn't know about reupholstery isn't worth knowing. A few months back I'd bought this pair of handsome circa-1915 leather armchairs with ball and claw feet, that looked like they'd come from a gentlemen's club somewhere, but needed quite a bit of work before we could sell them. They were missing the cushions and there was a problem with both the front panels sagging way more than they should be. I turned one upside down to get a better look and could see various layers of webbing. 'What happened there?' I asked. 'It looks like it's double-webbed.'

'It is,' Craig said. 'Somebody's gone over it again because a lot of the herring-bone has perished.'

The webbing is there to hold the metal springs in place and that gives the chair its comfort and structure. Craig pointed out what was wrong. 'You see the herring-bone's gone there and there. They've put in jute to support it.'

It didn't look good, something I hadn't noticed when I bought the chairs from a dealer I know in Yorkshire.

'The springs at the front have moved,' Craig went on. 'It's why the whole chair is sagging quite so badly. Problem is, I can't get them back in place without taking the sides off. That's a lot of work but it's the only way to do it.' He paused for a moment then pointed. 'The only other thing to do is try to pack the springs with something.'

I had to think about this because that sounded like a bit of a bodge and we don't bodge any restoration.

'Let's have a look at the other one,' I said, and turned it upside down to find it was in the same condition as the first. 'Craig,' I said. 'My brain says strip them down and do this properly.'

'It's not viable, economically.'

That was a blow because I'd already lost any profit I might've made and was not about to lose more money.

'Look,' he said. 'I can do some packing and it won't be a bodge.' He showed me where he meant to give the springs some support and I knew he would do it properly. 'We can make feather cushions and that'll look really good and both chairs will be good as new.'

'Just a bit of packing?' I said.

'Yeah, here and here.' He indicated.

'Will it last?'

'Of course, if I redo the webbing.' Again, he showed me. 'There might be some small issues with the front edge, but there's nothing we can do about that unless I strip them back completely.'

I took a moment to think, fully aware that if Craig said the repair would last then it would. If the seat still sagged a little at the front, that would be in keeping with the age and wear and was part of the charm I'd seen when I bought them in the first place. I'd paid 900 quid plus shipping, but I'd had them a while and Kevin had already done some work on the ball and claw. I was losing money like a leaking tap and I didn't want to lose any more. 'Do what you can,' I said. 'If I can get close to what I paid for them that'll be something.'

My attention switched to another chair Craig had been working on. Bespoke and semi-circular in design, it had been commissioned for a larger gentleman to kick back in. Its form was perfect and the construction reflected the design of a craftsman named Godwin, but I wanted to do some more research because it could also have been made by Holland & Sons. Either way, I'd bought it a couple of weeks earlier at auction and it needed a massive amount of work to restore correctly so I'd been prepared to pay a maximum of £1,500 plus VAT and commission. As it turned out, when it went under the hammer, I didn't have to pay anything like that. No one outbid my 200 quid and I came away thinking I'd nicked it.

'We'll make the money back here, Craig,' I said. 'Once this is up together, I'm asking six grand, and if it doesn't sell straight away there's a dealer who'll give me four for it.'

So, you win some and you lose some, that's the nature of this business. I had a good feeling about the Holland & Sons chair because there's always a solid market. As I turned to go, I took another envious look at the life-sized elephant head that hangs above the door to Craig's office. It came from the Indian restaurant on the prom in Llandudno and I used to covet it every time I went for a curry. 'You're never going to sell that to me, are you?'

'You know I can't,' he said. 'It's Nicky's.'

Nicky is Craig's wife, who's well known for buying and selling various stuff on the internet. One day a few years ago, a customer came in to check on the reupholster of some dining chairs and asked if Nicky could sell an elephant for him.

'A real one?' Craig said.

'Don't be silly, a model.'

'Sure. Nicky can sell anything.'

The guy went out to his van while Craig went back to work, thinking he was going to bring them a model of some kind. Moments later, the guy was back with another man, hefting the life-sized replica.

Craig stopped what he was doing and gawped. 'What the hell is that?' he demanded.

'It's the elephant I want you to sell for me.'

Nicky, who had been watching from the office, was off her chair and striding across the workshop. 'That's not for sale,' she said in a voice that sounds like chocolate being churned by gravel. 'I'm having it.'

'You what?' Craig said. 'What're you talking about?'

'I'll take it in lieu of the wages you owe me.'

She hadn't been working there long and was yet to be paid, so she took the elephant, which meant Craig had to upholster the dining chairs for nothing.

Having agreed a plan of action on the ball and claw chairs, Craig followed me out to the car. He's a massive petrolhead with both a 1976 Corvette in his shop as well as a 289 small-block Mustang and about forty old motorbikes as well. Given this was the second hottest day of the year I had left the four-by-four at home and was driving my 13-year-old Porsche 911. It's a cabriolet, but with the sun being so hot today I'd not been able to decide whether to have the roof down or use it as a parasol.

'So, you did get it back,' Craig said. 'You told me you found it before you went to Italy.'

I was gazing lovingly at the vehicle. 'I should never have let it go in the first place.'

He gestured to the sports exhaust pipes. 'Did you put those on?'

'Yeah, when I owned it the first time.'

I love that car and should never have sold it. A 997 C45 manual in triple black that I bought in 2012 with 18,000 miles on the clock from a woman who'd had it new from the showroom. The 15th 911 I'd owned, but it was the first cabriolet. I kept it for five years and put 50,000 more miles on the clock, because I'm not one of these people who has to have the mileage down to the minimum. People are fixated with low miles but, if the miles are low, you're not driving, and what's the point of a car if not to drive it? 911s will do 250,000 miles on one engine and most of the Porsche mechanics won't touch one that's below 100,000 because it takes that long for the motor to bed in.

For some reason I will never understand, I'd traded this car with a dealer in the Cotswolds for an Aston Martin V8 Vantage. I know Aston Martin make fantastic cars, but this one just didn't do anything for me. I was used to Porsche, Volkswagen and Mercedes and the quality of seamless Teutonic engineering. The way this drove was nothing like that, it felt cheap by comparison and it was just awful. That sounds ridiculous, I know, especially when we're talking about one of the most iconic names in the history of top-end sports car makers. But that's how I felt and, by the time I got home to Conwy, I knew I'd done the wrong thing letting the Porsche go, so I got on the phone to the dealer.

'The 911,' I said. 'I want to buy it back. I can't get on with the Aston Martin.'

'I'm sorry,' he said. 'It's gone already. I had a customer lined up. I've already sold it.'

I was gutted, kicking myself, and spent the next two years trawling the internet for another just like it. I never found one and had almost given up hope until the week before I went to Italy. I was in the shop when one of the girls asked me if I'd mind the till while she went out to get a sandwich. While she was gone, I logged on to the PistonHeads sales hub and typed in my usual search, *Black. Cabriolet. Manual.* The second car that popped up seemed to fit my requirements exactly: a 911 in triple black with sports exhaust and electronic performance chip. When I saw the number plate, I couldn't believe it: YN06 ZDT, my car, the one I'd sold two years previously. It was back with the same dealer, so I sent the guy a text telling him not to sell the car to anyone.

Five days went by with no response and I wasn't really surprised, as I hadn't had much time for the bloke in the first place. Five days to answer a call from someone he knows is good for the money – how do these people ever sell anything? I hadn't found the time to phone him back, as I was up to my neck getting stock we'd restored uploaded to the website. Then, just before I was about to leave for Italy, the dealer was on the phone talking as if I was the best friend he'd lost then found again. I asked if it was my car and he told me nothing had changed save a few more miles on the clock; it was in great condition.

'Right then,' I told him. 'I'll have it.'

What he said next completely changed my opinion of him. He had the car up for a decent price but told me he'd knock three and a half grand off because I'd sold it to him in the first place.

'You're a good customer,' he said. 'And I know you regretted it the moment you traded it. It's yours for what I paid for it.'

That was pretty good of him and I told him I'd pay for it over the phone then send someone down to collect it. I couldn't pick it up myself because I was going away, so Lee Blako went instead. Lee's a good lad I've known a while and he would trailer it back. He duly went down and, the day after I got home from the Italian trip, I woke up to it parked on my drive.

A 911 isn't just a car, it's a rolling work of art. After two long years I was desperate to get behind the wheel, so I took a drive out to see Chris Holt, an old friend who used to work for me. Sadly, he died from motor neurone disease at just 49 years of age and I owed a visit to his grave. He was a huge fan of Porsche and VW, the kind of guy who'd appreciate the story of how I'd sold this car and regretted it every day until I got it back. The last time I saw him was just before he died and, being away filming all the time, I'd neglected him a little. When I saw his dad, he made short work of telling me that his real friends had been there for him and where the hell had I been? It put me off going to the funeral. I wanted to because I'd known Chris and his family since 1986, but his dad seemed so bitter I couldn't bring myself to show up because I didn't want to annoy him any more than I already had. That was in 2017, so I drove to Chris's grave to have a chat with him. Holty, we called him; he was quite a character, with a three-legged cat called Tripod and a house called Holty Towers.

Sitting down beside his grave, I told him I'd got my 911 back. 'You know,' I said, 'the one I regretted selling the moment I drove away in the Vantage.'

Holty knew about my love of cars – Porsche, Volkswagen and particularly Bugatti. I've owned dozens of VWs and Porsches but never a Bugatti, though I've been in love with them since I first saw the T35. That's one of the most beautiful things a human being has ever created. They came out of the Automobiles Ettore Bugatti factory in Molsheim, a French city in Alsace that had been annexed by Germany in 1871. The factory was founded in 1909. Ettore was Italian by birth, an industrial designer by profession and his brilliance was personified in the detail of his engineering and artistry. His father, Carlo, was also a designer renowned for Art Nouveau furniture and jewellery.

I've owned bits of Bugattis and some very interesting pieces associated with the family but never one of their vehicles. For me the marque marries my love of cars and engineering with my appreciation of great design. If ever anyone got it right, it was Ettore: in every single aspect of everything he did, he just nailed it. He's one of the few designers I've come across who has stuck with me. As I said before, I was taught to appreciate design by my father, who is extremely adept at understanding design. When it's as natural, fluid, brilliant and in balance as it was with Bugatti, it creates an impression that never leaves you. When the T35 came out it was one of the most incredible things on the face of the earth. It was a fast car that won races, but also a masterpiece of design. The very first Monaco Grand Prix was won by an Englishman called William Grover-Williams driving a T35 Bugatti. A larger-than-life character, during the Second World War he was an agent with the Special Operations Executive (SOE) and coordinated a group of undercover operatives that gathered information in France and sent it back to London. A man both incredibly brave and calm, he was caught and executed by the Nazis.

So, when it comes to cars, it's Bugatti and Porsche, closely followed by Volkswagen. It is pronounced *Porsch-a*, by the way: sounds poncey, I know, but that's the correct way to say it.

The first time I saw a Porsche was at Oulton Park when I went to watch a race with my parents. It was the early 1980s and back then everybody parked on the grass verges. Just hovering there as we pulled in was an orange RS 2.7

911. With its big fat Fuchs wheels (first made as 'after-market' accessories for the Porsche 911 in 1965), the grass was brushing the underside of the sills and the car looked like it was floating. I utterly fell for it right there, one of the most beautiful things I'd seen, and that was saying something because my father was driving a Jaguar XK120 he'd restored to mirror the one Humphrey Smith was racing. My father's youth club instructor, Humphrey was a really nice guy who did a bit of private racing in an XK120. It's a stunning-looking car, one of the most beautiful designs ever, only topped when William Lyons cracked out the E-Type. That said, I still think the XK140 coupé in its early variation is one of my top five most beautiful cars of all time along with the Maserati Mistral.

I remember going with my father to buy his XK in Rugeley, Staffordshire. It was a 1950 right-hand drive and had been involved in a big accident that smashed up the side. He paid 1,100 quid for it, and I can't remember who else was with us, but I do remember it was night-time, pouring with rain, and we had to load the car onto a trailer. It was partly made of alloy: I think most of them had alloy bonnets, but this one had the bonnet as well as the front wings and boot lid and that made it much rarer. It was a classic even then, but it took my father 15 years to get it restored properly. He did it in Old English white with steel wheels and hubcaps, and, after that, a succession of XKs came through the house, culminating in a 150 drop-top.

The registration number was 9058 HG, in dark blue with blue leather, and had only ever been driven by the chauffeur.

It took me a long time before I was able to buy my first Porsche. I've had over a hundred VWs though. I bought the first one, a camper van, when I was 17 and driving a knackered old yellow Capri called the Flying Banana. A Mark II 1600L, the number plate was KED888P. I'd thrashed it to bits going to and from work in Abergele, so it was long past time for a change when I checked the ads in the paper.

VW SPLIT SCREEN VAN 1967 – £500

I'm having that, I thought, and rang the guy straight away. Three miles as the crow flies, I turned up in my Capri with 150 quid in cash and drove home in my first VW. Back then all my mates had them because they were cool, cheap and fun: you could fix them yourself and there was a big fashion for them. This one was rough as a dog's arse, 1500 single-port engine, and rusted to shit with a clutch that slipped like crazy. I didn't care. I can still remember the smell inside and I fell in love with it; I've not been without a VW since.

It was through the VW scene that I met Clive Holland, who is an extremely good friend and someone I trust implicitly. A couple of years older than me, he had some really cool cars, including the first Cal-look VW in North Wales. It was a style from California, where people had modified

Beetles and notch-back/square-back vans as well as Karmann Ghias with lowered suspension, polished Fuchs and whitewall tyres. It was a fashion thing that Clive latched on to; he was the first guy where we lived to take a really cool car and make it even cooler. I was about 18 at this point and still on the YTS scheme working for Gordon Stewart, but Clive and I decided we could make a few quid on the side if we combined our abilities. He's the kind of guy that can turn his hand to most things and, when he does, he's brilliant, a perfectionist, the most fastidious person I've ever known and especially when it comes to vehicles.

'Drew,' he said one day, 'you've got a knack of finding old cars, haven't you?'

'Yep. Throw me into a village anywhere and I'll do it.'

In those days there were a lot of old cars knocking about so we started driving around to see what we could come up with. We'd pick an area, Llan Ffestiniog for example, and drive up every side road, lane and dead end. What we came across was insane. Over a period, we found two right-hand-drive Type 34 razor-edge Karmann Ghias, and a 21-window right-hand-drive split-screen van. We found a Porsche 914 two-litre, a 356B as well as a 1974 Carrera Targa with a one digit, three-letter number plate and paid only £3,000 for it.

One of the best was a bay-window VW camper van I spotted while I was out and about working with Gordon Stewart. All I clocked was the pop-up roof behind a hedge, but I noted where it was and that weekend me and Clive drove over. We knocked on the door and asked the owner if he was interested in selling. It was a green and white Westfalia conversion, one of the first 1.7-litre fuel-injected models; solid but scruffy, and had clearly been lying for a couple of years. The owner told us it didn't start due to some recurring problem he hadn't been able to fathom. Clive got underneath, rummaged around for no more than 30 seconds then slid out and told me to buy it. I went to see the owner and said that if he had the V5 we'd take the van.

'It doesn't start,' he said. 'How are you going to get it out of here?'

'We'll give it a go,' I said. 'How much do you want for it?'

He took a moment to consider then came back with a figure of 500 quid.

I offered £400, he agreed, so I gave him the cash, signed the V5 and told Clive it was ours now.

'Great,' he said, then slid back underneath and came out another 30 seconds later. He told me it was only the fuel line and all he had to do was reattach it. He got in the cab, turned the key and the van started.

So, I love VWs and I'd righted a wrong with Holty and felt much better for doing it. Over the weekend I got most of the stuff from Carmarthen onto the website and met up with T to go to Cambridgeshire the following Monday.

He asked me how the book was going and I told him I'd managed a couple of chapters.

'Really?' he said. 'That's not bad, the last time we talked you had no idea where to begin.'

'Piccadilly Woods,' I said. 'I took your advice, went up there the other day, but you can't get in. The old fields have been fenced off so there's no way down from the top and you can't get past the houses at the bottom.

'I'll send my drone up,' he said. 'See if anything's down there.' We drove on for a bit, then he said: 'So, is it an autobiography?'

'Partly. I've been writing about the chapel, trying to get across the state it was in when I bought it.'

'Right,' he said. 'If it was a horse, you'd have shot it.'

'Where're we going exactly?' I said. I'd yet to look at the call-sheet.

'Ely, then Duxford. We're at Arabesque Antiques on Thursday.'

That all sounded good, although Arabesque might be a little expensive. It's run by Peter Whipps, a dealer I've known for years who had a stand next to mine in a warehouse emporium in Tetbury, Gloucestershire. Mine's long gone but his is still there, though we were meeting at his warehouse facility in the Midlands.

Ely was the first port of call, however, which involved a long cross-country drive from North Wales. 'Am I in the book?' T asked me.

'Do you want to be?'

'Not really. What's there to say, except we've known each other since we were kids in Glan Conwy?'

'There's plenty to say,' I told him. 'I could tell them your real name or how you're a vegetarian and all you eat is beige porridge wrapped in goat's cheese.'

'You're forgetting the Guinness.'

'Then there's your moniker: The Prince of Darkness.'

'My mum coined that,' he said. 'My superpower was sleep.'

'I remember. We'd roll out of the pub on Friday night and nobody could rouse you until half-time in the football on Saturday.'

We still had some distance to go and soon fell into the kind of comfortable silence born of a 40-year friendship.

I remember first seeing T as I cycled down to the bus stop in Glan Conwy. I was eight years old, riding the Raleigh Chopper I'd wanted for ages. That was the bike to have in 1978 but my parents couldn't afford to get me a new one. Instead my dad found a broken one and between us we took it apart and he resprayed it black – most choppers were orange but black was the colour I wanted. I'd taken the mudguards off, had a whip aerial on the back and only a back brake because I thought front brakes looked stupid. Black is still my thing; designs change and I've moved on from bicycles to cars but it's always been black for me.

CHAPTER 4

The bus stop was where the local kids hung out and one of my mates was talking to another lad riding an orange Raleigh Chopper. He'd just moved from Holyhead to Glan Conwy because his dad was a detective inspector who'd moved to the local station. I liked T immediately. Funny as fuck at eight years old, we hit it off right away. He became part of the gang that I mentioned before, only it had expanded now to include Glyn, Stephen Campbell, as well as Olly, Richard and Peter, and not forgetting Geraint Wellies. We called him that because he always wore welly boots. We were a gaggle of horrible little spotty fuckers who'd go setting fire to things, scrumping apples, letting car tyres down and riding through people's gardens. T was a skinny runt; he only put weight on after drinking too much beer. He was the year above me in school, but we were mates from that day at the bus stop. His surname is Tee, so we lengthened it to Teabag then shortened it to T and that's how he's been known ever since. He's the kind of guy who endears himself to everyone; my mother and grandmother loved him.

I'd like to be able to say we were golden children, but we were right little twats, always trying to get hold of cigarettes and finding dirty mags in hedges. We played at being in the Brixton riots, a bunch of skin-headed mods who were into the second wave of the ska scene with bands like The Specials and Madness. I was so into them; my dad painted the Madness M with Chas Smash dancing as a mural on my bedroom wall; it was brilliant. We grew up in a time when our parents kicked us out at nine o'clock in the morning and told us not to come back until teatime. I loved it. We had an absolute riot and our friendship only got stronger.

It wasn't all bliss, though. I'm not as thick-skinned as I might come across. After a couple of traumatic teenage moments, I started having panic attacks while I was in technical college, which was part of the YTS scheme when I worked for Gordon Stewart. I'd been going out with this girl called Emma, my first real proper love. It lasted about a year before she dumped me. It was unceremonious, I mean really. She dropped me from a very great height, probably because I didn't fit in with her social circle. Maybe that's why being accepted by the antiques trade (which is a tight-knit, often very snobby community) has been so important to me. Even as a kid, acceptance was something I think I yearned for, and it hurt like hell when Emma ditched me.

I tried to get over it by throwing myself into the rebuild of my first car, a Morris Minor two-door, which I bought in 1985 when I was only 15. It took a couple of years and when it was finished it didn't have any seat belts. I'd put massive 'Carlos Fandango' wheels on the back and a bucket seat which wasn't bolted to the floor properly. There was a tiny steering wheel with no horn and the first time I took it for a proper run was across the valley to see Chris Holt with T. It was raining hard and the road pretty slick when we came around the other side of the valley. The car was going really well, then these lads passed us in a MK II Ford Escort and I remember thinking, Fucking hell, I'm having them. I stamped on the accelerator pedal, caught them up and tried to overtake but the car skidded sideways before properly rolling over. Amazingly, we didn't have so much as a scratch. Later, T told me he knew exactly how many times we had rolled because the beanie hat he wore back then kept disappearing and reappearing. Two and a half times in all. We should've been dead, because the roof caved in, the back window was gone and the engine was still running. I could smell petrol and when I looked over my shoulder I saw that the fuel tank was leaking and petrol was filling up the roof. Instinct must've kicked in because I immediately turned the ignition off, got myself out and kicked in T's window. A man and his kids pulled up in their car after they saw what happened and drove us to T's parents' house, telling us it was like watching something from the telly.

Neither of us had been injured physically, but I had a delayed reaction. A couple of days after the crash I was at work in the cement shed when I started to feel sort of tingly and out of body. It was really odd. I couldn't understand what was going on. Suddenly I couldn't cope and I had no idea what was happening. It was very scary and it was only much later that I realised it was trauma, which had started with the breakup from Emma and then the car crash. But I didn't know it then. I was working on a piece of glass when something just welled up inside me. I couldn't breathe. I was trembling. I had this weird feeling of panic. I didn't know what to do; it got worse and worse, I started to hyperventilate, so I went outside to get some air. Gordon took one look and told me to go home. Someone gave me a lift and, when I got to the house, I told my father I was feeling really weird and couldn't understand what was happening.

'You're just mental,' he said.

Right, brilliant. That's really going to help. I don't know why I bothered to tell him.

I managed to calm myself down and, after a couple of days, I seemed to be OK. But as time went on it kept happening. I was at a loss. There was no internet to look things up on and I didn't want to go to the doctor and tell him what I was feeling because I really didn't know myself. How could I say that one minute I was alright and the next I felt like I was going to die? No doctor would understand that, not in the 1980s. So, I didn't see anyone, I just tried to deal with it myself and it took me years to figure out what was happening. I was suffering from anxiety and these were panic attacks. It began with my girlfriend and was exacerbated by rolling the car; two major disturbances that followed one right after the other.

That was 33 years ago and I still suffer from them today. When an attack hits I have to meter it through until I'm over it. I understand what's going on but it's debilitating and can completely stop you in your tracks. I'm not a weak man. I've had to deal with all kinds of setbacks, but when a panic attack hits, it can knock me right on my arse.

It's hard to identify exactly what sets it off; it can be all sorts of things, and some that creep up on you when you least expect it. Being around too many people can do it, being pulled this way and that either in business or emotionally. I think part of the attraction of buying the chapel was the remote location, which meant I'd be able to shut myself away and get on with it. I did that for years, but I still suffered from panic attacks and sometimes they'd hit when I was on the chapel roof and that was a bit scary. There was no one around to see what I was going through, though, and I didn't talk about it to anyone because I didn't want anyone to judge me. It took another ten years before I went to the doctor, and by then the world was a different place entirely. Men had finally started to talk about things that affected them, and mental health was no longer taboo. The doctor knew what was going on and was very sympathetic. Initially, she prescribed some drugs and taught me breathing exercises and different coping mechanisms.

Quite a few of my friends have suffered similarly and most of them have no clue what's going on. Rather than feeling ashamed now, I can explain what's happening and help them get through it. A close friend started having attacks about a year ago; she called me up and I just told her we'd stay on the phone until it was sorted. Panic attacks are not something I ever expected to suffer from, but they're part of my life, and I've learned to live with them. It's not easy but at least now there's no stigma attached and that makes talking about it much less difficult.

CHAPTER 5

LIFE, LOVE AND LOWS

With my previous girlfriend having left, I spent the years between 25 and 29 with Blue, my beloved collie, working on the church, and I was as happy as I've ever been. Other girlfriends came and went, but the only residents were the two of us. Slowly but surely, I realised the dream I'd envisioned when I first went up there with Andy. I created something out of the chapel house and, when it was complete, I let it out and moved into the derelict two-storey stable block. Gradually that morphed into a very nice holiday cottage that was so popular, by the time I stopped renting it out, it was occupied for 50 weeks of the year.

So, the house was done and that was followed by the chapel. I'd turned 28 by now and had two sets of paying tenants. Back to basics again, I moved into the chapel and slept on an old mattress. Every day after work, I'd be up on the roof working, and every day this same girl would drive by in a white VW Golf and beep the horn at me. I was very fit back then, thin and muscular: she must've liked what she saw.

One night I fancied some company so I went down to the local pub. As I walked in, I saw the girl from the Golf sitting in a corner with her mates. I found out her name was Kate and she was half-Irish. We got talking, one thing led to another and a few months after we started seeing each other I found out she was pregnant. A year older than me, she already had two boys and it came as a massive shock because I never had any thoughts about having children – it wasn't part of the plan.

I had to think logistics, though, and with the chapel house and stable block finished, I told Kate I'd ask the tenants to vacate and we'd move in. I liked her sons, both good lads, so it wouldn't be a problem. Decision made, a few weeks later we went for a scan at Bodelwyddan Hospital on the other side of Abergele. By now I was into the idea of fatherhood and looking forward to a way of life I'd not even contemplated. But something changed in Kate and the plans went right out the window.

These days, my son Tom works in the shop during the summer and he plans to go into the auctioneering business when he finishes his degree. We have a brilliant relationship but it's one I had to fight for. All those years ago when Kate told me she was pregnant we'd only been together six months and that's too short a time to really get to know someone you might spend the rest of your life with. I was still in shock the day we went for the scan, wondering how I was going to pull it together. It was daunting, but at the same time I was up for it. Now this had happened, all I wanted to do was be a good father. I didn't get the chance, though. Far from moving in together, by the time Tom was born, his mother and I weren't even seeing each other. For various reasons, the relationship broke down before it ever began, but I made sure I was at the birth, conscious that it might not be something I'd experience again. I remember just hoping there would be nothing wrong with him and, thankfully, there wasn't. He was fit and healthy, and we named him Tom James Hamilton-Pritchard, which was a combination of his mother's name and mine. Tom was my grandfather on my mother's side who fought in the Second World War. Back home in Wales afterwards, he was reunited with my grandmother 'Nin' only to drop dead in the kitchen of a brain aneurysm. Nin never married again; for 50 years she remained true to his memory, and that was something I really respected. A formidable, wonderful woman who was always 'Nin' because I couldn't pronounce 'Nainy' (what we call grandmothers in North Wales) when I was a young child. Five foot of fury, she used to 'force-feed' T whenever he came round, because he was so thin and pasty. Nin was a massive influence on my life; it's not exaggerating to say she shaped it.

After Tom was born, communication between me and his mother was non-existent. She'd gone from being the person I was going to share my life with to someone else. I was 29 and still working from the partitioned inspection pit underneath my dad's garage. In that tiny space I was restoring stained glass and stripping doors, as well as selling old fireplaces and windows. I had a lean-to shed at the bottom of the garden to store stuff and a little sign on the road that said 'Stained Glass – Architectural Antiques'. Things between me and Kate had completely broken down; Tom was five months old and I was fighting for the right to see him. I was living in the chapel and driving to my parents' house for work.

Looking back, I let that situation go on far too long, because years before my relationship with my father had broken down completely. It was one of those things that just happened. There was no single event to spark it off – it was just a gradual deterioration that I've never been able to get to the bottom of. Initially he really did encourage me, but the more I got into the business of antiques the more estranged we seemed to become. I didn't understand it then and I still don't now.

I used to work for him cutting log signs all day on a Saturday. We had a huge circular saw with no guard on it; a massive thing, it was fucking dangerous. A 60cm-diameter blade with teeth the size of a pair of adult thumbs, I'd use it to cut planks of yew for house names he'd sign-write for customers. I'd work until I was knackered, cutting and shaping, sanding the wood and varnishing. That saw was lethal, there's no way I'd go anywhere near it now and I was only 11 years old. Every Saturday and all through the summer holidays I'd work until I dropped, yet it felt like all he did was have a go at me.

I haven't seen him in 16 years. I see my mum all the time and she reckons all he talks about is how he wants to see me. I've tried to do that over the years, but we're at each other's throat within about thirty seconds of meeting. I think he believes I don't know anything that he didn't teach me, but the truth is I taught myself. It's a tragedy what's happened between us. I think he's an amazing man; he can play 13 different instruments and is a brilliant fine artist. He's completely self-taught in everything he does. I just wish he could acknowledge the same in me.

By this time my relationship with Kate was well and truly over. The deterioration began with the scan at the hospital, and it seemed to finish before it ever really got started. But I had a son, and within six months of him being born I met Rebecca.

I was in the workshop at my parents' house working with Darren restoring some glass, and the only natural light was the head-height window. I was taking a break when this knackered old Volvo 940 estate turned up, the driver's door opened and this woman got out with razor-cut peroxide hair. She was wearing a big baggy jumper, a pair of skin-tight black leather trousers and a pair of biker-style jackboots. As soon as I saw her I turned to Darren and said, 'I'm going to marry her.'

I went out to see what she wanted and she told me she'd bought a 40-acre farm near Betws-y-Coed and needed some shutters for the windows on the farmhouse. I didn't have anything like that, but I fancied the pants off her, so I showed her a few shitty old doors just to keep the conversation going. I found out later she was a few years older than me, but she didn't look her age, in fact she looked way younger than I did. Determined to see her again, I took a phone number and told her I'd find what she wanted.

A few weeks later I phoned her up and told her I'd located the stuff and would bring it out to the farm. By then I was driving a Jeep Cherokee, which was the first modern car I'd ever owned. When I found out I was going to be a dad, I thought I'd better have a sensible car, so I bought a four-litre, manual, left-hand-drive Jeep that did about three miles to the gallon. After loading the shutters and other bits and bobs I'd picked up, I put my last 20 quid's worth of fuel in the tank and drove out to her place at Betws-y-Coed. I'm not joking; that's the only money I had. I was skint now, completely. I had a mortgage to pay and didn't know how I was going to do it. Every penny I earned I spent on the chapel. If I made 50 quid, I didn't think about feeding myself, I bought roof slates or floor tiles. When I bought the place, I'd had a vision of what it would be, and if I spent 400 quid, I knew I'd be adding £4,000.

When I got to Rebecca's place, bizarrely, her mum and sister were there and we sat down and had a chat; I discovered she was divorced with two young daughters. A few weeks later she came over to the chapel and we spent the weekend together and that was pretty much the two of us from then on.

Six months after that first weekend with Rebecca, I moved to her farm in Betws-y-Coed, which was still a work-in-progress. What I loved about her was the can-do, no-fear attitude she always had: for Bec there was no such thing as an insurmountable obstacle. Spread over 43 acres was the farmhouse, campsite and holiday cottage, plus a B&B as well as two caravans. She'd taken on the project all by herself while trying to bring up two young children. I helped her do the place up and gradually it began to come together. What I'd told Darren that morning turned out to be true. I did marry her and she got involved with the business. Her daughters eventually changed their surname to mine and effectively became my children.

The next few years sucked the life right out of me. Whatever I tried to do for my son Tom, it seemed I was thwarted. I wanted him to go to a decent school, one I could afford to pay for, and it took a huge amount of effort and emotion just to get agreement for that to happen. I never said anything to Tom, whatever issues go on between parents should be kept well away from the children. Suffice to say, I'll do anything I can to support Fathers 4 Justice. That whole period was a real low point in my life and, unfortunately, it was to be repeated in terms of my relationship with Rebecca. The difference this time, though, was that what happened between us was entirely my fault, and I take full responsibility for it. People drift apart, and there are a lot of factors involved, one of which is not spending enough quality time together, and that was certainly the case with us. The travelling I have to continually do meant I was often away from home, which inevitably put pressure on the relationship, but the way it unravelled wasn't necessary. It could have been done in a much more grown-up manner, but I behaved like an idiot. I let the fact that nobody seemed to be saying 'no' to me any more go completely to my head, albeit only for a brief moment. It's not something I'm proud of and I regret my actions bitterly, but with hindsight we *were* growing apart and the decision to split was the right one.

By the time our marriage was over we'd long since moved from the farm at Betws-y-Coed to the converted chapel in the Conwy Valley. The hassle of running a B&B and campsite had taken its toll on both of us and we were fed up of people not treating the place with any respect. For some reason the customers didn't seem to care about their surroundings; they would try to cut down trees for campfires and leave litter all over the place; it was incredibly frustrating. Camp grounds have to be appealing and it was just too much work constantly clearing up after the guests. We'd be up at the crack of dawn and never in bed before midnight and every day just seemed to run into the next.

Once we moved on from Betws-y-Coed, things should have been great and for a while they were: we had a fantastic place to live, with everything I'd envisaged when I first bought the chapel having been completed. It wasn't just the buildings; I'd bought more land so there was a massive garden where I could take a day to mow the lawn if I wanted. I was around for the school run and I had all my old cars to mess about with. But by now the TV show was becoming pretty successful and, as a result, we were filming more and more episodes and that meant I started to be away more than I was at home.

Business was great, and not just because of the show: in those days I had almost a floor of my own at Liberty in London, which was pretty much unheard of. It took up so much time that we leased a flat in Chelsea so Rebecca could manage that part of the business. We would both be home most weekends, but that was the only real time we'd have together and I know I wasn't attentive enough. I didn't take care of our relationship. I loved being with the children, that was always great and I'd be there for them as much as I could, but problems started to arise between me and Rebecca. We both had a hell of a lot to do, with her in London and me filming, and trying to get back into the rhythm of dealing was getting ever more difficult. Initially, the show only took up 10 per cent of my time, but as the series grew more successful the demands increased and today it's more like 90.

That growth was exponential and so was the downward spiral in terms of my behaviour. By the time we got to series eight, I was on the road all the time, staying in a different hotel every night with nothing to do but hit the bar. I've never been one to shut myself away so, as I alluded to before, drinking started to become an issue. It was particularly bad at the weekends when I'd get stuck into the red wine, and that was the beginning of my downfall. The funny thing is I'd never been bothered about alcohol before. I didn't really start drinking at all until I was 29, it didn't interest me. I might have a couple of pints on a Friday night with the lads, but that was it. After we started making the show, though, I began to drink every night and for a while it was a little crazy; we were working hard during the day nailing every show, but come the evening it was a debacle, really. Almost overnight, I started drinking a lot of beer during the week and, come the weekend, I could open a bottle of red wine and ten minutes later it would be empty. I'd happily do another and sometimes start on a third and that was only the tip of the iceberg. Every Friday night, every Saturday and Sunday, I would neck bottles of red wine on my own and it did not go unnoticed.

Rebecca could see how it was beginning to get out of hand and it wasn't very long before she told me I needed to do something about it. I knew she was right, but I didn't want to listen. Her opinion no longer mattered because emotionally I'd already left the marriage. I was there in body but not much else and it was becoming apparent to everyone. My heart was no longer in it. I was unhappy and I don't know why. I loved the house and I loved the children, but things were changing in other parts of my life and I was trying to make the adjustment. I was no longer just an antique dealer. I had a TV show, and trying to balance the time and commitment between the two wasn't easy. The bottom line was I was unhappy in both my marriage and the business. It felt like the show was taking over and I was getting pulled further and further away from the day-to-day dealing. Rebecca and I argued about it. I was spread too thin and that creates a feeling of being out of control, which wasn't helped by the panic attacks. The arguments grew more frequent and heated and it was my fault. I was changing, becoming a different person, and the amount of red wine I was drinking had a profound effect on who that person turned out to be.

I tried to keep tabs on it while we were working but, as I said above, for a while at least, it did get a little out of hand. I remember one day when we finished filming, I got to the hotel before the crew as they had to pack up all the equipment and I wanted to get stock uploaded to the website. By this time, we were staying in decent hotels and this was a really swanky place. I hit the bar an hour before T got there and, when he walked in, I was already into a third or fourth pint. Dinner didn't happen, and by half-seven I was so hammered he had to walk me up the stairs, pour me into my room and point me towards the bed.

I always complied with the 12-hour ban on drinking in the run up to filming, but it carried on like that for a while. I made the call-sheet every day and did what I was being paid to do. When we started to go abroad it was harder. An away day in a different country with new people to meet and new places to see, it was a licence to drink and my life became a swirl of filming and booze then going home to a place I didn't want to be.

Somewhere in the middle of all that I made a massive mistake. I got involved with another woman and that really wasn't good for me. I knew I was messing up badly but that didn't stop me. I was out of control. I was hurting people I didn't want to hurt and it took far too long for the penny to drop. By the time it did, in 2016, my relationship with Rebecca was beyond repair, as it was abundantly clear I didn't want to be there. I knew I couldn't allow it to go on, so I got myself together enough to sit down with her and tell her I wanted a divorce.

'Fine,' she said. 'Me too.'

That conversation should've allowed me the space to think so the two of us could do what had to be done in a grown-up way, but it wasn't like that. Instead of calming me down, it was as if someone had taken the shackles off. I didn't have to pretend any more. I didn't have to be someone

I didn't want to be. I went wild, and I mean absolutely crazy. I began to party like there was no tomorrow. I had money in my pocket and I was on my own again. In a single month I spent £18,000 on hotel bills, hanging out with all sorts of people I really should've avoided. I was hammering it badly, drinking at least three bottles of red wine a night and beginning to make myself ill. It got so bad that eventually I went to the doctor, and he did a liver and kidney test to find out the kind of damage I was doing. When the results came in, he sat me down and told me that I would die if I didn't stop drinking immediately. I don't know whether I believed him or not. I probably thought he was exaggerating.

'Fine,' I said. 'Right, I'll pack it in then. I can do that, no problem.' But I didn't. I wasn't an alcoholic. I didn't need AA meetings or rehab. I *wanted* to drink; I didn't have to. I didn't stop. I pushed what had been said to the back of my mind and carried on just as before. That went on for a few more months, then, suddenly, something clicked and I knew I had to stop. I didn't pack it in altogether, but I immediately quit the red wine. That was my poison, it's what changed my behaviour, so I knocked it on the head and stopped partying every night.

With the consumption of red wine in check, I could see what this crazy lifestyle had done to me. I'd lost my house, my wife and my children. I was so out of it most of the time my buying instincts were all over the place and I nearly lost my business as well. The whole period is still a haze.

There are weeks that I can't recall and I don't know if that was caused by the drink or if I just don't want to remember what happened. It's as if it was happening to someone else where the timeline makes no sense, and I can't remember half the things people tell me I got up to. Drinking too much also brought on panic attacks – it was a real mess.

I hate myself for allowing the situation to get out of hand, and I bitterly regret the hurt I caused to Rebecca. To this day I don't have any idea why I behaved as I did. I have no real idea what made me start drinking so much. I have no idea why I went off with another woman or why I spent so much money on stuff that wasn't good for me. I can't explain why I caused so much pain to the people that were closest to me. I look in the mirror and have no answer to the questions I ask myself. It was just something that happened.

But self-destruction had run its course and I was able to save the business. Trade was crap – so bad, in fact, I was using my savings to pay the ten grand I had to shell out every month in wages. I was trying to make sense of the fact we weren't taking any money and it hit me when I walked into the warehouse one day and saw the quality of the stock. I had no idea how so much rubbish had got there and nobody could understand what was going on. When I took a moment to think it through, the answer was obvious. I'd been buying online while shit-faced on red wine and the result was an inventory we'd never get rid of.

It brought me up short and I started to sort things out both professionally and personally. I got back to buying the right stock and the business began to pick up again. At the same time, Rebecca and I went through the divorce proceedings. I knew I was at fault so I didn't want to fight her on anything. I basically told her she could have whatever she wanted and that included the chapel, which was already on the market with an asking price of £895,000. I remember standing up in court and telling her she could have it all. I wasn't going to contest anything. We had no mortgage and I was entitled to half the value of the marital home but I felt total guilt so I just gave it to her. The only thing she didn't take were my cars. She could have, they were part of our possessions, but she didn't seem to want them. Worth a lot of money at that time, there were 13 sports and vintage cars, and I still don't know why she left them. I bought her out of the business (which was a considerable sum in cash) and gave her an alimony settlement. It took months to sort out, a very difficult period for both of us, and during it all we were still filming the TV series.

Single again, I was on my uppers completely. Having had a stack of money in the bank, I had barely anything to my name now. I was out of the chapel and had to sell a car so I had enough cash to put a small deposit on a house in Conwy. That was it, though, an empty house where I had nothing but a single Howard sofa in front of the fire and

Enzo my faithful Jack Russell. For weeks he and I ate out of the same can and he curled up with me on that sofa.

I was still pretty unaware just how bad my behaviour had become; it was only much later that I realised how big an idiot I'd actually been. Maybe deep down somewhere there's a big red self-destruct button that's begging to be pressed and every so often I have to oblige it. I try to tell myself that it had no effect on the TV, but that's not true. Although I never missed a call, I know if I'd been in a better space, we would have made a better show.

To write it down like this is cathartic, but it's also pretty disturbing. Somehow, I got through it, and the irony is that during that 'blizzard' period, we had some of the best viewing figures we've ever achieved. It was rock 'n' roll and nobody was saying 'no' to me. I'd walk into a hotel and be recognised by the staff and there was nothing they couldn't do to make my stay more comfortable. A free upgrade on the room, Mr Pritchard? Sure. A bottle of champagne, Mr Pritchard? Why not? Anything I wanted they gave me. It was intoxicating and I immersed myself in the lifestyle completely.

The fact there was no rhyme or reason to any of it still bothers me. The way it just crept up with no warning is a worry, because if it happened once it can happen again. If I was able to see a sequence of events that led up to the blow-out, I know I'd be able to avoid it. But I can't. There is no point in time where I can say: That happened, and, as a result I did this, or X led to Y and so on.

CHAPTER 5

Anyway, it was all over thankfully, and I had to begin again. This time was different, though; there was no Rebecca to help me, I'd have to do it on my own. Now I'm out the other side I regret what happened and the way it happened, but I don't regret the decision to leave the marriage because it had run its course for both of us. Instead of getting hammered every night to mask my unhappiness, though, I should've acknowledged it for what it was and sat down with Rebecca much sooner.

CHAPTER 6

BEWARE OF
THE DOG

With no let-up in the TV shooting schedule, T and I spent a few days in Cambridgeshire in early August 2019 on a variety of calls, one of which was the Duxford Aviation Society Museum, which is right up there with the V&A in terms of a fantastic experience. As soon as I found out Concorde was there, I knew I had to have something from the period. That aircraft is iconic, spectacular in both engineering and design. It first flew in 1969 and, to this day, there hasn't been a better-looking commercial plane. At Duxford I was fortunate enough to take the pilot's seat, and to be able to sit in a place of such authority completely blew my mind.

Our guide for the day was a wonderful man called David who is chair of the DAS. I asked him if there were any items of memorabilia left from the plane, an ashtray or something, maybe. He told me all the stuff like that was long gone, but he did think he'd be able to come up with something. In the holding area he went through a set of drawers and found an unused pair of mechanic's overalls with 'CONCORDE' printed on the back. They were amazing: I knew I could sell them all day long and parted with 200 quid. We picked up four BOAC shoulder bags for twenty-five quid apiece; retro-looking, they'd either been for the cabin crew or first-class freebies. There was a lot of other stuff to look through and I found an original blueprint for a Lancaster bomber that took my breath away. 'Look at this, T,' I said. 'Once it's framed, I know collectors who'll be all over it.'

Something else caught my eye, a navigator's seat that I was sure came out of a bomber. 'What's this, David?' I said.

'I'm not sure.' He inspected the seat very carefully. 'The label says Haynes, and that might be from a test. I don't think it's actually from an operational bomber. By the look of it, it's more likely to be an engineer's seat from a test aircraft.'

Even so, there was something about it. 'How much d'you want for it?' I said.

'Three hundred.'

'I tell you what; it's not exactly what I thought it was – how about two-fifty?'

'That's fine,' he said, and we shook on it.

Prior to Duxford, we'd filmed from the spire of Ely Cathedral, T and I schlepping up so many steps my knees were screwed and I thought I was going to die of a heart attack. Ely is magnificent, a work of art in terms of architecture and built on the site of a church that dates back to AD 672. Again, our guide was called David and he told us the stone had been quarried at Barnack and bought from Peterborough Abbey. I could see elements of Purbeck marble from the fossil beds down in Dorset, as well as an ancient building material they call clunch, which is a chalky limestone only found in Normandy and the east of England. I was here to buy as well as study the architecture, though, and spotted something that stopped my breath. Two seven-foot wooden pews; one was very badly damaged but the other was complete and it was a belter.

'Is that Gilbert Scott?' I asked David.

'It is,' he said. 'We're very proud to have it.'

No wonder. This was a find-and-a-half, a pew from the Aesthetic/Gothic-style restoration and remodel of Ely by George Gilbert Scott, a prolific 'Revival' architect of the day. I knew his work, but what was more important to me was that the pew had been completed in the style of A.W.N. Pugin. To me, Pugin is pretty much God and I'd come across him when I began to appreciate the stained glass wrought by William Morris. I had to have this; it was just one of those pieces you never find and it wouldn't go to the shop or website. I wanted it for the house I knew I would buy as soon as I found it. Ever since I left the chapel, I've had the house I want in my head only – I've yet to actually locate it. Despite that, I'm already filling the rooms with various items I'll never sell, and the Gilbert

Scott pew was one of them. I asked David how much he wanted for it.

'We couldn't let it go for less than a thousand.'

'I'll give you a thousand,' I said. 'How about two hundred for the one that's broken?'

'Alright,' he said. 'We can do that.'

I'd been to Ely once before as a kid. Back then, however, I knew nothing of the history and that's what the antiques business is all about. You learn in steps; a little bit of this, a little bit of that, and as the years go by you amass a great deal of knowledge. I've said it before, but that's what grabbed me when I began to read the catalogues and Lyle books Mum and Dad had around the house. I mentioned them before, but I'm not quite sure I got across just how important they were to me and how much time I actually spent studying. Unlike schoolwork, where I couldn't see the point, I devoured every Lyle and catalogue I could get my hands on. They excited me then and they still excite me today because you can never learn enough, there's always something else going on. Knowledge is critical, not just so you have a handle on what an item is worth, but for the appreciation of the artistry and history. There's a soul to this business and I can't reiterate enough just how much that means to me. I take what I do very seriously. I still pinch myself when I think how far I've come in terms of understanding and appreciation.

I thought back to what T had said about flying a drone over Piccadilly Woods. There's no reason why the remnants of those old cars shouldn't be back there. It would've been hard to clear them from the farmland above and the builders of the housing estate completely ignored them. The idea that some bits and pieces might still be there really excites me because I relate the time when I saw cars floating in the air with the Gilbert Scott restoration at Ely Cathedral. Links in a chain; you understand *this* then you learn about *that* and, over time, those snippets of information start meshing together. One day you might be looking at nineteenth-century English furniture, and the day after that Georgian chimneypieces. You see a pattern form in terms of when things were made and what was in the mind of the people that made them.

Not all dealers have that level of appreciation; some are just there to turn a profit. One who does, though, is Peter Whipps, who we filmed with after a night at the Belfry, where we'd stopped on the way from Cambridgeshire. Though I hate golf with a passion, the Belfry makes a good burger, so I ate one of those then spent the evening loading more stuff onto the website, including the chest of drawers I'd bought from Sir James Shuckburgh. Kevin had completed the work and it looked fantastic. I stayed up late making sure everything had been taken care of, so I wasn't too bothered when I got a call telling me filming had been delayed in the morning.

Peter rents space from the Dugdale Estate in Warwickshire, a couple of barns next door to a lovely old Tudor farmhouse that's rented by a lady called June who keeps St Bernard dogs. The crew were due to get there before T and I showed up in the van and first on scene was Simon Jolly. He's the sound man and has been with us since the very first TV show; he's the third Salvage Hunter along with T and me. He's brilliant at his job and his being first on set wasn't unusual, but he had no idea the farmhouse didn't belong to Peter.

'What's up?' I said when the director phoned me. 'Why the delay?'

'It's Simon. Anna just took him to A&E.'

I was still in bed, adding yet more items we'd bought and restored to the website.

'He's been bitten by a dog. Peter Whipps found him; the dog almost took his hand off.'

'Is he OK?'

'I don't know. They've taken him to have an X-ray.'

'How did a dog manage to bite him?'

'He thought the farmhouse was Peter's. The dogs were loose and he stuck his hand over the fence to stroke them.'

Fucking idiot, the first thing I saw when we pulled up in the van later was a sign on the farmhouse gate. BEWARE OF THE DOG. ENTER AT YOUR OWN RISK. I could see two bloody great St Bernards locked up in a cage and they were barking at me. When Simon got there, they'd been loose and he'd been daft enough to reach over the gate. Not only that, he'd locked his keys in his van and we were waiting for the AA. When Anna, the assistant producer, brought him back from hospital with his hand all bandaged up, he looked pale and shocked and showed me a photo of the wound on his phone. A massive great gash across the top of his wrist, it looked as if the hand was about to fall off. Of course, I gave him all the sympathy I could muster.

'You didn't see the sign then?' I said to him.

'No.'

'It's right there on the farmhouse gate.'

'Yeah, but the dogs were friendly.'

'Evidently.' I nodded to the mass of bandage.

'No, I mean they were wagging their tails and everything. This is a dog-friendly show. I thought the dogs were Peter's; I didn't think anything of it.'

'How many were there?'

'Four.'

'Well, if it was going to happen to someone, it was going to happen to you. Four massive dogs and you put your hand in?'

He was looking sheepish. 'Well, no. I said hello first.'

'Oh yeah, cos dogs can understand that, can't they?'

I did feel for him, of course I did; but it was a stupid thing to do and the crew were taking the piss. Steve, the lead cameraman, located an advert for Jollyes Dog Food on the net which he immediately forwarded to Simon.

With Simon out of action for the day, we had to wait for another sound man but also the AA. In the meantime, T and

I took a look around the studio where Peter photographs his stock. He's only been selling online for about six years, prior to that he relied on people coming out here or visiting the shop in Tetbury. He's been in the business twenty-odd years, starting out in what we call 'Country' furniture, exemplified by the kind of untouched cupboards and cabinetry you see in old English country houses. After that he moved more into 'Original Paint', which are items that have been decorated. One of his mainstays is garden antiques and, as we walked in, a large terracotta urn caught my eye. I had a customer in mind with a particular set-up he wanted to exploit and I thought this might fit the bill exactly.

'So, it was you who found Simon then?' I said to Peter.

He nodded. 'The crew told me they'd be here between eight and half-past but he arrived before then. When I pulled up, there was blood everywhere.'

Peter's wife Dawn was making tea while the crew set up and Simon sat down to nurse his wounds and wait for the AA. Dawn is as much involved in the trade as her husband, having started a company called Arabesque Interiors years ago. Since then she's been a mural artist and worked on restoration with Peter, as well as designing interiors. Now she buys and sells twentieth-century paintings.

Peter had to make a couple of calls so T and I took a look at the stuff in his showroom, a really nice barn with a beamed pitch roof over a set of double glass doors that creates a feeling of light and space. He had some cracking stuff, including a George III washstand that had been dry-scraped to clear what was probably a dozen layers of paint. If you're lucky you can scrape a piece like that back to its original layer, but it takes a lot of man-hours. You might find unpainted pine in rustic pieces but not generally from those country houses. There the furniture was always painted: sometimes to enable a piece to fit with the room but sometimes it was just decorative. In the late eighteenth and early nineteenth century, country houses were flamboyant and whenever you find something like this you take a punt on whether you can take it back to the condition it should be. It's immensely time-consuming and costly but whoever worked on the washstand had done a great job.

Peter had another piece that looked freshly scraped, a George III cupboard that was missing its handles. I put it around 1780: good looking, well built with good proportions. Like most English cupboards of the period, it stood really well, with the kind of simplicity you don't find in European examples. I found a really handsome Regency Waterfall bookcase and Peter told me he'd already spent 600 quid on the dry-scrape and it barely looked like it had been touched.

'Where'd you get it?' I asked him.

He smiled a little wryly. 'I bought it in a sale. Someone had added a couple of drawers and it was catalogued as a kitchen dresser. I only paid four hundred quid for it.'

CHAPTER 6

It just goes to show that the salerooms don't always know what they've got. This was one of the best examples of a Regency Waterfall I'd seen. The form was excellent, and even with the cost of dry-scraping Peter would see an excellent profit.

He really does have a good eye. Standing against one wall was a great Welsh dresser in dark oak, the sort of piece I always look to buy. This one would probably be too expensive, but I did want a cabinet for an interior designer who was working on a house in Beverly Hills. That's the beauty of the website, since that Eureka moment with Rob Wilding 20 years ago, I've created a database that spans the globe. Peter's not been exploiting it for as long as I have, but he's one of the best architectural antique dealers in the country. He understands what he's looking at and loves things in the same condition as I do, which is pretty much untouched. Dry-scraping is a chore alright, but the result is worth it. Sometimes it's done with a very sharp chisel, sometimes something as simple as a two-pence piece. Peter's a purist; the way the stuff was displayed was clever and educated, it had a really good look that was reflected in the quality of each item.

He had a couple of urns set up on socles (which is the base they sit on). There was a pair of early-nineteenth-century stocks and a selection of glass cucumber straighteners. These were copies of originals that George Stephenson (of Stephenson's *Rocket*) had blown in his Northumberland factory. Like most Victorian inventors, Stephenson tried to adapt the natural world to his own design and had a thing about the curve in a cucumber. He wanted his to be straight so he had a competition with his neighbour to see who could grow the best one. He had the glass blown specifically with a hole in the top where a string was tied and the young cucumber attached to it. The glass was then hung in a greenhouse and as the cucumber grew it was shaped by the confines of the cylinder. Peter told us he'd found them in a derelict greenhouse in somebody's garden and now they were displayed in a hand-barrow made by William Woods of Taplow.

'How much do you want for them?' I asked him.

'The whole lot are up at fourteen hundred. I had a couple a few years ago but sold them and didn't think I'd see any more until I got the call about the greenhouse.'

That was too steep for me, so I took a closer look at the urns, which were Coade stone, the pinnacle of English terracotta. The name comes from Eleanor Coade, who was in the business of making garden statuary in the late eighteenth century. She created a process called Lithodipyra, the twice-firing of terracotta that was ground down so it could be poured into moulds to create neoclassical urns and statues. The designs were created by the cream of English sculptors, people like John Bacon, famous for his bust of George III in Oxford and Father Thames at Ham House near Richmond. If you walk across Westminster Bridge, you can see eight Bacon Coade stone urns on top of Somerset House. Eleanor Coade was a visionary; a businesswoman in the days when they were few and far between. She came from a family that were both wool merchants and weavers, though, so it was in her DNA. I checked out the Pulham urns that were Victorian from Suffolk, where James Pulham's company specialised in rock gardens and follies. They used terracotta and something they created called Pulhamite which had been inspired by Coade stone from the previous century.

We continued to look around and T spotted some Coalbrookdale cast-iron urns that were 'Naples' in design, meant to create an Italian feel. One other piece really stood out, a classic example of chinoiserie, a chest on a stand in black and gold; it was absolutely beautiful.

'Where's that from?' I asked Peter.

'Uttar Pradesh.'

'1850?'

'About then, yes. It's got the original key, the original folding stands so you can move it around. Lovely, isn't it?'

'It's a belter.' I opened the chest and it still had the original paint inside. This was the kind of thing you'd find in a stately home or country house; they're usually displayed in the hallway. Chinoiserie is a European style of decoration that mimics ancient Chinese and East Asian art. This one was textured; you could feel the way the decoration was raised and that made the chest even more interesting. He'd want two grand all day long and it was worth every penny, but there'd be no room to manoeuvre for me.

Outside, the AA man had arrived to try to get Simon's van open. A young buff guy, he looked like a red-haired Arnold Schwarzenegger. First, he tried to pick the lock, but that didn't work so he went around to the passenger side where Simon's keys were lying on the seat. The fob lay face up so he fetched some rubber wedges from his van and hammered them into the top of the door frame, then enlarged the space with a pump-up rubber balloon. There was just enough room to get a pair of metal rods inside and he spent the next five minutes trying to get at the fob. Finally, he managed to use the rods to press the button that popped the locks and the doors were open.

Job done, I joined Peter in the other barn where he kept the stuff he was waiting to restore, and this was decorative salvage at its finest. Windows, a pair of door surrounds he was going to turn into mirrors that would fetch between £8,000 and £10,000. I was considering two bronze wall lanterns from the eighteenth century and he was asking £900. They had a Greek key detail and a really crisp upside-down anthemion; that's decorative artwork from ancient Egypt that was adopted by the Greeks and highlighted again in eighteenth-century Europe. They were missing the glass and I was considering a reglaze in proper German mouth-blown, but that was really pricey. It's the sort of thing we used to do when we restored stuff for other dealers. I knew where to get the glass, what colour and style, but it was expensive and I doubted there would be much room left at the end. I decided to leave them for Peter to punt on to another dealer and turned my attention to a slim two-piece dresser/cabinet with a painted decorative finish.

'I do like this sort of thing,' I said. 'I know it's a bit whimsical but I fall for it every now and again.'

'It's pretty, isn't it?' Peter said. 'I only bought it two days ago. I really like the detail on the legs.'

I was thinking about the interior designer and the house in Beverly Hills. The cabinet was painted pine from the early twentieth century and I thought we might do quite well. I'd need Kevin to replace a run of cock-beading as well as a piece of architrave that would have to be manufactured and painted, but it was the only thing required by way of restoration. The cabinet looked like it might've been commissioned by an interior design company called Colefax & Fowler, who are still in business today. The paint was very good and, although it was English and early twentieth century, it looked like the style the French were creating back in the eighteenth.

'How much do I have to pay?'

'Eight-fifty,' Peter said.

I shook my head. 'Can't do that, not with the work. I'll give you seven hundred for it.'

He agreed to that and, with luck, I'd get £1,200 from the designer for the house in the USA. There wasn't that kind of room in the terracotta urn, though, I'd be lucky to see 100 quid profit. That said, there was nothing to be done to it either. It was English from around 1870 and would fit in the house I was thinking of perfectly. The house has various sets of double doors that open all the way through the ground floor and the urn would fit either outside on the approach or in the hallway. It came with a socle that looked 'associated' even though it wasn't the original. Associated is a term we use which means it looks as if the two pieces are meant to fit together or it's similar in age or maker.

'You're asking six-fifty?' I said.

'Yeah.'

'How about six?'

'Alright, I can do that.'

That was good, I knew I could move it on very quickly and there was no work to be done, maybe I'd see 150.

I've mentioned before that the very best antiques are those that strike an immediate emotional chord and there was one in particular I came across that just shouted 'history' at me. In about 2015, we were called to film a piece for the show at a castle on the Welsh/Cheshire border. T wasn't there; I was with Rob Black, who'd become a pretty good mate after our night out in west London. As it happened, it wasn't so much a castle as a turret, the last remaining section of what had been a massive, sprawling construction.

'Would you look at the place?' I said as we pulled up. 'Imagine living here, Rob, it's incredible.' It was beautiful, atmospheric, and I had a really good feeling about the day ahead. That feeling died the moment we walked through the door, however, because inside the place was awful. The owner was a man of vast means and absolutely no taste. He'd redone every single inch of the interior at great expense but the result was just appalling. God knows how much he'd spent; he had handmade rugs, curtains, wallpaper for every room and every bit of it was horrible. It was nothing like I'd expected; the guy had systematically ruined what had been a stunning house – it was a tour de force in bad taste.

I didn't tell him, of course, it was only my opinion and I might have been wrong, but I don't think so. He took us from room to room and it looked like it had been done by a Barbie doll with a tartan fetish. But he was a nice guy, so what could I do? We were filming and, no matter how bad a place might be, you can't tell someone they've got no taste. The owner was very proud and he was chatting away, but there was nothing there I'd put in my house. I was beginning to think this could turn out to be the shittiest call we'd ever made but we soldiered on in the hope of finding something. There was nothing inside I wanted, so I asked if we could look at the outbuildings.

He led us into the garden and, as we walked up the path, I clocked two marble pots just lying in the rosebed.

Ovaloid in form, I knew what they were despite the fact they were half-covered in brambles and had been used to toss cigarette butts in. Goose pimples broke out on my arms. The hairs went mad on the back of my neck. Fuck me, I thought. Two stone wine coolers, not a pair, but associated. One was full of sand, the other bits of rubbish and brimming with rainwater that soaked the fag butts into a mush of tobacco and paper. They were single-piece marble, like ovaloid sinks, one with a gadrooned body.

I didn't say anything because I still didn't quite believe what I was seeing. We were only just into the call and I decided I'd 'notice' them on the way back to the house, but Rob thought I'd missed them completely.

'Oi,' he said. 'Are you fucking blind, Pritchard? Good job you've got me here. You walked right past two wine coolers. What's wrong with you?'

I tried to shut him up with a look, but the owner of the house turned back to where Rob was pointing. I couldn't ignore the coolers now, so I asked the guy what he wanted for them.

'Huh!' he said. 'Those old things, I was going to chuck them in a skip. Give me two hundred quid and you can have them.' He had no idea what they were and he clearly didn't give a shit either. Dealer mentality kicked in and we shook hands on £100 apiece. Usually, if someone is seriously undervaluing something, I say so right away. I'm not in this business to rip people off, but this guy had all the money in the world and really didn't care about the wine coolers.

I had a gut feeling and already I knew there was no way I'd be selling them. I was pretty certain one was from the eighteenth century, but the one with the gadroon might be from a much earlier period.

'Tell me something,' I said to the owner of the house as he led the way to the outbuildings. 'This place is pretty old; I don't suppose there's any Roman involvement?'

'Oh, yeah,' he said. 'There used to be a building next door but it was demolished; some of the earthworks were Roman.'

'Did you find any bits and pieces?'

'Those two sinks you just bought. I've never had any use for them.'

Are you kidding me? Two hundred quid for the pair, I'd have paid two grand if he'd asked me. But he didn't. He knew where they came from so he must've had an idea they could be Roman. As we walked towards the outbuildings, Rob fell in alongside me. 'Fucking hell, Drew. Can you believe it?'

'I know,' I said. 'I clocked them as soon as we walked out the house. I didn't need you to tell me.'

'You're looking at thousands for them.'

'Maybe. I don't know. They're not for sale, Rob. Too interesting. I'm keeping them.'

I still have to pinch myself whenever I look at those wine coolers in my living room. The history, the years that have passed since anybody used them, just blows me away. You do not find Roman cellarettes lying around in people's gardens, but, somehow, I did. I've never actually had the age confirmed but I've shown them to some very knowledgeable dealer friends and they're all convinced the gadroon is Roman. I've had plenty of offers and I sell about 70 per cent of the stuff I buy to the trade, but there's no way I'm parting with the wine coolers.

CHAPTER 7

NOT FOR THE FAINT-HEARTED

As I said in the introduction, this is a business that's as exciting and diverse as the items we come across, but you have to fully embrace it and roll with those punches. It's varied enough that there are plenty of dealers who only deal with the trade. They don't sell to the public at all, and you see the same stuff passing from hand to hand in one long, continuous rotation. There's a joke among us that, if three antique dealers and a chair washed up on a desert island, all three would make a living.

I've mentioned how it used to be a closed shop but it's not like that any more. There are about forty or so dealers who think they're top of the tree and mixing with them is all about having the confidence to do so. That comes from the knowledge I've amassed over the years where I've had to learn to inhabit a lot of different worlds and deal with a lot of very wealthy people. Many are entitled, posh (for want of a better word), and being able to hold my own (which

I can) with them comes down to the first five seconds of meeting. I've had to learn to walk into very wealthy people's houses to talk about buying or restoring things that have been in their family for generations. That's something that took a little mastering because I left school with nothing and 'entitled' wealth can be intimidating to some people, but not me. That said, I've dealt with self-made men who can't even write their own name and have learned to make no distinction. I remember a day when I made one deal with a toothless scrap dealer, another with a billionaire Irish businessman and, finally, some drugged-up rock star who wanted to buy stained glass off me. I sell unusual things, which means unusual clients, and I've had to learn to live in that space along with them.

In the early days I made a point of watching people's nuances and got to be very good at understanding how to be around them. In this business you have to adapt to a given situation and learn how to handle egos. I don't care who anyone is or where they come from. If they have something I want to buy, I'll try to get it at the price that suits me. It's the same when they come to me. I know what I've got and how much it's worth and if you don't want to pay my price don't waste my time. I'm not being arsey. I just can't be bothered with bullshit. I do the TV shows because I want people to get involved and I'm happy to do as much as I can to assist the expansion of the antiques business.

It's not for the faint-hearted, though. You have to be prepared for the ups and downs; it's not some simple transition from hobby to business. The fact you're only making money if someone *wants* something and not if they have to have it can take its toll. Those who really do well are the people who fully comprehend that their particular take on the trade is bound to go in and out of fashion. It's a question of riding out the storms and surviving. My friend George at Brownrigg in Tetbury has a great eye and a great way of doing things. There's Spencer Swaffer in Arundel and Alex MacArthur in Rye. As far as I'm concerned, they're at the top of their own particular game and have been for a long time. I'm good friends with Russ and Mick of 17/21 up in York, as well as David Bedale and Will Fisher, all of whom are as good as anyone out there.

I've been near the very top of this trade, then dropped off only to climb back again, before dropping off a second time. It's like being on a seesaw: sometimes you're so high you're bouncing on the seat and others so low your arse is between your heels on the tarmac. I don't sell things people need, I sell what they want, and when money's tight that's the first thing to go out the window. By the time I was 38, back in 2008, I was worth about three and a half million quid with three good properties, a million quid's worth of antiques, a fleet of cars and three kids in private education. I'd converted the chapel into the most beautiful home and, businesswise, we were absolutely smashing it. I had a holiday place in Abersoch, along with a speedboat, even though I hate the sea. The first time I went out, we ran out of petrol and had to get towed in by another boat being sailed by people who actually knew what they were doing. I'm fine when it comes to engines on land, but I had no experience, and I really hate the water. Looking back, I have no idea why I bought the boat in the first place.

I'd also converted a Gothic church into a warehouse and showroom in Llandudno, and I had a massive warehouse in Glan Conwy, both of which were doing cracking business. Things were so good I took off for a couple of weeks, which is something I never do.

Buying that warehouse in Glan Conwy was a milestone, a purchase that changed the perception of my business but put a huge pressure on my resources. A disused garden centre, I bought it after driving past on a daily basis not long after Rebecca and I got married. It looked like it was rapidly going to rack and ruin, so one morning when I had a bit of time, I called in to see if it might be for sale. I was making money and had been looking for premises, so I thought I'd find out how the land lay. The doors were open and I could see a guy sweeping the floor, so I went over and introduced myself.

'This might be a bit cheeky,' I said, 'but I drive past here every day and I wondered if the place was for sale?'

He seemed to think about that as he looked me up and down. 'Are you in the market?'

'I don't know. I might be. How big is it?'

'The site's four acres and there are two sheds totalling forty thousand square feet.'

'That's pretty big.'

'Yes, it is.'

'I've been looking for warehouse facilities and there must be retail permission?'

'There is,' he said. 'We open seven days a week.'

'Are you thinking of selling?'

'I might be, depends what you'd be willing to pay.'

'How much do you want?'

He took a moment to think about that. 'Three hundred and forty thousand, it's yours.'

Not a bad place to start. 'How about two-forty?'

'Three hundred.'

'Two-sixty.'

'The best I can do is two-eighty.'

'Alright, I'll take it,' I told him.

That deal took no more than five minutes and I remember walking out thinking, I own a four-acre site having walked in with a simple question. It wasn't on a whim though; I just followed my instincts and seized an opportunity. I knew I could use one shed as a showroom and the other for restoration and storage. With something that size my business would be taken even more seriously. I was buzzing as I went back to the car, and when I got to the office Rebecca asked me where I'd been.

'I just bought the garden centre in Glan Conwy.'

'You're kidding?'

'No, I'm serious. We've got a four-acre site and two warehouses.'

With that purchase my portfolio came to four properties but, as far as available cash was concerned, I'd used up all my reserves. I was on my arse and that would come back to haunt me.

On that holiday in Abersoch in 2008 I was able to switch off the phone and chill out properly. We were doing between £2,500 and £5,000 per day, seven days a week, in each of the three warehouses and I'd been buying stock like there was no tomorrow. The most I spent in a week was £83,000, which was an absolute fortune. I had no fear. It wasn't a risk. We were making big money and big money needed big inventory. All was well, so I stretched that two weeks into two and a half, and when I got back I asked the lads how they'd been doing. Chris Holt was manager in Glan Conwy and Clive Holland in Llandudno. I went to see Clive first and asked how business had been and how much money he'd taken.

'Two hundred and fifty quid,' he told me.

'What, this morning?'

'No, in total.'

I stood there not quite taking it in. 'You mean that's all you've done since I've been away?'

'Yeah,' he said. 'I'm sorry, Drew. There's all that crap on the news about the banking crisis. Nobody's buying anything.'

Back in the car I drove to Glan Conwy and had the same conversation with Holty. 'How's it been?' I asked him.

He looked grim. 'It's been crap. We've done nothing. Not a sausage.'

It was like being smacked in the face. A big fat zero. 'You're telling me you haven't sold anything in two and a half weeks?'

'That's right,' he said. 'I don't think we've had anyone in the warehouse.'

The recession hit me hard and the banking sector was in crisis. They stopped lending money, some went bust, and governments propped up the rest. It wasn't just the lack of sales that worried me: in order to get the kind of architectural stock I was known for, houses had to be pulled down or renovated and that was about to stop happening. I knew my supply chain was going to be cut off at the knees and there was fuck-all I could do about it. It felt as if somebody just flicked a switch, the world went black and I had 12 employees working full time who had families and mortgages. The gravy train had stopped. I'd worked unbelievably hard to get where I was, so this was going to hurt, and badly. For years I'd be there at seven in the morning and I was still hitting the coalface come midnight. I'd been savvy, made some smart decisions, but in a few short weeks everything was taken away from me. Miles away in America the banks had lent to people on mortgage bonds that were going to cripple them. The wave of panic that created rolled across the Atlantic and smashed right into me.

I looked at the books, got a handle on exactly where we were, and knew I had to make a decision quickly. The day after the lads told me how little they'd done I woke up to Robert Peston, the business editor at the BBC, telling everybody this was the end of everything.

'Will you shut the fuck up,' I shouted at the television. 'You're making things worse. Just stop talking.'

I went into the warehouse, sat down at my desk and made the toughest decision of my life. That day I let all but two of the contracted employees go, but I made sure I looked after everyone and found them new jobs to go to. Only Gavin and Holty stayed and that was only for a while. I'd been back from holiday just one day but the writing was on the wall already. I knew, if I didn't act, I could lose everything. I paid what was owed in wages until the end of the month but that was all I could do. As soon as it was done, I got on the phone to anybody I owed money to and promised to settle their bills, but it would take longer than I'd expected. It was the same promise Gordon Stewart had made to me that Christmas Eve all those years ago. He made good on his word and I would too. I hate it when people go bankrupt and fuck everybody over. I've had it done to me on a couple of occasions and it sucks. I wasn't going to do that. I promised them I'd pay what was owed in full and made sure I did.

The bank didn't help; in fact, they were absolutely useless. Two weeks after the crash I had this snivelling piece of shit sit down in my office with the kind of look on his face that only bankers with final-salary pension schemes can display.

'OK, Mr Pritchard,' he said. 'Things aren't going to get better; we need to do something about it.'

'Hang on,' I said. 'I'm still servicing my loans; in fact, I'm overpaying on both of them.' I've always done that: if I borrow money and the repayment is £1,500 a month, I'll pay £2,500.

'You're paying now,' he said, 'but there's no money coming in. We need the deeds to your house.'

That put the fear of God into me, but it also made me angry. I'd never let anyone put a business charge on my house and I wasn't going to start with this guy.

'No way,' I said. 'That's never going to happen.'

'Alright, but we want our exposure reduced, so the only other option is to sell your commercial properties.'

I should've told him to go fuck himself right there, but I didn't. Instead, I did as he told me. I put some of the properties on the market and sold the storage place right away. The church in Llandudno was wanted by a guy I knew who'd made millions from some dot-com company. He showed up, took a look around and told me he'd pay the full price in cash, but I had to be ready in six weeks.

'Can you do that?'

'Course I can,' I told him.

It was much easier said than done, because the place was crammed full of stock and it cost me thousands to get it shifted. I might as well not have bothered because, just as we were about to complete, he started playing silly buggers and I had to pay the mortgage for another year. He'd gone back on his word but couldn't give a shit. Finally, we did complete but, in the meantime, I was losing a fortune paying the bills on both premises while we took in no money. They talk about a double-dip recession, but I was bitten once, then again before it came back for a third go. With one property sold and one supposedly sold, I had the garden centre, one Transit van and my old Mercedes estate, which was completely shot to shit. My Porsche went, all the other cars went, along with the holiday home and speedboat I'd never wanted in the first place. I still had help from Rebecca, Gav and Holty, but in terms of the day-to-day running I was on my own, working 15-hour shifts just as I used to. For years I'd delegated everything except buying the stock – now, once again, I was doing everything.

I had to organise the computer now and my skills were so shit I couldn't even switch the machine on. I'd employed people to set up the website and other people to run it for me. I was so inept I had to get written instructions from Holty. He looked after the computer in those days and, initially, I was glad I'd been able to retain him. But then he was offered another job so I had to let him go.

'I don't have to take it,' he said. 'I can stick around if you want me to.'

'Take it,' I told him. 'I want to keep you on because we've been friends for years and you've been brilliant. But I can't give you any guarantees so maybe you ought to take the job – just show me how to work the computer.'

He did and it was literal:

1) Press power button on bottom right-hand corner and hold for three seconds.

2) Release button and wait for computer to boot up.

I was that bad, honestly. I don't think I slept for days. I locked myself away and taught myself how to use it properly. A week later Holty was gone and I was modifying the database. Gavin took a job doing some double-glazing work but still restored for me on Saturday and Sunday. I was on my own but I could work the computer, and I'd remembered how Rob Wilding had done so much business on eBay. I started shoving masses of stock through there and gradually the money started coming in. I managed to keep the kids in school at £3,600 – per child – per term and I don't know how I did it.

Things improved, but there was something wrong and it went way deeper than just the business. It was like those panic attacks when they first happened, I didn't know what was up or how to fix it until one day in the warehouse a month into the recession.

The week after I bought the cabinet and urn from Peter, I travelled to Oxford to film the classic car show. It's a series I do with my mate Paul Cowland called *Salvage Hunters Classic Cars* that came about due to the success of my first TV series where my passion for cars became apparent. It's about finding cars from all eras that need restoration. We source them, fix them up so they look brand new, then reveal them later before they're sold on to, hopefully, very happy buyers.

We did some work in Banbury before revealing a 1970 Fiat 500 that had been a complete wreck when we bought it. It got even worse when we took the paint off as that had been holding the bodywork together. I restyled everything, changing the colour, the wheels, engine and gearbox, as well as the interior. It was transformed into a thing of beauty and, when we revealed it, we brought whole sections of Oxford city centre to a standstill. Hundreds of people stopped to stare at the deep black paint and chrome bumpers; it's one of the best transformations we've ever done. Not only that, it was the best day of filming I can remember. There was something really cool about driving this Modernist gem of a car around such a beautiful old city where the architecture dated back to the fourteenth century. People loved it; they were chatting away, queuing up to take pictures with us and the car. It was fantastic.

CHAPTER 7

There's a lot less pressure on me when I do that show because I don't have to go out and find lots of different things; I'm basically being paid to do my hobby. During the last series I bought a pre-airflow Mark I Ford Cortina manufactured in 1964 that came from South Africa. There's no rust. It's never had any welding or bodywork done, and, right now, it's in Dundee waiting to be collected. Paul's fun to work with, a man with a lifelong passion for cars; what he doesn't know would fit on a match-head. Really, we're just dicking around with old cars, but there's nothing better than seeing a beaten-up hunk of metal recreated as something both functional and beautiful. A rolling work of art (as I like to say); so it was with the Fiat 500.

We'd bought an MGA a few months back and that restoration was designed to create something an enthusiast could rally. It was painted duck-egg blue with a silver roof. I had to go to Telford to source some seats and had located a company called Cobra. That name intrigued me, because it evoked the car created by the late great Carroll Shelby, a racing driver and entrepreneur with a heart condition, who took on the might of Ferrari and beat them. It was something I brought up when I met Mark Dunsford, the managing director.

'So, tell me,' I said. 'The name Cobra, is that anything to do with AC?'

'Oh, yes,' he said. 'Very much so.'

He was a nice guy; a lot of fun and I could tell his workforce really liked him. He told me how his grandfather,

Len, was one of the foremost coach trimmers in the country back in the early 1960s. Working for AC Cars out of Thames Ditton, he built seats for racing cars driven by such luminaries as Jim Clark and Stirling Moss. Rising to be the company's head coach trimmer, Len was there when Shelby showed up to see if it was possible to squeeze a seven-litre Ford V8 into an AC Ace. With a few modifications it could be done; the subsequent car they created was bound for Le Mans and the rest is history. The first AC Cobra was completed in 1962 and tested on what was the brand-new M1 motorway. The story goes that in the early hours of a Sunday morning they took the car out to see how fast it would go and it was absolutely blistering. A combination of raw Ford power and an aluminium body, it's alleged it was down to that test that there's a 70mph speed limit on UK motorways.

Mark's dad served a short and eventful apprenticeship at AC working with his father. But he messed about so much Len told him he would have to leave before he got him the sack. He lasted six months then left for a job with Moto-Lita steering wheels. With a background in coach trimming, he tried to persuade the owners that they should make after-market car seats but they said there was no money in it. Mark's dad wasn't convinced, so he started his own company from a shed in Camberley and got an order for 50 seats from Gordon Spice Engineering. Pretty soon business was booming so he moved to Telford because it was a

New Town with an offer of free rent and rates. Every seat is hand-made and, 40 years later, the company is the biggest competitor to Recaro. They make all the seats you see in the dugouts at Premier League football grounds, having originally been approached by Manchester United. The headrest is removable so whenever they change sponsor a whole new seat doesn't have to be manufactured.

Mark took me upstairs, where he had a couple of seats for me to look at. 'This is the department we call Brushing and Bagging,' he said. 'The final inspection where each seat is brushed and cleaned; it's where my mum used to work, before she moved to the sales office.'

He showed me a bucket-style seat with a headrest that looked a little modern but was the sort of thing I wanted. It had a dog-tooth check, which he told me was the original Porsche pattern.

'Really?' I said. 'I'm just restoring a right-hand-drive 1968 911 and was tempted to go that way, but we've got the original seats so we'll stick with them.'

I took a good look at the other two seats, both variations on a theme, and could see the quality. They weren't quite right, though. I knew the kind of thing I wanted and would recognise it when I saw it. 'I like these,' I said. 'But they're too modern. I need something that feels MGA.'

'Right,' Mark said. 'No problem.'

'I want it to look classic but racy. We're selling the car and I think the kind of person who buys it will be at – let's call it – our time of life, so they need to be able to get in and out without it being a problem.'

'OK,' he said. 'Something that looks old but still gives lateral support without being too tall at the side so you don't give the driver a hernia.'

He came up with a classic-styled bucket seat that looked like it might've been made for a Cobra from the 1960s. It was low at the sides while still hugging the body and didn't have a headrest. I ummed and ahed about whether to opt for one, as Mark said they could figure something out if we thought it was necessary. I wasn't sure; it was more about the overall look of the seat and it had to be in keeping with the age of the car. In the end I plumped for the seats as they were and we decided to fit them with a Whillans-style four-piece rally harness. After that it was a question of the fabric, and Mark showed me just about every style and colour you could imagine. I chose a grey/blue plaid that would fit the age of the car and complement the bodywork properly.

'So, how much are we talking?' I asked him.

'We need to doctor the seats a little so they fit the car. With that and the fabric – four hundred pounds apiece.'

A pair of bespoke seats with full harness and trim for 800 quid, I'd shake on that all day. 'Great,' I said. 'When can I have them?'

A good chunk of what I've written about so far involves filming, but being on television was never something I envisioned. That said, a few years before *Salvage Hunters* started, I made a brief appearance on a BBC show called *The Reclaimers*. It was a one-off, though, not a career choice. The opportunity came up, and I took it so I could get some more exposure for my salvage business.

I certainly needed exposure in 2008: the recession was still hitting me hard, and I was determined to get back to where I'd been previously. That day in the warehouse I mentioned before was a watershed, and not just for the business. I needed something to get us rocking and rolling again, but I also needed something for me personally. I had to think of a way to inspire people and I had to express who I was within the trade, because I had no true identity, but I also wanted to be free from the shackles of convention and conformity.

For two days I couldn't sleep, I had this thing in my head about changing things up, and a day or so later I went to the photography area of the warehouse and stared at the white wall we used for the background. I had to change it. I don't know why, but I had to do something fresh, and black has always been my colour. I had some Farrow & Ball paint so I got a brush and painted the wall matt black. I liked it, a different look; now I had to set something against it. I dug out some 1970s Pagwood stacking chairs and placed two side by side on the floor then threw the rest on top. Taking a step back, I considered the jumbled result and thought it looked great, so I ought to take a photograph. The only camera I had was 40 quid's worth of digital from Tesco on a tripod I found in a skip, but it worked and I began snapping pictures.

After uploading them to the website, I went home and grabbed some sleep, and by the time I got up in the morning the chairs had sold. I thought, Fucking hell, how did that happen? I realised then that it wasn't just for sale purposes I'd done this; it was for me. I had to show people what Drew Pritchard was all about in terms of the antiques business. For so long this trade has been staid and steady, dominated by posh people looking to maximise their profit. It had never been that way for me. It was a love of things that were rusty or weathered, old and forgotten: it was beauty, poetry; even music. I'm a massive music fan and told you I grew up with Madness, The Specials and The Who. I have everything Paul Weller ever recorded from his time with The Jam, through the Style Council to his solo career. He's an icon, an innovator, a 'mod' in the truest sense of the word; and I totally identified with his music because he's an artist who really did go his own way. As far as I was concerned, the business that chose me wasn't staid and steady, it was rock 'n' roll. What I did with that pile of chairs was release all the frustration and tension; the *having to conform* to what everyone else in the antiques business thought. But I didn't think that way. I'd initially been grabbed by old cars floating in the air. I sought chairs that generations of people had sat on, desktops worn to the grain by elbows. No item was static, they all had a life of their own. In that moment of matt-black paint and Pagwood chairs, everything I'd been told, everything I'd learned about the antiques business was tossed out the window. I thought, Fuck it, I'm going to do this my way.

The next thing I did was get a chain and hang it from the ceiling. Then I found a really good Edwardian club armchair I'd bought and strung it up on the chain. I grabbed a bench and put Enzo on one end and took a photo. That's what went on the website, a shot of my dog that showed only a tiny section of the bench I was selling. I went from idea to idea and put all the pictures on the site and it felt like a dam had burst inside me. I'd allowed myself to become stymied by the recession and how this business was supposed to work, when all along I should have been doing it my way. I moved on to a mahogany chest of drawers that I turned three-quarter-ways on then pulled out half the drawers and dumped a couple of toy cars inside so they looked like they were falling out. I was invigorated, an artistic vent had opened and I was no longer defined by convention. The effect was incredible. I was doing what I wanted and I no longer gave a shit what anyone else was thinking.

I didn't know it then, but I'd announced myself to the upper echelons of the antiques business, and I mean people I really respected. As I was driving home one night not long after those first images hit the site, the phone rang and it

Above and below: Me aged two at my grandmother Nin's house near West Shore Beach, Llandudno

Me aged five outside my dad's garage in Glan Conwy

On one of our art gallery
holidays in Zermatt,
around 1980

Trying out my first BMX
in Glan Conwy, 1983

Cycling in France,
around 1982

With Mum in
Llandudno, 1970

Me and my
younger brother
Guy in Glan Conwy

Me and Nin at my
cousin Alison's wedding

The family at
Alison's wedding

Hanging around Dad's
shed in Conwy, 1975

On holiday in
France, 1986

At Butlin's
Pwllheli, 1979

At Oulton Park, where I saw my first Porsche

Dad's Jaguar XKs – he should never have sold the 150

Driving the MG TD in the Asda car park, 1985

Me with the Beacon Buggy in 1987

Dad's artwork

Collecting driftwood, 1987

Fitting a church window with my mate Gavin in Kinmel Bay, 1990

was Alex MacArthur from Rye telling me that what I was doing was brilliant. Alex is one of the dealers I really look up to and I didn't know what to say. The top of the tree, the best of the best in her chosen field. I'm like: *Are you kidding me? Alex MacArthur thinks what I did with the website is brilliant.*

We had a really in-depth conversation but I was driving and distracted so I stopped in a lay-by just down the road from the garden centre. Half an hour later I said goodbye and was about to pull back onto the road when the phone rang again.

'Hello?' I said, not recognising the number.

'Oh, hi.' An American accent. 'Is that Drew?'

'Yes.'

'This is Ray Azoulay from Obsolete in California.'

Fuck me. First Alex and now Ray Azoulay. These were people at the top of their game. I remember thinking, What the hell is going on? In the space of just a few minutes two major influences on my life in terms of antiques were on the phone. I was tongue-tied as Ray echoed everything Alex had said. 'You're doing great things, I'm really impressed.'

The hairs were prickling the back of my neck. 'Thank you,' I said. 'Thank you very much. You have no idea what that means to me.'

I'd grabbed his attention working with 40 quid's worth of Tesco camera and, as the weeks went by, he started buying stuff off me. Alex bought too, but not like Ray. He bought masses and shipped it out to California.

Looking back to those dark days of the recession, it's hard to believe I'm where I am today. Things could have gone completely pear-shaped but that moment in the studio changed everything. My outlook was fresh, I was no longer a slave to conformity. I felt free to really express myself and had found another way to reach people. I still had the garden centre but the whole operation was much leaner and I realised I preferred it that way. That didn't change the fact I was determined to get back to where I'd been, though, and in order to do that I had to rely on experience. In just under a month I'd gone from assets of three and a half million to minus-80 grand in my buying account. I'd put the properties up for sale so I could pay off my debts and I was trying to shift the inventory. By the end of that month I was back to £60,000 in the black and I was kicking on. Everything bar the garden centre had been sold (the long-winded deal in Llandudno not-withstanding). I'd kept the chapel and changed the way our stock was displayed on the website. I'd had a Eureka moment with Alex and Ray, and there was light at the end of the tunnel. But then there was more scaremongering on telly about double- and triple-dip recession and business fell off again.

I was struggling through when one Saturday afternoon I sat down at the desk in the Glan Conwy warehouse to leaf through the *Antiques Gazette*. It's the bible of the trade and I've been reading it for 20 years. Right at the back, I spotted an advert no more than 4cm square that was edged in black.

Are you a man with a van who drives around salvage yards and demolition sites collecting architectural salvage and antiques?

It had been placed by a TV production company with a number to call and, as soon as I read it, I knew I fitted the bill exactly. I'd already done *The Reclaimers* and remembered the director telling me I was pretty good and should do more TV if the opportunity ever presented itself. I'd enjoyed it; a piece of piss. I didn't have to impress anybody. I was just talking to camera about something I love.

I cut the advert out and pinned it on the blackboard but it was Saturday and nobody would be at the production company, so I decided to give them a ring on Monday. Of course, things cropped up, it went out of my mind and the advert remained on the board for weeks. Business picked up a little and I was out and about, then a dealer showed up at the warehouse.

'Drew,' he said, as he opened his wallet and brought out a copy of the same advert, 'have you seen this?'

I pointed to the one pinned on my board. 'Saw it weeks ago,' I said. 'Never got around to phoning.'

'You should. "A man with a van" – that's you.'

Again, it was Saturday, but after he left, I did pick up the phone. There was no one in the office to take the call so I left a message on the answer machine. When I got home, I told Rebecca and she said, if anything came of it, she'd back me.

I went into work on Monday and the production company was on the phone right away. 'Mr Pritchard,' the woman said, 'we'd like to film with you. I want to send a crew. Is tomorrow OK?'

'Sure,' I said. 'OK.'

They turned up early and I did a bit to camera outside the warehouse and they left again. Christmas came and went, then early in the new year I got a call from the office asking me if I would be interested in a series to be broadcast on the History Channel. Of course, I would; but nothing happened and I just carried on with my business. A year went by and it was the following Christmas Eve before I heard anything from the production company. I'd shut the shop and was on my way home when the phone rang.

'Hi, Drew. This is Izzy from the production company in London. Sorry it's been so long since we were in touch, but that's how it is in the television business. Anyway, I'm calling with good news. Congratulations, you've got a ten-part series with the History Channel.'

I wasn't in the least bit surprised. Despite the amount of time that had passed, when the film crew left, everything had felt right and I knew I was going to get it.

We started filming the following March. The money wasn't much but it would only take a few months and I thought it would be the easiest bit of cash I'd ever earn. As it turned out, it was actually the hardest work I'd done in years and that was down to the travelling. Until you're on the road day after day, week after week, you've no idea how gruelling it can be. Today we only do one location a day, but back then we did two or three with 100, sometimes 200 miles in between.

My motivation wasn't what you might think; it had nothing to do with being on TV. I've never wanted to be famous, but for me this was the best advertising I could get for my business. Hopefully, people would see the show and ring up to sell me stuff that I could restore and then sell on at a decent profit. This had already happened after I did *The Reclaimers* and I had no interest other than generating stock for the website. It never crossed my mind that the show might be successful enough to become an income stream in its own right, it was just another way of buying antiques.

So, I thought it was going to be a piece of piss, but I admit I was pretty nervous that first day. It's important to point out that this wasn't the production company that make the show today, but its predecessor and they're no longer in existence. But, that aside, it wasn't just one bit to camera; it was an entire series and everyone was much more experienced than me. It was a bit of a stuttered start in actual fact, and almost got derailed completely due to a clash of ideas between me and the director. The production company sent over a young, Swedish director who'd already had a worldwide hit. He was experienced and I wasn't and we took an instant dislike to each other.

Back then I was still driving an eight-year-old, beaten-to-shit E300 Mercedes estate which had done 180,000 miles. With rust in every corner it looked like the *Bismarck*. The director told me we'd rehearse how the first call was going to play out and he wanted a piece to camera in the car with me.

'We'll pretend you're travelling to the destination,' he said. 'Discuss how you're going to play it and what you're going to say.'

'Alright,' I said. 'Let's go.'

So, we jumped in the car with me driving and John Nutter, the cameraman, in the passenger seat. The director was in the back along with Simon Jolly. We got onto the A55 and had driven about two miles when the director starts in with the set-up.

'OK, Drew,' he said in a really annoying nasal accent. 'We're going to see this woman. Tell me how you're going to rip her off.'

'What?' I looked in the mirror at him.

'I want you to go in there and absolutely smash the price. I want you to rip her off.'

'No chance,' I said. 'I'm not going to do that.'

'What're you talking about?'

'I don't rip people off.'

'Yeah, but this is TV.'

'I don't care. It's not what I do.'

He took a moment to absorb that then told me that, whether I liked it or not, that was the show.

'Bollocks to that,' I said. 'I'm not going to rip people off, that's not what I do.' I was adamant and the guy was beginning to bug me. 'This might be your show and I don't mind taking direction, but I've got a business to run. How am I going to do that if all they see is me ripping people off on TV?'

'Yeah, but the contract.'

'Fuck the contract. I didn't sign up to rip people off.'

He would not let up, kept going on and on about this and that until I swivelled round in the seat and jabbed a finger at him. 'Listen, mate,' I said. 'You're missing the point if you think I'm going to rip people off. You can tell me until you're blue in the face, but I'm not going to do it. There's no fucking way.'

He just stared at me with his mouth open.

'I mean it. You keep on like this I'm going to lose my rag and things will really kick off, I promise you.'

He was smiling, shaking his head as if I was stupid and just didn't understand what he wanted. That was it. I really lost my shit and pulled over into a lay-by. I was in his face, telling him if this was what they thought the show was going to be about it was news to me. Clearly, they had no

CHAPTER 7

idea who I was, so I told him I'd spent years building up a reputation and I wasn't going to blow it all for the sake of TV. Whatever nerves I'd had were gone and I was fuming.

I'd had enough so I drove back to the yard in silence. I'd never come across anyone like this guy before and he'd never come across anyone like me. When we got there, I jumped out of the car, went around to open his door and was about to drag him out, but then a little bit of sense kicked in. I had a contract and I'm a professional. TV presenters don't go around fighting directors, but there was no way I was going to work with him.

'You see that building,' I said, pointing to the warehouse. 'That belongs to me and you're not allowed in there, OK? You've got me all wrong and you need to listen because, if you step inside, I won't be responsible for what happens to you.'

I had to get a handle on my temper and the only way I could do that was if he was nowhere near me. I had a contract with the production company but that contract wasn't with the director. The company would have to sort this out or just forget the whole thing and I knew they wouldn't do that because the channel was expecting a series. As far as I was concerned, that wouldn't include this director and I refused to let him inside the building. Looking back now, the crew must've been wondering what the hell they'd got themselves into. The director got on the phone to London and a little while later Philip Whelan, the series producer, called to tell me I had to do what I'd been asked to do. I told him straight, I don't rip people off and this was over if that's what they wanted me to do. We had a chat, then he said he'd come down and sort things out so I put down the phone, not quite sure what to expect when he got there.

Immediately he jumped in a car and arrived at the warehouse a few hours later. He calmed things down and the two of us tried to work out a way we could get on with the series. I was adamant I wasn't going to rip anyone off and I could not work with someone who wanted me to do that, so the director flew back to Sweden. I'd made it clear to Philip that the show would only work if I was allowed to do it my way. It had to be exactly as it was when I was buying without a film crew; open, honest and no bullshit. He agreed and we all took a couple of days for the dust to settle, then the crew came back with another director. His name was Mark and I don't know if he was expecting some firebrand Welshman but he was pretty wary around me. But only to begin with: I'd calmed down, and the bottom line was the show had to work, so we agreed to make that happen.

With Mark at the helm we made a plan of how things would play out with me just being me. After that we hit the road, heading for our first location in Lancaster. I was excited now, again a little nervous, but all that disappeared when we arrived at a real shit-hole of a hotel and that set me right back again. I could feel a panic attack coming on and it was made worse when we went to a steakhouse for dinner and the food was absolutely appalling. So much for bloody TV. This was 48 hours after the shit with the first director; the hotel was crap, we couldn't eat the food and I was so stressed I shut myself in my room. I had to deal with the panic attack and had learned how to do that, but it wasn't easy. Somehow, I managed to get myself together, but was plagued by attacks the entire shoot. I had one every single day. I could've set my watch by them. Philip could see how stressed I was, and he was able to defuse the situation completely. He's a very funny guy, always cracking jokes, and that lightened the atmosphere considerably.

'Drew,' he said, 'just be yourself. If you know about something and you're talking, just keep going. We want to know what you know. We'll cut what we don't need for the show.' That was the best piece of TV advice I've ever been given. It chilled me out and a relationship was forged that I still respect today. He became someone I trusted and I think he understands more about why people watch a particular programme than anyone else I know.

The next day we were filming with a dealer called Golly and I found a couple of really interesting items. It was a lot of fun and we got through it pretty unscathed. On the second day of filming we were in Blackpool at the Illuminations warehouse, so we stayed in a hotel attached to the Pleasure Beach. Gavin came up to join me and there was another film crew staying in the hotel, some of whom Philip knew. They came over for a drink and the director was a bit pissed by the time she talked to me. 'Whatever you do, don't turn into an arsehole,' she slurred at me.

'I've got no intention of turning into an arsehole.'

'Well, don't.' She poked a finger in my chest. 'That's what happens in this business.'

'I won't,' I promised, and she went off to annoy someone else.

'What was all that about?' Gavin said.

'She was telling me not to become an arsehole.'

'It's a bit late for that,' he told me.

CHAPTER 8

BUGATTIS AND BEETLES

Whenever I'm buying, no matter how far I am from Conwy, I always try to make it home at the end of the day. It's only if I'm in Scotland or the southeastern corner of Kent, maybe, that I stay in a hotel. When we filmed the first TV series, however, I lived out of a suitcase for four months solid and home seemed a long way away.

I only say this because, ten years later, I've spent my life in hotel rooms and it was the last thing I ever expected. There's so much glamour attached to TV, but the bit you see is only a small part of what actually happens. So far, we've made 250-plus shows and I'm just about to sign up for another two and a half years. I've still got 18 months of my existing contract to run, so that's another four years with four different hotels per week, which adds up to about 750. I'm not moaning, far from it; I'm only too aware what the TV series has done for the profile of my business and I wouldn't have it any other way. All I'm trying to say is that life on the road making show after show isn't necessarily all it's cracked up to be. It's draining, repetitive, you don't see your family and that can cause all sorts of problems. For example, at two o'clock this morning, I was pacing another strange room trying to breathe my way through a heart palpitation. I got there eventually, but it's debilitating to wake up covered in sweat with your heart racing in unfamiliar and often uncomfortable surroundings. I don't ask much of a hotel – a decent bed, a shower that works and reasonable food – but one of the things I've learned over the past ten years is that, in Britain, we do terrible hotels really well.

We began filming the first series on 22 March 2010 and it lasted 16 weeks. I still had a business to run and spent my evenings uploading stock onto the website. When we were finished and the crew went home, I returned to buying on my own as I'd done for years. Nothing changed but the show was yet to air; when it did, I was hoping I'd get people on the phone wanting to sell me stuff I wouldn't otherwise have come across. The schedule had been much tougher than I thought it would be, but I was happy that I'd dug my heels in and was able to do it my way.

I'm sure it's apparent by now that I have huge respect for the antiques trade as an entity in itself and every part of what I do has to maintain that authenticity. So long as the edit was done in the right way the viewers should see the reality and that might draw more people to the business. So much of what is shown on television doesn't portray this trade properly. Most programmes bear no resemblance to how it works: people don't walk into an antique shop and look at an item the dealer has up for £100 and offer £15. I've seen that on the telly and, after a bit of back and forth, the dealer accepts the £15. That just does not happen and it creates a false impression of what we do. I know for a fact that the second filming stops a runner is there with the other £85 to give to the dealer. What's the point of a 'reality' show if it's not going to deal with reality?

More often than not, the dealers you see are only posing as such; they're auctioneers and there's a fundamental difference between an auctioneer and an antique dealer. Auctioneers sell on behalf of clients and their knowledge of any particular item is generally nowhere near as extensive. Take that Regency Waterfall bookcase Peter Whipps bought that was catalogued as a kitchen dresser. As far as I'm concerned, many of the TV shows about the antiques trade do nothing but damage the industry. They do not represent me and they do not represent any of the people I know and respect.

Proper antique dealers have spent a lifetime learning their craft in exactly the same way as a great chef or musician. If you watch Marco Pierre White or Rick Stein, for example, when they're cooking and talking about food, you get the real deal. Equally, if you watch me talking about antiques, you get the real deal, just as you do with someone like Rupert Maas on *Antiques Roadshow* when he's describing a painting. It's obvious he knows exactly what he's talking about and has a genuine passion for it. To use food as an analogy, I equate the daytime antiques programmes with pot noodles. It's still food, it's still got multiple ingredients; you have to do something with it before you can actually eat it, but it's not food you want to eat. It's not real, it's fake, and that's how I feel about those programmes. They are 'boil-in-the-bag' television. That may sound harsh but think of it this way: if there was a programme out there that denigrated lawyers in the way some of those shows denigrate what I do, they'd be sued to high heaven. How can anyone take this business and all the nuances that go with it, not to mention the decades it takes to learn and be any good, then bring it down to that level? Being an antique dealer is like learning to play an instrument, you get to a point where you can do it but you have to keep on doing it and doing it if you want to get to any kind of serious level.

As far as our show was concerned, I'd done the first series, we were waiting for it to air and I was looking forward to seeing it. When I signed up, the production company were in talks with the History Channel where it was thought they'd put it on immediately before *American Pickers*. That was great, I'd seen *American Pickers* and, although it revolved around the same kind of subject, it was a very different show to the one we did. Just before the programme went out, however, I had a phone call from the production company telling me it wasn't going to be History now, but

Discovery. They had a new channel called Quest and the show would be broadcast on that platform instead. I wasn't sure about that; I'd never heard of Quest; it didn't bode well and I was beginning to dread what I might see. A TV show is all about the edit and we film hours and hours of material, most of which doesn't get anywhere near what is actually broadcast. The wrong cut here or there can completely alter the perception of a transaction and that's what I began to fear.

I needn't have worried; when the show finally aired what I saw was the real me. There on the screen was the bloke I'd been determined to get across and the one *I* recognised, let alone anyone else. They hadn't dicked about: what Philip Whelan had promised would be the show *was* the show and I was delighted with the result. He'd done right by me when he could've cut it any way he fancied and made me look like the kind of rip-off merchant the original director had wanted. He didn't do that and he has my lasting respect for honouring everything I was trying to achieve.

It was all very positive and the fact that it wasn't shown on the History Channel no longer mattered to me. Nothing really happened though; there was no great change in my life, people didn't start recognising me on the street; nobody stopped to shake my hand or tell me they thought I was rubbish. But what I'd hoped would happen did. Immediately, people started ringing in with stuff they wanted to sell and I had access to a whole new marketplace. I'd achieved my objective: made sure they saw the real me, and it was clear I didn't rip anyone off. 'Drew Pritchard': what you see is what you get, no frills, no bullshit, just someone who loves finding antiques to restore and sell on to someone else who will appreciate them. This is the best job in the world and you have to respect it. It's multifaceted and multilayered; it's interesting, beautiful, dangerous, rude and crude all at the same time. You immerse yourself to the point where you think you've found your place, then it changes completely and that happens again and again. What you thought was definitive isn't. There's another facet and another; you're learning something every day.

So, business kicked on, we were smashing it again, but I didn't hear anything from anyone to do with the TV show. I didn't think about it, it hadn't been a career choice; I was already doing what I wanted and, if that one series was it, I'd done what I set out to do. Then one day (when I least expected it) the phone rang and it was the production company telling me they wanted to do another series. That was great: I knew what I was doing now and they'd proved they were happy to do it my way. The only question was whether we were going to keep the same personnel. During the first series it had largely been me and a mate called Julian who worked with me, together with a few episodes where Gavin came along. By the time I got the call to do the second series, however, Julian was no longer working for me. The company asked me if there was anyone else I could think of who might fulfil the role, and get back to them as soon as possible.

It wasn't hard. All I had to do was ask myself who I'd want to hang out with in the cab of a van day after day for months on end, while staying in crap hotels. The answer was simple – T. I thought he might be up for it, because he'd worked as a roadie for years and could cope with all the travelling. He's my friend and he's rounded; interesting and a little bit punk like me. As soon as we knew Julian was out of the frame, I got on the phone to him.

'Hello, mate, how've you been?'

'I'm alright, keeping busy, you know.'

'How busy?'

'What do you mean?'

'I mean, what're you doing for the next three months?'

'I don't know yet, but I'm not going on that shit programme of yours.'

Typical T, I hadn't expected anything less. I told him it would be a laugh; we'd have a good crack and the company would give him at least what he was earning now.

'They'll pay your hotel bills, give us lunch and you'll get fifteen pounds in per diems a day.'

'Go on then,' he said.

T's been with me on the show ever since and the ease with which we work together is mirrored on the classic car show I do with Paul. When he first started out, Paul won't mind me saying he was what we call a tiny bit 'TV', but I knew what I was about and what was wanted. By then I'd been doing my show for nine years and it only took a couple of days to knock off the edges. I'd known Paul for a few years and his real persona is just like me and T. Paul is a pro, and once he relaxed into being himself, it was absolutely brilliant, easy, really good TV.

That show is about finding, fixing and selling classic cars, but with all things automotive there's 'classic' and then there's 'classic', and Paul and I don't always agree. That was the case with the Honda we bought the other day. A black two-door CRX VTEC that Paul had heard about from a guy with a warehouse on a farm outside Reading. We'd been in Banbury the day before so it wasn't very far to travel. We already had 20 projects going on, and the MGA was well on the way to its reveal, having been fitted with the seats from Cobra. I'd loved the Fiat 500 of course, and we had a beast of a Volvo 850 that needed a new headliner, the material that lines the inside of the roof. That was all good stuff, but this VTEC Paul was raving about was hardly a rolling work of art and didn't come anywhere near the classic brief for me. VTEC means Variable Valve Timing & Lift Electronic Control, and it's all about the profile of the camshaft that allows more air into the cylinders at higher speed, which generates more horsepower and hence you go quicker.

'A Honda?' I said. 'They haven't been around long enough to be a classic.'

'Of course they have. They made a pickup called a T360 in 1963.'

'So, what year's this hatchback?'

'Early nineties, it's the VTEC that makes it classic. The engine, it's very clever.'

I'm not as anal about the internal combustion engine as Paul, but I know enough to understand VTEC and, yes, it's clever, but clever doesn't make it classic.

'A 911 is a classic,' I said, as we drove through country lanes towards the location. '1960s short wheelbase or the 993; that's a fantastically engineered piece of design right up there with the T35.'

'Bugatti again, Jesus, you never stop banging on about them, do you?'

'That's because the man who designed them was a genius. His whole family were like that, amazing people, visionaries. There's never been another car like the Bugatti. I can't afford one but I've got bits and pieces, including the original sign from the factory.'

'So, where's the sign now?' Paul said as we turned.

'Hanging on the door of my living room in Conwy.'

A few years back, Rob Bellis, a dealer pal of mine from Llangollen, called me.

'Drew,' he said, 'you're not going to believe it, but I've found the original sign from the gates of the Bugatti factory in Molsheim.'

'Really?' I said, not even trying to hide the sarcasm.

'Yeah, really. I mean it. It's the actual sign.'

'How do you know?'

'I've got an old photograph that was taken outside the gates and the sign's right there and it's the same one. I'm telling you, this is the original.'

Rob's no bullshitter, and after ten years in the business his knowledge is pretty solid. He's a really good guy, I like him a lot and there was something in the tone of his voice that made me sit up and take notice. If he was right then this was something very special, and I trusted his judgement enough to make the drive to Llangollen. Like any good dealer, he didn't tell me where he got the sign, only that he was sure it was something I'd want to take a look at.

When I got to his place, he brought out the sign and I took a really close look and it seemed authentic to me. It was around 45cm wide and had the right patination; I knew there were copies out there, I'd seen them before and had been thinking that this might be one, but the moment I clapped eyes on it I was certain. That ain't a copy, I said to myself. That's exactly what Rob said it was on the phone. The wear was right, the colour and quality. The size, scale, fit and finish; just the general feeling told me this was the real deal. It was confirmed when he brought out the old photograph taken outside the factory gates where the sign that I held in my hands right then was hanging for all to see.

'What do you want for it?' I asked him.

CHAPTER 8

'Four hundred quid.'

'Yep, I'll have it. Thank you.'

I've had that sign for a few years now, one of those dis-
coveries that's up there with the gadroon wine cooler and
the 'Voyage to Vinland' stained-glass windows. It was on
my mind because I'd just come back from the Goodwood
Revival where there were Bugattis all over the place. In a rare
moment of downtime, I'd taken off to attend the motoring
festival that started in 1998, 50 years after the 9th Duke of
Richmond opened the racetrack in West Sussex. It's two and
a half miles of tarmac designed for both cars and motorbikes, and the revival recreates a period when Goodwood
rivalled Silverstone as Britain's number-one motor racing
venue. What's really cool is the fact that during the three
days of the festival no modern vehicles are allowed inside
the perimeter apart from ambulances and rescue trucks.

I wandered among short-wheelbase 911s and Bugattis. There weren't just T35s, but Type 55s, as well as a two-
seater Atalante coupé with rear mudguards that swamped
the wheels a bit like an Indian motorcycle. Long in the
bonnet and short in the boot, it's such an amazing piece of
design that was produced between 1934 and 1940. What I
love about those cars is the fact that they're not just hidden
away under a dust sheet in an air-conditioned garage while
the value goes up; the people who buy them use them and
race them.

To see so many in the flesh had all my senses tingling. One caught my eye that was covered in dead flies and dirt kicked up by a 1,000-mile drive from the French Riviera. It had luggage bags hanging off the sides in a real tribute to a bygone era. It was right-hand drive and I spent a good half-hour chatting to the owner. He shared my view that this was the highest form of art. Strong and light, designed with a simple yet absolute purpose, it stirs the same emotions today that I first felt when I was eight years old in Glan Conwy. Nothing has changed except my level of knowledge and experience.

It's raw, brutal, honest; and I'm convinced that without Ettore Bugatti we would never have seen the Modernist movement. To me, all aspects of design have some connection and that's a complex idea to try to get across, especially when you're not the most educated guy out there. But I talk about links in a chain and for me Ettore holds a special place in that chain. Modernism isn't just art, it's philosophical and cultural, and spawned trends that reverberated across the planet.

Goodwood is where I went to race my VW Beetle after it was finally completed back in 2010. It was something I'd always wanted to do, as racing is in the Pritchard blood. My grandfather John on my father's side was a bit of a wheelsman, and when he died I went through one of his old wallets and found more speeding tickets than you could imagine.

He even had one for riding a pushbike, can you believe that? He got fined for speeding on a bicycle. My father thinks he's a wheelsman, my brother too, as well as me; we all think we're a bit better than we probably are. When I was 19, I was sat in the pub with T and a lad called Crofty, all of us car-mad, and I told them I was going to design a black 1950s Beetle with BRMs, 356 brakes and a straight-cut gearbox linked to a 2.2-litre engine. I was going to hill-climb, sprint and circuit race … and 20 years later, I did.

Business was good, we were into the second TV series and I'd started to make a few quid. I was busy as hell but found the time I needed to think about racing and start making a few important contacts. They're everything in the racing world, and I made many of mine through a very good friend called Stewart Imber, who has become almost a father figure to me. I'd read about him when I was 17 in a classic sports car magazine: he had a farm in Hertfordshire with the most incredible collection of Mercedes Benz from the 1950s and 60s. There was an SE cabriolet, a coupé and a 600 series, as well as a Fintail and Ponton that he was racing. It seemed to me he'd bought the most beautiful cars at just the right time and in exactly the right condition, and that struck a chord with me.

Over 20 years later I arranged for us to film with Stewart at his farm in Hertfordshire. I'd wanted to meet him since I read the article and we clicked right away. Since then I've filmed with him maybe six or seven times and he invited me to a classic car race meeting. I jumped at the chance; it had always been an ambition to race classic cars but I never thought I'd have the opportunity.

Now I just might be able to do so. I had the money and the contacts I'd need to build the car I'd talked about all those years ago, but it was no small undertaking. Typical me, I wasn't about to get a Mini and start at the bottom to work my way up; I was going to build something that nobody had ever done before. At that time there was no competitive VW Beetle on the British historic racing scene. One project had been started by the managing director of Porsche UK but he couldn't get it finished. Since then there have been a few, and right now a young guy is building a car, but then there was nothing and I believed I could not only do it, but also win the 'Touring Greats' class. Stewart was a great help. He's been part of the Goodwood Revival since day one, together with Julius Thurgood, who runs the Historic Racing Drivers Club. I joined the HRDC and later I set about having the car built. Then the bills started coming in. My God, is it expensive to build a race car. I'd had no idea just how much I was going to spend if I wanted to do it properly, but I'd collated a team of individuals to do the work, having sourced the car in the southern states of America.

A '58 Deluxe in black that had been lovingly restored arrived in the UK and we immediately stripped out every mechanical part, taking it back to a shell. From that moment I was bleeding cash. I remember telling the lads to ring me every time they spent five grand, and in one week alone they rang three times. That's the nature of race cars, you have to have passion and you have to have the money. It took 18 months to complete and, once it was done, we wangled our way into the Goodwood members meeting. Prior to that Paul Cowland helped me get my racing licence in a hot Subaru, a process where you get the initial licence, which effectively gives you a set of 'L' plates, then you complete a dozen or so races before you're fully qualified.

Everything seemed to be falling into place and, the day before the members meeting, I was sitting on the start line in my full-spec 200bhp screaming VW Beetle about to do my test day. I remember thinking, How the fuck did I get here? Since then there's been a seven-page article in *Octane* magazine on the car, written by David Lillywhite. I've made loads of great contacts, and next year I'm commentating on the Monaco Historic Grand Prix for the second time with Marino Franchitti (younger brother of three-time Indy 500 winner Dario). He's spent a career racing sports cars and GTs, and I'm really looking forward to going. That morning at Goodwood, though, it was freezing cold but the car looked the absolute nuts and was getting loads of attention. I was completely blown away when Ivan Dutton, a Bugatti restorer who specialises in T35s, told me it was the best-prepared car in the paddock.

That was the test day, and in the members meeting that followed we were assigned a professional racing driver to take the car for qualifying. A professional and a privateer, those are the rules; he or she gets grid position and you do the race on Sunday. When we knew who our driver was going to be, I took him to one side and pointed out where he had to be careful because the car could get sideways and he just looked at me.

'It's a car,' he said, and walked away.

OK, I thought, this guy knows what he's doing so I'll just let him get on with it. With his knowledge and skill, I'd get my lap position and tomorrow it would be my turn.

For the previous 18 months we had poured blood, sweat and tears as well as a ridiculous amount of money into creating this car specifically to race at Goodwood. Together with a mechanic called Andy, the engine had been built by Ian Clark of Wolfsburg Performance Services and it was an absolute work of art. Ian's dad was a clockmaker who taught him that art, which he perfected and later started messing about with Volkswagens and Porsches. His skill as an engineer is beyond comparison; he works on his own from a farm in Lincolnshire and people fly their cars in from America so he can tune them.

Ian, Andy and I were in the pits with the rest of the team watching the monitor as the professional driver went out to get us our qualifying position. This was a very special moment, a VW Beetle racing at Goodwood; it had never been done before, and tomorrow I would achieve all that I'd told T and Crofty I would two decades previously. It was magical, we were surrounded by well-wishers who echoed Ivan Dutton's belief that ours was the best car out there. Our turn came and we watched with bated breath as the driver went from 13th to 3rd on the grid. It was amazing, the car was like a rocket and we were riveted to the monitor. It was going superbly well, better than any of us could've expected. Then, on the last corner, we saw the car scream into view with smoke pouring out the back. I remember thinking, What the fuck, then the driver pulled into the pits and told us it just went on him; he had no idea what happened. It wasn't his problem, it was ours, and when Ian checked underneath, he found a con rod had pierced the bottom of the engine case, smashing it to pieces.

That was it. The weekend was over. There would be no race tomorrow and it hit me like a ton of bricks. To say I was gutted would be the understatement of the year. It was so bad I couldn't actually be near anyone else; I just wandered off on my own. For the next three hours it felt as though my world had collapsed, I just could not believe it. So much effort, so much time, so much of my soul had gone into the project, it was beyond anything I'd ever done before. Finally, someone came to find me and, when I went back to the pits, they told me there was something I had to see. We had a GoPro camera inside the car and it had captured what actually happened. I watched the lap and saw the speedo hitting 80mph in fourth gear, then the driver changed down – but instead of hitting third he put the car into first. There was no way the drivetrain could cope with that, and it smashed everything to pieces. I can't begin to explain quite how low I felt, and the fault was nothing to do with me or the engineering crew – it was purely down to driver error but there was nothing we could do because he could not be held accountable.

As we pulled up onto a gravel road that led to a large industrial warehouse outside Reading, the guys selling the Honda were waiting and my first reaction astonished me. I like cars. I love cars, but I've never had such a visceral dislike for any vehicle ever. At first glance I hated it and it didn't get any better when we got out to take a closer look. As I walked around the thing, I thought it was the biggest pile of shit I'd ever seen. Paul, on the other hand, was purring. 'It's really cool, Drew,' he kept telling me.

'No,' I said. 'It's not. It's horrible.'

I love Paul, hopefully we'll be friends for the rest of my life, but when it comes to what's cool, he really hasn't got a clue. The car was just dreadful. 'I know it goes like stink,' I said. 'And I know the VTEC is an amazingly clever engine, but I really don't care. It's shit. Everything about the way it looks is awful.' I was shaking my head. 'I want nothing to do with this car; nothing.'

The wonderful thing about the car show is that from day one they let me do whatever I wanted. If I loved something, I could wax lyrical all day, and if I hated something I could say so. I hated this. It was absolute crap and I didn't pull any punches. Fortunately, the guys who were selling it were there on behalf of the owner so I wasn't hurting anyone's feelings.

'Paul,' I went on, 'the whole point of our show is motoring icons. We're trying to find cars that stir something in people.'

'Right,' he said. 'Like the VTEC engine, and that's what makes this iconic.'

'No. It doesn't,' I said. 'What's iconic is a Mark I, eight-valve Golf GTI or a Mini Cooper.'

'Or a Dodge Challenger,' he suggested.

'Exactly, that's an icon that goes all the way back to *Vanishing Point*. It stirs something deep in people and that doesn't happen with a little black Honda that might drive like a race car but wouldn't be seen dead on my drive. We're not looking for converts here. This show appeals to people who are already hooked; they'll laugh at us when they see this. It's not a car, it's an appliance like an iron or a toaster. It's got all the charm of a verruca.'

It was all to no avail. Paul was buying this shitty little car even if we had to pay the full eight grand they were asking. He thought it was the best thing since sliced bread but I just couldn't see it. The truth is he and I agree on three makes of car without question: Porsche, Volkswagen and Subaru. After that it's a grey area.

'Paul,' I said, 'he's asking eight grand, which is eight grand too much. I'd rather set fire to my feet than part with the money. That car is a blot on the landscape; if someone gave me a JCB I'd happily dig a hole and bury it.'

'So, you don't like it then,' he said.

'Get that, did you? I fucking hate it.'

'It's a landmark,' he said. 'A Honda CRX double-over-head cam SiR.'

'Which translates as Stupid Irrelevant Rubbish.'

'I reckon he'll take seven and a half,' he said. 'Wheels off, brakes changed and the suspension. I think we can get eleven grand, no problem.'

Oh sure, I thought. Hopefully it'll catch fire in the meantime.

Most of the time we're on the same page, though, so I suppose we can agree to disagree on what is and is not a 'classic'.

CHAPTER 9

THE POWER TO CREATE AND RESHAPE

Once filming for the day was over, Paul went home while I headed for yet another hotel where I had to get as much stuff uploaded onto the website as possible. After dumping my bag, I started work with the 6:00pm deadline rapidly approaching. Every Wednesday and Friday we send an electronic mailshot to 60,000 subscribers alerting them to the very latest wallop of stock I've put on the website. It has to be out by 6:00pm and it was already 5:40. That gave me just 20 minutes and there were some really nice items I wanted people to see. It's one of the moments in the week I really enjoy because it generates immediate interest. The stuff I was uploading was eclectic and that's been our signature since I had the moment with the Pagwood chairs and Tesco camera. The new items had only just been bought and restored, and it's a challenge to add real quality twice a week.

Equally, the timing is critical. I can't be late because by five past six we start getting emails from interested parties.

With just ten minutes to go I had a Welsh blanket uploaded as well as an abstract painting and two wooden lay figures, which was a great mix, but there were still another couple of items to go. When it comes to antiques, I'm a purist but also a bit of a magpie. I don't care if something retails for 15 grand or 150 quid so long as I'd be happy to own it.

The lay figures were interesting, not the best I've bought but still very good, and there was a kind of naivety in the manufacture that really appealed to me. I've got a passion for these articulated figures and I have three at home, one I bought by chance that's right up there with the Roman wine cooler in terms of just how special it is to me. The one I was uploading now I'd bought on the way back from Goodwood, having also stopped on the way down. Just as we got to West Sussex, in fact, I'd spotted a sign at the side of the road that said ANTIQUES and it turned out to be quite a find. I picked up some wonderful little Christopher Dresser brass pouring jugs for a couple of quid apiece as well as a whole stack of other stuff. I love Dresser; he was an interesting guy and considered to be a really important independent designer back in the nineteenth century. Born in Glasgow in 1834, he died in Mulhouse in the Alsace region, 70 years later. Mulhouse was both a city and artists' commune, and Dresser was both a designer and a design theorist (which is the philosophy behind design). He was a big part of the Aesthetic movement that focused on art and literature rather than the political themes of the time.

So, I already had a carload of stuff when we stopped for the night in Oxfordshire. On Monday morning we drove through the Cotswolds, where I always do well, and called on various dealers. By the time I was done, I'd spent more than 20 grand and had so much stuff I had to send a van down to ship it back to Conwy. I wasn't finished yet, though; there was one more place to stop and that was Baggott's in Stow-on-the-Wold. It has to be the most 'antique' of any antique shop in Britain and the owner is old-school like you wouldn't believe. He's incredibly knowledgeable, with a fabulous stock, and I call about four times a year. I rarely buy anything, but this time I spotted a lay figure in the window with a price tag of £1,800 and knew immediately I wanted to buy it. Inside, the owner and I got talking and it turned out he was a big fan of the show, though I had no idea. I mentioned the lay figure and told him I was interested; it was just a case of how much I'd have to pay. It was unusual in that it was pine not a hardwood, and it was nineteenth century not eighteenth, and it's eighteenth-century figures I collect. He said he could do it for £1,500 but I managed to get it down to £1,300. Since then it had been photographed and there was every chance I'd double my money. If it had been eighteenth century or earlier, I'd have kept it. Not forever, nothing is forever, but there's a time to buy and a time to sell and it's up to me to make that decision.

In 34 years of buying lay figures I've only come across three that were worth keeping and I've still got all of them. The best I've ever found was at a museum of rural life in Kent, which was a brilliant call where the curator was great and we had a right old laugh all day. They had a school-house there, so they sat me and T down and brought in this old schoolmaster to shout at us and I was reminded of my childhood in Glan Conwy. We bought a few bits and pieces, bric-a-brac mostly, nothing that had stood out spe-cifically but that was OK. The crew had a few last general-view shots to take care of and I wasn't required, so I had a wander around on my own. Not all areas of the museum were actually open and I took the opportunity to check out a couple of olde-worlde shops that we hadn't been into. I wasn't looking for anything; I wasn't even really thinking about anything, it was just a moment of downtime.

As far as I could see the shops had become storage sheds for the kind of tat museums don't really want but always get given anyway. You know the kind of thing: potato peelers and garden rakes, old stools that aren't very old, generally any old shit somebody wants to get rid of. Inside they were dark and dusty and one was partitioned by a counter. You never know what you might find in the recesses, though, so I stuck my head over just to be nosey.

CHAPTER 9

On the other side, lying on the floor covered in shit, was the single best lay figure I'd ever seen. About a metre tall, it was eighteenth century and just the kind of thing I collected. As I picked it up, I had to disengage a ravenous woodworm that was literally eating its head. Now I really was excited. This was English, with a trace of original paint on its face; the most enigmatic, sculptural, artistic and magical lay figure I'd ever come across. I knew I had to have it.

So, I went to track down the curator and showed him the figure. 'I just found this in one of your old shops,' I said. 'It was lying on the floor in a pile of dirt being eaten by woodworm. Is there any chance you'd sell it?'

Before he even opened his mouth, his expression told me everything. 'I can't,' he said. 'It was gifted to the museum.'

Shit, I thought. I'm not going to be able to get it. I couldn't believe it; gifted and yet lying in a pile of crap on the floor of a shop that was not even an exhibit. It would rot back there – if I hadn't come along the woodworm would have devoured it. I was gutted, but I understood that, if something has been given to the museum, the custodians can't just up and sell it.

'Alright,' I said. 'I get that, but if anything changes, I'll give you three thousand pounds for it.'

The man looked absolutely gobsmacked. 'Three thousand?'

'Right here. Right now, if you're prepared to sell it.'

'I can't,' he said. 'I'd like to, but I just can't. We'll clean it up and store it properly.'

'Don't clean it,' I told him. 'If I bought it, I'd want it just as it is, only without the woodworm. You need to keep that away or it'll be completely ruined.' Reluctantly, I handed the lay figure to him and departed.

I remember telling T just how pissed off I was at not being able to get it. It happens, though; you don't always get what you want, and so it was with that lay figure. But you move on and I did, and pretty much forgot about it. Then, two and a half years later, the phone rang.

'Mr Pritchard?'

'Yes?'

'This is the curator from the museum.'

Museum? I thought. What museum?

'Down in Kent, you were here a couple of years ago and we talked about a lay figure. You said you'd pay three thousand pounds for it; I don't know if you remember?'

'I do,' I said.

'Does the offer still stand?'

'Of course.'

'It's yours then, if you want it.'

Again, it was one of those moments you really never expect. I didn't think the figure would ever be for sale, but it was, and it's worth every penny of the £3,000, because I get a huge amount of pleasure every time I look at it.

*

The symmetry of a top-drawer lay figure reflects the level of industry and dedication, not to mention talent, it requires to become a great artist, and it is great artists who create different artistic movements. The way those movements tie in with other aspects of our culture has always held a huge fascination for me. For example, just as the Aesthetic movement was all about art and literature, so the term Modernism reflects the trends of another period in European history. If you look at the origins, you'll find references to the 'power of human beings to create, improve and reshape'.

Discovering and understanding the various artistic movements was part of the learning process that began when I was a spotty little kid. Some forty years later, I can't look at anything without thinking a thousand different thoughts and making a thousand different decisions, because my mind has become attuned to viewing things in a particular fashion. I instantly know why something was made in a specific way and where the manufacturer's influences came from. Instinctively, I understand what they were trying to say. The best antiques are pure, with the artist or artisan having travelled one particular road without veering from it one iota. It's both passionate and slavish. They have this idea in their heart that they want to show to you and that's exactly what you see. If you look at pieces from Art Nouveau or pure Aestheticism, English Regency, you get where the artist was and what they were trying to achieve in a deep, almost spiritual way. You amass more and more knowledge and the learning curve just keeps climbing. It affects every aspect of your life and you begin to understand why you think and feel in a certain way. One thing leads to another and you start to recognise how you've developed as a person and the influences that have shaped your own particular journey. Take music, for example; it's been a huge part of my life and has influenced my appreciation of this business that harks back to the origins of Modernism.

I already said that from a very young age I was obsessed with ska, two-tone and the whole mod scene. The 40th anniversary of the film *Quadrophenia* was marked with a cast reunion on TV on 21 September 2019. When I saw it advertised, it set me thinking about the way music has influenced my career right from the very beginning. I'm in love with scooters; I've got lots of them and for me it's Vespa rather than Lambretta. Scooters represent an explosive period in British culture that hit a second wave in the late 1970s. It was all about mod, a fashion statement and musical movement that has echoes harking back to the attitude displayed by the man I consider to be the greatest British artist ever: J.M.W. Turner. He was part of the Romantic movement, but anticipated both the French Impressionists and Modernism because he sought to break down conventional methods of representation; to my mind, that's exactly what the mod revival of the 1970s accomplished.

CHAPTER 9

You're probably thinking that it's quite a leap from Turner to The Who, but the way I learned to see things has enabled me to understand the passage of time and how one cultural or architectural movement links to another. 2-Tone Records was a label started by Jerry Dammers of The Specials that attempted to break down the barriers and racial tensions that existed in Britain during the years of Margaret Thatcher. Bits of the original Jamaican ska from the 1950s were mixed with punk rock and new wave and became a massive part of the Anti-Nazi League that grew up in urban centres all over the country. It was music and clothing: The Specials, Selector, The Beat, and a slightly edgier connotation from The Jam. Those bands were at the forefront of something that echoed the breaking down of traditional barriers that began with the Modernist movement. Rather than paintings and buildings, it was an audible and visual reflection of a change on the streets of Britain that I became part of as I grew up in North Wales. It was Crombie coats, Dr Marten boots and three-button suits. It was the two-tone bowling shoes The Jam brought into fashion when they first hit the scene with their single 'In the City'. I was only seven at the time but the energy of the whole thing was like being punched in the face. The very first record I ever bought was the 1980 'Too Much Too Young' EP from The Specials that I still have today.

It's a constant reminder of a time when my learning curve was growing exponentially and music culture was part of it. Mods, rockers, skinheads and soul boys; none of that tribalism exists any more but for me it was part of a surge of expression. Without the music there wouldn't have been such an interest in scooters, and they've become as big a part of my life as VWs and Porsches. The whole scene was incredibly British and I don't think it could've happened anywhere else; but the scooters, the coffee and fashion were all from Italy and that excited me.

Long ago I decided that, when the time is right, I'll knock all this on the head and fuck off to southern Italy. I'll buy a little house somewhere I can sit with a dog and watch the world go by while I dabble in antiques, because it's something I'll do until they box me up and burn me. I intend to slow the pace, listen to music and use a classic Vespa to get around on.

The Vespa – the word is Italian for 'wasp' – predates the first Lambretta, and the first model was on the market in 1946. It was made by Piaggio, who were an aircraft man-ufacturer before and during the Second World War. When the fighting ended, Enrico Piaggio, the son of the com-pany's founder, realised Italians needed a cheap and 'modern' form of transportation. Two years earlier two of the com-pany's top engineers had designed a motorbike with body-work that fully enclosed the drivetrain. It had a tall central section and a prominent headlamp that made it look like a duck, so they called it 'Paperino', which I'm told means 'Donald Duck' in Italian. It wasn't bad, but Enrico thought they could do better and the first fully fledged Vespa was launched in 1946 with sales of a couple of thousand. That steadily increased, and in 1950 they sold 60,000 of them. The model was given a massive fillip when Audrey Hepburn rode pillion to Gregory Peck in the 1953 film *Roman Holiday* and the Vespa quickly became the go-to ride for Hollywood superstars.

I was into scooters the first time I ever saw one. We always had loads of old motorbikes around our house and it was the age and patina that got me. My father had over thirty and knew everything about pre and post-war models, the flat-tanks and Nortons, BSAs, etc. One of his mates, a guy called Smutty, used to race the Isle of Man TT and another good friend made leathers – Alan Kershaw, he's still around; I bumped into him the other day and he's still got all the old patterns including the one for Barry Sheene's race leathers.

My father used to come across motorbikes in the most unlikely of places. I remember going with him in his old minivan to a house with an old barn somewhere above Llanrwst and that's when I first learned the art of 'knocking', which I used later when me and Clive Holland went car hunting. It's a term in the antiques trade for when you're driving around and get a feel for a particular place then knock on the door with a story ready. It would usually go something like this:

'Hello, my name's Drew and I'm here to see
Mr Roberts about the old motorbikes you've got for
sale in the barn.'
   'Mr who?'
   'Roberts.'
   A shake of the head. 'No, there's no Mr Roberts
here, I'm afraid, but we do have an old motorbike if
you want to look at it.'

That's exactly what my father did and invariably he'd find some gem that had been locked away for years. When we got to the house above Llanrwst, my father 'knocked' and, yes, there were motorbikes and we were welcome to take a look at them. The owner of the house led us to a shed/workshop attached to the barn but I couldn't see any motorbikes anywhere. He had a workbench about waist-height and 60cm deep running all the way around the shed, and underneath the bench were two motorbikes. I didn't see them because he'd taken the wheels off so he could sit them on the frames and slide them in, so they didn't look like motorbikes. But there they were, and I had no idea just how amazing a find this was until I was a lot older. Those two bikes were Brough Superiors, which is what Lawrence of Arabia was riding when he got killed on a road near Bovington. I don't know what my father paid for them, but he did some kind of deal and they were added to his collection. He must've had half a dozen Manx Nortons as well as other classic race bikes, including a trials Greeves that I burned my leg on when we went to a barbecue at Rowen in the Conwy Valley.

Motorbikes were everywhere, and me and my brother Guy would mess about with them, even though we were told to stay away in case one fell on us or something. There was one in particular that we had to steer clear of but never did, a late 1950s or early 60s Ducati race bike where the stand had been worn into a very sharp point. That was due to the standing starts where the rider would run to his bike and slide it off the stand before jumping on and bump-starting it. By the time that bike was added to my father's collection, the stand had been so badly worn it was little more than a spike. Me and Guy had been dicking about when we'd been specifically told not to, then I went off to do something else, leaving him with the Ducati.

The next thing I knew, bedlam broke out with my mum screaming, my father shouting and everyone running around because my brother was pinned to the floor by the stand on that Ducati. He'd been rocking it from side to side, lifting the spike off the ground, only for it to come down with all the weight of the bike on top of his foot and go right through it to pin him to the floor. Before I knew what was happening, I was in the back of my parents' Mark I Cortina estate with a black, blue and purple bathroom towel wrapped around my brother's foot and blood everywhere. We went to hospital and Guy was alright. Not long after, though, Smutty was killed racing at the TT and my mum told my father he had to get rid of his collection. He put them on the open market and a German collector came over and bought the whole lot to exhibit in a museum.

Maybe what happened back then is why bikes never held quite the same attraction for me as motor scooters. Simple and yet beautiful, functional and fun; the perfect combination of two-wheeled design and engineering. They were clean and stylish, suited to the city and easy to ride, with no exposed drivetrain to get oil on your snappy trousers. I think that was partially why they appealed to mods: a way of zipping through town in your best clobber without having to get changed after. As a statement the scooter went hand in glove with the music and clothing. It's personified in *Quadrophenia* where the first wave is explored in a uniquely British way. We didn't create Modernism and we didn't create Brutalism either. We didn't actually create punk rock either – Iggy Pop did that about three years before it exploded – but the mods were British through and through.

I was too young to own one but I wanted to be part of mod, i.e. modern culture. It was obvious to me when I was eight or nine and my mum took me to Blackpool with the youth club she used to run at Llandudno Junction. Already I was into The Specials and Madness and I used to cycle five miles to Llandudno along the main road to look for the kind of sunglasses Chas Smash wore, but could never find them. When I went to Blackpool, it was on a coach full of skinheads in donkey jackets and Dr Martens. We arrived at the Pleasure Beach fairground and everywhere I looked it was more skinheads as well as mods in suits and fishtail parkas. Everywhere I looked it was scooters. It was another Eureka moment, coming not long after I'd seen the cars at Piccadilly Woods, and I remember thinking, Oh my God, that's me. That's me done. That's where I want to be.

It grew and grew and that's when my dad painted the mural on the wall of my bedroom. I was already into ska, but I started listening to The Jam and the music got under my skin to the point that it stayed with me all through the 1980s. When I was older, Oasis came along with a British vibe that for me echoed The Kinks and Small Faces. It was something Blur tried to emulate but never quite managed. I know the Gallagher lads can be idiots at times, but no matter what you think about them, their music has an iconic feel and, as time goes on, I think they'll sit in the same uniquely 'British' space as The Kinks and Paul Weller. The music Oasis played reflected their roots on a council estate that I experienced for a while myself when I was growing up. It never leaves you. It doesn't matter where you live now or how much money you've made; the raw reality of a British council estate is inescapable. Oasis embraced that. It was a case of 'That's who we are and we're not going to apologise to anyone.' It's exactly the same with me and it was true of the entire mod movement.

Music and fashion, and the cultural changes they release, are as important to me as antiques, and it's in the Vespa that those two strands of my life come together. As far as I'm concerned, it will always be the best form of two-wheeled transport, personified in the 1959 GS. A perfect piece of engineering and design, its beauty is in its simplicity. There are no frills to a 150cc 1959 GS. Unfortunately, I don't own one, but my mate Dave has one that's absolutely beautiful. Just as the T35 is the most beautiful Bugatti and the 911 the best Porsche, the 1959 Vespa is the icon of all motor scooters. I have the 1960 model, and bought it because it was untouched, completely original and, although it just misses that purity of design, it's still a work of art. It's the best in my collection and five are GS Vespas. The Lambretta is actually better to ride; it's lower with a longer wheelbase, and Phil Daniels' character is riding one in *Quadrophenia*, but it's the Vespa GS that gets the iconic mention from The Who.

My 1960 model is painted cream and I bought it from a contact I still deal with in Sicily who specialises in hunting down classic scooters. An American girl called Lee, she called me on the phone ten years ago, then sent pictures and I just fell in love with it. I didn't need to fly out, I could tell how good it was and I parted with £4,000 in order to buy it. All my mates told me I was mental – four grand for a GS that wasn't the '59. What the fuck was I doing?

CHAPTER 9

I knew exactly what I was doing; that scooter has more than doubled its value, although I've backed off buying them these past few years as I've had to really concentrate on the business. I'll probably get back into it again, but for now that 1960 GS is not only the stand-out scooter, it's also part of my personal heritage.

CHAPTER 10

HOME AND AWAY

Over the past couple of years, I've been keen to really spread my wings in the search for a yet more varied range of antiques. It's a global business with no physical boundaries and the show is broadcast all over the world, so it's important to get out there where people can see what we do first-hand.

Filming abroad is a mammoth undertaking with the largest crew we ever assemble. There's Rob the director, Sean and Steve on the main cameras, Simon the sound man, our assistant producer Olly, as well as Carl who operates another camera, our runner Conor and Dan Trelford, the series producer. Hugely experienced and someone I have the utmost respect for, Dan was a fan of the show who wrote to the production company telling them he wanted to get involved, then he elevated what we do to a whole new level altogether. A man who can spot real talent, he's seen it in various members of the crew and helped them expand their careers.

Being on the road overseas is different to being on the road here, with an opportunity to meet new people and see new places. The trips are great fun and any issues that have arisen from the pressures of filming in the UK seem to get blown away. The only downside is that we have to get a lot done in a short space of time and travel vast distances. Imagine being in a rock band on tour without all the drugs and sex, but lots of beer and crap food, and you'll have an idea what we get up to.

It means I'm nowhere near the showroom, though, and sometimes it bothers me. I wonder what I'm doing. I mean, I used to be an antique dealer (and quite a good one) but what am I now, exactly? Am I still a dealer or am I someone who appears on TV? I've tried to combine the two and work very hard to keep a consistent flow of quality stock, as I have nine people on the payroll to consider. But the fact I'm no longer 'dealing face to face with clients' bothers me. The business is fine, we're smashing it again, but it's a continual balancing act and requires a lot of headspace and energy. The upside is that trying to perpetually do two things at once keeps me sharp, and sharp is where I need to be. That said, I really miss the day-to-day mixing with customers. You know the sort of thing; people walking into the shop for a bit of a look around.

'Hiya, mate. What you got? Oh, yeah. I'll have that.' Bosh, on to the next one.

There's a rhythm to dealing that's very important. Come March 2020, we'll have been doing the show for ten years and it's what I spend most of my time working on. Back when we first started, we'd film for three months and it would take a week to get back into the swing of dealing, but then I'd have six months solid on that before another round of filming. As the show became more successful, however, the intervals between filming grew less and the time it took to get back into the selling side of the business got much longer. I'm talking about the ebb and flow of the thing, and the more that rhythm is broken the harder it is to get back into. It's one of the many variables of the antiques trade that's quite difficult to get across, but it's something I've always been conscious of. I liken it to a cantering horse, constant movement at a speed that's both comfortable and manageable. If the stride is broken, it's hard to get it back and that's what I've had to give up in order to make the TV show. I still have all the buzz that comes with buying because that's what I'm doing day-in, day-out; it's the selling side, the interaction with regular customers, I miss out on.

Because no two items are ever the same, there's a fresh- ness to dealing that gets you out of bed every morning, but there's also the network of clients you've hopefully built a rapport with. Sometimes the customers who come into the shop are first-timers, but more often than not they're people you've dealt with before, and if you're clever you'll make sure you know the kind of thing they're in to. If you don't have what they want, you can plant a seed by letting them know what's coming in. If you've looked after them properly and gauged them right, they'll want to be the first to view and you're halfway to the deal already. That's how it works, a garden of clients and dealers you nurture in order to keep the business growing.

This whole trade is a series of relationships. It's an affinity with regular clients who might be members of the public or other dealers, auctioneers or interior designers (decorators, as they call themselves). As I've already said, my problem with so many of the shows about antiques is that they make it all about the sale, the bargain; and it really isn't like that. It takes years to get to the level of dealing where you've established those all-important relationships and it's something I strive to maintain despite the demands of TV.

You can't have it all, though, can you? I suppose the flipside of losing some of that rhythm is that I'm doing something else now as regards the antiques trade. As I said before, I never wanted to be a TV person because I've never sought the fame or notoriety that tends to go with it. What I wanted to do was get across my passion for antiques and bring more and more people into the business. You may not like me, you may not like the show, but I guarantee someone has walked into your shop or auction house because they watched us on TV. That expands the business and can only be good for all of us. These days I'm not just working for myself, but every antique dealer in the country.

Hopefully, what I do is a good influence on the trade and, from what most proper dealers tell me, it seems to be. I've been told that the show is authentic and I know it has inspired lots of people. But, remember: just because you buy a silly hat and open a shop doesn't make you an antique dealer. That takes years, and the important thing is to establish your own identity. What you shouldn't do is copy me. I've lost count of the websites that have sprung up that are a straight copy of mine; some are so close they look like they've been cut and pasted. If you are going to create a business, you need it to be individual.

I did that years ago when I had my moment in the warehouse with the Tesco camera. Since then my business has evolved and it's been helped by the TV show, but there's a downside to that because being in the public eye is crap. Honestly, it's shit. There are very few upsides. Everybody thinks you're an arsehole and I get so much flak, it's ridiculous. When someone watches an episode of the show, it's important to remember that it's a mere 46 minutes of my life and I shouldn't be judged by that alone. I make money, that's why I'm in business; but it's my money we spend and it's my risk and I have no spare minutes to call my own. Sometimes that can be really debilitating and it only adds to the panic attacks. It can get too much, particularly when you've just got back from a long trip away and you're in the car again facing a six-hour schlepp to another hotel. You've barely had time to toss your dirty clothes in the washing machine before you're back on the road.

The fact I do so much travelling is pretty ironic actually, given that when I was a kid my mum used to tell people

I hated going anywhere. If you put me in a car for half an hour, I was sick and had a headache. My eczema would flare up, I'd be tired and moaning and want to go home. Fortunately, that's not the case any more, particularly when it comes to travelling abroad. We're a team on the road, out of our comfort zone, and we all muck in. It's a period of bonding. If you ever bump into us, you'll soon see there are no 'stars' and no airs and graces. If I ever got too big for my boots, the entire crew would very soon let me know. There's a sense of togetherness that's forged not only from what we're trying to achieve, but from the fun we have as we're doing it.

The first foreign trip we made was to Norway back in 2012 and it was a great success, though an expensive place to stay as well as to buy antiques. Since then we've been to Spain and France, as well as a few other places, but we were yet to go to any of the old Soviet Bloc countries, so when a trip to Hungary in September 2019 was mentioned I jumped at the chance, as I'd never been there before. I love to travel, because it both improves my eye and expands my knowledge, and I was interested to see what might be about from the Soviet era. The night before, me and Simon Jolly stayed in a Manchester hotel then left for the airport in plenty of time to make the plane, only for Simon (who was born and bred in the city) to direct me the wrong way. I was travelling light as I always do. Generally, I'll prepare my bag then go through it and toss out everything that's not totally essential.

Hand luggage suffices for a couple of weeks; I've learned it's the best way to go. Despite heavy traffic and heading in the wrong direction, we made the plane and the buzz was in full swing when we landed in Budapest and hooked up with the lads who had flown from London. We got the hire vans packed with all the gear and I was really up for exploring.

Budapest is a fantastic city situated in the north of the country and bisected by the River Danube, with a population close to a couple of million. The sprawl goes on and on, covering over two hundred square miles of Gothic buildings and Soviet-era apartments. It's chock-full of cultural and historical icons; the Museum of Fine Arts, the Hungarian National Museum, the Franz Liszt Academy of Music and the State Opera House. But we weren't going to any of those, we were headed for a massive flea market to which no self-respecting dealer would venture alone.

Our assistant producer Olly had already been out for a recce and organised a fabulous secessionist hotel in the city centre that used to be a public bath house. He's brilliant, the kind of guy you can parachute in and know he's going to come up with something really special. I refer to him as our resident lunatic: boundless energy, but a huge amount of nous and enthusiasm, as well as a love of the antiques business, so that makes my job a lot easier. He had organised the first couple of calls and spoken to potential contributors, as well as doing the groundwork on where we'd stay. It's not a simple process, and obviously too big of a financial risk to wing it entirely, so Olly flies in armed with a small camera and a backpack and gets chatting to people. From those conversations he figures out where to go and who to talk to. That information is relayed back to the office and the trip set up with the kind of rough parameters that allow us to improvise still if we want to.

With a great hotel lined up for the first couple of nights, the crew was really happy and we were all happier still when we found a bar within spitting distance that charged 50p for a pint of lager.

'Fantastic, Olly,' I said when he came down to find me. 'This is really great, you've outdone yourself.'

'Glad you like it,' he said. 'The flea market tomorrow should be eventful.'

I had my notes on the table and was scribbling a couple of things down and he looked a little quizzical. 'What're you doing?' he asked me.

'Writing a book.'

'Really? T said as much. I thought he was joking.'

'No, it's true. I was working on it on the plane.'

'What's it about?'

'Me and the antiques business.'

'Is T in it?'

'We all are, Olly,' I told him.

He grabbed his pint and necked a mouthful. 'Well, if they want to know what I do, tell them I spend most of the time herding a flock of shit-faced ducklings.'

That's not a bad description, but it's much more than that really. With a bit of research already done, I know we'll get great stuff for the show and really enjoy doing it. We work very hard and the hours are long, but we also play hard and our tight-knit group is all the stronger for it. We make the most of every call and, hopefully, that comes across to the viewer. The camaraderie between us seems to rub off on the people we meet, and we met a lot of fans of the show this time, which is avidly watched in Hungary. I'm always amazed at how many people have seen it evolve from the early days when it was just me and T piling into places full of damp and dust to the expansive series it is today.

Having dumped our stuff and partaken of the odd 50p pint, we went out to eat at a restaurant Olly had scoped, where we were introduced to our fixer, Lazlo. Apparently, that's the most common name for a boy in Hungary, and I discovered that our Lazlo was a journalist who worked for the national press and was really into antiques. A big guy in his fifties with no hair and a handlebar moustache, he'd arranged to take us to the Ecseri flea market, which takes place every day in Budapest. But, as I said, it's not the kind of place any of us would venture alone, and there were dark-eyed gangsters all over the place looking to scam us. The moment Sean rocked up with the camera, one of them asked for his passport, telling him he couldn't get in without it. Sean's too long in the tooth for that kind of crap so he just shouldered the camera, looked the bloke in the eye and went on through.

I've been to one or two flea markets in my time, but this place was a world away from anything I'd ever experienced. Part indoors and part out, it was filthy, smelly, and the main warehouse looked as though it had been there since the 1920s. Most of the shops or stalls were about the size of three toilet cubicles and there were hundreds of them all over. Outside, people parked knackered old cars side by side and sold from their open boots.

Everywhere I went I was accosted by a gang of Romanians who were prattling in broken English. They'd obviously seen the show and kept grabbing me and trying to get me to go with them. 'Drew,' they said, 'come and look. We've got great stuff. Come and see.' They were pretty insistent and they didn't seem to be with ones we had to avoid, so I tagged along with them. The cameras weren't on yet, Sean was still setting up, but this place had such an atmosphere I dropped into dealer mould right away.

All my instincts kicked in when I spotted a painting that was 150cm tall by 60cm wide that just said something to me. Oil on canvas, it was a life-size portrait of a young boy dressed in a blue coat and white collar, holding a rifle. There was something in his face, the expression both angelic and yet a hint of devilment. A kid from Eastern Europe with a rifle, it wouldn't have been unusual for the period. Dated 1918, it was good, I mean really good, and I knew I had to do a deal right then otherwise I would lose it. I was still being mobbed by the Romanians but managed to speak to the vendor and asked him how much he wanted.

'Five hundred euros,' he told me.

No, I thought; that's not happening. I like it but not that much. 'How about three?'

He shook his head and held up four fingers.

'Four? Alright, I can do four hundred, but I can't take it now, you have to hold it for me because we need to film this for the television show.' He didn't understand at first but I managed to get the message across with hand signals and the international language of cash. Fair play to the guy, he did hold the painting and, when we came back, I bought it on camera. That's something we never like to do because the whole point of the show is to be natural, and the things I buy are the things I see when the camera is rolling, but I knew I'd lose this if we waited.

That first purchase set the tone for the whole of the day. We wandered from cubicle to cubicle and some were pretty good and others not so. A lot of the dealers were selling Soviet-era furniture, which has its own mid-century, morbid style, but we had to wade through lots of junk and crap in order to find the real items of interest. One guy operating out of a tiny shop looked like Father Christmas, but spoke good English. He'd seen the show and beckoned me over.

'Drew,' he said, 'come over here. Come on. There's something I want to show you.'

He looked like an interesting guy and his collection seemed pretty eclectic. The first thing that struck me was an eighteenth-century Japanese tapestry hanging on the back wall; the quality of the workmanship was fantastic. But it was rotten, so bad it looked as though it would fall apart at any moment. I loved it, it was a wonderful thing, but I doubted it would make it as far as the van without disintegrating completely. He clearly had a terrific eye, though, and knew his subject.

This was great, a real dealer in this sea of cubicles. I took a closer look at what else he had going on apart from that amazing tapestry. There were lots of great things but none that set the hairs standing on the back of my neck until I spotted a tiny drawing. Graphite on paper, it was an image of a man's head and that man was clearly going through some horrendous torment. No more than 15cm by 8cm in the frame, I flipped it over and on the back were stickers from all the galleries the picture had been through in the early part of the century, which meant it had already been recognised by the trade as quality. Fab, I thought, that's brilliant. I looked closely at the picture again, and only then did I realise there wasn't a curved line in the drawing. The artist had taken a pencil and used it to create tiny individual strokes that made up the image of a tortured soul who just spoke to me. There wasn't a line out of place, the skill quite incredible; it reminded me of how Picasso used a single line to draw an entire fighting bull.

'How much do you want?' I asked the guy.

'Sixty euros.'

Without thinking I offered 50 and we shook hands. It was ridiculous, the dealer in me had kicked in to get the price even lower when this was one of the best pieces of art that had ever crossed my path. It was one of those really rare moments that come along just a few times in your life … and I've seen some incredible artworks, believe me. I was angry with myself for dicking about on the price; this was insanely good and I'd offered ten euros less than the paltry amount he was already asking. I knew I had to make recompense because the drawing stirred something in my soul and it was one that would hang on my wall at home. A man in absolute despair; someone at the end of their tether completely. I knew there wasn't a person alive who could not identify with him and I asked the dealer how long he'd had it.

'Oh, ages,' he said. 'I bought it months ago.'

I couldn't believe it. In any art gallery anywhere in the world this drawing would fetch a couple of thousand easy. I was feeling really bad but the deal had been done, so there was nothing I could do except buy something I didn't want and make sure I paid full price for it. Spotting a nondescript load of other paintings the guy was selling as a job lot, I asked him how much he wanted.

'A hundred and fifty euros.'

'I'll have them,' I said. 'Thank you.'

I left his shop with the best piece of art I'd seen in a while and we hadn't even got started. It was a great omen and I was beginning to think Hungary might be as good a foreign trip as we'd covered. As soon as we moved on, I was grabbed by another bloke who'd been following us around all morning. He told me he was a massive fan of the show and I had to come and see his emporium. As we cut through the crowd, he started telling me about some of the things he'd found down the years and how he'd been in the market every day since he was 13 years old.

Instead of trading from one cubicle, he had about ten spread all over Ecseri. We walked into the largest and I immediately spotted a really good painting of a guy in his sixties. Clearly Hungarian in origin, the dealer told me it was one half of a framed pair and dug out the other. Standing side by side they showed an older man and his extremely stern-looking wife: 'Mr and Mrs Wagner'. Painted in the early nineteenth century, I liked them a lot but he wanted 150 euros, so I had a think about it. While I was doing that, I turned around and saw a collection of what looked like doll's furniture displayed on the back of the door. There was a sofa and two tubular steel chairs in red, as well as a circular coffee table. At first glance it looked like something a kid might play with, but I knew it wasn't doll's furniture. Another of those incredible moments, the second in a matter of minutes. I was looking at a collection of salesman's models created by a designer called Jindrich

Halabala in 1950s Czechoslovakia. I knew his work; one of the pre-eminent Eastern European designers of the time, he was born in 1903 and spent his early years as a cabinet maker before enrolling in the state-owned woodworking school in 1920. In his early twenties he joined the firm UP and became their development manager, where he was able to bring his belief that furniture should be functional, modular and mobile to the fore, and pioneered mass-market industrial furniture in Czechoslovakia.

This stuff was rare, very rare. To find Halabala models in a flea market was pretty much unheard of. Back in the day, the salesman couldn't throw a sofa in the back of their NSU and travel the country; instead they were issued with scale models and this was a complete set of living-room furniture. I bought that and I bought Mr and Mrs Wagner.

All day we went from shop to shop, and T was as surprised by the quality of the stuff as I was. The market just seemed to go on and on; there were literally hundreds of stalls and shops; no sooner did we get to the end of one row there was another and another. It wasn't long before I had a fantastic painting of some Russian ladies called 'The Gleaners'. It wasn't the kind of thing I'd seen before so I parted with 150 euros. By the end of the day I'd bought a dozen paintings, as well as the Halabala models and this amazing bronze of a man in the style of Giacometti, which cost me 50 euros. It was another item that really said something, a sculpture that had been welded together out of nuts and bolts and then cast in bronze. Why would someone do that? That's what interested me. Almost certainly because nuts and bolts were the only materials they had to work with.

The deeper we got into the place the larger the shops became. Now they were no longer just cubicles, they were a decent size packed with stock, and we stopped at one that looked about 15m square. At first glance it didn't seem very promising; the only thing that attracted me was a light hanging in the window. But when we walked in, it was like – *bang!* We were with somebody who really knew their job.

The sign outside said Pieta & Pieta and the owner couldn't speak any English. My Hungarian doesn't stretch further than the word 'Hungary', so we had to find a way to communicate. At first, there was nothing to say, because the quality of his stock just hit me and I had to take that in before we could strike up any kind of conversation. It was world class, chosen by a really intelligent, educated eye, and I was completely taken with it. Equally, I was wondering what a guy with this kind of education was doing in a place like Ecseri – no offence meant, of course, it just seemed so incongruous. The way he had everything displayed was really clever and thoughtful. It was something that takes a well-practised eye and a real understanding of the business. I could tell he'd been in the trade for a very long time and I was desperate to ask him about it. Like a kid in a sweetshop, I just started buying things: sculptures, bronzes, art and furniture, as well as a pair of hairdressing scissors in the Ascetic style, which I recognised because my auntie had been a hairdresser.

The more I bought, the more I wanted to talk to him. But we couldn't exchange a word and yet we had so much to say because we were coming at the same subject from completely different worlds, and yet with a commonality between us. A classic example of a shared passion that straddled completely alien cultures. I knew nothing of life in Hungary, either before or after Communism, and he had no idea what it was like to grow up in Glan Conwy. I wanted to know if he'd taught himself to appreciate the history and beauty in the same way I did, or had he been tutored by someone. We had such a similar eye there were bound to be things we had in common, so not being able to discuss them was incredibly frustrating. He reminded me of Jon Tredant, a man we were going to see the week after we got back to the UK. Old school, proper, knowledgeable: if you look up 'antique dealer' in the dictionary, you might see the definition as 'Jon Tredant'. He's a man who's been knocking around about as long as I have, and I had the same feel about that guy in Ecseri.

It was hard to communicate with any real authority. Lazlo did his best to interpret but so much gets lost in translation. It was a pity, but tempered at least by the quality of the stuff I was buying. Normally when we're buying in a flea market, T and I might spend ten minutes at a stall before we move on, but we were at least an hour and a half with this guy. As Olly said afterwards, I put my glasses on my head and descended into silence, and when that happens, he knows we're in for the long haul. As I said, the shop wasn't very big, but it was packed with such fantastic stuff I was immersed from the moment I stepped inside. He had a female marble bust from the Communist era, something I'd never seen before. That's the time to buy, but he wanted 600 euros so I passed on it and I don't know why; the bust would be three grand on the website and I was spending thousands anyway. I bought masses of other stuff, though, including four superb cigarette cases that had been gifts for the upper echelons of the Communist Party. They were just brilliant so I snapped them up at 300 euros for the lot when one alone would easily fetch that.

Finally, we had to move on, and I was still gutted that I hadn't been able to get to know the guy, but that's the language barrier for you. We took a look in the place next door where the dealer told us he'd cleared every Communist hospital after the Russians went home and left everything. Cabinets, tables, chairs; I bought his entire stock and picked up a pair of donkey-ear trench binoculars that were used for range-finding. Like a periscope, there's a series of mirrors that allow you to see over the top of the trench so you don't have to risk getting shot by sticking your head up. This was NOS (new old stock) that had never been used and was marked 'Made in 1950'. The case was missing, but the binoculars came with the tripod and both were in mint condition. The dealer also had some desktop toys made for the top brass that really appealed to me. Oddments, the kind of thing I'd not come across before and could only be bought from a place like Hungary. There was a train, a MiG fighter and the weirdest thing ever. I picked it up and it took me a moment to work out that it was a missile launcher. This was a real insight into how things must have been during the days when the Soviets ruled here. Beautifully made, the missile launcher was cast alloy that had been painted, with the rockets in chrome sitting on top of it. It was set on a multiple-wood timber base with an alloy inset and it was up for 50 euros. As I parted with the money, I imagined some high-ranking Russian army officer with this on his desk as he supped vodka and smoked Belomorkanal cigarettes.

It was an amazing glimpse of how the Soviet Union was so steeped in militarism they made missile launchers as desk toys to give to their officials. That was a first, but I already knew that back in the 1950s they used to make models of TV and radio towers, which have since become highly collectible. They're every bit as beautifully made as the launcher; 45–60cm tall, cast in alloy with clear plastic sections and timber bases, it's craftsmanship at its finest. Back then people in the Soviet Union would make long trips to visit the sites of the real TV aerials and come home with a model. I knew about that, so I started buying them up whenever I saw them in junk shops or on eBay. There are only so many out there and by the time I was finished I had a collection which I put on the website and sold in its entirety.

It had been an incredible first day and, after we packed up the gear, we piled back to the hotel to take a shower, then headed for that cheap bar I mentioned next-door to the hotel. We called it 'The Spoons' and got absolutely fucked on 50p pints of quality lager. We weren't working tomorrow, Saturday was a rest day; we were heading out on Sunday and were all full of the events at Ecseri. It was as perfect a start to any overseas trip as we'd made. I was in love with this place; the variety and quality of the antiques I'd bought would add a whole new dimension to our website. I spent Saturday organising shipping and liaising with Ruth and Michaela back in Conwy. They run things for me, make sure the money we bring in is taken care of, and ensure the whole operation runs like clockwork. I couldn't do what I do without them. Ruth sets up my entire life and I have no idea where I'm going or what I'm doing until she tells me.

That evening Olly took us to the food court at Szimpla Kert, where I had the best cheeseburger I can remember. I love cheeseburgers, one of my favourite things to eat, and this was as good as any. I've eaten in some top-notch restaurants all over the world but, if you get a good cheeseburger, there's nothing to beat it. After that we headed for a 'Ruins Bar'; they're dotted all over the old Jewish quarter.

They're called 'Ruins' because this part of the city was badly bombed in the Second World War and very few residents ever returned to their homes after. For years the area was left derelict, then the Berlin Wall came down and a few young mavericks reconditioned the empty buildings into eclectic 'Ruins' bars that are famous all over the world now. Courtyards stuffed with tables, balconies, shabby high-ceilinged rooms that have never been repainted, they were beautiful. It was just another facet of what was fast becoming a favourite city.

Heading southeast towards the Romanian border on Monday, we spent a few days on the road guided by a dealer called Balacz, who was running for mayor in the town of Vac close to the Slovakian border. That would be our last call before we flew back to Britain. In the meantime, we called on lots of places, where we found a raft of Soviet-era stuff, including industrial furniture. The language was pretty impenetrable but, as that week went by, I slipped into a rhythm of hand signals and the odd word from our interpreter. The contributors were great, but Balacz was going to be a long-term contact. He took us to an old grain mill where I picked up tons of stuff to add to what I already had. Most of it can best be described as house clearance, sort of Communist Bloc stuff that was beige and horrid and cheap, but there were a couple of engineering gems that were both architectural and industrial.

Balacz was really knowledgeable and a dealer I could connect with. He and I struck up a friendship right away and he told me he lived in a castle he bought for nothing when the Soviets moved out and everybody else moved in. Among his stock were lots of bits and pieces that made up architectural shop fronts, and I bought an entire façade for 650 euros.

On the way north again, we stayed the night at the most beautiful spot on the Danube after exhausting our collection of sing-along country music like one big happy, gypsy family. It personified the trip; outside Budapest the food had been terrible but the accommodation great and the company of Hungarians warm and friendly. The beer was cheap, which helped oil the wheels, and I was looking forward to seeing the last place Balacz had arranged for us to visit. As far as we could tell, it was the largest antiques warehouse in Hungary and run by a guy called Zsolt, which is pronounced Jol-T. I wasn't sure what to expect but he turned out to be one of the most switched-on people I've met and another guy I'll continue to do business with. When the lads arrived, he had schnapps and coffee waiting. This was 7:30 in the morning, but, apparently, it's the custom and if you don't partake it's very rude; so, of course, we all obliged him. Previously an old Soviet concrete casting factory, the place was so big Zsolt had motorised scooters for his customers to get around on. I kid you not, they were lined up before we got to the schnapps and we needed them because this place was enormous.

I bought everything from industrial ceiling lamps to an array of incredible furniture, including cupboards and cabinets, small tables, large tables, benches, stools and a whole array of glass hospital cabinets, as well as two massive wall signs. The place was stacked floor to ceiling with antiques, with a series of offices above accessed by metal stairs and walkways. I don't think I've ever seen such an eclectic range in any one place. Just about everything you can imagine was being sold, from ornaments and furniture to scooters, motorbikes and old bicycles, even a couple of horse-drawn carriages. It was one of the best days I've ever had buying. The flea market had been great but this was on another level. On top of the other stuff, I picked up a pair of folk-art dragons to fit on the end of water spouts and an eighteenth-century carriage seat. There were console tables, a marriage cabinet and a wonderful old zinc bath, as well as a couple of heavy industrial pieces that had been part of the casting factory. Having bought so much, I'd already upped the size of the van to ship it home to a 10-tonne truck, but I still wasn't finished. When the crew stopped filming, I carried on and bought another entire collection of medical cabinets.

It was a wrap, the Hungarian adventure almost over. We had a last meal on the banks of the Danube and reflected on a massively successful effort. Everyone had worked so hard, the hours for the crew were insane, and I'd had to be on it all day every day. Now we were leaving, it felt like a huge comedown and the change in atmosphere was tangible.

CHAPTER 10

It's an incredible thing I get to do. I travel the world meeting new people and buying beautiful things and I consider it a blessing, really. I know how lucky I am, but to be that lucky you have to work very hard and I'm on it 24/7. In the casting factory alone, I bought 39 different items and within that there were multiples of nine. I'd spent ten grand, which pushed the total for the trip well beyond £40,000, but I knew I'd get most of it back in the first few items that hit the website.

I had a lot to reflect on and not just the quality of what I'd been able to buy but the country itself, the people and contacts I'd made that would be great for future business. Balacz understood the kind of thing I was looking to buy, and if something really good came up, I knew he'd be on the phone to tell me.

CHAPTER 11

T'S A COCKNEY GEEZER

In the morning, I left Hungary for Manchester with Carl and Simon Jolly, each of us carrying a couple of large batteries. There are so many required for a shoot like that, they can't all be shipped as one unit, so they're split between us for the journey.

The flight was only two and a half hours and I took a moment to close my eyes and reflect on a really great buying trip, particularly that graphite on paper, which was my personal highlight of Budapest, something I would keep. There have been a few such items down the years and I've mentioned some, but there's one that stands out above all the others: a wall frieze from Thomas Bruce, the 7th Earl of Elgin, who removed half the surviving Parthenon sculptures from the *propylaea* (temple entrance) at the beginning of the nineteenth century. Classical Greek marbles, they were designed by the architect and sculptor Phidias 2,500 years ago.

CHAPTER 11

What made Elgin think it was alright to bring them back I don't know, but it caused a storm when they were shipped to Britain, with luminaries such as Lord Byron claiming it was an act of vandalism. In 1798 Elgin had been appointed as ambassador to Selim III, Sultan of the Ottoman Empire, who ruled over Greece. Before he left, Elgin asked the British government if they were interested in sending out artists to draw and cast the marbles. They weren't up for it, and whether that inspired him to bring the originals back instead, we'll never know. But the fact that he'd thought of taking casts had always been of interest to me. I'd read about Elgin years ago and I knew he'd not taken any casts in Greece because he acquired thirty-odd metres of the frieze instead. According to the research I'd done, though, when he got them back to London, he made two plaster casts of each individual piece and had them framed very simply.

So, I knew of the existence of casts, but I'd never actually come across them until one day when we were filming at a private girls' school down in Sussex. I can't remember where it was exactly – T will know – I just recall we'd been filming and picked up a few items, though nothing that really set the juices flowing. Old schools can be a good source of material and you never quite know what you're going to find, but we'd exhausted all possible areas except a couple of junk-filled garages.

They were stacked with defunct cookers and old washing machines, some doors and bits and pieces of shite, and we were about to call it a day when I noticed something about the way the floor was constructed. It was on two levels, one considerably higher than the other, and right at the back was some old furniture we were yet to go through, so I poked around a little. At the point where the floor met the wall the gap seemed a little over-wide and I realised something was stored there. Whatever it was had been stacked like crackers in a package so it was vertical; I could see what I thought was the corner of a piece of plaster about five centimetres deep and there was something unusual about it. The sixth sense I've cultivated since I was a kid kicked in, and I felt a tingling sensation.

'Hey, T?' I called. 'Come over here.'

He made his way to where I was standing.

'Can you see that?' I said. 'It's some kind of frame. That corner is definitely plaster.'

'D'you want me to get it out?'

'Can you? I mean, without breaking it?'

'I can try,' he said, and set about attempting to work it free.

Whatever was back there, it was pretty long and pretty deep and, as T began to lever it free, I could tell it was a large plaster casting. He got it to the point where I could take the other end and, between us, we started to drag it clear. It wasn't easy and we had to be careful. We had to move old doors and other bits and pieces to make sure we didn't damage it and it was only then I realised just how big it was. We had to slide it clear, so T took hold of his end and I leaned against the wall so I could push the other end with my foot. It was bulky and very heavy and my bad back had been killing me all day. I've got this disc that likes to pop out now and again, often when I'm in a car … and I'm in a car for long periods.

So, T did the donkey work but I helped as much as I could and we managed to get it free. It was facing the wall and I still didn't know what it was, but the way the frame had been constructed really intrigued me. This was some kind of frieze and the nails that held it to the frame looked right for the period. On closer inspection, I could see the same was true with the construction of the timbers themselves and the way they had been jointed. My mouth was dry and a surge of adrenalin seemed to rush through me. I thought I knew what it was and, when we turned it face on, I was certain. The frame, those nails, the way the timbers … I couldn't believe what I was looking at.

'Fucking hell,' I said.

'What is it?' T said.

I had my glasses on my head, standing with my hands on my hips. I looked it over very carefully.

'What is it?' he repeated.

'It's part of the Parthenon Frieze, cast by Lord Elgin when he brought them back from Athens.'

'You're kidding me.'

I was shaking my head. 'He made two of every section and I'm positive we're looking at one of them.'

It wasn't in the best of shape, a little damaged in places and damp from having been stored in the garage. I'd seen plaster reliefs like this go for three grand at auction, but not one of the marbles taken by Elgin. I was pretty sure this was one of his casts but I'd need to have it verified. Technically the history was questionable so I had to hedge my bets when it came to what I was prepared to pay for it. With that in mind I offered the school 1,600 quid, expecting them to come back at £2,000. But they didn't. They shook my hand on the £1,600.

Since then I've taken some flak online with people claiming I ripped them off, but I didn't. I thought I knew what I was looking at, but could not be sure, and £1,600 was only my opening gambit as none had been on the market before. Given the frieze was beginning to rot, the value would only go down the longer it sat there and it had already been hidden away for years. The school accepted the bid so I wasn't going to up it, but I'd already paid over the odds for the rest of the stuff I bought from them anyway. It's important to remember that the things you see me buy on TV are only what we can fit into that 15-minute slot, and some of what I come away with is purchased off-camera. I picked up plenty that day and paid handsomely for it, so we all won.

I love that cast and still have it at home in Conwy. It's my favourite thing in the house and I thought it was worth three grand all day long, and it still might be. But this business is fickle, and recently three similar pieces went through an auction house at only 600 quid. Those were also Elgin casts but smaller, and not the size of the originals. I think the price I paid was a fair reflection of condition and provenance. Right now, I'm not selling, but I still think I'll make money when the time comes because mine is exactly the same size as the original. I haven't had an expert out, but the nails are handmade and were manufactured around the turn of the nineteenth century, which was correct. The joints, the way the whole frieze was put together, tell me I wasn't wrong and the one I have was made by Lord Elgin. As a decorative object it's just fantastic. I know which piece of the Parthenon it is; I've been to see the actual marbles and checked every last detail. What bugs me is not the price the others were sold at, but the fact that I missed them. I only found out after they were gone, and if I'd known they were going under the hammer I'd have bid on them.

Elgin's removal of what were actually the 'Phidian Marbles' spawned a neo-classical British take on what the Greeks had been doing more than two thousand years previously. That era formed a period in architecture and design that's never been equalled and I'm proud to think I have an original cast in my collection.

Back home from Hungary, I barely had any time at all before I was on the road again, heading for the Cornish/ Devon border. Things had been so hectic I'd not had a moment to think. One day seemed to merge with the next and I had to count back before I could figure out this was Wednesday. Ahead of me was a five-and-a-half-hour drive without stops and traffic, so it could be as bad as seven. That's the worst bit of the job, but it has to be done if I'm to find the most interesting places and people.

I was tired before I even got started. Early in the week someone had hacked our bank account and stolen £14,000 before we were able to put a stop to it. It was something I could've done without, and there had been some other personal stuff flying around that I put down to bullshit stories peddled by a local rag of a newspaper whose name I won't bother to mention. Suffice to say, the crap they've printed over the years has caused me untold problems; sometimes living in the place where I grew up can be a real hassle. Every now and again it gets a little crazy and there's a part of me that yearns to disappear off to Italy or buy a flat somewhere nobody knows me.

In-car time, though, there's an awful lot of it, and lately I've been travelling alone on the way to shoot the TV show because T now lives a long way from Conwy. Whereas we used to take off in the van together, we can't always do that any more; sometimes we don't hook up until we get to the destination. Today I was in the Range Rover, which is a nice place to be, but I've put 72,000 miles on the clock in the 18 months I've had it. That's without van time, so you can see just how great the distances are we have to cover. Despite being knackered, I was looking forward to Dingles

Fairground Heritage, which was the call we'd make tomorrow. It was 2:30pm already and I was only just leaving Colwyn Bay but I had my office on wheels and my music. At 5:00pm I'd put on Radio 4 and listen to the news before the comedy half-hour at 6:30. That's sacrosanct, no matter where I am or what I'm doing, that's time I have to myself every day and nothing gets in the way of it. I switch off at 7:00pm because I can't stand *The Archers*, but I have to listen to the comedy.

After a night in another hotel, we spent a mad day at Dingles, which was something of a landmark moment. Just shy of ten years ago, we visited the place on the very first series and turned up (all of us and all the gear) in a single people carrier. A rabble, that's how Simon Jolly described us. Not really knowing what we were doing but full of enthusiasm anyway.

Dingles is an entire fairground that two old boys put together to create a heritage centre that's also used by schools as an educational facility. As Simon said, it was like gate-crashing an episode of *Scooby-Doo* where we showed up in our very own 'Mystery Machine' and were confronted with all the old rides and music. Ten years later we were back, and we were a little choked up with emotion. Neither Simon nor I had believed we'd come this far; for my part I'd never contemplated the idea of a second series, let alone still doing it ten years later. But the fact is we're still here and that's largely due to Simon. He was the one who saw the way I was in front of the camera and told me just to keep on doing what I was doing. Back then I was getting a little bit of flak from the producers because (despite the leeway Philip had given me) I was too honest and upfront, and they wanted that tempered a little. Simon didn't agree and he stuck his neck out to tell me. In fact, he could've got fired for what he said when he nudged me one day and told me it was really good and to ignore what everyone else was saying. That made up my mind and it's how I've done the show ever since.

To be back here where we'd filmed during that very first series resonated and we were both more than a bit nostalgic. So much had happened since; people had come and gone, and others had taken their place. Children had been born and some of us had been through messy divorces. All the while, though, the show grew in popularity and the only real constants were me, T, Simon Jolly and Gavin.

With nostalgia still trickling through our veins, we arrived at yet another hotel, then most of the crew went out for a curry at an excellent Indian restaurant in Exeter called Ganges. Afterwards we sat down for a drink and Simon and I reminisced about all we'd accomplished over the last ten years of the series. The beer was flowing, as were the war stories, when a guy came over to say 'hello', and he seemed to immediately personify all that we'd been trying to achieve with the telly. His name was Gary Churchward and he was in the bar later than he should have been, having promised his wife he'd be home by 11:00pm. It was well past that already and he still had a 20-minute walk ahead of him. He'd been about to leave when he spotted us rabble as we came through from the restaurant and decided to come over and introduce himself. A really nice guy, he was a fan of the show, the second person to tell us that night. Gary's been a guard on the railways for 32 years and was into railway memorabilia long before he started watching the series. He told us he'd been watching since the very beginning and, after he'd gone, I looked long and hard at Simon.

'Sums up everything we've been through today,' I said. 'Ten years on and who would've thought it?'

I know there are thousands of people out there like Gary whose interest in antiques has been taken to another level because they've watched the series. What really grabbed him was the time I came across a set of stacking (or modular) bookshelves made by Globe Wernicke, a firm formed in 1899 after Globe Files from Cincinnati bought Wernicke in Minneapolis. I don't remember where I found the shelves, but it was the fact that I knew what they were that piqued Gary's interest. He told me that since then he's done his own research on countless items we've come across and has been completely hooked by the learning curve that goes with the business.

Talking to him was liberating. This was exactly what I'd been trying to do when I agreed to make the show in the first place. Exeter was already special because of where we'd been today and Gary brought that home in a way that was obvious to the entire crew. For that alone the show has been a success, never mind the ever-growing viewing figures. It was the perfect end to a perfect day, only surpassed when we were finally able to flag down a cab big enough for all six of us. The driver recognised T the moment he climbed in and joined us in an Olly-led rendition of that famous old North-Walian ballad: 'T's a cockney geezer, mushy peas and liquor – eels, eels, eels. Eels, eels, eels.'

Yeah, I know – you really had to be there.

Up not so bright and early in the morning, it was back to business and a call to Jon Tredant, the guy I told you about who typifies what it means to be an antique dealer. He runs Carradale Antiques from a warehouse showroom close to Exeter Airport, but we were going to take a look at some of his overflow stock housed in a massive 1870s-built barn in the courtyard outside his farmhouse. The farm itself spans 77 acres and Jon's family moved in on 7 July 2007 – 07/07/07. Prior to that, the house he lived in was number 77, so it's no wonder he considers seven to be something of a lucky number, but it's one of the numbers I have trouble with, along with three and nine. I'm told it's something to do with a form of dyslexia, which wasn't diagnosed until I was 37. Anyway, I was looking forward to talking to Jon; he's a little older than me and wears a pair of ten-quid glasses perched on the end of his nose, though he should go to the optician because he really can't see anything through them.

CHAPTER 11

His history is not dissimilar to mine in that he came to appreciate the business early. When I first met him, he told me how he was dragged around antique shops pretty much from birth and absolutely loathed it. That changed, though, when he was eight years old and made money on a silver fish knife. Since then he's become as obsessed as I am, a real dealer who learned his craft over a number of years and shares my passion for things as 'untouched' as possible. His showroom/warehouse carries a lot of stock that's spread over three floors. He has a good eye and displays stuff with imagination. He's got another warehouse at the same location, plus a few containers he uses to store back-up stock, then there's the farm where the barns are stuffed to the rafters.

'You've got some stock here,' I said, as we climbed the steps to the upper floor of the first barn.

'It's what I call the overflow of the overflow, and there are a couple of pieces I think you might want to have a look at.'

He told me how he'd just put a new roof on the Exeter showroom and was keeping it awash with what he hoped was the right kind of stock. He has a passion for really old, really big cupboards and cabinets, but the market for that kind of thing really isn't there right now, so he's had to hold on to a lot of it. The market will come back, it always does, there's a revolving door to this business, but right now there's not much call for the big stuff. Most of what Jon sells has something going on and it would be interesting to see if the items he thought I might buy would be what I wanted to go for. That's how it works when it's dealer to dealer. We all think we know what someone will want to buy, but this business is full of surprises.

'I like this place,' I told him. 'It's got a great feel.'

'Yes,' he said. 'It reminds me of the farm my mother and father rented and the museum shop I created.'

'You had a museum shop? I was selling bits of old bicycle from the roadside.'

T was already looking around and the amount of stock Jon had on the upper floor alone was mind-boggling. It was packed with dining and club chairs, and tables of various sizes from England and France. There were mirrors, bookcases, even an old wooden canoe upside-down on the rafters. I spotted a grandfather clock and loads of cupboards and cabinets, most of which were early English. He had chairs on desks and a pair of old untouched leather armchairs he thought I might be interested in. We talked about what was selling right now and what wasn't. I pointed out a large carved walnut cupboard dating from the seventeenth century.

'There's another one to match it.' Jon nodded to the far end of the room where an even bigger cupboard was standing. 'I like them, I always have. I bought those in a sale fifteen years ago and they were disassembled. Someone had stored them in a barn since the Second World War and they were in a pretty poor state, but we restored them and put them back together.'

'They're beautiful,' I said. 'A matched pair, it's not often you see that.'

'Schranks, from Bodensee, they're dated 1660.'

'They're good,' I said. 'Really handsome.'

'But too big. Nobody wants them that big these days, but I don't care. I like them.'

I asked him how much he'd paid for them.

'All in all, with the restoration, they cost me £17,000 but I doubt they're worth that today.'

Another buy he'd made with his heart and not his head was a series of Mediterranean fishing floats, green glass spheres strung with thick netting, that were hanging from the ceiling in the stable block downstairs. Jon told me he'd bought a whole stack from a friend of his, years ago, and this was all that was left of them.

'How many did you buy?'

'Oh,' he said, 'at least seven or eight hundred. I regretted it right away and had to work really hard to get rid of them.'

'And what's left here is the profit?'

'Almost certainly.' He had a wry smile. 'I could've sold them a few times since I got rid of the others, but they remind me of a wild deal I made so I'm keeping them.'

I pointed out another cupboard and he told me he'd had that a long time, and had partially restored it. He doubted the market would come back but it didn't matter because the money had long since turned over and it was good background stock regardless. He had a Gothic oak wardrobe and bedroom set that he'd sold to a friend who had recently moved out of the large house where she was living. She phoned him up to see if he wanted to buy them back, and he did, though for only a third of what she paid; but that's how the market was right now so he couldn't give her what she wanted. Jon pointed out that smaller items like jewellery and Rolex watches have done nothing but go up in the last few years, but they're the things you really have to compete for.

I had a vintage Rolex on my wrist that had done nothing but increase in value since the day I bought it. It replaced one I'd been wearing for half my life that came (in a round-about way) from my grandmother Nin, the most important person in my life. She came to live with us in 1973 and was part of the family I grew up in. Winfred Alice Roberts, my mother's mother, she's the reason I'm the man I am today, the greatest influence on my life and the strongest person I've ever met. I said before, five foot of fury but also knowledge and love, and I adored every inch of her. Anything I've ever done is because of her. I don't mean the bad shit, that's my doing, but all the good stuff comes from her. It was she who instilled the 'Take it or leave it – Don't like it don't look' attitude, which I believe has stood me in good stead throughout my career. I don't take prisoners. I don't suffer fools and neither did Nin (or Ninja, as T sometimes referred to her).

When she died in 1992, she left me and my brother £500 each. He bought a Rolex Datejust with the money, but I had a mortgage to pay and nothing to pay it with, so I used her money for a month's worth. A year later I was back at Newark and the guy with the stall next to mine was a watch dealer. He was having a really bad day but he had a very nice Rolex Datejust I had my eye on. He was asking 1,200 quid and I couldn't afford that, but the fair lasted three days and the watch didn't sell, so on the final day I wandered over. 'Show's over,' I said. 'What's your best price on the Datejust?'

'Give me seven hundred quid and it's yours.'

I gave him the cash, took the watch and wore it every single day until I bought the one I have now, because I didn't want to damage it any further. I was 23 then and I'm 49 now and I consider the watch my inheritance from my grandmother. It's stowed away safely now and won't be touched again until it's passed down to my son.

Apart from those club chairs, Jon had a couple of other items in mind he wanted to show me, one of which was a glass tobacco sign he'd forgotten he had because it had been stored behind one of his large cabinets. There was a French farmhouse table he'd only picked up the day before and we'd have a discussion about it. T spotted a really nice English chess table from 1860 made in Verre Eglomise, that's 'gilded glass' where the underside of the top is painted with gold or silver leaf then partially covered in wax before being dipped in acid. That process creates recesses on more than one level, which are then decorated from beneath, giving it a three-dimensional appearance.

All Jon's stuff is quality; he has the eye of someone who's been in the business 37 years; if we weren't filming, I could spend a week here. But we were filming, and the crew was getting restless, so it was time to get down to business.

CHAPTER 12

THE BEST OF
THE BEST

By the time I got back to Conwy after filming with Jon, the lorry-load of stock was on its way from Hungary and I'd already been on the phone buying more antiques. Some of the items I was going to keep (like that pen-and-ink drawing, for example, because for me it was right up there with some of my best finds). There's something about having an item around that's really top quality that is immensely satisfying. It doesn't have to be wildly expensive – it can be as simple as a picture, some folk-art or what looks to some like a knackered old sofa.

The show had come so far since the early days and there's no doubt in my mind that part of the success was down to Rebecca. She's no longer involved in the business, of course, but she and I were together for a lot of years, and, if I hadn't let things slide, it's possible we still would be.

Hopefully, that's a period in my life I've left behind for good, and these days I'm in a much better place emotionally. I'm in a good spot as far as the TV series is concerned, and the business is smashing it. Because I'm writing this book it's been on my mind a lot and the full turnaround I've made since those dark times was exemplified when the quality stock arrived from Hungary. There was so much of it crammed into the warehouse we could no longer get the main doors shut, so whatever had to go to the first floor was shunted up the narrow staircase. Everything had to be photographed and I asked Eleri to begin with the smalls so I could get them onto the website as soon as possible. It would take weeks to get everything we'd bought into the public eye, and I knew I had to get started. That said, we were filming all the time with some big trips coming up, so the upload would be limited to Wednesday and Friday as always. Having cast my eye over the fresh inventory, I left the lads to figure out the issues with storage and drove back to Conwy to repack my bag for the following week.

Spending so many hours at the wheel of a car, I have a lot of time to think (when the phones not ringing, that is), and on the way back from seeing Jon I'd been thinking about this book and everything I wanted to get across. Searching out the best of the best is important to me – it's so integral to this business – and I'd been thinking about some of the other rare and precious items I've found, one of which was an old wooden box.

It wasn't just any old box, though. It belonged to one of my heroes and comes from a period of British achievement that's hard to surpass. Remember I told you I hated boats? Well, that goes for all but one: the *Bluebird K3*, which wasn't the one that broke up when Donald Campbell was killed on Coniston Water, but the one his father Malcolm raced on Lake Maggiore and Geneva when he broke the world water-speed record. Long before that, he'd already broken the record on land at Pendine Sands. A truly amazing man, he was the David Beckham of his era. At 21 he won the first of three consecutive London to Land's End races on a motorbike and by 1910 he was racing cars at Brooklands. When the First World War broke out, he enlisted as a despatch rider then worked as a ferry pilot for the Royal Flying Corps because his superiors thought he was too clumsy to be given control of a fighter. He broke the land-speed record for the first time in 1924 driving a V12 Sunbeam, and in 1927 and 1928 he won the Grand Prix de Boulogne driving a T37A Bugatti. It was on Lake Maggiore in 1937 where his twin-engine *Bluebird* surpassed the world water-speed record that had been set by Garfield Wood in a four-engine boat called *Miss America*. A year later he was back in the boat on Lake Geneva.

Malcolm Campbell had fascinated me since I was a kid and it was well known to my friends in the trade, so when I took a call from a couple of really good dealers I know, I pricked my ears up. John and Jonny from Liverpool, they're good friends I meet up with from time to time, a pair of dyed-in-the-wool dealers who have been in the trade for as long as me. The day they rang I was in the warehouse and I hadn't heard from them in weeks.

'Hey,' I said. 'What's going on?'

'We're at an auction and there's a really special item in the catalogue we think you might be interested in.'

'What is it?'

'Malcolm Campbell's toolbox from *Bluebird*.'

'You're kidding.' I was stunned. 'You're sure it's Malcolm not Donald?' I had to be certain because, if you mention the words Campbell and *Bluebird* in the same sentence, the first thought is Donald and Coniston Water.

'Yeah,' they said. 'It's Malcolm, alright, his name is on the box. It's the one his mechanic used on Lake Geneva.'

That was 1938 and I'd never seen anything like it come up in all my years as a dealer. 'Buy it,' I said. 'Buy it at any cost.'

I owned nothing from Malcolm Campbell and I didn't care how much I had to pay. To this day he remains an icon. A boy's own hero, but a real hard-arse of a guy who didn't seem to have been very loving towards his son. Perhaps that's why Donald was always trying to live up to him, I don't know, but a few years ago I started collecting early photographs of the cars used to break the land-speed record. I had one of Major Henry Segrave, the first person to break 200mph on land in a Sunbeam V12, which was the same car Campbell had used at Pendine Sands. It's a period that really interests me because the most incredible risks were taken with the most amazing machinery. If you see the cars in the flesh, they're mammoth, absolutely terrifying, with no safety aids whatsoever.

So, I wanted the toolbox no matter what it cost, and John and Jonny brought it over a couple of days later. It was a big old thing, planked and painted blue to match the boat and beautifully faded. Malcolm Campbell's name was stencilled into the wood, but the 'Sir' had clearly been added later. He was knighted in 1931 and he hadn't been on Lake Geneva until 1938 so his mechanic must've been using this box long before then. There was no question in my mind that it was the real deal and I wanted it, no matter how much I had to pay.

'How much d'you want for it?' I asked them.

'Twenty thousand pounds.'

Wow, that was a lot of money, especially as I knew they'd only paid £5,000 for it. But that's the trade, they had been there to bid and I hadn't and they knew this was a piece I really wanted.

'How about fifteen?' I suggested.

'No, it's twenty thousand or we're not selling it. It's worth all of that right now. Who knows how much it might be worth if we hang on to it?'

That was a shedload of money for an empty pine box, but it was a magical item. I had to be sure, though, so I gave it another really close inspection. Three things stood out: first, it was marked 'Geneva', which dated it to at least 1938, but I was sure it was used before 1931. It was also stamped with 'No. 1' and that suggested it was the original toolbox Leo Villa (who was Campbell's mechanic) had used on all their projects. I'd never seen another come on to the market, and it might very well have been the box they used on the car at Pendine Sands back in 1924. I'd never be able to prove that, but as well as the fact the word 'Sir' had been added later, there were two shades of blue paint, which denoted the colours of both *Bluebirds* Campbell commissioned. Technically, the box would've belonged to Villa and it looked as though it had also been used to store pots of paint in after he retired. I knew he had worked with both Malcolm and Donald Campbell, so it's possible this box had been used on *K7* as well as *K3* on Lake Geneva.

I had to make a decision, because John's dad (who had been in the trade since before his son was born) had already advised him not to sell it. In fact, he told him he was nuts even at £20,000, so I stepped up to the plate and bought it. Twenty grand for an empty box, it was a massive amount of money, but I've never regretted it for a moment. John and Jonny made a profit and I don't begrudge them a penny. If our roles had been reversed and I'd paid the £5,000, I wouldn't have sold it to them, even if they'd offered the £20,000. It's our job to make a profit and sometimes we're on different ends of that arrangement, that's just the nature of this business. They made good money then and I might make some later. Right now, it doesn't matter. Some things are worth more than money, they transcend profit, and the Campbell toolbox is one of them.

Over the years I've shown it to a few dealers I really respect and none of them thinks I paid too much. One guy who's right at the top of the tree told me it was one of the best things he'd ever come across. He's right. There's a certain magic about it. Look at that box and you don't have to guess at the history, you're there on the banks of Lake Geneva. You're there at Lake Maggiore and Loch Lomond, where *K3* was launched, and maybe even Pendine Sands.

There's been a resurgence of interest lately because of the 'Bluebird Project', where a team of enthusiasts raised the *K7* wreckage from Donald Campbell's fatal 1967 crash in 2001. The boat is now back on the water, having been painstakingly restored to the point where the new one is 90 per cent still the old. I planned to take the toolbox up on the day they first set it back in the water, but we were filming miles away and I wasn't able to do it. I've had various offers for it over the years, none of which I've accepted, though it's on the website if you want to buy it. It's iconic, up there with the sign from the Bugatti factory and the Elgin cast.

It happens with furniture sometimes, too. I've got a Howard sofa in my house that stands against the wall directly underneath the Elgin frieze. It's ratty and old and

I've done nothing to it since I bought it but it's perfect for what I wanted. When I saw it online, I didn't even have to think. I'd been in the house nearly four years and had been looking for the right sofa pretty much since I'd got there. It became an obsession, a bit like trying to find another Porsche after I sold my 911. I found one sofa I thought might work which was up for three and a half grand and I was prepared to pay that, but it had to fit exactly. It was being sold by a dealer I know and I asked to try it before I bought it, but he told me I had to pay for it.

'OK,' I said. 'But if I can't get it through the door it's no use to me. I'm not going to pay for it until I've tried it.'

'Well, you can't try it then,' he said, and that was the end of it.

I was on a mission now, so I sat down with my iPad and started hunting seriously. Literally five minutes later I found the Howard that's now in my living room. The company was started in London in 1820 and became the pre-eminent producers of 'seated' furniture throughout the nineteenth and early twentieth century. It's still going today and remains the best in its field because of innovative designs and the quality of workmanship and materials. It's nice to have something in your home that's considered to be 'the best': I already had two Howard Grafton armchairs and wanted the right sofa to complement them.

As I trawled the net, I found one from 1915 that had seen the kind of wear I was looking for and was exactly the right style. It was unusual because it had been covered by a kilim at the factory. Kilim is a rough type of carpet that fades over time and this had exactly the patination I wanted. I saw it on the Instagram site of another dealer I know, and was positive it would fit, but it seemed to have been on the page for months and I thought he must've forgotten to take it down after he'd sold it. Sure it was already gone, I sent him a quick text message.

You haven't got that still, John, do you?

A message came right back.

Shockingly yes.

How much is it?

To you – £2,600?

Right, I'll have it.

It was perfect: I had no problem getting it into the room and it fitted exactly where I wanted. No adjustment was necessary and I didn't have to move the Elgin frieze. It's in the style of the English country house and I think the best period for that look was around the 1920s. Later on, it was promoted by dealers and decorators like Sybil Colefax and John Fowler. The market quietened down for a while, then in the 1960s it came back with master decorators such as Geoffrey Bennison. More recently, it's been made popular again by people like Piers von Westenholz, David Bedale and Robert Kime. These are dealers who specialise in that really high-end feel and I'm far too much of a magpie to compete, because I have a strong tilt towards the industrial.

My own house, though, is the epitome of that bohemian style and the Howard sofa fits perfectly.

A Howard is the best of the best and, as I said, sometimes it's just nice to know you own something of that quality. It's the same with cars, and for me that's Bugatti or Porsche or the Mercedes AMG GT. Earlier I mentioned that, when I bought an Aston Martin in favour of my 911, I did nothing but regret it after; but for many people Aston Martin is the best of the best and I appreciate that. People love them, they evoke exactly the same emotions as I get from a T35, and every now and again you come across someone who loves them so much they have an entire collection.

During filming for the classic car show in early December, I went on a call to a really rundown area of Birmingham in search of some trim rings for the wheels on a Saab 96 we're in the middle of restoring. J. Hipwell & Sons in Greet is a company that's been supplying specialist car parts since 1898, which is almost as long as the industry's been going. I did a little research and discovered that the first four-wheel petrol-driven car made in Britain was built in 1892 by a man named Frederick Bremer in Walthamstow. The next one was made in 1895 in Birmingham by Frederick Lanchester, who at the same time patented the disc brake. Cars were in their infancy and the company I was going to see were there right at the very beginning.

CHAPTER 12

At their height Hipwell employed about forty staff, though that's dwindled to just a handful. They do a great job; everything is handmade and one of the things I want to do with the classic car show is bring in as many restorers and small businesses as possible. We'd bought this Saab and I wanted to have trim rings (or beauty rings as they were called back in the day) fitted to the wheels to give them that little 'extra'. Trim rings fit to the metal section of the wheel to aggrandise it a little and that's the look I wanted.

When I got to J. Hipwell & Sons, I was met by Paul, a man in his mid-sixties, who told me the company is the oldest manufacturer of trim rings in the world. It was brilliant, perfect, and I have no idea how the lads who work on the car show keep finding these places. Chris, James and Mike; they do an amazing job and this was incredible. An old building that really doesn't look anything from the outside, with one of those old-fashioned plastic 1970s signs where the lettering looks as if it's come off a bag of spangles. Inside, I found myself in a massive Dickensian workshop with wooden offices strung up in the timber A-frame and a floor full of lathes and other engineering equipment. They make air filters and badge bars, but their speciality is trim rings and hub caps, and I told Paul it was trim rings I wanted. Back in the day, Saab were always banging on about their aeroplane technological background and the 96 design was pretty much based on an aircraft wing. It's really fluid and harks back to a bygone era, and I wanted our car to look much older than it actually is. I told Paul I needed the hub cap/trim rings combination to be totally smooth, and he immediately got what I was talking about. We talked about the Saab 96, then he hit me with the fact that he'd made the very last set of hub caps for the very last run of Saab 96s ever made in 1980. Saab UK wanted to go out with a bit of a splash so they came to Hipwell to have the hub caps made specially.

'You're kidding me,' I said. 'You made the originals for the car I've just bought?'

'That's right, a one-piece disc that goes over the whole wheel.'

I couldn't believe it, this was perfect; exactly the sort of thing I'd been looking for. He said he still had some and wandered off to have a look while I took another moment to check out the rest of the workshop. A few minutes later he was back with one of the original discs, still in the wrapping. It had little vents, though, which I didn't want, so I asked him if he could do anything like that and he told me he had another one. Off he went again and came back with one just as I'd described in stainless steel and still in the original greaseproof paper.

I needed four and he could supply that: fantastic, job done. I was delighted. That was all we needed, though, so I turned to go then spotted the wheel of an Aston Martin DBS.

'Why've you got that?' I asked him.

'The wheel? I collect them.'

'You collect wheels?'

'No,' he said. 'Aston Martins.'

I looked at him a little dumbfounded. A Dickensian workshop with just a few people working, in a pretty shitty area of Birmingham. 'You collect Aston Martins?'

'Yes,' he said. 'I've got thirteen of them.'

'What?' I couldn't believe it. 'Thirteen Aston Martins? You don't have any DB4s, 5s or 6s, do you?'

'Yeah,' he said. 'I've got a couple of each. Do you want to see them?'

Of course I did, this was amazing. Paul led me through a side door into a much smaller room but instead of old-school lathes there was an original 1970s V8 Vantage, a DBS and a DBS kit with an alloy body built on the frame of a Vantage. Pulling back a dust cover, he showed me a right-hand-drive DB5 and the hairs stood up on the back of my neck. First made in 1963, the DB5 is the iconic car James Bond drove in *Goldfinger*. Paul told me he races them and, apart from this one, he had another that Aston built for Le Mans but was never actually used. It was the most incredible find in the most unlikely of places. I mean, the area was really run down and this factory a relic from the past, yet here were six of the finest cars ever made. The DBs were stacked on top of each other on four post hydraulic lifts, because there really wasn't enough space for three cars, never mind six.

'God, Paul,' I said. 'You'd have to sell a truckload of trim rings to afford a collection like this.'

'I've had them since the 1960s. When I was eighteen, I wanted to go racing and had the choice between an E-Type for £500 or an Aston Martin for £425. Money was tight, in racing it always is, so I chose the cheaper option.'

He told me he still has that original Aston, and after he went racing, his dad started buying Aston Martins and keeping them. The DB5 on the lift was one of those in metallic blue and absolutely beautiful.

'How long have you had this one?' I asked him.

'Thirty-five years. My dad bought it off a scrap dealer after it'd had a bang on the passenger side so I had to find a second-hand wing.'

'How much did your dad pay for the car?'

'Six hundred quid.'

I asked him how much he thought it was worth now and he told me around £400,000 but it was more like £575,000.

'Would you ever consider selling it?'

'No,' he said. 'None of them is for sale. We didn't buy them to sell. I just love them.'

I got that completely. Paul was an aficionado; he loved to race the cars and that's where the passion began, and it was still the same forty-odd years later. He told me his personal everyday car is a 1966 DB, 3.6-litre with a sun roof and Borrani wheels, which are the sexiest wires ever made and you find them from De Tomaso to Ferrari.

I came away from Hipwell with not just the perfect wheel trim for the Saab, but also an incredible story behind that trim and a whole history of one man's love affair with Aston Martin. It's what makes this job so special and it's why I made the point about the other TV shows and how much they grate with me. It's a special business and what I'd been party to today was just one of hundreds of experiences that this great trade has enabled me to share in. It's ever changing; no two items or experiences are the same and that's why I will always be so passionate about it.

CHAPTER 13

A SPECIAL PLACE TO BE

I spoke about Turner and his relationship to the Modernist movement, but the first time I saw one of his works was a copy my father painted. He really is brilliant, and quite often people would ask him to recreate great paintings such as Turner's *The Fighting Temeraire*. It's an incredibly famous painting that hangs in the National Gallery, depicting the last moments of HMS *Temeraire*, a 'second-rate' 98-gun ship, as it's towed by a tug to Rotherhithe, where it was broken up and used for scrap wood. Turner painted it in 1838 and it was exhibited at the Royal Academy a year later.

I saw my dad working on his version when I was a kid, and remember thinking, Oh my God, what is that? It was utterly brilliant and I just couldn't stop staring. The colours, the way the thin film of cloud is reflected in the water, he captured the whole image so evocatively it stayed with me. Afterwards he took me to a gallery and showed me some original Turners and I was just blown away. I could not believe what I was looking at. The whole visual effect was stunning. Back then I was too young and inexperienced to know why the paintings were so special; now that I do, I'd rather I didn't. The wonder I felt is what got me and sometimes the only way to maintain that wonder is to not understand, just appreciate what you've witnessed. Impressionism in its finest form; Turner was the first to really nail it. As far as I'm concerned, he did it better than anybody else until Van Gogh came along, maybe.

Turner was born in Covent Garden and died in Cheyne Walk, which is where I'd delivered the Empire cellarette that leaked all over that white carpet. By the age of 14 he'd been accepted into the Royal Academy, and was originally part of Romanticism, which was prevalent at the time, and emphasised intense emotion. That was exactly what I experienced when I saw my dad's version of his painting. From what I've read, Turner was a man who retained his cockney accent all his life and when he lectured at the Academy from 1807 until 1828, he was said to be really inarticulate. He travelled Europe in his twenties and you can see the influences in his paintings. He's one of a number of artists I really rate: Hockney is terrific and so is Edward Hopper, who painted *Nighthawks* in 1942. You'll know that if you see it, even if you don't know its name. It's a Modernist image of people at a downtown diner late at night, viewed from the street through a plate-glass window.

Turner was a reclusive figure who didn't have many friends, his best being his dad, who lived with him for 30 years and worked as his studio assistant. He never got married but is believed to be the father of two children by a woman called Sarah Danby. Later he moved into the Chelsea home of the widow Sophia Booth and lived as 'Mr Booth' for 18 years. His work fascinates me. It strikes the emotional chord I've talked about more than any other British artist. We had books about him around the house when I was a child and that's where I did my research.

A few years ago, I was at the National Gallery in Edinburgh where a couple of his paintings hang, and I saw another at a private house in northern Scotland, a castle actually. We were there for an episode of the show, and I got talking about art with the contributor, and told him how much I loved Turner.

'Oh,' he said, 'I've got one here. Come on, I'll show you.'

He had an original hanging on his wall, not the best I've seen, but who cares – it was still a Turner. In his later years he was championed by the critic John Ruskin and, when he died, he left over five hundred oil paintings, a couple of thousand water colours and some thirty thousand drawings. He lived for his art and allowed nothing to get in the way. I love that kind of passion, it speaks to me, and, as far as Turner was concerned, it was born from the copy my father painted. I remember the hazy background; the vision

Turner must've had in order to make it so atmospheric. The flashes of light here and there, it brought the composition to life in a way few other artists have.

It's so much more than a painting, it's a whole other world, a story all of its own and a piece of British history. It's the same with his landscapes, they suck you in so you're right there in the midst of everything. When I look at art, I try to do it from the perspective I had as a child when the whole composition just grabbed hold of me. That's not so easy to do, because the problem with being an antique dealer is that we don't see what other people see, we look at a piece and tend to see the faults before anything else. The best buys are the ones when you don't even have to think about faults; that happened with the drawing I bought at Esceri.

In my opinion Turner is the greatest British artist and I've always wanted to own something he created. The trouble is you can't buy Turner's work, can you? Not unless you've got a few million quid lying around, and I haven't. He left a couple of snuff boxes behind as well as a pair of glasses but you can't buy those either; one snuff box is part of an ongoing exhibition and I've no clue what happened to the other.

So, owning something of Turner's was a desire I thought would never be fulfilled until the day I got an email from someone I'd never met, asking if I'd like to buy his signature. I wasn't sure how they knew I liked him; I suppose it must have come out during an interview. I asked them to send me a photo of the signature so I could see the context and, when it came through, it looked like an entry in a diary or register. I'd have to do some work to find out where that might be from, but in the meantime, I took a long time studying the signature. It looked right, but I'm no expert and couldn't be sure so I sent it to a friend of mine who deals in fine art and asked him what he thought. The response was swift and positive. It was dead right – as far as he was concerned that was J.M.W. Turner's signature.

I immediately rang the seller who told me they wanted £400, and I had no idea if that's what it was worth, but I didn't care. It was worth it to me and that's all that mattered. With certain things there is no top and bottom price, it's all about what it's worth to you emotionally, and for me the emotion attached to Turner far outweighed 400 quid. I was happy to pay, and when it arrived it had that sense of magic about it. This was real and I'd achieved a lifelong ambition to own something by my favourite British artist. Having done some research, I now believe it dates back to his early days at the Royal Academy when he had to sign the register after dropping off a selection of paintings for exhibition. It's one of many signatures on a page from the diary of a well-documented annual event – but it really doesn't matter to me where the signature is from. After seeing my father recreate one of his most famous paintings, I finally had something from the hand of the master.

There have been lots of great British artists, of course, people like Gainsborough and Constable, but there's just something about Turner. When I look at his works, I can appreciate the toil and fight he had with himself to get what he wanted to express onto the canvas. It's what I call 'pure vision'. He knew what he wanted exactly but to be able to recreate what was in his heart like that wasn't easy. I see it in the brush strokes of every painting; the same kind of pain I picked up in the drawing I'd bought at Ecseri.

I understand that toil. I can draw and paint, although to nothing like that standard. When I was restoring stained glass, I would be drawing on a daily basis to design windows and create schemes we would manufacture. I understand the mental process, the way you have to fight to get something you feel out onto the paper. With fine art it's not just the idea, though, it's the entire construction. When I look at a painting, I see the pain and toil, but I also ask myself why the artist chose that particular size of canvas or those specific colours. In the case of *The Fighting Temeraire* I was in awe of how Turner had painted the clouds in such a thin film they looked like gun-smoke. The flashes of light look like explosions. This was a warship about to go to its grave and what he'd achieved was a single picture that brilliantly evoked its history.

That level of appreciation transcends the visual arts into all areas of my life and business. For example, I would put the musician Prince in the same bracket of genius as Turner.

That might sound mental, but in his particular field Prince was exceptional. I've already talked about how the whole mod thing had links to what Turner was doing originally, and the sculptor Henry Moore is up there with him in that respect too. I love Moore's work and have an original piece in my collection. He was born in 1898, died in 1986 and represented all things modern, abstract and surreal. He created the *Recumbent Figure* in 1938 and *Family Group* in 1950 as well as *Nuclear Energy*, which is a domed sculpture resembling a mushroom cloud and is displayed at the site of the world's very first man-made nuclear chain reaction. His stamp is all over that piece, though it's unlike most of the others he created. There's something ominous about it that just shouts at you.

Another guy you can't ignore is the genius that was Rennie Mackintosh, a man who just seemed to pull his work out of nowhere. Originally a water-colourist, he became an architect and designer whose work had links to European Symbolism. He died in 1928 and since then he's been copied and his name plastered over everything from tearoom chairs to shitty stained glass and car stickers. An artist who's been ruined by his own popularity, but if you look at his work, particularly Hill House, Helensburgh, just outside Glasgow, you see absolute genius. He designed the interior as well as the building and most of the furnishings for the publisher Walter Blackie.

It's the same with people like Alberto Giacometti, the Swiss sculptor who created some truly fantastic pieces.

No outside influences, a purity of vision where nothing is watered down, it's the artist at that particular moment, and – for the true greats – that moment spanned a lifetime. I think I've had that level of 'pure me' for about ten seconds in my entire life, but I'm able to get what they're doing and I think that's been evident throughout my career.

It's spanned 33 years so far and I hope it will continue for a lot longer. Year on year I've been climbing, not just in terms of my standing within the trade, but in terms of my knowledge and understanding. It's been a series of steps: you go up one and the next, then another until you get to a level where you stop worrying because you know more than enough to get by now. That's all well and good, but if you keep climbing you keep learning and that way you get to a point you never even knew existed. There the mist just clears and everything is obvious. Your thinking becomes a 360-degree experience. You see things in a completely different way to how you used to and for me that's reflected in houses, clothes, the design of cars, as well as music and the way trends are dictated. When I look at a building, I see how a bricklayer isn't just an artisan, but a visual artist. They have to be, otherwise they'd never be able to get the symmetry and beauty into a particular building. It's not merely the eyes of the architect: it's the vision of the people who actually build it that creates the thing of beauty, and it's the same with a joiner or gardener.

In my case that vision grew as I worked my way up the steps of my career until it all came together in one exceptional, unforgettable moment. A point of acceptance I'd craved ever since I first saw those antique dealers show up at my parents' house to have their vans sign-written. For years I'd held the trade in such high regard, I'd get annoyed when people would tell me they were antique dealers. I knew I was doing ten times the business they were and had a hundred times more knowledge, but I still didn't consider myself to be an antique dealer. Over the years I'd worked on multi-million-pound jobs in hotels and churches, I'd restored old schools with re-creations in stained glass. My whole life had been a constant stream of find, buy and mend old things; but I knew there was so much more to being an antique dealer than that and I strove to get to the point where I could accept *myself*, let alone be accepted.

It finally came to fruition a few years ago when the TV show was into its second or third series. I was 41 years old and we were nailing it as a business. The whole thing was going incredibly well but I still didn't consider myself to be a proper dealer. That changed when I was accepted to exhibit for the first time at the Decorative Antiques & Textiles Fair at Battersea Park in London. This was a way bigger deal than anything I'd done before, including Olympia, which I had done and probably falls into the second tier. Battersea is the crème de la crème when it comes to our business. You have to apply and they vet you to find out if you're good enough and if your stock is up to it. You really have to know what you're doing, have a style or look of your own, so I didn't hold out much hope when I stuck my application in. To my surprise they came back and said I could have a stand, and that was the moment I began to alter the way I viewed myself and my business.

I was a bit nervous because I knew what Battersea meant to the trade and the quality of dealer I would find there. Three days prior to the fair opening, I packed up the van and drove down to London, where I set up my stand. As I was working, I discovered that the dealers around me were the easiest people in the world to talk to. We spoke the same language. We had something in common and, for the first time in my life, I realised I was able to play at the level of most of them.

It was like dawn breaking, and the mist finally cleared for good on the final day of set-up when I walked to the hall through the foyer. In those days the café was off to the right and, as I passed, I spotted Peter Berg, Andrew Purchase, Russell and Mick from 17/21, as well as George from Brownrigg and Paddy Macintosh, David Bedale and Richard Nadin all sitting at one table. These were the best dealers in the country and I wasn't going to stop because I knew they'd have nothing to say to me. I carried on by and was almost back in the main hall when one of them called out to me.

'Hey, Drew,' he said. 'Come on over here. Come and join us.'

I remember thinking, Are they talking to me or is there another bloke in the hall called Drew I haven't come across?

No, there wasn't. Nobody else back there, it seemed that the elite group of antique dealers in the trade were asking me to sit down with them at the high table.

Wow! It was up there with the most important moments of my life and one I will never forget because, prior to that, if someone asked me what I did for a living, I didn't dare say I was an antique dealer, I'd just say I was involved in architectural salvage.

But how you see yourself isn't necessarily how others see you, and as I sat down it became clear that the best of the best had a level of respect for what I was doing that I'd only experienced once before after Alex MacArthur and Ray Azoulay phoned me. I had to pinch myself just to believe I was actually sitting with them. It was so easy, so comfortable, so natural. We were having a laugh, talking about the trade and the upcoming fair and it felt like a bunch of mates taking the piss out of one another and I was completely, deliriously happy. To this day those guys have remained some of my best friends, and I know I could ring any one of them at any time and they would be there for me.

The moment of acceptance, it was so dramatic I could've cried. I knew I was in because if you're going to exhibit at Battersea your gear had better be dead right or you'll be found wanting – and I wasn't.

After that first fair I had the confidence to start mixing in business circles I never dreamed I'd ever be involved with. I found myself in the company of the kinds of interior designers and decorators that cater for the largest country homes and multimillion-pound town houses and apartments. Businesswise I did alright, but when the next fair came around I took £60,000, and the next after that I took £120,000.

After so many years grinding away at the coalface, everything clicked into place and I went up another gear altogether. The moment I'd been looking for all my life; it cemented a fact that I know to be true, though it took a lifetime to get there. I'm not just a man with a van, I'm an antique dealer.

ACKNOWLEDGEMENTS

Jeff Gulvin, Gordon Stewart, Joe Sturgess, my team at DP HQ Ruth, Eleri, Michaela, Neil, David, Sam and all my friends and enemies in the antiques world.

Special thanks to Tee, Paul Cowland, Andy Jaye and Marino Franchitti for putting up with me.

INDEX

INDEX

INDEX

INDEX

Gloucester   Hereford   Worcester

THREE CHOIRS

A History of the Festival

For
Jonathan and Lucy

Gloucester   Hereford   Worcester

THREE
CHOIRS

A HISTORY OF THE FESTIVAL

ANTHONY   BODEN

with
ANNALS OF THE THREE CHOIRS
by
CHRISTIAN WILSON

ALAN SUTTON

First published in the United Kingdom in 1992
Alan Sutton Publishing Ltd · Phoenix Mill · Far Thrupp · Stroud · Gloucestershire

First published in the United States of America in 1992
Alan Sutton Publishing Inc · Wolfeboro Falls · NH 03896–0848

British Library Cataloguing in Publication Data

Boden, Anthony
Three Choirs: History of the Festival –
Gloucester, Hereford, Worcester
I. Title
782.5078

ISBN 0–7509–0082–2

Library of Congress Cataloging in Publication Data applied for

Endpapers: *front*: south-west view of the City of Hereford (*Hereford Cathedral Library*);
back: south-west view of the City of Worcester.

Typeset in 11/12pt Garamond.
Typesetting and origination by
Alan Sutton Publishing Limited.
Printed in Great Britain by
The Bath Press, Bath, Avon.

CONTENTS

Annals of The Three Choirs

ACKNOWLEDGEMENTS

Since starting out in 1989 to research and write this history the list of those to whom I turned for information, advice and help, steadily and inevitably increased. From the outset my closest companion and colleague was Christian Wilson, who not only took upon himself the task of updating the Annals of the Three Choirs which form the Appendices to this book, but also willingly volunteered to type out my manuscript. For this considerable labour, his encouragement, and countless cups of coffee, I am deeply grateful.

It has been my good fortune to meet many people whose memories of the Festival over long years have helped to enliven these pages. I am particularly indebted to Basil Butcher, Maurice Hunt and Reginald Woolford who were kind enough not only to lend me their valuable collections of Three Choirs photographs, press cuttings and memorabilia, but also to allow me to keep them by my side for many months as most useful sources of reference.

I have been helped greatly by the reminiscences of past and present organists of Gloucester, Hereford and Worcester: Melville Cook, Meredith Davies, Douglas Guest, Donald Hunt, Richard Lloyd, Roy Massey, Christopher Robinson, John Sanders, Herbert Sumsion and Sir David Willcocks. I also acknowledge with gratitude the help of many kinds which I have received from Wulstan Atkins, Jean Armstrong, Rodney Bennett, Ray Boddington, Vernon Butcher, Tony Clark, Hugo Cole, Pat David, Jeremy Dibble, W.A. DuBuisson, Alice Dyson, Sir Keith Falkner, Diana Feilden, Tom Fenton, the late Joy Finzi, Derek Foxton, Brian Frith, Patience Gobey, Mike Grundy, John Harris, Jenny Houston, Brendan Kerney, Jerrold Northrop Moore, Christopher Palmer, Arthur Pritchard, Peter Roberts, Rosemary Passmore-Rowe, Watkins Shaw, the late Edith Sterry, Alice Sumsion, R.S. Thompson, Canon David Welander, Sam Driver White, Howard Williams, Ursula Vaughan Williams, Francis Witts, and Percy Young.

I am most grateful to Robin Stayt who, having offered to assist in researching this work, accepted the specific but unenviable task of seeking out the precise origins of Three Choirs. His enquiries over many months and in many places included the study of numerous manuscripts, family correspondence and other documents, and interviews with several historians of the eighteenth century. Although unsuccessful in adding substantially to the store of Three Choirs knowledge, his efforts were of enormous value in eliminating from further consideration those areas of research which he had proved to be without profit, thus saving me many hours of fruitless labour.

My researches would not have been possible without the cooperation and assistance of a number of professional librarians and archivists. For their unfailing courtesy and consideration I would like to thank Sue Hubbard, Jill Voyce, Barbara Griffiths, Graham Baker, and the staffs of the City Libraries and Records Offices in Gloucester, Hereford and Worcester; the National Sound Archive; Christopher Bornet and his colleagues at the Library of the Royal College of Music; Ian Ledsham at the Music Library of Birmingham University; Godfrey Waller of the Manuscript Department, Cambridge University Library; Robert Tucker at the Barbican Music Library; and Meg Kimmins, Joan Williams and Ron Stratton at the Cathedral Libraries of Gloucester, Hereford and Worcester respectively.

I am grateful to the Oxford University Press for permission to quote from *Walford Davies* by H.C. Colles; *R.V.W. – A Biography of Ralph Vaughan Williams* by Ursula Vaughan Williams; and *Elgar on Record* by Jerrold Northrop Moore; and to Gollancz Ltd for permission to quote from *Elgar as I knew him* by W.H. Reed.

My thanks are also due to Gareth Rees Roberts for copies of his photographs of the 1991 Hereford Festival, and to Jack Farley for his care and photographic skill in copying, often from very poor originals, many of the illustrations in this book.

Finally, I must thank my wife, Anne, for her constant support and forbearance throughout the past two years.

A.N.B.
June 1992

Picture Credits

Unless otherwise stated, the illustrations in this book are taken from the Extra-Illustrated edition of the Annals of the Three Choirs, compiled by A.M. Broadley, and presented to the City of Gloucester Library Local History Collection by Alderman Edwin Lea in 1917.

CATHEDRAL ORGANISTS

The organists of Gloucester, Hereford and Worcester from the time of the earliest Music Meetings to date

Gloucester	Hereford	Worcester
1712/13 William Hine	1707 Henry Hall (II)	1688 Richard Cherington
	1714 Edward Thompson	
	1720 Henry Swarbrick	
		1724 John Hoddinott
1730 Barnabas Gunn		
		1731 William Hayes
		1734 John Merifield
1740 Martin Smith		
		1747 Elias Isaac
	1754 Richard Clack	
	1779 William Perry	
1782 William Mutlow		
	1789 Miles Coyle	
		1793 Thomas Pitt
	1805 Charles Dare	
		1806 Jeremiah Clarke
		1807 William Kenge
		1813 Charles Clarke
	1818 Aaron Hayter	
	1820 John Clarke-Whitfeld	
1832 John Amott	1832 S.S. Wesley	
	1835 John Hunt	
	1843 George Townshend-Smith	
		1844 William Done
1865 S.S. Wesley		
1876 C.H. Lloyd		
	1877 Langdon Colbourne	
1882 C. Lee Williams		
	1889 George R. Sinclair	
		1895 Hugh Blair
1897 Herbert Brewer		1897 Ivor Atkins
	1918 Percy Hull	
1928 Herbert Sumsion		
	1950 Meredith Davies	1950 David Willcocks
	1956 Melville Cook	
		1957 Douglas Guest
		1963 Christopher Robinson
	1966 Richard Lloyd	
1967 John Sanders		
	1974 Roy Massey	
		1975 Donald Hunt

BIBLIOGRAPHY

Three Choirs Published Sources

Lysons, Revd Daniel, *History of the Origin and Progress of the Meeting of the Three Choirs of Gloucester, Worcester and Hereford and of The Charity connected with it* (Gloucester, 1812)

Ibid. Carried on to 1864 by John Amott (Gloucester, 1864)

Ibid. Continued to 1894 by C. Lee Williams and H. Godwin Chance (Gloucester, 1895)

Lee Williams, C. and Godwin Chance, H., *Annals of the Three Choirs of Gloucester, Hereford and Worcester. Continuation of History and Progress from 1894–1922* (Gloucester, 1922)

Lee Williams, C., Godwin Chance, H. and Hannam-Clark, T., *Annals of the Three Choirs of Gloucester, Hereford and Worcester. Continuation of History of Progress from 1895 to 1930*

Shaw, Watkins, *The Three Choirs Festival* – The Official History of the Meetings of the Three Choirs of Gloucester, Hereford and Worcester, c. 1713–1953 (Worcester, 1954)

Further Reading

Atkins, E. Wulstan, *The Elgar–Atkins Friendship* (David & Charles, 1985)

—— *1890–1990 The Centenary of the Birth of a Friendship* (Worcester, 1990)

Barrett, Philip, *The College of Vicars Choral at Hereford Cathedral* (Hereford, 1980)

Bennett, Joseph, *Forty Years of Music, 1865–1905* (London, 1908)

Best, G.F.A., *Temporal Pillars* (London, 1964)

Brewer, Sir Herbert, *Memories of Choirs and Cloisters* (London, 1931)

Butcher, Vernon, *The Organs and Music of Worcester Cathedral* (Worcester, 1981)

Colles, H.C., *Walford Davies* (Oxford, 1942)

Cook, Andrea T., *A History of the English Turf* (London, 1905)

Dean, Winton, *Handel's Dramatic Oratorios and Masques* (Oxford, 1959)

Frith, Brian, *Gloucester Cathedral Organ* – 'The Organists of Gloucester Cathedral' (Gloucester, 1972)

Gaisberg, F.W., *Music on Record* (London, 1948)

Gee, Very Revd Henry, *Gloucester Cathedral, its Organs and Organists* (London, 1921)

Goossens, Eugene, *Overture and Beginners* (Methuen, 1951)

Hawkins, Sir John, *A General History of the Science and Practice of Music* (London, new edn 1875)

Heighway, Caroline, *Gloucester – A History and Guide* (Alan Sutton, 1985)

Holst, Imogen, *Gustav Holst – A Biography* (Oxford, 1938; reprinted 1988)

Hunt, Donald, *Samuel Sebastian Wesley* (Seren Books, 1990)

Jacobs, Arthur, *Arthur Sullivan, A Victorian Musician* (Oxford, 1984)

Moore, Jerrold Northrop, *Edward Elgar – A Creative Life* (Oxford, 1990)
—— *Elgar on Record* (Oxford, 1974)
Myers, R.M., *Handel's Messiah: a touchstone of taste* (London, 1948)
Phillips, Henry, *Musical and Personal Recollections During Half a Century* (London, 1864)
Plumb, J.H., *The Commercialisation of Leisure in Eighteenth-Century England* (Reading, 1974)
Reed, W.H., *Elgar* (Dent, 1946)
—— *Elgar as I knew him* (Gollancz, 1936; reprinted OUP 1989)
Rosenfeld, Sybil, *Strolling Players and Drama in the Provinces* (Cambridge, 1939)
Shaw, Watkins, *The Organists and Organs of Hereford Cathedral* (1988)
Walker, Ernest, *A History of Music in England*, 2nd edn (Oxford, 1924)
Welander, Revd David, *The History, Art and Architecture of Gloucester Cathedral* (Alan Sutton, 1991)
West, John E., *Cathedral Organists Past and Present* (London, 1899) (NB Now updated by Watkins Shaw, *The Succession of Organists of the Chapel Royal and the Cathedrals of England and Wales from* c. 1538 (Oxford, 1991))
Whyte, J.C., *History of the British Turf*, 2 vols (London, 1840)
Vaughan Williams, Ursula, *RVW – A Biography of Ralph Vaughan Williams* (Oxford, 1980)

Abbreviations

MW	*The Musical World*
MT	*The Musical Times*
(G)	Gloucester
(H)	Hereford
(W)	Worcester

following a year to denote the venue of a Festival (e.g. 1991(H) = the Hereford Festival of 1991)

CHAPTER ONE

LEGEND AND LEDGERS

H aving searched for the origins of Three Choirs, the Revd Daniel Lysons was forced in 1812 to admit that, 'It is in vain that I have endeavoured . . . to trace any thing like the time of their first establishment.'[1] More than 150 years later, in an historical note for a Worcester Festival programme book, the music critic A.T. Shaw pronounced that ' . . . any attempt to fix the date of the [first] meeting is predestined to failure'.[2]

The earliest record which Lysons had been able to trace was contained in an announcement in the *Gloucester Journal* of Monday 12 August 1723:

> All Gentlemen who are Subscribers to the Annual Meeting of the Three Choirs at Gloucester, Hereford and Worcester are desired to take Notice, That the Day and Place of Meeting this year is at Hereford, Tuesday, Sept. 3rd., in order to a performance of Musick the two Days following, pursuant to their subscription. Tickets to be had at Mr John Hunt's, Bookseller, and at Mr Ford's at the Redstreak-Tree, in Hereford.

In 1723 the *Gloucester Journal* was only in its second year of publication and no references to a Music Meeting at Worcester appear in the 1722 editions. However, the *Worcester Postman* had already then been in existence for more than a decade, and the edition dated 14–21 August 1719 contains the following notice, first traced by Sir Ivor Atkins:[3]

> The Members of the yearly Musical Assembly of these Parts are desired to take Notice, That, by their Subscription in September last at Gloucester, they are obliged (not withstanding a false and groundless Report to the contrary) to meet at Worcester, on Monday the last day of this instant August; in order to publick performance, on the Tuesday and Wednesday following.

Clearly an annual event was already established by 1720, but for exactly how long is far more difficult to determine. In searching for the seeds of Three Choirs it is necessary to look back much further – and to begin with a misty legend.

In his booklet, *1890–1990 The Centenary of the Birth of a Friendship, Edward Elgar – Ivor Atkins: Elgar and Atkins and their Influence on the Three Choirs Festival*, Sir Ivor Atkin's son (and Elgar's godson), E. Wulstan Atkins, recollected his boyhood years in the Worcester Cathedral Choir, 1913–19, and hearing from 'the oldest lay clerk, James Smith, then nearing eighty, about a "legend" which was handed down from one generation of lay clerks to the next, relating to the start at Worcester of the Three Choirs Meetings':

I was fascinated, and told my father, who said that he knew all about the romantic legend, but without confirmation it could not be treated seriously . . . Some years later I found that Elgar . . . knew all about it, having, he thought, been told it by his father when he was about 12. I asked him to tell me the version he had heard. It was almost word for word what I had been told in about 1918, and what my father had heard in 1897 when he first became organist at Worcester. All three versions stated definitely that it was Worcester who had started the Meetings in 1662, by the lay clerks inviting their colleagues in Hereford and Gloucester to join them in celebrating the recent full restoration at Worcester of daily sung services with organ. Neither Elgar nor my father, being good historians, would accept the legend without written proof; it sounding to them too much like 'an old monk's tale'. They admitted, however, that there were points of great interest to them in the story, particularly the date for the start of the Meetings at Worcester in 1662. Both knew that this would be the first year after the 1660 Restoration in which the lay clerks could have invited their colleagues, but in itself this did not prove anything.[4]

But why, in any case, should the Worcester lay clerks invite their colleagues from two other cathedrals to join them in 1662? Worcester and Gloucester are linked by a navigable river but travel to Worcester from Hereford would have involved a difficult journey on horseback or by horse-drawn cart along rutted tracks. What connections can we find to link the three cathedrals before 1662? Let us begin with Worcester and Gloucester, and with a celebrated English family of musicians.

Thomas Tomkins (1572–1656), master composer, was appointed organist in Worcester *c.* 1596. He was an old Gloucester boy, born probably under the shadow of the cathedral. His father, also named Thomas, who had been Precentor of Gloucester Cathedral and Vicar of St Mary de Lode in the city, died in 1627. The younger Thomas was a pupil of Byrd, and was made a gentleman and later organist of the Chapel Royal.

When in 1616 William Laud, afterwards Archbishop of Canterbury, became Dean of Gloucester with a mandate from James I to set right much that was amiss, he turned to Tomkins at Worcester for advice on the organ. Thomas Dallam, who had built a new organ at Worcester in 1613, came to see the Gloucester instrument. It was 'very mean and very far decayed'. On Dallam's advice, Laud decided to follow the example of Worcester Cathedral and appeal for funds for a new organ. On 12 March 1616 Laud wrote to 'the right worshipful our verry worthy and lovinge Friendes the Gentrey and others of the Countie and Citty of Gloucester':

> . . . We are at this time repayringe the decayes of the church, and by that chardge are utterly disinabled to provide a new organe without the helpe of such worthye Gentlemen and others well disposed as shall approve and indeavour herein within the countie and the city. Wee are ledd on upon this adventure by the example of our neighbour church of Worcester, which (though it be farr better able than ours is, yett found this burthen too heavye for them) and therefore took this course with good successe to the great honour of the Gentrye and other Inhabitants of that Shire. The countie of Gloucester is farr larger, and wee have noe cause to doubte but that this countie and citty wilbe as forward and bountifull as their neighbours have beene . . .[5]

There is no record of the response made to Laud's appeal. Perhaps in a Puritan city where Laud's liturgical changes were thought to smack of popery, money was deliberately withheld. The old organ was patched; nothing more was done, and by 1637 it was considered beyond repair and sackbuts and cornets were introduced to accompany the choir. Then in 1640, John Okeover (Oker) was appointed organist and master of the choristers. Okeover, finding himself organist without a useable organ, turned, like Laud before him, to Worcester for example. He sought the advice of Thomas Tomkins, who no doubt advised the Gloucester Chapter to negotiate with Thomas Dallam's son, Robert. The accounts show that six shillings was given to 'a messenger to Worcester two severall tymes to Mr Thomkins about the agreemt with Dallam for the new organ'.

Choral services continued for at least two years after the new organ was set up. But in 1642 the dark clouds of Civil War finally broke. Worcester remained loyal to Charles I; Puritan Gloucester supported the Parliament, and even John Okeover became a soldier and took up arms in Cromwell's cause.

In September 1642 the Parliamentary army under the Earl of Essex effected 'the profanation of the Cathedral' [in Worcester], wrote Sir William Drysdale, 'destroying the organ, breaking in pieces divers beautiful windows wherein the foundation of the church was lively historified with painted glass, and barbarously defacing fair monuments of the dead.'[6]

Tomkins must have succeeded in having his organ repaired after these atrocities but in 1646 Worcester was besieged. Parliamentary reformers again fell upon the cathedral. 'The organs being two fair pair, all the bishops' beards, noses, fingers, and arms and all, if they had any white sleeves, were broken'.[7]

Thomas Tomkins was deprived of his living, his life's work seemingly in ruins about him. He went to live with his son, Nathaniel, at Martin Hussingtree where, a disappointed man, he died in 1656.

Cirencester fell to Royalist troops in 1643. Prince Rupert then rode on to Gloucester to demand its surrender. Gloucester refused. In August, Charles I surrounded the city with thirty thousand men. A Parliamentary force arrived on 5 September, relieved the siege within two days, and the Earl of Essex entered Gloucester in triumph.

Tradition has it that Gloucester Cathedral was spared excessive damage, but an ordinance abolishing all choral services in England and Wales, directing the demolition of all organs in cathedrals and other churches, was passed by Parliament in 1644. Deans and Chapters were dispersed and for sixteen years the choirs fell idle.

Following the Restoration of Charles II in 1660, all confiscated church lands and buildings were given back. Surviving members of the Chapters, lay clerks and others returned and a massive programme of repairs was set under way. But it would be a long time before all was back to normal. Wulstan Atkins has summarized the situation at Worcester:

1660, Cathedral partly ruinous, no choir, no organ, no Master of the Choristers and no music. Morning Prayer was said for the first time on August 31st, 1660. The new Dean, Dr Oliver, President of Magdalen College, was installed on September 13th, and strenuous efforts were made to 'settle the church in order', including re-establishing the choral services, since it was understood that Charles II would visit Worcester on 3rd September, 1661, the anniversary of the Battle of Worcester. (The visit did not take place). Only four of the Minor Canons who had served the Cathedral in 1646 and six of the former lay clerks were still alive. The full complement of ten lay clerks was reached in April, 1661, but it was not until May, 1662 that the Minor Canons were up to the ten required by the statutes. The choristers had been formally admitted by November, 1660, but they would require many months' training before they could take their part in the choir.

   In June, 1661, the Chapter appointed Giles Tomkins, a nephew of the former organist Thomas Tomkins, as organist and Master of the Choristers. . . . In July, 1661, an organ loft was constructed, and George Dallam built an organ, probably from the remains of his father's 1613 organ and of the other smaller organs taken down in 1646.[8]

Giles Tomkins visited the Dean and Chapter of Gloucester in the latter part of 1661, no doubt to advise them in regard to the organ, thus re-establishing musical links between the two cathedrals. He would have found a city, unlike Worcester, under the deep suspicion of Charles II. If Worcester had been the 'Faithful City', the last to hold out in defence of the Crown, Charles 'had not forgotten Gloucester's earlier sympathies, and took steps to make sure the city would not oppose him again':

> By the Corporation Act of 1661, the town councillors, aldermen, and officers all had to take an oath of allegiance, and to forswear the Puritan's Solemn League and Covenant . . . The Council was also purged of all its anti-Royalist members: 10 aldermen, 25 councillors (more than half) and John Dorney, the town clerk, were all removed.[9]

It comes as no surprise, therefore, to learn that at the Bishop's Visitation of Gloucester Cathedral in February 1663, John Okeover had failed to return to his post:

> . . . there was lately an Organist in the said Church who is lately gone away, And that at present there is no organist there, & we further say that ever since his Majesty's most happy restoration the teaching of the Choristers or singinge boys, hath been committed by the Deane & Chapter to Richard Elliott, one of the Lay Clerks of the said Church for the said time, being two whole yeares, & we know not where it may be continued on him longer, & for his paynes and care, we leave it to your Lordshipps Consideration.[10]

In the absence of an organist the task of answering the Bishop's questions fell to two of the singing men: Robert Muddin and the aforementioned Richard Elliott, whose son was a chorister. From them we learn that there were seven singing men and eight choristers at Gloucester in February 1663 – the year following the first legendary Music Meeting at Worcester. Wulstan Atkins again:

> To replace the destroyed music books the [Worcester] accounts show that in 1661 the Chapter purchased a set of Barnard's 1641 '[The first Book of] Selected Church Music', and later other music was obtained from King's College, Cambridge. The accounts for 1662 have a number of entries of payments for copying music. Complete sets of music for all the choir were not available until 1662. The Chapter's troubles regarding the organist were not over, however, since the accounts show that Giles Tomkins absented himself before December, 1661 . . . Richard Browne, one of the Minor Canons, was elected in March and admitted as organist on 26th April, 1662. The Cathedral was, therefore, without an organist for about six months, though probably Richard Browne carried out the duties.
>
> From all these facts it is clear that the Chapter, who would naturally have wanted the music for the services to be of the highest standard, and the lay clerks themselves, would not have been in a position to invite their colleagues from Hereford and Gloucester to visit them before September, 1662.
>
> At first sight all this would appear to confirm the 'legend', but unfortunately, despite the detailed entries already referred to, no trace can be found of later entries making any reference to the three Cathedral choirs meeting at Worcester in 1662. It is true that the legend claims it was the Worcester lay clerks who issued the invitation and possibly therefore there was no expense to the Chapter, but nevertheless one would have expected some entry in the official archives, if only to record the date and that official approval had been granted.[11]

Thus, we have evidence of strong musical links between Gloucester and Worcester over half a century, firstly through Thomas Tomkins and, after the Restoration, his nephew Giles Tomkins. It is also reasonable to assume that Gloucester would be anxious to demonstrate loyalty to Charles II by sending a delegation and taking part in

Restoration celebrations in the 'Faithful City'. But these were hectic times for the Worcester Chapter. The Treasurer's Accounts reflect an immense amount of cathedral repair-work in progress, and the ledger is far less neatly maintained than in the settled days to come. Unless the visit of the Gloucester lay clerks involved expense, no entry would appear in the accounts. And what about the Gloucester Cathedral Accounts for 1662? Again, a complete blank; but not so for the following year. Here, at last, in an entry dated 24 August 1663, is strong evidence of a joint celebration:

> Given to the Worcester Choirmen and Organist with the consent of Dr Washbourne . . . £ 1 . 0 . 0[12]
> [Thomas Washbourne was a Prebendary.]

Then, on 6 November 1663, the Worcester Treasurer's Accounts show that five shillings was 'Paid for ringing when Mr Deane came from Gloucester'.[13]

Clearly, the Worcester lay clerks and Richard Browne were in Gloucester at about the time of the anniversary of the legendary Worcester 'Music Meeting'. If the Dean of Worcester, Dr Thomas Warmestry, was with them and returned at the same time, the visit must have lasted close to six weeks – and it seems unlikely that the Dean's return to Worcester would have been greeted by a peal of bells unless he had been gone for some time. In any event, evidence of such a visit from Worcester to Gloucester lends support to the strong possibility that there had indeed been a similar and initial celebration in Worcester in 1662. Such a legend is unlikely to have persisted over three centuries unless *some* sort of Meeting had taken place. However, not even fragmentary evidence exists to indicate that Hereford was involved in these first Meetings.

An undated entry in the Worcester Treasurer's Accounts for the year 1670 records:

> Given by order to Mr Elliott of Gloucester Choire . . . £ 2 . 0 . 0[14]

Elliott was paid £10 per year for his duties as a lay clerk at Gloucester. It is highly unlikely that he would have received £2 at Worcester entirely for himself, and it is reasonable to assume that this sum represented a payment to him as senior lay clerk on behalf of all the Gloucester choirmen. This entry is followed by another:

> A messenger to Gloster by Mr Tompkins order for a Singing man . . . 0 . 3 . 0

Had one of the Gloucester men failed to arrive in Worcester? Certainly two of Richard Elliott's contemporaries, Richard Broadgate and John Payntor, had been sacked in 1666, 'admonished to depart this church for often absences & contempt of the Dean and Chapter',[15] and their successors may well have been no more reliable. But the reference to 'Mr Tompkins' shows that the influence of that family was still strong. This was Nathaniel Tomkins, strong Royalist, High Churchman, amateur musician, Canon of Worcester Cathedral from 1629, and the son with whom the great Thomas Tomkins had lived for the last ten years of his life.

Throughout the years 1662 to the end of the century there is only one other ledger entry which might be significant. It appears in the Gloucester Treasurer's Accounts and is dated 21 November 1665:

> Paid to a Hereford Singing Man by Mr Deane's order . . . 0 . 5 . 0[16]

Was this a visit to Gloucester by a single singing man? He could have been in company with other Hereford choirmen; we can never know. What is clear is that no regular payments were made by the Chapters after 1663. This does not, of course, mean that Meetings did not take place. If arrangements for visits were made between lay clerks no Chapter expenditure would have been incurred and, therefore, no ledger entries made. Equally, although Chapter approval would have been required, no decision as such would have been entered in the Chapter Act books. From the few documentary fragments that *do* exist it is reasonable to conclude that *some* meetings between two, and possibly all three, of the cathedral's choirmen took place in the latter part of the seventeenth century, but no regular sequence can be deduced.

Unlike the cathedrals of Gloucester and Worcester, Hereford Cathedral had no monastic tradition. Having a secular (i.e. non-monastic) body of clergy, it underwent no constitutional change at the Dissolution of the Monasteries under Henry VIII. In the early middle ages the clergy of the cathedral included not only the Dean and twenty-seven canons, but also a number of chantry priests, or cantarists, who were employed to say Mass at the many altars in the cathedral. Richard II incorporated the vicars choral as a college in 1395, by which time their number had risen to twenty-seven, one of whom was elected custos. The Laudian statutes of 1637 provided for only twelve vicars, together with five lay members.

Shortly before the Civil War, a group of soldiers touring several cathedrals in different parts of the country, visited Hereford:

> Next came wee into a brave, and ancient Priviledg'd Place, through the Lady Arbour Cloyster, close by the Chapter House, called the Vicars' Chorall Cloyster, where 12 of the Singing Men, all in Orders, most of them Masters in Arts, of a gentile Garb, have their convenient severall dwellings, and a fayre Hall, with richly painted windowes Colledge-like, wherein they constantly dyet together, and have their Cooke, Butler, and other Officers, with a fayre Library to themselves, consisting all of English Bookes, wherein (after we had freelie tasted of their Chorall Cordiall Liquor) wee spent our time till the Bell toll'd us away to Cathedral Prayers. There we heard a most sweet organ, and voyces of all partes, Tenor, Counter-Tenor, Treeble and Base and amongst that orderly snowy crew of Queristers our Landlord-Guide did act his part in a deep and sweet Diapason.[17]

Over many centuries Hereford was served by its vicars choral: clergy specially chosen for their musical gifts; there was no parallel in Gloucester and Worcester. The buildings of the College of Vicars Choral at Hereford Cathedral, still inhabited, were begun in 1475. Until the mid-nineteenth century the vicars choral provided all the alto, tenor and bass parts in the cathedral choir, and the college was not dissolved until 1937.

During the Civil War the cathedral was closed and, in spite of the vicars choral sending a petition to the Committee for Sequestration, the college was disbanded. It did not re-open until 1660.

The Revd W. Cooke reported:

> The Buildings and Premises of the College had necessarily fallen into sad decay and dilapidation during the late Rebellion; and the Expences of reparation were a heavy tax upon the General Funds; to [Humphrey] Fisher [a vicar choral] was committed the superintendence of restoring the Common Hall and the Library.[18]

The College Hall and Library were finished by 1 September 1676, and soon, perhaps immediately, the hall became the focus for a college musical club — a venue for the performance and enjoyment of secular music which, of course, was banned from cathedrals — and it is certain that the vicars choral knew how to enjoy themselves; none more so than Henry Hall, successor in 1688 to the first post-Restoration organist at Hereford, John Badham.

Hall composed a great deal of music especially for the Hereford choir. 'But exclusive of musical talent,' wrote Cooke, 'Mr Hall had a great turn for poetry; and making allowances for the depraved taste and ribaldry, in those days still prevalent, there is considerable point and humour in his verses.'[19] The following catch by Henry Hall, written on King William's return from Flanders, proves Cooke's point that he was a rank Jacobite!

> Rejoice, ye fools, your Idol's come again,
> To pick your pockets, and to slay your Men.
> Give him yr. Millions — & his Dutch yr. lands,
> Don't *ring* ye *Bells*, you fools, but *wring* yr. Hands.

Of Mr Hall's secular music, little now remains; some of his catches may be found in Lampe's collection, a few are still in MS at Hereford; but since among his Poems several songs are inserted, it is presumed that in his two-fold capacity of Poet and Musician, he had no difficulty in giving proof of this combination of talent, by carolling those ditties in the *Black Lion Club Room*, where frequent carousals are spoken of among his jovial & political associates; compeers of those nightly revelries, which most likely diverted his thoughts from the greater duties of his professions, for which Education & Genius had so abundantly qualified him.[20]

Undoubtedly many of the Gloucester and Worcester lay clerks would have welcomed the opportunities for conviviality which the Hereford vicars choral seem to have enjoyed. The Chapter Act books give examples enough of admonishments meted out to lay clerks who dared to take their musical talents to town. Witness the following entry made at Worcester on 25 September 1684:

Whereas scandall has been given by Roger Fosbrooke the Elder a Lay Clerk of this Church, by his associating himself with the Town-Musick, it is hereby decreed, that he shall Determine and give his Answer before the first of March next, whether he will relinquish the Town-Musick, or resign his Lay Clerk's place. And if he shall presume after that time to play in any public house, or at any public meeting, or to associate himself with the Town Musick any more, that then be he hereby immediately, *ipso facto*, suspended from his sayd Lay Clerk's Place and from the benefitt and profitts thereof for the period of one whole year from the time of such offence committed. And to prevent all further scandall that may arise upon the matter, It is hereby decreed and enacted that for the future every Lay Clerk before his Admission shall with one sufficient Surety give Bond to the Dean and Chapter in the Summe of One Hundred Pounds, That neither he the said Lay Clerk to be admitted, nor his wife, nor any other from him shall keep any Tavern, Ale house or Victualling house; and that he will not accept or perform any service in any public Musick, nor at any time play in any public house whatsoever.[21]

Given that one hundred pounds in 1684 represented ten years' pay to a lay clerk, presumably the intention of this admonishment was not only to terrify Roger Fosbrooke into compliance but also *pour encourager les autres*. What it and other Chapter Acts like it show is that the pull of secular music for pleasure was very strong — but where was it to be heard? Even in London there were no specially designed concert halls, no true opera, no ballet, few theatres, and no musical festivals. In general, the best music was to be heard in inns.

By the time of Henry Hall's death at the age of fifty-one in 1707, however, a change was already well under way. Rising middle-class affluence, albeit at the price of a widening gap between 'haves' and 'have nots', increased the demand for popular entertainment of all kinds, and the exploitation of printing, which began in the middle of the seventeenth century and accelerated in the 1690s, was fundamental in bringing a scattered population to entertainment and vice versa.

Effective publicity, the availability of printed music, and the social and cultural aspirations of a rising middle class created ideal conditions for the steady expansion of provincial entertainment in the eighteenth century. The vicars choral at Hereford had been among the privileged few in having so splendid a hall in which to hear and make music from such an early date.

Henry Hall was succeeded at Hereford by his son, also named Henry, 'who possessed much of his Father's talent for music and Poetry, but unhappily [inherited] also the like Bacchanalian propensities'.[22] His counterpart at Gloucester was a kindred, albeit older, spirit — Stephen Jeffries.

Born at Salisbury, where he was a chorister and later assistant organist in the cathedral, Jeffries was appointed organist at Gloucester in 1682 when only twenty years old. Soon after his arrival he was admonished by the Dean and Chapter 'for manifold neglect and unreasonable absence from the Church without leave desired or obtained' in spite of having been given £2 by them shortly before 'for his encouragement'. In 1688 he was again admonished for playing on the organ 'a common Ballad' which caused female members of the congregation to dance.

Jeffries continued as organist at Gloucester until his death in 1712, aged fifty-four, although he appears to have been replaced in effect some five years earlier. The Treasurer's Accounts for 13 October 1707 record the payment of £6 5s. 0d. to 'Mr Hynde the new organist', yet the drunken Jeffries continued to be listed as organist. In 1709/10 Hine received £27 10s. 0d. for his year's salary, with an additional gratuity of two guineas, and continued to receive part-payment until Jeffries' death.

According to Hawkins, Hine was 'so much esteemed for skill in his faculty and his gentlemanly qualities, that his salary was, by the dean and chapter . . . increased twenty pounds a year'. Born at Brightwell, Oxfordshire in 1687, he became a chorister at Magdalen College, Oxford, and was later a pupil of Jeremiah Clarke. He remained at Gloucester until his death in 1730.

Henry Hall the younger, sharp-witted poet and *bon viveur*, and William Hine were almost exact contemporaries — both twenty or twenty-one in 1707 when they were appointed at Hereford and Gloucester. The Worcester organist at this time, Richard Cherington, was an older man. In 1697 he was ordered to do penance for quarrelling and fighting with a lay clerk,[23] but apart from this, little is known about him.

The earliest of the triennial Music Meetings are known to have been held during the tenures of Hine and Cherington. A manuscript note in the British Museum, dated June 1746, referring to the 'most noble Pile' of the cathedral at Worcester and 'those two elegant and adorned' cathedrals at Hereford and Gloucester, reads:

> . . . which three choirs have for abt these 30 years last past annually met in September reciprocally with their Choirs to perform ye finest Piece of Music England can boast of . . .[24]

The vagueness of this wording suggests that even in 1746 the date of the first Meeting could not be remembered with accuracy, and this is not surprising if, as seems to have been the case, the gatherings had evolved only gradually before settling into a formal arrangement supported by annual subscriptions.

There is no evidence to show that Richard Cherington took any part in the Music Meetings or that he collaborated in any way with Henry Hall or William Hine. On the other hand, there is no doubt that Hall and Hine worked closely together. They were the joint composers of the morning service known as 'Hall and Hine in E flat' – the *Te Deum* is by Hall, the *Jubilate* by Hine.

A collaborative composition is certainly unusual and the reason for its genesis arouses curiosity, especially as Hall and Hine were working upon it at around the time that the Music Meetings began. Could the service have been composed with a combined performance by two or more cathedral choirs in mind? If so, is there any evidence to show that either man took his singing men to visit the other's cathedral? Once again, the ledgers provide the only clue. An entry in the Gloucester Treasurer's Accounts shows that on an unspecified date in 1709 'the Organist fromward Hereford' was paid £2,[25] a large sum which could well have represented a payment for Hereford's participation in a combined service – possibly 'Hall and Hine in E flat'.

The regular Music Meetings began in music clubs. As Lysons explains:

> . . . the Meetings of the Three Choirs of Gloucester, Hereford and Worcester, originated in a compact entered into by members of certain musical clubs or societies in those cities, to make an annual visit to each other in rotation, and continue together two days, for improving themselves in harmony, by the performance of several concerts of music. These clubs consisted chiefly of members of the several choirs, with the addition of a few *amateurs* of music, in the several cities and their immediate neighbourhood.[26]

The closest link between cathedral and music club was, as we have seen, at Hereford. Indeed, one of the vicars choral, Peter Senhouse, who had been admitted to the college in 1691, was a regular performer in the music club. His name reappears in the records of the 1727 Music Meeting in Gloucester as one of the two Hereford Stewards of the charity. He was also the preacher of the annual sermon in that year, and again in 1728 when the dedication to his printed sermon alluded to the laying 'of the foundations of the good work' of the Music Meetings (see Chapter Two).

In his continuation of the *Annals*, John Amott showed that: 'Musical clubs existed in these cities anterior to the time of the first Meetings of the Choirs, and there is strong evidence to prove that they were in nowise connected'.[27]

Hence the lack of entries in cathedral records after 1709. Thereafter Deans and Chapters granted permission for the use of the cathedrals during Music Meetings; they did not initiate their use.

It is possible that during his 1709 visit to Gloucester, Hall discussed with Hine the notion of an annual Music Meeting. The long-established music club at the Hereford College of Vicars Choral would doubtless have been a great attraction, and it seems not unreasonable to postulate, as did Cooke, that the activities there formed the nucleus of the triennial Music Meetings. If 1709 did indeed mark a first embryonic Meeting, the timing would fit in perfectly with the three-year cyle of the known and documented 1719 Worcester, 1720 Hereford and 1721 Gloucester Meetings. And if a Meeting took place in that sequence at Hereford at Hall's invitation there is only one year in which that would have been possible: 1711. Henry Hall died in January 1714 at the age of twenty-seven or twenty-eight.

Notes

1. *Annals* 1812, p. 159
2. Worcester Festival 1966 programme book, p. 14
3. See Watkins Shaw, p. 1
4. E. Wulstan Atkins, *1890–1990 The Centenary of the Birth of a Friendship* (Worcester, 1990), pp. 1–2
5. See Very Revd Henry Gee, *Gloucester Cathedral its Organs and Organists* (London, 1921), pp. 7–8
6. See Vernon Butcher, *The Organs and Music of Worcester Cathedral* (Worcester, 1981), p. 9
7. Ibid., quoting Carte's letter, Worcester Cathedral Library (1.15)
8. E. Wulstan Atkins, *1890–1990 The Centenary of the Birth of a Friendship* (Worcester, 1990), pp. 2–3
9. Caroline Heighway, *Gloucester – A History and Guide* (Alan Sutton, 1985), p. 127
10. *Episcopal Visitations of the Dean and Chapter of Gloucester, 1542–1751*, Gloucester Cathedral Library
11. E. Wulstan Atkins, *1890–1990, The Centenary of the Birth of a Friendship* (Worcester, 1990), p. 3
12. Gloucester Records Office (D 936A 1/2)
13. Worcester Cathedral Library (A.26)
14. Ibid.
15. Gloucester Cathedral Library, Chapter Act Book (1 Feb 1666)
16. Gloucester Records Office (D 936A 1/3)
17. See Philip Barrett, *The College of Vicars Choral at Hereford Cathedral* (Hereford, 1980), p. 19
18. W. Cooke, *Biographical Memoirs of the Custos and Vicars* (1851), 2 vols (mss) in Hereford Cathedral Library
19. Ibid.
20. Ibid.
21. Chapter Act Book 1684. Worcester Cathedral Library
22. W. Cooke, op. cit.
23. John E. West, *Cathedral Organists Past and Present* (London, 1899), p. 90
24. Add. MS. 5811, f. 134, *Various Parochial Antiquities* (information given to Watkins Shaw by Sir Ivor Atkins)
25. Gloucester Records Office (D 936A 1/5)
26. *Annals* 1812, p. 159
27. *Annals* 1895, p. 13

CHAPTER TWO

A FORTUITOUS AND FRIENDLY PROPOSAL

The musical club which met in the hall belonging to the vicars choral at Hereford was, as Lysons points out, 'an establishment of little expence: the performances were all *gratis*, except that of Mr Woodcock, their leader, whose nightly pay was five shillings. The members were regaled with ale, cyder and tobacco.'[1]

The Woodcocks were a musical family. Hawkins, speaking of Robert Woodcock, famous as a flute-player and composer for that instrument, adds:

> He had a brother named Thomas, who kept a coffee-house at Hereford, an excellent performer on the violin, and played the solos of Corelli with exquisite neatness and elegance. In that country his merits were not known, for his employment was playing country-dances, and his recreation angling. He died about the year 1750.[2]

At some time before mid-century the Hereford musical club meetings had fallen into abeyance. They were revived in 1749 by William Felton, a vicar choral from 1741–69, who transferred the concerts from the College Hall to the Coffee House in St John Street, then owned by Frank Woodcock, which possessed the only room in the city large enough for the purpose. This new arrangement seems to have been quite profitable to Woodcock. The articles of the society, drawn up by Felton, show that Woodcock was to be paid seven shillings for his performance (presumably on the violin) and fifteen shillings: 'for the use of his Room, Fires, Forms & Candles for the two Sconces & Desks and Harpsichord'. In addition, Frank Woodcock's son, Francisco, was also to receive two shillings and sixpence as a performer, and the Treasurer of the society was one John Woodcock. In the face of a potential monopoly it was perhaps prudent of Felton to ensure that the articles allowed that: 'It shall be in the power of the Majority of the Performers (who are not paid) to remove this meeting to any other place they shall think proper.' Among the performers who *were* paid, apart from Woodcock and son, appear the Hereford Cathedral organist, Henry Swarbrick, who played the harpsichord and was also responsible for ensuring that it was tuned, and a Mr Dyer, both of whom received seven shillings and sixpence, and one Jemmy George, who was paid ten shillings and sixpence. The Treasurer was also required 'to provide a Hautboy to perform Each Night at as cheap a Rate as he can'; in 1749 a player named Clarke was paid one pound six shillings to come from Worcester.[3]

The Hereford musical club had its equivalents in Gloucester and Worcester. Lysons tells us that 'at Gloucester the meetings of the club were held in a large room within the walls of the Deanery',[4] an arrangement which continued until 1763. But an advertisement in the *Gloucester Journal* of Monday 17 September 1722 shows that from early in the eighteenth century music was also performed in the College Library.

Looking to Worcester, we find an advertisement in the *Worcester Postman* of 17–26 August 1720:

> This is to give Notice to all Gentlemen, Ladies and others that are lovers of music, that on Friday 26th August at the Green Room in the Tower, will be a concert for the benefit of Claudius Phillips, whereat he will perform several Pieces by himself. N.B. Tickets may be had at Mr Corfields at the Cross in the City of Worcester, at 2s and 6d each. Beginning at 6 in the evening.

The joining together once per year, in each of the three cities in rotation, of the members of the musical clubs had, at first, no purpose beyond that of the pleasure of listening to or sharing in the performance of music in a social gathering. The Meetings were, from the beginning, of two days' duration: extended Matins, accompanied by an orchestra, in the cathedral each morning, and performances in various secular buildings each evening.

Then, in 1716, Dr Philip Bisse, Bishop of Hereford, appointed his brother, Thomas, to the chancellorship of that diocese. Dr Thomas Bisse was a Gloucestershire man, born in 1675 at Oldbury-on-the-Hill, where his father was rector. He graduated at Oxford and held an appointment at the Rolls Chapel in London before joining his brother in Hereford. Thomas was an eloquent preacher with a genuine concern for the wretched condition of so many of his clerical brethren and their families. On 6 December 1716, he had preached a sermon at St Paul's Cathedral, before the Corporation of the Sons of the Clergy.

> Under this ancient and mysterious title, there is concealed a considerable company of Christian men and women, subject to no conditions of birth or status or education, whose only bond is a desire to remedy the distresses and to ease the struggles of the clergy, their widows, their unmarried daughters, and, perhaps above all, their boys and girls who are starting out to make their way in life.[5]

So wrote Ernest Pearce, later Bishop of Worcester and a Treasurer of the Corporation, in his study *The Sons of the Clergy*, published early in this century. Instituted in 1655, the Corporation was granted a royal charter in 1678. From the outset, its purpose was charitable even though over more than three centuries the Sons of the Clergy have been best known to the public for an annual festival held in St Paul's. However, as the Corporation's historian, Nicholas Cox, has pointed out, until relatively recently this was not strictly part of the Corporation at all.[6] This is the reverse of the original *raison d'être* of Three Choirs, which began as a Music Meeting with social rather than charitable ends.

In addressing the Sons of the Clergy, Thomas Bisse was following in his brother's footsteps. Philip Bisse had preached for the Corporation in 1708, and was its President from 1717 to 1721, thus retaining an association with that body after his appointment as Bishop, first to St David's (1710) and then to Hereford (about 1715).

It comes as no surprise, then, to discover that Thomas Bisse soon pressed forward the idea that the annual Music Meetings should embrace a similar charitable purpose to that of the Sons of the Clergy. His first sermon at Three Choirs was published in 1720:

> A Rationale on Cathedral Worship or Choir Service. A sermon preach'd in the Cathedral Church of Hereford, at the Aniversary Meeting of the Choirs of Worcester Gloucester and Hereford, Sept. 7, 1720. By Tho. Bisse, D.D., and Chancelor of the said Church. Printed for W. and J. Innys at the Prince's Arms at the West End of St Paul's. 1720.[7]

But in 1724, at the Gloucester Meeting, his sermon promoted the cause of the charity, details of which were contained in a handbill circulated on the previous day:

> These are to give notice, that tomorrow, viz. – Thursday, the 10th instant, (September,) there will be a collection made after morning service, at the Cathedral-door, for placing out, or assisting the education and maintenance of the orphans of the poorer clergy belonging to the dioceses of Gloucester, Worcester, and Hereford, or of members of the three respective choirs; to be disposed of by six stewards, members of the Society, a clergyman, and a gentleman respectively belonging to the said dioceses.

In the following two years, first at Worcester and then at Hereford, Bisse persisted in his purpose. His 1726 sermon at Hereford was based upon a text from Ecclesiastes II, viii: 'I gat me men-singers and women-singers, and the delights of the sons of men, as musical instruments, and that of all sorts.' And in a note to the sermon, he says: '. . . having first proposed this Charity with success at Gloucester, in 1724, and recommended it at Worcester in 1725, I thought myself obliged to promote it in this way, in the church and diocese to which I belong.'[8] Why he should have left promotion to the charity in his home diocese until the last is uncertain but is a further indication that the Music Meetings evolved only gradually from the occasional visits to 'sister' cathedrals by singing men and organists in the seventeenth century; then possible closer ties involving secular as well as sacred music-making early in the eighteenth century; the establishment of a formal subscription society by 1717; and finally the union of the Music Meetings with the charity in 1724. Only the date of this last can be certain, and to this extent Thomas Bisse may be considered the father of an institution which, as Daniel Lysons put it, 'at the same time that it provides relief for so large a portion of the children of misery [it] promotes the ends of social intercourse and affords the lovers of music an opportunity of hearing the most exquisite harmonic performances'.[9]

Among the earliest benefactors of the charity, two philanthropists deserve particular mention: Colonel Maynard Colchester of Westbury, and his neighbour Catharine Boevey at Flaxley, both of whom were also prime movers in inaugurating the Society for the Promotion of Christian Knowledge.[10]

Maynard Colchester succeeded to the manor and estates at Westbury-on-Severn in 1696. His near neighbour at Flaxley Abbey, the rakish William Boevey, a wealthy merchant of Dutch descent, died in 1704 leaving a widow. Well-educated, cultivated and still young, 'Catherine Boevey regularly spent winters in London and summers at Flaxley entertaining notable personalities, including bishops and the writers Steele and Addison, who were said to have portrayed her in *The Tatler* as the perverse widow wooed in vain by Sir Roger de Coverley.'[11]

There was an ancient link between Westbury and the College of Vicars Choral at Hereford, forged in 1384 when some of the vicars attempted to obtain the revenue of the church of Westbury. This led to a dispute about their right to hold property, settled in 1395 when Richard II incorporated the vicars choral as a college. In addition to enjoying the revenues of the church, the college also controlled the lease of the rectory at Westbury. Details of seventeenth- and eighteenth-century leaseholders are recorded in the Accounts Book of the college, which is lodged in the Hereford Cathedral Library, and include an entry showing that from 1675 to 1682 the lease was granted to Sir Thomas Brydges, later Lord Chandos.

Catherine Boevey died on 21 January 1726, aged fifty-seven, much mourned throughout Gloucestershire. At the Gloucester Music Meeting in 1728 the Revd Peter Senhouse preached a sermon on 'The Use of Musick'. It was printed later in the year, with a dedication to 'Mrs Pope', sometime companion to Mrs Boevey, and an acknowledgement 'how much is owing', in respect to the Meeting of the Three Choirs, 'to the wisdom and goodness of your late excellent friend, and our kind and memorable patroness, Mrs Boevey, who *laid the foundation of the good work*, and during her life liberally contributed to the support of it.'[12]

As the charity founded by Bisse was barely a year old when Catharine Boevey died, it appears clear that she had given substantial support to the pre-charitable Music Meetings since their inception. And, of course, only after she was widowed, aged twenty-two (thirteen years after Peter Senhouse was admitted as a vicar choral at Hereford) would she have enjoyed any financial independence.

The charity was soon proving its effectiveness. In the first year, 1724, the collection amounted to £31 10s. 0d., divided equally between the three dioceses for disbursement by the six Stewards.[13] The Minute Book (opened in 1612) of the Haberdashers Company in Hereford shows that on 5 November 1725, one Posthumous Whitney, son of Hester Whitney, widow of the vicar of Clifford, was bound apprentice to a local 'Barber Chyrurgeon and Perukemaker (by the Charity having paid out of the Contribution of the three Choirs of Hereford, Worster, & Gloster for ye assistance of Clergymens Widdows & Orphans).' It is heartening to find in the same venerable Minute Book that by 1758 Posthumous Whitney had risen to the exalted position of Master of the Haberdashers Company![14]

By 1778 the collections at the Music Meetings were proving inadequate for the relief of the widows and orphans in Worcestershire and so at the Worcester Meeting in that year a subscription scheme was begun whereby the beneficed clergy and some of the opulent laity donated an annual sum not exceeding one guinea each. The subscription in the first year amounted to £200. Similar schemes began in Gloucester in 1786 and in Hereford in 1791, building upon the strength of Bisse's initial proposal.

In 1729 at Hereford, Thomas Bisse preached once more for the charity and was able to say with some pride:

> In one thing our Society hath a perfect resemblance to that greater [the Corporation for the relief of the Widows and Orphans of the Clergy], that it sprang, too, from a very small and accidental origin. It was in like manner a fortuitous and friendly proposal, between a few lovers of harmony and brethren of the correspondent choirs, to commence an anniversary visit, to be kept in turn; which voluntary instance of friendship and fraternity was quickly strengthened by social compact; and afterwards, being blessed and sanctioned by a charity collection, with the word of exhortation added to confirm the whole, it is arrived to the figure and estimation as ye see this day. . . . Though the members of that communion we have entered into, being voluntary, may go off as their wills vary or

as their affairs require, yet, by the accession of others, the Society may subsist unto many years, yea, generations, tending to the furtherance of God's glory, in the exaltation of His holy worship, to the improvement of our choirs, the credit of our foundations; to the benefit of our cities, the comfort of the fatherless; to the delight of mankind, of ourselves, and all that come nigh us. Upon these grounds it commenced, and upon these let our brotherly love continue.[15]

Notes

1. *Annals* 1812, p. 161
2. Hawkins, *History of Music* (new edn, p. 826)
3. Hereford Cathedral Library, Minute Book and Accounts of the Hereford Musical Society, 1749–57 (MR.4.D.xii)
4. *Annals* 1812, p. 162
5. E.H. Pearce, *The Sons of the Clergy*, Preface, pp. ix–x
6. See Nicholas Cox, *Bridging the Gap, A history of the Corporation of the Sons of the Clergy over three hundred years, 1655–1978* (Oxford, 1978), Introduction, p. xi
7. See footnote by E.F. Rimbault, *Annals* 1864 and 1895, p. 3
8. Copies of the sermons of Thomas Bisse are held in Hereford City Library
9. *Annals* 1812, p. 139
10. See Joan Johnson, *The Gloucestershire Gentry* (Alan Sutton, 1989), p. 190
11. Ibid., pp. 196 and 197
12. See *Annals* 1895, footnote to p. 3
13. The Stewards of the Charity should not be confused with the Stewards of the Meeting, of whom there was only one in earliest years. For a short history of the Three Choirs Charity see: Brian Frith, 'The Festival Charity', an essay published in *Two Hundred and Fifty Years of the Three Choirs Festival* (Three Choirs Festival Association, 1977), pp. 25–6
14. Hereford City Library (338.6)
15. *Annals* 1812, pp. 127–30

CHAPTER THREE

A NUMEROUS APPEARANCE OF GENTRY

D etails of the music performed at Meetings of the Three Choirs in the first half of the eighteenth century are tantalizingly sketchy, even though local newspapers, published to serve the interests of the nobility and gentry, regularly carried notices advertising the dates and places of the Music Meetings. After the event a gushing paragraph could be expected, of which the following from the *Gloucester Journal* of Tuesday, 17 September 1728 is typical:

> Worcester, Sept 12.   On the 4th. and 5th. Instant was held here the Anniversary Meeting of the Three Choirs, Worcester, Gloucester and Hereford, when there was a numerous Appearance of Gentry of the first Rank. A very good sermon was preach'd upon the Occasion by the Revd. Mr. Brooks of Hanly; and the Musical Performances were executed to great and general Satisfaction. The Charity Collection for placing out the Children of the poorer Clergy, &c., amounted to 40£ the Mayor with the principal Gentlemen holding the Basons at the Cathedral-Doors.

Should a lord and his lady honour the Meetings with their presence this would be reported grandly, but many decades were to pass before the provincial press thought it any part of its duty to publish so much as one line of musical criticism in its very brief record, in spite of the fact that the Music Meeting quickly came to be regarded as an event of prime professional as well as social interest.

In the period from 1689 to 1713 England had, apart from an uneasy interval of four years, been at war with France. The signing of the Treaty of Utrecht, which in 1713 ushered in the long period of stability characteristic of eighteenth-century civilization, was celebrated throughout the land on 7 July of that year. The festivities in Worcester were reported in the *Worcester Postman*:

> Worcester, July 10.   Tuesday last, being the day appointed for a general Thanksgiving, the same was observed here with great Solemnity and Regularity in the following manner. The Bells began to ring as soon as day appeared; and about 10 in the Forenoon, the Right Worshipful John Frankcombe, Esq., our Mayor, was met at the Town Hall by the Aldermen and other Members of the Chamber; and the several Companies of this City met at their Halls, and meeting all together near the Cross, proceeded in great Order with their Streamers, and Musick before them to the Cathedral, where was performed Mr. Purcell's great *Te Deum*, with the Symphonies and instrumental parts, on Violins and Hautboys, and afterwards a Sermon, suitable to the Occasion, was preached by Mr Phillips.

Had members of the other two cathedral choirs been in Worcester for this splendid occasion, we might have had cause to believe that the celebrations for the Treaty of Utrecht signalled the start of regular Meetings. However, the Gloucester Cathedral Treasurer's Accounts clearly show that on 7 July 1713 £1 13s. 4d. was paid for a 'Thanksgiving for ye Peace to ye Preacher, Choir and Ringers.'[1] The Three Choirs were not in Worcester but at least the *Worcester Postman* piece confirms the contemporary popularity and esteem in which Purcell's 'great *Te Deum*' was held. When at last, in 1721, the *Worcester Postman* reveals which two pieces were to be performed in Gloucester Cathedral at the Music Meeting that year, we find mention of two *Te Deums*, one by Purcell and the other by William Croft.[2] Ten years later the *Gloucester Journal* makes its first mention of specific musical items at the Meetings – and Purcell is still supreme:

> **Worcester, Sept 9 [1731].** Yesterday being the first Day of the Annual Meeting of the Three Choirs, a suitable Sermon was preach'd by the Rev. Mr Philips, Sacrist of our Cathedral, before a grand and numerous Auditory. The same evening was perform'd a Concert of Vocal and Instrumental Musick at the Town Hall which was very much crowded, several Persons of Quality being present. And this Morning Dr Purcel's [*sic*] Great *Te Deum* was sung to Musick at our Cathedral, at the Doors whereof was collected upwards of 45£ for charitable Uses.[3]

A footnote to the *Gloucester Journal* notice advertising the Meeting starting in Hereford on Tuesday, 2 September 1729 shows that a day of rehearsal had by then been found to be necessary: 'N.B. The Performers have obliged themselves by a separate Article to meet on the Monday.'[4]

Lysons was unable to obtain very much information about the principal performers before the year 1755 other than that the Leader of the 'band' was Thomas Woodcock of Hereford, famous for playing the Fifth Violin Concerto by Vivaldi. Woodcock was paid up to one and a half guineas for his performance at the Meetings.

From 1733(G) onwards, Lysons believed 'the most eminent performers were engaged from the metropolis.'[5] A *Gloucester Journal* advertisement for that year notified that 'No Hands will be paid, but those that are apply'd to by the Steward, or his Assistants' and that 'We hear that the Steward of the Musick Meeting has engaged 2 French Horns, a Trumpet, and other Hands from London, a great many Persons of Distinction being expected here.'[6] The subsequent 'review' reported that:

> . . . there was the greatest Appearance of Gentlemen and Ladies of Distinction, and the best Performance that ever was known upon that Occasion; the Steward having collected out of London . . . the best Performers, both Vocal and Instrumental, consisting of French Horns, Trumpets, Hautboys, German Flute, and a fine Treble Harp, &c. The famous Mr Powell of Oxford, did us the Honour of singing in our Church on both Days . . .[7]

Walter Powell had been a member of the choirs of Christ Church and other colleges and was the principal male oratorio singer at Oxford during Handel's visit there in July 1733. Powell, apparently a counter-tenor, had made such an impression on this occasion that he was immediately appointed one of the gentlemen of the Chapel Royal. Following his death in 1744, an extravagant obituary appeared in the *Gentleman's Magazine*:

Is Powell dead? Then all the earth
Prepare to meet its fate:
To sing the everlasting birth,
The Choir of Heaven's complete.

It seems likely, even if proof is wanting, that the additional expense and effort on the part of the Steward in 1733 was directed towards the performance of some more than usually ambitious work, possibly by Handel. William Hayes, pupil of William Hine and an ardent Handelian, became organist at Worcester Cathedral in 1731. His influence on the Music Meetings remained strong even after his move in 1734 to Magdalen College, Oxford, in which year he served as Steward of the Meeting. He became Professor of Music at Oxford in 1741.

Our first certain knowledge of a performance of music by Handel at the Meetings appears in the *Gloucester Journal* of Tuesday, 17 August 1736. A notice states that 'Mr Purcell's *Te Deum* will be perform'd on the Wednesday Morning, and Mr Handel's on the Thursday morning.' Thereafter, new works by Handel were gradually introduced by William Boyce, composer to the Chapel Royal, who took over as conductor of the Three Choirs Meetings in 1737. Two advertisements in 1739(G) announce a performance of *Alexander's Feast*: 'an Ode written by Mr Dryden, and set to Musick by Mr Handel, with Trumpets, French Horns and Kettle-Drums'; and in a later edition of the paper the following is added: 'The two Evening Performances of Musick will be at the Booth-Hall, on one of which will be perform'd *Alexander's Feast*.'[8] Obviously, a larger venue for the secular concerts had become essential.

In the previous year, 1738, although not at a Music Meeting, Handel's *Esther*, composed in 1720 as a Masque, *Haman and Mordecai*, and revised in 1732 as his first English oratorio, was performed at the Town Hall, Worcester on 11 September for the benefit of John Merifield, the organist.[9]

Merifield's contemporary at Gloucester from 1730 to 1740, Barnabas Gunn, was a man of unusual versatility. Besides his musical responsibilities in Gloucester, Gunn supplemented his organist's salary of £35 per annum by entering into partnership with a dealer in timber from London, and they sold oak and deal at premises in Lower Westgate Street.[10] In 1736 he published two cantatas and six songs, settings of verses of Congreve, Prior and others, which, as Percy Young has pointed out, 'like some of his Harpsichord Lessons published by Robert Raikes in Gloucester and his Violin and 'Cello Solos later published by J. Johnson of Birmingham, may well have provided evening entertainment at Meeting time.'[11]

Gunn collected the remarkable number of 464 subscribers for this volume:

Among the names it was that of Mr Handel which shone the brightest. Why it may be asked, did Handel show such favour (as in 1745 he did in respect of Chilcot's Shakespeare songs)? There is, it may be felt, a possibility of *quid pro quo*.[12]

Before moving to Gloucester, Gunn had been organist at St Philip's, Birmingham, and in 1749 he returned there where, enterprising as ever, he combined his duties as organist with those of postmaster for the town, and also put on many concerts and theatrical performances in local theatres.[13]

The single Steward of the Music Meeting was always a musical man: a member of one of the musical clubs, generally either a clergyman or lay clerk belonging to one of the choirs. The Steward of the Meeting engaged and defrayed the expenses of the band, and was responsible for losses. Hardly an enviable task – by mid-century lavish productions at the secular concerts were proving expensive!

At Gloucester in 1745 a dramatic pastoral called *Love's Revenge, or Florimel and Myrtillo,* by Maurice Greene, and Handel's *Acis and Galatea* were performed at the Booth Hall. On 3 September the *Gloucester Journal* reported:

> **London, Aug. 29.**   This Day Dr Greene, Master of his Majesty's Band of Musick, with several gentlemen belonging to the Chapel Royal, Westminster Abbey and St Paul's set out for Gloucester, where they are to meet the Gentlemen belonging to the Choirs of Worcester, Hereford and Gloucester, in order to perform, at the last mentioned place, on Wednesday and Thursday next, a Grand Concert of Musick, both Vocal and Instrumental, for the Benefit of poor Clergymen's Widows and their Children.

Samson, composed by Handel in 1743, reached Three Choirs in 1748(G):

> . . . the musical Performance was greatly applauded, particularly the celebrated Oratorio of Samson. And the Assembly, each night, at the Bell, was so crowded, that there was scarce Room for the Gentlemen and Ladies to Dance . . .[14]

The Music Meetings and their attendant attractions – 'ordinaries', balls and horse-races – provided a focal point in the social calendar of nobility, gentry, better-off clergy, and any family the head of which could lay claim to the title 'gentleman'. Timed to follow the annual harvest, the Meetings provided an interlude of civic hospitality in late August or September, before the more serious business of winter hunting began.

In addition to the 'ordinaries' – lunches for patrons of the Music Meeting held in local hostelries – it became traditional by mid-century for the Steward to invite the performers to dine with him on the first day of the Meeting. This, in addition to all the other expenses, threatened the future of the Meetings for lack of volunteers to take up the heavy financial burden of Steward. In 1784 a contributor to the *Gloucester Journal,* writing under the pseudonym 'Philo-Harmonicus', suggested a solution:

> Having for many Years, attended your Annual Meetings, and being a sincere Well-Wisher to the Continuance of them, it gives me no small Concern to hear it frequently said they are likely to drop . . . [that] the Musical Performances were becoming so expensive as, sometimes, not be sustain'd by the Profits of the two Concerts, and that this made the Members of the Musical Societies diffident as to taking upon them the Office of STEWARD, and even to decline it.
>
> That all due encouragement may be given to Lay Members belonging to either of the Choirs . . . that the Organist of each Choir, and the Steward of each Musical Society, do nominate and appoint a moderate Number of Vocal and Instrumental performers, to attend the Rehearsals and Performances at every Meeting as well as the two others as that they belong to; and that their Expences be allow'd them, either by the Steward of the Annual Meeting, or by the private Society, as shall be deem'd most practicable. As this would be an Incitement to the younger Practitioner to study more in order to be distinguished, as would it, perhaps be a means of unclosing the Lips, and untying the Hands of some who are already qualified to be useful.
>
> . . . let the Steward disburse no more at Dinner, on the first Day of the Meeting, than will be barely sufficient to entertain such as are actual Performers; I mean such who are not only Performers

in their own Choirs or Concerts, but intend to assist in the Performances on the two succeeding Days . . . unless it can be prov'd that Dining together on that Day is of any particular Use or Emolument to the Society, it were far better abolish'd. This would, effectually, lessen not only the Expences, but the Trouble and Fatigue, of the Steward also.

At the heart of Philo-Harmonicus's letter was a suggestion of sound economic sense:

That each Subscriber instead of being entitled to Tickets Gratis, do pay, at the time of Subscribing, into the Hands of the Steward for the year ensuing, the Sum of Ten Shillings and Sixpence: In consideration of which he shall be entitled to a Ticket each Night, and his Ordinary paid each day by the Steward. But if he does not appear, that then the said Ten shillings and Sixpence shall be deem'd forfeited to the Society as usual.[19]

All of these ideas were endorsed the next week in a letter to the paper by a former Steward. The inclusion of 'Forfeits' in future statements of Music Meeting accounts suggests that they were taken up.

At the same time the balls, free to patrons of the Music Meeting, had become overcrowded by gatecrashers: a problem solved in Gloucester in 1757 by transferring the balls to the Booth Hall, where they followed immediately after the concerts. In 1752 the following advertisement appeared in the *Worcestershire Journal*:

City of Worcester, Sept 14. As it has been the desire of several ladies of distinction, that some method might be thought of to remove the many inconveniences which arise from the great number of people who crowd the ballroom at the Music Meetings, on account of their being admitted *gratis*, the Mayor (in order to carry on the balls with more decency and regularity) has taken the management of them into his own hands, and gives this public notice, that every lady, as well as gentleman, shall pay half-a-crown each night for their admittance, as is usual at the other meetings; and the money collected shall be disposed of in a proper manner. And, that the Stewards of the Meeting may not suffer by the necessary alteration, notice is hereby given, that no person shall have the liberty of coming to the balls without providing tickets (which will be given at the hall-door in exchange for concert tickets) for the satisfaction of the conductor of the ball, that they have favoured the concert with their company.

All this sounds to be entirely reasonable and businesslike – but it led to a major row at the next Worcester Meeting in 1755. In that year it had been decided that the number of Stewards should be increased to two, no doubt to ease the financial burden on any one individual. The Dean of Worcester, Dr Waugh, and the Honourable Edwin Sandys agreed to take on the task. Noting that the balls of 1752 had produced a profit of £178 3s. for the City Corporation – money, as they saw it, lost to the charity – they applied to the Mayor for the use of the Guildhall (or Town Hall) for the balls. Permission was refused. The distinguished but angry Stewards determined to hold the balls in the College Hall instead of the Guildhall, but not until they had inserted a lengthy notice, highly critical of the Mayor and Corporation, in the newspapers:

It is thought proper to state to the public the following facts, merely lest the Charity . . . should suffer by misrepresentation . . . That the taking separate pay for the balls, by persons who bear no part of the expenses of the musical performances, might not only hurt the collection, but reduce the number of concert-tickets so much, as not to raise a sufficient sum to pay the performers; by such means the Meeting itself would be ruined.
    That application was made to the Mayor by the Stewards, in the most respectful manner, for the use of the hall and ball-rooms over it, which, considering the benefits arising to the city by this

Meeting, and the charitable purpose for which they are asked, it was natural for them to expect would be granted; but some, it seems, of those in power in the city thought otherwise: *the request was not granted – the ball-room was refused*; and Mr Mayor transmitted to the Stewards a printed account how the money arising from the balls in 1752 had been applied: by which it appeared that not one shilling of it was given in charity . . .[20]

The Mayor, Benjamin Pearkes, clearly furious, responded with a document entitled 'The Corporation of the City of Worcester vindicated from a most injurious reflection', in which he said that the proceeds from the balls had never previously been applied in favour of the charity, and

> That several former Stewards of the Concert, and also of the *Balls*, whose minds have been actuated by the *Principles of Humanity*, have, in some Degree, applied the Surplus arising therefrom, to *charitable* Uses; but then have always discover'd the most passionate Regard for that valuable old Maxim – CHARITY *begins* at Home.[21]

The 'overplus' from the 1752 balls had, it seems, been spent on painting, gilding and lacquer-work, both inside and outside the Guildhall.

The Worcester Corporation hit back at the Stewards in 1755 by advertising rival balls and selling tickets at 2s. 6d. each from the two local coffee-houses. But peace returned in 1758 when the advertisements once again speak only of balls every evening, *gratis*.

From primitive beginnings, horse-racing grew rapidly in the first half of the eighteenth century and, as with the Music Meeting, newspapers played a vital role in its development. By 1722, 112 cities and towns in England were holding race meetings, and at large county towns the races were organized to coincide with their assizes.[22]

Worcester has one of the oldest race-courses in England. Horse-racing has taken place on Pitchcroft for more than 260 years and it may well have formed part of the city life from much earlier times.[23] A notice in the *Worcester Journal* for 20 June 1718 advertises that:

> On Friday the 27th June there will be run for in Pitchcroft, Worcester, a Saddle & Bridle £3 value by any Horse, Mare or Gelding carrying ten stones . . . the winning Horse to be sold for seven pounds . . . There will be at the same time, a pair of Silver Buckles run for by Men round Pitchcroft, Gratis: and a handsome Hat to be run for by young Women, the length of Pitchcroft. Also a very good Silver laced Hat to be won at Backsword, that Hat being 14s value. Those that are willing to enter their horses must enter the 26th of the instant, at the Crown in Broad Street, Worcester.

Racing at Hereford is first mentioned in the *Racing Calendar* as on 17 August 1731, and at Gloucester on 24 September 1734, but it was not until shortly after mid-century that the Race Meetings and the Music Meetings were timed deliberately to coincide. At Worcester in 1737 the Music Meeting was 'deferr'd a Week longer than the usual time, on Account of several Principal Performers being engag'd at Oxford Races',[24] and at Gloucester in 1748 the date of the Meeting was altered because it clashed with the Burford Races.[25] A sure way to ensure maximum attendance and to avoid divided loyalties was to bring the Race Meetings and Music Meetings together. In Gloucester, for instance, the races were advertised for Tuesday and Friday in the Music Meeting week. On Tuesday night there was always a ball at the Bell Inn, called the Stewards' Ball, 'at which the Lay-steward of the Meeting, who was also a Steward of the races, presided'.[26]

Although racing continues at Worcester and Hereford, it was already in decline at Gloucester by 1793 when the link with the Music Meeting was severed there. Thirty years earlier, the Revd Robert Gegg, a Gloucester man, had been unimpressed:

Sep 6th 1763.   A great deal of company in Town; the Meeting of the 3 Choirs of Gloucester, Worcester and Hereford, being held here this Week. An Horse-race in Maisemore Meadow this Afternoon, but (unfortunately for the Fools of Fashion) poor Sport.[27]

J.C. Whyte, writing in the following century, described the Gloucester course: 'The races take place in a meadow, on the banks of the Severn, the course being an oblong of about a mile and a half, with a straight run in of 400 yards.'[28]

So great a gathering of eighteenth-century wealth in one place drew to the Music Meetings an unofficial 'fringe' of attractions, as well as a fair number of the light-fingered gentry who continued to stretch police patience and resources well into the reign of Queen Victoria. Side-shows such as the following, noticed in 1748, would have been commonplace: 'We hear that Mr Bridges designs being here at the Music-Meeting on the 13th of next Month, to exhibit, to the Gentlemen, Ladies, &c., his Curious MACHINE, call'd the MICROCOSM.'[29] Not least of the attractions would have been the presence, in the Three Choirs cities, of groups of strolling players. One of the earliest provincial theatres was built in Bath in 1705. Its company spread wide its nets, and strolling players from Bath soon included Devon and Wiltshire, as well as Gloucester, Hereford and Worcester, in their itinerary. On 15 July 1729, a Hereford Music Meeting year, the *Gloucester Journal* announced:

The Bath Company of Comedians are building a large commodious Booth in the White Lyon Yard, near the Market-Place, to entertain the Public at the Approaching Assizes, Races and the Triennial Meeting of the Three Choirs: they have with them Mr. Hippisley, and other Actors from both of the Theatres in London; their Cloaths and Scenes far exceed any yet seen here. They will open on 28th Instant with the Beggars Opera, or Provok'd Husband.

The company in its summer progress was evidently strengthened by recruits from London.[30]

Some few years later Joseph Yarrow, a York comedian and playwright, recounted in verse 'An Epilogue, made by a Gentleman of Hereford, occasioned by meeting a Company of Strolers [*sic*] on the Road':[31]

> From Hereford the Jovial Crew departed,
> Kings walk'd on Foot, the Princesses were Carted:
> In pure Compassion to the Maiden Queen
> That wanted but a Month of Lying-In.
> Thus on a Heap lay pil'd; there the Brandy Bottle,
> Here the Child.
> Great Montezuma hir'd an humble Hack,
> And he that grasp'd the World bestrid a Pack:
> Great Orronoko from his Privy Purse,
> Cou'd not afford Imoinda poor a Horse:
> Young Amon, staying late behind the rest,

Was in great Danger too of being prest.
But Faith it would have made the Greatest laugh,
To see the Truncheon knuckle to the Staff.
Thus, on the Road, no more but common Men,
Once got to Ludlow, then all Kings again.

Notes

1. Gloucester Records Office (D 936A 1/5)
2. *Worcester Postman*, 9–16 June 1721 (Worcester City Library)
3. *Gloucester Journal*, 14 September 1731 (Gloucester City Library)
4. *Gloucester Journal*, 19 August 1729 (Gloucester City Library)
5. *Annals* 1812, p. 163
6. *Gloucester Journal*, 14 August 1733 (Gloucester City Library)
7. *Gloucester Journal*, 11 September 1733 (Gloucester City Library)
8. *Gloucester Journal*, 7 August 1739 and 4 September 1739 (Gloucester City Library)
9. *Gloucester Journal*, 12 September 1738
10. *Gloucester Journal*, 12 October 1736 and 8 August 1738
11. Percy M. Young, 'The First Hundred Years', an essay published in *Two Hundred and Fifty Years of the Three Choirs Festival* (Three Choirs Festival Association, 1977), p. 11
12. Ibid., pp. 11–13
13. See Brian Frith, *The Organists of Gloucester Cathedral* (Gloucester, 1972), pp. 58 and 59
14. *Gloucester Journal*, 20 September 1748
15. *Worcester Journal*, 23 July 1752
16. Watkins Shaw, *The Three Choirs Festival* (Worcester, 1954), pp. 8–9
17. *Worcester Journal*, 27 August 1752, and *Gloucester Journal*, 25 August 1752
18. *Worcester Journal*, 27 December 1753
19. *Gloucester Journal*, 30 August 1748. *Ordinary* – 18th century usage: living expenses, i.e. for meals or, perhaps, dinner
20. See *Annals* 1812, pp. 174 and 181
21. See Watkins Shaw, op. cit., p. 26
22. Andrea T. Cook, *A History of the English Turf* (1901–5), pp. 160 and 199
23. See E.J. Whitt, *Racing at Worcester* (1981), Worcester City Library (WG 798.4/255227), T.S.
24. *Gloucester Journal*, 9 August 1737
25. *Gloucester Journal*, 19 July 1748
26. *Annals* 1812, p. 182
27. Diary of Revd R. Gegg (1763) (Gloucester City Library)
28. J.C. Whyte, *History of the British Turf* (London, 1840), 2 vols, vol. 2, pp. 242–3
29. *Gloucester Journal*, 23 August 1748
30. See Sybil Rosenfeld, *Strolling Players and Drama in the Provinces* (Cambridge, 1939), p. 176
31. *A Choice Collection of Poetry* (1738), quoted by Rosenfeld, p. 19

CHAPTER FOUR

'THE MUSICK OF MY ADMIRATION HANDEL'

F ollowing the first known Three Choirs performance in 1736(G) of one of his *Te Deums*, the music of Handel rapidly rose into a position of absolute command at the Music Meetings. *Alexander's Feast* was repeated, and *L'Allegro, Il Penseroso* introduced at Gloucester in 1751. In the following year the *Worcester Journal* gave a detailed programme for the 1752(W) Meeting:

> On Wednesday will be perform'd, at the Cathedral, in the Morning, Purcel's [*sic*] Te Deum and Jubilate, an Anthem by Dr. Boyce, and Mr. Handel's celebrated Coronation Anthem; and at the Town-Hall in the Evening, a concert of Vocal and Instrumental Musick. On Thursday will be perform'd, at the Cathedral, in the Morning, Mr. Handel's Te Deum and Jubilate, A New Anthem by Dr. Boyce, and the same Coronation Anthem; and at the Town Hall, in the Evening, the Oratorio of Samson.
>
> J. Arnold, Steward[1]

The *Te Deum* and *Jubilate* of Purcell would be that in D which he wrote for St Cecilia's Day 1694, the year before his death. Handel wrote a set of four anthems for the Coronation of George II in 1727, but the 'celebrated' one is most likely to have been either of the two most popular: 'The King shall rejoice' or 'Zadok the Priest'. Handel's *Te Deum* and *Jubilate* could have been either that written in 1713 for the Treaty of Utrecht or, more likely, that written in 1743 for the victory of Dettingen which, according to Lysons, was introduced to the Music Meetings at Gloucester in 1748. But, as Watkins Shaw has pointed out, 'one notices that whereas in 1752, for example, we hear of a *Te Deum* by Handel, in 1755 and 1756 the announcement speaks of the "New *Te Deum*" by Handel. (Those dates, however, refer to Worcester and Hereford Meetings.) After 1755 there is no doubt that the "Dettingen" setting was in regular use.'[2] The anthem by Boyce would have been either 'Lord, thou has been our refuge' or 'Blessed is he that considereth the poor'. But it was the performance of *Samson* which incurred the greatest expense.

Mr Arnold was feeling the pinch, and one month after the initial notice of the Meeting appeared in the newspapers, it was followed by another:

> The *additional Expence* in preparing for the ORATORIO of SAMSON, and the larger Demands of the *London* Performers and Others, make it absolutely necessary to raise the Price of the CONCERT TICKETS from *Half-a-Crown* to *Three Shillings*. And that it may not be imagined that the Steward proposes any *Advantage* to himself, he assures the Publick, that if there be any *Overplus*, it shall be faithfully applied towards continuing the Charitable Meetings of the THREE CHOIRS which cannot be supported, unless the Stewards are to be indemnified . . .[3]

Arnold was careful to ensure that his full accounts were published in the *Worcester Journal*[4], thus proving that far from gaining any 'advantage to himself', the *overplus* remaining after meeting all expenses amounted to the princely sum of one shilling and fivepence halfpenny! Furthermore, the accounts show that he had made a loss of £10 16s. 8d. on the Meeting held as far back as 1744 and that these arrears had only been recouped after the 1752(W) Meeting. Income from tickets and books of words for the two nights amounted to £234 12s. 0d. against expenditure relating to the musical performance of £149 14s. 6d., including:

Performers –	£120
Transcribing the Oratorio of Samson, Paper and Binding	£22 18s. 6d.
Mending a Tenor Fiddle	10s. 0d.
Purchas'd a Pair of Kettle Drums	£6 6s. 0d.

Further expenditure was incurred on 'Stewards' Dinner, Wine, Ale, etc. used at the several Rehearsals and the Performance', printing costs, and an assortment of items, including Mayor's officers, candles, sconces and snuffers, and even a bill for fifteen shillings for mending the Guildhall windows.

At Hereford in 1750, a proposal had been made by friends and supporters of the music club to rebuild and enlarge the College Hall. The necessary amount was raised through voluntary contributions and the hall opened in time for the evening concerts at the 1753(H) Music Meetings. As a result of this initiative, Hereford now extended the Meeting to three evenings, an example not followed by Gloucester and Worcester until 1757 and 1758 respectively. Thereafter, either two or three evening concerts were given at each Meeting until 1770, after which three became the regular number.

The first evening in 1753(H) was devoted to a Miscellaneous Concert, the precedent for what was to become a long-lived tradition of Three Choirs; the second to Handel's oratorio *Samson*; and the third to a dramatic piece called *The Shepherd's Lottery*, written by Moses Mendez and set to music by William Boyce. And, as at Worcester in the previous year, the high costs involved in presenting *Samson* necessitated an increase in the price of tickets to three shillings.

William Hayes acted as Deputy Steward at Gloucester in 1754. In addition to *L'Allegro, Il Penseroso, Judas Maccabeus* was given twice: on Thursday evening and, in aid of 'the laudable Undertaking of erecting a County-hospital', a repeat performance on Friday morning at which a sum of just over £50 was collected.

From the year 1755 we have a regular account of the performers. The notice for the Worcester Meeting of that year states:

The Oratorio of Sampson [*sic*] by Mr Handel, and Dr Boyce's Solomon, with several other Pieces of Musick, will . . . be perform'd in the Great Hall in the College at Worcester, the Corporation of Worcester having refused the Stewards the Use of the Ball-room in the Town-hall, which they requested that all the Profits arising from the Meeting might be applied to the Charity for which it was instituted.

Care has been taken to engage the best Masters that can be procured. The Vocal Parts (beside the Gentlemen of the Three Choirs) will be perform'd by Mr Beard, Mr Wass, Mr Denham, Mr Baildon, Miss Turner, and others; the Instrumental Parts by Mr Brown, Mr Millar, Mr Adcock, Mr Messing &c. The Musick to be conducted by Dr Boyce . . .[5]

The first name among the singers is that of John Beard, the leading tenor of his day and the man who established the popularity of that type of voice in England, taking the principal part in numerous pieces, and being the original tenor in Handel's *Esther*. Beard was one of the singers in the Duke of Chandos's Chapel at Cannons. In 1739 he caused a great scandal by marrying Lady Henrietta Herbert, only daughter of James, Earl of Waldegrave, and widow of Lord Edward Herbert, second son of the Earl of Powis – a thing unheard of. In *The Wealth of Nations*, published in 1776, Adam Smith summed up a contemporary view of opera-singers and other entertainers:

There are some very agreeable and beautiful talents of which the possession commands a certain sort of admiration; but of which the exercise for the sake of gain is considered, whether from reason or prejudice, as a sort of public prostitution. The pecuniary recompense, therefore, of those who exercise them in this manner must be sufficient, not only to pay for the time, labour, and expense of acquiring the talents, but for the discredit which attends the employment of them as the means of subsistence. The exorbitant rewards of players, opera-singers, opera-dancers, etc. are founded upon those two principles; the rarity and beauty of the talents, and the discredit of employing them in this manner.[6]

Aristocratic reaction to Beard's marriage to Lady Herbert provides an unclouded glance at contemporary social attitudes. Lady Mary Wortley Montague, in one of her letters to Lady Pomfret, wrote:

Lady Herbert furnished the tea-tables here with fresh tattle for the last fortnight. I was one of the first informed of her adventure by Lady Gage, who was told that morning by a priest that she had desired him to marry her the next day to Beard, who sings in the farces at Drury Lane. He refused her that good office, and immediately told Lady Gage, who (having been unfortunate in her friends) was frightened at this affair, and asked my advice. I told her honestly that since the lady was capable of such amours I did not doubt, if this was broke off, she would bestow her person and fortune on some hackney-coachman or chairman, and that I really saw no method of saving her from ruin, and her family from dishonour, but by poisoning her, and offered to be at the expense of the arsenic, and even to administer it with my own hands, if she would invite her to drink tea that evening.

Her relations have certainly no reason to be amazed at her constitution, but are violently surprised at the mixture of devotion that forces her to have recourse to the church in her necessities, which has not been the road taken by the matrons of her family.[7]

Lady Herbert's 'friends' were disappointed. Beard was a man of liberal attainments, pleasing manners, good principles and respectable conduct. He and his wife enjoyed much happiness together. After her death Beard married a daughter of Rich, and eventually became one of the proprietors of the Covent Garden Theatre. He sang at Three Choirs in 1755(W), 1758(W), 1760(G) and 1761(W). He died in 1791.

Among the instrumentalists named in 1755(W) was Abraham Brown, Leader of the band before the arrival of Giardini in 1770. Brown succeeded Festing as Leader of the king's band and most of the public concerts. He is said to have had 'a clear, sprightly, and loud tone, with a strong hand, but was deficient in expression'.[9] The other performers mentioned were Miller and Adcock, both celebrated bassoonists, and Messing, an eminent French horn player.

At Hereford, in 1756, the great attraction at the Music Meeting was the first Three Choirs appearance of the Italian singer Giulia Frasi who came to England in 1743,

> young and interesting in person, with a sweet and clear voice: though she never ranked as first woman at the Italian opera, yet, by learning English, she became of much importance at our oratorios, theatres and public concerts, when singers of a higher class, without qualification, could be of no use. She pronounced our language in singing with a more distinct articulation than native performers; and her style being plain and simple, with a well-toned voice and a good shake, she delighted the ignorant and never displeased the learned. She became, in consequence, an established favourite with the public, and sang at the Meetings of the Three Choirs nine successive years. Frasi, after many years' residence in this country, where she made from £1100 to £1800 *per annum*, was obliged to retire to Calais, in order to avoid being arrested for debts, the consequence of her want of economy; and after subsisting for some time on small pensions from her friends in England, which gradually diminished, died almost literally for want of bread.[10]

Accepting the truth of notices which appeared in the papers that 'the City is very healthy, and quite free from the Smallpox', the crowds descended upon Hereford, three noblemen and twelve members of Parliament among them, and £182 was collected at the doors for the charity.[11] However, this figure was greatly exceeded in 1757(G) when Handel's *Messiah* was given at Three Choirs for the first time:

> . . . by a numerous Band of Vocal and Instrumental Performers from London, Salisbury, Bath, Oxford, and other places; particularly Signora Frasi, Mr Beard, Mr Wass, and Mr Hayes; Three Trumpets, a pair of Kettle-drums, Four Hautboys, Four Bassoons, Two Double-basses, Violins, Violoncellos, and Chorus Singers in Proportion. The Musick to be conducted by Dr Hayes.[12]

Messiah immediately became an indisputable favourite at Three Choirs, performed complete or in part at all but two Music Meetings until 1963(W). In 1757 the large sum of £300 was collected at the doors, but in addition there was an unprecedented 'overplus' of £60 added to the charity. A full statement of accounts was published in the *Gloucester Journal*:[13]

Received from Oratorio Tickets,			
1st Night [*Judas Maccabeus*]	162.	00.	0
2nd Night [*Acis and Galatea*]	136.	00.	0
3rd Night [*Messiah*]	207.	00.	0
Forfeits	024.	19.	0
From the Sale of Oratorio Book, Printing and Dispersing Expences cleared	000.	05.	0
Received	530.	04.	0

Disbursed to Singers and Instrumental Performers	267.	04.	6
To Doctor Hayes for Singing, and conducting the Musick	22.	01.	0
For collating, writing and adjusting Parts	005.	05.	0
For Advertisements and Carriage of Parcels, paid by Dr Hayes	006.	09.	0
To Frasi	052.	10.	0
Frasi's and Beard's Expences	046.	05.	9
Ball-Musick	022.	01.	0
To R. Raikes for Advertisements and Tickets	007.	02.	0
Wax Candles	021.	10.	6
Stewards' Dinner	012.	06.	6
To Officers and Porters	007.	08.	9

Disbursed	470.	04.	0

Received	530.	04.	0
Disbursed	470.	04.	0
Balance to be added to the Charity	60.	0.	0

George Talbot
Norborne Berkeley

At Worcester in 1758, the band was led by Thomas Pinto, a prodigious violinist of whom Dr Burney wrote that, 'With a powerful hand and a marvellous quick eye, he was so careless a player, that he performed the most difficult music better the first time he saw it, than ever after.'[14]

In 1759(H) the Revd Benjamin Mence joined Frasi and Wass as a principal singer. Recording the death in 1796 of this remarkable clergyman, the *Gentleman's Magazine* described him as one 'in whom the classical world have lost a scientific genius, and whose vocal powers as an English singer remain unrivalled'. In addition, 1759 was the second year in which the famous oboist Thomas Vincent, a pupil of Sammartini, played at Three Choirs. In that same year we also find the name of Storace, a double-bass player and father of the composer Stephen Storace, a friend of Mozart, and that of the soprano Ann Selina (Nancy) Storace.

Of greater significance than the names of the performers in 1759 was the venue for *Messiah*, transferred from the evening concerts to the cathedral – previously the exclusive preserve of services and anthems. But why should this change have happened? Certainly, the Hereford College Hall would have been too small for the scale of *Messiah* performances given in the public halls at Gloucester and Worcester, even though it was adequate for a 'Grand Concert of Vocal and Instrumental Musick' on the Thursday evening in 1759.[15] Why could *Messiah* not have been performed in the Hereford Guildhall?

The answer is to be found in a document still preserved in the City of Hereford Records Office, recording an agreement between the Mayor, aldermen and citizens of Hereford, that:

The Guildhall of the City of Hereford being ruinous and necessary to be rebuilt and it having been proposed that by the voluntary Contributions of the Gentlemen and Clergy within the County and Diocese of Hereford added to the fund raised by the Corporation of the said City, a Guildhall should be built upon a more extensive plan, and in a more Convenient Situation than the present, so as to have a Room proper for the reception of the Company at the Meetings of the Choirs of Hereford,

Gloucester and Worcester as well as for the General Convenience and use of the said City *Be it known* that for the satisfaction of all parties who are or may be concerned in so Generous an Undertaking *We* the Mayor Aldermen and Citizens of the said City *Do* Grant and agree to and with the Lord Bishop of Hereford and his Successors that the said Room when built as aforesaid shall at all times be free for the use of the said Meeting whenever requested by the Stewards thereof *Given* under our Common Seal the Twentieth day of July in the Year of Our Lord One Thousand seven hundred and fifty nine.[16]

Three weeks after this agreement was reached, notices were placed in the papers advertising that *Messiah* would be performed in the cathedral, the only building in Hereford of sufficient size which was not 'ruinous'. Surely, the deal struck with the Bishop for free use in perpetuity of the new Guildhall for the Music Meeting, with its implied advantage in terms of income to the charity, was of paramount significance in the granting of reciprocal approval for the use of the cathedral for oratorio performances. There was also another compelling reason why, in September 1759, the Stewards of the Music Meeting at Hereford would not have wished to be seen as the poor relations of Gloucester or Worcester in their *Messiah* performance: Handel had died the previous April.

Although at Gloucester the Meetings were conducted by William Hayes in the decade from 1754, and at Worcester by William Boyce (according to Lysons, from 1737) until his appointment as organist of the Chapel Royal in 1758,[17] the first of the cathedral organists to be recorded as conductor on his home ground is Richard Clack, organist at Hereford from 1754 to 1779, who was in charge of the 1759 Meeting. Perhaps he too used his limited influence to gain access to the cathedral for *Messiah*. Worcester followed Hereford's example in 1761, but Gloucester barred the cathedral to *Messiah* until 1769.

The 1760 Meeting at Gloucester was devoted to the memory of Handel. Hayes conducted *Esther* on Wednesday evening, and on the second night: '*The Passions*, an Ode written by Mr. Collins and set to music after the Manner of an Oratorio by Dr. Hayes, to which will be added an ODE to the Memory of Mr Handel; with a Variety of Instrumental Pieces between the several Parts.'[18]

Elias Isaac (1734–93), the Worcester organist, took over as conductor of the Worcester Music Meetings from 1761 and at Gloucester from 1769. He also conducted at Hereford in 1777, two years before the death of Richard Clack.

The principal tenor at Three Choirs was, for many years, Charles Norris, organist at St John's College and Christ Church, Oxford. As a boy, Norris was a chorister at Salisbury Cathedral, and it was as a treble that he first appeared at Worcester in 1761. Norris was greatly admired, particularly for the great feeling and expression with which he sang in *Messiah* and in Purcell's 'From Rosy Bowers'. He died in 1790 at little more than forty-five years of age, a victim of alcoholism. As Rimbault put it:

. . . from an early disappointment in love, [he] unhappily gave way to excesses falsely glossed over as *convivial*, to which he fell a premature victim. At Westminster Abbey, in 1790, he could not hold the book from which he sang, and excited emotions of pity in place of the rapture that was wont to follow his performance. He died at Himley Hall, the seat of Viscount Dudley and Ward, Sept 5th, 1790.[19]

Norris sang at Three Choirs for the last time in 1788(W).

In 1765, Giulia Frasi was replaced by Charlotte Brent, a pupil of Arne, in whose opera *Eliza* she made her first appearance in 1755. She was the original Mandane in

Arne's opera *Artaxerxes*, and in 1766 became the second wife of the violinist Thomas Pinto. Charlotte Brent spent the latter part of her life at 6 Vauxhall Walk, London, where in 1802 she died in poverty.

In 1769, at Gloucester, John Crosdill, the best English cellist of his time, made his first Three Choirs appearance, as did Johann Christian Fischer, the celebrated oboist. Fischer appeared regularly at Three Choirs for more than twenty years. In 1780 he married the daughter of the painter Thomas Gainsborough, but the match was an unhappy one. Fischer toured the Continent between 1786 and 1790, playing before a less-than-admiring Mozart in Vienna in 1787. He died in London in 1800.

Among the portraits of musicians painted by Gainsborough are studies of both his son-in-law Fischer, and of Elizabeth Linley, the daughter of Thomas Linley, a singing-master, composer and organist of Bath Abbey who with his son, also Thomas, wrote the music for Sheridan's play *The Duenna*. Elizabeth Linley first sang in her father's concerts in Bath and made her London and Three Choirs débuts in 1770(W). Considered to be the most accomplished singer that this country had produced, she enjoyed huge popularity wherever she appeared. But in 1773, between the time of her engagement for Three Choirs and the Meeting at Worcester, she eloped with Sheridan, having already married him in secret. It was feared that she would not fulfil her engagement, but Sheridan not only allowed his wife to appear but also presented one hundred pounds to the charity: the sum which was to have been Elizabeth Linley's fee.

In 1770(W) also, Felici Guardini became the Leader of the band – a position he filled for seven years – and the Italian castrato soprano Giusto Ferdinando Tenducci returned to Worcester, where he had first appeared in 1767.

Tenducci came to England in 1758, toured Scotland and Ireland with Thomas Arne, but later returned to Italy to escape his debts. Rimbault describes how Tenducci was engaged to sing at Worcester in 1767 for fifty guineas:

> When the money was paid to him, with true operatical dignity he refused to give a receipt for it, alleging 'that he should be sent for to sing at all the *horse-races* and cock-fighting in the kingdom; and that he would rather *give* his performance.' The stewards, the Right Hon. W. Dowdeswell, Chancellor of the Exchequer, and the Rev. Sir Richard Wrothesley, Bart., Dean of Worcester, being informed of his objection and the terms in which it was made, conveyed a hint to him that 'they should be thankful to him for the fifty guineas.' The hint was not lost upon him; he condescended to give a receipt for the sum for his own use.[20]

Tenducci, who married three times, died in Genoa in 1790.

Mary Linley, the younger sister of Elizabeth, sang at the Meetings from 1771 to 1773 and in 1775 and 1776. From 1774, her more famous sister's place was taken by Cecilia Davies, an Englishwoman who had won a great reputation in Italy, where she was called 'L'Inglesina'. In July 1832 Rimbault visited Cecilia Davies at her home in London. She was then ninety-two years of age. He was 'surprised to find that she retained all her faculties, was very communicative, and recollected the former events of her life perfectly, which she related with great distinctness and vivacity. She died a few years after, in the extreme of old age, disease and poverty.'[21] – a recurring theme, it seems.

At Gloucester in 1775, Handel's *Israel in Egypt* was performed at Three Choirs for the first time. Between the first and second parts of the oratorio a 'Miscellaneous Act' was given, consisting of songs performed by Mary Linley and the Italian castrato soprano, Venanzio Rauzzini, and instrumental pieces by Guardini, Fischer and Crosdill.

Rauzzini sang at three Meetings: 1775 to 1777, after which he regularly appeared as a member of the audience until his death in 1810. He had made his operatic début in Rome in 1765, and two years later entered the service of the court of the Elector of Bavaria in Munich. In 1772 he created the leading role in Mozart's *Lucio Silla* in Milan, and Mozart wrote the *Exsultate Jubilate* for him. In 1774 he settled in England, appearing both as singer and composer, and his opera *Piramo e Tisbe*, performed as an oratorio, was given in full at Hereford in 1777. From 1778 he lived in Bath where he gained a high reputation as a singing teacher, numbering among his pupils Gertrud Mara, John Braham, and Nancy Storace and Michael Kelly, both of whom sang in the first performance of Mozart's *La Nozze di Figaro*. Nancy Storace appeared as a 'juvenile performer' at the 1777(H) Meeting: she was not quite twelve years old!

In addition to the three cathedral choirs, additional choral singers from 'London, Salisbury, Bath, Oxford and other places' had been mentioned in the notice for the first *Messiah* performance in 1757(G), and such augmentation became the norm at Three Choirs. By 1772 it was acknowledged that the choirs at the Meetings lacked balance due to a shortage of trebles. Then, in 1772(H), 'were engaged this year, for the first time, to assist the trebles in the choruses, Miss Radcliffe and others, of the celebrated female chorus singers, as they were called, from the North of England'.[22] The *Gloucester Journal* reported that their 'exact and spirited accompanyment added greatly to the grandeur of the several choruses'.[23] The 'Concert of Ancient Music', an annual royal and aristocratic affair during nearly three quarters of a century from 1776, used also 'to import mill-girl sopranos from Lancashire and Yorkshire, and maintain them in London throughout the concert season'.[24] And the northern ladies were engaged regularly for Three Choirs throughout the last quarter of the eighteenth century.

Among the singers from the North who appeared at Gloucester in 1772 was one Miss Harrop. Six years later this lady returned to Gloucester as a soloist, able to command a fee of one hundred guineas. She had married Joah Bates, a Yorkshireman – 'one of the Commissioners of the Victualling Office, a scientific amateur in music'[25] – who had taken her from her music-master, Sacchini, and completed her musical education himself. According to Burney, Mrs Bates's 'seraphic voice and disposition for music were so highly cultivated by him as to render her one of the most enchanting singers ever heard; and that her performance of Handel's pathetic songs, in particular, had made it impossible to be pleased with her successor in them [Madam Mara] at the concerts of Ancient Music.'[26]

Joah Bates (1741–99) was the conductor of the Concert of Ancient Music in London from its inception in 1776. He conducted at the Handel Commemoration of 1784 at Westminster Abbey when, strangely, he employed Madam Mara and not his wife.

Samuel Harrison was one of the treble soloists with the Concerts of Ancient Music. His voice remained unbroken until the age of eighteen when it failed at once in a single day – the day of his engagement at the 1778(G) Music Meeting. Harrison went on to become a much sought-after tenor.

In 1778 Lamotte led the band, and 'the matchless Cervetto', as Burney styled the famous cellist, appeared as an instrumentalist for the first time. Two years later, at Hereford, William Cramer took over as Leader, beginning a long association of the

Cramer family with Three Choirs. He was a brilliant violinist, a member of the Elector's orchestra at Mannheim from 1752 to 1772, after which he settled in London. He was nominated chamber musician to the king and appointed Leader at the Ancient Concerts.

Following the transfer of *Messiah* to the cathedrals at Hereford in 1759, Worcester in 1761 and Gloucester in 1769, three morning events – *Messiah* and two church services – became a regular pattern at Three Choirs until 1784. In that year the (inaccurately calculated) centenary of Handel's birth was, as we have seen, celebrated at Westminster Abbey under the direction of Joah Bates. Similar celebrations were held elsewhere in the country, including at Gloucester where, on the second morning in the cathedral, 'on which till this time the church services had been repeated, and to which admission was gratuitous, there were substituted the music which had been performed in Westminster Abbey on the first day of Handel's commemoration; and the admittance to this performance was fixed at 5s. 6d., the same as the other concerts'.[27] The 'Westminster Abbey Selection' now became the regular item for the second morning at each Meeting (except in 1787(G) when *Israel in Egypt* was performed). After 1791 it became a 'Grand Selection of Sacred Music by Handel'.

The famous Madam Mara made her Three Choirs début in 1784(G), fresh from her huge success at Westminster Abbey, of which Burney said:

> She had the power of conveying the softest and most artificial inflexions of her sweet and brilliant tone to the remotest corner of that immense building, whilst she articulated every syllable with such neatness, precision and purity, that it was rendered as audible and intelligible as it could possibly have been in a small theatre by mere declamation.[28]

Gertrud Mara (née Schmeling) was born at Cassel in 1749 and was taken on tour by her father as a child prodigy violinist. While visiting England her talent as a singer was discovered and she had lessons from Domenico Paradisi. She sang under Hiller in Leipzig in 1769, and in 1771 married the cellist Mara and entered the service of Frederick the Great in Berlin. When, in 1780, she tried to leave Prussia she was imprisoned for her attempt – a fate which also befell Voltaire when he had tried to leave Frederick's Court! When, at last, she was able to get away, she appeared with great success in Vienna, Paris and London.

Among the singers who made their first Three Choirs appearance at Gloucester in 1784 were, in addition to Mara, Miss Cantelo, a young singer who later married Samuel Harrison, and James Bartleman, the leading bass of his generation, but appearing in 1784, as Harrison had done before him, as a treble.

On Easter Monday 1786, the whole of the west end of Hereford Cathedral collapsed, taking with it several bays of arches in the nave. Quite obviously, there was no possibility of using the building for the morning performances at the Music Meetings in the following September. The two gentlemen who had been nominated as Stewards, fearing a large financial loss, withdrew from office and others could not easily be found to take their places. At last, James Walwyn Esq. and the Revd Canon Morgan agreed to accept nomination. The Meeting took place as usual; the morning performances, the 'Westminster Abbey Selection' and *Messiah* were transferred to St Peter's Church. On the first and third evenings there were Miscellaneous Concerts; and on the intermediate evening 'a Concert of Ancient Music' on the plan of those held in London. What might the audience have heard at these Miscellaneous Concerts?

Only one printed programme of an eighteenth-century Three Choirs Miscellaneous Concert is known to survive. It is to be found in the Painswick House Collection held in the Gloucester City Library and refers to the year 1790 when, among other artists, the young son of the Gloucester organist, William Mutlow, appeared as a treble in a melodramatic ballad, 'The Ghost of Edwin', written by one Colin Roope Esq.

A Selection of Songs
for the
Performances at the Booth Hall
on Thursday Evening
September 9, 1790

Gloucester: Printed by R. Raikes

Act I

Overture, 'Ariadne'	
Song, Madame Mara *Gia trionfar*	(Anfossi)
Concerto Oboe, Mr. Parke	
Song, Miss Parke *Dove sei*	(Handel)
Concerto, *Corelli*	
Song, Madame Mara 'Softly sweet'	
Recit, 'Search round the world' – Solomon	
Chorus, 'May no rash intruder' – Solomon	

Act II

Grand Concerto, Handel	
Glee, 'Sigh no more Ladies' – *Stevens*	
Song, Master Mutlow 'Pale was the Moon' – The Ghost of Edwin (new)	(Hayes)
Quartetto, Pleyell	
Song, Miss Parke 'The prince unable'	(Handel)
Concertante, Wilton	
Song, Madame Mara 'Dunque corri'	(Giordanielli)
Chorus, 'The many rend the skies'	

In June 1788, George III suffered a particularly bad series of bilious attacks and his physician, Sir George Baker, advised him to visit Cheltenham for a course of treatment, taking the spa waters there. The king arrived in Cheltenham on Saturday 12 July, accompanied by Queen Charlotte, the Princess Royal, the Princesses Augusta and Elizabeth, Lord Courtoun (comptroller of the Royal Household), Lady Weymouth (in charge of the ladies-in-waiting) and other members of a large party, including Fanny Burney.

While in Cheltenham, the king learned that the triennial Music Meeting was to be celebrated at Worcester on 27, 28 and 29 August. He signified his intention of being present at the Meeting, provided that it could be brought forward to the 6, 7 and 8 of that month – and the alteration was accordingly made. Two days before the Meeting, the king wrote to his daughter, Princess Sophia, opening his letter with the following paragraph:

My Dearest Sophia,

    The account of this Day of Mary is so charming that it has quite put me into Spirits and prepared me for going tomorrow after Dinner to Worcester where I shall remain till Friday Evening that I may attend the three Mornings at the Cathedral the Musick of my Admiration Handel.[29]

The royal party arrived in Worcester on the evening of Tuesday 5 August as planned and took up residence at the Bishop's Palace. The next day at 5 a.m. the king walked out to view incognito many parts of the city before returning for various levees, followed by Divine Service in the cathedral. This included the overture to *Esther*, the Dettingen *Te Deum*, *Grand Jubilate*, an anthem and two coronation anthems. The following morning, the 'Westminster Abbey Selection' was performed; and on the third morning, an audience of almost three thousand attended *Messiah*.

Up until 1834 all cathedral performances at Three Choirs were given in the quire, but for the royal visit of 1788 the nave of Worcester Cathedral was handsomely fitted up for the occasion. A gallery for the royal family was erected under the Great West Window: 'It was spread with a rich Worcester carpet, lined and faced with crimson silk, and shaded with a lofty canopy of the same material and surmounted with a crown.'[30] On the right hand of it was a seat for the Bishops of the three dioceses, and on the left another for the Dean and Chapter of Worcester. Behind these seats were others for the Stewards of the Meeting and for the royal suite. 'The orchestra was at the opposite end of the Nave. Below the Royal Gallery were rows of seats raised one above another for the Nobility and persons of Distinction. There was also a small Gallery on each side of the Nave for the Corporation and their families. The area was filled with seats for the audience in general.'[31]

At seven o'clock on the Friday evening the royal family went to the College Hall to hear a Miscellaneous Concert. An elegant box had been prepared in the centre of the gallery for their reception.

The King was dressed in a Blue and Gold uniform. The Queen and Princesses in royal purple gowns with silver tissue petticoats. The Queen's head dress was a cap decorated with purple ribbands and studded with beads of polished steel as brilliant as the finest diamond . . . The Princesses wore their hair ornamented very gracefully with gauze and flowers; their slippers adorned with polished steel rosettes, lately invented by Bailey of Gloucester.[32]

Fanny Burney attended the concert and recorded in her diary:

I was much more pleased than in the morning [*Messiah*], but was obliged to come away at the end of the first act, as it was already ten o'clock . . .
    The box for the Royals was prepared upstairs and made very handsome; but there was no sort of resting-place considered for the attendants who were forced to stand perpendicular the whole time. Miss Hawkins, Betsy and myself had places behind the Royal Box. The King, Queen, and Princesses had very handsome large chairs; their poor standing attendants were Lady Harcourt, Lord Oxford, Mr Fairly, and the two Colonels to fill up, for in form and order the Equeries are never admitted to the Royal Box, but in the country this etiquette is cast aside . . . Poor Lady Harcourt was so weakened by her influenza that she was ready to drop, and after the first act was forced to entreat permission to resign her place to Lady Pembroke, who was in the gallery; and, being another Lady of the Bed Chamber, was equally proper for it.[33]

The principal singers at the royal Music Meeting were Gertrud Mara and Mrs Ambrose (née Mahon); Charles Norris, singing for the last time at Three Choirs; Hindle and

Wilson, counter-tenors; and the basses Sale and Griffiths. The instrumental performers, according to Lysons, were:

> Mr Cramer, leader, Fischer, Mara [the cellist husband of Gertrud Mara], Mahon, Ashley, with the double drums &c., &c., aided by the powerful support of His Majesty's private band. The music was conducted by Mr Isaac.[34]

In 1789(H) the principal soprano was the celebrated Elizabeth Billington, daughter of Carl Weichsal, a German oboist who had settled in London. She was a pupil of J.C. Bach, appearing first in public as a child pianist in 1774. She married the double-bass player, James Billington, in 1783. 'When I first heard her in 1783,' wrote Lord Mount Edgcumbe,

> . . . she was very young and pretty, had a delightful fresh voice of very high compass, and sang with great neatness several songs composed for Allegranti, whom she closely imitated . . . yet something was wanting; for she possessed not the feeling to give touching expression, even when she sang with the utmost delicacy and skill . . .[35]

But Haydn, in his Diary of 1791, spoke of Mrs Billington as a singer of genius. Like Cecilia Davies before her, Elizabeth Billington gained the rare distinction of acceptance as a first female singer in Italian theatres, and she was a great favourite at Three Choirs for many years. Although advertised to appear at Worcester in 1791, Mrs Billington did not appear and her place was taken by Gertrud Mara. John Marsh, an amateur composer, writer about music and diarist, was present at the first evening performance:

> . . . After seven I hurried to the performance of Acis and Galatea at the college-hall, fearing I should lose the overture, but found they had not begun, though much after the time announced for the beginning, being waiting for Madam Mara, who was to sing the first song, and who, when she thought proper to make her appearance, did not choose to sit in the orchestra with the other singers, but with the company in the room, whence she never went to the orchestra without being waited upon, to be handed up by Mr. Wigley, the member for Worcester. As she notwithstanding this behaviour met with great applause after every song she sang, Miss Poole, the next singer, to shew her satisfaction, also joined in the applause by wrapping [sic] with her fan; which (it seemed) much displeased Mara, who observed that it was as much as to say she sang almost as well as Miss Poole did herself, and that she had a great mind to box her ears for her impertinence.[36]

As the eighteenth century drew towards its end Europe was in turmoil. The American Revolution had ended in 1783, dealing a crushing blow to the policies of George III, forcing him to make concessions to public opinion in England. The French Revolution began in 1789, and Louis XVI was guillotined in January 1793. Napoleon rose to power – and Britain was at war with France.

Against this background, the following statement appeared in the *Hereford Journal* of 26 July 1798:

> **Hereford.**   The Dean and Chapter having no expectation, in the present exigencies of the country and in the absence of many of the principal inhabitants of the diocese, that any gentleman will undertake the large and increasing expenses of conducting a Music Meeting, submit to the consideration of the Nobility, Gentry and Clergy, the propriety of raising a subscription to answer the charitable purposes of it . . .

The idea was a failure and the subscription unproductive.

Fortunately, the Duke of Norfolk had gathered together a large number of singers and instrumentalists at his Holm Lacy country house, all of whom offered their services free at two performances in aid of the charity on 5 and 6 September. When this plan was published in the *Hereford Journal* it prompted a meeting of the gentry of the county at which it was resolved that, in preference to accepting this benevolent offer, the Meeting of the Three Choirs should go ahead as usual on 26, 27 and 28 September, and that the number of Stewards should, from then on, be increased to two or more lay and two or more clerical. In fact, six Stewards accepted office in 1798, one of them being Canon Morgan, who had stood forward in a similar way in 1786.

John Marsh paid three more visits to Three Choirs, in 1808(G), 1819(H) and 1821(W). His description of the first of these will serve to take us into the Music Meetings of the nineteenth century, and into the congenial company of William Mutlow, organist of Gloucester from 1782 until 1832; Marsh travelled into Gloucestershire from Monmouth:

I made a famous breakfast; and about eleven we set out for Ross, eleven miles, to which we had a very pleasant ride, great part of the way by the river, Wye, the scenery about which was delightful. Here we went, to see the fine view from the church-yard; after which, we got our dinner at the inn, and about three set off again for Gloucester, which we did not reach till near seven o'clock, when we took possession of a small lodging in St. Mary's churchyard, taken for us at a great price, three guineas and a half for cooking, for the music meeting week by Mr. Mutlow, the organist.

On Tuesday, the sixth, we got in to the rehearsal at the cathedral, and were much pleased, the principal vocal performers being Mrs Billington, Mr and Mrs Vaughan, Mess. Harrison, Goss and Bartleman, and the principal instrumental Mess. Cramer, leader, Lindley, Griesbach, Mahon, Holmes, Boyce etc. With all these, except the females and Harrison, and near twenty others I dined this day at Mr Mutlow's, who gave us a fine turbot, turtle soup, venison, and plenty of game, which was sent him by the stewards of the meeting. On the next morning we went immediately after breakfast to the cathedral to get good places; and at eleven the service began with the overture of Esther, performed by the band, and afterwards were introduced the Dettingen Te Deum, one of Dr Boyce's charity-anthems, and the coronation anthem; beside which the full band and chorus joined in the Gloria-patri of the psalms, which had a very striking effect. After the prayers there was an appropriate sermon, and a collection at going out for the widows and orphans of the clergy of the three dioceses; for which one of the plates being held by the bishop, Dr Huntingford, he was so good as to recognise me, as we passed. At a quarter before six we went to the room and were much entertained with the oratorio of Alexander's Feast, finely performed. On the next morning we went to a grand selection at the cathedral, of which the first and third parts were mostly from Handel, and the second consisted of the first act of Haydn's Creation. In the evening, the room being much crowded, we did not enjoy the concert so much as on the evening before, neither did it go off so well, as in consequence of the heat of the room the performers were much oppressed, and found it expedient to shorten the concert by leaving out a concertante of Mozart's for six obligato instruments and the concluding full piece. We here took our leave of the music at Gloucester, as instead of going to the Messiah the next morning at the cathedral, which we had so often heard, we devoted this our last morning at Gloucester to going to see the new jail there, built on Mr Howard's plan with a penitentiary, and proper distinction between the debtors and felons, and Mr Weaver's pin-manufactory.[37]

Notes

1. *Worcester Journal*, 23 July 1752
2. Watkins Shaw, *The Three Choirs Festival* (Worcester, 1954) pp. 8 and 9
3. *Worcester Journal*, 27 August 1752
4. *Worcester Journal*, 27 December 1753
5. *Gloucester Journal*, 8 July 1755
6. Adam Smith, *The Wealth of Nations* (Penguin, 1986), p. 209
7. See MW 1860, p. 584
8. Rimbault, *Annals* 1895, footnote to p. 31
9. *Annals* 1812, p. 183
10. *Annals* 1812, pp. 184–5
11. *Gloucester Journal*, 14 and 21 September 1756
12. *Gloucester Journal*, 12 July 1757
13. *Gloucester Journal*, 1 November 1757
14. *Annals* 1812, p. 188
15. *Gloucester Journal*, 14 August 1759
16. Hereford Record Office (AE 75)
17. Boyce conducted at Worcester in 1755 (see *Gloucester Journal* notice, 8 July 1755). Deafness forced him to give up much of his work during his later years. He died in 1779.
18. *Gloucester Journal*, 29 July 1760
19. *Annals* 1895, footnote to p. 39
20. *Annals* 1895, footnote to p. 47
21. *Annals* 1895, footnote to p. 51
22. *Annals* 1812, p. 203
23. *Gloucester Journal*, 14 September 1772
24. Percy A. Scholes, *The Mirror of Music* (London, 1947), vol. 1, p. 49
25. *Annals* 1812, p. 210
26. *Annals* 1895, footnote to p. 55
27. *Annals* 1812, p. 218
28. *Annals* 1812, pp. 218–19
29. Gloucester City Library
30. *Gentleman's Magazine*, 3rd no. of vol. LVII, pt. II, p. 756
31. Revd James Nankiwell, *The Royal Visit to the Three Choirs Meeting in 1788* (Worcester, 1950), p. 13
32. *European Magazine*, vol. XIV, pp. 150–1
33. Fanny Burney, *Diary*, vol. IV, pp. 76–8
34. *Annals* 1812, pp. 227–8
35. *Annals* 1895, footnote to p. 70
36. Diaries of John Marsh (ms), 16 vols, Cambridge University Library (Add. ms 7757)
37. Ibid.

CHAPTER FIVE

THE GENTLEMEN AND THE PLAYERS

F ollowing the rescue of the Festival by the Duke of Norfolk in 1798, the number of
Stewards rose to six, three clerical and three lay, in each city. Even so, rising costs
and falling receipts placed an increasingly formidable burden upon these
gentlemen. After 1817(G), when receipts exceeded expenditure and the Stewards were
able to invest a surplus in consols, the Festival made a loss every year until 1853(G). In
1836 it was rumoured that at a meeting of the Worcester Stewards 'some good round
sums were offered by certain of them to be released from their impending responsibility'.[1] This is hardly surprising: deficits in the previous decade had exceeded £750 per
annum, reaching a peak of £1,365 1s. 0d. in 1832(G).

Between 1836 and 1838 three meetings took place at the Episcopal Palace in
Worcester of a committee appointed 'to consider the best means of ensuring a more
enlarged and efficient support of the Triennial Musical Festival in Worcester'.[2] The
result was the setting up in Worcester of a guarantee fund amounting to £746 in which
thirty-two gentlemen and members of the clergy, including the Bishops of Worcester
and Rochester and three members of Parliament, agreed to subscribe the whole, or such
proportions as necessary, of amounts from £5 to £20 each towards the Worcester Music
Meetings. This sum, together with £50 from each of the, by then, eight Stewards was
used to defray expenses; the payment from each subscriber being made in proportion to
the amount of their subscriptions.

In 1844 a guarantee fund was opened in Gloucester too, but there the preferred
method of raising an extra subsidy was to increase the number of Stewards. In 1847
James Henry Brown took over as Secretary of the Gloucester Festival. Not only was he a
first-class administrator but he also had a gift for attracting men of means and influence
to the ranks of the Stewards; in 1853 there were twenty-three, in 1862 fifty-four, and by
1868 there were no fewer than one hundred and six.

If anything, the difficulty was greater at Hereford than at either of the other cities.
Although the Hereford Stewards made every effort to keep Festival expenses down, they
could do nothing to increase the number of seats in the smallest of the three cathedrals.
In consequence, financial losses at Hereford were often greater than at Worcester or
Gloucester. In 1858 their plight was so severe that the Secretary of the Hereford Festival

Committee wrote to his counterpart in Gloucester to ask if there was any possibility of changing the Festival of that year from Hereford to Gloucester and delaying Hereford's turn until 1859. The Gloucester Committee refused to accept this proposal but suggested instead that Hereford too should increase the number of Stewards serving the Festival.[3] By the end of the century at both Gloucester and Worcester the Stewards numbered around two hundred, and at Hereford three hundred.

While to have a large number of generous Stewards was financially advantageous, the arrangement created its own problems. The possession of a noble title, wealth, civic status or a seat in Parliament is not necessarily a guarantee of musical sensitivity. On the other hand, a Steward pledging large sums of personal money might expect to have his opinions heard in the process of Festival decision-making. Inevitably, committees grew larger; sub-committees were formed to debate even minor matters; meetings grew in number and duration; stress on the Secretary and conductor increased; and the resulting decisions were sometimes patently wrong.

The Reverend F.E. Witts (1783–1854), vicar of Wick Rissington in Gloucestershire, left in his diary a delightful pen-picture of the activities of a Festival Steward in the early nineteenth century. On 13 September 1826 Witts wrote:[4]

> The town was all alive with company, some crowding towards the college, some arriving at the inns and lodgings, all in gay attire and nothing could be more lovely than the weather. A large posse of constables under the able generalship of a Bow Street Officer was posted at the Cathedral door, and their services were likely to be needed for the admission this morning was free. Each Steward's share of tickets for the galleries was 25, and the lay and clerical galleries held about 60 persons and were each day almost exclusively occupied by the first ladies in point of rank and connection, who attended the meeting, a most beautiful sight and the present style of female dress tended to justify the appelations affixed: a *parterre* – a bed of roses.
>
> My own ladies were each day accommodated in the first row of the clerical gallery, and from the extent of my acquaintance I was each morning soon drained of my tickets, and had I twice as many could have disposed of them to various applicants. By 11 o'clock the inner choir of the Cathedral was fearfully crowded . . . an occasional scream or groan indicated distress or fainting, some were carried out, some struggled into the outer choir, the most persevering stood their ground . . .
>
> The concert at the Shire Hall was very fully attended, nearly a thousand persons were present and the pressure at the upper end of the room was great. Lady Lyttleton and the Misses Witts were there and as soon as I had provided for their accommodation by a fresh bench between those already occupied and the orchestra,[5] the well-known and obtrusive Alderman Matthew Wood[6] of London, coveting similar accommodation addressed himself to me. I explained it had been the constant rule with the Stewards to reserve accommodation for their own parties, and with very few forms kept back and the Lord Lieutenant not yet arrived he would have to find accommodation in the seats already placed. In reply the Alderman (who since the death of the sister of his namesake the eccentric and wealthy Jemmy Wood, Banker of Gloucester, has been a summer resident here where the old lady left him a good house in consideration of his championship of the late Queen Caroline, and where he hopes to worm himself into the good graces of Banker Jemmy) dilated on the ill-usage of the public by the Stewards: then exit in rage.
>
> When the conversation reached the ears of Bowles[7] the following day when we were summing up the receipts at the Cathedral door, the poet extemporised:
>
> > What money our music produces;
> > For surely a meeting is good
> > Where are Beauforts and Sherbornes and Ducies
> > And Lansdownes and Alderman Wood.

In the following year, 1827, royal patronage was extended to the Music Meetings by King George IV, a privilege continued to the present day.

Though generally courteous in helping the public to their seats at Festival performances, the Stewards could often be guilty of a pompous arrogance, especially to the gentlemen of the Press:

So long as the Gloucester Festival has the good fortune to retain the services of such a secretary as Mr. J.H. Brown there is no fear of any paucity of stewards; but with all respect to these public spirited gentlemen I would venture to suggest that the administrative [*sic*] should be in fewer hands. We all know the proberb about 'Too many cooks,' and this week it has been most painfully exemplified. Personally speaking I am making no complaint – on the contrary, so far as I am concerned individually, I have received the greatest possible courtesy and politeness from every steward with whom I have been brought in contact; but it has not been the case with all my London *confrères*, one of whom was told on Friday, upon requesting a seat, that 'no one had asked him to come there, and if he did come it was either for his own pleasure or profit.' . . . On Thursday, while Mr. Reeves was touching the heart of everyone by his exquisite singing of 'Total Eclipse,' one of the stewards (the most exalted functionary of Gloucester), was moving about, whispering in the ear of one or other of his colleagues, to the annoyance of everyone in his neighbourhood, who wished to listen to the greatest treat of the whole Festival.[8]

Of the grand dress ball at the Shire Hall last night, I am not in a condition to send you a report. On entering the Hall, I presented my ticket, as usual, and entered the room, when a gentleman tapped me on the shoulder, and requested to know if I belonged to the London press. I told him I had that honour; whereupon he expressed a desire that I should follow him to the orchestra, whither he had received orders to show gentlemen of the press who might think proper to attend the ball. I was too indignant to remonstrate – 'surprise held me mute' – so I left, convinced that the stewards of the Hereford Festival were not by any means courteous to strangers, and this was my last impression of the Meeting of the Three Choirs in 1855.[9]

In his autobiography published in 1908, Joseph Bennett describes the ordeal of a young and inexperienced reporter attending the Festival for the first time:

In 1865, for some months before the Gloucester Festival took place, I had acted as a reporter of concerts, and such like, for the *Sunday Times*. . . . The paper was of no weight in the councils of music, and I was absolutely unknown – a mere waif, or stray, that had drifted by accident into the area of the art, and, like all such things, liable to be swept up and cast into the fire. But I felt none the less ambitious on that account, and as the Festival drew near, my mind was made up to attend it. So, one day, I presented myself before Mr Seale, the proprietor of my first journal, and enlarged upon the fitness with which the *Sunday Times* might place itself among other important papers in the Festival jury-box. My eloquence, though very sincere, proved of none effect. Seale remarked that the *Sunday Times* was a London weekly, and that musical doings in Gloucester did not concern it. He graciously added, however, that as I seemed to wish it, he would accept a report of the Festival, provided it cost him nothing. Let me confess that, for the moment, I was staggered by the preferred conditions. But only for a moment. My resolve to go held fast, though I had to support a wife and family upon means which left nothing to spare. I 'pinched' to do it – pinched myself, that is; going to Gloucester by the cheapest way, and securing a bedroom in one of a row of cottages some distance from the centre of the city. My food I could get as opportunity offered, but, of course, I was outside the zone of hospitality in my character as a friendless stranger. That, however, troubled me not at all, so long as I had a shilling in my pocket.

The next morning saw me bowing before the majesty of the Festival secretary, and pleading for a ticket of admission to the performances. The official's name was Brown; his ordinary rôle, if I rightly remember, was that of drawing-master at an important school hard by, and he lived in a quaint old house on the eastern side of the cathedral yard. Said Mr Brown, as I approached him in his secretarial office, 'Well, sir, what can I have the pleasure of doing for you?' That was promising, and I could see, further, that I had to deal with a kindly little man. 'I represent the *Sunday Times*, Mr Brown, and shall be obliged by a ticket of admission for the week.' A cloud of doubt settled on the secretary's face. Opening a drawer, he took out a note-book and examined a particular page. Then he spoke again: 'I don't find the name of the *Sunday Times* in the list of papers to which admission has been granted.' 'No, sir,' I replied, 'but I have lately been appointed its critic, and I want to change all that and much else.' 'That's right,' said Brown; then, after a pause for consideration, he filled up, and handed to me a ticket for any vacant seat in the north aisle. That second-class place I took to be a compromise between good nature and official strictness, but anyhow it served my purpose very well; and, as none of the critics knew me, and I was equally ignorant of them, there was no occasion for false shame. . . .

Here let me say that Festival authorities forty years ago were not always remarkable for politeness or suavity when dealing with members of the press. I quite agree that allowance should be made for them in this regard, because it sometimes happened that members of the press were as lacking in the graces of behaviour as themselves; standing too much upon an unduly heightened sense of their own importance, and so on. Since the time of which I speak, a great change for the better has taken place, but still there is room for improvement, and much further good might be done by abolishing the journalist's free pass, which, I have always thought, degrades him in the common eye. I could say much on this question, but I touch it now only in passing.

Forty years ago the Festivals at Gloucester, Worcester, Hereford and Norwich (all these being cathedral cities) ended with a ball, the sole survivor of various 'side shows,' which clung more or less tenaciously to the main attraction. . . .

The ball of the Three Choirs I never cared to witness, and I came too late on the scene to refuse the Gloucester 'Ordinary' – not a Bishop but a sort of public dinner – together with Gloucester Races, both functions being left-handed appendages of the Festival. Lastly, the ball vanished also. The air of the seventies was not good for it, but that its demise was lamented by the county Misses I can well believe.

Do you ask how the free press-tickets affected the amenities between festival officials and festival reporters? The answer is that fifty years ago, and for a good while later, journalists who attended festivals in the provinces, and received free tickets, were not looked upon as gentlemen, albeit, when referred to as a body, they were sometimes styled 'gentlemen of the press,' that form being employed as a sort of compliment if toasts were about. They may have been famous critics in London, but, generally speaking, the provincial mind recognised no difference between them and the newspaper men whose ordinary vocation it was to attend coroner's inquests, and make notes of police court proceedings. This was not all. Your festival official, in the long-past time to which I refer, appreciated in a wonderful manner his four days' brief authority, and exerted himself to the extent of unblushing impudence; without deliberate purpose, in many cases, I firmly believe, but simply because he thought it the proper course to take with a journalist. I remember how, on one occasion, I walked to a certain cathedral, rather carefully 'made up' for the part of a gentleman, and was received by a local magnate, acting as steward, with pleasant smiles and a friendly mien. I showed him my ticket, which was prominently marked 'Press,' and, alas! the smiles vanished, and the bearing became stiff and hard as, waving his hand, he cried 'Pass up.' I did not blame the poor man, because there was the question whether he knew any better, and likewise was there the fact, avowed on the ticket, that I had entered as a mere dead-head. [10]

For the great majority of nineteenth-century Stewards, Three Choirs was a highlight of the social calendar, presenting an opportunity to meet and to be seen with a larger number of the nobility and gentry than at most other occasions in the three shires. For the ladies there was always the task of assisting as plate-holders in the collections for the Festival charity. This simple duty could be quite an ordeal for an aristocratic young lady unused to public exposure in Victorian England. In her memoirs, written a century ago, the Margravine of Anspach recalled her experience at a Gloucester Festival. This lady was the youngest daughter of Augustus, fourth Earl of Berkeley. Her first husband was

Lord Craven, and her second the Margrave of Anspach. But the extract has to do with her maiden days, when she was the 'toast' of Gloucestershire:

> In the summer after the grand *fête* at Berkeley, there was a music-meeting at Gloucester, to which I went with Lady Berkeley [her stepmother]. An unexpected summons came to me to request that I would leave the pew where I was, and hold one of the plates for the money collected for the poor, at one of the doors of the Cathedral. This requisition was made by desire of the Bishop of Gloucester, and to this door all the gentlemen of the three counties rushed to get a sight at the young novelty. As I naturally must have felt abashed at such a situation, where I was so very conspicuous, the consequence was that I averted my face when I curtsied for the guineas that were given, and they all fell sliding from the plate, to the entire dismay of the two beadles who attended. So great was my confusion at this unlucky circumstance that, on my return to the Bishop's palace, where I was staying, I was obliged to retire to my bedroom, where I remained to cry and sob at my misfortune. It was only Lord Berkeley [her brother] who could rouse me, by telling me peremptorily that I must go to the ball, where I was again mortified because he scolded me for refusing to dance with an odious Baronet, whom he liked and I hated because he had ventured to tell me that he was in love with me; and as there were others who talked love to me I disliked them all.[11]

Given the Victorian perception of women as guardians of the home, consigned to a subordinate, domestic role, it is not surprising that the notion of ladies becoming Stewards at the Festival was not even discussed until the latter part of the century. The Gloucester Secretary suggested in 1889 that the Executive Committee might invite ladies to be Stewards. The proposal was considered but rejected several times in the remaining years of the century, and nothing more was done until 1907 when it was agreed to confer with the Hereford and Worcester Stewards. A resolution was then made that invitations should be sent to 'Ladies who are Householders, and whose husbands, brothers or sons, would have been eligible to become Stewards'.[12] Even so, no lady actually became a Steward until after the First World War, by which time an irreversible change in the social order was, in any case, under way.

Throughout the nineteenth century, although the main burdens of the musical direction and administration of a Festival fell to the conductor and the Secretary respectively, there was no question of them being treated by the gentlemen of the Executive Committee as their equals. Rather, their status appears to have been that of highly respected senior servants. A glimpse into the Committee Room will prove the point.

After Secretary Brown's death, his place in Gloucester was taken by a young man called F. W. Waller. Brown's honorarium had been £50 per Festival; but on Waller's appointment in 1874 the Stewards immediately halved this sum. The new Secretary soon found himself in difficulties and, before the 1877 Festival, took the courage to write formally to his Chairman:

> I must ask your consideration of one point . . . before the year gets too far advanced in case you desire to make any change in consequence of what I have to put before you.
> When I first accepted the duties of the office, it was fully represented to me by the Stewards that the payment was very small & quite out of proportion to the work & I took it for the year 1874 on that understanding . . .
> Though I was influenced by the very small remuneration, still I hoped to clear my expenses for as I am dependent on my own exertions I cannot afford to be a loser by the Festival, but such was the case on the last occasion from the following cause.
> The duties of the Secretaryship absorbed so much of my attention especially just before & at the

time of the Festival that it became absolutely necessary for me to employ an additional clerk in my office to do work, all of which I should have easily accomplished myself under ordinary circumstances.

The payment for this assistance amounted to over £40, thus it will be seen, as I received £25 from the Festival, that in addition to the time & labour expended upon the work, I was out of pocket £15 besides incurring many incidental expenses quite inseparable from the Secretaryship.

Under the circumstances, I hope I shall not be considered unreasonable in asking the Stewards to increase the payment sufficiently to recoup me for any outlay to which I may be put in the coming year so as to ensure my not being out of pocket by the undertaking.[13]

The Stewards were gracious enough to see Waller's point of view and to award him the same honorarium as his predecessor. They were less gracious in 1880 when the Gloucester Cathedral lay clerks refused to accept the terms offered to them, i.e. £6 for singing at all the oratorios, the special service on Friday evening and the usual services, except the three evening services for which 15 shillings would be paid by the Dean and Chapter. Two lay clerks, Thomas and Hargrave, attended a meeting of the Music Committee to explain their views. They had, they said, received from Dr Wesley in 1874:

For Oratorios	£5 0s. 0d.
For Special Service	£1 1s. 0d.
For three Evening Services	15s. 0d.
Total	£6 16s. 0d.

They now required £7 7s. 0d., being 11 shillings extra, and if the Stewards would give them that amount they would give their assistance at the Friday evening service. The Stewards pointed out that the evening service would be paid for by the Dean and Chapter; the lay clerks would not be moved: 'They said that the £7 7s. 0d. was the sum which they must have and that they considered that [they] had been unfairly treated in the matter of the Festival Charity.'[14] (The widows and orphans of lay clerks had originally benefited from the charity but this was discontinued when the services of the lay clerks ceased to be gratuitous.)

The special service on Friday evening, introduced at Gloucester in 1874 in place of the traditional ball, had not been universally welcomed:

The Ball is as dead as a dodo, and the 'light fantastic toe' now reposes, with the foot to which it belongs, on cathedral hassocks . . . As regards the musical service, I am bound to write severe things. The members of the Three Choirs, clad in surplices, made a great show on the lower benches of the orchestra; but their singing was almost beneath criticism, lacking, as it did, the very elements of such merit as alone could satisfy reasonable expectations.[15]

Perhaps remembering this slovenly performance, the Committee refused to discuss the lay clerks' grievance; Thomas and Hargrave left the room. When they had gone it was agreed that no increase on the £6 would be allowed but that the Friday evening service would be optional – a clear sign of their belief that the service could hardly suffer!

The attitude of polite nineteenth-century society towards musicians was much the same as the attitude towards tradespeople. Performers were considered as purveyors of music just as grocers were purveyors of food and wine. Music could be enjoyed as food and wine could be enjoyed; but the musician and the grocer would not be invited to tea.

By 1811 Three Choirs had already begun to assume much of the aspect which it would have for the rest of the century. It had progressed from a small gathering of amateurs and cathedral choristers to become a major national festival engaging celebrated singers, solo instrumentalists and orchestral players, and augmenting the choral forces of Gloucester, Hereford and Worcester with choral societies and choirs from other cities.

The size of the orchestra varied year by year in the early part of the century. In 1812(W) there were twenty-two violins, eight violas, four cellos and four double-basses; two flutes, two oboes, two clarinets, two bassoons, two trumpets, two horns, drums and a 'double trombone', which is the standard 'Mozart' orchestra,[16] plus a bass trombone. In 1831(H) we read that 'the instrumental band, with Mr F. Cramer as principal first violin, was small but select'.[17]

Following the transfer of the oratorio performances from the quire to the nave [1834(H)] an expanded orchestra could be accommodated, comprising more or less the same players who performed at other major festivals and drawn 'from the Concert of Ancient Music, Philharmonic, Italian Opera and other establishments from London'. In 1839(W) 'the band, judiciously selected . . . consisted of the following performers:

Violins:	F. Cramer, Loder, Blagrove, C. Reeve, Wagstaff, Griesbach, Guynemer, Kearns, Loder, jun., N. Mori, Patey, Piggott, Watkins, Anderson, Mackintosh, W. Cramer, J. Marshall, Hope, Perry, D'Egville, J. D'Egville, Martin, Newson, Newsham, Holmes.
Violas:	Moralt, Daniels, Nicks, S. Calkin, Abbott, Glanville, Davis, Marshall.
Violoncellos:	Lindley, Crouch, W. Lindley, C. Lindley, Hatton, Piggott.
Double Basses:	Dragonetti, Anfossi, Howell, G. Smart, Flower, Griffiths.
Flutes:	Ribas, Hill.
Oboes:	Cooke, Keating.
Clarinets:	Willman, Williams.
Bassoons:	Baumann, Tully.
Horns:	Platt, Rae, Kielbach, C. Tully.
Trumpets:	Harper, Irwin, T. Harper, jun.
Trombones:	Smithies, Smithies, jun., Allbrecht.

Drums: Chipp. *Organ*: Mr. Amott. *Pianoforte*: Mr. Hunt.[18]

Among these players were some of the finest instrumentalists of the first half of the century. F. Cramer, Loder and Blagrove all belonged to famous musical families and each performed the duties of Leader at different concerts.

Francois Cramer (1772–1848) first played at a Music Meeting in 1788, the year of George III's visit, succeeded his father as Leader in 1800, and continued to appear at Three Choirs until he retired in his seventy-sixth year. In 1830, on his way to the Worcester Festival with his wife and daughter, Cramer narrowly escaped serious injury or worse. The coach on which they were travelling from London was heavily laden with baggage which was much too high on the top; more was put on at Cheltenham and Tewkesbury. The Cramers and one other person were inside the coach but there were eleven passengers and the coachman outside. They had reached Severn Stoke, seven miles from Worcester, by ten o'clock on the night of Saturday 11 September. Coming down a steep hill the coachman failed to lock the wheel and lost control of the horses. The coach careered down the hill and 'after going for a few minutes at a rapid pace, came to a curve on the road, when, from the immense weight of passengers and luggage at the top, the coach swung, and was thrown to the earth with a tremendous crash'.[19] Few of the passengers escaped injury, and two of them were killed: Joseph Hughes, a maltster from Sidbury, and Frederick Bennett, the organist of Christ Church and New College, Oxford.

Robert Lindley (1777–1855), a Yorkshireman, was the principal cellist at the Italian Opera House in London where he played at the same desk as the great double-bass player, Domenico Dragonetti (1763–1846). For half a century the two were seen playing together not only at the opera but also at the Ancient Concerts, the Philharmonic, and all the provincial festivals; and Dragonetti's dog Carlo was often to be seen sitting beside them.

> Next came that 'Concertante duett' of Corelli's by Lindley and Dragonetti. This was a treat to which all lovers of harmony had been for some time looking forward, and the whole audience and orchestra were on tiptoe in anxious expectation. The veterans, on coming in front, were greeted with loud cheers by all parties, and then, after a 'majestic silence,' the strain began. Words would fail us if we endeavoured to express our admiration of this wonderful performance; the tone, expression, and taste displayed by Lindley in the slow movement, and his execution in the allegro were 'beyond compare.' As to Dragonetti, it will ever remain a wonder with us, how he could move his fingers with such astonishing rapidity on his unwieldy Behemoth of an instrument. The performance of this work of Corelli's was in the musical sphere one of those 'angel visits' which are few and far between. It was finished amid thunders of applause.[20]

Lindley and Dragonetti were remembered in the autobiography of the baritone Henry Phillips:[21]

> Giants they were in talent, such as had never existed before, and possibly may not again. The tone of Lindley's violoncello it is far beyond the power of words to convey, it was so pure, so mellow, so harmonious. He was so perfectly skilled in all he had to do, that you might as well have tried to confuse an automaton as turn him from his path. One of his great achievements was accompanying Mr. Braham in Arne's celebrated cantata 'Alexis.' Many a listener must have left the concert-room fevered with wonder at the marvellous execution of the two artists. Another quality Lindley possessed, which I have never found in any other violoncellist, viz. that when accompanying a recitative, he gave the full chord, and frequently the note on which the singers were to commence. Some one or two tried to imitate his mode, but all failed. When accompanying a song, his last symphony would be most elaborate; he would play wonderful harmonies, and running roulades that one thought could not possibly terminate in the proper key. I well remember, at a musical festival, his accompanying Mr. Braham in that beautiful air, 'Oh, Liberty, thou choicest Treasure.' At the morning performance in the cathedral, when he came to the concluding symphony, he played, to the astonishment of the whole orchestra, in harmonics, 'Over the hills and far away.' This, I presume, was his idea of Oh, Liberty! The bishop and nobility present were delighted, and a repetition was immediately demanded. Lindley laughed to such a distressing degree, and took so much snuff, in both of which offices Dragonetti joined, that he said he couldn't play it again, and he wouldn't, and he didn't.
> Then Dragonetti! in him what a strange being I shall have to describe: he was a kind-hearted man, abounding with eccentricities; by nature a lover of the fine arts; and on his instrument, the double bass, *perfection*. The power and tones he produced from his unwieldy instrument were wonderful, and to this he added great and rapid execution. The ends of his fingers had become, by practice, broad, covered with corns, and almost without form. Take him out of his profession, he was a mere child, given to the greatest frivolities. He led a single life, and occupied one lodging for years; which lodging, consisted of a bed-room, sitting-room, and a vacant apartment, which contained his collection of paintings, engravings, and dolls. Dolls – do not start, reader! a strange weakness for a

man of genius to indulge in, but so it was; white dolls, brown dolls, dark dolls, and black, large, small, middling, and diminutive, formed an important feature in his establishment. The large black doll he would call his wife, and she used to travel with him sometimes to the festivals. He and Lindley generally journeyed together inside the coach, and when changing horses in some little village, he would take this black doll and dance it at the window, to the infinite astonishment and amusement of the bystanders. Such was one of the strange eccentricities of this really great man. So powerful was the tone he could produce from his instrument, that I have frequently heard him pull a whole orchestra back with one accent if they wavered in the least.

One of his and Lindley's great performances was a duet of Corelli's for violoncello and contra-basso, a surprising performance, and one which never failed to elicit an encore. The copy, in Dragonetti's handwriting, was played from, for nearly fifty years; it eventually fell into my possession, having been presented to me by Vincent Novello after Dragonetti's death.

Thomas Harper (1787–1853) was a Worcester man with a national reputation as the leading performer on the slide trumpet in the country. When in his prime his playing was said to need 'no praise of any critic – it speaks indeed "trumpet tongued"'.[22] After his death he was succeeded as principal-trumpet by his son. Another father-and-son partnership in the Festival band was that of the Smithies, senior and junior – the most accomplished trombonists of their time.

Before the invention of the bass tuba the lowest brass notes were provided by the ophicleide,[23] a player being hired as required. Liberties were sometimes taken with the orchestration of works in order to include the impressive ophicleide sound. An example of this was Edward Taylor's adaptation of Mozart's *Requiem*, the *Redemption*: 'In the score which Mozart has made perfectly symmetrical, an ophicleide had been intruded, and an oboe substituted for one of the *corni di bassetti*. These liberties . . . are highly reprehensible.'[24] The most respected ophicleidist of the nineteenth century was a Mr Ponder who, having been engaged for the 1841 Festival, arrived in Gloucester by coach from London, immediately burst into a fit of violent coughing, and died within minutes.

The demise of the ophicleide itself followed only a very few years afer Ponder's death. During the nineteenth century the technology of the valve brought to all brass instruments an advantage previously available only to trombone players: every note in the range of each instrument could now be played.

Before 1840 there were comparatively few amateurs in Britain with an extensive knowledge of music. By mid-century a steady increase in the number of brass bands and choral societies had begun. Collective music-making was thereby extended for the first time from the upper to the 'respectable' members of the lower classes – and smiled upon by society as a virtuous and moral activity.

Increased access to music and music-making was boosted by the introduction of modern methods in the production of instruments and sheet music. In 1850, for example, the possession of a piano was a rare luxury; by 1871 it was estimated that there were 400,000 pianos and a million pianists in Britain. By the end of the century the availability of the three-year hire purchase system had brought less-expensive pianos within the budgets of many thousands more. At the same time, sheet music was becoming increasingly affordable. The cost of a vocal score of *Messiah* in 1837 was a guinea; in 1887 it was one shilling.

An equally important factor in the increasing practicality of establishing choral societies was the introduction of classes for choral singing. John Hullah (1812–84) was a

Worcester man who went to Paris in 1839–40 to study G.L. Wilhelm's method of teaching singing in classes. On his return he started similar classes in this country, and in 1841 began to teach schoolmasters at Exeter Hall in the Strand, London, demonstrating successfully that everyone might learn to sing – a completely new notion at the time. Although Hullah's was the first attempt in England to spread a general knowledge of music, his system ultimately gave way to Curwen's Tonic Sol-fa.

Exeter Hall was home to the Sacred Harmonic Society from 1834 to 1880. In the early years of the Society's life there were so few amateur performers available in London that singers were brought from Yorkshire and Lancashire to strengthen the chorus, and were found employment in the capital. By 1842, professional members of the Sacred Harmonic Society were beginning to resent the influx of amateurs, and *The Musical World* took up their cause when singers from Exeter Hall were engaged to perform at the Worcester Festival:

> **Worcester Festival**. We promised to afford the Exeter Hall amateurs the advantage of as much notoriety as we could procure for them – the strictures we have from time to time felt it our duty to publish, on the unfairness of unprofessional persons supplanting artists in their legitimate engagements, have had the double effect of considerably reducing their numbers, and inducing every possible means of disguise, change of name, and incognito – we, however, have the pleasure to gratify the following gentlemen, to whom this public announcement will, doubtless, prove more satisfactory than the several fees of six pounds each, suborned by them from the pockets of the regular chorus singers, for filling, but certainly not supplying their places: – Mr. H. Withers, pastry cook, Blackfriar's Road – Mr. T. Carmichael, coal clerk – Mr. A. Carmichael, coal clerk – Mr. W. Pocock, stock broker – Mr. J. Taylor, plumber, Clement's Lane – Mr. W. Cowell, tailor and draper – Mr. Robert Bowley, boot maker to the Duke of Cambridge, Charing Cross – Mr. J. Windsor, oil and colourman – Mr. Benjamin Ward, retired painter and glazier – Mr. H. Paine, coach trimmer – Mr. H. Muggeridge, custom house clerk. We shall hope to extend this list in our next.[25]

By 1850 the band and chorus at Exeter Hall had increased to seven hundred and the Society had built up a high reputation for the performance of complete oratorios, especially those by Handel and Mendelssohn.

The tradition of importing additional singers had, as we have seen, been established at Three Choirs long before the foundation of the Sacred Harmonic Society in 1832. By 1850 the advertisements for the Gloucester Festival could boast proudly and in heavy type that the 'Instrumental Band and Chorus' comprised 'nearly three hundred performers, selected with care from the Orchestra of the Philharmonic, and from the Choral Societies and Choirs of Exeter Hall, Bristol, Norwich, Windsor, Worcester, Hereford, etc.' During the second half of the century the visiting choral singers came from many other towns and cities, including Leeds, Bradford, Liverpool, Huddersfield, Cheltenham and Birmingham.

The Crystal Palace, built in Hyde Park to house the Great Exhibition of 1851, became a venue for Sacred Harmonic Society performances of Handel's oratorios in 1857 and 1858. In the following year, 1859, the centenary of Handel's death was marked by a festival at the Crystal Palace. At each performance the choir exceeded 2,700 and the orchestra 450. So popular were these large-scale productions that the Handel Festivals became a triennial event. An era of monster oratorio performances had arrived; so much so that by the 1880s, the peak of the Handel Festivals' popular appeal, the chorus numbered 4,000 and the orchestra 500.

Three Choirs performances of *Messiah* never reached the excesses of scale which so delighted Victorian audiences at the Crystal Palace; lack of space in the cathedrals would, in any case, have limited the numbers of choir and orchestra to a smaller army. None the less, the same version of the oratorio, reinforced by Mozart's 'additional accompaniments', was demanded by provincial festival audiences. Handel was distorted for mass effect. As Winton Dean has pointed out, 'the Victorians worshipped Handel; they did not know him.'[26]

Visiting choral singers continued to swell the ranks of the Three Choirs until the closing years of the nineteenth century. Many of these, along with professional orchestral players from London, travelled the circuit of major music festivals each year; a system which in 1872 brought them very close to disaster when the passenger train in which they were travelling from Worcester to the Norwich Festival collided with a luggage train. By good fortune, the only casualties were musical instruments, destroyed in the crash; the performers, including leading soloists, escaped with nothing worse than bruises and shock.

Until 1864 the custom at Three Choirs was for the organist of the host cathedral to act as Festival conductor, for one of the visiting organists to play the piano, and for the other to play the organ. For at least the first thirty years of the century the word 'conductor' had a very different meaning from that understood today. In purely orchestral works the direction of the orchestra was the responsibility of the principal violinist while another musician 'at the pianoforte', with a full score before him, played or made gestures as necessary. In choral works the role of the 'conductor' was that of beating time and indicating entries with a roll of paper – and a sketch of William Mutlow, drawn by Maria Malibran in 1829, shows him doing just that (see illustration).

The change to modern conducting practice began in 1820 when Louis Spohr visited England to take part in a season of Philharmonic concerts. While rehearsing a manuscript symphony of his own, billed in the programme to be 'Conducted by the Composer', Spohr, instead of taking his place 'at the pianoforte', carried a music desk to the front of the orchestra, drew a baton from his pocket and began to direct the players in the manner already gaining popularity in Germany. When Mendelssohn conducted in London in 1829 he too used a baton. The old method gradually gave way to the new.

But the new method was a severe trial for provincial organists whose training came from their predecessors, who lacked any experience of directing professional players and singers, and who were required to don an uncomfortable mantle for only one week in every three years. Add to these difficulties the severe lack of rehearsal time available to the conductor, who was unable to drill his resident and visiting forces together until the day before the Festival, and it would be surprising if the invariable outcome had been a polished performance. Only the perennial repetition of *Messiah* and, later, *Elijah* engendered confidence through familiarity. 'Novelties' could present a worrying challenge.

While the gentlemen of the local Press were more often than not enthusiastic about Three Choirs performances, it was inevitable that London critics, accustomed to the panache of professional conductors, such as Joseph Surman and Sir Michael Costa, should make unfavourable comparisons and question the contribution of Three Choirs to the cause of art. What *is* surprising is how frequently, in spite of daunting obstacles, the cathedral organists of the nineteenth century so very often *did* succeed in drawing their disparate forces together to achieve highly creditable results.

The tenure of William Mutlow at Gloucester spanned half a century and the reigns of George III, George IV and William IV. Throughout these many years he was much-loved as a kindly, good-tempered and eccentric character with a zest for living and a pointed disregard for the use of the king's English. Something of the waggish Mutlow can be gauged from the following anecdote recorded by the Gloucester historian and attorney, George Worrall Counsell (1758–1843), referring to an incident which took place in 1824:[27]

Gloucester Pedestrianisms

On Saturday evening last a most extraordinary feat of pedestrianism was exhibited at the Mitre in this City by two very singular personages. Mr Mutlow, the fat Organist of our Cathedral, 64 years of age, five feet in height and four feet in circumference, challenged an old gentleman of this City of the name of Rogers who is in his 70th year, who has been for a long time past a martyr to the gout, subject to flatulence and bending under the weight of age and infirmities, (and who) agreed to run for a wager ten times round the landlord's garden, a distance of 500 yards.

The Organist . . . had unfortunately that day partaken of a most splendid dinner and an extra quantity of wine to which he super-added two pints of Goodwin's ale. His friends were therefore apprehensive of his falling down with his load during the race, in which case he would most likely have burst asunder, notwithstanding which he appeared quite in glee, being screwed up to Concert pitch and, jumping up like the jack of a harpsichord, went off at (speed) . . . but the old gentleman, his antagonist, being perfectly sober, shook off the gout and appeared to gain strength at every round, whilst the Organist's bellows were soon out of wind and, being a bar behind, he lost his time, began to shake, was out of tune and, looking like a flat between two naturals and his pipes being nearly choked, came to a finale, and his opponent then after a few eructations took the lead, went forwards *con spirito* and, although he suffered so much from an accumulation of wind as the Organist did for want of it, he finally won the bet.

A behind-the-scenes side-light on the Festival of 1826 is given in a letter from Mutlow to 'Mr. Hedgley, 20 Castle Street, Pimlico, London,' a well-known music copyist and librarian. It was published in *The Musical Times* of October 1901:

Dear Sir,
    Respecting Mr. Bond, I am sorry to say I cannot comply with his terms. I have Dragonetti, Philpots, and Chattaway. If Mr. Bond will come for Twelve Guineas, I shall be glad to see him, if not I shall see for one on less terms. Harper is engaged. I have his answer saying he will come – 25 guineas. I will thank you to see him. I cannot take three of the Lindleys and Marshall of Warwick. Respecting the London chorus singers, my terms are eight guineas each, and if either of the following should object to the terms, you must engage others in their room – Taylor, Lewis, Tett, Hennies, Birt, Doane, Buggins, and Fisher. Say nothing to Doane on the subject.
    Have you the vocal principals and chorus parts of the new words of the Creation? I want but 4 *st*, 4 *2d*, 3 [?] violas, 4 violoncs. Of anything you may send with the flutes, oboes, etc., will you send two cantos and two tenors of 'He sent a thick darkness'?
    I wish you would spend a week with me before the Meeting – you would relieve my mind very much.

I am, yours truly,

W. MUTLOW

Gloucester, August 20, 1826

Mutlow's last Music Meeting was that of 1829. After his death on 1 January 1832, in his seventy-second year, Counsell wrote of him, '. . . it may with truth be asserted, that few men died more sincerely regretted'.[28]

The stability afforded to Gloucester by Mutlow was not enjoyed by Hereford until 1835. Charles Dare made no significant contribution to the Festival, was dismissed his post due to 'bibulous tendencies',[29] and died in 1820. His successor, Aaron Hayter, also disgraced himself, and was dismissed after only two years in post, during which he was the conductor at the Music Meeting of 1819 and, after serving as organist of the Collegiate Church of Brecon for fifteen years, emigrated to the United States where he became organist of the most important churches in New York and Boston, and where he was much esteemed.

John Clarke-Whitfeld was already fifty years old when he relieved Hayter at Hereford. Born in Gloucester on 13 December 1770, John Clarke assumed the additional surname of Whitfeld in 1814 on the death of his maternal uncle, H.F. Whitfeld, in anticipation of receiving an inheritance. Unfortunately his only gain was a name; the inheritance never materialized.

Clarke-Whitfeld was a composer as well as an organist. He presented two of his own oratorios at the Hereford Music Meetings: *The Crucifixion* in 1822 and *The Resurrection* in 1825. Although neither work was successful, Clarke-Whitfeld had set the precedent which would form a pattern later in the century of cathedral organists composing sacred works specifically for Three Choirs performance.

Soon after his arrival at Hereford, Clarke-Whitfeld had been dogged by ill health. He tendered his resignation in April 1823 but withdrew it in June. In 1832 the Chapter were reluctantly obliged to relieve him of his responsibilities as a result of an attack of paralysis, and he died, aged sixty-five, on 22 February 1836.

In October 1832 the ailing Clarke-Whitfeld was replaced by a young man of a very different stamp. Samuel Sebastian Wesley (1810–76), twenty-two years old when he came to Hereford, had already held various organist posts in London during the previous six years as well as gaining valuable experience of secular music-making in the capital. The illegitimate son of the composer Samuel Wesley (1766–1837), Samuel Sebastian's grandfather was the hymn-writer Charles Wesley (1707–88), and his great-uncle was the religious reformer and founder of Methodism, John Wesley (1703–91). Samuel Sebastian soon set his sights on reform too: reform of the abysmal state into which cathedral music had slumped in the nineteenth century.

Wesley remained at Hereford for only three years (1832–5). After London he found provincial life lonely and unrewarding. His income was insufficient for his needs, forcing him to take on a widespread teaching commitment. He was already a superlative organist whose ambition was to devote his life to composition, and at Hereford he completed his famous anthem *The Wilderness*. But an organist at that time depended upon the Church for his livelihood – the same Church whose low musical standards he was bravely prepared to attack; turbulence lay ahead.

At the 'away' Music Meetings of 1833(W) and 1835(G), S.S. Wesley took his place at the pianoforte, but in 1834 the Meeting at Hereford was under his direction. The programme included three pieces by the conductor: a *Sanctus*, a sacred song *Abraham's Offering*, and a *Manuscript Overture*. Also in 1834 a major Three Choirs innovation, aiming to make the Meeting more attractive, was announced in the programme:

. . . in furtherance of this view, as well as in compliance with scruples to which [the Stewards] willingly defer, they have concurred with the Dean and Chapter in a determination to transfer the scene of the musical performances from the choir to the nave of the Cathedral, where the more ample accommodation for the auditory, the impressive character of the architecture, and the improved sphere for the undulation of harmonious sounds, will combine to augment that unspeakable fascination which is the never-failing effect of the grand compositions selected for the occasion.[30]

Surely it must have been S.S. Wesley, with his sure ear for the diagnosis of ills in the performance of cathedral music, who suggested to the Stewards how 'the undulation of harmonious sounds' should best be heard.

Wesley resigned his post at Hereford in September 1835 and his next contribution to Three Choirs followed after an interval of full thirty years; years spent in turn at Exeter Cathedral, Leeds Parish Church and Winchester Cathedral; years too in which his finest music was composed; but years in which he was frequently dispirited in searching for a higher level of discipline and excellence in the choral services of the Church of England by the lack of understanding shown to him by a seemingly indifferent clergy. In 1865 Wesley was appointed Organist and Master of the Choristers of Gloucester Cathedral where he remained until his death.

Following Wesley's resignation, the Hereford Chapter appointed John Hunt to take his place. He too was a young man – only twenty-eight years old when he took up his post on 1 October 1835. Hunt had been brought up as a chorister and articled pupil at Salisbury, moving to Lichfield, where he was a vicar-choral, in 1827. At his first Music Meeting at Hereford, Hunt impressed not only as a conductor but also as a singer:

Mr. Hunt, the organist of the cathedral and conductor of the festival, possesses a sweet counter-tenor voice; and which appears to be a real chest voice – not often the quality of an alto. It is unfortunately not always audible; but when heard, the effect is very agreeable. Moreover the style is chaste and correct. We heard him to the best advantage in the leading solo to the last chorus of the *Dettingen*, 'Lord in thee have I trusted'.[31]

Considerable difficulty had been experienced in obtaining Stewards for the 1837 Meeting. 'On 26th June an advertisement appeared in the Hereford newspapers stating that the stewards of the preceding Hereford Meeting had made every effort to obtain successors, but had only procured the names of three gentlemen who were willing to act.'[32] The 1834 Meeting had made a loss of £933 8s. 0d. as a result of Wesley's decision to include only a selection from *Messiah* instead of the complete work. Within four weeks sufficient Stewards had been found, but meanwhile Hunt had persuaded the soloists to appear at reduced fees. The Stewards were so grateful that they presented him 'with some articles of plate, as an acknowledgement of his zeal and exertions on behalf of the Meeting'.[33]

During Hunt's time as organist, the fabric of Hereford Cathedral once more gave cause for concern. In 1841, at the request of Bishop Musgrave, a survey was carried out. The piers of the central tower were found to be in a dangerous state, and the eastern gable of the Lady Chapel was about to collapse. Restoration and repair, superintended by Dean Merewether (S.S. Wesley's brother-in-law) and his successor Dean Dawes, continued for over twenty years, but John Hunt did not live to see the outcome. He died, aged thirty-five, on 17 November 1842 after having fallen over a dinner wagon, laden with plates and glasses, which had been left in a dark part of the cloisters after an audit dinner. Three days later his adopted nephew, a chorister, died from the shock of his uncle's death and was buried in the same grave.[34]

At Worcester, the early years of the nineteenth century were marked by three fairly rapid changes in the incumbent of the organ loft. Thomas Pitt resigned in 1806 and was relieved by Jeremiah Clarke (not to be confused with the more famous composer of the same name who committed suicide in 1707). Clarke had been a chorister at Worcester, was a noted violinist and first played at Three Choirs in 1800(W) as principal second violin, a position which he filled at other national festivals also. Following his death in 1807, Clarke was replaced by William Kenge. Clarke conducted only one Music Meeting, 1806, and Kenge two, 1809 and 1812. Long-term stability was then achieved by the appointment of Charles Clarke in 1813.

Clarke was born in Worcester in December 1795 and was a chorister at the cathedral. He was appointed Organist of Durham Cathedral when still only sixteen years old but resigned that post in 1813 in order to return to Worcester to take over from Kenge, and there he remained until his death on 28 April 1844.

A royal visit made to the Worcester Music Meeting of 1830 by the Duchess of Kent and her twelve-year-old daughter, Princess Victoria, must surely have been a highlight of Charles Clarke's career. George IV had died in June 1830, and was succeeded by the 'sailor king', William IV, who, alone among George IV's six brothers, enjoyed a measure of popularity with the public. Victoria's father, the Duke of Kent, was a soldier; hated by the army for his love of severe punishments; and hated by George IV for his hypocrisy and intrigues. Her mother was a princess of Leiningen.

Excitement mounted during the week preceding the Music Meeting as first one and then another royal or noble guest arrived to take up their quarters in Malvern:

> There has been a great influx of rank and fashion at Malvern during the week. The Duchess de Berri and suite arrived there yesterday; after visiting St. Ann's Well, the Church, and Library, her Royal Highness partook of refreshments at the Foley Arms, and continued her route to this city. Her Royal Highness arrived last evening at the Hop Pole Inn, where she slept, and proceeded, at an early hour, this morning, to Birmingham. The Marchioness of Bute and family are amongst the recent arrivals; the Marquess is shortly expected, and likewise Sir Robt. Peel, on a visit to his brother, Colonel Peel, who has been for some time past residing at this delightful spot.
>
> Directions have been received at the Foley Arms for apartments to be prepared for the reception of Prince Leopold, whose arrival is daily looked for. It is expected that her Royal Highness the Duchess of Kent will prolong her stay until the month of October, Earl Beauchamp will display his accustomed hospitality by entertaining the Princess Esterhazy and a host of fashionables during the ensuing week, at his seat at Madresfield.[35]

On Tuesday 14 September the royal visitors arrived in Worcester:

> The Mayor and Corporation on receiving an intimation of the intended visit, eagerly embraced the opportunity of evincing that loyalty and attachment to the Royal Family, for which this city has at all times been so eminently conspicuous; and preparations were accordingly ordered, on an extensive scale, for the suitable reception of the illustrious visitors at the Town Hall.[36]

Their efforts and expense were quite wasted. On arrival in the city the Duchess of Kent announced that she wished to avoid a public reception, and the Body Corporate was asked to attend an audience at the Deanery instead. But the people of Worcester saw their future queen as she drove by in an open landau:

Thomas Bisse (Hereford Cathedral Library)

William Hayes

Thomas Norris

John Beard

November y⁵·ᵗʰ 1725

[Handwritten manuscript entry in 18th-century script]

Entry dated 5 November 1724, in the Minute Book of the Hereford Haberdashers Company recording the apprenticeship of Posthumous Whitney to a local 'Barber, Chyrurgeon and Perukemaker' with funds provided by the Three Choirs charity (Hereford City Library)

Eighteenth-century catch singers

North-west view of the City of Gloucester

The City of Worcester

Giusto Ferdinando Tenducci

Giulia Frasi

AN ACCOUNT

Of the DISTRIBUTION of

One Hundred and Sixty-nine Pounds, Eighteen Shillings
and One Penny,

Being Part of the Money collected at the Meeting of the *Three Choirs*, at GLOCESTER, *September* 1772,

Allotted for the Relief of such CLERGYMEN's WIDOWS and ORPHANS, within the Diocese of *Worcester*, as should be deemed proper OBJECTS of this CHARITY,

By the Stewards,

Sir HERBERT PERROT PAKINGTON, Bart.

The Rev. Dr. DIGBY, Dean of *Worcester*.

Widows Relieved.	Husbands' Appointment.	£.	s.	d.
ANN Samwell	*Leigh,* Curate of	6	10	0
Elizabeth Chellingworth	*Churchill,* Rector of	6	10	0
Mary Nash	*St. Peter's, Droitwich,* Vicar of	6	10	0
Ann Steel	*Yardley,* Vicar of	6	10	0
Margaret Protheroe	*Martley,* Curate of	6	10	0
Sarah Lea	*Oldbury,* Curate of	6	10	0
Annabella Hart, with six Children	*Broughton Hacket,* Rector of	11	5	1

Orphans.	Fathers' Appointment.			
Elizabeth Southall	*Kempsey,* Vicar of	3	0	0
John Sanders	*Broom,* Rector of	4	15	0
Elizabeth Martin	*Throckmorton,* Curate of	6	10	0
Samuel Medens	*Knightwick,* Rector of	4	15	0
Mary Thrup	*Wichenford,* Curate of	4	15	0
Utrecia Gibbons	*Stretton,* Rector of	4	15	0
Anna-Maria Jenks	*Inkberrow,* Vicar of	4	15	0
Alethea Willim	*Eldersfield,* Vicar of	4	15	0
Constantia Broughton	*Rushock,* Vicar of	4	15	0
John Rastall	*Abberley,* Curate of	4	15	0
Ann Stokes	*Dudley,* Rector of	4	15	0
Elizabeth Mogridge		3	7	8
Charles Thomas Mogridge	*Himbleton,* Rector of	3	7	8
Samuel Renatus Mogridge		3	7	8
Elizabeth Lodge		4	15	0
Sibil Protheroe	*Cherrington,* Rector of	4	15	0
Elizabeth Protheroe	*Martley,* Curate of	4	15	0
Margaret Protheroe		4	15	0
Sarah Bate		5	5	0
Elizabeth Bate	*Claines,* Curate of	5	5	0
Margaret Bate		4	15	0
Ann Cooke		4	15	0
Hannah Jones	*Bayton,* Vicar of	4	0	0
Catherine Elt		4	15	0
Mercey Watkins	*Knightwick,* Vicar of	4	15	0
	Cropthorne, Vicar of	4	15	0
Elizabeth Owen	*Offenham,* Rector of	4	15	0

Paid as above — *L.* 169 18 1

The Clergymen's Widows and Orphans fund (The Foley Collection, Worcester Records Office)

Johann Christian Fischer by Thomas Gainsborough

Mrs Richard Brinsley Sheridan, née Elizabeth Linley, by Thomas Gainsborough

Hereford Cathedral, 18 April 1786 (Hereford City Museum)

King George III

Worcester Cathedral at the beginning of the nineteenth century – J. Powell (Worcester Cathedral Library)

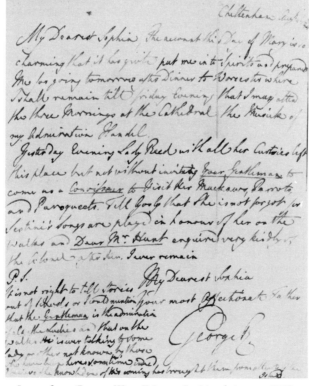

Letter from George III to Princess Sophia, 4 August 1788

Worcester Music Meeting. *1791.*

The MEETING of the THREE CHOIRS, *WORCESTER, HEREFORD,* and *GLOCES-TER,* for the Benefit of the *Widows* and *Orphans* of the Poor *Clergy* of the Three Dioceses, will be held at WORCESTER, on *Wednesday,* September the 14th, and the Two following Days.

AT the CATHEDRAL, WEDNESDAY MORNING, a SERMON will be preached by

The Rev. Mr. A N D R E W S;

And, in the Course of the Service, will be performed, Mr. HANDEL's *Overture to Esther; Dettingen* Te Deum; Dr. BOYCE's Anthem, *Lord thou hast been our Refuge;* and the Coronation Anthem, *Zadock the Priest.*

In the EVENING, at the COLLEGE HALL,

A C I S AND G A L A T E A,

BETWEEN THE FIRST AND SECOND ACT,
A CONCERTO on the O.BOE, by Mr. FISCHER,

THURSDAY MORNING, at the CATHEDRAL,
The following GRAND SELECTION of SACRED MUSIC, from HANDEL,

PART THE FIRST.

OVERTURE OCCASIONAL.

SONG.	*Shall I in Mamre's*	} JOSHUA.
CHORUS.	*For all these Mercies*	
RECIT.	*Thrice happy Israel*	} ISRAEL IN EGYPT,
SONG.	*When the Sun*	
CHORUS.	*O God who in thy*	JOSEPH.
SONG.	*Total Eclipse*	} SAMSON.
CHORUS.	*O first created Beam*	
SONG,	*Holy, holy, Lord*	NABAL.
CHORUS.	*He gave them Hailstones*	ISRAEL IN EGYPT,

PART THE SECOND.

OVERTURE *and* DEAD MARCH — SAUL.
FUNERAL ANTHEM.

SONG.	*In sweetest Harmony*	} SAUL.
CHORUS.	*O fatal Day*	
SONG.	*O magnify the Lord*	ANTHEM.
CHORUS.	*Hear, Jacob's God*	SAMSON.
RECIT.	*O worse than Death*	} THEODORA,
SONG.	*Angels ever bright*	
CHORUS.	*Gird on thy Sword*	SAUL.

PART THE THIRD.

SECOND HAUTBOY CONCERTO.

SONG.	*Lord remember David*	NABAL.
CHORUS.	*Fall'n is the Foe*	JUDAS MACCABEUS.
SONG.	*Tune your Harps*	ESTHER.
CHORUS.	*The mighty Pow'r*	ATHALIA.
RECIT.	*Ye sacred Priests*	} JEPHTHA.
SONG.	*Farewel ye limpid Springs*	
CHORUS.	*The Lord shall reign*	ISRAEL IN EGYPT.

IN THE EVENING,

L'A L L E G R O, I L P E N S E R O S O;

BETWEEN THE FIRST AND SECOND ACT,
A CONCERTO on the O BOE, by Mr. FISCHER,

FRIDAY MORNING, at the CATHEDRAL,

The M E S S I A H,

AND IN THE EVENING,

A GRAND MISCELLANEOUS CONCERT,

After each EVENING PERFORMANCE, a BALL.

PRINCIPAL VOCAL PERFORMERS,
Madame Mara, Miss Poole, Master Welsh, Messrs. Saville, Griffith, Barthelemon, Spray, &c.

PRINCIPAL INSTRUMENTAL,
Messrs. G. Ashley, (Leader of the Band,) Fischer, Myers, C. Ashley, Mara, Boyce, Mahon, Flack, Patria, Clark, Bird, J, Ashley, with the Double Drums, &c. &c. &c.

The ORGAN by Mr. PITT.

The BAND will be considerably enlarged, and the CHORUSSES very numerous and complete,
The Whole to be conducted by Mr. ISAAC.

EDMUND WIGLEY, Esq; M. P. } STEWARDS.
Rev. Mr. FOUNTAINE,

The Performers are requested to be at Worcester on MONDAY EVENING, the 12th of SEPTEMBER,
The ORDINARIES will be, on WEDNESDAY, at the HOP POLE; on THURSDAY, at the CROWN; and on FRIDAY, at the BELL.
N. B. There will be a PUBLIC TEA DRINKING on TUESDAY AFTERNOON, the 13th; and on SATURDAY MORNING, the 17th, a PUBLIC BREAKFAST at DIGLEY GREEN, as usual.
TICKETS for the Performances at 5s. 6d. each, and Books of the Words at 1s. each, to be had at Mr. SKYNNER's, No, 103, Mr. HOLL's, No. 54, both in High-street; and Mr. SHUCK's, No, 66, Broad-street.

J, TYMBS, PRINTER,

Handbill for Worcester Music Meeting, 1791 (The Foley Collection, Worcester Records Office)

John Braham

Gertrud Elisabeth Mara

James Bartleman

Angelica Catalani

Elizabeth Billington

Nancy Storace

Robert Lindley and Domenico Dragonetti

Francois Cramer

Maria Malibran

Charles de Beriot

Caricature of William Mutlow drawn by Maria
Malibran at Gloucester in 1829 (British Museum)

William Mutlow

During their progress through different parts of the city they proceeded at a slow pace, with the laudable view of gratifying the eager desire of the assembled populace to approach the carriage – a condescension which was duly appreciated; indeed, the courteous demeanour of their Royal Highnesses won the affections of all classes. The Princess . . . possesses a most intelligent and interesting countenance, and displays at this early age intellectual powers of no ordinary kind. The incessant care with which these powers are cultivated, and the maternal solicitude with which the best feelings of the heart are fostered, are clearly perceptible, and open a bright prospect for the future. A feeling of deep interest is naturally excited for the welfare of this Princess who will, in all human probability, one day rule over the destinies of this country.[37]

After more than a century under the first four Georges there must have been many fingers crossed for 'a bright prospect'!

The arrangements in the cathedral and Chapter House were elaborate and carefully planned:

As the Duchess of Kent and the Princess Victoria would necessarily be the principal objects of attraction, the seats prepared for them are so situated and so much elevated, that their Royal Highnesses are visible from almost every part of the Church: they occupy that space which is between Prince Arthur's Chapel, and the doorway into the south aisle of the choir; the whole compartment is covered with scarlet cloth; two antique chairs are provided for the Duchess and her interesting daughter; the cushions were those used by the revered George III, and his Consort; they have been recently found. The royal arms are in the centre, richly emblazoned in gold. The approach to the seats is from the garden of the Deanery; a staircase is erected up to a window in the Dean's Chapel; this window being taken out, forms an entrance to a raised platform which leads directly to the seats, so that their Royal Highnesses and suite have an opportunity of passing into the choir without interruption. The Chancel Gallery extends from the back of the altar to the east window, and is capable of accommodating 800 persons; it is a beautiful piece of carpentry; when filled with company, the effect is singularly fine; two other galleries extend over portions of the north and south aisles. In the Chapter Room (which is appropriated to the entertainment of the Nobility and Gentry invited by the Bishop of Rochester and Lady Sarah Murray) the arrangements are equally good. Round this fine apartment tables are laid with convenient intervals, and round the column in the centre there is a table for the Duchess and the Princess and those distinguished individuals who may accompany them. Their Royal Highnesses and suite enter the Chapter Room from the Deanery, one of the windows of which is taken out, and a covered way made to one of the Chapter Room windows, whence a staircase descends into the apartment.

TUESDAY, SEPT. 14 – At an early hour this morning, persons began to assemble about the Cathedral, and before the hour of opening the doors (half past nine), a considerable crowd was waiting for admission; by half past ten there was scarcely a place vacant, though the accommodation was so ample. Their Royal Highnesses the Duchess of Kent and the Princess Victoria arrived with their suite at twenty minutes before eleven at the Deanery, where they were received by the Bishop of Rochester and Lady Sarah Murray; they soon after passed into the Cathedral. Our venerable Diocesan conducted the Duchess of Kent, and the Bishop of Rochester led the interesting Princess Victoria. Both their Lordships wore their robes. A long train of Nobility occupied seats near the Royal Highnesses, towards whom every eye was directed. At this moment the Church presented an appearance equally striking and beautiful; the magnificent chancel gallery was filled in every part.[38]

During the Opening Service, while the choir was singing 'When thou had'st overcome the sharpness of death', the cathedral grew dim; a thunderstorm blackened the sky outside; '. . . and the rolling peals mingling their awful sounds with the music, added to the solemnity of the general effect'.[39]

In contrast, a short distance away at Worcester County Gaol the same thunderstorm underlined the despair of William Haydon, George Bromfield and Richard Ray, awaiting transportation for seven years; and of Joseph Fletcher, James Rastall, John Reynolds and William Workman sentenced to transportation for life. All seven men were removed to a ship at Chatham the next day.

After William Mutlow's death in 1832 his place at Gloucester was taken by John Amott, a pupil of Mutlow who, from 1820, had been organist of the Abbey Church, Shrewsbury. Amott seems not to have been a very distinguished musician: one of his old choristers told Sir Herbert Brewer that Amott's ability as an organist was '. . . of an elementary character. The pedals were rarely used, and when he did play on them he would allow the choristers, as a special favour, to go to the organ loft to see how it was done. As a rule a board was placed over the pedals on which his feet rested.'[40]

To Amott and his contemporaries fell the task of adapting to the new method of conducting with a baton at the Festivals. Even after a quarter of a century of experience, the Gloucester organist still clearly lacked an adequate technique. In a review of the 1856 Gloucester Festival, the music critic of the *Press* put his finger on the causes for less than satisfactory performances at Three Choirs:

> The execution of the works at these festivals has not kept pace altogether with musical advancement in other places. It is true that the *Messiah* and *Elijah* were better performed than on previous occasions, but on the whole, with the materials of principals, chorus, and band, engaged for the four morning performances in the Cathedral and the three evening concerts in the Shire-hall, greater precision, more delicacy, and a finer *ensemble* ought to have been secured. Where the deficiency lies is patent to everybody. So long as the conductor's baton at these festivals remains in the hands of the inexperienced local organist, so long must there be mishaps, mistakes, and contrarieties. It is not reasonable to expect that, once in three years, a provincial professor, however respectable his talents may be, can bring together a mixed body of choralists and instrumentalists, and a cosmopolitan phalanx of leading singers, and with one rehearsal insure a steady and finished interpretation of most intricate oratorios, and of selections from the music of operatic masters and concert composers of every school. . . . How is it, that when the orchestra, with Sainton and Blagrove as leaders, and conductors too, thought proper to run away from the 'traditional' beat, the overtures and symphonies went so briskly, as in the *Zauberflöte*, *Anacreaon* and *Der Freischütz*, and in Haydn's sparkling No. 8 Symphony? But when the *baton* of the conductor and the bow of the *chef-d'attaque* came into collision, as in the accompaniments to many of the vocal pieces, what a 'confusion worse confounded' ensued! As instances, let Mendelssohn's *Lorely* finale, and Beethoven's 'Crown ye the altars,' from the *Ruins of Athens*, be cited. What a 'gachis' were the accompaniments to 'Casta Diva,' sung by Viardot, and 'Il segreto,' sung by Alboni. What must foreign amateurs have thought of these exhibitions at a great English musical festival – a time-honoured institution fast approaching to an existence of a century and a half?

In 1856 the Stewards paid Amott £130 for his services, plus 20 guineas travelling expenses, £5 for the special instruction of choristers, and 6 free tickets for each performance. At the next Gloucester Festival, in 1859, his terms were unchanged except that the allowance of free tickets was reduced to two – 'For Mr and Mrs Amott only'![41] Amott's popularity with the critics was unchanged too. Describing how the position of the organ in the Gloucester Shire Hall prevented members of the audience sitting at its side from getting a good view of the conductor, the critic of *The Musical World* added: 'Not that the latter fact need be such a matter of regret, as far as the gentleman who wields the baton at Gloucester is concerned.'[42]

In fairness to Amott it must be said that what he lacked as a musical director he more than made up for in his aims for the development of the Festival. At his first

Music Meeting in 1832 he re-introduced 'the full band of trombones' which had been a feature of the Handel commemoration of 1784. The expansion of choral and orchestral forces at Gloucester from 1835 must have resulted from Amott's initiative. And above all, we owe a debt of gratitude to him for continuing the *Annals* of the Three Choirs, from the point at which Lysons had left them in 1811, to the year before his death, 1864.

Happily, at Amott's last Festival as conductor (1862(G)) providence granted him a real success. Even though three of the oratorios were performed without any rehearsal at all the critics of the national and musical Press were united in their praise for his direction of *Elijah*. Amott was able to reproduce proudly and in full in the *Annals* a glowing report which appeared in *The Times*, and must have been delighted with what he read in *The Musical World*:

> We can with . . . justice make the *amende* to Mr. Amott, for the really admirable manner in which he directed his forces in *Elijah* . . . Not only were the respective times correctly taken throughout, Mr. Amott merely adopting the medium course, and neither following the example (of which we have such frequent instance in London) of accelerating the speed, with the mistaken notion of increased brilliancy, nor of dragging the time, as has been generally the case with the conductors of the festivals of the [three] choirs. Taken altogether, it is hardly too much to say that this was one of the most unexceptionable performances of *Elijah* ever heard.[43]

Amott was the last to live in the Gloucester organist's house within the Palace Garden by the Infirmary arches, demolished in the 1860s, and the first to occupy what has been designated the organist's residence in Miller's Green since 1861. He died there on 3 February 1865.

Twelve days later a General Meeting of the Stewards was called at which the Secretary read out a letter from W.P. Price Esq., who was unable to attend. In it he suggested 'the present time would be a favourable opportunity to apply to the Dean and Chapter for permission, in future, to employ a London Conductor, instead of the Organist, for the time being, of the Cathedral.'[44]

Faced with such an important decision the Dean and Chapter determined to seek the advice of England's most eminent cathedral organist, Samuel Sebastian Wesley. To their astonishment and pleasure Wesley offered to take the Gloucester post himself and, even though they must surely have known that the long-suffering Winchester Chapter had asked him to resign as a result of neglect of duty, his offer was gratefully accepted.

Wesley was fifty-five years old when he arrived in Gloucester and, although only middle-aged, had suffered from ill health for many years, was lame, having broken a leg badly while crossing a stile in 1847, and was embittered by his long and discouraging experience of cathedral life.

In spite of concern about the safety of the Great West Window, Wesley persuaded the Stewards that the orchestra should be relocated at the west end of the cathedral for his first Festival — a layout which had been introduced successfully at Hereford in the previous year. This necessitated the hire of an organ from Henry Willis. The arrangements proved far more expensive than they had anticipated and, although receipts were larger than any since 1853, at a General Meeting of the Stewards on 11 October 1865 it was resolved that:

The conductor should be kept in due subordination to the Stewards. This important point was only secured after a series of struggles which threatened more than once to impede the Festival and the Stewards should be careful now not to give the staff out of their own hands. It was thought by more than one that too much was left to the discretion of the Conductor at the last Festival, e.g. in the engagement of the principals, the alteration of the position of the orchestra, involving the expense of hiring a special organ, etc. etc., and thus contravening the principle of scrupulously avoiding all unnecessary outlay.[45]

To be fair to Wesley, in the engagement of the principals he had *tried* to economize. The finest British tenor of the day, John Sims Reeves, had asked for a fee of £315, would not accept less, and so was not engaged. Another Festival favourite, the contralto Charlotte Sainton-Dolby, was also dropped, as was her husband, the violinist Prosper Sainton who often led the evening concerts. Unfortunately, this was precisely the wrong area in which to try to save money. The substitute tenor, Herr Gunz, was a German who had never before sung in English and who proved totally inadequate for the position of a principal. Two young ladies engaged to replace Sainton-Dolby, the Misses Wilkinson and Elton, were unequal to the task. *The Queen* magazine, acknowledging that the Festival had been a commercial success, summed up its artistic achievement:

With respect to the receipts, it is expected that the stewards will be relieved from any liability, although the 'penny wise and pound foolish' system of making the engagements will tell more heavily than was anticipated, by the getting rid of Sims Reeves, M. Sainton and Madame Sainton-Dolby. The financial success is cited by the superficial and interested as an approval on the part of the public of the musical arrangements. A greater fallacy cannot exist. If the argument of receipts be worth anything, it would be to assert that let the engagements be ever so bad, the execution ever so indifferent, success must attend these meetings from extraneous causes, such as the splendid sermon preached by the Rev. Canon Kennaway, the glorious weather of the week, and the determination of the county not to submit to the clerical intolerance. As regards public opinion of the week's musical doings, how is it to be gathered? If you read the local organs here, there never was such a conductor as Dr. Wesley, nor such perfect performances. If you look at the reports supplied by 'manifold' copy by one single reporter to the *Morning Post*, *Daily News*, *Advertiser*, and *Star*, although not quite up to the provincial puffery, success sanctifies the musical *mistake*. Indeed, the *Times*, cautious as it is with respect to Dr. Wesley's conducting and his programme, thinks it may fairly . point to the result to whitewash him. The *Morning Herald* and *Morning Advertiser*, and some of our weekly contemporaries, are more outspoken; they state, without equivocation or qualification, that the programmes, the performances, and the conductor, were altogether a complete mistake; in other words, that the festival was artistically a failure. Now, any impartial person, whose opinion is entitled to the smallest consideration as a critic, whether professor or amateur, will endorse the statement as perfectly accurate, that the selections were never worse conducted, that the order of their execution displayed a total want of judgment as to light and shade, and that the engagements of the chief artists were not judicious or up to the mark.

All was not quite so black as painted by *The Queen*. In his programming of the evening concerts Wesley had initiated an important change of emphasis from popular and often trivial miscellanies towards the performance of more serious and complete major works. The real problem was less concerned with the selection of works than with their execution – especially when Wesley took up the baton.

In 1865 the pianist Arabella Goddard was engaged to play in Beethoven's Choral Fantasia at the first evening concert and Mendelssohn's Concerto in G minor at the second. Reviewing both concerts, the critic of the *Morning Herald* reported on the Beethoven that:

. . . the chorus was too numerous for the band, and worse than that, did not know their parts. The conductor [Wesley] whose affection for his score is so great that he can never take his eyes off the copy, was not the general who by a glance of his eye could call together dispersed troops. It was an awful *gachis* . . . How disheartening for a pianiste to perform the obbligato of the fantasia under such circumstances may be conceived.

On the following evening 'the conductor resigned his baton, and permitted Mr. Henry Blagrove [the Leader] to conduct with his violin bow.'[46] Joseph Bennett was present:

The music went on well enough in such accustomed hands as those of the pianist and the 'leader,' the Doctor's beat being little regarded – a circumstance which did not appear to trouble him. Gradually Wesley's face lightened and beamed. The music having hold of him, presently took entire possession. He swayed from side to side; he put down the baton, treated himself to a pinch of snuff with an air of exquisite enjoyment, and then sat motionless, listening. Meanwhile Blagrove conducted with his violin-bow.[47]

By the end of Wesley's first Festival the Gloucester Stewards were probably beginning to lament the passing of even the unremarkable Amott. At least he, unlike his successor, had not been encumbered by temperamental genius, and his ability as a conductor was hardly any worse. Brewer tells us that:

Wesley was essentially an organist and composer and not a choir trainer or conductor. In fact, towards the end of his time the training of the choristers was left in the hands of one of the lay clerks. When a full rehearsal of the choir took place the men made no attempt to sing out but just whispered their parts.[48]

In 1866, even though acknowledged as the finest organist and the greatest composer of church music in the country, Wesley was not invited to compose anything for the Worcester Festival. On the eve of the Festival he withdrew, suggesting to the Committee that his place at the organ should be taken by Hamilton Clarke of Queen's College, Oxford:

Mr. Townshend Smith, of Hereford, was again at the organ, the Festival Committee having declined the substitute proposed by Dr. S.S. Wesley, of Gloucester, whose absence is being accounted for in all sorts of ways, not one of which, however, approximates to the truth. We have reason to believe that the learned Doctor is busily engaged in bringing through the press his long-expected great Psalmody book – *The European Psalmist* – which at present engrosses his exclusive attention . . . From another point of view the absence of so eminent a professor is, perhaps, less significant. Not a single composition of his was put down in the programme; nor was he asked to play an organ voluntary . . . Whether Dr. Wesley felt piqued, it is impossible for us to know.[49]

To add insult to injury the organist of St Paul's Cathedral, John Goss, *was* invited to compose an anthem for the 1866 Festival. It would be difficult to defend Wesley's action but honour was restored at Hereford in 1867. The first performance in the cathedral included Wesley's anthem *Ascribe unto the Lord* conducted by the composer.

The eccentric Wesley continued to be an equally eccentric Festival conductor. During Beethoven's *Mass in C* in 1868(G), 'an unfortunate breakdown at the commencement of the Kyrie, owing to the uncertainty of the tempo adopted, created an uneasy feeling that more disasters were in store and, by the time Miss Edith Wynne came in with her solo, hopeless confusion reigned supreme, so that the movement came to a sudden collapse, and was recommenced.'[50] *The Musical World* decided that the week's performances included 'points of excellence which not even Dr. Wesley could spoil'.[51] Once again, Joseph Bennett had been in the audience:

> On the Saturday of the Festival week at Gloucester (1868), all the music being ended, and all who helped to make it at rest from their labours, myself and a friend ventured upon a visit to the conductor-organist, and found him at home in the old house which was once the residence of Robert Raikes. After some desultory chat, the Doctor was begged to go into the cathedral and play to us anything he pleased. It was a bold request, for the poor man must have been suffering more or less from fatigue. He protested that he could not play if he would, and that he would not if he could; but the chance of hearing him was too good to be lost, and we pressed him hard. In the end, and perhaps thinking that assent was the quickest way to get rid of us, he agreed to go into the cathedral, sent for the blowers, flung off his slippers, put on a pair of thin boots, and led the way, keys in hand. 'Mind,' he said, 'you are not to come up into the gallery with me. You are to go and sit on the steps leading to the altar rails, and wait there until I have finished.' We took up our positions forthwith, but as he turned to the foot of the gallery stairs, the Doctor cried out: 'Mind, I can't play; haven't touched the organ for months, and the instrument is in a very bad state.' With this damper upon our expectations, Wesley began his display. There was a great deal of noise with the stops – ungainly things, as long as a man's forearm – and the Doctor started upon one of Bach's fugues. He made a bad beginning, stopped and shouted to us: 'I told you I couldn't play!' 'Never mind, Doctor, go on.' Another attempt ended much as did the first, after which we called out: 'Extemporise, Doctor.' We could hear him grumbling, but in a minute or two he began, and soon got into the mood. His performance was lengthy, but quite magnificent. My companion had heard Mendelssohn extemporise, and even he, with such a comparison to make, expressed his astonishment at the Doctor's wonderful resources. The organ became silent after a fugal climax, and we waited for more. We waited long, so long that we feared something had happened. What had happened was this: The Doctor had crept behind the front of the gallery, stooping so that he was not visible below; then silently descended the stairs, and, giving word to the blowers, left the cathedral. We called again and again, and there was no reply. We returned to the organist's house, and found our runaway once more in his slippers, and chuckling over the little joke he had played upon us. But for the sake of that extemporaneous performance, we would have put up with twenty jokes.[52]

The arrival of Wesley at Gloucester in 1865 broke up a triad of Three Choirs conductors who had worked together for over a decade: John Amott, George Townshend Smith and William Done.

Townshend Smith was born at Windsor on 14 November 1813, the son of Edward Smith, a lay clerk of St George's Chapel, Windsor, where he became a chorister under Highmore Skeats. Afterwards he studied under Samuel Wesley senior. Before he was chosen as organist of Hereford on 5 January 1843, Townshend Smith was organist of the Old Parish Church, Eastbourne and of St Margaret's, King's Lynn.

Of the three contemporaries, Townshend Smith seems to have been the most energetic and able in the cause of Three Choirs. Of his first Festival in 1843 *The Musical World* was pleased to report that:

> As a *whole*, we never witnessed a meeting go off more successfully, and praise, well deserved, sits brightly upon the conductor, Mr. Townshend Smith, who in this, his first essay as conductor of the Triennial Festival in this city, has earned the applause of every well-wisher to the meeting, as well as the true lover of sterling music.[53]

Townshend Smith not only conducted at Three Choirs but also acted as Festival Secretary – a prodigious double burden. On several occasions during his thirty-four years in office the Hereford Festival was in danger of winding up due to lack of financial support. The zealous exertions of Townshend Smith were always able to save the day. Unlike Amott, who never enjoyed personal popularity, owing perhaps to a stiff reserve of manner,[54] Townshend Smith was held in great affection. His was a genial and kindly presence in Hereford, a man of antiquarian interests and greatly admired as a musician. Joseph Bennett said of him:

> Smith had strength. The orchestra would follow him without any sense of risk; he knew what he wanted, and, generally, how to get it – a state of things highly valued because singularly rare . . . I can give an instance of his energy and alertness. After conducting a long morning performance it was not his custom to sink into an easy chair, crying, like the despairing lover in 'Solomon's Song': 'Stay me with flagons, comfort me with pomegranates.' Rather would he make up his returns of attendance and collections, then himself starting out to leave copies at the hotels where musical critics were lodging. We always looked for Townshend Smith within an hour of his laying downthe bâton; and he, with his zeal and devotion to duty, never failed us.[55]

After Smith's death there was a genuine sense of loss which, as *The Musical Times* put it, 'evidenced the high estimation in which he was held, even by those whose attachment to him could in no degree be influenced by local position'.[56] Samuel Sebastian Wesley died on 19 April 1876, and George Townshend Smith on 3 August 1877.

For fifty-one years from 1844 William Done was the organist at Worcester, where he was born on 4 October 1815, a few months after the Battle of Waterloo. He was a chorister in the cathedral and a pupil-assistant to Charles Clarke, whom he eventually succeeded. Done never sought a post away from the city of his birth and, although he made great improvements in the cathedral services at Worcester, was an unremarkable but reliable Three Choirs conductor, considering himself to be primarily a teacher of music. He lived quietly in the organist's house in College Green where the attic was fitted up as an aviary for his many canaries. Describing the quiet, plodding Done, Joseph Bennett said that he was a 'good, amiable man – as feebly built as a suburban villa'.[57]

Although Done received his share of mixed reviews for his efforts with the baton, *The Musical Times* balanced the record in a report of the 1881 Worcester Festival:

> Looking back upon the artistic results of the week, we cannot but feel that very much of the success of the Festival was owing to the exertions of the local Conductor, Mr. Done. It is too much the custom to underrate the services rendered at these meetings by the Cathedral organist simply because some experienced Conductor might be brought from London who, it is said, would exercise more control over the executants. But, apart from the ungracious act of placing a stranger in a Cathedral where the musical arrangements are always presided over by one well known to the residents, is it fair to ignore the hard work which has devolved upon the organist for many months before the performance? We happen to know, for example, that Mr. Done had for a very long period toiled hard with different sections of the choir, and even journeyed to Leeds, in order to insure an adequate rendering of Cherubini's Mass; and we emphatically say that the choral singing in this work would have done honour to any Conductor. The general performances under his direction, too, were very far above the average.[58]

Francois Cramer's long reign as Leader of the Festival orchestra ended in 1844, four years before his death at the age of seventy-six. His place was taken by John Loder at William

Done's first Festival as conductor in 1845(W). Loder (1788–1846) had relieved Cramer at the evening concerts for many years but predeceased the older man by two years.

The Leader at the Festivals of 1846(H) and 1847(G) was Thomas Cooke (1782–1848), the Irish tenor, violinist and composer who at the age of seven had performed a violin concerto in public 'with an effect and precision rarely equalled by so young a performer'.[59] Cooke was an amazingly versatile musician: for twenty years he had not only sung at the Drury Lane Theatre, but also led the orchestra, played nine different instruments, managed the house and composed musical stage pieces for it.

No British musician of the nineteenth century was more versatile than John Liptrot Hatton (1809–86). Born in Liverpool, Hatton was a violinist, pianist, organist, singer and composer.

At the Hereford Festival in 1846 Hatton appeared as both singer and pianist. At the first of the Miscellaneous Concerts in the Shire Hall he played the piano part in Beethoven's early Quintet in E flat for piano, clarinet, oboe, horn and bassoon. In the second part of the concert Charlotte Dolby, accompanied by Hatton, sang two songs, 'The Chapel' and 'The Shepherd's Winter Song', both announced as the compositions of P.B. Czapek (*czapek* being the Hungarian for 'hat on'!). Hatton himself sang a chansonette, 'Le Savoyard', acknowledged as his own composition: 'a piece of drollery which was vociferously encored, and the words of which consisted in a mixture of the French and Italian languages common to the Italian frontier',[60] and Miss Birch accompanied herself in Hatton's cavatina, 'The Syren's Invitation'.

The music critic of *The Times*, J.W. Davison, took Hatton to task concerning his 'Czapek' songs:

> These songs are the compositions of Mr J.L. Hatton, an English artist of distinguished talent, who should know better how to regard his art and respect the public, than to adopt an uncouth hyperborean signature 'Czapek.' They are exceedingly clever and musician-like, and will win favour on the score of their own merits, without the subterfuge of pseudonymous parentage.[61]

But the same critic was much kinder to Hatton when, in the third evening concert, he played the solo part in what was then a rare performance of Mozart's Piano Concerto No. 22 in D minor, K. 466:

> These works of the immortal master who has enriched the repertory of the piano to a greater extent than any other composer, except the universal Beethoven, are too much neglected by our performers, and Mr. J.L. Hatton deserves credit for endeavouring to bring them to notice.

After Thomas Cooke's death, Henry Blagrove (1811–72) took over as Leader; he too had been a prodigy, appearing before the public from the age of five. His brother, Richard Manning Blagrove (1826–95), became the leading British viola player and professor of this instrument at the Royal Academy of Music. He was also an accomplished and celebrated concertina player, formed a Concertina Quartet, published a *Concertina Journal* (from 1853), and composed fantasias, etc. for concertina and piano. Richard Blagrove remained the leading viola at Three Choirs until 1890(W) and also played the concertina occasionally at evening concerts. Two of his sons, Arthur and Stanley, were also musicians, playing cello and violin respectively in the orchestra at the 1893(W) Festival.

During Henry Blagrove's long reign as Leader – 1845 to 1870 – the evening concerts were often led by Prosper Sainton (1813–90). Sainton was born in Toulouse where, in 1840, he became a professor at the Conservatoire. In 1844 he visited London and played under Mendelssohn, returning in the following year to settle in England as a member of the Beethoven Quartet Society, an orchestral leader and teacher. In 1860 he married the contralto Charlotte Dolby, and in 1871 succeeded Blagrove as sole Leader of the Festival orchestra at Three Choirs.

At the third evening concert of the 1866(W) Festival, Sainton and Blagrove were joined by J.T. Carrodus and Henry Holmes in a performance of Ludwig Maurer's Symphonie Concertante for four violins. This proved so popular that it was repeated at the Festivals of 1867(H) and 1868(G). Although once famous, by the 1860s the Maurer work was already considered showy and trivial. None the less, the brilliant playing of the four violinists was such 'that all idea of its triviality was lost in the admirable ensemble of its execution'.[62]

In 1869(W) Carrodus returned to thrill the Three Choirs audience with a performance of the first movement of the Beethoven Violin Concerto, into which he introduced a cadenza by Molique: 'For purity of tone, finished correctness of mechanism, delicacy of expression, and thorough comprehension of the composer's intentions, Mr. Carrodus stands second to no living English violinist.'[63]

John Tiplady Carrodus (1836–95) was the head of yet another family of musicians. He was a Yorkshireman who appeared before the Keighley public at the age of nine, and before the London public four years later. His foreign-sounding surname is thought to be a corruption of the Scottish 'Carruthers'. He had been a pupil of Bernhard Molique and became the Leader of the orchestra of the Philharmonic Society. In 1882 Carrodus took over from Sainton as the Leader of the Three Choirs Festival orchestra and in 1894, at Hereford, his family possibly set a record: in the orchestra were J.T. Carrodus and his five sons.

Without doubt, the family name to emerge as the most famous from among the members of the Festival orchestra through the late-Victorian years was that of Elgar. William Elgar and his brother Henry played second violin and viola respectively in the orchestra for many years. And at Worcester in 1878, William was joined among the second violins by his son, Edward.

Notes

1. MW 1842, p. 305
2. *Annals* 1895, p. 135
3. Gloucester Festival Minute Book, 1858
4. Revd F.E. Witts (ed. D. Verey), *The Diary of a Cotswold Parson* (Alan Sutton, 1978)
5. The word 'orchestra' referred to the platform upon which the musicians (i.e. the 'band') performed.
6. Two silver cups presented in 1820 and 1821 to Sir Matthew Wood, MP, Lord Mayor of London, for the part he played in championing the cause of Queen Caroline, are now in the possession of the City of Gloucester. (Caroline, Princess of Brunswick, married the Prince of Wales in 1795. Described by the historian Dr J.H. Plumb as 'eccentric . . . coarse-fibred . . . flamboyant, dirty and highly-sexed', Queen Caroline was subjected to a House of Lords trial, accused of adultery and scandalous behaviour when the Prince ascended to the throne as King George IV in 1820.)
7. The Revd W.L. Bowles, another Steward

8. MW 1868, p. 652
9. MW 1855, p. 562
10. Bennett, *Forty Years of Music, 1865–1905* (London, 1908)
11. Quoted in MT, 1 October 1897, pp. 668–9
12. Gloucester Festival Minute Book, 1907
13. Ibid., 1877
14. Ibid., 1880
15. MW 1874, p. 621
16. See Watkins Shaw, p. 40
17. *Annals* 1895, p. 119
18. MW 1839, p. 307
19. *Worcester Herald*, 15 September 1830
20. *Worcester Herald*, 14 September 1839
21. Phillips, *Musical and Personal Recollections During Half a Century* (London, 1864)
22. MW 1836, p. 56
23. The ophicleide was made from a metal, wide-bored conical tube 8–9 feet long, with a U-bend about half way. It was played with a cup-shaped mouthpiece, had holes covered with keys in the side, and had a compass of about three octaves.
24. MW 1846, p. 431
25. MW 1842, p. 310
26. Winton Dean, *Handel's Dramatic Oratorios and Masques* (Oxford, 1959)
27. Now deposited in the Gloucestershire Records Office
28. *Gloucester Journal*, 7 January 1832
29. Gretton, *Memories Hark Back*, reproduced in Watkins Shaw, *The Organists and Organs of Hereford Cathedral* (1988)
30. *Annals* 1895, p. 123
31. MW 1837, p. 54
32. *Annals* 1895, pp. 130–1
33. *Annals* 1895, p. 132
34. See Watkins Shaw, *The Organists and Organs of Hereford Cathedral* (1988), p. 23, and John E. West, *Cathedral Organists Past and Present* (London, 1899), p. 43
35. *Worcester Herald*, 10 September 1830
36. Ibid.
37. Ibid.
38. *Worcester Herald*, 15 September 1830
39. Ibid.
40. Brewer, *Memories of Choirs and Cloisters* (London, 1931)
41. Gloucester Festival Minute Book, 1856 and 1859
42. MW 1859, p. 612
43. MW 1862, p. 582
44. Gloucester Festival Minute Book, 1865
45. Ibid.
46. *The Morning Herald*, 7 September 1865
47. Bennett, op. cit.
48. Brewer, *Memories of Choirs and Cloisters* (London, 1931)
49. MW 1866, p. 599
50. *Annals* 1895, p. 239
51. MW 1868, p. 645
52. Bennett, op. cit.
53. MW 1843, p. 310
54. See obituary notice in *The Times*, 4 September 1865
55. Bennett, op. cit.
56. MT 1877, p. 427
57. Bennett, op. cit.
58. MT 1881, p. 512

59.   *Annals* 1895, footnote to p. 134
60.   *Annals* 1895, p. 155
61.   Reproduced in MT 1909, p. 644
62.   MW 1866, p. 601
63.   MW 1869, p. 641

CHAPTER SIX

AVOIDING SHIPWRECK

In its long history, Three Choirs has not always sailed in untroubled waters. In the nineteenth century it sometimes appeared that the Festival was steering an uncertain course between the opposing fleets of High and Low Church, and in danger of foundering upon the rocks thrown up by those who sought to banish it from the cathedrals altogether.

It is difficult for us to imagine that a music festival should generate controversy and rancour; but Three Choirs is as inseparable from the cathedrals of Gloucester, Hereford and Worcester as religion was from nineteenth-century England. It was religion, the Christian religion, which permeated every aspect of life: political, educational, social, artistic and scientific. Some discord was inevitable.

One of King George IV's subjects whose opposition to the Festival was expressed almost as strongly as his protest against the way in which the country was being governed, was the Radical, William Cobbett.

For a decade after the rout of Napoleon at Waterloo, depression and political reaction gripped England. Poverty and distress were widespread. Between 1822 and 1826 Cobbett made a number of journeys through the southern counties, on horseback, to see for himself the condition of the people and the changes in the countryside. His arrival at Gloucester in 1826, recorded in his diary account *Rural Rides*, coincided with Three Choirs.

From Stroud I came up to PITCHCOMB, leaving PAINSWICK on my right. From the lofty hill at PITCHCOMB I looked down into that flat and almost circular vale, of which the city of GLOUCESTER is in the centre. To the left I saw the SEVERN, become a sort of arm of the sea; and before me I saw the hills that divide this county from Herefordshire and Worcestershire. The hill is a mile down. When down, you are among dairy-farms and orchards all the way to Gloucester, and, this year, the orchards, particularly those of *pears*, are greatly productive. I intended to sleep at Gloucester, as I had, when there, already come twenty-five miles, and, as the fourteen which remained for me to go, in order to reach BOLLITREE, in Herefordshire, would make about nine more than either I or my horse had a taste for. But, when I came to Gloucester, I found, that I should run a risk of having no bed if I did not bow very low and pay very high; for, what should there be here, but one of those scandalous and beastly fruits of the system, called a 'MUSIC MEETING'! Those who founded the CATHEDRALS never dreamed, I dare say, that they would have been put to such uses as this! They are upon these occasions, made use of as *Opera-Houses*; and, I am told, that the money, which is collected, goes, in some shape or another, to the *Clergy of the Church*, or their widows, or children, or something. These asemblages of player-folks, half-rogues and half-fools, *began with the small paper money*[1] and with it they will go. They are amongst the profligate pranks which idleness plays when fed by the sweat of a starving people. From this scene of prostitution and of pocket-picking I moved off with all convenient speed, but not before the ostler made me pay 9d. for merely letting my horse *stand* for about ten minutes, and not before he had *begun* to abuse me for declining, though in a very polite manner, to *make him a present* in addition to the 9d. How he ended I do not know; for I soon set the noise of the shoes of my horse to answer him. I got to this village, about eight miles from Gloucester, by five o'clock; it is now half past seven, and I am going to bed with an intention of getting to BOLLITREE (six miles only) early enough in the morning to *catch my sons in bed if they play the sluggard*.

He was obviously in a foul temper! Fortunately his sons *were* up when he arrived the following morning and the beauty of the Herefordshire countryside soon calmed him down.

The year 1832 was a time of crisis. The previous September a Reform Bill to abolish rotten boroughs, widen the franchises and introduce representation in Parliament for the new industrial towns was defeated in the House of Lords by forty-one votes (twenty-one of which came from the bench of bishops); revolution seemed imminent. Serious rioting took place in London and elsewhere; in Bristol the mob ran riot for two days. Finally, in May 1832 William IV threatened to create sufficient new peers to push the Bill through the House of Lords. The Reform Act of 1832 was passed and the crisis was averted; but, by then, so was the courage of many to travel to Gloucester for the Music Meeting.

In addition to the political turmoil in the country, cholera broke out in 1832 and spread widely, reaching Gloucester in June: 'its ravages, though not so great as in many other places, did not finally cease until about the period of the [Music] Meeting'.[2] Cancellation was expected but, in spite of public nervousness, it ultimately went ahead on 11 September.

Then another blow fell: two of the principal singers engaged – Maria Caradori and Henriette-Clementine Meric – failed to turn up. The Festival was so poorly attended in that year that a huge shortfall in income had to be made up by the hapless Stewards. Only the generous donation of one hundred pounds from Lord Redesdale prevented the Festival charity from suffering.

All these problems beset the new organist at Gloucester Cathedral, John Amott, on taking up his duties as conductor of the Music Meeting for the first time in 1832. In the preface to his continuation of the *Annals* from 1812 to 1864, Amott wrote that 'the meetings of the Three Choirs have, upon several occasions, narrowly escaped shipwreck'. In 1832 the Festival was sailing towards very choppy waters indeed.

In his review of the 1836 Festival at Worcester, the critic of *The Musical World* commented on the audience's behaviour at the first concert in the College Hall:

So far as the audience were concerned, it was of little consequence how the band performed . . . for the indifference manifested by the auditory was most uncomplimentary both to their own understandings – to say nothing of good education – and to the efforts of the performers . . . The English people have no doubt made considerable advance of late years in musical taste and knowledge; but the good folks of Worcester are leagues in the rear of the general improvement. They are mere Goths, for instance, compared with their Birmingham neighbours.

The same critic, reporting from Hereford in 1837, wrote:

> The effect of the orchestra appeared to be almost poverty-stricken after having emerged from the great volumes of sound that had been ringing in our ears at Birmingham . . . The Birmingham performances have damped the zeal of many amateurs in this neighbourhood: added to which Hereford in itself is not of sufficient importance to uphold a festival on a grand scale.

The Birmingham Festival had originated in 1768 with performances in aid of the funds of the General Hospital; by 1800 it had become a triennial event. The rapid growth of the city, fuelled by industrial expansion, caused a doubling of the population during the nineteenth century, to reach 437,000 at the census of 1881. The Birmingham Town Hall was opened in 1834: a symbol of civic pride which, quite naturally, became the grand new venue for the Birmingham Festival.

England was steadily pacing from a rural to an urban society. By 1851, for the first time, more than half of the population lived in towns and cities; thirty years later the figure had risen to 70 per cent. Industrialists and businessmen were founding a new aristocracy. A desire to give expression to that status, along with the presence of an increasing number of choral singers and, as at Birmingham, a new town hall, ensured that in the industrial towns and cities of the Midlands and northern England there were the will and the resources to develop existing festivals and to establish new ones. Not one important city wished to be outdone by another for very long.

Although Three Choirs had provided the example for others such as Birmingham, Liverpool, Leeds and Norwich to follow, the three cathedral cities now found themselves in competition with their large industrial neighbour – a neighbour who could afford not only to engage the same soloists at the same enormous expense, but could also provide a larger venue and larger orchestra under the batons of celebrity conductors for both secular concerts and oratorio performances. Nor did the managers of the Birmingham Festival have to consider the problem of ecclesiastical censorship.

At the Worcester Festival of 1836, the third morning began with a performance of Mozart's *Requiem*, adapted by Edward Taylor under the title of *Redemption* for performance in English:

> Not only was the title of *Requiem* altered by Mr. Taylor, but additional music was introduced, some of which was not by Mozart. This, together with the substitution of English words for the original Latin to which the music had been expressly composed, justly excited the opposition of the critics, so that the strange mixture has since been very properly rejected.[3]

In addition to this massacre of Mozart's *Requiem*, anti-Catholic feeling was manifest in a number of late alterations to the printed programme. On the third morning, Miss Hawes sang Cherubini's *O salutaris*: English words were substituted – an objection being taken to the Catholic ones. The next day, in a Miscellaneous Selection, Clara Novello had been announced to sing Cherubini's *Ave Maria* and Hummel's *Alma Virgo*, but an objection had been raised against the words of these pieces too. Handel's 'Holy, holy' and Haydn's 'With verdure clad' were substituted.

But why this censure in 1836 when, only three years earlier at Worcester, Maria Malibran had delighted her audience with Cherubini's *O salutaris* sung in the original Latin, and when Mozart's *Requiem* had been performed in full in 1834 at Hereford?

The Worcester Stewards were so grateful to Clara Novello in 1836 for agreeing without fuss to substitute non-contentious works at short notice, that they presented her, by the hands of Lady Harriet Clive, with an ornament costing fifty guineas: 'If our Church are afraid of Popish words biting them, why', asked *The Musical World* angrily, 'do they not quash the whole of our Liturgy?'

In the century before the 1830s, evangelicalism − 'the call to seriousness' − had established itself in a dominant position in British Protestantism. Then, in the 1830s and 1840s, evangelicalism was challenged, under the impetus of the Oxford Movement, by a re-awakening of the Catholic spirit within the Anglican communion. Evangelicals, resisting a revival of the Catholic tradition, took up the fight with zealous energy for the next forty years; only at the end of the nineteenth century was it possible for compromise to still this bitter struggle.

Against such a background the choice of items for performance at the Music Meetings became a matter requiring great delicacy. When, for instance, a selection from Beethoven's Mass in C was performed in 1847(G) it was called then, and for some time, Service in C − 'to suit Protestant tastes!'[4] When the same work was performed in 1850(G), a large proportion of the audience walked out, 'marking painfully the schism in the High and Low Church'.[5]

The first Festival appearance of Beethoven's *Mount of Olives (Christus am Olberg)* in 1842(W) was in an English adaptation and with a changed title: *Engedi*, or *David in the Wilderness* because the original libretto includes a conversation between Our Lord and an angel, which was considered 'unthinkable except to an audience of sceptics or freethinkers',[6] with the result that 'Beethoven's intentions were outraged from the beginning to end, and, in spite of the perfection of the performance, the effect was nearly lost from the absurd inapplicability of the words to the music'.[7]

In 1871(G), S.S. Wesley conducted the *St Matthew Passion*. It was the first complete performance of an oratorio by Bach ever to be heard at Three Choirs, and even this was censored. 'Mr. Bayly and Mr. Gambier Parry consulted with the conductor as to certain parts of the Passion Music which the stewards desire to be omitted, especially that of Our Lord's Words on the Cross.'[8]

Having become accustomed to navigating carefully around the shoals and breakers of censorship, in 1838 the Festival sailed into the cannon-fire of a powerful opposition which threatened to scupper it completely.

At Hereford in 1834, possibly in response to the competition of the Birmingham Festival and regular financial losses, the 24-year-old S.S. Wesley had obtained approval for the nave of the cathedral to be used for the first time for oratorio performances. A similar arrangement was adopted by Gloucester in the following year, and by Worcester in 1842. The Festival was now expanding to meet increased audience expectations: by 1838, the year following Queen Victoria's accession, the orchestra and chorus at Gloucester had grown from two hundred to three hundred, and the Meeting was designated a 'Festival' in the programme for the first time. Huge and expensive efforts were made to present a perfect setting for the performances:

The preparations in the cathedral, for the accommodation of the audience, presented a splendid *coup d'oeil* from the orchestra. At the bottom of the nave, embracing the whole extent between the pillars, ran a long sloping gallery, reaching from the bottom of the large window to about ten feet from the ground. This gallery was fitted up with rows of benches having backs, each bench containing numbered seats; by which means places might be secured by a timely application, and by ballot, in any part of the gallery. The whole of the nave, from the front of the gallery to that of the orchestra, contained rows of benches without backs. Here twelve shillings and sixpence purchased a seat; those in the gallery cost a guinea. On the side of the nave next to the choir, rose a splendid orchestra, affording easy accommodation for three hundred performers. It was on a level with the gallery, and rose as high as the foot of the organ, which formed the background of the picture. The seats were decorated with scarlet cloth, which, with the scarlet and gold ornamental work on the fronts of the gallery and orchestra, formed a rich and bold contrast with the quiet tint of the noble nave and its massive columns. The aisles were fitted up with plain seats for the accommodation of persons of humbler pretensions than the occupants of either the gallery or the nave. The arrangements at the Shire-hall Evening Concerts were made upon a scale as liberal as those of the cathedral, and with equal attention to the comforts of the audience.[9]

If William Cobbett's complaints of a dozen years earlier had failed to blow the Festival ship off course, his line of attack was now followed up by a highly influential clergyman whose salvo opened up a breach which had still not been fully repaired by the end of the century.

A sermon given by the Revd Francis Close, a staunchly evangelical clergyman, at Cheltenham Parish Church on the Sunday before the 1838 Festival was reported in the *Cheltenham Journal*:

There are other amusements, less obviously inconsistent with 'the love of the Father,' in which the great majority of pious persons think it wrong to participate. They are aware that the specious garment of a charitable object is cast over them; that the hallowed sanction of religious services is in measure imparted to them, by introductory prayers, and even the preaching of a sermon: – but when they view the Music Meeting as a whole, – when they investigate more narrowly its details and its accompaniments, they are forced to the conclusion that it is 'not of the Father, but of the world.'

Strong condemnation of the Festival followed. 'May the eyes of many', said Close, 'be opened to see "the end of these things".'

A meeting of the Stewards was called in the ensuing week at which Baron Segrave made the following speech which was reported in the *Gloucestershire Chronicle*:

I have attended these meetings now for thirty-six years, and have been absent from none, with one single exception. I have afforded them, during that time, the best support in my humble power to give, and have been under the impression that in so doing, I was pursuing a praiseworthy and charitable line of conduct. I, therefore, admit that I should not feel satisfied with myself if I omitted to notice a very severe attack that has been made on this institution from a neighbouring pulpit. I should have hoped that the countenance given to this charity and these meetings, by the stewardships of Bishop Ryder, Bishop Bethell and the present Diocesean, would have been sufficient to have protected us from the charge of irreligion; but that charge has nevertheless been deliberately and gravely made. If it had been made by an obscure or ignorant individual, it might have been suffered to pass by unnoticed. But Mr. Close is neither the one nor the other. He is a clergyman of undoubted talent and acquirement, and of considerable influence in the large and populous town of Cheltenham. He is not a contemptible adversary. I have therefore thought this a proper occasion to call the attention of the friends of the charity to this question, but I am of opinion that it would be not only a very unfit opportunity to discuss it, but more, that we are not the tribunal by which it ought to be settled. But as a member of the Church of England, I most respectfully submit that, those clergymen who are friendly to this institution should refute the charge brought against it, and fairly tell us whether we are upholding a system of folly and sin, or whether we are supporting, by laudable means, a charity, the ends of which are beneficial.

The effect of this appeal was quite the opposite to that desired by the Revd Francis Close. Fearing for the future of the charity, the clergy rallied around the Festival. Pointing out that they had, in the past, failed to give the charity the support which it deserved, either by their presence or their contributions, the Dean of Hereford, the Very Revd John Merewether, wrote to every clergyman in the diocese requesting their attendance in gowns on the first day of the Festival:

> You are probably aware of the difficulties which have attended the continuance of the Festival for another occasion. What would the poor recipients of its funds do if they were deprived of its support, which is actually, in some cases, almost all they have to depend upon? Might they not cast an upbraiding look on those who have not lent their aid and countenance in promoting its valuable object? That object is peculiarly one which the Parochial Clergy are interested in promoting, and when the Bishops of each diocese, the Archdeacons, the Cathedral Clergy, all concur in giving it their sanction, can we justify our unconcern without impropriety? . . . The whole may be regarded, and ought to be conducted, as an occasion of innocent enjoyment, sanctified by its dedication at the outset, and endeavouring to obtain a result of the most benevolent and charitable kind.

The Stewards breathed a sigh of relief: a considerable number of clergy appeared in gowns at the Opening Service of the 1840(H) Festival; and for the next thirty-four years, although frequently beset by financial difficulties, the Festival enjoyed a period of relative calm, punctuated by the periodical pricking of clerical conscience. Had there been no charitable purpose behind the Festivals, it is certain that they would not have survived the mid-nineteenth century. As it was, the income from the charity was essential to the maintenance of the widows and orphans of the poor clergy of the dioceses. In the absence of any other source of support, the clergy felt obliged to continue their sanction of the Festival. In October 1852 the Bishop of Gloucester and Bristol wrote:

> I feel it my duty to continue to extend to this charitable scheme all the support and encouragement in my power; unless any other plan for securing similar benefits to the families of our poorer brethren could be suggested, which should be equally efficient and less exposed to objections . . . I can only say that my determination remains unaltered, and that no substitute for the Music Meetings has been proposed.[10]

Any alternative proposal would have necessitated the raising of £1,000 in each diocese every three years. Not surprisingly, none could find support.

And the Revd Francis Close? He became the Dean of Carlisle on the recommendation of Lord Shaftesbury to Palmerston and, after his death, the Cheltenham school which bears his name was dedicated to the memory of Dean Close.

In 1863 Charles John Ellicott was appointed Bishop of the united See of Bristol and Gloucester[11] by Lord Palmerston on Lord Shaftesbury's advice because of his opposition to answering *Essays and Reviews*, the work of six distinguished Broad Churchmen.[12] Dr Ellicott was not a lover of music. On first encountering Three Choirs in 1865(G) he selected Festival week to cross 'from Lauterbrunnen over the Tschingel glacier to Kandersteg'. The Dean of Gloucester, Henry Law, who was appointed in 1862, also absented himself, as did two of the cathedral canons. So marked a disapproval of the Festival prompted a lively exchange of correspondence in the columns of the musical, national and local press. One 'Button of Birmingham' wrote to the *Birmingham Daily Post* and *The Musical World*:[13]

> Musical Festivals are not always so harmonious as they seem to be. While band and chorus pour forth a swelling flood of sweet sounds in cathedral or hall, there may be a dreadful squabble going on in the Committee Room. It is in cathedral towns, I believe, that these little difficulties happen with the greatest frequency; and here another element of discordance comes in, by the necessary interference of the clergy. Either the Bishop won't preach, or the Dean has doubts about the lawfulness of oratorio music, or an eccentric canon goes off with a highly Protestant bang – and then what is called a 'scandal' arises, and the Festival which ought to be the perfection of harmony, becomes an occasion of strife and a source of bitterness. Something of this kind, it seems, but lately happened at Gloucester.

The correspondent of *The Times*, reporting on the Festival, had noted that:

> Although the Dean is absent, the Deanery is occupied by Lord Ellenborough, who exercises the accustomed and expected hospitality; and although Bishop Elicott – also absent – objected to preach on behalf of the widows and orphans, he has found a most admirable substitute in the Rev. C.E. Kennaway, Canon of Gloucester and Vicar of Chipping Camden, whose sermon of this day, built upon the text 'For *all* are thy servants' (Psalm 119, v. 91) is the talk of every one. Never was good cause more eloquently supported from the pulpit. Mr. Kennaway not only pleaded for the charity, but for the Festival; and not merely for the Festival in the abstract, but for the performances of sacred music in the Church.[14]

Three Choirs survived the Festival of 1865 but Dr Ellicott's lack of interest in music could never be reversed, not even by his wife who was a keen amateur musician, an able contralto, a founder-member of the Handel Society (f. 1882) and of the Gloucestershire Philharmonic Society. In spite of the Bishop's absence at Festival-time, she restored the tradition of throwing open the Palace with generous hospitality. On 3 September 1886 she wrote to A.M. Broadley:

> I am sorry to say the Bishop will not be at home for the Festival . . . I shall be most happy to see you after the oratorio on Tuesday afternoon. I am 'at home' all through the week so pray look in whenever you like. Besides Lady Westbury and Miss Simpson my guests are as follows: Lord and Lady Norton and Miss Adderley, Mr. and Mrs. Power, Mr. and Mrs. Travers, Revd. H.R. Haweis, Mr. Frederic Cowen, Mr. Lionel Monckton, Professor Thomas Wingham, Mr. Alfred Barnett, Mr. Henry Lazarus, Mr. William Wing and Mr. W. de Manby Sergison. So you see music is well represented – all these seven gentlemen being artists – with the exception perhaps of Mr. Monckton who wishes to be considered an amateur for fear of spoiling his career as a Barrister – but he writes charmingly.[15]
>
> Perhaps you are not aware that I have an artist in my own daughter. She is bringing out an Overture (her second Orchestral work) at the Tuesday Evening Concert and to judge from its reception by the band at the rehearsal on Wednesday morning I think it is likely to produce a sensation. She calls it 'dramatic' because one of its leading features are *recits* for celli – I hope you will be able to go and hear the work on Tuesday evening.
>
> My daughter was a student at the R.A.M. and is in all respects a member of the musical profession and *not an amateur*.
>
> You may be amused by my emphatic underlining but she is always annoyed at being spoken of as a 'talented amateur'.[16]

The *Dramatic Overture* by Rosalind Ellicott (1857–1924) was well received and praised by *The Musical Times* as a work of exceptional merit. Her other compositions for Three Choirs, all performed at Gloucester, included a song, 'To the Immortals' sung by Hilda

Wilson in 1882; *Elysium* for soprano, chorus and orchestra in 1889; Fantaisie in A minor for piano and orchestra in 1895 (Sybil Palliser was the soloist); and in 1898 a choral ballad for men's voices, *Henry of Navarre*, a setting of verses by Macaulay.

Like her mother, Rosalind Ellicott was a good singer – a soprano who often sang at charitable concerts in Gloucestershire. Sir Herbert Brewer recalled an occasion when the unmusical Bishop arrived home one winter afternoon to find his wife and daughter entertaining some friends:

> They were singing a duet. The fire was black and cheerless; the Bishop took up the poker and began to stir it vigorously. Mrs. Ellicott stopped singing and, in reproachful voice exclaimed, 'My dear, my dear!' The Bishop, holding up his hand in a becalming manner, replied, 'Don't stop, my love, don't stop! You don't disturb me in the least!'[17]

When Dr Ellicott died in 1905 his had been the longest episcopate in the history of the diocese of Gloucester – forty-two years. But even during the boycott of his first Three Choirs in 1865 rumour was spreading that Worcester would be compelled, through powerful outside influence, to give up *its* triennial Festival. *The Times*, reporting on the extraordinary success of the Gloucester Festival, suggested that the large turnout of inhabitants and supporters represented a protest against 'clerical interference', adding that the people had 'little mercy on their Bishop, less on their Dean, and least of all on Lord Dudley, who is generally supposed to be harbouring unfriendly intentions towards the Worcester Festival of 1866'.[18] The Dean of Gloucester, in granting the use of the cathedral, had yielded, against his own conviction, to the force of public opinion. At Worcester, opposition to the Festival was led by one of the richest noblemen in the land, the great Worcestershire magnate Earl Dudley who, writing to *Berrow's Worcester Journal* on 4 October 1865, had said:

> When a better religious feeling banished the festival from the choir – from the Holy of Holies – where it had degenerated from a service by the united choirs, to a performance of works on sacred subjects by English and foreign artists – of indifferent reputation, greedy of pay then as now, and the latter barely able to pronounce the language they were paid to sing in – when this took place, the nave, the neglected, dusty, broken-floored, never-used nave – a mere ante-chapel to the choir, was suggested as a convenient place, and has been so used ever since. Is this any reason that it should go on? Warmed, lighted, fitted for service, used for it, ordinarily and specially restored to Divine use – is it again to have any work – however great and good in itself – performed in it, save service alone? Ask the candid, even of those who attended the Gloucester Festival in a spirit of opposition, if the Cathedral was not desecrated? and if it was, as I know it was, you will not be a party to ours being so used and misused.

The argument rumbled on for the next few years but the Festival continued.

The year 1873 marked the beginning of the so-called Great Depression in Victorian Britain; the year in which, following decades of industrial omnipotence and boom, British manufacturers were faced for the first time by competition from abroad. The following year brought depression to the Three Choirs Festival.

In April 1874, Worcester Cathedral was re-opened following extensive restoration. The Gloucester Festival in September of that year ended with a service in the cathedral instead of the usual ball; the sermon was given by the Revd Dr Barry, a canon of Worcester Cathedral. In it he implicitly confirmed a rumour which had been circulating for some weeks: that the Dean and Chapter of Worcester would not permit the Festival of

1875 to take place in its traditional form. At the end of the sermon Dr S.S. Wesley made his comment in music: he played the Dead March from *Saul*.

The reasons put forward by the Dean and Chapter of Worcester for withholding permission for the use of the cathedral for the Festival were twofold. Firstly, the cathedral having been completely restored, and the nave as well as the choir being devoted to public worship, they no longer felt at liberty to transfer the charge and control of it to other hands. However, their real motive was revealed in the second reason alleged – that the Dean and Chapter 'are of the opinion that musical performances which are unconnected with any religious service, and to which admission is given only by purchased tickets, should no longer take place in the Cathedral'.

In fact, Lord Dudley had offered a sum of £10,000 towards the restoration of Worcester Cathedral on condition that the Music Meetings should no longer be held there. In the face of strong public opposition to such a condition Lord Dudley retracted his first offer and subscribed £5,000 on condition that Lord Hampton would raise the rest. The result was a subscription, not of £5,000, but of £11,000.

In Lord Hampton's view, this large sum was subscribed and bestowed upon the cathedral on an understanding that the Festival would not be discontinued. The newly-appointed Dean of Worcester, Dr Grantham M. Yorke, remained unmoved. The Stewards of Gloucester and Hereford were dismayed, as were the citizens of Worcester, not a few of whom would suffer financial loss if the Festival were cancelled. Protests poured into Worcester Cathedral.

The issue was taken up in the national as well as the local press and the musical journals:

> It seems, on the face of it, a great pity that a beautiful Musical Festival, which a custom of a century and a half has rendered little less than an institution in the West, should be so summarily put an end to, and the reasons ought to be very strong on which the Dean and Chapter rely. It is easy to see that the feeling which has dictated the refusal is connected with the novel sentiments of ecclesiastical propriety which have gained so much ground of late years among the clergy, and the moment for thus enforcing a strict ecclesiastical standard has, at least, been very unfortunately chosen. It would have been more graceful if the new Dean had exerted his influence to permit the holding of the first Festival which occurs since his appointment, and he could have interfered afterwards with much greater effect. [19]

An 'indignation' meeting was held in Worcester at which the Mayor presided and deputations from Gloucester and Hereford attended. In a series of resolutions which were forwarded to the Dean and Chapter, the meeting regretted that the friendly relations which had 'so long subsisted between the Dean and Chapter and the City of Worcester should be imperilled'. Lord Hampton insisted that the Chapter were morally bound by the understanding which he contended was arrived at in 1870, when the public raised £11,000 for the completion of the cathedral – that the Festivals should be continued. It was this latter point upon which the response of the Dean concentrated:

> (The Dean and Chapter) desire to call special attention to the second resolution, in which they observe, with much surprise and regret, that the Stewards have thought it fit publicly to accuse them by implication, of taking advantage of the absence of a 'literal obligation' to depart from an 'honourable understanding', and have thus encouraged those ignorant of the circumstances to represent the Dean and Chapter as 'having obtained money under false pretences'.

The Dean maintained that in seeking subscriptions towards the restoration of the cathedral 'every condition was withdrawn, and that every question of opinion, whether with respect to Musical Festivals or otherwise, was left entirely open and unprejudiced'. In support of his argument he quoted the text of a letter from the Lord Bishop of Worcester dated 3 October 1874:

> I always understood that, when contributions were solicited on the last occasion for the restoration of the Cathedral, it had been agreed on all sides that the question of the continuance of the Musical Festivals was to be considered open, the Dean and Chapter being left free to decide it one way or the other, as they might think fit, without reference to the opinions of the persons contributing. My own contribution certainly was given on this understanding.
>
> I am yours, very truly
>
> sgnd: H. Worcester

What Dean Yorke failed to say was that he had quoted only an extract from a much longer letter. The rest of the Bishop's text was as follows:

> Lord Hampton and other contributors might, perhaps, fairly encourage the hope that the Dean and Chapter, being relieved from the pressure of Lord Dudley's offer and the apparent difficulty of completing the restoration without accepting the conditions, would eventually decide in favour of continuing the Festivals, but I do not think that they have any ground for saying that the Dean and Chapter are under any obligation to continue the Festivals because the liberal contributions of some who wished them to be continued relieved them from the embarrassment of returning an answer to Lord Dudley's offer.
>
> My own opinions about the Festivals have been always the same. I enjoy the oratorios in the Cathedral very much myself, and I think that they are edifying and profitable to the great mass of people who attend them. I do not see any objection to such use of the Cathedral, nor to the admission of hearers by paid tickets. But I admit a very great evil in the erection and removal of the huge platform hitherto thought necessary, and I hope that if the Dean and Chapter will allow the use of the Cathedral for oratorios they will insist upon some other arrangement. My feeling on this subject is so strong that, if the oratorios cannot be performed satisfactorily without turning the cathedral into a carpenter's shop for many days before and after the Festival, I would rather that they were discontinued.[20]

(The problem of noise in constructing and removing the complicated wooden platforms had been a source of irritation to the Dean and Chapter at Gloucester as well as at Worcester. The Dean of Gloucester had asked the Stewards there if screws, instead of nails, could be used in the construction so as to reduce the noise to a minimum. The problem was solved by asking the contractor, Mr Clutterbuck, to prefabricate all the parts required to make the staging and then to assemble the timbers in the cathedral using iron bolts.)

The Musical World was forthright in its condemnation:

> The Dean and Chapter of Worcester Cathedral have, at last, taken a decisive step and positively refused the use of the Cathedral for the next Festival of the Three Choirs. Their decision can only take by surprise those who are ignorant of the capacity of clergymen for doing the wrong thing. With some bright exceptions, clergymen only in name, the 'parsons' have gone on blundering from the beginning, spoiling every good work to which they have put their hands, and only succeeding when the object has been to do mischief. So, now, the clerical trustees of Worcester, for the sake of a principle waived by scores of men as good or better than themselves, fly in the face of public opinion,

and shut the doors of a national building against their neighbours and the public. Be it so. The new Dean will have his reward from those among whom he has just gone as a stranger, and the Chapter must look forward to a day of reckoning. The temper of these times is not in favour of clerical assumptions, and Church dignitaries should remember that what the nation gave it can also take away. In possession of handsome incomes (for doing little) and comfortable residences, they, no doubt, think themselves 'lords over God's heritage,' whose power nothing can touch. But every such act as the one under notice lengthens an already formidable indictment against a rotten ecclesiastical corporation, which will ere long tumble about the ears of those who wax fat and kick beneath its shadow. When that event happens, the nation, and not a sect, will possess the national buildings, and all danger of their refusal for an innocent and laudable purpose will have passed.[21]

A final conference between the Worcester Stewards and the Dean and Chapter took place just before Christmas 1874. The Stewards described it as 'a useless ceremony'; at the request of the Mayor of Worcester they sent a petition to the queen in Council, together with one to the same effect from the citizens of Worcester, protesting that:

Application has been made to the present Dean and Chapter of Worcester for the Cathedral as heretofore for the festival of the year 1875, but the Dean and Chapter have declined to grant the use thereof, and have proposed to substitute for a festival, such as those which have so long and so satisfactorily been held in the Cathedral, religious services and sermons, which some sections of your Majesty's subjects would be unable to attend . . . Your petitioners, therefore, humbly pray that your Most Gracious Majesty, as the head of the Church of this realm, will be pleased to use your influence with the Dean and Chapter of Worcester to induce them to permit the holding of the triennial festivals in the Cathedral Church of this city, under such arrangements as will best promote the object in view.[22]

One last skirmish took place before the end of 1874: an exchange of carefully controlled civilities between the Bishops of Worcester and Gloucester:[23]

> Hartlebury
> Kidderminster
>
> Dec. 9th. 1874

My dear Bishop of Gloucester,

At a general meeting of subscribers to the Society for the relief of Clergymen's Widows and Orphans in the Archdeaconry of Worcester, held this day, the secretary informed them that the usual remittances had not been received from the Stewards of the Musical Festival held this year at Gloucester. As the meeting was further informed that the remittance was withheld under your sanction and advice, I was requested by the members present to write to your Lordship on the subject in the hope that further consideration may induce the Stewards to follow the course which has been usual on such occasions. . . . In the advertisement of the Festival of 1874, it was announced to the public that the money collected would be devoted to the benefit of the Widows and Orphans of the Clergy of the three Dioceses. It is to be presumed that money was given on this occasion for such purposes, and it is contended that money so given cannot properly be diverted from the object for which contributions were solicited. Again, the members of the Worcester Choir were invited to take part in the performances, and did actually take part, on the understanding that the Festival was for the benefit of the three dioceses in common; and it is contended that if the share due to the Worcester Diocese be now withheld, such withholding is as much a breach of faith as if the understanding had been a contract executed under hand and seal between the Stewards of the Festival on the one hand

and the members of the Worcester Choir on the other. Our Society entertains no doubt that if the question was submitted to a Court of Equity, the Court would direct the Stewards of the Gloucester Festival to pay the Worcester Charity its third as usual.

The reasons which I have stated appear to be sound and good, even on the supposition that no Musical Festival may be held in Worcester next year. But I may mention that the question of the continuance of the Festivals at Worcester is not yet settled, arrangements having been recently made for a conference between the Stewards of the Proposed Festival of 1875 and the Dean and Chapter of Worcester, with the view of determining the conditions under which the Festival may be held satisfactory to both parties.

I am, my dear Bishop,

Yours very faithfully,

(sgnd.) H. Worcester

Reply from the Bishop of Gloucester and Bristol:

I thank you for your kind letter. Having heard from our local Treasurer (a) that it appears by documentary evidence that the cycle of Festivals commenced with Gloucester and (b) that an assurance (now in my judgement equitably necessary) had not been received that the sum usually sent from Worcester would be forthcoming next year for our widows and orphans, I approved of our Treasurer waiting till such assurance should be received. Feeling, however, that the advertisement to which you refer may carry with it technical liability, I wrote to our Treasurer suggesting that he should invite our Stewards to a meeting, place before them your letter, take their decision thereon and report to me. I will then have the pleasure of writing to you again.

December 11th. 1874

The Gloucester Stewards met and, with considerable reluctance, authorized the Treasurer to pay over forthwith to the Treasurer of the Worcester charity the one-third of the collection of the 1874 Festival.

The 'reformed' Festival of 1875 went ahead in an atmosphere of civic gloom and anger. No solo performers or orchestra were engaged, no platform was erected in the cathedral, no tickets were sold, and no secular concerts were held. Only about sixty people turned up for the Opening Service on 28 September. The music performed during the three days of the 'Festival' – quickly dubbed as the 'Mock Festival' by the unhappy townsfolk of Worcester – was less than exciting: no oratorios, not even *Messiah*, were heard. Three choral services were held on the second day (at 8.30, 11.00 and 3.30) and the Festival was brought to a close on the third day with services at 11.30 and 3.30. The music consisted almost entirely of settings of the canticles, with anthems by Ouseley, Wesley, Mendelssohn, Spohr, Handel, Attwood and others.

Thus ended the Worcester Festival of 1875. Amongst other signs of disapprobation it was noticed that the cabmen had crêpe bows tied to their whips, and one or two black flags were displayed in the streets.[24]

Years later Sir Edward Elgar described the prevailing gloom to Sir Ivor Atkins: how the only redeeming feature had been S.S. Wesley's wonderful organ playing at the end of evening services of Bach's *Wedge* and *Giant* Fugues, and how, to Elgar's delight, it had rained incessantly during the Mock Festival, though it had been fine up till then, and brilliant sunshine returned the day it was over.[25]

The atmosphere of mourning prompted the following epitaph which appeared in the *Birmingham Town Crier*:

IN MEMORY OF THE

WORCESTER MUSIC FESTIVAL

Died September, 1875

Though of humble origin
And for years having only
A very
Modest existence
It tried to attain
Great importance,
And to
Achieve many great and good works,
When in the height of its
Influence and prosperity,
And after ministering to the
Wants of hundreds,
And elevating the
Minds of thousands,
It was unfortunately discovered that it was
Unfit to live.
It was fired at by a
Noisy Canon,
Attacked by a
Military Dean,
And denounced by a
Religious nobleman.
Persecuted by prigs, Puritans and parsons,
Choked by a highly Christian Chapter,
It faintly and feebly
Breathed its last
Before the eyes
And in the presence of its
Chief assailants and assassins.
Weep, Worcester, weep,
Thy lyric glory's gone
No more, alas, to be
Till Dean and Chapter
All translated are
Into the silent see.

The Festival went ahead as usual in Hereford in 1876 and Gloucester in 1877, and by 1878 the Dean and Chapter of Worcester had thought fit to capitulate. The Worcester Festival was re-born. At the Opening Service the sermon was preached by the Bishop himself, and the scruples of the clerical authorities were effectively satisfied by the introduction of prayers before the performance of sacred works in the cathedral.

Since 1875 the only interruptions in the otherwise unbroken annual Three Choirs tradition have been those caused by the two world wars, but an element of opposition to the Festival continued until well into the twentieth century.

Notes

1.   The Stamp Act, requiring a government stamp to be fixed to newspapers, advertisements and various legal documents, was introduced in 1765. In 1802 Cobbett started the *Weekly Register*, a Radical newspaper, but in 1810 was fined £1,000 and sent to gaol for two years for having criticized flogging in the army. In 1816 he reduced the price of the paper from one shilling to twopence so that it escaped the stamp duty.
2.   *Annals* 1895, p. 120
3.   *Annals* 1895, p. 129, footnote 1
4.   *Annals* 1895, p. 156
5.   *Illustrated London News*, 14 September 1850
6.   *Worcester Journal*, 8 September 1842
7.   MW 1842, p. 308
8.   Gloucester Festival Minute Book, 1871
9.   MW 1838, p. 37
10. *Annals* 1895, p. 171
11. The Sees of Gloucester and Bristol were joined in 1836, and divided in 1897, with effect from 1 January 1898.
12. See Welander, *The History, Art and Architecture of Gloucester Cathedral* (Alan Sutton, 1991)
13. MW 1865, pp. 594–5
14. *The Times*, 6 September 1865
15. Lionel Monckton (1861–1924), composer of *The Quaker Girl*, etc.
16. Letter from the Broadley Collection in Gloucester City Library.
17. Brewer, *Memoirs of Choirs and Cloisters* (London, 1931), p. 86
18. *The Times*, 8 September 1865
19. *The Times*, and reported in MW, 31 October 1874, p. 715
20. MW 1874, p. 755
21. MW 1874, p. 705
22. MW 1875, p. 4
23. Gloucester Festival Minute Book, 1874
24. *Annals* 1895, p. 265
25. E. Wulstan Atkins, *The Elgar–Atkins Friendship* (David & Charles, 1985) p. 474

CHAPTER SEVEN

PRIMA VOCE

F or the first three-quarters of the nineteenth century, Britain was the unchallenged supplier of the world's goods, skills and services. Although one-third of the people lived in a residuum of wretched poverty, the nation as a whole attracted unprecedented wealth, in the wake of which the finest foreign singers were drawn to London opera houses and concert halls to perform alongside the best British artists.

At a time when the notions of the radio and the gramophone were less than dreams, a public hungry for music was prepared to pay high prices for opera and concert tickets, and national and international celebrity singers could demand huge fees for their appearances. At the end of the London season each year, these stars would tour the country, singing at regional music festivals such as Leeds, Liverpool, Norwich, Birmingham and Three Choirs.

To enable provincial concert-goers to see and to hear as many of their renowned favourites as possible, it was customary for the solo parts of a work performed at Three Choirs to be divided between a first and second singer of the same voice, the former receiving a higher fee than the latter. Not surprisingly, this division sometimes led to rivalry and to contractual problems.

In addition to singing in performances of sacred works in the cathedrals, the same stars would take part in the evening Miscellaneous Concerts in secular venues. To modern tastes these concerts would seem to have been over-long and indigestible mixtures of operatic arias, ballads, humorous songs and instrumental and orchestral pieces. However, they gave people living in rural communities the occasional opportunity to experience a cross-section of the entertainment enjoyed regularly by their London cousins. To them it seemed not the least bit incongruous that, as at Gloucester in 1847, Marietta Alboni should share the bill with, among others, John Parry — a comic singer and 'shaker of sides' — and that following her performances of operatic arias and duets with the great bass Joseph Staudigl, Parry was 'received uproariously, was in unproarious humour, and was uproariously encored in both his ingenious pasticcios'.[1]

In the early years of the nineteenth century Three Choirs soloists included a few whose reputations had been made in the eighteenth century. Gertrud Mara sang for the last time at a Music Meeting in 1801(H) and Elizabeth Billington in 1809(W). James Bartleman carried on until 1817(G):

> It is melancholy to record that many of the latter years of Bartleman's life were passed in almost unremitting pain. His ardent mind long struggled against disease, and he was often delighting crowded audiences with his performance, while the dew of bodily agony stood upon his brow.[2]

Bartleman was so ill by 1819 that he was unable to attend his own benefit concert. He died on 15 April 1821 at the age of fifty-one and is buried in Westminster Abbey. Dr Rimbault records that 'after his decease, his large and valuable library of ancient music was sold by auction, and the respectable auctioneer ran away with the proceeds, which thus became lost to his two sisters who survived him'.[3]

Throughout the nineteenth century Three Choirs was notable for the engagement, year after year, of a galaxy of star singers which, to a later age, would have been the equivalent of regular appearances by Caruso, Melba and Chaliapin; or to today's audiences, performances in the western shires by Domingo, Pavarotti and Jessye Norman.

The Italian soprano Angelica Catalani (1780–1849) was among the foreign celebrities whose first appearances at the Music Meetings were made in the early years of the century. She sang at Gloucester in 1811 and at Worcester in 1812. Catalani came to England in 1806 and, with performances at Covent Garden and elsewhere, had in less than six months earned almost £10,000. Her fee to sing in Gloucester was the highest ever before paid by Three Choirs: 450 guineas! However, she was famous not only for her magnificent voice but also for her generosity: while in Gloucestershire she visited the county prison and donated a large sum to the prison charity. She then proposed and took part in a concert, held in the Cheltenham Assembly Rooms, which was so successful that there was money to spare for the county infirmary too. Furthermore, she donated 50 guineas of her Three Choirs fee to the Festival charity.

Maria Malibran (1808–36) sang at three Music Meetings in the last few years of her short, brilliant and tragic life: 1828(G), 1830(W) and 1833(W). Taught by her Spanish father, Manuel Garcia, and by Hérold in Paris, she made her London début in 1825 as Rosina in *The Barber of Seville* before she was seventeen. At the end of that season she went to America with her father where, one day after her eighteenth birthday, she married Malibran, an elderly Frenchman. 'The marriage proved to be a ghastly failure. Whatever may have been M. Malibran's musical attainments, his only known composition was a composition with his creditors. The bankruptcy of the elderly bridegroom took place within a year of the nuptial ceremony, and Maria left him.'[4]

In 1930 she found love with the Belgian violinist Charles de Beriot whom she married in 1836 and with whom she appeared at the Music Meeting of 1833(W).

The glorious voice of Malibran was contralto in quality, with a compass of three octaves. She was a woman of remarkable personality and amazingly varied accomplishments:

> She was an intrepid horsewoman, a capital dancer, an inimitable caricaturist,[5] a humorous concocter of charades and riddles, and – though some 'superior' persons may regard this as a weakness in her character – she could make a very good pun. Yet, upon the slightest indication, she would . . .

discuss with discriminate enthusiasm the genius of Dante or Shakespeare, Raphael or Michaelangelo. She was an excellent pianist, and composed many very creditable songs . . . in short, her versatility was quite phenomenal.[6]

Reporting on the Music Meeting of 1829(G), the *Gloucester Journal* records that a great crowd attended the morning service, at which 'many females were carried out in a fainting state'. The prayers were read by the Revd W. W. Mutlow, a son of the cathedral organist and a minor canon of the cathedral. Of Malibran's achievements at the Music Meeting we learn from the paper that:

> To remarkable powers of voice, she unites singular clearness of articulation; and her style of singing is strongly characterised by that depth of feeling which constitutes the very soul of the music. There is something in her demeanour, too, which is very pleasing; and we were delighted to observe that both she and Mrs. Knyvett invariably took a prominent part in the responses of the day – a point not always attended to by the principal singers on such occasions as the present . . . The whole company was enraptured by Madame Malibran's execution of the Bishop air, 'Should he upbraid', and a general encore was the natural consequence. Madame Malibran still further charmed the company by the ready and obliging manner in which she complied with the request of one of the Stewards to favour them with another song, when she instantly took her seat at the piano, and with a degree of archness and good humour peculiarly her own, gave the lively and playful air 'Rampataplan', which was loudly commended.[7]

Following her triumph in Gloucester, Malibran was invited to sing at Worcester in the following year, 1830, the year in which Princess Victoria and her mother, the Duchess of Kent, attended the Music Meeting.

In the spring of 1836 Malibran, by then pregnant, fell from her horse. In spite of the seriousness of her condition, she insisted upon travelling from Paris to Manchester in the following September in order to fulfill an engagement at that city's music festival. Though weak and ill she sang on both the morning and evening of Tuesday, 13 September and again on the following day. At the Wednesday evening concert she took part in a duet with Maria Caradori Allan – 'Vanne se alberghi in petto' from Mercadante's *Andronica*. It was received with immense enthusiasm, and she even repeated the performance; but at its end, while the concert room was still ringing with applause, she was fainting in the arms of her friends. Nine days later – 23 September 1836 – at the Mosley Arms Hotel, Manchester, Maria Malibran passed away at the age of twenty-eight.

The life of Malibran's brother, Manuel Garcia (1805–1906) was as full of years as Maria's was deprived of them. He was an eminent singing teacher and the inventor of the laryngoscope, who retired at the age of ninety-five and lived for five more years.

Malibran's sister, the mezzo-soprano and composer Pauline Viardot-Garcia, sang at the Music Meetings in 1841(G), 1854(W) and 1858(H). She too was a woman of formidable talents who married a much older man: the French writer Louis Viardot was twenty-one years her senior. In 1843 she met the novelist Turgenev in Paris and formed an intimate relationship with him. When both men died in 1883, Pauline withdrew from society and lived as a semi-recluse until her death in 1910 at the age of eighty-nine.

It was Malibran who sang the role of Leonora in the first performance in English of Beethoven's opera *Fidelio* at Covent Garden in 1835. Eleven years earlier the soprano parts in Beethoven's *Missa Solemnis* and Ninth Symphony (the *Choral*) had been sung at their first performances by Henriette Sontag in the presence of the, by then, profoundly deaf composer. In 1823 Weber had chosen her to sing the title-part in *Euryanthe*. After her marriage to the Count de Rossi in 1828 she retired but, following the revolutions of 1848 in Europe, returned to the stage. Her re-appearance in London after twenty years caused a sensation, and in 1850 she sang at the Gloucester Festival:

> . . . the anxiety to hear Madame Sontag was so great that all other considerations were overlooked. Her first song, Donizetti's cavatina, 'Se crudele il cor', is by no means a remarkable composition, but the original and perfectly executed cadenza which Madame Sontag introduced at the end of the largo, and the exquisite fancy with which she embellished the cabaletta, raised the greatest enthusiasm. In Arne's 'Soldier tired', Madame Sontag obtained a unanimous encore: . . . Madame Sontag has made an indelible impression on the Gloucesterians, who never gave a stronger proof of their good taste than by the unbounded applause they bestowed upon the efforts of this gifted and accomplished artist.[8]

In 1852 Henriette Sontag went to America. While in Mexico City she contracted cholera and died there on 17 June 1854.

A contemporary of Sontag and Malibran, the Scottish soprano Mary Ann Paton (1802–54) appeared at the Festivals in 1825(W), 1828(H), 1829(G) and 1830(W). She had made her first stage appearance in 1822 and married Lord William Pitt Lennox in 1824, but they separated later and she married Joseph Wood, tenor, of the Covent Garden Theatre, ultimately settling in Manchester and then Leeds as a teacher of singing. Mary Paton was the first Rezia in Weber's *Oberon*; and it was with an aria by Weber, 'Softly sighs' from *Der Freischütz*, that she thrilled the Gloucester audience in 1829. She died at Radcliffe Hall, Yorkshire on 23 July 1864.

The Worcester Festival of 1842 brought to prominence a young contralto who was to remain a Three Choirs favourite for a quarter of a century. Charles Clarke, the cathedral organist, was too ill to conduct and the Stewards engaged Joseph Surman of the Exeter Hall in London to take his place. The Stewards had by this time already engaged the principal soloists, among whom was the contralto Maria Hawes whose first Three Choirs appearance had been at Hereford in 1834. Surman wrote to Miss Hawes, sending her the programme, in response to which she replied in a letter:

> . . . containing sundry protestations against the (as Miss H. terms it) unwarrantable distribution of various solos and duets, which she has been accustomed to sing, among sundry other vocalists – also containing certain *commands*, that such and such a song should be placed in such and such a place – that such a duet should be reversed – that so and so should not sing this or that – and that she (Miss Hawes) insisted upon doing this or that, or the other.[9]

Surman suggested various compromise solutions to Miss Hawes but she wrote back immediately to him, and later to the Festival Committee, insisting upon having her own way or declining her engagement. The committee despatched a Mr Rogers to London forthwith to obtain a replacement for Miss Hawes, and he engaged the 21-year-old Charlotte Dolby who had recently made her début there following her studies at the Royal Academy of Music.

Miss Dolby rushed to Worcester without knowing anything of the music which she would have to perform and without the advantage of a single rehearsal. Her appearance was a triumph.

Miss Hawes never sang at Worcester again, and only once more in a Three Choirs Festival: at Gloucester in 1844. However, Charlotte Dolby (who became Madame Sainton-Dolby on marrying the French violinist Prosper Sainton, Leader of the Festival orchestra from 1871 to 1882), achieved fame and distinction. In 1845 she was invited by Mendelssohn to sing with Jenny Lind at Leipzig; and on 26 August 1846 she sang in the first performance of *Elijah* under the direction of the composer at the Birmingham Festival, along with Maria Caradori-Allan, Charles Lockey and Joseph Staudigl.

Three Choirs had a vintage year in 1847. Not only did the four soloists who had performed in the Birmingham première of *Elijah* repeat the work in Gloucester but also the famous contralto Marietta Alboni (1822–94) was engaged to sing in the second and third Miscellaneous Concerts. Alboni, a pupil of Rossini, had made her début at La Scala, Milan in 1843. In London she shared star-billing with Jenny Lind at Her Majesty's Theatre.

> Alboni, the gorgeous Alboni, with her portly frame and winning smile, came forward and sang 'Una voce poco fa' after her own peculiar fashion, and at once produced an impression which has had no parallel in the musical annals of Gloucester . . . She was rapturously encored, and repeated the allegro with increased brilliancy. There was scarcely a note of Rossini's text, but the thing had a charm of its own that was quite irresistible . . . Alboni is the whole theme of Gloucester *causerie*: you cannot pass up and down the streets without hearing an earnest discussion of her merits in almost every corner, nor can you approach a house where there is a piano, without hearing some young lady endeavouring to emulate [her] fervour and *intensity*.[10]

Alboni was not only celebrated for her beautiful voice but also for her bodily size. Madame Girardin was once asked by someone who knew nothing of opera: 'What is Alboni then?' Madame Girardin replied: 'What is she? Why, she is an elephant who has swallowed a nightingale!'[11]

Another and more slender nightingale became the most sought-after of all sopranos. Jenny Lind (1820–87), 'The Swedish Nightingale', studied with Garcia in Paris and came to settle in England in 1847. Within a very short time she established a huge reputation.

In December 1847, the Bishop of Worcester wrote inviting her to appear at the Worcester Festival of 1848. To this she replied that she would have great pleasure in being able to aid so excellent a charity. The only condition Jenny Lind made was that a sufficient interval should be allowed to elapse between the end of the London opera season and the Festival, so as to be able to recover from the fatigue of her opera engagements.

William Done was despatched to London to make the necessary arrangements, and had an interview with Jenny Lind, who referred him to Mr Lumley, the director of Her Majesty's Theatre, to ascertain when the opera season would close. However, Done was obliged to return to Worcester with nothing settled.

The Festival Secretary, the Revd Robert Sargeant, wrote to Jenny Lind reminding her of her letter to the Bishop and advising that the start of the Festival had been deferred to 5 September for her convenience. He received a letter from Mr Lumley expressing regret that Mlle Lind's previous engagements would not permit her appearance at Worcester. Sargeant went to see Lumley but was unable to change his mind; a little later he received a letter from Lumley containing a cheque for £50 from Jenny Lind, as a donation from her towards the Festival charity.

In the second week of August 1848, advertisements appeared in the newspapers announcing that Jenny Lind had accepted engagements to sing at Birmingham and Cheltenham during the same week that the Worcester Festival was to be held. The indignation of the Worcester Stewards was extreme. Sargeant wrote to Jenny Lind pointing out that her appearance at the two towns 'must inevitably be productive of the most serious injury that the festival can sustain'.[12]

It is not known if he received any reply. However, for Lumley the seasons of 1847 and 1848, thanks to Jenny Lind, were a huge success. It was rumoured that in 1847 alone he had pocketed £22,000 clear of all expenses.

In 1852, Jenny Lind married the composer and conductor Otto Goldschmidt and toured widely with him. For the 1856 Festival, the Gloucester Stewards authorized John Amott to negotiate with her for a sum not exceeding £500 (in that year Alboni received £275 and Viardot £180), but he was not successful. He tried again for 1859 but 'she declined to enter into any engagement to sing at the Festival'. Finally, in 1862 the Festival Chairman, Sir George Jackson, High Sheriff of Gloucester, was asked to approach Jenny Lind. This time her reason for refusal became plain: in her letter declining yet again to sing at the Festival she added that in any engagement she might make, she would reqire Mr Otto Goldschmidt to be the conductor.[13]

At last, in 1867, Jenny Lind-Goldschmidt agreed to sing in her husband's oratorio *Ruth* at the Hereford Festival in a performance conducted by him. While there she also sang in *Elijah* and *Messiah*. In these two long-established masterpieces she scored a fair success:

> Those who know the intense absorption of Madame Goldschmidt in her work, and the wonderful combinations of earnestness and intelligence she brings to its performance will not require to be told what an effect she made in the impassioned music of her part [in *Elijah*]. Years have produced their inevitable effect upon the voice which once cast a spell over every listener, but the instinct of the artist remains strong as ever, and asserted, this morning, all its old power.[14]

> The rendering of the sublimest of airs, 'I know that my Redeemer liveth' by Madame Goldschmidt . . . was a marvel of artistic skill and profound expression.[15]

The 'instinct of the artist' was insufficient to make a success of *Ruth*, a work described by *The Musical World* as 'an unsymmmetrical corpse'. *The Times* noted that not one of the many choruses was gone through from end to end without impediment, and the *Hereford Journal* reported that 'Madame Lind-Goldschmidt's exertions in the part of Ruth were almost painful to witness; her once fine voice is gone'.

Giulia Grisi (1811–69) was an Italian prima donna with an international reputation. She sang in the Festivals of 1838(G) and 1855(H), and was considered by many to be the finest dramatic soprano of her generation. She was typical of the many singers of both sexes who rose to fame on the stages of the world's opera houses and who, although not specialists in oratorio singing, were in huge public demand to sing at the regional festivals. To opponents of the Music Meetings the very fact that these stars were theatrical performers was anathema: a cathedral was a House of God, not an opera house. At the same time, within the musical establishment there was a rising tide of opposition to the policy of engaging foreign stars at huge expense in preference to British singers for so absolutely British an institution as the Three Choirs Festival.

Pre-eminent among the English women singers of the mid-nineteenth century was the soprano Clara Novello (1818–1908), daughter of Vincent Novello, the composer and founder of the famous music-publishing firm. Clara Novello made her début at the Worcester Music Meeting of 1833 and sang regularly at Three Choirs for almost three decades. During her career she earned the praise of both Mendelssohn and Schumann, and her reviews read like a litany of praise. For her final performance in 1860, again at Worcester, *The Musical World* reported:

> To say that she sang to perfection would be faint praise . . . It made everyone feel a regret that we are so soon to lose such a voice from among us, and that future festivals must look long and far before they again find any one conveying the sensations produced by those clear ringing bell-like notes.[16]

It was seventeen years before the Festivals found such a voice again.

The first principal soprano from 1861 to 1876 was the Hungarian Therese Tietjens (1831–77), who settled in England in 1858 and first sang at Three Choirs in the evening concerts in 1859(G).

Although engaged to sing at Gloucester in 1877, Tietjens fell ill in the June of that year. The Stewards, fearing that she might be unable to sing at the Festival, authorized Charles Harford Lloyd to negotiate for a possible stand-in. He considered Madam Helen Lemmens-Sherrington, who had not sung at Three Choirs for five years, but found that she was already booked to appear in a series of concerts during the Festival week. To obtain her services would have involved buying up those concerts at a cost of £130, in addition to paying her fee of 150 guineas for singing with Tietjens, or 200 guineas if she took on all the work alone. The Stewards considered this to be out of the question.[17]

On 12 July the manager of Her Majesty's Theatre in London, Col. J.H. Mapleson, who was Tietjen's agent, wrote to Lloyd saying that she was very much better and that her medical attendant had authorized him to announce that she would be fit to perform before the close of the opera season. Even so, Lloyd continued to plan for the possibility of her not being able to appear, He had, in any case, determined to engage a soprano of the finest quality for this, his first Three Choirs Festival. He contacted Frederick Gye, the agent of Mademoiselle Emma Albani,[18] a Canadian singer who had settled in England in 1872 after making a successful début at Covent Garden. Gye wrote to Lloyd saying that as Three Choirs had agreed to pay Tietjens 350 guineas, he presumed that there would be no objection to paying 'such an Artiste as Mdlle. Albani considerably more'. He asked for 450 guineas: far more than the cost of engaging Helen Lemmens-Sherrington *and* buying out her previously booked concerts.

On 11 August 1877, just three weeks before the start of the Festival, Mapleson wrote to Lloyd:

> I am very sorry to say that Mdlle Tietjens is not making the progress we had all wished. Her medical attendant Dr Spencer Wells up to last Saturday gave me a full assurance that her services were to be relied upon. During the last three or four days she has become much weaker and feels she will be unable to undertake the engagement.[19]

Lloyd persuaded the Stewards to engage Emma Albani, in spite of the cost. We are told

'She threw her whole soul into *Elijah*'[20] and so began her 34-year association with Three Choirs. Therese Tietjens died on 3 October 1877.

Madam (afterwards Dame Emma) Albani became the 'Queen of Song' of this and all the English musical festivals of the day. The impression she made was vivid many years later. In reminiscences communicated to Watkins Shaw in 1952, Sir Ivor Atkins recalled the magnificent effect of her singing of the aria 'Hear ye, Israel' at the beginning of Part II of *Elijah*, particularly her soaring phrases at 'I, thy God', an effect enhanced by her practice of requiring the earlier soprano music of the oratorio to be sung by a soloist of lesser calibre. He recalled, too, how she would not come on the platform until Part II was about to begin, when she entered with her copy of the music tied in ribbon, and held up the proceedings while she knelt for a moment in prayer. He mentioned also her ostentatious reluctance – and refusal – to rehearse, even to use her singing voice; and her elaborate progress in carriage and pair even if it were only the eighty yards from where she stayed, at what was later for a time the Worcester Deanery and is now the King's School office, to the south cloister gate of Worcester Cathedral. But as Dr Shaw has pointed out, 'before her active career was over, a style came to be required which demanded more personal effacement, a greater degree of artistic and intellectual subtlety', and H.C. Colles notes that her instinct was right when in 1902 she was reluctant to sing in Walford Davies's *The Temple*.[21]

Janet Patey, née Whytock (1842–94), a Scottish contralto, appeared regularly at Three Choirs from 1866(W), the year following that of her first concert tour, and the year of her marriage to John Patey, the English baritone. There was great disappointment when in 1877(W) Madame Patey was not invited to sing at the Festival. Both she and Charles Santley were dropped 'from motives of economy'.[22] Although Santley was back in the following year Patey never returned.

Of the second rank of female principal singers in the latter half of the nineteenth century, mention must be made of the soprano Anna Williams and the contralto Hilda Wilson; both were Festival favourites for many years, Williams appearing regularly from 1878(H) and Wilson from 1880(G) until 1904(G). In fact Hilda Wilson (1860–1915) was a local girl, the daughter of James Wilson 'professor of music' and bandmaster, who also seems to have kept 'The Running Horse' at 38 Barton Street, Gloucester. Her younger sister Agnes was a soprano, and her brother, H. Lane Wilson, a well-known song-writer, accompanist and bass-singer who appeared as a soloist at Three Choirs in 1898(G) and 1902(W).[23] Hilda Wilson's musical training had been generously paid for by Gloucester ladies.[24]

Among the famous foreign male opera singers to appear at Three Choirs in the first sixty years of the nineteenth century were the tenors Giovanni Rubini and Giovanni Mario, the baritones Antonio Tamburini and Giovanni Belletti and the great bass Luigi Lablache.

Lablache (1794–1858) was born in Italy of French and Irish parents, made his début in Naples in 1812 and quickly became world famous. In 1827 he was a torch-bearer at the funeral of Beethoven and in 1830 made his first appearance in London, returning to England every year except 1833 until the closure of Her Majesty's Theatre in 1852. He sang at Three Choirs for the first time in 1835(G) and in the following year was appointed singing-master to Queen Victoria. He returned to the Festival in 1838(G), 1840(H) and 1848(W). In 1850 *The Musical World* heaped praise upon Lablache:

Lablache's voice is an organ of extraordinary power. It is impossible by description to give any notion of its volume of sound. He is an ophicleide among singers. One may have some idea of the power of tone, when it may be asserted, that, with the entire opera band and chorus playing and singing *forte*, his voice may be as distinctly and separately heard above them all as a trumpet among violins.[25]

The German bass, Theodor Formes, sang at Three Choirs each year from 1850 to 1854 and again in 1857. His voice was described as colossal and impressive but, in common with other stars of the day, he sometimes saw no purpose in attending rehearsals of works he had sung many times. On one occasion (1851(W)), he failed to turn up for an evening concert, sending word that he was indisposed. Rumour had it that 'Formes was off to sing somewhere else that night' and when 'towards the end of the evening the Stewards came up in solemn file and announced that Herr Formes was got better [sic] and would certainly sing the morrow morning in the *Messiah* . . . there was a good deal of laughing, and it was pronounced to be a case of a very sudden cure.'[27]

The only counter-tenor of distinction to be heard at Three Choirs in the nineteenth century was William Knyvett (1777–1856), a member of a famous family of English musicians, who was appointed a Gentleman of the Chapel Royal in 1797. Knyvett was a conductor and composer as well as a singer; he first performed at a Music Meeting in 1799(G) when he was described as 'a most chaste counter-tenor singer' and 'one of the very few English singers remarkable for correctness in the musical enunciation of the words of the English language'.[28] Knyvett's wife, Deborah, was also a singer and they performed together for many years, making their last Three Choirs appearance in 1838(G).

One other albeit reluctant counter-tenor made his brief mark in the period. At the Opening Service of the Worcester Festival in 1854, Charlotte Dolby became suddenly unwell. At a moment's notice the alto parts were taken 'and most creditably executed' by Mr Jones, the organist at Tewkesbury.[29]

John Braham (1777–1856), whose real name was Abraham, was a Jew of German extraction: a small man (he was 5 ft 3 ins tall) with a huge, trumpet-like tenor voice. His singing career began as a treble at the Covent Garden Theatre in 1787 but in 1794 he made his début as a tenor at Rauzzini's concerts in Bath. He appeared in London and at the Gloucester Festival in 1796. The composer Stephen Storace was so impressed by Braham's singing that be began writing *Mahmoud* for him, but died in 1796, at the age of thirty-three, before completing the score. Shortly afterwards, Braham left for the Continent with Storace's sister Nancy, the first Susanna in Mozart's *Le Nozze di Figaro* (1786) who had been a pupil of Rauzzini and who had become Braham's mistress. He returned to England in 1801 following huge acclaim in France and Italy, and in the next twenty-five years is said to have earned an average of £14,000 per annum.

Braham reappeared at Three Choirs in 1809(W) and sang at the Music Meetings until 1838(G). He was greatly admired as an opera singer but less so in oratorio and popular ballads which he tended to 'Italianize'. At Gloucester in 1817: 'The performance of *Messiah* was considerably marred by Mr Braham, who sang 'Comfort ye, my people' in a manner so ill-fitting the subject, and with such redundancy of false ornament, as to draw upon himself the censure of the critics of that period, who were naturally disposed to indulgence, especially towards one whose popularity was then at its zenith.'[30]

When Braham was nearly sixty years old, the critic of *The Musical World* was kinder to him in reviewing the Worcester Festival of 1836:

After nearly forty years of acquaintance with Mr. Braham's public life, it was delightful to hear him pour out with such youthful vigour the 'Sound the Alarm!' It is good to listen to him, if it be only to cheat oneself into the belief that both we and he are the same as when we used to think that there never had been such a voice and such fine singing since the creation of our first parents.[31]

Braham frequently sang with Maria Malibran and with the baritone Henry Phillips. In his autobiography, *Musical and Personal Recollections During Half a Century* (1864), Phillips describes Braham as 'a rare mimic, and at times very witty':

He would often refer to one of [Angelica] Catalini's weaknesses, viz: boasting of the various articles of jewellery she possessed. Certainly they were very costly, and she would walk round our room saying, – You see dis brooch? de Emperor of Austria gave me dis. You see dese earrings? de Emperor of Russia gave me dese. You see dis ring? de Emperor Napoleon gave me dis,' and so on. Mr. Braham, in imitation of this, would say, pointing to his umbrella, – 'You see dis? de Emperor of China gave me dis.' Then, pointing to his teeth, 'de King of Tuscany gave me dese.'

Phillips tells another story about Braham which refers to a Three Choirs performance in which, under the baton of William Mutlow, Maria Malibran, Braham and Phillips took part. In his book, *Cathedral Organists* (1899), John West suggests that this anecdote should be taken *cum grano salis*. Even so, it is a good tale:

Mr. Braham was a man generally of most reserved manners, which gave the impression of pride, yet no one entered more into jest than he did, whether practical or otherwise. One of a laughable character occurred at a celebrated triennial festival, in connection with the conductor, who was organist of the cathedral. He chanced to be a gentleman of eccentric habits and appearance, very short and fat, an epicure of no ordinary stamp, the length of whose arm was as near as possible the measure of his baton. Though an especial favourite with Madame Malibran, she delighted to play him all sorts of tricks, at which he never took offence. On one occasion of a morning performance, of selected sacred music, Madame Malibran and Braham had to sing a duett, John Loder being leader of the orchestra; the three consulted together as to what trick they could play the conductor, and one having been agreed upon, the morning performance arrived, all went very well, the band and singers going on smoothly in one time while the conductor beat another – that was of little consequence in those days. At length came the duett by Malibran and Braham, which had a long symphony preceding it; the conductor, with more than ordinary energy in honor of so grand an occasion, waved his baton in the air, till down it came as a signal for the first chord, but not a semblance of sound issued from the orchestra. 'Hallo!' shouted the conductor, with a raised head, in amazement, 'can't you all see? Now, then, we'll try again.' He did, and the result was the same. 'Why, what the devil's the matter? – are you all mad?' cried the little fat man, the huge drops falling from his forehead, which, as he drew his handkerchief to remove, the symphony began, to his great astonishment, and almost defied his beating a bar correctly till it had nearly finished, the singers nearly fainting with suppressed laughter at the success of the trick they had so ingeniously planned.
    When this little conductor gave a lesson on the pianoforte, it was always in a room next to the kitchen: in the middle of the lesson he would say, 'There, go on; I can hear ye, I'm only going to baste the air' (hare), so he walked into the kitchen, did what he proposed, came back, and finished the lesson. The Queen's English was a matter sadly disregarded by this gentleman: luckily, not being at court, he escaped the condemnation it must otherwise have brought upon him; when going out he would call to the servant, 'Hann, where's my 'at?' He was, however, a kind, good-tempered soul, took all that happened in the best part, and when the festival had terminated said, 'Some very droll things have occurred this week; but never mind, come and dine with me, and we'll enjoy the haunch of venison and drink success to the next festival in some of the finest port wine in England.'

The most prominent British tenors for the remainder of the nineteenth century were Charles Lockey, John Sims Reeves and Edward Lloyd.

Charles Lockey (1820–1901) first sang at a Music Meeting in 1846(H), the year in which he came to prominence by taking the tenor part in the first performance of Mendelssohn's *Elijah* in Birmingham. He repeated this success in Gloucester in 1847, for which he received £42, and continued to sing at the Festivals until 1856(G), by which time his career had been rather eclipsed by that of Sims Reeves.

John Sims Reeves (1818–1900) was the king of tenors in this country for over thirty years from his first London appearance in 1847. He sang regularly at Three Choirs from 1848(W) until 1877(G) and was equally popular and successful in the performance of operatic arias and oratorios. He also endeared himself to the British public as a singer of ballads such as 'Tom Bowling', 'The Death of Nelson', 'The Bay of Biscay' and 'My pretty Jane'.

Sims Reeves would never agree to sing unless he was in good voice, and once stated that he had lost £80,000 during his long career through his conscientiousness. He always preferred to disappoint an audience than to turn up and sing to them 'with a throat', and Three Choirs audiences were often disappointed. As early as 1849(H) he failed to turn up for *Messiah* and Charles Lockey was obliged to substitute without notice. His absences from concerts became so notorious that *The Orchestra* magazine suggested that promoters resort to a new form of advertisement:

> ON THIS OCCASION THE AUDIENCE WILL POSITIVELY HAVE A * CHANCE OF HEARING MR. SIMS REEVES
>
> * Here insert 'good', 'fair', 'small', or 'poor' as the case may be

So used did the Three Choirs Stewards become to Sims Reeves' absences that they were not prepared to be sympathetic when, genuinely ill, he left the platform halfway through the Wednesday evening concert in the Shire Hall at the Gloucester Festival of 1859; a shocking and faintly comic scene ensued, and was reported the next day in *The Times*:

No less than four speeches were adventured in the course of about one hour last night – three short, and little to the purpose; one not very long, but *much* to the purpose. Of the short speeches one was delivered by Mr. T. Gambier Parry,[32] a 'steward', and two were furnished by the Mayor of Gloucester: the not very long speech flowed gently from the lips of Madame Clara Novello. The origin of all these improvised orations may be briefly stated. The indisposition of Mr. Sims Reeves has been alluded to. It was observed on all sides during the performance of *The May Queen*, and no one ought to have felt surprise, however he may have experienced disappointment, at the omission of a ballad allotted to this gentleman in the second part of the concert. When, however, Madame Novello had sung 'Prendi per me' out of its place, and on her retiring there were no signs of Mr. Reeves, the audience began to be restive, and would not be pacified until one of the stewards (Mr T.G. Parry) came forward and addressed them. He said (as clearly as we can remember), 'Ladies and Gentlemen, – It seems to be the principal duty of the stewards to make apologies for Mr. Sims Reeves. The stewards have done all in their power, but as Mr Sims Reeves has quietly walked off, the stewards cannot fetch him back, and I hope they will not be blamed. He has found a good friend in Madame Novello, who has kindly consented to sing a song in his stead.' This address was received with mingled applause and hisses. It did not, however, satisfy Mr Reeves's substitute, who, protesting that it conveyed an erroneous statement of the facts, declared that she would not sing until it had been corrected. The Mayor of Gloucester (on the refusal of his colleague to set matters right) then volunteered a further explanation, which amounted to this: –

'Ladies and Gentlemen, – I have the pleasure to inform you that Madame Novello will give another song in place of Mr. Sims Reeves.' Cries of 'Not enough' – 'We know that already' – greeted the ears of his worship as he left the platform, having delivered himself of this weighty piece of information. Being apprised of the inadequate manner in which he had accomplished his self-imposed task, the Mayor returned to the charge, and addressed his turbulent co-citizens afresh: – 'Ladies and Gentlemen,' he said, 'I am to state that Mr. Sims Reeves, being ill, was compelled to leave.' This speech, a worthy pendant of the other, was answered by shouts of laughter, and it seemed unlikely now that the disturbance would be quelled at all. After a long interval, during the progress of which the Shire hall threatened to be turned into a bear-garden, Madame Clara Novello made her appearance on the platform, to fulfil as was generally surmised, the task she had undertaken as deputy. Shouts, cheers, and plaudits greeted her from every part of the room, and when these subsided, she opened her lips – but not to sing. Instead of 'Bonnie Prince Charlie' it was 'Ladies and Gentlemen.' Calmly, unaffectedly, yet firmly, Madame Novello, like a musical Portia, admonished her hearers. She spoke to the following purport: – 'Before he went away, very ill, Mr Reeves explained to the conductor his total inability to sing his ballad in the second part; but, with a desire that the audience might not be losers through his indisposition, which was not his fault, he applied to me to introduce something in its place, and even sent for a copy of the ballad I am now going to have the honour of singing to you, with much less ability than he would have shown.

'Mr. Amott, with whom alone the artists engaged at the festival can communicate on business, was consulted, and gave his approval; and, not satisfied even with this, Mr. Reeves spoke with one of the stewards, who also consented to the change. Had this been stated, no fault could possibly have been laid at his charge. I thus take the liberty to address you, Ladies and Gentlemen, because I will not allow a brother artist to be unjustly accused, as Mr. Reeves was – of course unintentionally – in the explanation given this evening, or to be blamed when he is entirely innocent, and especially when he had taken all the precautions in his power to compensate for any disappointment.' The tones of this nightingale had more persuasive eloquence in them than the voices of the steward and the Mayor. The fair apologist (who speaks, by the way, quite as musically as she sings) was completely overwhelmed with the demonstrations of complete satisfaction that her quiet speech had elicited, and the peace of her 'brother artist' was made with the public. We do not remember a more graceful act on the part of one artist to another – an act implying a strong sense of right, no little moral courage, and the total absence of a certain feeling of jealous rivalry from which even the most distinguished members of the profession are not invariably exempt.

The next day, Sims Reeves was confined to bed, but was able to sing in *Messiah* on the Friday. The reason for his illness was made clear in the Press: one night in the week before the Festival, he had been staying in a London hotel which had caught fire. He had joined in the efforts to extinguish the blaze which threatened to destroy the whole building. Then, with his family, he had been obliged to spend the night camping on the wet grass of a nearby park and had caught a cold.

The Gloucester Stewards made a public apology for their blunder and Sims Reeves donated 25 guineas to the Festival charity to compensate for the disappointment, pointing out that he would have given more, but that he had in any case charged 50 guineas less than his usual terms.[33] He was known for his generosity: following *Messiah* in Hereford in 1867, the collection plate was found to contain a cheque for £100 from Sims Reeves.

Although he must have earned vast sums, Sims Reeves was never a saver and ended his days in poverty. In 1896 he was reduced to appearing at music halls, and in April 1900 he was given a Civil List pension of £100; six months later he was dead.

Edward Lloyd (1845–1927) had been a choirboy at Westminster Abbey until 1860 and one of the Gentlemen of the Chapel Royal from 1869. His first important public appearance was at the Gloucester Festival of 1871 when S.S. Wesley chose him to sing the part of the Evangelist in the first Three Choirs performance of Bach's *St Matthew Passion*. His beautiful singing brought him the approval of the critics, a fee of 30 guineas, and a foothold on the ladder to fame. Lloyd retired from public life after the Hereford Festival of 1900.

The leading British singers to perform the bass solos at Three Choirs in the nineteenth century were Henry Phillips, W.H. Weiss and Sir Charles Santley.

Phillips (1801–76) was born in Bristol, appeared on the stage when still only a boy, sang in the chorus at the Drury Lane Theatre in London and gradually worked his way up to become the leading British baritone of his generation. He appeared not only on the opera stage and concert platform but also in table entertainments. After performances at Three Choirs, where he sang between 1826 and 1852, he would sometimes take to the boards in local theatres, singing parts such as that of Tom Tug in Dibdin's *The Waterman*.

Willoughby Hunter Weiss (1820–67) was considered to be second only to Joseph Staudigl (1807–61) as an interpreter of the name-part in *Elijah*. He first sang at Three Choirs in 1844(G) where an eighteen-year-old soprano from Gloucester, Georgina Ansell Barrett (1826–80), was making her début. Weiss and Barrett became man and wife, frequently sharing the concert platform until her last Festival appearance in 1864(H).

In 1859 Weiss came into collision with the Gloucester Stewards as a result of a bungle by John Amott who had engaged Giovanni Belletti to share the bass parts with Weiss. In accepting his engagement, Weiss wrote to Amott on 28 June making the condition that there should be a fair arrangement of the music between Belletti and himself. On 9 July he wrote again saying: 'I hope I shall have the Elijah'. Unfortunately, Belletti had insisted that he would only appear 'on the understanding that he would not be called upon to learn music or English words with which he was not already perfectly acquainted'.[34] As Belletti *was* acquainted with *Elijah*, Amott gave the part of the prophet to him. The fat was in the fire; the Festival Committee received a spiky letter from Weiss:

> . . . the terms on which I accepted the Engagement at your Festival, have not been complied with, and any person conversant with musical matters will, I feel convinced, agree that I have not been fairly dealt with – and that in justice to my own professional reputation I cannot do otherwise than refuse to go into the Engagement with the music allotted to me, which certainly is not that of first principal Bass, for which I expressly stipulated.

Gloucester had to manage without Weiss in 1859 but he sang at the next five Festivals and again for the last time, magnificent as 'Elijah', at Hereford in 1867, the year of his death at the age of forty-seven. W.H. Weiss is still remembered as a writer of lyrics and composer of ballads, the best known of which is *The Village Blacksmith*.

A Gloucestershire man who built a successful international career, the baritone Robert Watkin-Mills was born in Painswick on 5 March 1856, studied in London and Milan, and made his first public appearance at a Crystal Palace concert in 1884. He was back in Gloucester for the Festival of 1886 and appeared frequently as a Three Choirs principal soloist until 1906(H). Watkin-Mills finally settled in Toronto where he died in 1930.

But the greatest British baritone of the latter half of the nineteenth century was Sir Charles Santley (1834–1922). Trained by Gaetano Nava in Milan and by Manuel Garcia in London, his career spanned the five decades from 1857. Enormously successful as an opera-singer, Santley sang the role of Valentine in the first performance (in Italian) of Gounod's *Faust* in England at Her Majesty's Theatre on 11 June 1863.

Following this success, Santley was engaged for Three Choirs and became the principal bass soloist at all the major festivals until the beginning of the twentieth century. In January 1864 he again sang Valentine at Her Majesty's Theatre in an English version of *Faust* prepared by Henry Chorley. Gounod composed a new aria especially for Santley, 'Even bravest heart may swell', and this was destined to become one of the most popular numbers in the opera. However, after 1877 he was heard only in concerts and oratorios – and at the start of the new century in a medium which would make his voice immortal: the gramophone.

There can be no doubt that throughout the nineteenth century, audiences had been attracted to Three Choirs chiefly by the appearance at the Festival of star-artists. The double-cast system, coupled to the enormous fees of soloists, had regularly plunged the Festival into deficit, generously underwritten by the hard-pressed and sometimes reluctant Stewards. The cost of engaging principal singers in three typical years is of interest: 1865(G) – £1,058; 1866(W) – £1,220; 1867(H) – £1,208. Under pressure from the Stewards, the Festival conductors made periodic attempts to economize: at Gloucester in 1871, S.S. Wesley engaged neither Sims Reeves nor Santley – to the disappointment of public and critics alike. Even so, the fees of the principal singers during the three days of the Festival amounted to £915, the equivalent of some £20,000 in real terms today.

As the nineteenth century drew to a close so too did the provincial clamour for international star singers. 'Taste and education in music were developing with such rapid strides, that Festival Committees had to realize that the chief attraction was the music itself.'[35] The gramophone played an important part in developing taste and education in music. The demand for miscellaneous concerts of operatic arias, ballads, humorous songs and instrumental pieces, already fading out of fashion by mid-century, declined further as the public were enabled to listen to their favourite artists on records at home. The opera star who also sang in *Messiah* and *Elijah* gave way to the specialist oratorio singer – the path chosen by Charles Santley in 1877. And in the year in which Santley was knighted, 1907, the first sod of earth on the site of the future Gramophone Company[36] factory at Hayes, Middlesex, was cut by a famous tenor whose career had begun at the Three Choirs Festival of 1871: Edward Lloyd.

Notes

1. MW 1847, p. 616
2. *Annals* 1895, footnote p. 63
3. Ibid.
4. MT 1901, p. 585
5. See illustration of Malibran's caricature of William Mutlow.
6. MT 1901, p. 586
7. *Gloucester Journal*, 26 September 1829. The 'Rampataplan' was Malibran's own composition – her 'Rataplan'.
8. MW 1850, p. 593
9. MW 1842, p. 308
10. MW 1847, p. 629
11. MW 1855, p. 544
12. MW 1848, pp. 567–8
13. Gloucester Festival Minute Book, 1862
14. MW 1867, p. 576
15. Ibid., p. 592
16. MW 1860, p. 587
17. Gloucester Festival Minute Book, 1877
18. Albani's real name was Marie Louise Cecile Lajeunesse. She later married Gye, after which she was known as Madam Albani-Gye.
19. Gloucester Festival Minute Book, 1877
20. *The Times*, 4 September 1877
21. H.C. Colles, *Walford Davies* (London, 1942), p. 73
22. *Annals* 1895, p. 289
23. I am indebted to Mr Brian Frith for this information.
24. See Watkins Shaw, p. 79
25. MW 1850, p. 617
27. *Worcester Herald*, 30 August 1851
28. *Annals* 1895, p. 79
29. MW 1854, p. 610
30. *Annals* 1895, p. 101
31. MW 1836, p. 56
32. Father of Sir Hubert Parry.
33. Gloucester Festival Minute Book, 1859
34. Ibid.
35. Sir Herbert Brewer, *Memories of Choirs and Cloisters*, ch. VIII, p. 91
36. Makers of *His Master's Voice* gramophone records; now EMI Records Ltd.

CHAPTER EIGHT

FAVOURITES AND FLOPS

hroughout the eighteenth century the music of Handel had dominated Three
Choirs and, supreme among all his works, *Messiah* remained safely anchored to
the Festivals for the whole of the nineteenth and much of the twentieth centuries.
It was a brave S.S. Wesley who, in his first Festival as conductor at Hereford (1834),
dared to present only a *Selection from Messiah* instead of the whole work – an experiment
which he was not allowed to repeat. However, the Handelian domination did slowly
subside as successive Festival conductors, by patient persistence, gradually stimulated
the appetites of their provincial audiences to accept a more varied oratorio diet. The
turning point came in 1800(W).

Joseph Haydn (1732–1809) had attended the Handel Festival at Westminster Abbey
in 1791. The experience had an enormous effect upon him. After one performance of
Messiah he said of Handel: 'He is the master of us all' and, as a result of this Festival,
began to consider the possibility of composing an oratorio of his own. Haydn completed
The Creation in 1798. The work occupied him for two whole years, of which time he
said, 'Never before was I so devout as when I composed *The Creation*. I knelt down each
day to pray to God to give me strength for my work'; and when urged to bring it to a
conclusion, he calmly replied, 'I spend much time over it, because I intend it to last a
long time.'

The Creation was published in 1800, performed in London in March and heard for only
the third time in England at the Worcester Music Meeting of that year. The
individuality of Haydn's genius was not at first fully understood by Three Choirs
audiences nurtured on the style of Handel, but selections from *The Creation* became ever
more popular as the century progressed.

There was less of individuality or genius in the oratorio *Palestine* by Dr William
Crotch (1775–1847) and yet the work was in great demand for a short time. Extracts
from it were given in 1827(W) and 1833(W). Following a complete performance in
1839(W), *The Musical World* even went so far as to describe it as 'the best specimen of
oratorio writing in this country'.[1] When it was repeated in 1840(H) the same journal
acknowledged that *Palestine* contained much that was plagiarized Handel, and adjusted
its earlier assessment: 'it is the oddest mixture of great talent and servile, drivelling

imitation that can be conceived'.[2] Following Crotch's death in 1847, a poorly attended performance of the work was given in a final salute at the Worcester Festival of 1848. As far as Three Choirs was concerned, the oratorio died with its composer.

Even more rapid obscurity awaited Neukomm's *Mount Sinai* (extracts 1832(G)) and Schneider's *The Deluge* (extracts 1833(W)), neither of which survived to a second Three Choirs performance. The same fate befell two oratorios by Dr John Clarke-Whitfeld, the Hereford organist, and presented under his own direction: *The Crucifixion* (1822(H)) and *The Resurrection* (1825(H)). The ever-outspoken critic of *The Musical World* was cruel enough to describe a piece by Clarke-Whitfeld as 'grave though sapless twaddle'[3], and it is inconceivable that modern listeners will ever be given the opportunity to judge for themselves.

At the Music Meeting of 1832(G), John Amott introduced not only the ill-fated *Mount Sinai* but also Mozart's *Requiem* and extracts from the best-known oratorio of Louis Spohr (1784–1859), *The Last Judgement*. Other choral works by Spohr were taken up by Three Choirs: *The Fall of Babylon* (1846(H)), *Calvary* (1849(H)) and *The Christian's Prayer* (1855(H)), each of which received a handful of performances in succeeding years but failed to achieve the sensational success of *The Last Judgement* which was demanded time and again until 1901.

Now almost completely forgotten and ignored, in its day *The Last Judgement* was considered to be 'the mighty conception of a master-mind'.[4] Composed by Spohr in 1825, it was first performed in this country at the Norwich Festival of 1830 when, as in a full performance at the Worcester Festival of 1836, the bass solos were sung by Edward Taylor, who was also responsible for preparing the English adaptation of the original German libretto (*Die letzten Dinge*). It was Taylor who adapted Mozart's *Requiem* under the title of *Redemption* for the controversial performance in English at Worcester in 1836.

Sir Herbert Brewer recalled an incident at one of the Three Choirs Festivals when a Steward gently informed a lady that she was occupying the wrong seat. With indignation she replied: 'I sat in this seat for *The Creation* and I intend to remain here for *The Last Judgement*'![5]

In the first half of the century Beethoven's *Mount of Olives* (1842(W)) and Mass in C (1847(G)) were introduced to Three Choirs, both with altered titles, *Engedi* and Service in C, and 'protestantized'. But the coming man was Felix Mendelssohn (1809–47) whose oratorio *St Paul* (1837(H)) and the sinfonia-cantata *Hymn of Praise* (1841(G)) became immediate Festival favourites. His next choral work proved to be the most popular of all – a masterpiece which marched in step with *Messiah* at all but two of the Festivals between 1847 and 1929, was programmed many times thereafter and remains a firm favourite to the present day. In the spring of 1846 Mendelssohn wrote to Jenny Lind about his new oratorio: 'I am jumping about my room for joy! If it only turns out half as good as I fancy it is how pleased I shall be!'

Mendelssohn's *Elijah* was given a triumphant first performance at the Birmingham Festival on 26 August 1846 under the direction of the composer. Its repetition at the Gloucester Festival of 1847 was sufficient incentive to bring the correspondent of *The Musical World* hastening back from his first-ever assignment in 'the ancient, celebrated, and never-enough-to-be-extolled city of Paris' – a city which within the year was plunged once more into revolution.

The journey from Paris to Gloucester involves a distance of between three and four hundred miles. I left Paris on Sunday morning, and (after sleeping on Sunday night at Boulogne) arrived here on Tuesday morning, in the middle of the night – to employ an Irishism – by the mail train from London. You will say that I am a great amateur of festivals to travel such a long way for the sake of assisting at one, and to leave such a city of delights as Paris for an out-of-the-way corner of the world like this very ancient and venerable city of Gloucester – and in such strong stormy weather especially. But 'business before pleasure' is an axiom from which I have so often swerved, that the novelty of sticking to it, for once in a way, amuses me. And I have not been ill repaid for my trouble, since I have listened once more to *Elijah*, the greatest masterpiece of modern music – and exceedingly well rendered, by the way. . . . The sensation produced by *Elijah* justified all that the Gloucester amateurs had anticipated. Its success, both in an artistic and pecuniary point of view, was triumphant. There was but one opinion about it. Worcester, next year, and Hereford, the year after (unless Mr Done and Mr Smith, the organists of either cathedral, be not the men for whom I take them) will imitate the example of Gloucester, and make the *Elijah* the prominent attraction of the Festival.[6]

Elijah marked the culmination of Mendelssohn's career: he died on 4 November 1847 at the age of thirty-eight, leaving unfinished a third oratorio which could well have been something beyond *Elijah*, just as *Elijah* had been something beyond *St Paul*. This was *Christus*, the fragments of which were performed in 1853(G) and 1870(H).

Contemporary music found eager audiences in Victorian Britain, and the first name among popular contemporary composers was that of Mendelssohn. For more than a generation after his death it was the genius of Mendelssohn which dominated the musical taste of this country, during which time any new oratorio fell inevitably under the shadow of *Elijah*. The *Stabat Mater* of Rossini (1792–1862) was given eight Three Choirs performances between 1849(H) and the end of the century, but his *Petite Messe Solenelle*, given in 1869(W) and 1874(G), found less favour. Sir Michael Costa's *Eli* (1856(G) and 1857(W)) and *Naaman* (1866(W)) made no lasting impression.

The most prominent British composer of the early Victorian period, also well known as pianist and conductor, was Sir William Sterndale Bennett (1816–75). A friend of Mendelssohn and Schumann, his music was strongly influenced by the former. Sterndale Bennett's popular cantata, *The May Queen*, received three performances at the Festival in secular evening concerts (1859(G), 1860(W) and 1878(W)) but his only oratorio, *The Woman of Samaria*, was not given until 1888(H). After long neglect, his music is now enjoying a limited revival, but England owes an especially important debt to Sterndale Bennett for his promotion here of the proper appreciation of Bach and other great foreign composers. He founded the Bach Society in 1849 and gave the first performance in England of Bach's *St Matthew Passion* in 1854.

Pieces by Bach had occasionally been included in Three Choirs Miscellaneous Concerts much earlier: in 1836(W) the chorale from the *St Matthew Passion* was encored – not by cheering and stamping but by a gesture from the Bishop's finger! It was the initiative of S.S. Wesley which was responsible for the introduction of the complete *St Matthew Passion* to the Festivals for the first time in 1871(G). Sadly, the performance was under-rehearsed, badly conducted and at one point broke down completely. The cathedral was barely half-filled for a programme which began at 11.30 a.m and did not finish until nearly 5.00 p.m. It included not only the Bach and the first, and last, Three Choirs performance of *Gideon* by William Cusins, but also a selection from Spohr's *Calvary* 'performed to a weary and vanishing audience'.[7]

In spite of all, the wonder of the *Passion* shone through, and William Done was successful in recommending it to the Worcester Committee for the following year. Five more years passed before the newly-appointed Charles Harford Lloyd included the *St Matthew Passion* in the Gloucester Festival programme of 1877. Two years later at Hereford, Langdon Colborne introduced the *Christmas Oratorio*, which was repeated in 1894(H) by George Robertson Sinclair and, in 1896(W), by Hugh Blair. And it was Hugh Blair who, standing in for William Done, gave the first-ever performance at Three Choirs of Bach's Mass in B minor in 1893(W). The work had been given in Leeds in 1886 and 1892, and the Leeds Choir of a hundred voices formed half the chorus at Worcester.

The bounds set by the first Three Choirs performances of the *St Matthew Passion* and Mass in B minor mark a span of more than two decades, during which innovation slowly gained pace. In 1880 *The Musical Times* was able to say of the Gloucester Festival:

> Mr C.H. Lloyd having felt his power at the Festival three years ago, when but recently appointed organist at the Cathedral, was evidently ambitious on the next occasion to present us with a work of acknowledged high interest, but one not generally known; and in choosing Beethoven's Mass in D (*Missa Solemnis*) we think he made a wise selection. The rage for novelty should not blind us to the fact of the existence of several excellent works which not only the general public, but many musicians, are entirely unacquainted with, and we therefore, in addition to Beethoven's Mass, cordially welcome Leonardo Leo's *Dixit Dominus* and Palestrina's *Stabat Mater*, not only for their intrinsic merits, but as proof that the programmes of the Three Choirs Festivals are not, as many persons tell us, always composed of works which everybody knows!'[8]

The veteran William Done sought to match Lloyd's success when planning the Worcester Festival of the following year. The Mass in D minor by Luigi Cherubini (1760–1842) had been brought to the notice of the English public at a Bach Society concert under the direction of Otto Goldschmidt in 1881. Done wasted little time in deciding to bring the Cherubini work to Worcester.

> Mr Done deserves every credit for affording us the opportunity of hearing the effect of this sublime composition in its true home – a Cathedral. Comparable only in power and grandeur to Beethoven's Mass in D, which was one of the great attractions at the last Gloucester Festival. Pedantic amateurs, who are sometimes apt to cast a slur upon these 'country meetings', may now perhaps begin to think that if they wish to hear the greatest sacred works rendered amidst the greatest sacred architectural surroundings, they must journey to one of the Three Choirs Festivals.[9]

Thirty years after the death of Mendelssohn a major choral work by a living foreign composer was once again introduced to Three Choirs. *Ein Deutsches Requiem* (*A German Requiem*) by Johannes Brahms (1833–97) received its first public performance in England in 1873 and was repeated brilliantly by Lloyd at his Gloucester Festival début in 1877, with Sophie Lowe and Charles Santley in the principal solo parts. *The Times* described the work as a 'colossus' which had been 'rendered with the greatest fluency and precision'.

The oratorios of Charles Gounod (1818–93) enjoyed some popularity at Three Choirs, particularly *The Redemption*, in its day universally acknowledged as a masterpiece, which was introduced by Charles Lee Williams in 1883(G) and repeated in 1884(W), 1885(H), 1887(W), 1892(G) and 1897(H). Williams also brought forward Gounod's *Mors et Vita* and *Messe Solenelle* to Gloucester (in 1886 and 1889) but neither work struck root, and today all memory of *The Redemption* has withered away.

Worcester celebrated in grand style at the 1884 Festival to mark the eight-hundredth anniversary of the founding of the cathedral. The full Festival orchestra and chorus took part in the Opening Service on Sunday 6 September; Monday was taken up by rehearsals, and on the Tuesday morning Gounod's *The Redemption* was accorded the position usually occupied by *Elijah*, which was deferred until the Wednesday evening. William Done repeated his success of 1881 with Cherubini's Mass in D minor in the first part of the Wednesday morning concert. But the chief interest of the Festival centred on the next day when the largest audience of the week assembled in the cathedral to hear the second performance in England of the *Stabat Mater* by Antonin Dvořák (1841–1904), conducted by the composer and with Albani, Patey, Lloyd and Santley in glorious voice.

The Musical Times awarded Dvořák's oratorio the accolade 'one of the greatest compositions of modern times' and recorded how the silent audience had been visibly moved by the performance.

At the secular concert in the Shire Hall in the evening the audience were released from all restraint when Dvořák appeared again to conduct his Symphony in D major.[10]

> On his entry into the orchestra, the applause was so overwhelming that it was many minutes before he was allowed to give the signal for commencing; a similar demonstration followed the end of each movement, and at the end of the work he received such an ovation as we trust will convince him that English people are ever ready to recognise and give welcome to, the highest representative men in art, whatever may be the country of their birth.[11]

It is unlikely that Dvořák spotted this hint of misplaced chauvinism. In any event, he returned to England five times in the next two years and in 1891 was asked by the Birmingham Festival Committee to compose a setting of John Henry Newman's poem *The Dream of Gerontius*. Instead he gave them his colourful and dramatic *Requiem Mass*, a work which was repeated at the Hereford Festival of 1894 under the direction of George Robertson Sinclair. Birmingham had to wait until 1900 for its Newman setting, and it came from a composer born no further away than Broadheath in Worcestershire and destined to become the first name in English music.

Meanwhile, the nation was content to lionize the prodigious son of a military bandmaster and 'probably the most widely popular English composer who has ever lived'.[12]

By the time he was twenty-five, Arthur Sullivan (1842–1900) was well known as a song-writer, the composer of a fine symphony (the *Irish*), and had achieved considerable success with a suite of incidental music to *The Tempest*. Collaboration with W.S. Gilbert was two years in the future and a knighthood twelve more, but already he was the respected member of a circle which included Alfred Tennyson, John Millais, George Grove, Henry Chorley, Jenny Lind and her husband Otto Goldschmidt. Sullivan's overture *In Memoriam* had been performed at the Norwich Festival of 1866 under the direction of Sir Julius Benedict, and now he was ready to strengthen his links with the major festivals – the *sine qua non* at that time for a British composer wishing to present large-scale choral works to the public.

Sullivan completed his oratorio *The Prodigal Son* in only three weeks. The biblical texts, selected by himself, were arranged by George Grove. The first performance, under the composer's baton, was given at the Worcester Festival of 1869. Otto Goldschmidt, still smarting from the failure of his *Ruth* in 1867, wrote a cautionary note to Sullivan:

> In the case of Hereford two years ago, the chorus – numbering about 160 – came from Hereford, Worcester, Gloucester, Bristol, Bradford [and] London. They had not met together until the general rehearsal [for both choir and orchestra] in the Cathedral on the Monday. Your choruses may be so well written and easy that this single hasty rehearsal is sufficient. As a rule I should say it was not. Certainly it did not prove so in my case. I had again asked for one joint rehearsal, but the answer was that it was impossible . . . Experience, however, has shown me that though the chorus may not be able to meet collectively before the Monday noon, they *can* meet after, viz. in the evening of that day . . . You will know how to profit by this friendly hint . . .[13]

Perhaps the hint was heeded – *The Musical World* review of *The Prodigal Son* tells us that 'our most rising English composer conducted his own work as he had already done at the *rehearsals*'. In any event, the work was hailed as a triumph of originality; 'the principal parts were sung to perfection by Mdlle. Tietjens, Madame Trebelli-Bettini, Messrs. Sims Reeves and Santley, the band and chorus went marvellously well, and altogether a more perfect first performance could hardly have been possible'.[14] Sullivan had passed the critical Rubicon.

The Prodigal Son was repeated at Hereford in 1870 and again, under Sullivan's baton, at Gloucester in 1889 when his overture *In Memoriam* was substituted for the National Anthem at the beginning of the programme in testimony to the memory of Thomas Gambier Parry who had died the previous year.

By 1889, with his reputation firmly built not upon the oratorios but the outstanding success of the Savoy operas, Sullivan was at the height of his fame. *The Prodigal Son* had already fallen into neglect and it had been a decade since he had conducted the only Three Choirs performance of his oratorio *The Light of the World*, a work described by Ernest Walker as having 'hardly any vitality, even to be vulgar'.[15] However, he achieved huge popular acclaim for his secular cantata *The Golden Legend*, composed for the Leeds Festival of 1886 and repeated under his own direction at the Worcester Festival of 1887 when the chorus was composed entirely of the Leeds contingent of the Festival Choir. Sullivan returned to conduct *The Golden Legend* at Hereford in 1888 – and did so with no rehearsal at all; his diary entry for 11 September 1888 reads: 'Left Paddington 12 . . . arrived Hereford 5.31 . . . Eight o'clock, conducted performance of *Golden Legend* in Shirehall – crammed house. Very good performance – only band *rough*, a lot of fossils amongst them.'[16] *The Golden Legend* was performed at Three Choirs for the last time in 1898(G) when the conductor was Herbert Brewer.

Posterity has decreed that Sullivan will be remembered above all for his light operas, but there were many other British composers of the late Victorian period whose contributions to the corpus of oratorio- and cantata-writing lie forgotten under the dust of more than a century and whose names are barely remembered at all. The following list covers the years from 1869 to 1895; works performed at secular concerts are distinguished by (s).

| 1869 | Sullivan | *Prodigal Son* (repeated 1870 and 1889) |
| 1870 | Barnby | *Rebekah* |

1871	Cusins	*Gideon*
1873	Ouseley	*Hagar*
1876	Barnett	*Raising of Lazarus*
1878	Armes	*Hezekiah*
1879	Sullivan	*The Light of the World*
1880	Holmes	*Christmas Day*
	Parry	*Prometheus Unbound* (s)
1881	Caldicott	*Widow of Nain*
	Mackenzie	*The Bride* (s)
	Barnett	*Building of the Ship* (s)
1882	Garrett	*The Shunammite*
	A.M. Smith	*Ode to the Passions* (s)
1883	Stainer	*St Mary Magdalene*
		(repeated 1891)
	Arnold	*Sennacherib*
	Lloyd	*Allen-a-Dale* (s)
	Parry	*The glories of our blood and state* (s)
1884	Lloyd	*Hero and Leander* (s)
1885	J. Smith	*St Kevin* (s)
	Lloyd	*Song of Balder* (s)
1886	Rockstro	*The Good Shepherd*
	Lloyd	*Andromeda* (s)
	Cowen	*Sleeping Beauty* (s)
1887	Cowen	*Ruth*
	Sullivan	*The Golden Legend* (s)
		(repeated 1888, 1889 and 1898)
	Stanford	*The Revenge* (s)
1888	Bennett	*Woman of Samaria*
	Colborne	*Samuel*
	Cowen	*Song of Thanksgiving*
	Parry	*Blest Pair of Sirens*
1889	Parry	*Judith*
	Lee Williams	*Last Night at Bethany*
		(repeated 1890)
	Mackenzie	*Dream of Jubal* (s)
	Ellicott	*Elysium* (s)
1890	Bridge	*Repentance of Nineveh*
	Parry	*Ode to St Cecilia* (s)
1891	Edwards	*Praise to the Holiest*
	Lloyd	*Song of Judgement*
	Parry	*De Profundis*
	Stanford	*Battle of the Baltic* (s)
	Sullivan	*Te Deum*
1892	Bridge	*The Lord's Prayer*
	Lee Williams	*Gethsemane*
	Parry	*Job*
		(repeated 1893 and 1894)

1894	Bridge	*Cradle of Christ*
	Mackenzie	*Bethlehem*
	Lloyd	*Ballad of Sir Ogie and the Lady Elsie* (s)
1895	Parry	*King Saul*
	Cowen	*The Transfiguration*
	Lee Williams	*Dedication*

Of all these works, only Parry's *Blest Pair of Sirens* is heard with any regularity today.

In the main, the volume of compositions resulted from the demand each year to include one or more 'novelties' in the Three Choirs programmes – and after 1880 that demand was fuelled by a clearly increasing rivalry between the three cathedral cities to attract the first names in contemporary music to compose substantial pieces specifically for the Festivals. One example will suffice: Sir Frederick Cowen (1852–1935), a West Indian by birth, was celebrated as both composer and conductor and was knighted in 1911. His Symphony No. 3 (the *Scandinavian*), composed in 1880, had been hailed by *The Times* as 'the most important English symphony for years'; his operas, orchestral pieces and many songs were filled with delightful melodies of the lighter kind. The announcement that Cowen had been commissioned to write an oratorio for the 1887 Worcester Festival excited widespread interest and a great demand for tickets. In view of Goldschmidt's experience in 1867 it is perhaps surprising that Cowen, with Joseph Bennett as librettist, chose *Ruth* as the subject and title of his oratorio. Over 2,600 people packed into Worcester Cathedral to hear it, prompting *The Musical Times* to comment:

> *Ruth*, therefore, appeared in the light of a good investment on the part of the committee, and the fact may have an important influence on future policy. At the same time, we must bear in mind that composers with the special popularity of Mr. Cowen cannot be 'turned on' at any time, nor can musician and subject be always so admirably suited to each other as in the present case.[17]

Unfortunately, the libretto of *Ruth* caused eyebrows to raise, and Joseph Bennett explained why:

> The public [applied] to an innocent Bible story the rigid conventionality of the suburban mind. As it stands in the Sacred Book, the tale of Ruth and Boaz is as chaste as anything from the pen of Jane Austen, but knowing the tendency of nice people towards ideas which are the reverse, I made slight changes to humour their nicety. But they took their old stand – that is to say, they would have an Eastern tale only after it had been brought as far as possible into conformity with the notions of their 'straitest sect.' I really could not prevent Ruth from paying a nocturnal visit to Boaz. Had I done so I should now be recording my own shame, and inditing apologies to the Bible.
>   *Ruth* was produced at a Festival of the Three Choirs, and I greatly fear that Dr Cowen's extremely beautiful dance-music in the festival scene was grievous to the 'unco guid.' I wonder why they have not called a meeting, and passed a vote of censure upon King David for dancing before the Lord in Gilgal.[18]

Cowen was not writing in his most comfortable *métier*; he regarded himself primarily as a symphonist. His best works have not survived the eclipse of Victorian musical taste and, unlike Sullivan, he found no collaborator of the genius of W.S. Gilbert to whose words he could wed his melodic gift.

Not all the 'novelties' presented at Three Choirs were even so well received as those by Sullivan and Cowen; there was much which was banal. Commenting on the 'musical platitudes' in Rockstro's *The Good Shepherd*[19] the reviewer of *The Musical Times* asked why the composer was 'permitted to arrest our attention when greater men are waiting for a hearing?'[20] But at least new British works were being heard in increasing numbers. It *was* possible for a newly-appointed cathedral organist like Charles Lee Williams to make his début as a Festival composer in 1889 before an immense audience with his cantata *Last Night in Bethany*, to have it performed by the leading soloists and finest choral singers of the day, and to have the satisfaction of knowing that the piece was booked for performance in several places as an immediate result of its Three Choirs success. This was in startling contrast to the lack of adventure in Festival programmes at the beginning of the century; and even if much of this music did little more than give devotional sentiment to words culled from a multitude of biblical texts, a chance was given for much rarer gold to shine through.

As a direct result of that more adventurous spirit the 'greater men' eventually found an audience and modern English music was born. Even so, the first precious glimmerings were not discovered in a packed cathedral but in the far less auspicious surroundings of a secular concert in the Gloucester Shire Hall.

Notes

1. MW 1839, p. 326
2. MW 1840, p. 203
3. Ibid., re the spirit scene from Charles Whitfeld's *The Lay of the Last Minstrel*.
4. *Gloucester Journal*, September 1835
5. Brewer, *Memories of Choirs and Cloisters* (London, 1931)
6. MW 1847, pp. 614–29
7. *Annals* 1895, p. 250
8. MT 1880, p. 498
9. MT 1881, p. 511
10. Originally published as his first symphony, the D major opus 60 was, in fact, Dvořák's sixth.
11. MT 1884, p. 584
12. Ernest Walker, *A History of Music in England*, 2nd edn (Oxford, 1924)
13. Arthur Jacobs, *Arthur Sullivan, A Victorian Musician* (Oxford, 1984)
14. MW 1869, p. 641
15. Ernest Walker, *A History of Music in England*, 2nd edn (Oxford, 1924)
16. Arthur Jacobs, op. cit.
17. MT 1887, p. 601
18. Joseph Bennett, *Forty Years of Music, 1865–1905* (London, 1908)
19. William Rockstro (originally Rackstraw) (1823–95)
20. MT 1886, p. 592

CHAPTER NINE

SACRED AND PROFANE

'Ⓘf we seek for a definite birthday for modern English music, September 7, 1880, when *Prometheus* saw the light at Gloucester and met with a mixed reception, has undoubtedly the best claim.'[1]
With his dramatic cantata *Prometheus Unbound*, Hubert Parry (1848–1918) strode into the midst of all that was conventional and 'safe' in English choral music and unwittingly became, in the words of Herbert Howells, 'a near revolutionary'.[2] Every conceivable obstacle stood in the way of his success.

In spite of his championship of Three Choirs as a Steward over many years, Parry's father, Thomas Gambier Parry, squire at Highnam Court near Gloucester, would not tolerate music as a profession for his children and forbade his eldest son, Clinton, to pursue it. Following his education at Eton and Oxford, Hubert was obliged against his will to take up a career in insurance and to limit his musical activities to those of an amateur. His first offering to Three Choirs was an *Intermezzo Religioso* (1868(G)) which, in the judgement of the *Pall Mall Gazette* of 12 September 1868, 'in no way belied its amateur origin'. In 1877, following seven years at Lloyds Register of Shipping which ended in financial disaster, he was at last able to take up music as his chosen profession. Meanwhile, in 1873, he had begun regular lessons with the concert pianist Edward Dannreuther who introduced Parry to the music of Wagner and provided him with free tickets to visit Bayreuth for the first performance of *The Ring* there in 1876.

Parry returned from Bayreuth aglow with inspiration; but many of the English critics were scathing about the 'so-called Prophet of the Future, Richard Wagner'.[3] Except for Dannreuther, Parry's friends pilloried him for turning towards 'the music of the future' in his own composition. By this time he had also further alienated himself from his father and contemporary society by renouncing Christian doctrine. Even so, uncomfortable isolation was no deterrent from his boldness in choosing to set scenes from Shelley's epic poem for his first major choral work. Alas, the performance was under-rehearsed and quite beyond the bass soloist, a Mr Francis, who sang the title role:

> The chorus of 250 voices, selected from Worcester, Hereford, London, Huddersfield, Oxford, Bristol, and other towns, as well as with the Gloucester choir, was, together with the already practised band, kept at rehearsal yesterday [Monday, the day before the concert] from ten in the morning till five in the afternoon, and again from half-past seven in the evening until past midnight. As a matter of course the 'three choirs' assembled for cathedral service this morning [Tuesday]; but independent of this duty, there was a return to the previous night's work of rehearsal solely on account of Mr. Hubert Parry's work.[4]

In low spirits following the late-night rehearsal and unaware that the chorus, on the initiative of the Huddersfield contingent, would volunteer to rehearse again the next day, Parry wrote in his diary for Monday 6 September 1880:

> Rehearsal of *Prometheus* in the evening which was literally agonizing. Not time to do much more than go through it. Everything at sixes and sevens and chorus literally bewildered. Everybody tired with rehearsing other things all day, and general misery all round.[5]

On top of this, Parry was depressed about his difficulty in finding a publisher for the work.

The secular concert in which *Prometheus Unbound* was performed began with Beethoven's overture to *Fidelio*, followed by four arias by Mozart, Gluck and Gounod before Parry's piece was heard. After the interval, an over-long evening continued with a Mozart symphony, several arias, and Gounod's Jupiter Festival March from *Polyeucte* for orchestra and choir.

> A generous welcome was accorded to Mr. Parry on his taking the conductor's place. Any pleasure which his work may have afforded was not demonstrated with enthusiasm. That the second part of the concert was a very late affair needs hardly to be said . . . the most extremely adverse judgements do not deny the composer a strength which he may apply at will, and which, if applied with less inveterate determination to out-Wagner Wagner, would no doubt be capable of greater, if not of more elaborately artificial, work than this most ambitious essay.[6]

Players, singers and audience were all weary; the parts were peppered with mistakes and difficult to read in the dim gaslight; but thanks to the Huddersfield Chorus and the magnificent singing of Edward Lloyd, the performance held together and, at the end, Parry was called forward and loudly applauded. The critics took up positions which ranged from the generously defensive to the pointedly hostile. But nearly forty years later Sir Henry Hadow remembered the significance of 7 September 1880; 'No-one seems to have had any idea that, on that evening in the Shirehall, English music had, after many years, come again into its own and that it had come with a master-piece in its hands.'[7]

Parry's biographer, Dr Jeremy Dibble, has re-assessed that significance:

> There can be little doubt that *Prometheus Unbound* excited many scholars and critics (including Bernard Shaw) because, in embracing, at least in part, Wagnerian techniques of declamation and leitmotif, Parry's cantata automatically set itself apart from other contemporary English works in the same idiom. The association, however, of the revolutionary vision and intellect of the atheist Shelley and Parry's apparent literary audacity has tended to overemphasise the work's true musical quality. In fact, along with the extraordinary juxtaposition of Wagner and Brahms, one is also aware of some areas that are entirely indebted to the traditionally conservative Handelian and Mendelssohnian conditioning of his early musical training. The work suffers from stylistic inconsistency and suggests more readily someone with an admirable technical proficiency, but with as yet insufficient conviction. Moreover, with its obvious eclecticism, *Prometheus* bears all the symptoms of immaturity, experiment, and the uncertainty of a composer who had not yet found himself.'[8]

Whatever the musical quality of *Prometheus Unbound*, it is certain that so powerful an expression of humanitarian ideology would not have been granted admission to a cathedral. If Gloucester *can* lay claim to the birth of modern English music, no matter how immature the work, then the essential condition of the delivery of that birth, and the single advantage available to Parry, was the existence of the Three Choirs secular concerts.

The hugely-popular secular evening concerts were given splendid new venues in the nineteenth century when Shire Halls were built in each of the Three Choirs cities. The one at Gloucester, designed in the Greek Revival style by Robert Smirke, architect of the British Museum, was constructed between 1814 and 1816. The secular concerts were transferred there from the old Booth Hall in 1817 when, on the second evening of the Music Meeting, upwards of 1,400 tickets were sold. The exterior of the building, with its four heavy, unfluted Ionic columns, is most impressive. Unfortunately, the interior of the Grand Hall, approached via a staircase rising from the vestibule, was not ideal for concerts: the acoustic was dry, and the organ occupied too large a space in the centre of the platform to allow a satisfactory arrangement of the chorus and orchestra. (In 1910 Sir Hubert Parry donated £1,500 towards the cost of improving the hall, his wishes being that the platform should be reconstructed, side seats removed, and a gallery erected facing the platform. This was done, and at Herbert Brewer's suggestion, the organ was moved, rebuilt and bracketed on the wall.[9])

Robert Smirke was again engaged to design the Shire Hall in Hereford which was built, immediately following completion of the Gloucester Shire Hall, between 1817 and 1819. This time Smirke gave the façade a noble portico of eight pillars in Doric style imitation of the temple of Theseus at Athens. The Three Choirs secular concerts moved to the Shire Hall from the Hereford Music Room in 1819 but again, as at Gloucester, there were shortcomings in the hall's usefulness as a concert venue. Various improvement schemes were put forward during the nineteenth century: the question of alterations arose as early as 1846, strenuously advocated by George Townshend Smith. By 1854 a definite scheme was drawn up, which then lapsed owing to lack of funds but was revived and successfully carried out in 1862, in good time for the Hereford Festival of 1864.

Since the Festival of 1861 important changes and modifications have been made in the large room in the Shire Hall. The space formerly given to the orchestra is now absorbed by the auditorium; while a new orchestra, occupying a recess under an arched roof, exactly opposite the portico, or great entrance, and fitted up alike with taste and simplicity, is an object as grateful as the former one was ungrateful to the eye. Besides this, the old raised benches are discarded, which not only enlarges the accommodation but imparts freedom and boldness to the general appearance of the area. The acoustic properties of the building are wonderfully improved by the alterations, and the Hereford people may now lay claim to the possession of a room for their festival and evening concerts, balls and other such entertainments far superior to the Shire Hall at Gloucester, and at least equal to College Hall at Worcester.[10]

The Shire Hall at Worcester was built between 1834 and 1835 to a design by Charles Day, the County Architect, who chose to emulate the Greek Revival style favoured by Smirke and faced his building with a portico of six fluted Ionic columns. Worcester's secular concerts remained at the College Hall for almost half a century more until a fine organ by Nicholson was installed in the Shire Hall. The change was made in 1884 in time for Dvořák's visit to Worcester; but surprisingly, with an ideal instrument available, no organ works were included in the secular concert programmes for that year.

The secular evening concerts, which had become such a popular feature of the eighteenth-century Music Meetings, continued regularly to be three in number until

1870. The balls which followed these concerts were gradually reduced to one only on the last night until, as part of the 'call to seriousness', they were dropped altogether in 1874(G).

> People whose judgement is not warped by excessive religious sentiment have often gravely shaken their heads at the Ball. Why? Is dancing sinful *per se*? . . . But a chorus arises on all hands protesting that to dance in the evening, after hearing *Messiah* in the morning, is 'improper'. At what time is it proper then? Has anybody, armed with a gauge of propriety, investigated the subject, and ascertained exactly how many minutes after the 'Amen' chorus one may, without sin, stand up for a quadrille?[11]

The programme of the secular concerts contained a mixture of lightweight frivolities, glees, songs, assorted arias, overtures and instrumental showpieces; but gradually classic works of substance began to appear. Beethoven's Symphony No. 1 in C and the overtures *Prometheus* and *Egmont* were heard at Three Choirs in the composer's lifetime, and by 1853 all of his first eight symphonies had been performed. A limited selection of the symphonies of Haydn and Mozart were played, and the overture to *The Magic Flute*, first heard in 1807(H), became a popular favourite, as did Cherubini's overture, *Anacreon*. Of Schubert there was nothing. Vivaldi was all but forgotten.

Typical of these programmes before mid-century is that for the first secular concert in Gloucester in 1841:

Part I

Overture: *Anacreon*	Cherubini
Prize Ballad 1841 (Mr Hobbs)	Hobbs
Glee, 'Blow gentle gales', The Slave	Bishop
Air: *Robert le Diable* (Madame Dorus Gras)	Meyerbeer
Aria: 'Lord remember David' (Signor Brizzi)	Handel
Duetto: *Il Fanatico per la Musica* (Madame Viardot Garcia and Signor Tamburini)	Fioravanti
Solo, Violoncello (Mr Lindley)	Lindley
Ballad: 'I feel that thou art changed' (Miss Marshall)	Balfe
Duetto: 'Vanne se alberglie' (Mesdames Dorus Gras and Viardot Garcia)	Mercadante
Song: 'The Sailor's Journal' (Mr H. Phillips)	Dibdin
Preghiera: *Mose in Egitto*	Rossini

Part II

Symphony No. 8[12]	Haydn
Ballad: 'I'll speak of thee' (Miss M.B. Hawes)	Hawes
Terzetto: 'Tremati, empi tremati' (Miss Birch, Signori Brizzi and Tamburini)	Beethoven
Finale: *La Cenerentola* (Madame Viardot Garcia)	Rossini
Aria: 'Cruda funesta smagnia' (Signor Tamburini)	Rossini

Ballad: 'Auld Robin Gray' (Miss Birch)	trad.
Duetto: *Le Nozze di Darina* (Madame Viardot Garcia and Signor Tamburini)	Mosca
Ballad: 'The three Ages of Love' (Mr J. Bennett)	E.J. Loder
Glee: 'The Chough and Crow' (Guy Mannering)	Bishop

London critics visiting the provinces found these programmes extremely tiresome. Even so eminent a musician as Robert Lindley (1777–1855), the leading cellist of his day, could become a target for their barbs when playing in such an indiscriminate setting:

> Mr Lindley, by courtesy 'the veteran', seems determined always to remind us how very long he has been the sole supreme, the great arch-violoncellist; for it is only to such archness that we can attribute his invariably choosing for his solos such antediluvian twaddle, as must have sounded old-fashioned and common-place to our mothers' grandmothers: of course he *delighted* his audience tonight.[13]

But if the concert itself lacked interest, at least the unrestrained chattering of 'the élite, the wealth and the beauty of the three counties' could provide a source of innocent merriment; in this case at a concert in 1837:

> On Wednesday evening, the hall was exceedingly full, the attendants anticipating, if not a delightful concert, a *most* delightful dance; and this was evidently expressed upon numerous countenances during the former parts of the two last evenings' entertainment. Very shortly, therefore, after the commencement, endurance rather than enjoyment of the music began to be manifest. The Jupiter Symphony, excellently played, was scarcely noticed. Seeing at once how the game was likely to go, we amused ourselves with minuting down the remarks made around us upon the several pieces as they went off. First, on Hobbs' ballad, 'Oh, weep not mother.' – 'Ah, very pretty, but *very* long.' (Critique by a gentleman in jappaned pumps.) Rondo from La Cenerentola, 'Non piu mesta,' by Mme. Albertazzi. – 'The sweetest thing she has sung. That's the length now I like for a song.' (Gentleman, in an uncorrugated cravat.) Glee, 'With sighs sweet rose,' Calcott. – 'Sweet thing, if I could have heard Mr. Hunt. Sung *rather too slow*.' (The gentleman in pumps.) Lindley's violoncello concerto. – 'Very wonderful fiddling; but it was all so up and down – and *very long*.' (A flower-girl; at least a girl with flowers – in her hair.) 'Machin always chooses such long songs. That 'Pirate crew' will never be over.' (Flower-girl aforesaid.) Ballad, Mrs. Knyvett, 'The auld wife,' Greisbach. – 'Sweet thing; but too many verses. I applaud because it's over.' (A dancing gentleman.) Quartett from the Puritani, 'A te, o cara.' – 'Sweet thing indeed. Havn't [*sic*] they nearly done?' (Ditto.) 'Bonnie Prince Charlie,' Miss Clara Novello – 'Dear – that's a sweet thing indeed. We must have that again. But O la! there are two pages more to come.' (The flower-girl.) Overture, Euryanthe. – 'Well, now that long thing's over, we have a chance.' Cavatina, Miss Woodyatt, 'Il braccio mio,' Nicolini. – 'Charming voice! Belongs to Hereford. Sweet thing! Oh, she's not done yet. – There, now that's done.' Song, 'Invocation to Spring,' Mr Phillips. – Oh Lord, are they going to have that again? It's quite ridiculous.' Ballad, Miss Hawes, 'The mermaid's cave,' Horn. – 'Sweet thing! Oh, no! no!! no!!! we can-*not* have that again.' Grand Septuor, (Beethoven), Blagrove, Moralt, Williams, Platt, Denman, Lindley, and Anfossi. – 'Very hot, ain't it? I wish those good people thought so. How they do go on! Look, how he is blowing with the horn. Why, we had a long overture before.' Glee, Mrs. Knyvett, Messrs. Hunt, Hobbs and Machin, 'Sweet thrush,' Danby. – 'Dear, dear! a thing with four verses at this time o'night!' Duet, Mme. Albertazzi and Miss Clara Novello, 'Deh con te.' – 'I could almost give up dancing, to hear that girl's voice. Bravo, bravo! No, no! not again – go on.' Serenade, Mr. Bennett, 'Look, forth, my fairest,' Balfe. – 'Six verses at *any* time are a bore – but NOW, twenty minutes after eleven!' Finale, Clemenza di Tito, 'Tu, e ver.' – 'Well! *at* last. Very fine! Bravo! bravo!! Now then for clearing away the benches. Sweet music, but too much of it. A devil of a bore; though I am partial to music. But dancing is more merry like.'[14]

At which point Mr Adams and his celebrated Quadrille Band took their places on the platform.

The orchestral items with which each part of these concerts opened were frequently drowned out in the hubbub, augmented by the voices of the helpful but noisy Stewards, as members of the audience searched for their seats. Applause between the movements of a work was expected. The benches were uncomfortable; the lighting and ventilation poor; and the halls frequently packed to suffocation, with many people standing.

At Worcester in 1848 a crowd of 1,100 attended a concert in which Alboni, Castellan, Sims Reeves and Lablache were singing. So great was the crush that the doors of the College Hall had to be removed.[15] And in 1860 upwards of 300 people were turned away when not even standing room was available.

A further problem arose in the late 1850s due to the prevailing fashion for ladies to 'make broad the borders of their garments'. The College Hall at Worcester could normally hold about 900 people (600 in the body of the room and 300 in the gallery) but the wearing of crinoline dresses meant that over 100 seats at half a guinea each were lost at each concert:

> Perhaps when the present fashion is discarded (it cannot last for ever, that's one consolation), and ladies return to the straight and limp costume of their grandmammas . . . the 'consummation devoutly to be wished' may be accomplished.[16]

It is impossible to avoid the impression that until the latter part of the nineteenth century the secular concerts were as much, if not more, occasions for society display as well as for musical appreciation. Rarely was this so evident as at Worcester in 1857: the second evening concert was particularly well attended because it was known that the Duke of Cambridge would be present. He had not arrived by the time the concert started with a selection from Weber's *Der Freischütz*. Indeed, several numbers had already been performed and Madame Weiss, wife of the bass W.H. Weiss, was in the middle of singing Agatha's lovely Act III cavatina 'And though a cloud the sun obscure' when the duke entered the hall. The music immediately stopped; the National Anthem was played, with Clara Novello and John Sims Reeves joining in as soloists; the audience applauded loudly; and, after all that, Mme Weiss was obliged to resume the abandoned aria from the beginning.

By mid-century these pot-pourris were in any case becoming less popular, and it was George Townshend Smith at Hereford who laid the foundations for a more serious form of secular music-making. In 1861 he introduced an extra event on the fourth evening of the Festival: a Chamber Concert at the College Hall. His programme for the first of these included Mozart's Quartet in D minor, Mendelssohn's Quartet with Canzonet Op. 12, and the second movement of Beethoven's Septet; the soloists were Messrs H. Blagrove, Clementi, R. Blagrove, G. Collins, Blakestone, Williams (clarinet), Mann (horn) and Woetzig (bassoon). These pieces were interspersed with arias and duets by Buononcini, Haydn and Spohr, sung by Madame and Mr Weiss.

This recital was so well received that at the next Hereford Festival, in 1864, Townshend Smith repeated the experiment and presented a programme which included Mozart's Quartet in G, Beethoven's Quartet in A and a Quintet in D by George Onslow.

The Hereford Chamber Concerts continued for many years, following the pattern of a series of Monday Popular Concerts which Arthur Chappell had successfully organized at the St James's Hall in London, but they were not taken up by Gloucester or Worcester.

The arrival of S.S. Wesley at Gloucester in time for the Festival of 1865 heralded a significant change in the content of the secular concert programmes. Mendelssohn's incidental music to *A Midsummer Night's Dream* had been popular at Three Choirs for thirty years and *The First Walpurgis Night* for twenty: Townshend Smith had conducted the 'Italian' Symphony in 1861. But Wesley, in his first Gloucester Festival programmes, included Mendelssohn's Piano Concerto No. 1 in G minor and Beethoven's Choral Fantasia in C minor, both with Arabella Goddard as soloist, thus beginning the trend away from the performance of unsatisfactory miscellanies and towards that of an increasing number of complete works from more or less classical masters, along with carefully selected shorter items.

As the century progressed, this same trend was to be seen in a gradual departure from the practice of devoting one day of the festival to 'A Grand Selection of Sacred Music' in the cathedral. As in the evening concerts, these performances had comprised an over-long and unrelated mixture of overtures, airs and choruses, but extracted from popular sacred, rather than secular, pieces. Although the works of Handel had dominated these selections in the early years of the century (in 1816(H) for instance, of twenty-one items performed all but three were by Handel) it eventually became possible for a greater but hardly more satisfactory variety to be chanced.

William Mutlow at his last Music Meeting in 1829(G) went so far as to present the following seemingly interminable programme on the second morning:

Part I

Opening Movement	Te Deum	Graun
Recit. and Air	'What, tho' I trace'	Handel
Duett	'Qual Anelante'	Marcello
Quartett	'For this God'	Marcello and Knyvett
Recits. and Airs	'O liberty' 'From mighty kings' 'Shall I in Mamre's'	Handel
Chorus	'For all these mercies'	
Recit. and Air	'With verdure clad'	
Recit.	'In splendour bright'	Haydn
Chorus	'The Heavens are telling'	

Part 2

First Grand Concerto		Handel
Offertorio	'The Hymn'	Dr. Chard
Chorus	'Kyrie Eleison'	Rhigini
Air	'Agnus Dei'	Mozart

Chorus	'Rex Tremendae'	
Quartett	'Recordare'	Winter
Chorus	'Lachrymosa'	
Air	'Gratias agimus'	Guglielmi
Recit. and Air	'The snares of death'	Stevenson
Recit.	'So will'd my father'	
Trio and Chorus	'Disdainful of Danger'	Handel
Chorus	'If guiltless blood'	
Chorus	'Cum sancto Spiritu'	Mozart

Part 3

Luther's Hymn		
Air	'O magnify the Lord'	Handel
Scena	'The last man'	Callcott
Recit. and Air	'Ah! parlate'	Cimarosa
Chorus	'Glory to God'	Beethoven
Air	'O my God'	Ciampi
Quartetto	'Domine Jesu Christi'	Winter
Chorus	'The Lord shall reign'	Handel

Forty years later, in 1869(W), the Three Choirs audience on the second morning was well contented to hear Sullivan's *Prodigal Son*, extracts from Handel's *Judas Maccabaeus* and nothing more.

The Festival was of three days' duration until 1836, when Worcester added a fourth morning event (reverting to three days for the Festival of 1845 only). Gloucester followed this precedent in 1838 and Hereford in 1849. Typically, after 1847 *Elijah* would be performed on the first day (Tuesday), *Messiah* on the last, and Miscellaneous Sacred Concerts on the second and third days.

At Hereford in 1870, for a royal visit by Prince and Princess Christian, George Townshend Smith dropped the first evening secular concert altogether and replaced it with an oratorio performance in the recently gaslit cathedral. An even more important precedent, set in 1870, was the performance of a symphony for the first time in the cathedral. (As late as 1870 some clergymen were doubtful about the propriety of allowing even a Beethoven symphony to be played in a cathedral.) Townshend Smith's success may well have been due to his canniness in obtaining approval to include Mendelssohn's *Reformation* Symphony in a programme which also contained the same composer's setting of Psalm 42 and part of *Christus*.

In the year following this innovation, Canon Tinling, preaching at the Opening Service of the Gloucester Festival, pleaded for 'more reverence in the Cathedral during the oratorio performances, and a higher religious tone and character to all that takes place within the sacred walls during Festival Week'.[17] He had good reason to rebuke his listeners: a not insignificant factor in the hardening anti-Festival mood among many clergymen was the behaviour of Three Choirs audiences. It was not unusual for a large number of visitors to the cathedrals 'feeling that they had come to a concert, and consequently disregarding the nature of the building in which it took place, complacently [to] lunch during the interval, and sometimes during the performance, even occasionally hanging their hats upon the recumbent figures on the tombs within their reach, and adopting a manner which seemed to show that they had come out for a holiday and were resolved to enjoy themselves.'[18] Many of those who did not remain in the cathedral for lunch would think little of stampeding out to nearby hostelries before the end of the morning performance.

Since the Music Meetings originated through the coming together of the three cathedral choirs to sing the daily Offices, it is perhaps surprising that details of the music sung at the services, which marked the opening of each Festival in the nineteenth century, are often only briefly referred to in the *Annals*; in the account of the Festival in some years no mention is made at all. It is, however, clear that the morning services followed the form of Matins: reference is made to the singing of the responses (for a long period to the setting by Tallis) while throughout the first half of the century Handel's Dettingen *Te Deum* and Utrecht *Jubilate* continued to hold pride of place. Also included were anthems – occasionally as many as three or four – by Boyce and Handel, and later by Knyvett, Kent, Attwood, Croft and other composers of their day.

Lysons, in a footnote to the *Annals* for 1812(W), complained about the interpolation of a song from Arnold's *The Redemption* (an adaptation of music by Handel) into the Dettingen *Te Deum*:

> The extremely bad taste in allowing the song 'Holy, Holy, Holy' to be thrust into a sublime composition, already perfect in itself, amounts to an act of positive desecration, and an insult to the Divine Majesty, when the fact is declared that the original words of this beautiful air in the opera of *Rodelinda*, are those of a love song, *Dove sei, amato bene?*[19]

His objection was apparently not shared by others, the records showing that the same 'desecration' was repeated regularly until at least mid-century.[20]

It was not until mid-century that the music of J.S. Bach was heard at the services. Other so-called 'novelties' were heard later: the *Annals* for 1855(H) list no fewer than eight musical items at the Opening Service. Quite early in the century, though not regularly, an orchestral or organ overture preceded the service; for example, in 1823(G) Handel's overture to *Esther* and in 1825(H) his overture to *Saul* were performed. Tradition was broken at Gloucester when, in 1874, 'the concluding act of the Festival was a grand Chorus Service in the nave . . . on Friday evening'.[21] At Gloucester in 1853, choral Matins sung by the cathedral choirs at 8 a.m. on the second and subsequent mornings of the Festival were introduced, presaging the Choral Evensong of the modern Festival. Not only did these services remove the 'scruples of many persons who were hostile to the musical performances in the Cathedral on the ground that they interfered with the legitimate object of the sacred edifice . . . that of divine worship',[22] but they were extremely well attended by the 'humbler classes', admittance being free.

In 1876, for the first time, the Mayor of Hereford issued 'an earnest invitation . . . to his brethren at Gloucester and Worcester to come over (for the Opening Service), and thus enable the great desire of the civic bodies of each city for the continuance of the

Festivals on the old lines'.[23] We read that this invitation 'was heartily responded to'; and it is a practice which civil dignitaries, both of the three cities and of the counties, now regularly follow.

At Worcester in 1881 the Opening Service began at 3 p.m. on Sunday 3 September and took the form of Evensong instead of Matins.

> The convenience of the hour, no doubt, helped to secure the attendance of an enormous crowd for all of whom indeed the great church was far too small. On going into the cathedral close, while the bells were still chiming, I found hundreds of people standing vainly before gates closed and guarded by policemen. 'Too late, too late, ye cannot enter now.' The refrain of Tennyson's mournful song may have occurred to some of the disappointed ones as they turned away. But a reference more distinctly scriptural possibly occupied the minds of others, who, having tickets for the reserved portion, found the way narrow and the gate straight. It was only too evident from the arrangements made that the cathedral authorities have little experience in dealing with crowds. They actually constructed at the doors for ticket holders a kind of funnel, through the narrow mouth of which applicants for admission had to filter one at a time. The result was unseemly crushing and crowding, so much that when the press was over the policemen congratulated one another on the close of a 'hot job.' Still worse were the regulations for the exit of the congregation. At one of the doors attempts were made to prevent persons from leaving, not only before the offertory but after it. In this instance a particularly zealous verger had more than he could do to carry out what I am bound to assume were his instructions. If he left his post for a moment the imprisoned people began to escape, seeing which he would push rudely through the throng with anything but solemn calm on his countenance, and interpose the barrier of his body and the authority of his gown. Under these circumstances a gentleman requested permission to retire, and being refused, flung the door open by main force. The verger grappled with him, and for a few moments a struggle of the liveliest description went on, ending in the discomfiture of the official, who, however, expressed himself much consoled by reflecting that as the outer gates were locked his opponent could not get off the premises.[24]

Among the large crowds pouring into the ancient cities at Festival time were several visitors who had indeed come out for a holiday, and the expansion of the railway network by mid-century considerably increased their numbers. Of Gloucester in 1853 *The Musical World* reported that:

> We hear, upon the best authority, that there are at this moment only a few of the least desirable of the numbered tickets for the four morning performances left unsold. These places occupy about two-thirds of the whole area of the nave of the Cathedral, in which the morning performances of sacred music take place, and it is an unprecedented circumstance, that the majority of the holders of these tickets are strangers. Gloucester is peculiarly well placed for travellers, forming, as it does, an important centre of the western and south midland district, railways on both gauges meeting here. The Midland, Great Western, Gloucester and Dean Forest, and South Wales Railways meet here at one common station. At the last Gloucester Festival, in 1850, the South Wales line was not opened direct to Gloucester, a *hiatus* of twenty-seven miles having to be travelled by coach. There is, however, now a length considerably over one hundred miles of this line open – Gloucester to Carmarthen – and there can be little doubt that Taffy will avail himself of the opportunity of witnessing an English 'cwmrygeddion.' The South Wales Company, by way of encouraging the traffic, intend conveying passengers to and from Gloucester in one day for a single fare. The Midland Company also issue return tickets, available for the week; and the Great Western run special trains.[25]

In addition to local and visiting nobility, gentry and clergy who occupied the raised seats and nave, 'in the aisles were observed a strong muster of the humbler classes'.[26] And outside the cathedral on the last day, 'owing to the enormous press of individuals anxious to be present [at *Messiah*] . . . the police – whose regulations for preserving order and for avoiding collisions and mistakes, were admirably carried out — underwent no small difficulty in disposing of the equipages of the country visitors.'[27]

In 1843 Hereford Cathedral was in such a state of dilapidation that the Festival had to be held in All Saints' Church. By 1846 the nave had been sufficiently restored for the cathedral to be used again. Something of the very special atmosphere of Victorian Hereford at Three Choirs can be gathered from *The Times* of 11 September 1846:

> The town of Hereford is now, perhaps, as full of gaiety and bustle as it is possible for it to be under any circumstances. The streets are thronged — that is, thronged for Hereford, for a Hereford crowd and a London, or even a Birmingham crowd, are very different matters. Still there is little doubt that an average of two out of three of the comfortable population of 10,000 may be reckoned upon as interested, profitably or pleasurably, in the progress of the festival, which once in three years awakens the ancient city from its slumbers. And so, yesterday, a motley army of lookers-on covered the area on either side of Broad-Street, right up to the very mouth of the Cathedral, watching the more favoured children of fortune, as they entered the sacred edifice, to listen to the second morning's performance.

At the next Hereford Festival, in 1852, on the second morning came the news of the unexpected death of the Duke of Wellington:

> The solemn tolling of the Cathedral bell, which announced that England's most honoured son had quitted this world for ever, was not at first comprehended; but as soon as the cause was explained it became the theme of conversation and remark in every circle . . . at the Cathedral, before the oratorio commenced, the Dead March from Handel's *Saul* was performed in honour of the illustrious dead, the audience (the most crowded since the festival began) all standing. It was a most impressive and affecting scene. The simplicity of the music, which has so often commemorated the decease of great princes and greater soldiers; the measured blows of the drum, each, as it were, a warning to mortality; the significant expression upon every countenance, which told in unmistakable terms the deep regret of all, were not mere parts of an empty ceremony. There was nothing of show in the manifestation. It was a gratuitous and unanimous exhibition, in which the heart was prime mover, of sorrow for the loss of a great and good man, of sympathy and veneration for England's champion and the benefactor of the world.[28]

By 1855 the railway had come to Hereford by the extension of the Great Western, via Gloucester and Ross, and the completion of the Shrewsbury and Hereford Railways. As at Gloucester, the trains brought larger than ever crowds to the Festival and a marked increase in demand for accommodation in the city:

> The Herefordshire Militia, for some time quartered on the inhabitants of the town, has been ordered to Aldershot, and is expected to leave early on Wednesday morning. It was thought, I do not know why, that their presence might interfere with the conduct of the Festival. More likely the rooms occupied *gratis* by the men were in request.[29]

The pride and interest shown in the Festival at each of the three cities ensured that there would be an impressive display of street decorations during Three Choirs week. Although the smallest city, Hereford's effort was often the most spectacular. In 1882, for example, triumphal arches were erected in most of the important streets, one of them representing Cleopatra's Needle and one near the Merton Hotel bearing the message: 'Welcome to our city'. Venetian masts were erected around High Town and part of

Commercial Street at intervals of sixteen yards, and on each of these masts the name of a composer whose work was to be performed at the Festival.[30]

So, on to Worcester, and let us discover what the correspondent of *The Musical World* thought of that city in 1854:

> Worcester is not altogether the *beau ideal* of a cathedral city, nor is its church one of the very first class. . . Consistently with its clerical reputation, it is not so much put out of its way by these triennial festivals as some people would imagine. It gets up its excitements in a grave and sober way. Of course, on these occasions, there is an extraordinary influx of visitors, and, we believe, never more so than at the present festival. So, at least, goes our experience; for we can vouch that 'good accommodation for man and horse,' during this week has been a thing not to be sought without patience under much denial, both in the city and neighbourhood. Yet with all this great extra population leavening the whole lump, as it were, and forcing the sober old city into a holiday mind, – with all the crowding about the streets, and gay dresses, and constant paradings to and from the Cathedral and College Hall, with a great deal of interpolated visiting and sight-seeing besides, there is no noisy and vulgar bustle. There is a brim-full but quiet happification about the whole scene that, to our taste, contrasts most favourably with the riot, heat, and turmoil emitted by those surging and crushing masses of humanity, which usually represent public beatitude in more populous places.[31]

This was the city which, in 1841, drew William Henry Elgar from his native Dover to earn a living as piano tuner, teacher and organist; the city where he met his wife Ann, and where their first three children were born. In 1856 the Elgars moved to a rented cottage in the village of Broadheath, two miles west of the river, and there, on 2 June 1857 a fourth child, Edward, was born. By the time Edward was two years old the expansion of his father's business necessitated a reluctant move from Broadheath back to Worcester; back to the city where W.H. Elgar now supplied music to the cathedral and played the violin in the Three Choirs Festival orchestra, and where young Edward Elgar grew up to become the finest composer of English music since Henry Purcell.

Notes

1. Ernest Walker, *A History of Music in England*, 2nd edn (Oxford, 1924)
2. Herbert Howells, Crees Lecture delivered at the Royal College of Music on 7 October 1968
3. MT 1880, p. 499
4. MW 1880, p. 515
5. Jeremy Dibble, *Parry: Some Fresh Thoughts*, Gloucester TCF Book Programme 1989, p. 24
6. MW 1880, p. 576
7. *Proceedings of the Musical Association*, vol. XLV, 1918–19
8. Jeremy Dibble, op. cit.
9. Gloucester Festival Minute Book, 1910
10. MW 1864, p. 569
11. MW 1874, p. 621
12. Symphony No. 8 of the 'Salomon Symphonies', i.e. No. 98 in B flat.
13. MW 1841, p. 179
14. MW 1837, pp. 56–7. Part of a review of the Hereford Festival.
15. *Annals* 1895, p. 160

16.	MW 1860, p. 586
17.	*Annals* 1895, p. 247
18.	MT 1884, p. 584
19.	*Annals* 1895, footnote pp. 96–7
20.	See Watkins Shaw, p. 31
21.	*Annals* 1895, p. 256
22.	Ibid., p. 174
23.	Ibid., p. 267
24.	MW 1881, pp. 575–6
25.	MW 1853, pp. 589–90
26.	MW 1853, p. 591
27.	MW 1853, p. 609
28.	MW 1852, p. 597
29.	MW 1855, p. 542
30.	*Hereford Times*, 16 September 1882
31.	MW 1854, p. 609

Giovanni Mario

Giulia Grisi

Antonio Tamburini

Luigi Lablache

Henriette Sontag

Clara Novello

John Sims Reeves

Joseph Staudigl

Mary Ann Paton

Therese Tietjens

Jenny Lind

Henry Phillips

Marietta Alboni

Samuel Sebastian Wesley

George Townshend Smith
(Hereford Cathedral Library)

Hereford, 1852 (*Illustrated London News*)

MUSIC.

GLOUCESTER MUSICAL FESTIVAL.

(From our own Correspondent.)

GLOUCESTER, WEDNESDAY.

GLOUCESTER CATHEDRAL.—THE SUPPOSED PILGRIM'S DOOR.

THE GRAND MUSICAL FESTIVAL IN GLOUCESTER CATHEDRAL.

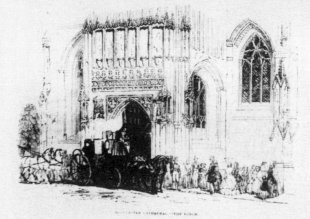

GLOUCESTER CATHEDRAL—THE PORCH.

Gloucester, 1850 (*Illustrated London News*)

William Done (Worcester Cathedral Library)

Worcester, 1863. Probably the last photograph taken before the fine screen surmounted by the organ was removed (Worcester Cathedral Library)

William Done (wearing top hat), Hugh Blair (wearing mortar-board) and choristers, Worcester, 1890 (Worcester Cathedral Library)

THE FESTIVAL OF THE THREE CHOIRS IN WORCESTER CATHEDRAL.—

Worcester, 1866 (*Illustrated London News*)

Gloucester, 1841

A railway poster from 1883

Iron Bridge over the River Wye at Hereford, from a drawing by J. Clayton (Hereford Cathedral Library)

Gloucester, 1865. The nave of the cathedral, looking west (*Illustrated London News*)

Gloucester, 1853. The Secular Concert in the Shire Hall. The three solo vocalists are Mme Castellan, Miss Dolby and Theodore Formes (*Illustrated London News*)

Bishop Ellicott. A caricature by 'Spy'

Lord Dudley. A caricature by 'Spy' (1875)

Rosalind Ellicott

The Very Revd Francis Close

Langdon Colborne (Hereford Cathedral Library)

Sir Hubert Parry (photograph courtesy of Tom Fenton)

Sir Frederic Cowen

Sir Arthur Sullivan

Hereford, 1891. G.R. Sinclair (*standing*). *Seated (left to right)*: J.T. Carrodus, W.H. Eayres, R.M. Blagrove, and C. Ould (Worcester Cathedral Library)

'The Metamorphosis of Dan' (*The Musical Times*)

G.R. Sinclair and Dan (photograph courtesy of Basil Butcher)

Left to right: Ivor Atkins, George Robertson Sinclair and Herbert Brewer, *c.* 1899 (photograph courtesy of Basil Butcher)

Hereford, 1900. G.R. Sinclair conducting a rehearsal. C.V. Stanford is seated at right of rostrum (with hat on lap) (Hereford Cathedral Library)

Hereford, 1897 (Hereford Cathedral Library)

Percy Hull

Emma Albani (1902) (Worcester Cathedral Library)   Marie Brema (1899) (Worcester Cathedral Library)

Sir Charles Santley   Edward Lloyd

Worcester, 1902. Concert in the Public Hall (Worcester Cathedral Library)

Worcester, 1902 (Three Choirs Festival Association)

CHELTENHAM CHRONICLE AND GLOUCESTERSHIRE GRAPHIC, SEPTEMBER 10, 1904.

Photos by Miss Wheeler, Churcham, near Gloucester.

GLOUCESTER MUSICAL FESTIVAL.

Corporation Procession to Opening Service on Sunday Afternoon.
Very Rev. Dean Spence-Jones, Mrs. Spence-Jones, and Sir John Dorington in
    Deanery Gardens after the "Elijah."
Going to Opening Service.

Entering South Transept Door on Sunday.
Leaving after Morning Recital on Tuesday.

Mr. J. Dearman Birchall arrives on Motor-Car on Tuesday.

Printed and Published as a Gratis Supplement by the Cheltenham Newspaper Company.

Gloucester, 1904 (*Cheltenham Chronicle and Gloucestershire Graphic*)

Gloucester, 1901. Herbert Brewer conducts a rehearsal in the cathedral. C.H. Lloyd is seated at left of rostrum (Gloucester Cathedral Library)

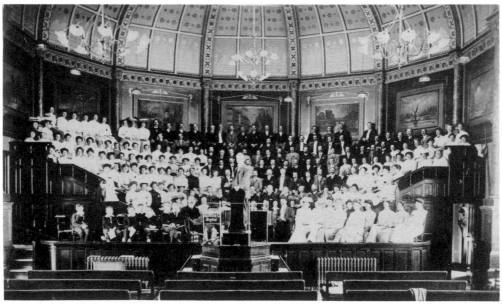

Hereford, 1906. G.R. Sinclair conducts a rehearsal in the Shire Hall. Dan is lying by his side on the rostrum, and Ivor Atkins is at the piano (photograph courtesy of Roy Massey)

Hereford street decorations, 1906 (photograph courtesy of Derek Foxton)

Gloucester, 1907. Festival breakfast at the New Inn. Pictured (*left to right*) are (*front row*): – Lawrence, – F. Phillips, – Harman, – Tidmarsh, E. Rowley Lewis, R.H. Hillyard, J. Collins, – Fletcher, – Dickinson, – Lane and – Bubb; (*second row*): Precentor Fleming, G.R. Sinclair, Herbert Brewer, Sir Edward Elgar, Canon St John, Dean Spence-Jones, Archdeacon Hayward, C.H. Lloyd, Charles Lee Williams, Revd G. Ryley and the Revd A. Porter; (*third row*): – Dyson, George Smith, G. Banks, – Harden, – Proctor, Nigel Haines, P. Barrett-Cooke (Secretary of the Gloucester Festival), H.W. Young, G. Lewis, Howard Gray, W. Batey and – Tyrell; (*back row*): – Somerton, Percy Hull, – Carden, – Davis, Burton Barnes, Hatherley Bubb, H.N. Pitt, C. Rowles, Ivor Gurney, A. Castings and – Miller

GLOUCESTER MUSICAL FESTIVAL, SEPT. 8-13, 1907.

1. Mr. Ivor Atkins (on left) and Mr. P. Barrett Cooke (secretary to the stewards).
2. Group including Sir Hubert Parry (on left), Mrs. F. W. Waller, the City Member, and Miss Marie Brema (on right).
3. Mr. Lee Williams (on right), with Mr. Brevel, of Cardiff.
4. Mr. Ivor Atkins (on left), Sir Edward Elgar, Mr. W. H. Reed, and Mr. John Coates.
5. The Very Rev. Dean Spence-Jones.
6. Mr. Granville Bantock (on left), Dr. A. H. Brewer, and Dr. Harford Lloyd.
7. Mr. Gervase Elwes.

Gloucester, 1907 (*Cheltenham Chronicle and Gloucestershire Graphic*)

A Festival reception given at Highnam Court by Sir Hubert Parry (seated at centre of front row, holding hat and cane). Probably 1907 (photograph courtesy of Basil Butcher)

CHAPTER TEN

FROISSART

D uring William Done's fifty-one years at Worcester he had worked with
Gloucester colleagues John Amott, S.S. Wesley, Charles Harford Lloyd and
Charles Lee Williams; and George Townshend Smith, Langdon Colborne and
George Robertson Sinclair at Hereford.

Lloyd made his Three Choirs début in the organ loft at the Hereford Festival of
1876. Selections from *Samson* and *Creation* in the gaslit cathedral provided a special
attraction at an evening concert: 'Lurid glares of gas fell upon the stately pillars, and
pierced through gloom to the far-off roof, giving a weird-like appearance to nave and
aisle.'[1]

A Gloucestershire man, born at Thornbury in 1849, Lloyd had graduated in Arts and
Music at Magdalen Hall, Oxford. At his first Gloucester Festival in 1877 it quickly
became apparent that the young new cathedral organist was a musician of ability,
distinction and moreover, one who seemed 'to possess the right stuff for a conductor,
combining those essential attributes of firmness, quietude, and self-control, in the
absence of which any hope of reaching eminence as a ruler in this particular sphere of
art-demonstration must be altogether illusory.'[2] *The Musical Times* reserved to the end of
a review of the week's events a notice of especial praise for Lloyd's conducting, praising
'not only his skill in conveying . . . an accurate knowledge of the tempi of the several
pieces, but his evident intimate acquaintance with the scores, and the intelligence he
evinced in the endeavour to realise every point indicated by the composer.'[3]

Lloyd was an innovator. We have already noted his introduction at the Gloucester
Festivals of Brahms's *Ein Deutsches Requiem* in 1877 and of Beethoven's *Missa Solemnis* in
1880, both drawing much-needed oxygen into the suffocating ultra-conservatism of
nineteenth-century provincial taste. We have seen too that Parry's *Prometheus Unbound*,
accepted by Lloyd for performance in the 1880 Festival, was later identified as the work
which marked the birth of the renaissance of English music. But 1880 was to be Lloyd's
second and last Festival as conductor. In 1882 he reluctantly resigned his post at
Gloucester on appointment as organist at Christ Church Cathedral, Oxford. Ten years
later he succeeded Sir Joseph Barnby as organist and precentor of Eton College, and in
1914 he was appointed organist at the Chapel Royal, London.

In his memoirs, Sir Herbert Brewer remembered Lloyd with affection:

> He was the most unselfish and generous of men with an intensely keen sense of duty, and he consistently lived up to the very high ideals he had of life . . . His was an extremely highly strung, nervous temperament . . . I remember an occasion on which he was conducting in the nave of Gloucester Cathedral and his assistant at the organ failed to follow his beat. Throwing down his baton, Lloyd rushed up to the organ-loft and flung aside the assistant who came in audible contact with the floor, and played himself.[4]

Curiously, during his six years at Gloucester Lloyd wrote no major work for the Festival. Then, having left, over a period of fifteen years he became a most prolific Three Choirs composer. His contributions were: *Hero and Leander*, 1884(W); *The Song of Balder*, 1885(H); *Andromeda*. 1886(G); *A Song of Judgement*, 1891(H); *Sir Ogie and Lady Elsie*, 1894(H); Concerto in F minor for organ and orchestra, 1895(G); *Hymn of Thanksgiving*, 1897(H); and an eight-part motet, *The Souls of the Righteous*, 1901(G) – in memory of Queen Victoria.

It is curious too that although an organist all his life, as a cantata composer Lloyd was most drawn to secular subjects. Charles Harford Lloyd died at Slough on his seventieth birthday, 16 October 1919.

If Lloyd had been an excellent Festival conductor, the efforts of his contemporary at Hereford on behalf of Three Choirs from 1877, Langdon Colborne, can perhaps at best be described as capable.

Born at Hackney in 1835, Colborne was a pupil of George Cooper before being appointed organist of St Michael's College, Tenbury, in 1860. The foundation stone of St Michael's was laid in 1854 and the college opened in 1856. The founder was the Revd Sir Arthur Gore Ouseley who, in 1855, was elected Professor of Music at Oxford and, in that same year, appointed precentor of Hereford Cathedral. Colborne remained at St Michael's College for fourteen years before moving to Beverley Minster in 1874, Wigan Parish Church in 1875 and, briefly, Dorking Parish Church in 1877, the year of George Townshend Smith's death at Hereford.

At Colborne's first Festival as conductor in 1879 *The Musical Times* reported that 'he endeavoured to earn, rather than to force, his position', and that 'if he did not venture any new readings of the standard works, he at least averted any catastrophe in ensuring the old ones.'[5] *The Musical World*, reviewing the performance of *Elijah*, noted that Colborne depended 'wisely on the occasional indications of Mr. Weist Hill, first violin in the orchestra, and a thoroughly experienced musician'.[6] Nor did Colborne, like Townshend Smith, attempt to fill the shoes of the Festival Secretary in addition to those of the conductor; the Revd Berkeley L.S. Stanhope took on those duties.

It is to Colborne's credit that he introduced the first and second parts of Bach's *Christmas Oratorio* to the Festival in 1879, and the same composer's *Magnificat* in 1882, but some of his choices were far less inspired: Dr G.M. Garrett's *The Shunammite* and Molique's *Abraham* in 1882; Dr Joseph Smith's *Saint Kevin* – which tells how a young monk, tempted by the love of a maiden, from whom he attempts to fly, eventually saves himself by hurling her, shrieking, into a lake – in 1885; and Colborne's own church cantata *Samuel* in 1888. *The Musical Times* suggested that Colborne's piece was 'on a par with a book written for children . . . the music taxes nobody's powers of comprehension . . . the work was manifestly out of place'.[7]

The Hereford Festival of 1888, Colborne's last, must have been a great disappointment to him. Not only did his *Samuel* fail to hit the mark but his conducting of a selection from Handel's *Samson* was judged a double failure:

> The choice of pieces omitted some of the best numbers, and included a lot of recitative in the vain hope of sustaining the continuity and interest of the story, while in the performance all was confusion, even the Conductor seeming not to know, at times, what should come next. This state of things reached a climax when Dr. Colborne and the orchestra went on to the second part of an air which it was agreed with the singer should be omitted. The singer declined to follow, and a collapse ensued.[8]

The following day, Thursday, a fairly large audience assembled in the cathedral to hear Cherubini's Mass in D minor; Frederic Cowen's *Song of Thanksgiving*, written for the Centennial Exhibition at Melbourne and receiving its first performance in England; Hubert Parry's *Blest Pair of Sirens*; and Sir Frederick Ouseley's *Martyrdom of St Polycarp*. Cowen and Parry conducted their own works and scored significant successes. Colborne conducted the Mass in D minor and 'supported by the influence of the sacred place, Cherubini's strains subdued the audience till tears came unbidden to many eyes'.[9] But the Ouseley piece, a Degree exercise written thirty years previously, was a disappointment of which no mention is made in the *Annals*, even though the performance, in which Anna Williams, Hilda Wilson, Edward Lloyd and Charles Santley took part, was considered one of the best of the week:

> This is partly explained by the comparative easiness of the music; and it is clear that Dr. Colborne's natural desire to do the most possible for his old friend and patron met with sympathy on the part of the performers.[10]

Colborne received the Lambeth doctorate in music in 1883.

Ouseley had been something of a prodigy, recognizing at the age of five the key in which his father blew his nose; and at six playing a duet with Mendelssohn. He succeeded to his father's baronetcy in 1844. Ernest Walker, in his *History of Music in England*, summed up Ouseley's achievement as a composer: he

> always wrote with a lofty ideal; but inspiration, or anything approaching thereto, visited him rarely. His work is massive and sincere, but it is usually very dull; however, he deserves a word or two of commendation not only for his excellent technical workmanship, sometimes of a brilliantly elaborate kind, but also for one or two emergences into a really vitalized atmosphere.

As the precentor of Hereford Cathedral, Ouseley seems to have taken little interest in the Three Choirs Festival. In 1858, a year in which Dean Dawes was said to have expressed his hostility to the 'abominable festival' by taking away the key to the choir, Ouseley absented himself from Hereford along with Archdeacon Freer and Lord Saye and Sele, one of the canons. It was rumoured that the precentor was sulking at St Michael's College, Tenbury, because he did not want his anthem, *The Lord is the true God*, performed on Tuesday!

Thirty years later Ouseley agreed to preach at the Opening Service at Hereford. The congregation looked forward to the sermon being a 'vindication of sacred music in its widest sense. But Sir Frederick Ouseley said not a word regarding the art, limiting himself exclusively to the virtue of charity, and the opportunity then afforded for its particular exercise.'[11] In the event, the collections for the charity in 1888 were below average.

Sir Frederick Ouseley died on 6 April 1889 at the age of sixty-three. The following September, Langdon Colborne made his final Three Choirs appearance, playing the organ at the Gloucester Festival. A few days later, on 16 September 1889, he too died.

> **Gloucester 1883** At the request of the Stewards 'rigid economy' was the text preached at this Festival, and the inevitable results of such preachment were speedily seen in the falling off in the sale of tickets.[12]

The period from 1873 to 1896, generally termed the Great Depression by economic historians, was a time in which agriculture in England was in sharp decline. A series of bad harvests and the challenge of imported wheat threatened the long-held supremacy of the landed gentry, the very men who in the Three Choirs counties had volunteered for Stewardship of the Festival year after year, regularly underwriting deficits, compelling them to share their pre-eminence with financiers and industrialists. At Hereford the recession was felt more sharply than at Gloucester and Worcester because, then as now, the cathedral was smaller, resulting in a wider gap between ticket-income and expenditure. Consequently, the Festival there depended upon some three hundred Stewards contributing £5 each to a guarantee fund. In 1882 half of those Stewards refused to join; the Festival was a financial failure of such proportion as to excite comment in the national Press: London audiences wanted new works and famous conductors; provincial audiences wanted only old favourites; the Festival needed to draw its audiences from both London and the provinces, *and* to attract a large privately-funded subsidy through the Stewardship scheme.

This was the dilemma facing Charles Lee Williams when he took over from C.H. Lloyd in Gloucester in 1882.

Williams was thirty-one years old when he arrived at Gloucester. He was born at Alton Barnes, Wiltshire on 1 May 1851, and had been a chorister in New College, Oxford; a pupil of Dr G.B. Arnold, and assistant organist of Winchester Cathedral; organist of Upton Church, Torquay, 1870; music-master of St Colomba's College, Rathfarnham, 1872; and organist of Llandaff Cathedral, where his uncle was Dean, from 1876.

At a General Meeting of the Gloucester Stewards held on 15 March 1883, Williams faced thirty-seven gentlemen, among whom were several whose principal concern was to 'curtail the expenses and prevent the deficits which had occurred at the Festivals at Gloucester of 1877 and 1880'.[13] (The deficit in 1877 had been £136 15s. 5d., but in 1880 it had leapt to £470 0s. 7d., the highest amount for thirty-three years. Furthermore, in 1865, 1868 and 1871, the S.S. Wesley years, the Gloucester Festival had shown a worthwhile surplus.) The conductor presented his proposed list of principal singers and their anticipated fees; at the top of the list was Emma Albani.

She would, said Williams, require a fee of at least 420 guineas. Opposition was immediate, and several around the table were fully prepared to dispense with the services of the star attraction altogether. Charles Harford Lloyd, still a committee member, was present to support Williams – perhaps a compromise could be reached by engaging Albani for fewer performances. The gathered wisdom was unable to make a decision on the number of principals to be engaged or the levels of fees to be paid. A Music Committee would have to be formed. Could it, Williams asked, please sit immediately after the present meeting – time was running short?

The Music Committee met: Albani must be offered no more than 150 guineas for one oratorio and one concert; Edward Lloyd had asked for 150 guineas for five performances – he must be offered that amount for *six* performances; and reduced fees must be offered to Anna Williams and Hilda Wilson.

Not surprisingly, Frederick Gye would not allow Albani to appear on these terms. Undeterred, Charles Lee Williams pressed on with an ambitious plan to introduce a greater number of new works than ever before at the Gloucester Festival of 1883. The Stewards commissioned three short pieces from local men: one from Hubert Parry – *The Glories of our Blood and State*, a setting of James Shirley's Poem *Death the Leveller*; one from C.H. Lloyd – *Allen a Dale*, to verses from Scott's *Rokeby*; and a choral setting of Byron's lines *I wish to tune my quivering lyre* from Dr A.E. Dyer of Cheltenham College. Williams's teacher, Dr G.B. Arnold, the organist of Winchester Cathedral, was invited to compose and to conduct a choral work. The result was *Sennacherib*, of which not even Williams could say more than that 'the composer's great knowledge of fugal writing and elaborate counterpoint was apparent throughout the cantata'.[14] *The Musical Times* judged it simply tedious. From more famous pens came the first performance of Sir John Stainer's *St Mary Magdalen*, thereafter known as his 'Gloucester Oratorio', and the second performance of Dr (later Sir) Charles Villiers Stanford's *Elegiac* Symphony, both conducted by their composers.

Richard Wagner died on 13 February 1883. Four weeks later Charles Lee Williams proposed to the Music Committee that the first Miscellaneous Evening Concert of the 1883 Festival should end with *Tannhäuser* (presumably the overture).[15] But no, the work actually played was Cherubini's overture to *Anacreon*. The Stewards were not yet ready for Wagner.

None the less, Williams had achieved a great deal at his first Festival. London critics could not accuse him of neglecting new works; eminent composers had conducted their own pieces; and as a conductor himself, Williams was thought really rather good. If only the Stewards had allowed him to engage Albani, the Festival might have been a financial as well as an artistic success, instead of which the deficit amounted to £330 2s. 10d. – more than the saving in artists' fees.

While planning his next two Festivals, Williams determined to increase standards and to reduce costs – but not to compromise in the selection of soloists. He was acutely aware that lack of rehearsal time for both orchestra and chorus was the most effective brake on the artistic advancement of the Festival. The chorus, drawn from many towns, did not rehearse as a body until the day before the Festival, and the conductor was limited to only one orchestral rehearsal in London.

Williams tackled this second problem first; an entry in his notebook records: 'London rehearsal Aug 28 & 29 [1889] at St. Andrew's Hall, Newman Street, at 9 for 9.30 a.m. Extra day put on in London at my urgent request. Quite impossible to do it with less – even with two days *more than half* the programme was performed *without any rehearsal at all*.'[16] He also noted his opinions on the orchestral players, marking down against each name, 'good', 'bad', 'too old', etc., concluding with, 'N.B. As vacancies occur in band, terms must be reduced – *especially* in *string*. There are any amount of excellent players ready and willing to attend the Festival. Good wind players are difficult to get and good terms must be offered.'[17] The problem of chorus rehearsal was more complex.

The approximate numbers and costs of the chorus members for the 1886(G) Festival were as follows:[18]

Worcester	37	incl. Lay Clerks & 4 boys	£166. 8. 0
Tewkesbury	9		15. 1. 0
Cardiff	20		57. 7. 0
Bradford	24		109. 10. 0
Gloucester	68	plus Lay Clerks & boys	145. 19. 0
Bristol	20	incl. 6 Lay Clerks	94. 10. 0
Hereford	29	incl. 8 Lay Clerks & 4 boys	134. 8. 0
Cambridge	4	Lay Clerks	16. 0. 0
Oxford	8		40. 0. 0
Single engagements	9		38. 0. 0

At a meeting of the Music Committee in Gloucester on 13 March 1886, Thomas Gambier Parry said that he had been asked to suggest that the choruses should be selected from Gloucester, Hereford and Worcester.[19] Williams promised to consider the matter but no changes were made until 1892. It seems probable that it was Joseph Bennett who made this suggestion to Parry; he had joined the Music Committee in 1886 but was absent on 13 March. Bennett certainly raised the subject again immediately following the very successful 1889(G) Festival. 'The chorus' he said, 'relatively, was the most expensive in the kingdom, inasmuch as its 200 voices cost £800. There were means by which this expense could be lessened, and he should be prepared to lay before the committee a scheme which, without impairing its efficiency, would lessen the cost by £300. (Applause).'[20]

In 1892(G) the Festival Chorus was, for the first time, drawn entirely from the counties of Herefordshire, Worcestershire and Gloucestershire, the last including nearly a hundred voices from Bristol. 'It was', *The Musical Times* said, 'a capital body of singers, fit for anything.'[21]

In the three Gloucester Festivals of 1886, 1889 and 1892, Lee Williams continued to champion new music, including the first performances of Hubert Parry's *Judith* (1889) and *Job* (1892). Williams himself contributed two cantatas: *Last Night at Bethany* (1889) and *Gethsemane* (1892).

Meanwhile William Done, at the age of seventy-five, had decided that it was time to hand his baton to a younger man and asked Charles Lee Williams to direct the Worcester Festival of 1890. On 1 January that year Done replied to a letter from Edward Elgar, who had asked if he would consider including a composition of his in the 1890(W) Festival:

> I shall be much pleased to receive the score of your new composition . . . and I shall study it with much pleasure as the work of one whose talent I have always recognized and admired. It will be a pleasure to you to know that the proposal to introduce your orchestral piece at the Festival met with

no opposition. I must not take the credit of it to myself, as it scarcely required a recommendation from me. I will take care to give you a good orchestra and fair opportunity of rehearsal.

Will you kindly tell me whether any extra instruments will be required. I hope not as the orchestra is so small.[22]

Three days later Done wrote again:

The score of your little work arrived safely. Many thanks to you for it. At the last Festival we had both Tuba and Contra Fag. but I do not intend to go to the expense of both this time. I myself much prefer the Contra Fag. One of the two we must have, but as Mr. Williams will conduct throughout the Festival I must leave him to decide which and will let you known as soon as I hear from him . . .[23]

Elgar was thirty-two. In the previous year he had married his beloved Alice in London. On 24 June 1889 he was present at a St James's Hall concert conducted by Hans Richter in which the first performance of Parry's Symphony No. 4 in E minor, written at Richter's request, had been given. This splendid work, so shamefully neglected and so filled with just the sweep and brilliance which we now identify as 'Elgarian', must surely have had a seminal influence on a composer already mature in years but yet still feverishly seeking to establish his artistic reputation.

On 2 July 1890, Done wrote to Elgar once more:

Mr. Wheeler [the Worcester Festival Secretary] has forwarded to me your note. I will take care to have your piece properly inserted in the programme.

The London rehearsals will take place at St. George's Hall on Wednesday and Thursday – September 3rd. and 4th. Our conductor has sent me a rehearsal programme, and I find that he has put you down for 3 o'clock on the first day – *Wednesday 3rd*. I hope to hear that that arrangement will suit you. You shall have a programme as soon as they are ready. I hope you are well.[24]

On 14 August the Elgars' only child, Carice, was born. Three and a half weeks later, on Wednesday 10 September, at the single evening secular concert of the 1890 Worcester Festival,[25] Edward Elgar's overture *Froissart* was heard for the first time. The occasion was vividly remembered by the 21-year-old assistant organist at Hereford Cathedral, Ivor Atkins:

Never before had I heard such a wonderful combination of a first-rate Chorus and Orchestra. I was naturally specially interested in Elgar, knowing that he was to produce a new Overture whose very title attracted me, for I had just been reading Froissart's *Chronicles*. Sinclair pointed Elgar out to me. There he was, fiddling among the first violins, with his fine intellectual face, his heavy moustache, his nervous eyes and his beautiful hands.

The Wednesday evening came. I had no dress clothes with me, having come over from Hereford for the day, so crept up the steps leading to the back of the Orchestra and peeped from behind those on the platform. The new Overture was placed at the end of the first half of the programme.

The great moment came, and I watched Elgar's shy entry on to the platform. From that moment my eyes did not leave him, and I listened to the Overture, hearing it in the exciting way one hears music when among the players. I heard the surge of the strings, the chatter of the wood wind, the sudden bursts from the horns, the battle call of the trumpets, the awesome beat of the drums and the thrill of cymbal clashes. I was conscious of all these and of the hundred and one other sounds from an orchestra that stir one's blood and send one's heart into one's mouth.

But there was something else I was conscious of – I knew that Elgar was the man for me, I knew that I completely understood his music, and that my heart and soul went with it.[26]

Writing in the *Daily Telegraph*, Joseph Bennett said: 'Mr. Punch's memorable advice to persons about to marry [i.e. 'Don't'] is that which true charity dictates in nine cases out of ten when young men propose to write overtures and symphonies. I regard Mr. Elgar as an exception. Let him go on. He will one day 'arrive'.' *The Musical Times* 'hoped, and, given opportunity, even expected' that Elgar would 'make his mark'.[27] And of Charles Lee Williams's direction of the Festival, 'no better man could have been found . . . enough cannot be said in acknowledging the unobtrusive efficiency which made the voyage of the Festival ship safe and pleasant . . . He is just such a conductor as these Festivals have long wanted.'[28]

Notes

1. MW 1876, p. 645
2. MW 1877, p. 600
3. Ibid., p. 480
4. Brewer, *Memories of Choirs and Cloisters* (London, 1931)
5. MT 1879, pp. 528 and 535
6. MW 1879, p. 578
7. MT 1888, p. 603
8. Ibid., p. 604
9. Ibid.
10. Ibid., p. 613
11. Ibid., p. 603
12. *Annals* 1895, p. 280
13. Gloucester Festival Minute Book, 1883
14. *Annals* 1895, p. 281
15. Gloucester Festival Minute Book, 1883
16. C.L. Williams's notebook, Gloucester City Library
17. Ibid.
18. Ibid.
19. Gloucester Festival Minute Book, 1886
20. Ibid., 1889
21. MT 1892, p. 598
22. Worcester Records Office
23. Ibid.
24. Worcester Records Office
25. A second evening concert in the cathedral was introduced in 1890.
26. E. Wulstan Atkins, *The Elgar–Atkins Friendship* (David & Charles, 1985)
27. MT 1890, p. 598
28. Ibid., pp. 596 and 599

CHAPTER ELEVEN

THE UNREASONABLE MAN

The reasonable man adapts himself to the world: the unreasonable one persists in trying to adapt the world to himself. Therefore all progress depends on the unreasonable man.

George Bernard Shaw

At the time of Langdon Colborne's death in 1889, Charles Lee Williams had been in post at Gloucester for seven years and William Done at Worcester for forty-five. Both men were, in their different ways, much liked and respected: Done, quietly persuasive and undemonstrative; Williams, clear in his purpose and firm but diplomatic. The new man appointed to Hereford was of a very different personality.

George Robertson Sinclair (1863–1917) was born at 3, Devonshire Villas, Sydenham Road, Croydon on 28 October 1863. His ancestors were of Scottish descent but had for several generations been settled in Ireland, at Killiney near Dublin. His father, Dr Robert Sharpe Sinclair held the appointment of Director of Public Education in Bombay, and it was owing to the temporary residence of his mother in England that Sinclair happened to be born in Croydon. But he was extremely proud to call himself an Irishman, proclaiming his nationality during the Hereford Festival week by hoisting the Irish flag outside his house.

At the age of eight Sinclair entered the Royal Irish Academy of Music, where he studied under Sir Robert Stewart, who was an old friend of his father's and of Sir Frederick Gore Ouseley. Thus, in 1873, young Sinclair – aged ten – gained a choral scholarship at St Michael's College, Tenbury, where he was the only boy known to have been taught personally by Ouseley. His parents intended that he should take Holy Orders; but the death of his father when Sinclair was seventeen threw him upon his own resources. When Bishop (afterwards Archbishop) Benson, of Truro, asked Ouseley to recommend him an organist for the proposed Cornish cathedral, he at once nominated Sinclair.

In 1880, at the age of seventeen, he was appointed to Truro Cathedral as the first organist and choirmaster.[1] Even though still only twenty-six when he succeeded Langdon Colborne at Hereford, Sinclair already possessed an unusual degree of experience in addition to prodigious ability.

At the Worcester Festival of 1890 Sinclair shared the organ music with Done's assistant, Hugh Blair, and thus, would have been present to hear the Three Choirs début of the brilliant young Irish baritone, Harry Plunket Greene; to hear the première of Elgar's overture *Froissart*; and at the same secular concert to hear Charles Lee Williams conduct, for the first time at a Three Choirs concert, a work by Wagner: the Prelude to Act III of *Lohengrin*.

The 'new music' of Wagner featured again in Sinclair's first Festival as conductor at Hereford in 1891. Not only did he include the overture and Preislied (sung by Edward Lloyd) from *Die Meistersinger* in the single Shire Hall secular concert on Tuesday evening; the next morning in the cathedral he conducted a programme in honour of the centenary of the death of Mozart, beginning with that composer's *Requiem* and followed by Beethoven's Symphony No. 3 in E flat (the *Eroica*); the first performance of a motet, *Praise to the Holiest*, by Dr H.J. Edwards – a setting of words from John Henry Newman's poem *The Dream of Gerontius*; then, for the first time in an English cathedral, the prelude to Wagner's *Parsifal* – 'a fact which elicited some comment'.[2] The concert ended with Sullivan's *Te Deum* for the recovery of the Prince of Wales.[3]

The two principal main works of the 1891(H) Festival were C.H. Lloyd's *Song of Judgement* and Hubert Parry's *De Profundis*, both performed under their composers' direction at the Thursday morning concert before a disappointingly small audience – only 921 tickets were sold. Of the Parry piece, a setting for soprano solo, orchestra and three choirs of four parts each, *The Musical Times* reported that 'shining through all, and giving it glory and splendour, are noble imaginings and exalted emotions . . . Men of varying tastes and judgement conceded to one another that in its way a great thing had been born into the world.'[4]

In addition to the musical achievements of the 1891 Hereford Festival, Sinclair was able to share in the satisfaction of a successful royal visit. On the first day of the Festival, the Duke and Duchess of Teck and their children, Princess Mary (later the Duchess of York, then queen to King George V) and Prince Alexander, attended a performance of Mendelssohn's *St Paul* in which Emma Albani, Hilda Wilson, Edward Lloyd and Charles Santley were the soloists, and 'the conductor Mr G.R. Sinclair . . . showed much skill and tact'.[5]

But tact was the one quality which not everyone in Hereford would have attributed to Sinclair. In 1891 he had trodden on toes in order to get his own way with the Stewards. In spite of the poor audience for the premièr of Parry's *De Profundis*, the total attendance at the Festival was 8,978, an increase of 2,343 on the figure for 1888. Sinclair must have felt complete justification in his selection of music and was determined, like Charles Lee Williams at Gloucester, not only to meet the insatiable demand for stock oratorios, *Messiah* and *Elijah*, but also to support and encourage performances of new works. Unfortunately, his single-mindedness could all too easily be construed as obduracy and his determination as petulance.

As preparations for the 1894(H) Festival got under way, an 'atmosphere' began to develop. The Chairman of the Executive Committee was Mr J.H. Arkwright, and the Festival Secretary the Revd Prebendary G.G. Ashley (whose predecessor, the Hon. and Ven. Berkeley Stanhope, was now the Archdeacon of Hereford).

On 22 January 1894, Stanhope wrote to Arkwright:

You will probably receive a letter from Ashley tomorrow, on the subject of 'Sinclair'. He has been here this morning, & I feel there is not any probability of harmony between them. They cannot, and will not work together, which is essential. . . .

Ashley is bent on resigning – & who is to take up the work? For it needs a strong man to keep Sinclair in his proper place.

If the breach cannot be permanently settled – better to have a fresh hand now, than later on when the work of Sec. is heavier.

But perhaps with the aid of the Dean something may be done – Sinclair is a spoilt child.

Sure enough, Arkwright *did* receive a letter from Ashley the following day:

. . . The Hon: Sec: and the Conductor have each their own special business to transact, and it seems a pity that they cannot each do their own work in harmony & good temper without the one interfering with the work of the other. I am sure that no one would resent more keenly my interference with the Band and Chorus than Mr Sinclair, and I think courtesy and good sense demands, if nothing else, that he should show to the Hon: Sec: the consideration he would expect to be shown to himself.

During the Festival of 1891 on many occasions Mr Sinclair interfered with the duties which devolved on me as Hon: Sec: and if the same line is to be adopted by him in reference to this festival it is obvious that we cannot work in harmony. I was in 1891 much annoyed by Mr Sinclair's interference but I had hoped no further unpleasantness would have occurred; I regret to find . . . that this is not the case.

I feel much interest in the Festival work and I am ready and willing to do my best in the interests of this excellent charity but I see clearly that unless harmony exists between the Hon: Sec: and the Conductor that the Festival cannot be a success. Whilst I am quite willing to continue to act as Hon: Sec: I cannot do so except on the understanding that my duties are not interfered with. I shall be glad to hear your views before taking any decided action in the matter, or, if possible, the view that the Executive Com: hold on the subject.

Arkwright replied to Ashley on 26 January:

I am extremely sorry that you have been again annoyed by Sinclair having reopened the question which I thought had been settled on the simplest grounds of common sense . . . unless Sinclair will shut up the Executive must be our referee. If you like I will write to him a very plain letter and submit it to you and the Archdeacon, which ought to settle it. And I hope this would put all thoughts of your resignation out of possibility *or* we three might wait on the Dean in camera and plan an escape.

Ashley wrote back from a London address on 30 January:

I am very glad to find by your letter that you hold so strong an opinion on the matter in question. I prefer the second of your suggestions – for this reason – because Mr Dean has a real authority & power over Mr Sinclair beyond any that the Com: could assume. If the Dean spoke in earnest it would probably do more than anything else. I shall be at home after next Friday. If however you & the Archdeacon think the letter best, I will fall in with your views at once. Indeed I don't mind what course is adopted if only matters could be put on a footing of peace and harmony. I detest disagreement & quarrels; and it takes away all pleasure in doing my work, as I dread something unpleasant at every turn. I have no wish to resign unless it is forced upon me, but it is clear that if our respective duties cannot be carried out without constant friction the Festival must suffer.

Arkwright decided to write at once to the Dean, who replied on 2 February:

I will see Sinclair & try & arrange matters. I fancy it would not be amiss if Berkeley Stanhope would call & talk the matter over with him – often there are faults on both sides.

Then both Ashley and Sinclair respect & trust the Archdeacon.[6]

The Dean's arranging seems to have been successful. Ashley was persuaded to carry on. Sinclair pressed his purpose home, injecting new vigour into the Festival, raising the standard of music at Hereford Cathedral to new heights, gaining professional distinction and attaining high office as a Freemason. When still only twenty-nine years old, he received the Lambeth degree of D. Mus., an honour not accorded to William Done until the celebration of his Golden Jubilee at Worcester in 1894, the year before his death.

In 1899 Sinclair was appointed conductor of the Birmingham Festival Choral Society, and in that same year Elgar's *Enigma Variations* were performed for the first time. Among the 'friends pictured within' to whom Elgar dedicated his masterpiece, 'G.R.S.' (Variation XI) bursts energetically in between the intimate delicacy of 'Dorabella' and the meditative cello solo of 'B.G.N.' (Basil Nevinson). Elgar insisted that the variation had nothing to do with organs, cathedrals or, except remotely, G.R.S., but that the first few bars were suggested by the boisterous antics of Sinclair's bulldog Dan. Even so, the music seems to match Dan's mercurial master remarkably well.

Away from the pressures of the cathedral and the Festival, Sinclair could be a kind and sociable man. He was a welcome guest at the home of the DuBuisson family from early in 1890. Margaret DuBuisson records in her diary[7] the pleasure she found in Sinclair's visits when she was a young girl. He frequently dined with them, as did a Miss Holland, and Sinclair entertained them himself and joined in other musical parties. Margaret DuBuisson shared his love for music and was fascinated by the skill with which he would improvise at the piano. He used to join in the games with the younger DuBuisson boys and was himself given dancing lessons by the family. In turn, he would play when a guest at parties and used to enjoy an evening pipe with his friends.

Sinclair's hobbies were cycling, yachting and photography. A bachelor, he shared his house with six cats and Dan, who followed closely in his master's footsteps, waiting patiently at the cathedral door whenever Sinclair went in. Dan was present at all Sinclair's lessons and at his rehearsals in the Shire Hall. A member of the Hereford Choral Society drew a caricature of Sinclair – 'the Metamorphosis of Dan' – which was passed quietly around during a rehearsal but was never intended to be seen by the conductor (see illustration). As one London critic observed: 'Dan deserves to be made a Dogter of Music!'

Although by no means everyone in Hereford found Sinclair an unreasonable man, as the years passed by he became ever more set in his solitary ways. Percy Hull's wife, Molly, remembered the days when she had been Sinclair's pupil. She found him a fussy, typical bachelor. Dan had been succeeded by Ben, who snuffled, snorted and slobbered; the whole house smelt of a mixture of dog and general stuffiness. Hardly an atmosphere in which a young girl could enjoy a music lesson.

Worcester 1893 It was hoped that Worcester, at the 170th meeting of the Three Choirs, held there in 1893, would follow the excellent lead set by the conductor at the Gloucester meeting the year before, and dispense with other voices than those supplied by the three counties; but Worcester decided to walk in the old ways, and Mr Broughton's Leeds Choir of a hundred voices formed half the chorus.[8]

The continued dependence on a large and well-trained contingent of singers from Leeds was felt to be an increasing cause of shame to the Worcester Festival Choral

Society, as was the humiliating fact that very few of their number were asked to take part in the Gloucester and Hereford Festivals. The debate, which had remained an internal matter within the committee and chorus, became public during 1893 when a visitor to the Festival wrote to *The Times*:

THREE CHOIRS FESTIVAL

Pray allow me to protest as publicly as possible against the further use of the above title at this festival. Out of a chorus of 200 voices (more or less) I observe the astounding statement that a large contingent – viz. nearly 100 voices – has been imported from Leeds. In these days of advanced musical knowledge, and with colleges and schools of music as plentiful as blackberries, do the authorities really mean to assert that in the combined counties of Worcester, Gloucester and Hereford 200 competent singers cannot be found to sing the very ordinary programme that the committee offer for performance this week? . . . Musical readers may recollect that at Gloucester last year the committee resolved, apart from the voices very properly contributed by Hereford and Worcester, to find their chorus exclusively within the bounds of the county. They made the experiment and were not disappointed. The Gloucestershire singers, with a comparatively small number of allies from the sister shires, answered all requirements, and so was removed a long-standing provocation to criticism. I am told that some sort of agreement was come to among the organists of the three cathedrals with a view to make the festival dioceses sufficient unto themselves in the matter of chorus-singers, but this, if it ever existed, could not bind the committee, and the Worcester managers have here a hundred voices from Leeds . . . it may be of interest to state that Gloucestershire has just formally united its vocal resources for festival purposes. A meeting of representatives of choral societies within the county was held last week, under the presidency of Mr C. Lee Williams, with the result that festival performances may henceforth be organised anywhere within the shire in full assurance of a competent chorus . . . The example of its sister county is worth, at any rate, the serious consideration of Worcestershire.

The 1893 Festival was the first at which Hugh Blair took charge. The programme included only two new works: Parry's *Overture to an Unwritten Tragedy*, and a symphonic poem, *Gretchen im Dom*, by a Dresden organist called Fischer who had died in the previous December. (It was a flop – 'Enough of *Gretchen im Dom* and good-bye!' wrote *The Musical Times* critic.) The one bold choice of the Festival was Bach's Mass in B minor, which had been performed at Leeds in 1886 and 1892 and which, therefore, was dependent upon the northerners for its success. Blair's tempi were too slow but Sinclair 'did capital work at the organ'.[9]

Blair, born on 26 May 1864, was a Worcester man; a pupil of William Done and afterwards of George Macfarren and Dr G.M. Garrett. He became organ scholar at Christ's College, Cambridge in 1883 and assistant organist of Worcester Cathedral in 1886, taking over from the elderly Done as acting organist in 1889 and succeeding to the full office on the death of Done in August 1895.

It is perhaps understandable that Blair would choose the path of safety in his first Festival – but there is a hint in Charles Lee Williams's 1895 update of the *Annals* that the acting organist at Worcester might just have lacked a sufficient level of commitment. Writing of the 1893 repetition of Parry's *Job* and of Spohr's *Last Judgement*, both performed on the third day of the Festival, he says: 'band and chorus showed such perfect familiarity with the work as to reduce Mr Blair's labours and responsibility to a minimum'.[10]

This suspicion was confirmed by an anonymous letter published in the *Birmingham Daily Gazette* following the 1896 Festival:

Sir, it is all very well to lament over the small number of engagements sent to the Worcester choristers when the festivals are held at Hereford and Gloucester. No persons are more anxious for the entire chorus to be drawn from the three counties than the authorities in those two cities last named; but as one who may perhaps be allowed to speak on behalf of those authorities may I throw out a hint to our friends at Worcester? Some conductors do not consider that a few rehearsals of 40 minutes' duration are sufficient to prepare the Worcester contingent for the Festivals held in Gloucester and Hereford, and until they are assured that the Worcester singers are well versed in the works to be produced, it is not surprising that the 'powers that be' at the two sister cities send so many engagements to a town where 60 rehearsals are not considered too much for a festival. We have had ample proof this week of what the three choirs are capable of, and it is a crying shame that such talent is not made the most of. – yours, &c.,

ONE FROM HEREFORD

Worcester 1896   'An excellent programme had been arranged for the Festival [Blair's second], but owing to insufficient rehearsal the imposing array of executants went into action more or less unprepared.'[11] 'Mr Blair, it is true,' reported *The Musical Times*, 'rehearsed his orchestra in London, where, also, some of the principals met him; but soloists, orchestra, and chorus were together in Worcester only one day and an evening – the last, it should be explained, being mainly devoted to the preparation of the music for the Opening Service.'[12]

The 1896 Festival included the introduction to Three Choirs of the *Requiem* by Verdi, then in his eighty-third year; Schumann's 'Rhenish' Symphony (No. 3); a cantata, *Blessed are they who watch*, by Blair himself; and the first performance of Elgar's *The Light of Life* (*Lux Christi*).

Hugh Blair and Edward Elgar were friends. Blair conducted the Worester Festival Choral Society; Elgar had been the Leader of its orchestra. On 20 December 1891, Elgar wrote to his Yorkshire friend, Dr Charles Buck: 'Blair and I are pulling together & making things lively here.' And Elgar's diary contains many references to visits by Blair during 1892. Blair had provided much-needed encouragement to Elgar at a time when recognition of his talent seemed the remotest possibility. Now Blair was to be the first conductor to bring forward an Elgar choral work – and his preparations for the Festival were defective.

Fortunately, *The Light of Life* escaped the worst embarrassments of the lack of rehearsal. Elgar himself travelled up to Yorkshire to rehearse with the Leeds Choral Union and also directed the Festival premièr. All ran smoothly, and the soloists, Anna Williams, Jessie King, Edward Lloyd[13] and Watkin Mills, were excellent.

The Musical Times was unusually enthusiastic in its review of the new oratorio:

Mr Elgar's *Light of Life* failed to secure a large audience on Tuesday evening. So much was expected. Does not the composer live near Worcester, and has he not yet to make a famous name? Facts of this kind were against him, but Mr Elgar, I hope, understands how 'to labour and to wait.' Time is on his side, and my trust is that, as years pass, he will make the best use of increasing experience in all that concerns the character and method of his art . . . It is now clear that Mr Elgar has endowments sufficient for important results. He is no wayside musician whom we can afford to pass and forget, but one to be watched, encouraged, and, as he is still a young man, counselled. I think there is need for counsel, which, if tendered from a proper quarter in a fitting spirit, will not be spurned. Mr Elgar is not yet a master of oratorio, and the reason is partly to be discovered, perhaps, in the fact, indicated by his new work, that his sympathies are much more with the orchestra than with voices.[14]

Elgar's friendship with Blair continued, but in a letter to Charles Lee Williams written thirty-six years later, he made it clear to whom he had felt equally indebted in 1896:

Worcester, 1st September 1932

I am deeply touched by your kind letter which brings back the happiest memories of your connection with the festivals: *you* made my first choral incursion into that somewhat *close* domain of the music meetings a pleasant experience. That was in 1896 & you have ever been the true friend you then proved yourself to me & to us all in the happy festival crowd.[15]

In 1897 Blair resigned his post at Worcester and became organist of Holy Trinity, Marylebone.

Charles Lee Williams, for some years troubled by a throat condition, also resigned in 1897, becoming an Examiner for the Associated Board of the Royal Academy of Music and Royal College of Music.

The year of Queen Victoria's Diamond Jubilee, 1897, brought new men to take charge of the Gloucester and Worcester Three Choirs – men whose abilities would match those of Sinclair at Hereford and who would lead the Festival strongly into the new century.

Notes

1. The building of Truro Cathedral, assisted financially by the Freemasons, began in 1880. The cathedral was completed and consecrated in 1887.
2. *Annals* 1895, p. 300
3. In December 1871 the Prince of Wales caught typhoid, from which he recovered.
4. MT 1891, p. 598
6. All of this correspondence is contained in the Arkwright Collection, City of Hereford Records Office.
7. I am grateful to Mr W.A. DuBuisson for this information.
8. *Annals* 1895, p. 306
9. MT 1893, p. 599
10. *Annals* 1895, pp. 307–8
11. *Annals* 1931, p. 16
12. MT 1896, p. 666
13. Edward Lloyd described *The Light of Life* as 'one of the finest English works composed for some time' (*Worcester Daily Times*, 7 September 1896).
14. MT 1896, p. 666
15. C.L. Williams' scrap-book, Gloucester City Library

CHAPTER TWELVE

THE DREAM

———————

At Hereford in 1897 Sinclair broke with the tradition of an Opening Service and sermon on the Tuesday morning, and followed instead the example set by Worcester in 1881. An 'immense congregation' was present to hear the Festival Chorus, orchestra and some of the principal soloists take part in a special Opening Service on Sunday morning, 12 September. The music was magnificent. At Sinclair's request Elgar had composed a *Te Deum and Benedictus* especially for the occasion, pieces instantly recognized by the critics as masterpieces of their kind. There were Schubert's Symphony No. 8 in B minor ('The Unfinished'); 'How lovely is Thy dwelling-place' from Brahms's *German Requiem*; Elgar's *Imperial March*; and the 'Hallelujah' chorus from Beethoven's *Mount of Olives*. Here was a blazing fanfare to herald not only a celebration for the Diamond Jubilee of a queen, but also the beginning of a new era for Three Choirs.

For the first time at Hereford, the chorus was drawn entirely from the Three Choirs cities. Sinclair, with customary energy and commitment, arranged combined rehearsals from months in advance. Highlights of the Festival included a new *Magnificat* by Parry; the Good Friday music and the Finale to the first act of Wagner's *Parsifal*, with Lloyd Chandos and Harry Plunket Greene; the Symphony No. 6 in B minor (*Pathetique*) by Tchaikovsky; and Beethoven's *Missa Solemnis* with Emma Albani, Hilda Wilson, Edward Lloyd and Watkin Mills – 'Rarely has that difficult music been attacked with greater spirit or more signal success.'[1]

Named in the programme for the first time in 1897 were the newly-appointed organists of Gloucester and Worcester: Herbert Brewer and Ivor Atkins. There, too, was Sinclair's eighteen-year-old assistant organist, Percy Hull, who had been present at Sinclair's house on 5 June 1897 when Elgar had taken over his MS of the *Te Deum and Benedictus*:

> I was privileged to hear Elgar play over his *Festival Te Deum and Benedictus* in Sinclair's house to see whether the work would be acceptable for the programme of the Festival at Hereford . . . He was as nervous as a kitten and heaved a huge sigh of relief when Sinclair said: 'It is *very very* modern, but I think it will do; you shall play it again after supper when Hull and I will give you our final verdict.' All this in Sinclair's stammering and somewhat patronising fashion.[2]

Within eight years the works of Elgar had established themselves as unassailable Festival favourites, equal in popularity to *Elijah* and *Messiah*.

The pulse of the Festival now began to quicken. By perceptible degrees the Steward-dominated conservatism of the past gave way to a greater reliance upon the tastes of conductors with a broader vision allied to a keen sense of purpose.

Orchestral standards were rising too. The Queen's Hall had opened in London in 1893; two years later Henry Wood instituted his famous Promenade Concerts. Some seventy players from the Queen's Hall orchestra were engaged each year for Three Choirs under their Leader, Alfred Burnett (J.T. Carrodus died in 1895). In 1900 A.W. Paynes took Burnett's place; then in 1904, the bulk of the players from the Queen's Hall orchestra left Henry Wood and formed the London Symphony Orchestra – a case of good coming out of bad – Wood had insisted upon abolishing the practice of sending deputies to rehearsals and concerts. So began the long association of the London Symphony Orchestra with Three Choirs.

When Herbert Brewer took over as organist at Gloucester on 15 December 1896, he found the Stewards preparing once more to sharpen the knife of economy. The 1895(G) Festival had left them with a large deficit, and a special committee had been set up to consider and report on the best way to ensure future financial success:

> In their report they drew attention to the fees paid to the principal singers, which, they said, were increasing year by year and a stand would have to be made. They also found that the Friday evening Cathedral service was undoubtedly prejudicial to the funds of the Charity and recommended that the Festival should close with *Messiah*.[3]

They also recommended that only one new work should be given at the next Festival – 'novelties' always incurred a financial loss.

Brewer *was* able to economize on principal singers in 1898. Only Albani could have been considered an extravagance – but a necessary one. His other choices included Ella Russell, Hilda Wilson, Ben Davies, Hirwen Jones, Watkins Mills and David Bispham, the total cost for whom, including Albani, was little more than half of the fees paid to the four principal singers in 1895.

Cancellation of the Friday evening service was a more thorny problem. A general meeting of the Stewards was called on 30 June 1897 to discuss the proposal – but the Dean of Gloucester, Henry Spence, always took his holiday in June and July. A letter from him to the Festival Secretary, P. Barrett Cooke, was read out at the meeting:

> I am very sorry the 30th June is fixed for the Standing Committee meeting to consider the Report. For several years past I have always been away for the last part of June and for July. I am still utterly opposed to giving up the 'free Service', and I hope nothing will be decided on that point until I can be present. Indeed, in my opinion, such a movement would be disastrous to the Festival.[4]

In spite of this, the committee unanimously resolved to retain the proposal that the Festival should close with the Friday evening oratorio, but the Stewards were 'willing to consider financially any suggestion from the Dean and Chapter as to the holding of the Sunday Service similar to the Opening Service at Hereford and Worcester'. Brewer tells us that this was his recommendation – and it averted the danger of re-opening old wounds. The committee met again in October and were so enthusiastic about the success of the Opening Service at the recent Hereford Festival that the Dean fell in with the wishes of the Stewards and agreed to preach the sermon at the first Sunday Opening Service held at the Gloucester Festival of 1898.

On the question of 'novelties', Brewer took a firm stand – and got his way: 'I pointed out that if musical interest was to be maintained and if the programmes contained no novelties, the Festivals would soon cease to attract and would pass away like other worn-out institutions.'[5]

The Stewards invited Sir Hubert Parry, Sir John Stainer, Charles Harford Lloyd, Charles Lee Williams, Rosalind Ellicott and Brewer himself to write new works. Such invitations customarily included a statement that the Stewards could offer no re-muneration and that the works must be produced in print at the expense of the composer to the librarians of the Festival.[6] The financial worries of the Stewards concerning 'novelties' were nothing at all to do with commissioning fees, but rather with the loss of income due to poor attendance whenever new works were performed. In the view of the Stewards, merely to be invited to compose for Three Choirs was a privilege which might do much to establish the reputation of a composer and his work. Such terms could hardly be attractive to a penniless unknown or to an eminent and established composer.

Sir John Stainer declined his invitation. Parry accepted reluctantly: 'It has been almost impossible for me to write anything at all now, so constant are the claims upon every hour I have to dispose of. But undoubtedly I shall be proud to attempt something for the honour of my native County if I can possibly find time for it.'[7]

On 1 April 1898, Rosalind Ellicott wrote to Barrett Cooke regretting that she had no opportunity of composing a new orchestral work but offering her choral ballad, *Henry of Navarre*, written for Queen's College, Oxford, instead. Two weeks later, at a meeting of the Finance Committee, Brewer asked that an invitation be sent to Elgar to write a short orchestral work in place of Miss Ellicott's piece. He received a reply by return of post:

> Forli
> Malvern
>
> April 17, 1898
>
> Dear Mr Brewer,
>
> I have received a request from the Secretary to write a short orchestral thing for the Evening Concert. I am sorry I am too busy to do so.
>
> I *wish, wish, wish*, you would ask Coleridge-Taylor to do it. He still wants recognition and is far away the cleverest fellow amongst the young men. *Please* don't let your Committee throw away the chance of doing a good act!
>
> Yours sincerely
>
> Edward Elgar[8]

A month later Brewer received a letter from A.J. Jaeger, head of the publishing department at Novello & Co.:

London

May 12, 1898

Dear Mr Brewer,

My friend Mr Elgar told me a week ago that he has refused an offer to write an orchestral work for your Festival. I am glad to hear it for *his* sake for he has his hands full with *Caractacus* and the haste with which most of you good men have to compose their Festival works is on the whole the great bane of English music. Everybody seems to write under fearful pressure (especially Parry) and the consequences we all know, alas! Well, it is not my business, but I am awfully sorry it is so.

My object in writing is to draw your attention to a young friend of mine, S. Coleridge-Taylor, who is most wonderfully gifted and might write your Committee a *fine* work in a short time. He has a quite Schubertian facility of invention and his stuff is always original and fresh. He is the coming man, I'm quite sure! He is only 22 or 23 but there is nothing immature or inartistic about his music. It is worth a great deal to me – I mean I value it very highly, because it is so original and often *beautiful*. Here is a real melodist at last.

Why not try him and make the '98 Festival memorable by the introduction of young S. C-T. He scores very well, in fact he conceives everything orchestrally and never touches the P.F. when composing! I suppose you know that his father is a negro. Hence his wonderful *freshness*.

Why not give him a commission? He would rise to the occasion and do something good.

His symphony in A major is a most original work. We are doing a short Cantata of his, *Hiawatha's Wedding Feast*; delightful stuff! Won't that do for your Festival? You want a secular work don't you? I'll send you the M.S. score (P.F.) if you like (though at present in the printer's hands).

At any rate you keep your eye on the lad, and believe me, he is *the* man of the future in musical England.

Yours faithfully

A.J. Jaeger[9]

Brewer was obviously still not quite convinced about Coleridge-Taylor because on 21 April he suggested to the committee that Edward German be invited to write a new piece for the Festival. Nothing came of thhis, and it was not until 28 May 1898 that he recommended Coleridge-Taylor – leaving the young composer just three months to complete his work. The result, an Orchestral Ballade in A minor, caused a sensation at the 1898(G) Festival secular concert, and Coleridge-Taylor, who conducted his own piece, received a tremendous ovation. The programme also included Wagner's overture to *Die Meistersingers*; Rosalind Ellicott's *Henry of Navarre*; and Sullivan's *The Golden Legend*. The Gloucester Shire Hall was packed and 'the audience . . . expressed their appreciation . . . in a very forcible manner, despite the almost disabling heat'.[10]

Sir Hubert Parry's contribution to the 1898 Festival was his *A Song of Darkness and Light*, performed at the beginning of the Thursday morning concert, which also included Beethoven's Symphony No. 3 in E flat ('Eroica'); the Adagio and Finale from Stanford's Symphony No. 5 in D major (*L'Allegro ed il Penseroso*), conducted by the composer; and Parts 1 and 2 of Bach's *Christmas Oratorio*.

The other 'novelties' were included in the Opening Service on Sunday 11 September. C.H. Lloyd had written a *Festival Overture*; C. Lee Williams a *Magnificat and Nunc Dimittis*; and Brewer a setting of Psalm 98. And for the first time at the Gloucester Festival a work by Elgar was performed: 'The Meditation' from *Lux Christi*.

But the most interesting item in Brewer's first Festival crept in almost by accident. He had intended that the Wednesday concert should include Brahms's *Ein Deutsches*

Requiem (Brahms died in 1897) and asked Barrett Cooke to hire copies from Novello & Co. However, the German publisher refused permission for the work to be performed from hired copies, and to purchase the music would have cost £20 – too much in the Stewards' view. An alternative suggestion, to perform Stanford's *Requiem*, was also considered, but for that Boosey's wanted a 16-guinea hire fee. Precious time was passing. Then a third possibility presented itself.

The first performance of Verdi's *Four Sacred Pieces* had been given at the Paris Grand Opera on 7 April 1898. Three weeks later Dean Spence proposed that this work should be included in the Festival programme. Barrett Cooke wrote to Verdi's publisher, Messrs Ricordi, but the hire fee which they quoted exceeded the cost of performing either the Brahms or the Stanford. He asked for a reduction, and on 16 May received a telegram from Messrs Ricordi:

> Price quoted exceptionally low considering importance of Works and right of first performance. However, relying on your securing thoroughly good performance will reduce to 15 guineas. Reply requested before Friday.[11]

Barrett Cooke accepted these terms. Three of the four Verdi pieces were hired for one guinea less than the cost of the Stanford *Requiem*, and received a 'thoroughly good' first performance in England under Brewer's baton on Wednesday 14 September 1898. The *Stabat Mater*, *Laudi alla Vergine* and *Te Deum* were given 'in a manner with which the composer himself might well have been satisfied. The beauty of the quartet . . . made a deep impression, while the two choral and orchestral pieces . . . went to the hearts of all who listened. The effect was profound – as deep as the solemn stillness which reigned everywhere among the audience.'[12] Verdi wrote to Brewer – 'a letter full of gratitude' – and the following Christmas sent him a signed photograph. The pieces which were Verdi's farewell to the earth helped to launch Herbert Brewer's reputation as a Three Choirs conductor. His labours, reported *The Musical Times*, 'carried him to a recognised place among those who wield the baton as to the manner born'. And the 1898 Festival was a financial as well as an artistic success – the deficit was less than £50 instead of over £600 as in 1895.

In taking up his appointment at Gloucester, Alfred Herbert Brewer was returning home. He was born in Gloucester on 21 June 1865 and was a chorister in the cathedral from 1877 to 1880. Brewer began his musical studies, alongside G.R. Sinclair, under Charles Harford Lloyd. The two boys were so alike that they were often mistaken for each other – a confusion which persisted into their later lives.

Brewer obtained the first organ scholarship at the Royal College of Music (April 1883), where he studied under Sir Walter Parratt and other professors. His church organistships were St Catherine's and St Mary de Crypt, both in Gloucester (1881), St Giles, Oxford (1882) and St Michael's, Coventry (1886–92). He was organ scholar of Exeter College, Oxford, from 1883 to 1885 and then, briefly, organist at Bristol Cathedral. From 1892 to 1897 he held the post of music-master at Tonbridge School. While there he had a curious experience:

> The organistship at Liverpool Town Hall became vacant through the resignation of W.T. Best. I applied and was chosen with two others to compete . . . After hearing that I had been selected I dreamt most vividly that my friend, Lee Williams, was retiring from the organistship of Gloucester Cathedral, the post of all others which I wished to hold. The dream occurred on three successive

nights and so unsettled me that I wrote to Liverpool to request that my name might be withdrawn from the list.[13]

A month later the organistship of Gloucester became vacant through the resignation of Charles Lee Williams due to ill health. Brewer obtained his FRCO in 1897 and took the degree of Bachelor of Music at Dublin University in the same year. In 1905 he received the Lambeth degree of D. Mus., and in 1926 he was knighted.

Brewer's contemporary at Worcester, Ivor Atkins, made a shaky start at his first Three Choirs Festival in 1899. The orchestra under its Leader, Alfred Burnett, was praised for the excellence of its playing, but the chorus was badly criticized – and the blame was laid at the feet of the inexperienced Atkins for not being fully in touch with his singers. Lack of experience was also evident in some of the programme planning. At the Opening Service, for instance, Wagner's *Kaisermarsch* was played during the offertory. Even the most ardent of Wagner's admirers might well have thought this piece of unrestrained jingoism, composed to celebrate the defeat of France and the founding of the German Empire in 1870 and 1871, somewhat out of place in an English cathedral on a Sunday afternoon.

The concert on Tuesday evening began with Charles Lee Williams's little piece *A Harvest Song*, during which the organ broke down. *Die Vätergruft* followed – an unaccompanied setting of Uhland's poem by Peter Cornelius for bass soloist and chorus. 'The solo was artistically interpreted by Mr Plunket Greene, who sang it in the original German, but the chorus appeared to be singing in an unknown tongue.'[14]

Coleridge-Taylor scored another Three Choirs success conducting the only 'novelty' of the Festival, his *Solemn Prelude*, at the beginning of the Wednesday morning concert. But the performance of Brahms's *German Requiem* which followed, conducted by Atkins, was a disappointment. After the interval Elgar conducted *The Light of Life*, in which the soloists were Esther Palliser, Marie Brema, Edward Lloyd and Andrew Black, and a very long programme ended with Dvořák's *Te Deum*.

Had Atkins's original intentions been realized this concert would have included the first performance of a symphony by Elgar; something which Elgar had been keen to do when, in 1898, he had suggested to Atkins the idea of a symphony written round the subject of Gen. Gordon. But by November 1898 Elgar was having second thoughts – which were passed on to his friend A.J. Jaeger: 'Then *unofficially*, poor old Worcester wants a symphony! . . . Now as to Gordon: the thing possesses me, but I can't write it down yet: I *may* make it the Worcester work if that engagement holds.'[15]

The 'Gordon' symphony was never written. Elgar could not afford to spend many months working on a composition which brought no fee and, in any case, he had not reached the stage in his development where he was ready to write a symphony.

That evening, in the Worcester Public Hall, Elgar conducted the first performance of his *Enigma Variations* with the new coda written in response to a request from Jaeger that he should make more of the Finale. Jaeger had expressed his own faith in Elgar in the columns of the July edition of *The Musical Times*:

Effortless originality – the only true originality – combined with thorough *savoir faire*, and, most important of all, beauty of theme, warmth, and feelings are his credentials, and they should open to him the hearts of all who have faith in the future of our English art and appreciate beautiful music wherever it is met.[16]

The next morning 'tip-toe expectation was rife' in the cathedral. For the first time in Three Choirs history an American composer was to conduct his work in the Festival. Atkins had invited Professor Horatio Parker of Yale University to conduct his oratorio *Hora Novissima*, a setting of part of a twelfth-century Latin poem, *The Rhythm of Bernard de Morlaix on the Celestial Country*. Elgar was in the audience.

For some years he had been considering *The Dream of Gerontius* as a possible subject for his music. At the heart of Newman's poem, Gerontius releases his hold on earthly life with that same cry: 'Novissima hora est'. Elgar was ready. There could be no doubt about the source of inspiration for his next major work.

Between Atkins's first Worcester Festival in 1899 and his second in 1902 the Boer War had begun and ended, Queen Victoria had died, and King Edward VII had ascended to the throne. In those three years Atkins had gained in confidence and conducting ability sufficiently for him to follow the examples of Sinclair and Brewer in drawing his Festival Chorus only from the Three Choirs cities, and for *The Musical Times* to conclude that, 'Mr Atkins has enormously improved since three years ago; he has got the grip of the thing well in hand now, and will develop assuredly into a really admirable conductor.'[17]

Ivor Algernon Atkins was born on 29 November 1869 in Cardiff, where his father, Frederick Pyke Atkins, was organist of St John's Church. He received his earliest training in music from his father and took organ lessons from Charles Lee Williams, at that time organist of Llandaff Cathedral. As a boy-organist he officiated at two churches, Marstow and Pencoyd. In 1885, aged fifteen, he went to Truro as a pupil of, and assistant to, G.R. Sinclair, whom he followed to Hereford in 1890. Two years later Atkins took the degree of Mus. B. at Oxford, and soon afterwards gained the FRCO. He became a D. Mus. by examination at Oxford in 1920 and was knighted the following year.

Ivor Atkins and Edward Elgar were particularly close friends for over forty years, meeting almost every week until Elgar's death in 1934. The story of this friendship has been told in vivid and accurate detail by Atkins's son, E. Wulstan Atkins, in a book which gives greater insights into this relationship, and its bearing on Three Choirs, than is possible in the present history.[18]

The Festivals of 1900 and 1901 reflected the mood of the country: of patriotism born of the Boer War and of mourning following the death of Queen Victoria on 22 January 1901.

New works introduced at the Hereford Festival in 1900 included Horatio Parker's setting of Psalm 107 and Samuel Coleridge-Taylor's song cycle *The Soul's Expression*, for contralto and orchestra. The Tuesday morning concert was termed a 'Patriotic Performance', and included two 'novelties' – Parry's *Thanksgiving Te Deum*, 'composed . . . to commemorate the noble achievements of the British Forces in South Africa', and a setting by Stanford for chorus, orchestra and bugle *obbligato* of W.E. Henley's poem *Last Post*:

> The day's high work is over and done,
> And these no more will need the sun:
> Blow, you bugles of England, blow!

The Parry and Stanford pieces were both conducted by their composers, and in the same concert 'Dr Sinclair brought his forces through with flying colours' in performances of Brahms's Symphony No. 2 in D and the Verdi *Requiem*, in which the soloists were Emma Albani, Marie Brema, Edward Lloyd and Andrew Black. After the performance a telegram was despatched to the composer:[19]

> Maestro Verdi   Busseto
> Saluti affetuosi da tutti dopo una recita splendida del Requiem Festival di Hereford.
> [signed] Albani-Gye, Brema, Lloyd, Sinclair, Elgar, Santley, Stanford

Determined to press ahead with innovations, Sinclair not only repeated the performances of Tchaikovsky's Symphony No. 6 in B minor (*Pathetique*), and the Good Friday music (Act III) and Finale (Act I) of Wagner's *Parsifal* which he had given in the cathedral in 1897, but also conducted a fine performance of Beethoven's *Choral* Symphony with Albani singing in the work for the first time in her career. Even in a new century, Sinclair's audacity was seen as too much by some, including the critic of *The Musical Times*:

> [The *Parsifal* extracts were] as much out of place – if not actually irreverent – in a Cathedral as Tchaikovsky's Symphony. Another attempted Cathedralisation was that of Beethoven's Choral Symphony, with a sacred (!) version of Schiller's words. Here again, while fully acknowledging Dr Sinclair's splendid qualities and the valuable services he has rendered to the cause of music in Hereford, I must part company with him on a question that has caused many misgivings in the minds of not a few thoughtful people in regard to the wisdom of admitting essentially non-sacred works into cathedrals.[20]

The year 1900 marked the farewell appearance at a Three Choirs Festival of Edward Lloyd. A Hereford lady presented him with a beautiful Jersey heifer named 'Symphony', and the Hereford Festival Choir a pair of silver candlesticks. In return, Lloyd wrote to members of the choir:

> My dear Friends,
>   I much appreciate your kindness in presenting me with those handsome Candle Sticks & thank you most sincerely for the tangible proof of your regard & good will.
>   You may rest assured that I shall greatly value your gift & all the pleasant associations it will bring back to my memory.
>   It was at Gloucester under Dr S.S. Wesley that I made my first appearance at a Three Choirs Festival. That was in 1871 when Dr Sinclair was a nice little boy of four in pinafores. I have therefore been connected with these famous music meetings on & off – mostly on – for the long period of nearly thirty years, during which time I have endeavoured to pursue the even tenor of my ways.
>   I am very grateful for the kindness that has been shown to me during all those long years, & which has reached its culminating point in the presentation to me of this token of your regard.
>   I am forwarding each of you a signed photograph which I hope you will honour me by accepting.
>   With every good wish & sincere congratulations on your excellent singing at the recent Festival.
> I am
> Yours very truly
> Edward Lloyd[21]

The first, disastrous, performance of Elgar's *The Dream of Gerontius* was given under Richter's baton at the Birmingham Festival on 3 October 1900. Everything had conspired to ruin a work, the worth of which Elgar knew only too well. The chorus-master, Swinnerton Heap, who understood Elgar's music, died in May before the rehearsals began, and in the interval before G.R. Sinclair took his place, the elderly W.C. Stockley took over. Stockley did not share Elgar's vision. The choir took a dislike to the music and failed to make an effort: Richter dragged the tempi. For Elgar the occasion was a nightmare. In spite of all, the critics hailed *The Dream of Gerontius* as a great work. An article by Otto Lessman for the *Allgemeine Musik Zeitung* was translated for *The Musical Times* of 1 January 1901:

> If I mistake not, the coming man has already arisen in the English musical world, an artist who has instinctively freed himself from the scholasticism which, till now, has held English art firmly bound in its fetters, an artist who has thrown open mind and heart to the great achievements which the mighty tone-masters of the century now departed have left us as a heritage for the one to come – Edward Elgar, the composer of *The Dream of Gerontius*.

No plans were made to include *The Dream of Gerontius* in the 1901(G) Festival, but Brewer invited Elgar to conduct the Prelude and 'Angel's Farewell' as part of the Opening Service, as well as his *Cockaigne* overture in the secular concert – part of a programme which included new works by Sir Frederick Bridge, W.H. Bell, Cowen and Hervey. But Elgar also played a vitally important part in ensuring the success of Herbert Brewer's own 'novelty' contribution to the 1901 Festival – his cantata *Emmaus*. Brewer, in his autobiography, recounted how this came about:[22]

> On receiving the invitation from the Stewards to write a work for the Festival I consulted my friend, Joseph Bennett, who, as is well known, had considerable experience and great gifts as a writer of libretti. His books are numerous and amongst them are to be found at least three Operas, some twelve Oratorios and half a dozen Cantatas. Who then could give better advice or help in such a matter? The fact that he was a Gloucestershire man was another attraction to me. His reply to my appeal was that he would put on his thinking-cap and would do all he could to provide me with the necessary book.
>
> I had not long to wait, for within a few days it arrived. It was on the subject of the Disciples journeying to Emmaus, and *Emmaus* was to be the title of the work.
>
> With the words in my possession, I travelled to North Wales for a holiday, where I hoped to stay until the Cantata was finished.
>
> The surroundings were so congenial and I became so interested in the subject that I finished the work within four weeks.
>
> I took the first opportunity of going through it with Mr. Bennett before submitting it to a publisher, and as it satisfied his critical ear I lost no time in placing it in the hands of Messrs. Novello & Co.
>
> Everthing went smoothly until the programme was publicly announced in the early spring preceding the Festival. The final proofs had been passed and I was about to score the work when I received crushing news from the publishers. They had had a communication from another composer to the effect that he had noticed in the programme that my new work was a setting of Mr. Joseph Bennett's words entitled *Emmaus*. He went on to say that he had purchased these words from Mr. Bennett some years previously.
>
> It transpired that Bennett, when searching through his manuscripts for a subject for my work, came across some loose sheets of paper on which was written a scene entitled *At Emmaus*, and forgetting all about the former transaction sent them to me as suitable material for a Cantata.
>
> In reply to a letter of distress from me Bennett wrote that he had been in many a worse mess and all would come right! He would re-write the words.
>
> This, however, entailed the re-writing of a great part of the music.

When this difficulty had been surmounted we were within a few weeks of the Festival – the chorus had their part to learn and not a note had been scored.

I was seriously thinking of withdrawing it from the programme when I received the following letter from Elgar:

Bettws-y-coed
N. Wales
June 14, 1901

My dear Brewer

Good! If I *can* I'll conduct *Cockaigne* for you but you would do it all right if I cannot come. I'll look out for you in town next week.

Jaeger – who has been in Malvern – but of course you know that – tells me by this post that you are somehow worried – (the exact *nuance* I don't quite understand – about getting your work ready) – he said something before we left home and I told him you must not be worried and that if necessary to make things smooth I would orchestrate some for you – that's all – I know it's a cheek to offer but if I can save you a little worry let me do so.

Yours ever
Edward Elgar

A more generous act could not be imagined. The proof copy of *Emmaus* was sent to him, and in a few days I received a letter which serves to prove the infinite trouble he took over the score:

Malvern
June 30, 1901

My dear Brewer,

I have scored Nos. 1, 4, 5, 6, 9 and 10. If that's not enough you must let me know. I send on my MS. I *hope* it will please you but I feel much at sea as to your wishes and I am sadly afraid you will not like my interpretation – the Tuttis may be all right.

No. 1 – see p. 7 of MS. (p. 2 in vocal score).

I *fattened* out the p.f. arrgt here – see strings especially last three bars, and on – you can easily sacrifice any of my orch: devices by a stroke of the pen.

I took the *bar before B* to be the actual 'chord of climax' and worked up to that: hence the brass alone and cumulative effect 3rd bar 3rd line.

See Andante Moderato p. 16 – I didn't know how much *force* you want and I have made you a fine burst, which will sound jolly but you may want to be more austere – It can easily be cut out.

p. 17, line 2, I gave this wholly (except final chords) for strings – I don't think it wants *colour* but you may have meant it for *wind* – but I give the soft wind a chance (contrasting) at letter R.

At O are these chords what you want? or do you want strings? at P I have to carry on the *flow* of the parts added a few notes for Vio: I – knock 'em out if you like.

2 bars before S. I've stuck *c* in first Vio: to avoid clashing with vocal part – also in the *rall*. near end – I have carried celli down to A.

The harp is effective but *ad lib.*

Thinking you will use the organ in other more likely places I've not put it in except a ped: or two in introduction.

I *have not* revised any of it I fear, as usual, there may be many errors but one of your pupils could look it thro': the first thing however is to know if it will *DO* at all for you.

Kind regards
Yours ever
Ed. Elgar

P.S. – I find I cannot send the parcel by post to-day: but will despatch it to-morrow. Send me a wire *in the a.m.* saying if you want me to continue any other numbers – *spell* the number (seven not 7) to avoid mistakes. If you are at liberty come over to see me, if necessary, and have lunch or something, let me hear if you are coming. I'm not let out on account of my chill.

I should be glad to see you. In haste.

A few days later he writes:

Malvern
July 7, 1901

My dear Brewer

I shall hope to despatch by an early post to-morrow the remainder of your score – it's all ready now but Sunday's a *dies non* with us as far as business posts are concerned.

I have taken great pleasure in trying to interpret your thoughts and feelings and only hope I have not grossly misrepresented them. Now: please *accept* my work on your score and never think I want any return whatever: keep a kind thought for a fellow sometime – that's all.

Please look very carefully thro' all the parts especially – once more – the transposing things.

I have enjoyed your themes immensely and they lend themselves to colour famously. I am especially pleased with No. 7 and (as far as I am concerned) with the first part of No. 11 – the end is good (as far as you're concerned) but I think you might have instrumented it better than I have.

I wish the work every success and if you have been saved any pin-pricks and have had a good rest I am happy in having done it!

Our kindest regards to your both.

Yours always
Edward Elgar

In the vocal score of *Emmaus* Elgar wrote – Began June 27, 1901. Ended July 7, 1901.

What this unselfish act meant to me it is difficult to describe. It not only relieved me of an enormous amount of work at an anxious time, but the scoring of my work by the master hand has been an invaluable lesson to me and I feel that what measure of success *Emmaus* has attained is largely due to the effective orchestration. When one considers the number of big works Elgar then had on hand and the physical strain alone of the actual writing, one has some slight conception of the generosity of this most friendly act.

And here I would record my gratitude to Lady Elgar for her untiring energy in preparing the score for her husband to work upon – work behind the scenes, unknown, unrecognized, yet how valuable!

In spite of all these efforts to avoid the infringement of copyright the lawyers were not to be so appeased, and a week before the Festival we were warned that the performance of *Emmaus* would render us liable for heavy penalties.

This cheering (!) news greeted me on my arrival in London for the rehearsals of soloists and orchestra. Madame Albani, who was to be one of the soloists in the work, said that if imprisonment was to be the result, she would accompany me to prison!!

Legal interviews ensued and permission was given for the work to be performed on condition that it was afterwards withdrawn and the plates destroyed.

To such terms I naturally could not consent. The work must be given a chance to live or not be performed at all.

Eventually, through the good auspices of Messrs. Novello, the claim was withdrawn and the work allowed to be published and performed.[23]

Emmaus was given on Thursday evening, 12 September 1901, with Albani, Sobrino and Ben Davies, and was repeated in 1907(G). Brewer is said to have been so proud of the compliment which Elgar had paid him in orchestrating *Emmaus* that the MS score remained displayed in a place of honour in his music-room thereafter. The original MS and orchestral parts of the work remained lost after Brewer's death, in spite of numerous attempts by scholars particularly interested in the Elgar scoring to find them. They were re-discovered quite by accident while researching this history, together with the original MS scores of Brewer's other works, wrapped in brown-paper parcels in the basement archive of the Gloucester City Library.

By 1902, the engagement of choral singers from outside the Three Choirs counties having ended, the Festival settled into a regular annual pattern. The choral contingent from the Festival city of the year was normally the largest, but each was taught the music of the coming programme by its own conductor in the early part of the year, and the complete Festival Chorus met for combined rehearsal before the summer holiday. Rehearsals for the orchestra with solo voices were held in London in the week before the Festival. The orchestra came down on the Saturday in time for a hasty rehearsal with the chorus of the music for the 'Grand Opening Service' held in the cathedral on Sunday afternoon. Monday, from about 9.30 a.m. to 5.30 p.m., was given to the general rehearsal in the cathedral; this was known to the chorus as 'Black Monday' – four days' music had to be hurried through in one day! *Elijah* was performed on Tuesday morning and *Messiah* on Friday morning. Other choral and orchestral works were given in the cathedral on Tuesday evening, Wednesday and Thursday morning and Thursday evening. Morning performances in the cathedral were interrupted by an interval of one hour for lunch and continued in the afternoon. On Wednesday evening there was a secular concert in one of the public halls and, at Hereford only, a chamber concert on Friday evening.

In spite of some opposition Sinclair, Brewer and Atkins were prepared to force the pace of change in Festival programming while retaining the ever-popular *Elijah* and *Messiah*. These two pieces were, in any case, so familiar to the chorus and orchestra that little of the precious rehearsal time was needed each year to polish them up – a poor excuse but a practical one for falling in with public demand. In 1904 Brewer managed to increase the London orchestral rehearsals from two to three, but this was still inadequate to deal with the number and complexity of new and often difficult works.

Consider the pressures on Atkins during his two orchestral rehearsal days in London in 1902, the year of King Edward VII's coronation. His programme included Beethoven's Fifth, Brahms's Third and Tchaikovsky's Sixth symphonies; the first performance at Three Choirs of a work by Richard Strauss – *Tod und Verklärung*; a Bach cantata – *The Lord is a Sun and Shield*; Percy Pitt's *Coronation March*; and Handel's coronation anthem *The King shall rejoice*. Then there was the music for the Opening Service. And time had to be found for composers who would be conducting new works at the Festival: Granville Bantock, *The Witch of Atlas*; Horatio Parker, Part III of *The Legend of St Christopher*; Walford Davies, *The Temple*; and Edward Elgar, directing *The Dream of Gerontius* personally for the first time – the highlight of a Festival which would also include his *Sursum Corda*, composed in 1894 for a special cathedral service honouring a visit to Worcester by the Duke of York (the future King George V), *Cockaigne*, the national anthem arrangement, and three of the *Sea Songs*.

Just as he had recommended Coleridge-Taylor to Brewer, Elgar suggested to the Worcester Festival Committee that Henry Walford Davies (1869–1941) should be invited to write a new work for them. The result, *The Temple*, is an oratorio in two parts which tell two stories, one of David's desire to build 'an house unto the name of the Lord', and the other of Solomon's accomplishment of the task. In his biography of the composer, H.C. Colles described the problems and anguish which faced Walford Davies in bringing his work to performance at Worcester – an experience not unlike that of Elgar in Birmingham two years earlier:

Walford had spent a good deal of time going to and fro to the sectional rehearsals earlier in the year, and in the process had made friends with the conductors, Atkins, Sinclair and Brewer, with officials and with the members of the choir. That was all to the good. They were all anxious to do their best for him, but none could disguise from themselves or him that he had unwarily piled up the obstacles to success.

Mme Albani, the reigning star of the moment, was offered him as his soprano soloist. He took his score to her; she asked at once to see her 'Prayer', was disappointed to find it was only two pages long, found it 'beautiful but not her *tessitura*' She was not keen to sing the narrative part which was all to be mixed up with choir. This was in May; later she was cajoled into compliance. But her instinct was right; it was not essentially her part. Walford succeeded in persuading the Committee to engage Gregory Hast for his tenor. They were a little doubtful of Hast's power to fill the Cathedral (either with people or with tone). But here Walford proved himself right. He got in Hast a tenor who understood him and his music intimately, and 'Solomon's Prayer' was the most impressive movement in the whole work. He would have liked to have had Forington too; the baritone solo is clearly written for his voice. But this was not allowed. Lane Wilson was chosen; he took great pains with it and sang it very well.

The chorus had shown promise in their several rehearsals with the piano, but the clouds began to gather when Walford faced the orchestra in London. His orchestral experience, as either orchestrator or conductor, was still rudimentary, and he was naturally anxious. He talked too much. He tried to explain what the work was about when the hard-bitten orchestral players only wanted to know what they had to do, to do it, and pass on to the next feature of their long programme. There were mistakes in the parts, and time was wasted in correcting them. There were obvious miscalculations in the scoring and emendations had to be made at the last moment. These are the troubles which every young composer-conductor encounters at the outset, but Walford took them more hardly than most. From the rehearsals of *The Temple* he gained the reputation of being what an elderly critic called 'a worrying man', a reputation which it took him a long time to live down.

By the time that they all arrived at Worcester Walford certainly was worrying, and knew that he had cause. He realized too late that his music was very much more difficult than it ought to have been for such a purpose. The choir half knew their job, knew it in that way which allows all to go well in the practice-room and risks it going awry when the singers are placed on the tiers of a tall rostrum with a cumbersome orchestra between them and the soloists with whom they have to collaborate. Walford's ideal had been a chamber music *ensemble* on an immense scale. The anomaly was exposed in the result.

He begged for more rehearsal time, got it, but took more than he was given. His exigence did not increase his popularity with the overdriven choir. Ivor Atkins was patient, but when he tried to comfort Walford by suggesting that things were better than they seemed, Walford received his words merely as a confession of the low standard which it must be his mission to raise.

Atkins, however, was proved right. Walford had made no allowance for that innate capacity of Englishmen to pull themselves together in the face of the enemy. In our slipshod musical life it has become proverbial that a bad rehearsal means a good performance and *vice versa*. Never fully prepared, the semblance of preparedness which a lucky final rehearsal gives often leads to complacence in the subsequent performance, while a bad rehearsal puts everyone on their mettle to display their British phlegm. It is splendid, though it is not art.

On the day everyone played up (to use the sporting vernacular) extraordinarily well, and much of the work had its intended effect. Mme Albani led the narrative sections with a surprising amount of dramatic energy, and that scene of the consecration of the Temple which had first inspired Walford to the task was the most stirring moment in the narrative. The big choral numbers too did not fail of their effect. Any unprejudiced person could perceive that the choral writing was masterly and that there was strong lyrical feeling in the big solos, baritone and tenor. *The Temple* was in fact all good music, and some of it was quite evidently great music.[24]

The first Three Choirs performance of *The Dream of Gerontius* was hardly free from problems either. Ivor Atkins realized that there would be doctrinal difficulties; principally that the Invocations to the Blessed Virgin Mary and to the saints in the poem were contrary to the Thirty-nine Articles of the Anglican Church. Although, in informal discussions, both the Dean of Worcester, Dr R.W. Forrest, and Canon T.L. Claughton, Chairman of the Festival Executive Committee, were anxious with Atkins for the performance to take place in the cathedral, written representation to the Bishop had to be made.

Elgar understood the difficulties and agreed that if changes to the text of the poem were agreed he would approach his friend Father Richard Bellasis of the Birmingham Oratory, and through him, Father William Neville, Cardinal Newman's executor and owner of the copyright.

By late April 1902, the Bishop of Worcester had given his approval to modifications to the text of *Gerontius* on the basis of omitting the Litany of the Saints, and of a substitution of 'Jesus', 'Lord' or 'Saviour' for 'Mary'; of 'souls' for 'souls in purgatory'; and, in the Angel's Farewell, of 'prayers' for 'Masses'. More than a month later Elgar had still not approached the Birmingham Oratory with the proposed changes, and the printing of Word Books for the Festival had become an imminent necessity. When on 16 May the Elgars had to leave for Germany to attend rehearsals of *Gerontius* at the Lower Rhine Festival, Atkins took the initiative, preparing two sets of drafts, the first embodying the word modifications approved by the Bishop, and the second to a plan of his own of omissions only, which would be indicated by asterisks, which he rightly felt might be more acceptable and which he had already agreed with Elgar.

Father Neville gave his approval of the omissions; the Bishop concurred; and printing of the Word Books went ahead. 'The libretto', said *The Musical Times*, 'had been purposely mutilated to suit Anglican tastes: but that was surely a deplorable blunder; at this rate how many works of art, when given in cathedrals, would "escape a whipping"? Surely this thing was too narrow and childish – as though the work were given from any sectarian standpoint!'[25]

But in spite of modification, the performance itself was deeply moving. William Green was to have taken the title-role but was unable to attend the London rehearsal and so, at short notice, John Coates sang *Gerontius* for the first of what was to be very many times. Muriel Foster was memorable as the Angel, and Harry Plunket Greene took the part of the Priest and the Angel of the Agony. The chorus sang wonderfully well – only at the end did 'the tremendous strain of the work' begin to tell on them. Elgar, whose mother had died a few days earlier, conducted in mourning black. Granville Bantock wrote to his friend Ernest Newman on 11 September 1902:

> Never have I experienced such an impression before, as I did on hearing 'Gerontius' this morning in the Cathedral. If Elgar never writes another note of music, I will still say that he is a giant, & overtops us all. His music moved me profoundly . . . It is a great work, & the man who wrote it, is a Master, and a Leader. We were all deeply affected, and gave way to our feelings. While Elgar was conducting, the tears were running down his cheeks. I want to hear nothing better. I have felt as if transfixed by a spike from the crown of my head to my feet. Once on hearing *Parsifal* at Bayreuth, when the dead swan is brought on, & today, at the words 'Novissima hora'.[26]

After the performance, Alice Elgar gave lunch to several friends. One of her guests was Henry Walford Davies. Later, she wrote in her diary: '*Crowds* of people came all the aftn. & to tea – & in the evening . . . A most wonderful day to have had in one's life. D.G.'[27]

Notes

1. MT 1897, p. 678
2. 'Elgar at Hereford', in the *RAM* magazine, 1960, p. 6
3. Brewer, *Memories of Choirs and Cloisters* (1931)
4. Gloucester Festival Minute Book, 1897
5. Brewer, *Memories of Choirs and Cloisters* (1931)
6. See Gloucester Festival Minute Book, 1885, p. 92
7. Gloucester Festival Minute Book, 1897
8. Brewer, *Memories of Choirs and Cloisters* (1931), p. 92
9. Ibid., p. 93 Jaeger's memory is perpetuated by Variation 9 ('Nimrod') in Elgar's *Enigma Variations*.
10. MT 1898, p. 667
11. Gloucester Festival Minute Book, 1898
12. MT 1898, p. 667
13. Brewer, *Memories of Choirs and Cloisters* (1931)
14. MT 1899, p. 669
15. Worcester Records Office
16. MT 1899, pp. 464–5
17. MT 1902, p. 676
18. E. Wulstan Atkins, *The Elgar–Atkins Friendship* (David & Charles, 1985)
19. MT 1900, p. 661
20. MT 1900, p. 660
21. A.M. Broadley Collection, Gloucester City Library
22. Brewer, *Memories of Choirs and Cloisters* (1931)
23. For the complete correspondence between Elgar and Brewer on *Emmaus* see Jerrold Northrop Moore, *Edward Elgar, Letters of a Lifetime* (Oxford, 1990) pp. 97–100
24. H.C. Colles, *Walford Davies* (Oxford, 1942), pp. 73–4
25. MT 1902, p. 676
26. See E. Wulstan Atkins, op. cit., pp. 80 and 89
27. See Jerrold Northrop Moore, *Edward Elgar, A Creative Life* (Oxford, 1990), p. 375

CHAPTER THIRTEEN

BEYOND THESE VOICES

I
n September 1900 Granville Bantock (1868–1946) was appointed Principal of the Birmingham and Midland Institute School of Music, and for the next thirty years was a regular visitor to Three Choirs. A number of his works received their first performances at the Festivals, many under Bantock's own direction. Some, such as *The Time Spirit*, a rhapsody for chorus and orchestra, performed at Gloucester in 1904, showed his gift for melodic charm and orchestral colour to pleasing effect; others missed the mark. Bantock's 'Fantastic poem for orchestra, in the form of a Prelude', *The Pierrot of the Minute* (1908(W) and 1924(H)) struck one young Festival-goer, Arthur Lloyd-Baker[1] as 'light but elaborately shapeless'.

Bantock was well known for his oriental proclivities, of which a setting of Fitzgerald's translation of *Omar Khayyam* is the most noted example. But such pieces found no place at Three Choirs. In 1909(H) he conducted his *Old English Suite*, an arrangement for small orchestra of sixteenth-century airs, which prompted *The Musical Times* to suggest that '. . . its example might be followed. Other suites as distinct from rhapsodies formed of old English airs, and particularly of folk songs, which have yet to be treated in this fashion, might be devised by British composers in search of new fields.'[2]

Ralph Vaughan Williams had already formed the Folk Song Society in 1904, writing in the *Morning Post* that 'whatever is done in the way of preserving traditional music must be done quickly; it must be remembered that the tunes, at all events, of true folk songs exist only by oral tradition, so that if they are not soon noted down and preserved they will be lost forever.'[3]

In his *Old English Suite*, Bantock 'lengthened lines and deepened shadows' in his adornment of airs by Orlando Gibbons, John Dowland, John Bull, Giles Farnaby and William Byrd, but 'all in the colours of the original'. The piece which followed in the programme was as refreshingly in the style of the twentieth century as Bantock's was rooted in that of the sixteenth: the first performance of the *Dance Rhapsody No. 1* by Frederick Delius, conducted by the composer in his single Three Choirs appearance.

Bantock's attempts at religious music were given a hearing at Three Choirs but none achieved a second Festival performance. Separate sections of his oratorio *Christus* were given over a period of eight years: an orchestral interlude entitled *The Wilderness*

(1903(H)); *Christ in the Wilderness* (1907(G)) for soprano, baritone, chorus and orchestra, with Agnes Nicholls (afterwards Lady Harty, CBE) and David Ffrangcon-Davies; and *Gethsemane* (1910(G)) – a cantata for baritone, chorus, orchestra and organ in which Frederick Austin was the soloist. These were deeply serious pieces – sometimes dreary, sometimes thrilling, and even occasionally stirring, as in the soprano solo in *Christ in the Wilderness*, scored for harp, woodwind and tambourine – but overall they were failures. 'Mysticism' said Ernest Walker, was 'not part of his endowment.'[4] Perhaps if the whole of *Christus* could have been heard at a single sitting, the totality of Bantock's design and the appropriateness of his music would have made more of an impact. As it was, *Christus* remained a mysteriously hinted-at large work. It was, in any event, too late. The first performance of Elgar's two oratorios inspired by the story of the life of Christ had been given in Birmingham within the same few years: *The Apostles* in 1903 and *The Kingdom* in 1906. Knighted in 1904, Elgar had been appointed Peyton Professor of Music at Birmingham University the following year. He resigned in 1908 and Granville Bantock, who remained in Birmingham until 1933, took his place. Bantock was knighted in 1930.

Samuel Coleridge-Taylor (1875–1912) made his last Three Choirs appearance in 1903(H), conducting the premier of *The Atonement* – a work which suffered badly from the libretto of Mrs Alice Parsons. The following day Arthur Lloyd-Baker was at Hereford to hear Sinclair conduct *The Dream of Gerontius*, with Muriel Foster, John Coates, Lane Wilson and Plunket Greene as soloists, and the first performance of Sir Hubert Parry's motet *Voces Clamantium*. In his view 'The Dream was very fine indeed. Sir Hubert's was more "popular" and easier to listen to.' *The Musical Times* expressed it rather more wordily: the Parry piece was 'an excellently written work, possessing a deeply true and intimate musical spirit, and constructed with a singular sense of fine equipoise.'[5]

The year 1904(G) was an important one for Three Choirs for many reasons: the first performance of Parry's *The Love that casteth out Fear* and Brewer's *The Holy Innocents*; Elgar conducting *The Apostles* and his overture *In the South (Alassio)* for the first time at the Festival; and the unrehearsed and unpredictable appearance of a young Gloucester boy who was to grow up to become not only one of the half-dozen finest composers of song whom England has produced, but also a poet of rare individuality.

The principals in Part I of *Elijah* included Mesdames Sobrino, Hicks Beach and Foster. For Part II, after the luncheon interval, Albani was down to take over from Sobrino as first principal soprano, and Daisy Hicks Beach was not required. The part of the Prophet was taken by David Ffrangcon-Davies. Lloyd-Baker recorded his impressions: 'The best performance of *Elijah* that I've heard. Ffrangcon-Davies magnificent & looked the part: sang without book. Muriel Foster very good indeed. Sobrino rather painful. Albani better than 3 or 6 years ago, owing to visit to S. Africa: quite magnificent.' But when the soloists returned for Part II there was no second soprano with them. Brewer began none the less. Lloyd-Baker continues: 'For "Lift thine eyes" Sobrino didn't turn up, owing to some misunderstanding. Daisy Beach was not to be found, & so the boy was hauled down to sing.'[6]

The 'boy' was the fourteen-year-old chorister who had accompanied Ffrangcon-Davies in Part I in the small part of the Youth in 'O Lord thou hast overthrown' – Ivor Gurney. Writing to Marion Scott at the Royal College of Music years later, Gurney's mother recalled the excitement of the occasion:

> . . . Ivor was top dog he sang with Madam Albani 3 Madams had to sing the trio lift thine eyes and the one when she was fetched down from the Bell Hotel said she didn't know it was time and so it had to be done and Dr Brewer said Ivor was to do it and Madam Albani would have him by her and he looked such a boy to her but they said he done it beautiful an unrehearsed piece and he was frightened at his success when he got home he hid in the kitchen everybody saying Ivor Gurney had been singing with Madam Albani . . .[7]

Sobrino, it seems, had taken lunch at the Bell Hotel and lingered too long over the decanter.

The audience for *Elijah* in 1904 was 2,324 – just one hundred less than for *Messiah*: but by far the largest turnout of the week, 2,784, was for *The Apostles*. The popularity of Elgar's music had, for the first time, topped that of the old traditional favourites. And in 1905 his music occupied fully a quarter of the entire programme at Worcester: *The Dream of Gerontius*, *The Apostles* and the recently written *Introduction and Allegro* for strings (Op. 47). *Gerontius* displaced *Elijah* from its traditional place at the beginning of the Festival, and before the performance Elgar was presented with the Freedom of the City of Worcester. Among the crowd of people lining the High Street from the Guildhall to the cathedral was a young violinist from the orchestra who had also appeared as a composer, conducting his own *Scenes from the Ballet* at the 1904(G) Festival – W.H. Reed:

> . . . the procession making its way from the guildhall to the cathedral with the mayor, the high sheriff and all the aldermen in their civic robes and Elgar walking solemnly in their midst, clothed in a strange gown which puzzled most of the onlookers. Upon enquiry this turned out to be the Yale University gown and hood which Elgar hastened to wear on the very first occasion that a Doctor of Music's robes were needed at any of his public engagements.
>
> Remaining in the memory is another thing in connection with this procession and civic honour, and that is that Elgar turned as he passed a certain house in the High Street on his way to the cathedral and saluted an old gentleman whose face could just be seen looking out of an upper window. It was his father, who was watching the honour being paid to his son by the city of his birth. Being very old and feeble, he was unable to leave his room; but what must his feelings have been on looking out of that window and seeing before his very eyes the fulfilment of his wildest dreams![8]

Back in the cathedral, 3,053 people heard Ivor Atkins conduct *The Dream of Gerontius*. After lunch Part 2 began with Atkins's own *Hymn of Faith*, in which Elgar had assisted with the orchestration. The concert ended with Brahms's Symphony No. 4 in E minor which, as with other symphonic works now being heard freely in the cathedrals, gained immensely from the absence of interruptions by the customary applause between movements.

A precedent was set in 1907(G) when the sixteen-year-old Mischa Elman, who had been engaged to play Beethoven's Violin Concerto in the Shire Hall secular concert, was invited to perform Beethoven's Romance in F as an 'extra' item in the cathedral on Thursday evening:

> The performance of the Romance in the crowded cathedral was a rare and memorable event in the long history of the Three Choirs Festival, and as from the organ loft I gazed at those magnificent Norman pillars in the nave, this thought crossed my mind: What would the earliest worshippers in Gloucester's stately nave have said to such a wonderful exhibition of a boy's skill on an instrument of music?[9]

In 1908(W) Mischa Elman returned to repeat his performance of the Beethoven Violin Concerto – but now that too was admitted to the cathedral. The same programme included a performance of *Everyman*, the cantata which secured Walford Davies's reputation following its premier at the Leeds Festival of 1904 and which for a few years enjoyed great popularity. Sir Charles Villiers Stanford, whose *Stabat Mater* preceded Elman's playing of the Beethoven Concerto in the concert, considered that Walford Davies had reached a high level of creative ability in *Everyman*, but the work fell out of vogue even before the start of the First World War.

Throughout the early years of the present century, the old argument about the suitability of cathedrals for Festival performances ground on, but with generally a little less venom than before. In his sermon at the Opening Service of the 1906 Festival at Hereford the Dean of Gloucester, who had been known to label Three Choirs critics as 'cranks', unearthed a precedent for church festivals which was as obscure as it was irresistible. He had discovered that a sacred mystery play by Roumanos had, as early as the fifth century, been given in the great cathedral of St Sophia in Constantinople. Its title was *The Apostles*!

In 1907(G) Arthur Lloyd-Baker found himself sitting next to the Bishop of Gloucester, E.C.S. Gibson, during tea at the Palace. Gibson had been appointed in 1905 following the death of Bishop Ellicott. 'The Bishop said that he had not been able "to rise to the heights of the Apostles". He expressed no opinion as to the Festival, but it is generally understood that he approves of it so far: it is in a way on its trial, as the Bishop's decision carries great influence even though he has no power to stop it.'[10]

From the point of view of its contribution to art, this would have been no time to stop the Festival. Under Atkins, Brewer and Sinclair Three Choirs had taken on a new lease of life. By 1909(H) *The Musical Times* was able to report that:

> . . . directed by earnestness and energy, the festivals have been gradually working up to a high pitch of excellence. The efforts of three organists may be said to have reached a definite stage on this occasion, for no better choral singing has ever been heard before at this festival. It reflects the condition of the day which finds choral singing in England in a higher state of efficiency than it has been for centuries. The possibility of securing notable results with the choir has been grasped, and to Dr Sinclair belongs the credit of being the first conductor to have charge of the best choir heard at these meetings.[11]

The Festival of 1910(G) opened with Sullivan's *In Memoriam* overture in memory of King Edward VII. For the first time at Gloucester, Dean Spence-Jones permitted a complete performance of *The Dream of Gerontius* – but in the 'Protestantized' version. And at the same concert a new work was heard, the significance to British music of which was immediately apparent to a young student of music from Lydney in the Forest of Dean – Herbert Howells (1892–1983):

> In that year I had become an articled pupil of Dr (later Sir) Herbert Brewer. (In that classification I became a fellow musician with the unforgettable but tragic Gloucester-born composer-poet, Ivor Gurney). At the time I still feared Dr Brewer as much as I revered him. But round about April I was brave enough to ask him whether there was to be any 'new work' at September's Meeting. He seemed puzzled, slow to answer. He had, he admitted, heard of 'the strange composer' . . . who would be bringing a strange work, 'something to do with Tallis'. Lovely first week of September came. With it came the composer from Chelsea, a magnificent figure on the rostrum, a younger but more

commanding version of the then Foreign Secretary, Sir Edward Grey. He was nearly thirty-nine. I gazed at him from the sixth row of the 'stalls' in the nave. (Beside him – in a crowded audience – an empty chair). I was seeing him for the first time. But what mattered was that it was Tuesday night, an Elgar night; a dedicated Elgar audience, all devotees of the by then 'accepted' masterpiece – *The Dream of Gerontius* . . . But there, conducting a strange work for strings, RVW himself, a comparative (or complete?) stranger; and his Fantasy would be holding up the *Dream*, maybe for ten minutes? In fact, for twice ten, as it happened.

He left the rostrum, in the non-applauding silence of those days, thanks be! And he came to the empty chair next to mine, carrying a copy of *Gerontius*, and presently was sharing it with me, while Elgar was conducting the first hearing I ever had of the *Dream*. For a music-bewildered youth of seventeen it was an overwhelming evening, so disturbing and moving that I even asked RVW for his autograph – and got it! I have it, still . . . And I still have what I now know to be a supreme commentary by one great composer upon another – the *Fantasia on a Theme by Thomas Tallis.*[12]

In 1910(G) there was also another deeply significant first performance – but one given before a small and very private audience. W.H. (Billy) Reed had taken over in that year from Frye Parker (Burnett's successor in 1905) as Leader of the Festival Orchestra. On the Saturday following the London rehearsals he called at Herbert Brewer's house. Sir Edward Elgar had finished his new Violin Concerto during the summer:

At once I knew that something exciting was afoot, because Sir Edward had been twice to see if I had arrived.

At all the Festivals of the Three Choirs it was customary for Sir Edward to take a house for the week and have a house-party of music-lovers. On this occasion he had taken one in College Green, a house normally used for the cookery school. It had a very large room containing a grand piano and several pictures. What these represented I never discovered, as they all had their faces turned to the wall. In many of the houses that Sir Edward had lent to him, or that he had taken for a short period (furnished), the pictures were either turned round the wrong way or covered over with some hanging material – even newspaper. No comment was ever made about the odd effect produced in the room. He just didn't want these family portraits, or whatever they were, staring at him; so he turned them round or covered them up.

As soon as I heard I was wanted, I quickly found Sir Edward and learned that Frank Schuster had made a grand suggestion, which was: to invite a select number of people to come to that nice large room at the cookery school on the Sunday evening, when we – Sir Edward and I – could play them the Violin Concerto right through. I said it was an excellent idea, although I must confess I had some inward qualms. I knew every note of the concerto, and exactly how he liked it played: every nuance, every shade of expression; yet I felt a little overwhelmed at being asked to play the solo part at what would actually be the very first performance before an audience. It was one of those facts that you cannot annihilate by just calling it private.

When the time arrived I went over to the house and found the guests assembled. Nearly all the prominent musicians engaged at the Festival were there: the three Festival conductors, Sinclair, Atkins and Brewer; the past organists of Gloucester Cathedral, Harford Lloyd and Lee Williams; some of the musical critics, and the house-party. The room was full; and all the lights were turned out except for some device arranged by Frank Schuster for lighting the piano and the violin-stand.

Sir Edward took his seat at the piano, and after a tense whisper to me – 'You are not going to leave me all alone in the *tuttis*, are you?' – we began. My qualms vanished: I became so thrilled by the atmosphere created, by the evident appreciation of the listeners and the magnetic force that flowed from Sir Edward, that I threw my whole heart and soul into the performance, realising that the soloist is, after all, but the servant of the composer, and that he must strive to render, not merely the notes and brilliance of the passage-work, but the inmost thoughts and the most subtle shades of meaning expressed in the music. That evening is a never-to-be-forgotten memory to me; and I always, as I think of it, feel deeply grateful to him for giving me such an artistic experience.

The orchestration of the concerto was already finished (on August 5th). Fritz Kreisler arrived towards the end of the Gloucester Festival week and at once began to study the concerto for the first public performance, which took place at Queen's Hall in London on November 10th of that year. Such was the energy of Elgar at this period that, as soon as the concerto was finished he was writing another *Pomp and Circumstance* March and correcting proofs of the concerto and other things, besides lending a helping hand and giving the benefit of his advice to Ivor Atkins . . . who was engaged upon a new edition of Bach's *St Matthew Passion.*[13]

Herbert Howells also heard something of Elgar and Kreisler working together:

> On the Wednesday evening Dr Brewer gave me a telegram for Sir Edward Elgar, who, for that week, was renting a lovely house near the Cathedral. 'Take it across to Sir Edward,' he said. 'But give it to him yourself.' I took it . . . waiting for the front door to open, I could hear the sounds of a violin and a piano. The door opened. I told the factotum I must give the telegram to Sir Edward myself. He asked me in, but with a polite warning. 'It might mean waiting. Sir Edward is upstairs with Mr Kreisler, practising.' He added, conspiratorially: 'I suggest you sit quietly at the top of the stairs, by the drawing-room door.' I did just that, for about forty minutes, entranced by hearing what I later knew was the slow movement of the Violin Concerto . . . I carried out instructions.
> Thursday, in the magical week, belonged to Kreisler in triplicate: sartorially, in public gesture and performance. And in historic misadventure. The initial white-tie array had to give way to a change into morning dress. As to gesture, the illustrious soloist bowed low and gracefully to the Cathedral audience, for the first time by any performer in Three Choirs history, and contrary to customary observance on holy ground. Finally, in performance, Bach's E major Concerto began as a matter of temperature-versus-stringed-instruments. In the very earliest phrase Mr Kreisler's E string snapped. Redemption was miraculously swift. The leader of the orchestra (beloved Billy Reed) handed his acclimatised fiddle to his great friend. Fuss was avoided, continuity maintained. Mr K. smiled, enchanted and at ease . . . and there was no final bow. (And no applause, in that day, in any of the three Cathedrals. Silent thanksgiving is a lost art. But 1910 still clung to it in the Three Choirs).[14]

Brewer tells us that when Reed had put a new string on Kreisler's violin he handed it to Kreisler who refused it and continued to use Reed's. 'The two instruments were twins – both being made by Joseph Guarnerius.'[15]

Parry was represented in 1910(G) by his motet *Beyond these voices there is peace*, which had been given its first performance under his baton at Worcester in 1908. The secular concert was given in the newly enlarged and decorated Shire Hall, the improvements to which, made possible by Parry's generosity, consisted mainly in the provision of an extensive balcony. During the evening Sir Hubert was the recipient of a grateful address from the Corporation of the city. In his reply Parry said that he looked to music as an antidote to socialism, hoping that people from the slums would be elevated by the power of the music. Brewer again:

> I had hoped that the gratitude of the city would take a more tangible form and that the Freedom of the City would have been conferred on Sir Hubert. I took steps to bring this about, but unfortunately Parry's political views were very pronounced . . . Party feeling, alas, runs very high in Gloucester as in most cathedral cities, and, as these views did not coincide with those of the party in power at the time, I was unable to achieve my project and secure this recognition of Parry's munificence.[16]

By 1911(W) the Festival had reached a new peak of confidence and artistic balance. The choir consisted of 63 sopranos and 24 boy choristers, 54 contraltos and 13 male altos, 56 tenors and 65 basses – 275 in all. The orchestra under its Leader, W.H. Reed, comprised 97 players selected mainly from the London Symphony Orchestra and included 14 first violins, 12 second violins, 10 violas, 8 cellos, 9 double-basses, 8 flutes and a piccolo,

8 oboes (the extras being required for the *St Matthew Passion*), a cor anglais, 4 clarinets, 5 bassoons, 3 trumpets, 3 trombones and a tuba, percussion and 2 harps.

Wagner had by then, thanks to Sinclair's persistence, become an established name at the Festivals. Extracts from *Parsifal* were regularly included in the cathedral programmes; other works at secular concerts. In 1911 the whole of the Third Act of *Parsifal* was given in Worcester Cathedral with John Coates, William Higley and Robert Radford.

Elgar's hard-won reputation was now established. His first Symphony (1909(H)) and *The Kingdom* (1907(G)) had taken their places among the regular Festival favourites. And in 1911, the year of King George V's coronation, the second Symphony, the unaccompanied six-part motet, *Go song of mine*, the *Coronation March*, and the Violin Concerto, with Fritz Kreisler as soloist, were added.

Another work only previously heard at the coronation was Parry's *Coronation Te Deum*, and there were new compositions by Walford Davies – *Five sayings of Jesus*, with the tenor Gervase Elwes, and Vaughan Williams – *Five Mystical Songs*, in which Campbell McInnes was the baritone soloist.

The Five Mystical Songs, conducted by the composer, preceded the Elgar Violin Concerto at the Thursday evening concert. Vaughan Williams, baton in hand, received something of a shock as his eyes ranged around the orchestra: 'I was thoroughly nervous. When I looked at the fiddles I thought I was going mad, for I saw what appeared to be Kreisler at a back desk. I got through somehow, and at the end I whispered to Reed, "*Am* I mad, or *did* I see Kreisler in the band?" "Oh yes", he said, "he broke a string and wanted to play it in before the Elgar Concerto and couldn't without being heard in the Cathedral."' Years later RVW was telling this story to some players and one of them completed it. 'I was sitting next to Kreisler, one of our people had been taken ill, so he slipped in beside me: just before we started, he said, "Nudge me if there's anything difficult and I'll leave it out."'[17]

Kreisler also played the violin obbligato to the solo, 'Have mercy' in the performance of the Elgar-Atkins edition of Bach's *St Matthew Passion* given on the Thursday morning. His playing, reported *The Musical Times*, was 'one of those perfect things rarely heard'.[18]

Inspired by a visit to Rothenburg-on-Tauber in Germany where he had heard a brass band playing from the top of the church tower, Atkins suggested to Elgar that an effective way to introduce their edition of the *St Matthew Passion* would be by playing before each part a Bach chorale from the top of the cathedral tower. He had it in mind that 'O Man, bemoan thy grievous sin' and 'O Sacred Head surrounded' should be used, and Elgar agreed to orchestrate them for brass instruments.

The playing of the chorales created a deep impression, and for many years they introduced the performances of the *St Matthew Passion* at Three Choirs.

Elgar was at the bottom of another enterprise in the form of a handbill entitled 'Side Shows' (see illustration) which he circulated among his friends on the opening day. Wulstan Atkins has explained its significance:

> The allusions were to well-known public figures, festival personalities and members of the Elgars' house-party. Most of them will be obvious, but perhaps a few need explanation.
>   'Burning of Heretics' refers indirectly to Granville Bantock, who was conducting his new work, *Overture to a Greek Tragedy* at the festival. Bantock was a co-founder of the STP Society, and signed himself the 'Arch Heretic' in their initiation ceremonies.

'Dr Elizabeth Pastoral' was Dr Herbert Brewer, the organist of Gloucester Cathedral, whose *Two Pastorals*, dealing with Elizabethan times, were being performed.

There had been a recent railway strike, with an orderly procession of banners and marching round 'Pitchcroft', a local open space by the river.

Canon J.M. Wilson, the cathedral librarian and a great authority on the architecture and history of the cathedral, had recently written an article about the probable origins of a stone coffin found during the cathedral restorations.

The local papers had reported the story of a fisherman who had caught a perch, which on being cleaned was found to have swallowed a gold ring.

St Kentigern, better known as St Mungo, lived about 518 to 603, and had ascribed to him a number of miracles, including the resuscitation of St Serf's favourite robin after it had been cooked in a pie, but alas, with no golden treasure.

A town house in Worcester had recently been bought for the Bishop, whose main residence was Hartlebury Castle, which was some miles outside the city.

'Bearpit in College Yard' – archaeological excavations were in progress outside the north side of the cathedral.

Worcester was gayer than ever before, with coronation decorations adding to the usual festival flags. The city and the county houses were full of guests, including royalty, and there was a festive mood over everything.[19]

The members of royalty present were the Princess Henry of Battenburg and Prince Leopold, and King Manoel of Portugal and his mother, Queen Amelia.

Another celebrated Festival prankster was the tenor John Coates, whose exploits were recounted in Sir Herbert Brewer's autobiography. One incident involving Coates and Billy Reed apparently fooled a large crowd of people outside Worcester Cathedral before a *Messiah* performance one Friday morning:

They were both staying with me . . . and in the drawing-room of the house which I had taken for the week was a brass hearth-brush which looked uncommonly like a large telescope. Reed, on catching sight of it, exclaimed, 'What an excellent thing for a practical joke!' They immediately proceeded to action and took up their position in College yard and appeared to look through this imaginary telescope at the tower of the Cathedral. Very soon a huge crowd of people collected round them trying to discover what it was they were watching so intently . . . This continued for several minutes, the traffic meanwhile becoming very congested. Then Reed suggested to Coates that it was time for the crowd to see the business end of the hearth-brush. When they saw the bristles appear and spread out at the end of the brass tube and realised how they had been fooled there was a roar of laughter, the crowd rapidly dispersed and . . . proceeded on their way to the Cathedral.[20]

At Hereford in 1906 another tenor had been engaged to sing in *Elijah* and so John Coates had a day off:

But not being of an idle nature he occupied his time in other ways that morning. I had taken a house in the corner of the Close – Harley Court. There was a passage way in front of it leading from the Close to another part of the town. To the surprise of Herefordians and visitors to the Festival they saw, on leaving the Cathedral for the luncheon interval, some notice-boards in front of my house which had not been there earlier in the day. One was placed on a privet hedge warning people 'Not to pluck the flowers'. On a few blades of grass and weeds was another, advising people to 'keep off the sward', and on a door leading to a rubbish heap near the house was the following notice – 'You are requested not to feed the wild Zigmollicans'.

It was highly amusing to watch these well-dressed people walk on tiptoe to the door and peer over cautiously, expecting to see some kind of wild beast in the pen; and then, on discovering only a heap of dead leaves, slink away, casting furtive glances around to see if their action had been observed.[21]

In the next edition of *The Musical Times*, the following comment appeared:

> Much interest was aroused at Hereford by some specimens of that rare animal, the Zigmollican. They were kept in confinement by an eminent brewer residing near the Cathedral, and passers-by who managed to catch a glimpse of the elusive little creatures greatly admired their subtly-tinted coats. It was reported that they had been recently imported by Herr Johann von Ueberrock, the well-known zoological specialist!

By 1912 the days of innocent fun were fast coming to an end. Emma Albani, a Festival institution for thirty-four years, had made her final Three Choirs appearance, in *Messiah*, in 1911(W). In the two years of peace remaining, her place was taken by Ruth Vincent. 'It is not often' recorded *The Musical Times*, 'that we hear the *Messiah* solos sung so truly in tune.'[22]

Muriel Foster also retired after the 1912(H) Festival in which she sang the solo cantata *O amantissime sponse Jesu* by Christian Ritter; the solo in Brahms's *Alto Rhapsody*; the *St Matthew Passion*; the first performance of Elgar's orchestrated version of (supposedly) Eastern European folk-songs, 'The Torch' and 'The River'; and finally, her consummate artistry was joined with that of Gervase Elwes in a memorable performance of *The Dream of Gerontius*.

Walford Davies had been invited to compose a piece for the 1912 Festival, but was unable to complete his promised work. Elgar conducted the first concert performance of his orchestral arrangement of *The Crown of India* suite; Vaughan Williams presented his *Fantasia on Christmas Carols*, in which Campbell McInnes was once again his soloist; and Billy Reed was present in his new capacity as Leader of the London Symphony Orchestra.

So to 1913 – and Gloucester was to experience both a shock and an honour. The shock, remembered by the late Edith Sterry (née Deavin) who first sang in the chorus in that year, was the sight and sound of the soprano Aïno Ackté, who came from Finland to sing in the Verdi *Requiem*, the first performance of *Luonnotar*, Op. 70, by Sibelius, and the closing scene from Richard Strauss's opera *Salome*. Not surprisingly the Dean would not allow this last piece to be given in the cathedral, and so both the Sibelius premier and the Strauss were included in the secular concert alongside such varied fare as Sullivan's overture *Macbeth*; the Hans Sachs monologue from Wagner's *Meistersinger*; Debussy's *Danse sacrée et danse profane*; Herbert Brewer's conventional ballad, *Sir Patrick Spens*; a scherzo caprice, *Will o' the Wisp* by W.H. Reed; and Mozart's Piano Concerto No. 27 in B flat, K. 595 played by a most distinguished visitor.

Edith Sterry remembered how the chorus were hustled out of the Shire Hall when Aïno Ackté arrived to rehearse. Brewer described the same scene in his autobiography:

> At the rehearsal she [Ackté] caused much resentment by the way she insisted on the withdrawal of the audience, which consisted chiefly of the members of the chorus . . . who were naturally anxious to hear the Finnish star. Her action was fully justified, for the music that she sang required so perfect an understanding between orchestra and singer that a detailed rehearsal was more than necessary. In fact parts of the score of *Luonnotar* were 'still in his head' a fortnight before the Festival, so the composer said. The orchestral parts were hastily copied out and full of errors.[23]

But Edith Sterry overcame Ackté's ban: she crept back in to the balcony and lay flat on the floor throughout the rehearsal![24] Brewer surmounted all the difficulties and in performance the piece made a great impression. Brewer received a letter from Sibelius thanking him for an excellent performance and congratulating him on his success.

> Still more sensational was [Ackté's] singing of the closing scene from Strauss's *Salome*. Never in living memory had such singing in such music been heard at a Three Choirs Festival. It was electrifying and the audience was worked up to a wild state of enthusiasm.[25]

The pianist in the Mozart Concerto was none other than the French composer Camille Saint-Saëns (1835–1921), who had honoured the Festival with the première of his new oratorio, *The Promised Land*, which he was to conduct in the cathedral the next day. Since Saint-Saëns was the first living Continental composer to conduct at Three Choirs since Dvořák visited Worcester in 1884, it was perhaps appropriate that the secular concert should end with Dvořák's *Carnival* overture.

The Promised Land failed to meet expectations, but none the less a glowing review appeared in the Paris *Figaro*:

> It is certain that in assigning the work to an English musical Festival, the French musician took means to ensure its production under the best conditions, and the most auspicious for an understanding of its true merits. Nowhere else, least of all in France, could he have discovered the magnificently sonorous choirs for which his finest and most significant pages were designed. Moreover, nowhere else would a presentation of the work so thoroughly in accord with its spirit have been realised.[27]

The Festival ended as usual with *Messiah*. The soloists were Ruth Vincent, Ada Crossley, John Coates and Robert Radford.

When Herbert Brewer laid down his baton on the afternoon of Friday 12 September 1913 the Three Choirs fell silent for seven years.

Notes

1. Lt. Col. Arthur Barwick Lloyd-Baker of Hardwicke Court, Gloucestershire. (His diaries are deposited in the City of Gloucester Records Office.)
2. MT 1909, p. 665
3. 4 October 1904. See also Ursula Vaughan Williams, *RVW – A Biography of Ralph Vaughan Williams* (Oxford, 1964) pp. 69–70
4. Ernest Walker, *A History of Music in England* (Oxford, 1924)
5. MT 1903, p. 671
6. Lloyd-Baker Diaries
7. Ivor Gurney Archive, Gloucester City Library
8. W.H. Reed, *Elgar* (Dent, 1946)
9. MT 1907, p. 654
10. Lloyd-Baker Diaries
11. MT 1909, p. 664
12. Herbert Howells, 'Memories from the Twentieth Century', an essay published in *Two Hundred and Fifty Years of the Three Choirs Festival* (Three Choirs Festival Association, 1977)
13. W.H. Reed, *Elgar as I Knew Him* (Gollancz, 1936; rep. OUP 1989), pp. 29–32
14. Herbert Howells, op. cit.
15. A.H. Brewer, *Memories of Choirs and Cloisters* (1931)
16. Ibid.
17. Ursula Vaughan Williams, *RVW – A Biography of Ralph Vaughan Williams* (Oxford, 1964), pp. 97–8

18. MT 1911, p. 666
19. E. Wulstan Atkins, *The Elgar–Atkins Friendship* (David & Charles, 1984)
20. Brewer, *Memories of Choirs and Cloisters* (1931)
21. Ibid.
22. MT 1912, p. 666
23. Brewer, *Memories of Choirs and Cloisters* (1931)
24. Recollections of Mrs Edith Sterry
27. *Le Figaro*, 15 September 1913

CHAPTER FOURTEEN

AN ESSENTIALLY ENGLISH INSTITUTION

A s the First World War drew to a close, speculation began about the future of the great national musical festivals. On 14 September 1918, a lengthy article appeared in the *Saturday Review*:

> Is the Musical Festival, triennial or otherwise, a thing of the past? For our part we think and hope not; but some people, who claim to speak with knowledge, are rather confident in their opinion that after the War there will be no regular resumption of these gatherings, which have naturally been suspended since the Autumn of 1914. And one thing is certain: if not held regularly they may as well not be held at all; for it is precisely because their occurrence hitherto has been as calculable as a solar eclipse or the landlord's demand for rent that they have been of real value in an artistic sense.

Going on to describe the provincial Festival as having been 'one of the prime glories of musical life in this country', the article stressed the key role which it had played in maintaining England's old supremacy in the department of choral singing, and ended with a plea for its future life.

> After all, at a Festival it is not the band, nor the soloists, nor the novelties, nor the conductor, but the choir that's 'the thing'. We could ill spare the institution that created the brilliant constellation to surround such a glorious central orb.

Since the last Three Choirs Festival had been held in Gloucester in 1913, it was the turn of Worcester to lead off after the war – but the choral members in each of the three cities were all keen to accept the challenge. On the third Saturday in January 1919, Lord Coventry presided over a meeting of the Worcester Executive Committee. Four questions had been submitted to the Deans and Chapters and Festival Committees of Worcester, Hereford and Gloucester: (1) Should the Festivals be revived; (2) if so, what should their form and character be; (3) what should be the limit of expenditure incurred; and (4) where should the next Festival be held?

The Dean and Chapter of Worcester had passed a memorandum to the meeting in which, in answer to the first question, they said they did not think the Festivals should be revived in the form they had come to assume before the war, the cost involved amounting to considerably more than £3,000. In order to meet this expenditure the Dean and Chapter thought:

> it became necessary to push the sale of tickets and advertise for patronage in a manner which they considered was not in accord with the character of the Cathedral, and which destroyed the idea that the Festivals were religious in character and a noble illustration of God's gift of music employed for sacred objects.[1]

They were also worried that in the austere post-war climate it would be difficult to raise sufficient money for the Festival and, while they did not wish to see it abandoned altogether, suggested that it could be continued in a modified form:

> They suggested that the Festivals should be revived as a three-days' Festival, in which music would be rendered by the members of the Three Choirs, reinforced by local voices, orchestra, and one or two solo voices, and that at one meeting each day the main object should be the choral rendering of the highest degree of perfection of music – the finest examples of English Church music being selected.[2]

Lastly, the Dean and Chapter proposed that in any form in which the Festivals were revived the expenditure should not be allowed to exceed £1,000.

The Worcester Executive Committee postponed a decision on holding a Festival in 1919 until the Dean and Chapter had given a definite decision upon whether they would be willing to permit the Festivals to continue in traditional style or not.

Although the Press had been excluded from the meeting, a report of it was supplied to them later. The danger was rising of a repetition of the filleted Festival of 1875. Then a letter from Sir Charles Villiers Stanford appeared in *The Times*:

> Sir,
>   May I express an earnest hope that the Committee of the Three Choirs Festival should see their way to re-establishing that essential English institution on at least its former basis of efficiency and excellence? It is not wise to start again tentatively or hesitatingly. British music deserves and demands more than that; it has struggled successfully through four years of unexampled difficulty and is waiting for its reward. The Three Choirs Festival has the unique chance of taking the lead at a most important juncture; and I feel sure there will be forthcoming a surprising amount of outside support if it takes a large view and advances without flinching.

This brought a response, also in the columns of *The Times*, from the Revd Arthur T. Bannister, Canon Residentiary and Precentor of Hereford:

> Sir,
>   May I express my cordial agreement with Sir Charles Stanford's opinion that the Three Choirs Festival should be re-established *on its former basis*.
>   I am sorry that the Worcester proposals should have been published before they had been thoroughly discussed by the Chapters and Stewards of Gloucester and Hereford. It may be that circumstances will prevent our making a start this year; but we in Hereford, both Dean and Chapter and Stewards, are full of hope that in 1920, at any rate, the festival may be as efficient and excellent as of old.

The Times itself took up the question of the future of Three Choirs in the issue of 8 February 1919:

Musical festivals seem to be coming into the region of practical politics again . . . [they] can hardly be regarded as local institutions, and their warmest friends are concerned to defend their existence on national rather than on local grounds. The question is not so much what part the triennial performance of oratorios and symphonies in the cathedral can play in the musical life of the place as whether the performances have a character of their own, some quality which musicians . . . value for its own sake and fail to find elsewhere. Is [Three Choirs] to be maintained, widened, and improved (all admit the possibility of improvement), or is it to be allowed to lapse in the hope of building another tradition in its place? That is the decision which the authorities have to face at this moment after the compulsory standstill of the past four years. Two parties, the musical purist and the unmusical reactionary, join in favouring the latter decision. The former says honestly, Let the cathedrals study great Church music; the latter echoes him, but means, Let us cut down the expenses, because great Church music requires neither orchestra nor expensive soloists. What the purist forgets is that every cathedral in the land has maintained for centuries a permanent establishment solely for the cultivation of great Church music in its appropriate setting of the daily offices. If these establishments are not doing their duty (and many of them one knows are not), let him press his case against them with all vigour. A triennial or an annual festival could do little to supply their defect.

Looking at the financial side of the Three Choirs Festival, it appears that for many years a large deficit was borne annually by the stewards of the festivals, who were the wealthier residents of the neighbourhood, because they felt the music to be worth paying for; while many thousands of pounds taken in collections at the doors have been given to a deserving clerical, not musical, charity. We learn, however, that in recent years the festivals have paid their expenses. It seems clearly, then, a case on which musical people should have the decision. Do they still want this sort of music; is it vital to them, and if so, will they risk something to have it? The pause of four years may have given occasion for many a reflection, resulting in many a reform of detail and the casting off of some outworn conventions. So much the better, if the answer to the question is affirmative, that festivals have before them now a clearer course and a richer future.

In the face of indignation and opposition the Worcester Dean and Chapter decided to permit the Festival to go ahead as of old provided that three hundred Stewards could be found. Ivor Atkins personally wrote one thousand letters; an action which produced 90 per cent of the guarantors needed to allow the Festival to be restarted, and the Bishop of Worcester set the seal of approval upon the proceedings by not only preaching at the Opening Service but by singing as a tenor in the chorus too.

The long Three Choirs tradition resumed and old friends met once more in Festival sunshine to celebrate the successful resuscitation of the ancient Meeting and to express sympathy for the very many who had sung and played for the last time at Gloucester in 1913. Apart from the victims of war, the intervening years had claimed the lives of Sir Hubert Parry, Charles Harford Lloyd and, at the early age of fifty-four, George Robertson Sinclair. For Elgar too, lodging alone, the Festival was a sad and mournful time. Lady Elgar had died on 7 April 1920.

Before the war the Festivals were numbered from the year 1724, when the charity collection was first made. Thus, the Festival of 1913 had been correctly described as the one hundred and ninetieth Meeting of the Three Choirs for the benefit of the charity. However, Ivor Atkins decided to acknowledge the earlier beginnings of the Music Meetings. Settling somewhat arbitrarily upon 1715 as a starting point, and allowing for the suspension during the years 1914–19, he accorded the distinction of the two-hundredth Meeting to the Worcester Festival of 1920. He also decided wisely that the time had come to dispense with the old system of engaging individual players for the orchestra, albeit that the majority of them had for some time past been members of the

London Symphony Orchestra. In spite of the higher overall contract cost, Atkins engaged the LSO as a complete ensemble.

Elijah was back on Tuesday – with Captain Herbert Heyner singing the role of the Prophet. On Wednesday morning Elgar conducted *The Dream of Gerontius*, with Kirkby Lunn superb as the Angel, John Coates in the title-part, and Heyner singing the two baritone solos. For the afternoon there was 'a solemn music' in memory of Parry, Lloyd and Sinclair. It opened with Beethoven's *Three Equali* for four trombones, conducted in the Lady Chapel by Brewer:

> These solemn chords, played . . . at the eastern end of the building, and softening along the whole length until the instruments sounded much like the diapason notes of an organ, revealed the length of the building as nothing else had done, and made one realise anew the interdependence of music and architecture.[3]

Then followed Parry's motet, 'There is an old belief', from the *Songs of Farewell*, a setting of James Lockhart's lines wholly appropriate to the occasion:

> There is an old belief
> > That on some solemn shore
> Beyond the sphere of grief
> > Dear friends shall meet once more . . .

Parry's *Blest Pair of Sirens*; Walford Davies's *Fantasy*, founded on an episode in Dante's *Divina Commedia* – scored for tenor solo, chorus and orchestra and composed for the abandoned Festival of 1914; with the Symphony in D minor by César Franck completing the concert.

At the 1920 secular concert in the Public Hall, place was found for the music of no fewer than five West Country composers. Apart from songs by Brewer and Atkins, and Elgar's *Introduction and Allegro for Strings*, there were *Four Worcestershire Sketches* by Julius Harrison and Alexander Brent Smith's *Worcester Rhapsody*. This last, conducted by its elegant young composer, impressed both critics and public.

Alexander Brent Smith (1889–1950) was born in the village of Brookthorpe near Gloucester and was educated at the King's School in Worcester, was a cathedral chorister, studied music with Atkins and became his assistant organist. In 1912 he was appointed Director of Music at Lancing College in Sussex. While there he was an extremely popular master, not only engendering an interest and love of music in his charges but also organizing 'Rag Concerts' for the last night of term. Among these were his 'Rag Operas': *Bacchus* in 1917; *Iphigenia* in 1921; *Circe and the Swine* in 1922; *Dido and Aeneas* in 1924; and a repeat of *Iphigenia* in 1926 in which sixteen-year-old Peter Pears made his stage début. Pears also took part in Brent Smith's stagings of scenes from *HMS Pinafore* in 1927 and *The Mikado* in 1928(H).

At Lancing, Brent Smith served under C.H. Blackistone, a headmaster whose popularity was as low as that of Brent Smith's was high.[4] Financial difficulties within the college led to staffing reductions, and 1934 saw the end of its much-admired Director of Music's work there. He returned to Brookthorpe, taught for some years at Pate's Grammar School in Cheltenham and continued to serve Three Choirs as a member of the Music Committee of the Gloucester Festival. He was a regular contributor to several journals, including *Music and Letters* and *The Musical Times*, and composed a large body of works in most forms, a number of which were first performed at Three Choirs.

In addition to *Messiah*, the 1920 Festival included the Elgar-Atkins edition of the *St Matthew Passion*, Verdi's *Requiem* and the first performance of Vaughan Williams's *Four Hymns* for tenor and string orchestra, written for and sung by Steuart Wilson, the youngest son of Canon J.M. Wilson of Worcester Cathedral, whose two elder sons were both killed in the First World War. Steuart Wilson suffered injuries in the war which affected one of his lungs and permanently damaged his health. Even so, his beautiful voice became one of the treasures of British music during the inter-war years, and his interpretations of *Gerontius* and the Evangelist in Bach's *Passions* were greatly admired.

In 1920 all three of the singers whose voices were most closely associated with the name-part in *Gerontius* during Elgar's lifetime appeared in the same Three Choirs Festival: John Coates, Gervase Elwes and Steuart Wilson. The styles of the two elder tenors were very different from each other but equally valid. Coates, whose career had begun as a baritone, brought the dramatic intensity and power to *Gerontius* which suited his voice so perfectly to the Wagnerian *Heldentenor* roles in which he also excelled. He was, said Gerald Moore, an aristocrat among singers. Elwes was noted for the spiritual commitment of his interpretations, especially, like Steuart Wilson after him, in *Gerontius* and the Bach *Passions*. Wulstan Atkins remembers him as a devout, almost saintly figure. But by 1920 Gervase Elwes was fifty-four years old and planning to retire from the profession on his return from an approaching tour in America.

Two other voices destined for stardom were heard at the Festival for the first time in 1920: the soprano Carrie Tubb and the superb bass Norman Allin, who dominated the British music scene for many years with his even, sonorous, flexible voice, and of whom Sir Henry Wood in his autobiography *My Life of Music* wrote:

> I have always thought it a pity that Allin is of such a retiring disposition, for, had he cared, he might have become one of the world's finest operatic basses. I believe his operatic roles numbered fifty. I imagine he loved the English countryside and his home too well, and who can blame him?

Charles Lee Williams, who had responded to Ivor Atkins's appeal for guarantors with a cheque for £10 ('put me amongst the *tenners* which you may think *base* of me'), wrote to Atkins on 14 September:

> My dear Atkins,
>   I can only once again say that above all praise which rightly comes to you this week you will I know value the now well established fact that you have resuscitated & guided the Festival ship into harbour off your own bat most admirably.
>   Please convey to your wife too my kindly greetings & say how much I appreciated being allowed to come in and out like a tame rabbit. It is just the spirit combined with tact & good humour that has carried you both through.
>   In a quiet way I have propagated propaganda for you and your interests as much as I could, for I realised the big importance of a success *now* or never! – Thanks too dear boy for doing 'Williams in D'. 'Pon my life I didn't know I had a tune left in me. Lord! how they all played and sang it!
>   *Don't write*: but get away right now & take a rod with you.
>
> Kindly greetings old Bean!
> Yours ever
> C.L.W.[6]

In November 1920 Ivor Atkins became a D. Mus. by examination at Oxford, and his work in re-starting the Festival after the war was recognized by the announcement of a knighthood in the New Year's Honours List of 1921.

Two weeks later the many friends and admirers of Gervase Elwes were stunned to learn that while travelling to an engagement at Harvard University he had been killed in a train accident.

Notes

1. *Gloucester Journal*, 1 February 1919
2. Ibid.
3. MT 1920, p. 667
4. Memories of Mr B.W.T. Handford
5. Memories of Mr R.S. Thompson
6. Letter in the possession of E. Wulstan Atkins

CHAPTER FIFTEEN

THE ELGAR FESTIVALS

The inter-war years were, above all, the years of the 'Elgar Festivals'. At a time when his music was out of fashion elsewhere in the country, Elgar was lionized at Three Choirs, and he in turn honoured the Festivals by regular appearances, usually conducting his own works. As *The Musical Times* put it in 1921, 'his world-wide fame finds its focus in the Three Choirs Festival, and if he owed something to them in his youth, he is now paying back the debt with interest.'[1] But world-wide fame and popularity are different things. Britain chose to neglect Elgar. Following a 1922 performance of *The Apostles* in a half-empty Queen's Hall, George Bernard Shaw, writing to the *Daily News*, apologized 'to posterity for living in a country where the capacity and tastes of schoolboys and sporting costermongers are the measure of metropolitan culture':

> *The Apostles* is one of the glories of British music . . . It places Britain once more definitely in the first European rank, after two centuries of leather and prunella.
> It would be an exaggeration to say that I was the only person present, like Ludwig of Bavaria at Wagner's premieres. My wife was there. Other couples were visible at intervals. One of the couples consisted of the Princess Mary and Viscount Lascelles, who just saved the situation as far as the credit of the Crown is concerned, as it very deeply is. I distinctly saw six people in the stalls, probably with complimentary tickets.[2]

On the other hand, Three Choirs audiences for *Gerontius*, *The Apostles* and *The Kingdom* frequently exceeded in number those for *Elijah* and even *Messiah*. Nowhere else were his works performed with quite such dedication, and nowhere else so regularly under Elgar's own direction. At no other national festival or concert venue could performers and public alike mingle socially and meet so easily with leading composers – and the familiar figure of Elgar, often in company with his friend and champion Bernard Shaw, could hardly be missed, especially when he chose to wear full court dress with orders. His was a kindly presence too, remembered by one who observed Elgar going into a store to buy sixpenny jewellery and then giving it to children he might pass on the way to the cathedral;[3] and by another who was a chorister in 1925: 'And here am I singing under the great Sir Edward himself – how majestic he looks on the rostrum – what a strangely nervous beat, and look at that delicate left hand resting on the score – now he's placing it over his heart and his face beams on Billy Reed as a favourite orchestral theme approaches.'[4]

Elgar was, in each sense, at home at Three Choirs; and his Festival friends were real friends, acknowledged not only in the *Enigma Variations* and the help he gave to Brewer with *Emmaus*, but also in the dedication of other works to Three Choirs conductors: the *Wand of Youth Suite No. 1* to C. Lee Williams; *The Black Knight* to Hugh Blair; the *Pomp and Circumstance* Marches Nos 3, 4 and 5 to Ivor Atkins, G.R. Sinclair and Percy Hull respectively; a setting of Lady Elgar's poem *A Christmas Greeting* to Sinclair and the Hereford Cathedral choristers; and to 'my friend, Percy Hull', a *Serenade*, a setting of a Russian text for unaccompanied choir.

Percy Clarke Hull (1878–1968) was the only ex-chorister of Hereford Cathedral, other than John Bull (1562–1628), to become its organist. He became a chorister in 1889 and was afterwards a pupil of Sinclair and assistant organist from 1896. In recognition of his service to music he was awarded an honorary FRCO in 1920, the Lambeth degree of D. Mus. in 1921 and, in 1947, a knighthood.

In 1914 he had been on holiday in Germany and at the outbreak of war was interned by the Germans. He spent the next four years at Ruhleben Prisoners-of-War Camp. Like Sinclair, Hull was a Freemason, and as such played an important part in bringing to the notice of the Grand Lodge the privations and sufferings of the Freemasons interned at Ruhleben, so that a large sum of money was raised for their assistance. He was appointed Deputy Assistant Grand Organist of England in recognition of his activities. On his release in November 1918, a sick man, he took over as organist at Hereford relieving Gordon Brown, an articled pupil of Sinclair who had deputized since February 1917. Although dogged by continuing illness Hull conducted his first Three Choirs Festival in 1921, achieving an unqualified success. 'His tempi' remarked *The Musical Times*, 'were on the side of vivacity, which afforded a contrast with those of his predecessor.'[5] Elgar assisted Hull, conducting *The Dream of Gerontius*, *The Apostles*, and the Cello Concerto, in which Beatrice Harrison, who had recorded the work in 1919, was the soloist. The chamber concert on Friday evening was all-British, including Ethel Smyth's Quartet in E minor and Elgar's Piano Quintet in A minor with Henry Ley, organist of Christ Church, Oxford, joining W.H. Reed's quartet of players as pianist. The Festival also included pieces by Benjamin Dale, Edgar Bainton and Frederick Keel, all of whom had been Percy Hull's companions in captivity at Ruhleben. But the most strikingly original choral work of the week was the first Three Choirs performance of Gustav Holst's *The Hymn of Jesus*, conducted by the composer.

The Hymn of Jesus was heard for the first time, under Holst's baton, at a Philharmonic concert at the Queen's Hall in March 1920; it was an 'overwhelming success'. Holst 'knew that it was the best thing he had written, but this was the first time that his opinion and public opinion coincided'.[6] Although performed several times in the months following its premier, it was at Hereford in 1921 that the work was first heard under the most favourable and fitting conditions. It has since been heard thirteen times at Three Choirs – the last in 1988(H).

Before directing his first Festival in 1891 Sinclair had spent some time with J.T. Carrodus, gaining insights into the technique of conducting. After the 1921 Festival,

Percy Hull acknowledged the great help of a similar sort which he too had received – from W.H. Reed. Under Hull, Hereford soon gained the reputation among members of the chorus as the most rigorously disciplined of the three Festivals, and the concentrated effort was well justified by remarkable results. Paying tribute to the choir in 1927(H) Harvey Grace wrote:

> It had much of the brilliance and vitality usually associated with the crack Northern bodies, together with the even greater virtue of beautiful tone for which we usually have to come farther south. And there can be no better tribute to these singers and their trainer than the fact of their being recruited on the 'let 'em all come' principle; for I am assured on the best authority that there is practically no voice trial. The singing would have been notable from a stringently chosen choir; from one that was simply collected it was astonishing.[7]

Herbert Sumsion also acknowledged Percy Hull's boundless energy:

> This took the form in music of a capacity for work, both on and off the platform, which has certainly not been exceeded by any other Festival Conductor within my knowledge . . . He was short in stature and by nature quick in all his movements – he always seemed in a hurry to get somewhere and to do something. As an administrator he took almost too much on his own shoulders, chiefly because he enjoyed being busy but also because he was so impatient to get a job done. It will be no surprise to learn that he was an early riser and could do with much less sleep than most people. His conversation was equally high powered, with most of the firing coming from his side. This developed into a manner which over the years became distinctly brusque. If you were unwise enough to greet him with 'Hello, Percy, how are you?' he would more than likely answer with 'What's that got to do with you?' – which could be disconcerting until one accepted that it was badinage and not meant to be taken literally. He was emphatic to a degree and things were either black or white – subtle tints of grey were not for him. This led to a certain rigidity in his personality and outlook, but he said what he meant and meant what he said and such an attitude can, and in his case did, pay handsome dividends.
>
> Particularly was this the case in his role as Conductor. Chorus, Soloists and Orchestra were never in any doubt as to what they had to do. Verbal instructions were clear, concise and unequivocal, and those given in writing were underlined, double underlined or even triple underlined and put in capital letters so that there could be no excuse for misunderstanding. The Orchestra liked his direct manner, the Soloists accepted their instructions (whether they agreed with him or not) and the Chorus, of course, loved being ordered about. It is almost superfluous to add that his beat was as clear as daylight, and under the conditions which inevitably prevailed at Festivals in his early days – chiefly lack of rehearsal time – such a beat was worth gold. Works such as Holst's *Hymn of Jesus*, with its complicated time patterns and unusual rhythms would have come to grief completely without that rock-firm and emphatic beat which steered everyone safely through what in those days were untravelled waters . . . He had such an affection for Bach's B minor Mass that it became a 'must' at all Hereford Festivals. It also led to the one main criticism which was levelled against him – that he took some of it too fast. This applied almost entirely to the Choruses. In his desire to whip up his singers to give all they'd got he probably allowed excitement to get the better of him, and he took things faster than he realized.
>
> . . . On the personal side friendship meant everything to him . . . He was affectionately known to everyone as 'P.C.' – which in itself speaks volumes – and this is a distinction which he shared with only one other musician of his generation, namely V.W.[8]

In a flash of sharp wit hardly intended to offend his Gloucester and Worcester colleagues, Percy Hull once described Three Choirs as 'the three Ms', a reference to the magnificent headgear worn in the mayoral procession at Worcester and Herbert Brewer's keen business-sense at Gloucester. 'The three Ms were', he said, 'at Worcester – Millinery; at Gloucester – Money; and at Hereford – Music!'[9]

Brewer's close attention to box-office receipts was well rewarded at the Gloucester Festival of 1922. Attendances exceeded those of any previous Festival and the sum of £2,110 was made available to the charity. It is also much to Brewer's credit that he was prepared to include many new works in his programmes even when they were alien to his own taste. This was certainly the case in 1922.

Once again, it was Elgar who suggested to the Festival Committee that they should invite three promising young men – Arthur Bliss, Eugene Goossens and Herbert Howells – to compose new pieces for the Festival. Charles Lee Williams, by then affectionately known as 'the Father of the Festival', had taken over as Chairman of the Gloucester Executive Committee, which promptly agreed to commission new works from all three. The results were more than Lee Williams or Brewer had bargained for, especially in the work from Bliss: *A Colour Symphony*. Influenced by Stravinsky and *Les Six*, Bliss had painted a dazzling sound picture: superbly orchestrated, frequently dissonant, vigorous and forward-looking – but barely understood by many in the audience. Yet again, rehearsal time was woefully inadequate and, worst of all, just before the actual performance it was found that there was too little room on the platform to seat all the orchestra and the chorus. Even though the chorus were not required during the symphony, it was orchestral players who were ejected, leaving Bliss without several key instruments. None of this was mentioned by Brewer in his autobiography but he does tell us that it was not until a fortnight before the Festival that the copies of Goossens' work, *Silence* (a choral setting of the poem by Walter de la Mare) were placed in the hands of the chorus, who agreed to a daily rehearsal to become acquainted with it. In his autobiography Goossens recalled the outcome:

> . . . I went to Gloucester for the Festival and stayed at one of the oldest inns in England, the New Inn (fifteenth century). I had rehearsed *Silence* with the London Symphony Orchestra two days previously in London, and the fine choir had mastered its part quite satisfactorily at separate rehearsals under the late Dr. Brewer, organist of Gloucester Cathedral. All that remained, therefore, was to join the two forces at a final rehearsal. The chorus, unused to my chromatic idiom, was experiencing difficulty in arriving at the unison *pianissimo* B flat at the end of the piece anywhere near pitch. Brewer therefore installed a small harmonium at the back of the chorus to sound the crucial B flat as an aid to the chorus, and undertook to play it himself. He could as well have used the organ; as things transpired, it's a pity he didn't. The actual concert, with chorus and orchestra arranged picturesquely in the organ loft over the sanctuary, an impressive sight, began with a most inappropriate work for performance in a church – Scriabine's erotic *Poem of Ecstasy*. Awaiting my turn to conduct *Silence*, I sat with Elgar in the choir stalls, where, hidden from sight, we discussed the proceedings. 'To think that Gloucester Cathedral should ever echo to such music,' sighed Elgar. 'It's a wonder the gargoyles don't fall off the tower. Heaven forgive Brewer!' The *Poem of Ecstasy* drew to a noisy, disorderly close, and the groined vaultings of the Cathedral turned the blare of trumpets into a shattering infamy. I started to leave for the choir-loft. 'Write a festival Mass, Eugene, and atone for this outrage.' 'All right, Sir Edward, but Mother Church won't approve of my modernisms.' 'Never mind. I'll be in Heaven by then; I'll make it all right for you! Don't forget, plenty of percussion in the *Sanctus*!'
>
> One of the most impressive things about a Three Choirs Festival is the great silence of the audience at the Cathedral concerts. The Scriabine finished in shocked silence, and I faced a silent audience to start my own *Silence*. All went well until the final unison (and perfectly in tune) *pianissimo* B flat, when, just as Brewer started to play his helping note on the harmonium, a deep rattling boom shook the awe-inspiring silence of the church and persisted till the end of the piece. One of the low pedal bourdon pipes of the organ had ciphered, and broken the very silence which was the whole point of my work. Elgar, when I returned to the choir stalls, said he thought the piece atmospheric ('and the

cipher was very effective'), but too short. 'All you youngsters are in far too great a hurry nowadays.' 'If that's what you think, just wait till you hear the next piece,' I replied. This was the première of Arthur Bliss's *Colour Symphony*, which lasted forty minutes. Elgar had to admit there were exceptions, and immensely admired Bliss's vivid symphony. After the concert we ate an enormous roast-beef lunch at the New Inn, and with Arthur Bliss and Willie Reed, concert-master of the L.S.O. and close friend of Elgar, spent the afternoon walking in open country along the banks of the Severn. Elgar not only outwalked us all, but completely out-matched us in matters of local history and topography. That evening, as proof of his energy, he conducted a Festival performance of his *Second Symphony*. An amazing, lovable man. . . .[10]

The Gloucester audience failed to understand the new works:

> . . . the two compositions of Mr Arthur Bliss and Mr Eugene Goossens contained such terribly harsh progressions and positively ugly idioms of the ultra modern school, that opinions were freely expressed about the propriety of admitting such music into the programme for the Cathedral, where at any rate we may hope and expect to be edified by music suitable to the solemn and mysterious atmosphere of religious exaltation.
>
> The *Colour Symphony* . . . and . . . *Silence* are obviously 'experiments' for secular concert halls only.[11]

On the other hand, Herbert Thompson, writing in *The Musical Times*, 'was not troubled by any sense of incongruity, for the music is not frivolous or distinctively secular in character. What I did feel was its intense vitality.'[12]

Bliss had to wait nearly forty years before his *Colour Symphony* was given a worthy performance at Three Choirs – again with the LSO and again under his own baton – at Hereford in 1955. Eugene Goossens' *Silence*, a work deserving of revival, never received a second chance. Herbert Howells's piece, a 'fantasy' for wordless soprano and tenor soloists, wordless chorus, large orchestra and organ, *Sine Nomine*, will receive only its second performance at the 1992 Gloucester Festival. In 1922 it was ridiculously placed – as a precursor to *Elijah*.

At luncheon immediately following *A Colour Symphony*, Howells, who always considered *Sine Nomine* to be one of his best works, received a two-edged compliment from the trumpeter J.J. Solomon: 'Well, young man, after the Symphony this morning, even *Sine Nomine* seems tolerable.'[13]

The 1922 Festival was remembered locally less for the music performed than for the unveiling of a memorial tablet to Sir Hubert Parry during the afternoon of Wednesday, 6 September by Viscount Gladstone, a friend of Parry's from Eton days:

> The ceremony was simple and appropriate. A procession was formed of musicians in their doctor's robes, who, with the Bishop and Dean, proceeded to where the tablet is placed on the west wall of the south aisle. Lord Gladstone, Sir Edward Elgar, Sir Charles Stanford, Sir Hugh Allen, Sir Henry Hadow, Professor Granville Bantock, and Dr Brewer took part in the procession. The tablet was formally presented to the Cathedral and unveiled. The Bishop read a couple of prayers, and then Lord Gladstone, returning to the conductor's desk, spoke to the congregation of what Parry had been in the musical life of his time and of his character as a man . . .[14]

The ceremony ended with a moving performance of *Blest Pair of Sirens* – Sir Hugh Allen refusing to conduct until every choralist's copy was thrown to the ground.

The memorial tablet bears an inscription by the then Poet Laureate, Robert Bridges:

HUBERT PARRY
Musician

1848–1918

From boyhood's eager play called by the English Muse
Her fine scholar to be then her Masters' compeer
A spirit elect whom no unworthy Thought might wrong
Nor any Fear touch thee joyously o'er life's waves
Navigating thy Soul unto her holy Haven
Long these familiar Walls shall re-echo thy song
And this Stone remember thy bounteous gaiety
Thy honour and thy grace and the love of thy friends

It is surrounded by a decorative border into which are set the coats of arms of the thirteen institutions with which Parry was connected. Charles Lee Williams was as baffled by Bridges' words as he had been by *A Colour Symphony*, describing them as 'ten lines . . . from the Poet Laureate . . . which no one can understand or punctuate!'[15] And Robert Bridges excused himself from attending the ceremony, saying in a letter to Brewer: '. . . I am better away, because the tablet in the Cathedral is not what I wished it to be, and my disappointment and dissatisfaction, which I should not well disguise, would be out of place.'[16]

The 1922 Festival included one new Elgar work – the only one to receive a first performance at Gloucester – the transcription for orchestra of Bach's Fantasia and Fugue in C minor. In the previous year Elgar had said, 'Now that my poor wife has gone I can't be original, and so I depend on people like Johann Sebastian for a source of inspiration.'[17] At Worcester in 1923 there was the transcription of Handel's overture in D minor (from Chandos Anthem No. 2) and orchestrations of anthems by S.S. Wesley and Battishill. Among twenty-one British composers represented there were first performances of Alexander Brent Smith's *In Glorious Freedom* and, most importantly, a choral work by Arnold Bax, *To the Name above every Name*, a setting of a poem by the seventeenth-century writer, Richard Crashaw. And an exciting young soprano made her Festival debut: Elsie Suddaby, 'who sang on five different occasions, and in all kinds of music, giving striking proof of her versatility and musical intelligence'.[18]

The great innovation of the 1923(W) Festival proved to be one of its most memorable features. Instead of ending with *Messiah* on Friday, an additional chamber concert, as at Hereford, was given on Friday evening in the College Hall by thirty-five players from the LSO. Symphonies by Haydn and Mozart; Wagner's *Siegfried Idyll*; the Scherzo from *A Midsummer Night's Dream*; Debussy's *Danses Sacrées et Profanes*: and songs by Megan Foster and Norman Allin made for a concert enjoyable from beginning to end. In 1925 Gloucester followed Worcester's lead, so that all three Festivals ended with a Friday evening secular concert.

Since Sinclair introduced it in 1897, the 'Grail' Scene from *Parsifal* had been included in every Hereford Festival programme – a tradition which continued until 1930. Atkins included it at Worcester in 1923 with, as at Hereford, a small semi-chorus of choirboys, hidden away in the central tower. Part of the tradition, and an object of pride, was the ability of the young singers to keep the pitch perfectly so that the entry of the orchestra which followed made a superb effect.

When, in 1926, Atkins decided to include the Prelude to *Parsifal* in his Festival programme, Dr Lacey, one of the Worcester Cathedral canons, wrote to the *Worcester Daily Times* protesting that Wagner was a 'sensualist'. Elgar replied angrily:

> The Canon quotes 'His emotions and spiritual experiences were those of the ordinary sensual man.' But 'Aren't we all?' If the Canon really believes that such emotions in early life debar a man from taking part in the services of the church in riper years he should at once resign his canonry and any other spiritual offices he is paid to hold. [19]

The Canon replied:

> Sir Edward Elgar misses the point. The writers whom I quoted were not criticising Wagner's life or character, but his art, in which they found sensuality of pietism matching the sensuality of his erotics. It was this that attracted my attention, for in my work as a priest I have had acquaintance with both kinds of sensuality, and I know what kind is the more dangerous. [20]

Canon Lacey seems to have missed the point, made so well by Samuel Langford following the 1920(W) Festival when comparing Walford Davies's *Fantasy* on the *Divine Comedy* of Dante unfavourably with Elgar's *Gerontius*:

> Where ideas transcend, the power of the composer must transcend equally or the result is doubtful. Perhaps after all it is the strongly sensuous imagination, as in the example of Wagner, that can most safely attempt these heavenly flights, for there music is in little danger of losing its hold on our human feelings. [21]

For the opening of the British Empire Exhibition at Wembley on St George's Day, 1924, Elgar had composed the *Empire March* but, because the massed bands had been unable to rehearse the new piece separately, he was asked to conduct the old *Imperial March* instead, along with *Land of Hope and Glory*, Parry's *Jerusalem* and the National Anthem. The *Empire March* was played later in the year at the Exhibition Pageant and repeated at the 1924 Hereford Festival: 'a brilliant work, more distinguished in its very effective development than in its themes.'[22] Sir Charles Villiers Stanford, Sir Frederick Bridge and Sir Walter Parratt, the Master of the King's Music, all died in 1924. As a tribute to their memory, Beethoven's three *Equali* for four trombones preceded *Elijah*. It was the new Master of the King's Music, Sir Edward Elgar, whose works again dominated the Festival but all was far from well when Elgar took up the baton to conduct *The Kingdom*. Sir Adrian Boult was present:

> It was at once apparent that the choir were perhaps resting too much on last year's laurels. . . . Bad intonation was evident near the start, and I felt that Sir Edward was losing interest, as he began to drive the performance, getting faster and faster as if the one thing he wanted was to get out of the Cathedral and forget about music. We endured this for nearly an hour when we came to the wonderful scena 'The sun goeth down', which was written for that great soprano, Agnes Nicholls. She had, if I remember rightly, practically retired at that time, but returned at short notice to take over the part which she had made her own many years before. I shall never forget the intense concentration with which she began that gentle opening phrase, and the way the orchestra seemed instantly to spring to life and, immediately after, the disgruntled composer's interest quickened, and from that moment the performance returned to the extraordinary beauty of the year before.

There were no problems in *Gerontius* – Astra Desmond, John Coates and Robert Radford joined a chorus determined to give of its best.

A short postscript to the 1924 Festival appeared in *The Musical Times*:

> No festival is without its anxieties, especially to the conductor, and even Dr. Hull's good humour must have been singularly tried at times by the requests launched at him from all quarters. The most embarrassing was, I imagine, a letter which reached him addressed to 'Dr John Bull, First Gresham Professor of Music, c/o Three Choirs Festival, Hereford Cathedral, Hereford.' It had also the superscription, 'Kindly forward', which Dr. Hull was unable to comply with, having unfortunately mislaid the address. The letter emanated from a press-cutting agency, which offered to supply Dr. Bull with references to himself and his compositions, and advised him that it had 'a large theatrical and musical department, under competent (*sic*) supervision.'[24]

To mark the tercentenary of the birth of Orlando Gibbons, Brewer decided to include an anthem by him in all but one of the 1925(G) Festival programmes. It was now Brewer's turn to receive letters addressed to Orlando Gibbons with a request that they should be forwarded![25]

Brewer had much else on his mind in 1925. Troubled for some time by the angina which forced him, when ascending to the organ loft, to climb slowly, one step at a time, and which prevented him from joining the choir at the top of the cathedral tower on Rogation Days,[26] he was immersed in planning a Festival which was to include more new works than ever before.

Sibelius had accepted an invitation to write a symphony for the Festival but was unable to complete it in time or to visit Gloucester, so the *Variations on the St Antoni Chorale* by Brahms were substituted along with Sibelius's *Finlandia*. Thirty-four British composers, twenty-five of them living, were represented in the programmes and services. Fifteen of these conducted their own works. There were ten 'novelties', the most important among which were Sir Walford Davies's choral suite *Men and Angels*; Basil Harwood's motet for chorus and orchestra, *Love Incarnate*; and two motets for unaccompanied chorus, *Glory and Honour and Laud* by Charles Wood who, in 1924, had succeeded Stanford as Professor of Music at Cambridge and who died in 1926, and *The Evening Watch* by Gustav Holst. New orchestral works included Thomas Dunhill's *Three Short Pieces* for strings and organ, and *Paradise Rondel* by Herbert Howells. The poet F.W. Harvey, a fellow Gloucestershire man and a close friend of Brewer's former pupils, Herbert Howells and Ivor Gurney, provided words for four old Irish airs under the collective title of *A Sprig of Shamrock*, which Brewer arranged for contralto or baritone voice with string quartet or piano accompaniment and which were performed by Flora Woodman and four players from the LSO. Described by Charles Lee Williams as 'a tasty feast of double-Gloucester', this cycle and pieces such as his most popular song, *The Fairy Pipers*, show the lightness of touch and delight in melody which, had his career taken a different direction, would have equipped Brewer for success as a composer of light opera.

One of the works chosen by Brewer for the 1925 Festival, Parry's *Job*, had been performed earlier in the year at the Royal College of Music. The Director of the College, Sir Hugh Allen, had selected a young bass-baritone, Keith Falkner, to sing the title-role which Harry Plunket Greene had created at Gloucester in 1892. Dr Emily Daymond, who had been Parry's amanuensis, asked Plunket Greene to help Keith Falkner.

'Help is hardly the word for it. He opened up a whole new world of declamation, colour and interpretation.'[27]

Though Keith Falkner didn't know it, Sir Hugh had asked Brewer to come to the college to hear the performance. The next day Sir Hugh told Falkner that Dr Brewer had engaged him for the performance at the Gloucester Festival.

'It was a great moment in my life . . . My father and mother were there and of course Dr Emily Daymond who gave me a conducted tour of Highnam. We stayed at "The Dog" at Over, just outside Gloucester. The following day, in the bar, the landlord read out the critique in the Gloucester paper. In broad dialect he shouted, "Ee called thee a tenor. 'Ee don't know the difference 'tween a tenor an' a bass. 'Ee don't know the difference 'tween a sow 'na hog!'[28]

In his *Musical Times* review of the Festival, Herbert Thompson said that 'Special mention should be made of Mr Keith Falkner, a young baritone who essayed the exacting part of Job, and, in spite of his youthful personality and voice, sang it with remarkable intelligence.'[29]

Following the First World War, one of Herbert Brewer's sons, Charles had become a member of the BBC production staff and through his influence the first-ever radio transmissions from the Three Choirs Festival were made in 1925. Both of the secular concerts were broadcast and during the interval of the first of these Sir Hugh Allen, unveiling a memorial to Sir Hubert Parry in the Shire Hall, said that 'for the first time a Three Choirs Concert was accessible in a way which Sir Hubert could not foresee, since thousands of people all over the British Isles and beyond were listening to it by wireless, via London.'[30] Loudspeakers were positioned in various parts of Gloucester and proved a great attraction to the crowds of people who gathered around them to listen to the concerts.

Other 'firsts' at the 1925(G) Festival included the performance of part of a Vaughan Williams symphony under the composer's baton: the last movement of the *Sea Symphony*, and the first appearance in the cathedral of Dame Ethel Smyth, who directed the Kyrie and Gloria from her Mass in D. She also won enthusiastic applause at the first secular concert with her overture *The Wreckers*.

Members of the chorus present at a rehearsal of Dame Ethel Smyth's Mass in the Chapter House of Gloucester Cathedral were treated to an amusing sample of her eccentricity. The sun, shining through a window directly opposite to her with intense brilliance, dazzled Dame Ethel who was unable to see the choir. 'Could one of the ladies please lend me a hat?' she asked. A hat was produced and Dame Ethel put it on, pulling the brim down over her eyes and, because her long hair was piled up into a bun, pulling the hat out of shape at the same time. Gradually, as she conducted, the hat was pulled further and further down, to hilarious effect. Then the wide belt which supported the skirt of her suit began to ride up. Brewer was sitting close by. 'Dr Brewer,' called out Dame Ethel, continuing to conduct, 'could you please attend to my belt?' So there was Brewer, usually the epitome of dignity, embarrassedly tugging at Dame Ethel Smyth's waist while the choristers were hardly able to sing through their mirth.[31]

The 1925(G) Festival marked the climax of Brewer's career and new peaks in both attendance (19,973) and receipts. The number of Stewards was a record 434 and profits from all sources amounted to £3,700 which, because Brewer had been able to persuade the Tax authorities to exempt Three Choirs from the payment of entertainments tax, was handed in its entirety to the charity.

Messiah drew the largest audience of the week: 3,410 tickets were sold. As Brewer conducted the 'Amen' chorus unrestrained tears rolled down his cheeks.[32] Perhaps he had been in pain, and certainly Lady Brewer recorded that 'after the 1925 Festival there were signs of failing health and walking became more and more of an effort. The Festival had undoubtedly been too great a strain, but his enthusiasm for work did not lessen and, in 1926, on the resignation of George Riseley from the conductorship of the Bristol Choral Society, he was invited to undertake and accepted the duties of that office.'[33] On New Year's Day, 1926, Brewer's name appeared in the Honours List, and on 5 February the king conferred the honour of knighthood upon him. Brewer was present at the 1927 Hereford Festival, taking his place in the organ loft for the historic recordings made during the week by The Gramophone Company.

Negotiations to record at the Three Choirs Festival had begun early in 1927. The Dean and Chapter had been somewhat doubtful about granting approval but, thanks to the intercession of Elgar and the enthusiasm of Percy Hull, finally agreed. The mobile recording van arrived in Hereford before the Opening Service on Sunday, 4 September and took up its position at the west end of the cathedral. The first item to be recorded was the most important of all: a Fanfare which Elgar had written especially for this Festival:

> At previous Three Choirs Festivals it had been the custom for the orchestra to play the National Anthem as the Mayor of the City and the Civic Party entered the Cathedral. During preparations for the 1927 Festival it had been pointed out that the National Anthem should properly be sounded at the appearance of the Sovereign's representative – in this case the Lord Lieutenant of the Shire, who made his entrance after the Civic Party. So Dr. Hull, as an old friend of Elgar's, had asked if he would compose a Fanfare to accompany the entry of the Civic Party. This Elgar had done, designing his music to lead up to the National Anthem. The performance at the Opening Service would therefore be an Elgar world premiere under the composer's direction.[34]

In spite of considerable difficulties of timing and balance, the recording engineers produced a total of twenty-five sides from the Festival performances. Many of these had to be destroyed but among the items issued are memorable performances by Margaret Balfour, Tudor Davies and Horace Stevens, the Festival Chorus, LSO, and Sir Herbert Brewer (organ), conducted by Elgar in excerpts from *Gerontius*.

Audience noise had been a particular problem in this essentially experimental recording project. One of the Gramophone Company men at Hereford was Bernard Wratten. In a letter to the editor of *The Gramophone* (2 October 1972) he recalled:

> One evening, after the day's music making was done, Dr. Hull invited us round to his house, where we found an impressive assortment of English composers, singers and musicians. Whilst we were there he told us that the wife of a local baronet, a lady with a considerable reputation for silliness, had been so taken with the hat of another member of the audience sitting just across the aisle during a rehearsal that she leant over to ask, under cover of combined choir and orchestra, where the hat had been bought. She had to raise her voice and at that moment the music stopped. She was clearly heard all over the Cathedral.
> The tale acquired its widely circulated form from our Public Relations Officer. It had nothing whatsoever to do with our recording but he felt there was a good news-story in it, and after decorating it he sent it out to the newspapers, most of which published it.[35]

But in his book *Music on Record*, Fred Gaisberg, The Gramophone Company's pioneering chief recording engineer, recalled another intrusion by fashion: '. . . at the

Three Choir performance of *Gerontius*, during a sudden silent pause after a *forte* climax, a lady's voice talking about "a lovely camisole for 11s 6d" was clearly exposed when the record was played back, and so ruined a fine set'.[36]

The Gramophone Company attempted to negotiate with the Dean and Chapter of Gloucester Cathedral to carry out recordings at the 1928 Festival but, in spite of pleading by Elgar, this was refused. The opportunity to establish a regular pattern of rare and valuable recording was thus stopped.

Brewer's plans for the 1928(G) Festival were as ambitious as ever and intended to please all tastes, including hoped-for new works from Ravel, Honegger, Bantock, Holst and Ireland. He invited Zoltán Kodály to conduct his *Psalmus Hungaricus*; Dame Ethel Smyth, a complete performance of her Mass in D; Elgar, *The Dream of Gerontius* and *The Kingdom*; and Vaughan Williams, *The Lark Ascending*. Among the works which Brewer was to conduct himself was Verdi's *Requiem*, the work 'of all others [which] would have been his choice for his own requiem. He had been heard to say that if he was told to choose two works to hear before he died he would choose Verdi's *Requiem* and *The Dream of Gerontius*.'[37]

Sir Herbert Brewer suffered a heart attack and died at his house in Miller's Green, Gloucester on 1 March 1928.

> It is a strange coincidence that on the first Thursday in March, 1897, Herbert Brewer began his duties as organist in Gloucester Cathedral by playing the organ at a Free Recital, and it was on the first Thursday in March, 1928, thirty-one years later, whilst the Concert of the Gloucestershire Orchestral Society was in progress, that he lay dying. Almost his last words were, 'I feel as if I were conducting the symphony.' Mozart's Symphony [No. 39] in E flat was then actually in progress.[38]

The *Daily Mail*, 30 August 1928

> One of the chief events of the English musical year – the Three Choirs Festival at Gloucester next week – will be conducted by a virtually unknown musician, Mr Herbert W. Sumsion.
>
> Sir Herbert Brewer's sudden death in the spring left vacant the conductorship of the festival and the organistship of the cathedral post which he had held for more than 30 years.
>
> Names of many well known musicians, including a City organist who is of the first eminence as a conductor and choir-trainer, were canvassed; but the Gloucester Cathedral authorities did the unexpected thing in appointing a young man who has yet to win his spurs . . .
>
> He has a very heavy week before him . . . Sir Herbert Brewer made a point of introducing into the Gloucester programme more unconventional music than is heard at Worcester and Hereford.
>
> Thus the staid Three Choirs audience is on Thursday afternoon to have the shock of a performance of Arthur Honegger's *King David*. This is a particularly taxing work for a young conductor to take charge of at the last moment; but Honegger cannot come, and so it falls to Mr Sumsion.

Herbert Whitton Sumsion was born in Gloucester on 19 January 1899, became a probationer in the cathedral choir in 1908 and a chorister two years later. From 1914 to 1917 he was an articled pupil to Brewer, becoming an ARCO in 1915 at the age of seventeen and an FRCO (Turpin Prize) in the following year. In 1917 he was commissioned in the Queen's Westminster Rifles and saw active service in the Flanders trenches. On his return to Gloucester in 1919 he was appointed assistant organist at the cathedral.

An excellent piano accompanist, Sumsion played for Elgar's Festival Chorus rehearsals, becoming an ardent admirer of his music. He learnt exactly what Elgar wanted and how it was achieved. He never forgot how, after a rehearsal of *Gerontius*, the composer came across to the piano to shake his hand and nod his thanks – from Elgar such gestures of appreciation were rare.

In 1922 Sumsion became organist at Christ Church, Lancaster Gate in London and in addition, in 1924, accepted the post of Director of Music at Bishops Stortford College and became an assistant instructor at Morley College. He also found time in 1924 to take lessons in conducting from Adrian Boult at the Royal College of Music. Boult was so impressed that he told Sumsion there was little that he could teach him which he didn't already know. At the RCM Sumsion met R.O. Morris, the professor of counterpoint and composition, and when, in 1926, Morris was appointed to a similar post at the Curtis Institute of Music, Philadelphia, USA, he invited Sumsion to join him as his assistant.

Sumsion sailed to America with R.O. Morris and his wife Emmeline, whose sister Adeline was married to Ralph Vaughan Williams. On the voyage they were befriended by Professor W.B. McDaniel and his wife, returning home following a year of teaching Classics at the American Academy in Rome. Walton McDaniel was Professor of Classics at the University of Pennsylvania, Philadelphia, and it was on a visit to the McDaniels' home that Sumsion met their niece, Alice Garlichs. Herbert Sumsion and Alice were married in Philadelphia on 7 June 1927. One year later, on 10 June 1928, they embarked for England.[39]

Although appointed organist at Coventry Cathedral, Sumsion was released in order to return to Gloucester as Brewer's successor. He was plunged immediately into preparations for the 1928(G) Festival while Alice, seven months pregnant, struggled to set up home at 7 Miller's Green. Fortunately, following Brewer's death, Samuel Underwood, organist of Stroud Parish Church and a first-class choir-trainer, stepped into the gap and trained the Festival Chorus until Sumsion's return.

Shortly before his death, Sir Herbert Brewer had said to the Dean of Gloucester (Dr Henry Gee); 'If anything happens to me, I want Herbert Sumsion to take over from me.'[40] His choice was now vindicated. There were uneven performances of course, but there were triumphs too. No little credit was due to the Gloucester assistant organist, Arthur Pritchard, whose playing was a notable feature of the Festival. And an old friend came to Sumsion's aid: Adrian Boult, by then the conductor of the City of Birmingham Symphony Orchestra, had driven down to Gloucester before breakfast one morning and helped Sumsion with his scores – a kind and unselfish act.

The new works from Ravel, Honegger, Ireland and Holst had not materialized, and perhaps as well under the circumstances. Sumsion gave an assured performance of Honegger's *King David*, a work described by Harvey Grace as suggesting 'the unnecessary discomfort of a progress over broken bottles',[41] but who, after the performance, declared that 'the Ayes clearly had it'. Kodály conducted an excellent performance of his *Psalmus Hungaricus*, and Dame Ethel Smyth caused a stir conducting her Mass in D.

Required by the Dean to cover her head while conducting in the cathedral, Dame Ethel wore her doctoral cap and gown – but quickly found the cap to be an irritating encumbrance which she discarded with a jerk of the head – and legend variously has it that it landed either on Billy Reed's desk or Dean Gee's lap![42]

At the Opening Service, Sullivan's *In Memoriam* overture was played in memory of Sir Herbert Brewer, and the Thursday evening programme was also made a special memorial performance by the inclusion of Lee Williams's unaccompanied anthem, *Thou wilt keep him in perfect peace*, sung in the distance by the cathedral choir, followed by a motet written by Brewer early in 1928 but never heard by him, *God Within*; these preceded Verdi's *Requiem*.

Vaughan Williams conducted *The Lark Ascending* and, of course, there was Elgar — conducting *The Dream of Gerontius*, *The Kingdom*, and the Cello Concerto with Beatrice Harrison as soloist.

Soon after the Sumsions' arrival in Gloucester, Elgar called on them at Miller's Green. Daisy, the parlourmaid and for many years a servant to Lady Brewer, opened the door to him. 'Oh! I know your face so well,' she said, 'but I can't put a name to it.' Elgar was shown in to Alice's sitting room where he presented a large bouquet of roses to Herbert Sumsion's shy young bride.[43]

Among the soloists who appeared at the 1928(G) Festival were many established favourites: Dorothy Silk, Elsie Suddaby, Margaret Balfour, Muriel Brunskill, Astra Desmond, Steuart Wilson and Robert Radford, but there were even more newcomers who, in turn, would become famous names. The sopranos Dora Labbette and Joan Elwes had made their Three Choirs débuts in 1927(H) and returned in 1928. The tenors Parry Jones, Frank Titterton and Walter Widdop, and the baritones Roy Henderson, Stuart Robertson and Harold Williams appeared at the Festival for the first time. Horace Stevens, the outstanding 'Elijah' of his generation, repeated the part of the Prophet as well as singing in *Gerontius*, infusing dramatic intensity into his interpretations and, word-perfect, singing without a score.

The ordeal faced by Sumsion in 1928 prompted Harvey Grace to question the accepted Three Choirs custom and to make a suggestion which presaged present practice:

> . . . the way in which the three Cathedral organists have risen to the occasion has long been a matter of admiring comment. But need the ordeal be so severe? Is it necessary to limit their opportunities of conducting a professional orchestra to one week and a few odd rehearsals in three years? Surely the strain would be less, and the conducting better than it is, if the work were shared annually. Each Cathedral organist would then have the advantage of regular yearly experience of conducting under Festival conditions. Even that is little enough, seeing how much complex and unfamiliar music the programmes now contain. But it would be just three times better than the present arrangement, under which a conductor puts in a week of hectic struggle, and then says goodbye to first-class orchestral experience for three years.[44]

But the time for change was not yet and, under the circumstances, Sumsion had coped remarkably well, calling from Elgar his famous remark: 'What at the beginning of the week was an *assumption* has now become a certainty.' And Charles Lee Williams sent Sumsion a dozen bottles of Champagne.

Elgar had considered writing a new work for the 1929 Worcester Festival, a setting of two poems by Shelley, *The Demon* and *Adonais*, but this was vetoed by the Dean (Dr Moore Ede) on the grounds that *Adonais* 'is frankly pagan'.[45] Sir Ivor Atkins tried hard to persuade Elgar to make the Festival 'memorable by a great work'[46] but was only able to interest him in orchestrating Purcell's motet *Jehovah, quam multi sunt hostes mei*. This was given, along with a Byrd five-part motet *Laetentur Coeli*, before *Elijah* on the Thursday morning; Steuart Wilson and Horace Stevens were the soloists. Elgar also conducted *Gerontius*, *The Kingdom*, *Introduction and Allegro for Strings*, and his Second Symphony.

The outstanding event of the 1929 Worcester Festival was the first performance at Three Choirs of Bach's *St John Passion* in the edition prepared by Sir Ivor Atkins. Canon Lacey of Worcester Cathedral, who three years earlier had crossed swords with Elgar over the issue of Wagner's sensuality, assisted Atkins by providing a new translation of the verses. The performance proved to be one of the best of the week. The soloists were Dorothy Silk, Muriel Brunskill, Steuart Wilson, Roy Henderson, Archibald Winter, and the bass-baritone Keith Falkner who had created such a great impression in 1925(G). From 1929 until the outbreak of the Second World War, in which he served with the Royal Air Force, Falkner sang regularly at Three Choirs. He succeeded Sir Ernest Bullock as Director of the Royal College of Music in 1960 and was knighted in 1967.

Another singer who became a much-loved personality at the Festivals and far beyond, Isobel Baillie, made her first Three Choirs appearance in 1929(W). Her voice, instantly recognizable, and described by Richard Capell in *Grove*, had 'treble-like purity, "angelic" was sometimes applied to it; not so much personal as brightly and serenely spiritual, made by her soaring and equable tones'. She sang at every Three Choirs Festival from 1929(W) to 1955(H) with the exception of 1933. Isobel Baillie was made a DBE in 1978 and returned to Three Choirs in the following year to give an autobiographical talk at the Hereford Festival.

It was in 1929(W) also that Myra Hess made the first of several appearances at Three Choirs, playing Beethoven's Fourth Piano Concerto in the cathedral. In 1941 she too received the DBE for her work in organizing the National Gallery wartime concerts.

New works presented in 1929 included Alexander Brent Smith's Choral Concerto and Sir Walford Davies's *Christ in the Universe*, a setting of a mystical poem by Alice Meynell, for soprano (Dorothy Silk), tenor (Steuart Wilson) and orchestra, in which there is a prominent part for piano, on this occasion played by the composer himself. There was also an Idyll for small orchestra and violin obbligato, *At Valley Green*, by Herbert Sumsion – a piece which showed him to have 'a feeling for gracious melody'.[47]

For Herbert and Alice Sumsion this was the first Three Choirs at which they could enjoy to the full those house-parties which were such a delightful feature of the pre-war Festival. Along with Percy Hull's wife, Molly, Alice Sumsion rented a house in College Green, Worcester, for a week. Among their guests were several musicians including Vaughan Williams, at the Festival to conduct his *Sancta Civitas* and *The Wasps*. Billy Reed brought Elgar to join in the fun – such as the rare sight of R.V.W. trying desperately to play ping-pong and not once succeeding in hitting the ball! This accompanied by roars of laughter. And more laughter as Elgar reminisced about his younger days: stories such as the one about him and his brother meeting in a Worcester street an acquaintance who was the worse for drink, taking him home and putting him to bed, only to discover later that it was in the wrong house![48]

Sir Keith Falkner recollects with particular pleasure how, apart from the music, the Festivals of the 1930s were great social affairs:

. . . tea parties, daily luncheons, with Receptions given by the Mayor, clergy and laity. Of this last category, two hostesses were famous: Mrs Holland-Martin (Worcester, Overbury Court) and Mrs Gwyn Holford (Gloucester, Hartpury House).

The latter, a delightful eccentric with strong convictions regarding her Anglo-Catholic religion, was a stickler for social behaviour. A large hat always topped her tall and graceful figure at both breakfast and luncheon. One night, at dinner, a guest seated on her right poured his sherry into his soup announcing, 'I always have sherry in my soup!' The retort came: 'This will be the last time you dine in my house' (The cook had prepared a delicious consommé).

With others Heddle Nash and I were at lunch. Halfway down the table I heard Heddle exclaim, 'It's alright! Gerontius is mine! Elgar has told me I'm the one!' Mrs Gwyn Holford, black hat a-tremble, said 'Mr Nash what did I hear you say?' 'Oh,' replied Heddle 'Elgar has told me I'm Gerontius.' 'Mr Nash you don't have the slightest idea what Gerontius is about!'

Deathly silence followed, everyone wondering what was to happen next. Heddle, of course, rose to the occasion saying: 'What's wrong with it? Can I come and talk with you about it?'

Later when we sang the work together I found he was the best *bel canto* Gerontius I ever heard of his time, following in the steps of Gervase Elwes, John Coates and Steuart Wilson. And certainly in 1936 at Hereford – with Percy Hull – it was the finest *Gerontius* performance I ever took part in.

The hospitality at Overbury Court with Mrs Holland-Martin for Worcester was equally luxurious and generous. One year the other guests included Sir Hugh Allen, Sir Walford Davies, Elsie Suddaby, Mary Jarred, Joyce Grenfell and Steuart Wilson:

The gardens and lawns were spacious, while tennis and croquet provided relaxation from the Festival atmosphere. One evening, after dinner, Sir Hugh produced a copy of the 'notorious unintentionally comic' oratorio *Ruth* by George Tolhurst (1864). The evening became hilarious as we stood round the piano: Allen and Walford playing four hands, the rest of us singing the various parts. At moments we became quite hysterical, breaking many times for laughter and repeats. Joyce Grenfell pleased us enormously with her resonant voice and sense of fun.[49]

Another whose hospitality at Three Choirs was celebrated among regular Festival-goers was Charles Lee Williams. At every Gloucester Festival he and his son kept 'open house at College Green, and the happy family feeling that pervaded the Festival was due very largely to his hospitality, and not least to his constant care, shown in a hundred little ways, for the comfort and happiness of visitors'.[50] In 1929(W) Lee Williams conducted his *alla capella* setting of the Lord's Prayer at the Opening Service.

He had [said Herbert Thompson in *The Musical Times*] grown old in the service of the Three Choirs, from the time of his appointment to Gloucester in 1882, and one of the pleasantest incidents of the Festival was when Sir Ivor Atkins announced, at the concluding concert, in the College Hall,[51] that the Archbishop of Canterbury had declared his intention of conferring upon Mr Williams the degree of Doctor of Music. It is an honour long delayed, but most appropriate. He has been styled the Grandfather of the Three Choirs, and one trusts he may live long enough to be hailed as their Great-grandfather.[52]

When he died on 29 August 1935 in his eighty-fifth year the music critic of *The Times* wrote, 'The Three Choirs Festival was the passion of Lee Williams's life.'[53]

The surprise of the 1930(H) Festival was less a matter of what was performed than of what was not. For the first time since 1847, excluding the 'mock' Festival of 1875(W), *Elijah* was dropped from the programme, and its inclusion was no longer an inevitability. *Elijah* was omitted in 1934 and 1936, and was performed only once or twice in each succeeding decade.

Elgar, Hereford Festival, 1909 (photograph courtesy of Wulstan Atkins)

Handbill circulated by Elgar at the 1911(W) Festival – see page 151

Hereford, 1912 (photograph courtesy of Roy Massey)

C.H. Lloyd, Brewer, Elgar and (*seated*) Saint-Saëns. Gloucester, 1913 (*The Musical Times*)

Percy Hull, Herbert Brewer and Sir Ivor Atkins –
Hereford, 1921 (photograph courtesy of Derek
Foxton)

Dedication of the Parry Memorial – Gloucester,
1922 (photograph courtesy of Alice Sumsion)

Elgar and Brewer – Gloucester, 1922

Arthur Bliss, Herbert Brewer, W.H. Reed, Sir
Edward Elgar and Eugene Goossens (the name of
the lady is not known) – Gloucester, 1922

Gloucester, 1922. Following the Dedication of
the Parry Memorial. *Standing (left to right)*:
Herbert Brewer, Sir Hugh Allen, Granville
Bantock, Sir Henry Hadow. *Sitting*: Sir Edward
Elgar, Bishop Gibson, Lord Gladstone, Dean Gee
and Sir Charles Villiers Stanford

Dorothy Silk, Agnes Nicholls and Elsie Suddaby
– Worcester, 1923 (*The Musical Times*)

Harry Plunkett Greene

Original ms of Elgar's *Civic Fanfare* for Hereford,
1927 (reproduced courtesy of Richard Lloyd)

The Gramophone Company Ltd van parked
outside Hereford Cathedral, 1927 (photograph: E.
diCusati – *Music on Record*, by F.W. Gaisberg
(London, 1948), p. 171)

THE THREE CHOIRS FESTIVAL AT GLOUCESTER CATHEDRAL.

Musical Celebrities of the Festival.

8.—Sir Ivor Atkins, the talented composer and organist of Worcester Cathedral, and Mr. Brent Smith.
9.—Miss Dorothy Silk, who sang the soprano parts in the " Elijah " performance.
10.—Mr. Herbert Heyner and Mr. Norman Allin, both of whom took principal parts.

11.—Mrs. Hathaway, Dr. Hathaway, and Dr. Lyon.
12.—Miss Margaret Balfour, the principal contralto in the " Elijah " and other performances.

13.—Mr. Horace Stevens, who has made a great name by his fine bass singing in many principal parts.

" Cheltenham Chronicle " Photos. Copies 1s. each, postage 2d. extra.

Gloucester, 1925 (*Cheltenham Chronicle and Gloucestershire Graphic*)

Sir Ivor Atkins, Percy Hull, Herbert Sumsion and
(*seated*) Sir Edward Elgar – Hereford, 1930
(photograph courtesy of Derek Foxton)

Dorothy Silk, Alice Sumsion, G.B.S. and Herbert
Sumsion – Gloucester, 1931 (photograph courtesy
of Alice Sumsion)

Standing (left to right): Alexander Brent Smith,
Sir George Dyson and Ralph Vaughan Williams.
Seated: Herbert Sumsion, Percy Hull and Sir
Ivor Atkins – Hereford, 1933

George Bernard Shaw, Elgar and Sumsion –
Hereford, 1933 (photograph taken by Harriet
Cohen and reproduced courtesy of Alice Sumsion)

Percy Hull and Elgar – Hereford, 1933
(photograph: Vivians Studio, Hereford)

Frank Titterton and his chauffeur – Hereford, 1933
(photograph courtesy of Basil Butcher)

Elsie Suddaby, Bishop Lyle Carr and Astra
Desmond – Hereford, 1933 (photograph
courtesy of Basil Butcher)

Gustav Holst

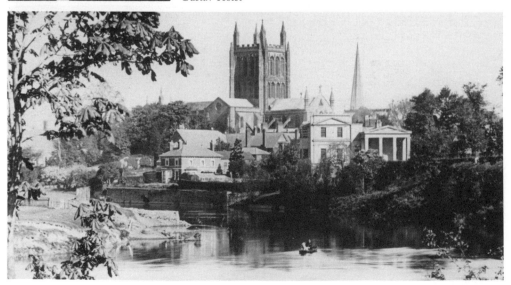

Hereford Cathedral (Hereford Cathedral Library)

THREE CHOIRS FESTIVAL AT WORCESTER

The 215th meeting of the Three Choirs of Gloucester, Worcester and Hereford began on Sunday afternoon in Worcester Cathedral, and was attended by the Mayor and Corporation of that city.

1.—Mr. George Bernard Shaw, who attended the Festival.
2.—Canon Hereford (Capetown), Rev. G. V. Blois, with Miss Blois, from Hanbury Rectory.
3.—Mr. Francis Brett Young, the author, and his wife.

4.—The memorial window to the late Sir Edward Elgar, which was unveiled by Lord Cobham.
5.—Dr. Robertson and Dr. A. W. Davies (Dean of Worcester).

6.—A scene outside the Cathedral on Tuesday.
7.—Mr. A. K. Nicholson (designer of memorial window), Mr. John Stallard (Mayor of Worcester) and Dr. Perowne (Bishop of Worcester) and Lord Cobham.

Worcester, 1935 (*Cheltenham Chronicle and Gloucestershire Graphic*)

Kodály rehearsing with Mary Jarred and Keith Falkner – Gloucester, 1937 (photograph courtesy of Sir Keith Falkner)

Vera Wood, Ralph Vaughan Williams, Alice and Herbert Sumsion – Worcester, 1938 (photograph courtesy of Alice Sumsion)

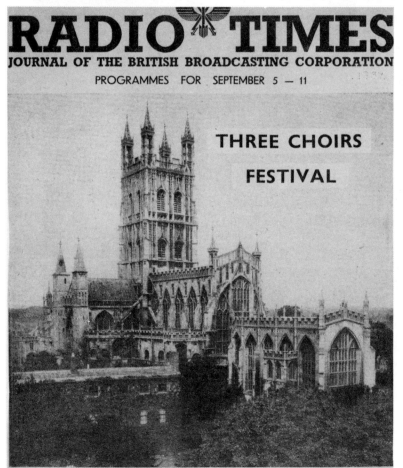

RADIO TIMES
JOURNAL OF THE BRITISH BROADCASTING CORPORATION
PROGRAMMES FOR SEPTEMBER 5 – 11

THREE CHOIRS

FESTIVAL

From Gloucester Cathedral, scene of this year's Three Choirs Festival, Elgar's oratorio 'The Dream of Gerontius' will be broadcast on Tuesday

Radio Times, 5–11 September 1937

Instead of *Elijah*, the opening work of the 1930(H) Festival was *The Apostles*, a performance vividly remembered by Sir Keith Falkner who appeared with Elgar, together with Elsie Suddaby, Astra Desmond, Heddle Nash, Roy Henderson and Norman Allin:

> Elgar took a piano rehearsal in the Close. All went normally until the Judas solo of his betrayal.
> Judas begins his marvellous song of anguish in which, to quote Elgar, 'a proud sinner is swayed by all sorts of feelings' while he sings to music that ranks among the most movingly intense that Elgar ever wrote.
> Norman was half-way through, singing magnificently. Elgar burst into tears. Leaning on the piano he said 'I can't go on'. The rehearsal stopped. I had never seen him in such an emotional state. Whenever I hear this great aria now, I'm reminded of that occasion.[54]

At the actual performance Elgar, who was suffering from sciatica, 'had to be helped to the conductor's rostrum, where he *sat* to conduct through the performance and then was helped down again'.[55] At the Opening Service on the previous day. Percy Hull had to conduct the *Introduction and Allegro* in Elgar's place. But as the week went on Elgar's condition gradually improved and on Thursday evening he conducted a beautiful and memorable performance of *Gerontius* with Steuart Wilson singing the name-part.

Only three new works were performed at Sumsion's second Gloucester Festival, in 1931. Holst had arrived for one of the chorus rehearsals soaked to the knees, having walked through mud and mire while following an ancient Roman trackway, and directed the rehearsal of his *Choral Fantasia* in a pair of Sumsion's trousers; there was a short orchestral work by R.O. Morris – the Sinfonia in C major; and an excellent performance under Sumsion's baton of Robin Milford's *A Prophet in the Land*, a 'Dramatic Oratorio' for soprano, tenor and baritone soloists and a large orchestra, including *ad lib* parts for treble recorder, harpsichord and organ.

George Bernard Shaw and his wife were accompanied at the Festival by T.E. Lawrence (Lawrence of Arabia, who by 1931 had rejoined the Royal Air Force under the name of Shaw, serving in the ranks until 1935, when he was killed in a motorcycling accident). On the Thursday, Alice gave lunch to a party of about twelve guests including the Shaws, R.O. Morris and his wife, and Dorothy Silk. Herbert Howells was also there: his song-cycle *Green Ways* with Isobel Baillie as soloist had scored an outstanding success at the Wednesday evening concert. Sumsion had reverted to tradition and opened the Festival with *Elijah*. Howells remembered the conversation around the lunch-table:

> . . . Most of the company had heard *Elijah* on the Tuesday. So had G.B.S. And they had now gone to the luncheon just after hearing a famous and masterly Holst work [*The Hymn of Jesus*]. At table Shavian certitude galvanised proceedings. The voice of *The Perfect Wagnerite*, serenely infallible, was heard declaring both Mendelssohn's and Holst's weaknesses in their orchestration. In the constrained silence there was only one casualty. A glass of lemonade was knocked over. It was G.B.S.'s own.[56]

During the week, Vaughan Williams conducted *The Lark Ascending* and *Job*, and Elgar *Gerontius*, the Violin Concerto (with Albert Sammons as soloist) and the *Nursery Suite*, composed in 1930 to celebrate the birth of Princess Margaret Rose to the Duke and Duchess of York.

Percy Hull's predilection for rapid tempi in his interpretation of Bach's Mass in B minor had earned for the Hereford Festival performances of that work the epithet 'the

Hereford Stakes'. In 1931 it seemed as though Herbert Sumsion wished to take a leaf from Hull's book. He had conducted the Mass in B minor at a morning performance and 'In order to be over in time for the Mayor's luncheon he took it at a very fast speed. As it ended, I think at 12.55, Sir Hugh Allen was to be seen walking furiously towards us – "Disgraceful – all much too fast." Steuart Wilson shouted, "By the way, what *is* bogey for the B minor?"'[57]

When the week was over Sumsion felt ill and somewhat depressed. Once more it was Adrian Boult who came to his aid, giving Sumsion an Hanovia ultra-violet lamp which he thought might be an effective pick-me-up – and it was![58]

William Walton first came into prominence in 1923, when his String Quartet was chosen for performance at the Salzburg Festival of the International Society for Contemporary Music. In the same year the first performance of *Façade*, at the Aeolian Hall, caused a scandal. In 1926 Walton's overture *Portsmouth Point*, was performed at the Zürich Festival of the International Society and next year it was heard in London at one of the 'Proms'. There followed the *Sinfonia Concertante* for piano and orchestra, performed under Ansermet in 1928, and the Viola Concerto (with Hindemith as soloist) in 1929. Then, at the Leeds Festival of 1931, came the most excitingly original choral work of a generation – *Belshazzar's Feast*, conducted by Sargent. 'Every note hit its mark,' said *The Musical Times*, 'and the composer had very definite notions of what those marks should be':

> Walton's first attempt to handle voices on a large scale showed an enormous increase on his already considerable grasp of saying something forceful and original without any kind of conscious striving to be like or unlike anyone else. His theme – expounded in a libretto by Mr. Osbert Sitwell, which balanced rapid dramatic narration with two big choruses of praise, one ironical to heathen gods of metal, wood and stone, and the other fanatical to the God of Israel – allowed him ample scope to depict with extreme vividness that barbaric mixture of monotheism and nationalism which lies just beneath the Bible narrative of the Captivity.

The shock of *Belshazzar's Feast* had, as Sir Adrian Boult put it, shattered the English musical world. Walton was invited to conduct at the 1932 Worcester Festival – but not *Belshazzar*, against which the Three Choirs cathedral doors remained bolted for a further twenty-five years.

Instead, Walton conducted his *Portsmouth Point* overture and, with Lionel Tertis as soloist, the Viola Concerto; Holst conducted the ballet music from his *Perfect Fool* as well as *The Hymn of Jesus*; and Vaughan Williams directed the first performance of his *Magnificat*, as well as his *Benedicite*. Sir Ivor Atkins presented a profoundly moving performance of Szymanowski's *Stabat Mater*, marred only by Muriel Brunskill's breakdown, losing her place in the *Agnus Dei* – the sensation of the Festival, but no more than an unfortunate accident. The bicentenary of the birth of Haydn was marked by Part I of *The Creation*, the *Te Deum* in C major, a string quartet, and a performance of the Symphony No. 93 – during which all the lights in the College Hall failed for quite a long time but the LSO astonished everybody by continuing to play without interruption.

In 1930 Elgar had been persuaded to compose a piece to celebrate the twenty-fifth Brass Band Competition Festival, held every year at the Crystal Palace. The result was the *Severn Suite*. He later scored this work for orchestra and conducted the first public performance at the 1932 Worcester Festival, having recorded the new version with the

London Symphony Orchestra the previous April. G.B. Shaw was impressed: 'What a transfiguration! Nobody will ever believe that it began as a cornet corobbery. It's extraordinarily beautiful.'[59]

Elgar also conducted performances of his First Symphony; *The Music Makers* with Muriel Brunskill as soloist; 'For the Fallen', from *The Spirit of England*, with Isobel Baillie; a superb *Gerontius* with Astra Desmond, Frank Titterton and Harold Williams; and at the chamber concert Myra Hess and the Griller String Quartet played Elgar's Piano Quintet in A minor.

'Who will ever love these Festivals as you and I have?' wrote Elgar to Atkins during the First World War.[60] In 1933 that love was as strong as ever:

> During these latter-day Festivals he is usually seated, but he's determined that the choir shall not fail him at the great outburst of 'Praise to the Holiest'. At rehearsal he is unimpressed – '*It wouldn't scare a mouse*'! On repetition, the choir responds with such vehemence that the Cathedral almost rocks![61]

Elgar and his daughter, Carice, rented a large house, 'The Priory', for the 1933 Hereford Festival. There was 'a convenient garden in front which was daily thronged with people coming to tea. They came in and out, and one hardly knew who they all were; but the Festival spirit prevailed – it was open door and hospitality throughout the week.'[62] Herbert and Alice Sumsion were among the throng. Elgar 'had the full score of *Elijah* by him and would show Bernard Shaw and others his pet points in it: things which appealed to him and of which he never tired'.[63] Sumsion joined Elgar and Shaw in this discussion, looking at the score over their shoulders – a moment captured by the camera of pianist Harriet Cohen (see illustration).

At the Opening Service Elgar, wearing full court dress, conducted his March in B flat – a transposition from C of his Triumphal March from *Caractacus*, and the *Civic Fanfare*. Astra Desmond, Frank Titterton and Horace Stevens were the soloists in *Gerontius* under Elgar's baton on Tuesday evening; and in the Kemble Theatre on Wednesday evening he conducted the viola arrangement of his Cello Concerto with Lionel Tertis as soloist.

Elgar mounted the Three Choirs rostrum for the last time at 11.30 a.m. on Thursday 7 September 1933. The work was:

> . . . a better performance of *The Kingdom* than one had dared to hope. Miss Elsie Suddaby, Miss Astra Desmond, Mr Frank Titterton, and Mr Harold Williams formed a team of soloists second only to the first unforgettable interpreters of this masterpiece. And repeated hearings only confirm that this *is* a masterpiece, incomparably ahead of anything else which has been written this century . . . The use Elgar makes of the harp alone would repay long study. But we do not prize and admire music because it is well-written. We prize it according to the degree of delight it gives us, and I am moved by *The Kingdom* as I am moved only by the greatest and noblest creations of musical art.[64]

Sir Edward Elgar died at his home, Marl Bank, Worcester, on Friday 23 February 1934. One week later, on Friday 2 March, a national memorial service was held in Worcester Cathedral. The players of the London Symphony Orchestra and the soloists Elsie Suddaby, Astra Desmond and Harold Williams gave their services freely as a mark of their affection and respect for a great musician. Elgar's two dearest friends, Sir Ivor Atkins and Billy Reed, along with the Dean of Worcester, made all the necessary arrangements. The choir was made up of the Festival Chorus and members of the choirs of the three cathedrals.

The service opened with the Prelude to Part 2 of *The Apostles* and included the *Enigma* theme, Variation I (C.A.E.) Variation IX ('Nimrod') and Variation XIII (***); the Prelude to the *Dream of Gerontius* and the final pages of Part I; the Angel's Song and the Angel's Farewell; the Virgin's Meditation from *The Kingdom*, and the music from the Lord's Prayer to the end of the work.

Prayers and Lessons were read by the Archdeacon, the Dean, and the Bishop of Worcester, including the following words taken from a prayer read by the Dean:

We give Thee humble and hearty thanks that it pleased Thee to endow our fellow citizen EDWARD ELGAR with that singular mastery of music, and the will to use it in Thy service, whereby he being dead yet speaketh; now filling our minds with visions of the mystery and beauty of Nature; now by the concert of sweet and solemn sounds telling our hearts secrets of life and death that lie too deep for words; now soaring with Angels and Archangels and with all the company of Heaven in an ecstasy of praise; now holding us bowed with the broken and contrite heart before the throne of judgment.

We thank Thee for the great place he holds in the glorious roll of England's Masters of Music. We thank Thee for the love and loyalty which ever bound this her son to the Faithful City.

Notes

1. MT 1921, p. 692
2. The *Daily News*, 9 June 1922
3. Herbert Howells, 85th birthday broadcast (BBC) October 1977
4. Melville Cook, *Notes from my Three Choirs Diary*, Hereford Festival programme book, 1988
5. MT 1921, p. 692
6. Imogen Holst, *Gustav Holst – A Biography* (Oxford, 1938 – reprinted in OUP paperback, 1988)
7. MT 1927, p. 922
8. Herbert Sumsion, *Percy Clarke Hull – A Tribute*, Hereford Festival programme book, 1970
9. Memories of Watkins Shaw
10. Eugene Goossens, *Overture and Beginners* (Methuen, 1951) pp. 193–4
11. *Annals* 1931, p. 86
12. MT 1922, p. 706
13. Herbert Howells, 'Memories from the Twentieth Century', an essay from *Two Hundred and Fifty Years of the Three Choirs Festival* (Three Choirs Festival Association, 1977)
14. *The Times*, 7 September 1922
15. C. Lee Williams scrap-book, Gloucester City Library
16. A.H. Brewer, *Memories of Choirs and Cloisters* (1931)
17. Eugene Goossens, *Overture and Beginners* (Methuen, 1951) p. 298
18. MT 1923, p. 717
19. *Worcester Daily Times*, 18 March 1926
20. Ibid. 18 March 1926
21. MT 1920, p. 667
22. MT 1924, p. 908
23. *Elgar Centenary Sketches* (1957), pp. 9–10
24. MT 1924, p. 910
25. A.H. Brewer, op. cit.
26. Memories of Dr Arthur Pritchard
27. Memories of Sir Keith Falkner
28. Ibid.
29. MT 1925, p. 924
30. *Annals* 1931, p. 92
31. Memories of Dr Melville Cook

32. Ibid.
33. A.H. Brewer, op. cit.
34. Jerrold Northrop Moore, *Elgar on Record* (Oxford, 1974), p. 72
35. Ibid., pp. 74–5
36. F.W. Gaisberg, *Music on Record* (1948), p. 171
37. A.H. Brewer, op. cit.
38. Ibid.
39. Memories of Mrs Alice Sumsion
40. Memories of Dr Arthur Pritchard
41. MT 1928, p. 898
42. Memories of Mrs Edith Sterry and Miss Patience Gobey
43. Memories of Mrs Alice Sumsion
44. MT 1928, p. 898
45. See Wulstan Atkins, *The Elgar–Atkins Friendship* (David & Charles, 1985), pp. 408–09
46. Ibid., p. 410
47. MT 1929, p. 895
48. Memories of Mrs Alice Sumsion
49. Memories of Sir Keith Falkner
50. MT 1928, p. 901
51. The use of the College Hall for a secular concert in 1929 was a revival. The hall had ceased to be a Three Choirs venue after 1878.
52. MT 1929, p. 895
53. *The Times*, 3 September 1935
54. Memories of Sir Keith Falkner
55. W.H. Reed, *Elgar as I knew him* (Oxford, 1936), p. 105
56. Herbert Howells, 'Memories from the Twentieth Century', an essay from *Two Hundred and Fifty Years of the Three Choirs Festival* (Three Choirs Association, 1977)
57. Memories of Sir Keith Falkner
58. Memories of Mrs Alice Sumsion
59. 11 July 1932. Worcester City Records Office
60. E. Wulstan Atkins, op. cit., p. 447
61. Melville Cook, op. cit.
62. W.H. Reed, op. cit., p. 106
63. Ibid.
64. F. Bonavia in MT 1933, p. 942

CHAPTER SIXTEEN

DONA NOBIS PACEM

The year 1934 robbed English music not only of Sir Edward Elgar but also of Gustav Holst and Frederick Delius. Without Elgar or Holst there was a sense of grievous loss to the musical and social round of Three Choirs, and this was reinforced at the 1934(G) Festival by the additional absence of Vaughan Williams, who had cut his foot while bathing and was suffering from a poisoned abscess.

In 1933(H) Percy Hull, continuing a policy of gradual change, had decided to include *Elijah*, dropped in 1939(H), but to perform only an abridged version of *Messiah*. Sumsion, in 1934(G), omitted *Elijah* but followed Hull's lead by presenting only the abridged *Messiah*, thus making room on the Friday morning for W.H. Reed's Symphony for Strings, Haydn's *Te Deum*, and the Brahms Violin Concerto, with Jelly d'Aranyi as soloist. In place of *Elijah* on Tuesday, *The Kingdom* conducted by Sumsion, was given 'In Memoriam Edward Elgar', followed by Kodály's *Psalmus Hungaricus* and Vaughan Williams's *Pastoral Symphony*, conducted by Gordon Jacob in the composer's absence. Other contemporary pieces heard during the week included *Summer Music* and *St Patrick's Breastplate* by Arnold Bax; *Elegy for Strings* and *Procession* by Herbert Howells; *Two Ballads* for baritone and orchestra by Howard Ferguson, in which Roy Henderson was the soloist; and Cyril B. Rootham's setting of Milton's *Ode on the Morning of Christ's Nativity*, with Isobel Baillie, Trefor Jones and Roy Henderson joining chorus, semi-chorus and orchestra under the composer's baton.

On Thursday evening, before a performance of *Gerontius*, G.D. Cunningham, the organist of Birmingham Town Hall, played Handel's Organ Concerto in F major. When he had finished, 'an embarrassing gap appeared in the proceedings whilst waiting for the B.B.C. to relay the final part of the programme'. Herbert Sumsion summoned his assistant organist, Melville Cook, successor to Arthur Pritchard in 1932:

Cook, what about playing an organ solo till they're ready to broadcast? Bach's D minor will fill the time nicely.' Me on to the organ bench in a jiffy, all stops drawn, now for it – diddle-de – and we're off, with the help of Sir Ivor Atkins to turn the pages. A great game of guessing after the concert – was it Cunningham? No, it was Cook, making his Festival debut without rehearsal![1]

Leaving Melville Cook's side, Sir Ivor Atkins made his way to the rostrum to conduct *Gerontius*, unrecognized by 'Crescendo' whose review in the *News Chronicle* commended 'Mr Sumsion, the orchestra, the chorus and the soloists, Mr Heddle Nash, Mr Harold Williams and Miss Astra Desmond, [who] have all sat under Elgar in the past and so know well his ways and wishes'. On the Tuesday evening Percy Hull had also taken a share in Sumsion's burden, conducting the Mozart *Requiem*. Elgar gone, the conducting load was shared for the first time, each of the two visiting organists directing one work; a sensible precedent for future Festivals.

Shortly after Elgar's death, the Dean of Worcester and Sir Ivor Atkins launched a successful appeal for funds to erect a permanent memorial in the cathedral in the form of a stained-glass window. A design by Archibald Nicholson was chosen, drawing its inspiration from *The Dream of Gerontius*. The window, placed in the north aisle close to the spot where Elgar so often stood during performances at the Festivals, was unveiled by Viscount Cobham, the Lord Lieutenant, in a short ceremony at 11 a.m. on 3 September 1935, immediately before a Festival performance of *Gerontius*.

George Dyson (1883–1964) was a popular figure at the Festivals from 1933(H), in which year he conducted the first performance of his setting for tenor, chorus and orchestra of *St Paul's Voyage to Melita* with Trefor Jones as soloist. It was repeated in 1934(G), 1937(G) and 1952(H). The music of Dyson, owing nothing to Elgar and, unlike that of Vaughan Williams, barely influenced by folk-song, casts back to the models of Stanford and Parry. A superb orchestrator, his work invariably drew contemporary critical praise. In addition to *St Paul's Voyage* two other compositions by Dyson for solo voices, chorus and orchestra received their first performances at Three Choirs: *Nebuchadnezzar* in 1935(W) and *Quo Vadis?* – Part I in 1946(H) and Parts I and II in 1949(H). Describing *Quo Vadis?* as 'a rare beauty . . . perfect exposition in poetry and music of a deep spiritual longing for human harmony with the divine', *The Musical Times* of October 1946 concluded that 'Sir George Dyson showed . . . a masterly command of his art, all the more admirable because at no point did he allow his superb craftsmanship to take on the appearance of conscious cleverness.'

In 1937 Dyson was appointed Director of the Royal College of Music in succession to Sir Hugh Allen. He was knighted in 1941, and conducted for the last time at Three Choirs in 1952(H), the year of his retirement from the RCM. The work was *St Paul's Voyage to Melita*, given a moving performance with Eric Greene as the tenor soloist. But its beauty ·was lost on two of the ladies in the audience, overheard on leaving the cathedral. 'Do you know where Melita is, dear?' one said. 'No', was the reply, 'but I was *so* grateful when he eventually got there'![2]

Three Choirs seems to have been affected little by the strikes and depression of the inter-war years. There was no shortage of applicants who, wishing to gain access to priority booking, were prepared to pay 5 guineas at Gloucester and Hereford, and 4 guineas at Worcester, for the privilege of Stewardship. In the three years immediately preceding the Second World War the sale of Stewardships amounted to:

	Gentlemen	Ladies
1936(H)	117	123
1937(G)	205	187
1938(W)	237	286

For many years, separate conditions of Stewardship were offered to ladies and gentlemen. When George Bernard Shaw first applied to become a Steward the Gloucester ticket secretary wrote to him 'to explain that he would not be able to sit with his wife as the Gentlemen Stewards were given seats in a separate reserved section. Shaw wrote back on a postcard, "Those whom God hath joined together, let no man put asunder."'[3]

It is interesting to compare the expenses of the Festival in these years with those of the nineteenth century. In 1886(G) Emma Albani had been able to demand 450 guineas; Edward Lloyd, 180 guineas; Anna Williams, 100 guineas; Janet Patey, 150 guineas; and Sir Charles Santley, 200 guineas. Even the lowest-paid principal, Watkin Mills, had received 50 guineas. Fifty years later, the payment of such astronomic sums would have been inconceivable: at Hereford, in 1936, Percy Hull was authorized to engage the artists chosen by the Music Committee – twelve singers and four solo instrumentalists – at fees not exceeding a total of £483. The lowest-paid principal singer received 10 guineas per performance, and even artists at the top of their profession, such as Astra Desmond and Heddle Nash, were offered only 18 guineas. The London Symphony Orchestra was engaged by the Festival at a total cost of £1,121, exclusive of railway fares; each of the orchestral players received 12/6d per performance and one guinea for the Leader.[4]

The Hereford Festival of 1936 was held under the patronage of King Edward VIII, whose abdication in December added crisis to uncertainty: Hitler had ordered his troops into the Rhineland in March, and the Spanish Civil War had begun in July. The composers who conducted their own works at the Festival were George Dyson – *Nebuchadnezzar* and the first performance of his Prelude, Fantasy and Chaconne for cello and orchestra, with Thelma Reiss as soloist; W.K. Stanton – an eight-part unaccompanied setting of Addison's *The Spacious Firmament*; and Vaughan Williams – his *Pastoral Symphony*, Part IV ('The Explorers') from the *Sea Symphony*, the Viola Suite and, composed for the Festival, two Hymn Preludes for small orchestra. At the Thursday morning concert an additional item was inserted into the programme: Roy Henderson sang 'Fare Well' from Stanford's *Songs of the Fleet* in tribute to Harry Plunket Greene who had died three weeks previously.

Zoltán Kodály returned to Gloucester in 1937, making the second of four visits to the Festival. He conducted his *Dances of Galanta* and the *Budavari Te Deum*, written for the celebrations at Budapest in 1936 of the two-hundred-and-fiftieth anniversary of the city's liberation from the Turks – a wildly colourful piece which was much enjoyed by the chorus. Alas, their enthusiasm evaporated the next day.

Kodály had been described by 'Crescendo' in the *News Chronicle* as 'a little man, with thick flowing hair, and a keen face with bright eyes, and he seems rather shy, and probably is, for the surroundings must be very strange to him'. Certainly Kodály must have felt a great strangeness when conducting his unaccompanied motet, *Jesus and the Traders*, a work considered difficult in those days. At rehearsals the chorus had struggled to master Kodály's complex harmonies. They continued to feel insecure about the opening of the piece, and on the morning of the performance were very apprehensive. Melville Cook, the assistant organist, aware of the problem, had agreed to play a short organ improvisation immediately before *Jesus and the Traders*, giving the chorus a strong lead by ending on the same chord with which the Kodály work begins. Sadly, the chorus was caught unawares. That last, precious chord faded away unnoted as Kodály stepped on to the platform and raised his baton. A look of crumpled disappointment crossed his face as the chorus plunged into a ragged opening from which recovery was both slow and painful. At least one member of the chorus felt as if she was 'on a ship going down'. For another, the stress was altogether too great – she simply fainted away![5]

Characteristic of Kodály's music are a profound sincerity and the unmistakable influence of the music of his country's folk-song. In 1906 he had written his university thesis on Hungarian folk-song, afterwards collecting folk-songs in collaboration with Bartók. He was, therefore, in some measure a Hungarian counterpart to Vaughan Williams, even though there is no similarity in their idioms.

Kodály met Vaughan Williams at Gloucester in 1937 and asked him 'searching questions about the reason and objects of the Festivals, and Ralph explained, with solemnity, that they became necessary after the Reformation, for in the days of celibate clergy there were neither widows nor orphans to support.'[6]

Vaughan Williams's own contribution to the 1937(G) Festival were the overture and songs from his opera *The Poisoned Kiss*, and the cantata for soprano and baritone soloists, chorus and orchestra, *Dona Nobis Pacem*, which had received its first performance at Huddersfield under Albert Coates on 2 October 1936. At Gloucester, and again at Worcester in 1938, the soloists were Elsie Suddaby and Roy Henderson. The text of *Dona Nobis Pacem*, formed of a fragment of the Latin Mass, conflations from the authorized version of the Bible, an extract from a parliamentary speech by John Bright, and three poems by Walt Whitman, presents a clear message. Vaughan Williams, like Whitman, had seen war at first hand, saw its deathly hand reaching out once more, and sought to warn –

> I see a sad procession,
> And I hear the channels of coming full-keyed bugles;
> All the channels of the city streets they're flooding,
> As with voices and with tears.

The winter of 1937 brought the death of Ivor Gurney at the age of forty-seven – following fifteen years of asylum, locked away from his beloved Gloucestershire in a Kent mental hospital and haunted by the horrors of the First World War. Gurney's memory was honoured at the 1938(W) Festival in a performance, by Mary Worth, of *Spring*, one of his five exquisite *Elizabethan Songs*, as part of a group which included songs by Clifton Parker, Hubert Parry and Gurney's friend and teacher from the RCM, Ralph Vaughan Williams. The accompanist was Edgar Day, who held the post of assistant organist at Worcester with distinction for half a century from 1912.

The orchestral concert at the 1938(W) Festival was given in the Gaumont Theatre, Worcester, by seventy members of the London Symphony Orchestra, joined by other orchestral players. The Leader was W.H. Reed, and the soloist in a performance of the Rachmaninoff Piano Concerto No. 2 in C minor was Benno Moiseiwitsch, who had become a British subject in the previous year.

By 1938, Thursday was generally known as the 'modern' day. The concert on the morning of 8 September began with Kodály's *Budavari Te Deum* and also included *The Blessed Damozel* by Debussy, the first performance of Lennox Berkeley's setting of Psalm 24, *Domini est terra*, conducted by the composer, and Vaughan Williams's *Dona Nobis Pacem*.

Seven weeks later Neville Chamberlain flew back from meeting Hitler in Munich, to tell cheering crowds that he had brought 'Peace for our time'.

Arrangements for the 1939 Festival at Hereford went ahead as usual. Tickets and programmes were printed, sold and distributed; soloists and orchestra engaged; and a full schedule of rehearsals completed. New works planned for performance included Sir George Dyson's *Quo Vadis?* Part I; the *Elegy* in memory of Edward Elgar by Alexander Brent Smith; and *Dies Natalis*, a cantata for high voice and strings by Gerald Finzi to words by the seventeenth-century Herefordshire poet, Thomas Traherne.

The dates for the Festival were set at 3, 5, 6, 7 and 8 September. In August Hitler signed an agreement with Russia, and war seemed inevitable. At midday on 28 August the Finance Committee of the Hereford Festival met, 'to decide whether or not to hold the Festival and, in the event of hostilities involving this country breaking out, what steps should be taken'.[7] Col. Pateshall proposed that the Festival should immediately be abandoned, but his proposition did not find a seconder. Percy Hull had gone to London for rehearsals with the orchestra and principals on the previous day, not knowing until he got there whether or not the rehearsals would be held. He promised to telegraph the committee, but the telegram failed to arrive while they were in session.

The committee resolved that the Secretary, R.A. Symonds, after consultation with the Chairman, E.R. Dymond, should be authorized to cancel the Festival should hostilities break out before 30 August. On Thursday 31 August an announcement was broadcast that the government had decided to proceed with evacuation plans which, inevitably, involved restrictions on transport. Also, a ban was placed on the congregation of large assemblies for the time being. It was now impossible to carry on with the Festival. The next day German forces invaded Poland and, on Sunday 3 September, the date set for the Opening Service, Britain and France declared war on Germany.

One man remained undeterred. At the instigation of the Hereford Chapter and Three Choirs Festival Committee, the Archbishop of Canterbury had on 1 May 1939 conferred the Lambeth degree of honorary Doctor of Music on W.H. Reed. Three Choirs Festival musicians, musical organizations and friends throughout the country subscribed towards his doctorate robes, and it was intended that they should be presented to him during the Festival. They were presented instead at a small ceremony at the Hereford Deanery on the afternoon of Tuesday 5 September. Under the heading 'Little Festival', the *Hereford Times* reported that:

> Ever since 1902 Dr Reed has been coming to Three Choirs Festivals, and he related this week . . . that when Dr Hull telephoned him and said that the Festival was 'off', he recalled his long innings and asked himself, 'Am I stumped?' answering, 'No, I will not be put off.'
>
> He accordingly packed up his fiddle on Friday and came to Hereford, deciding that as this was Festival week he would play at it. 'I had always played at the Festival before,' said Dr Reed, 'so I proceeded to the Cathedral on Sunday and played. So I think it is true to say I played at the Festival, though it may have been a small Festival lasting only five minutes.'

Billy Reed had played Mackenzie's *Benedictus* during morning service in the cathedral: "'I don't feel that my innings are at an end," he said. "I made one run on Sunday and my wicket is still up.'"

Billy Reed never returned to Hereford; his wicket fell on 2 July 1942. But his long years of service to Three Choirs and his friendship with Elgar were marked by his burial in Worcester Cathedral, close to the Gerontius window.

Notes

1. Melville Cook, *Notes from my Three Choirs Diary*, Hereford Festival programme book, 1988
2. Memories of Mr Rodney Bennett
3. Herbert Sumsion, 'Random Reminiscences' from *Two Hundred and Fifty Years of the Three Choirs Festival* (Three Choirs Festival Association, 1977)
4. Hereford Festival Minute Book, 1936–69
5. Memories of Mrs Diana Feilden
6. Ursula Vaughan Williams, 'Ralph Vaughan Williams at the Three Choirs Festival' from *Two Hundred and Fifty Years of the Three Choirs Festival* (Three Choirs Festival Association, 1977)
7. Hereford Festival Minute Book, 1936–69

CHAPTER SEVENTEEN

RECOVERY

The grim austerity of post-war Britain – shortages of food, petrol and paper, the continued requisitioning of city hotels, and greatly increased costs – could easily have deterred the Hereford Three Choirs Committee from embarking upon a resumption of the Festival in 1946. In spite of Percy Hull's confidence that all of the problems could be overcome, there were pessimistic voices at a meeting of Stewards and supporters held on 27 October 1945. Once again the Festival was saved by the needs of the charity, whose fortunes at Hereford, according to Prebendary P.A. Lushington, were 'absolutely on the rocks'.[1] The Deans of Gloucester and Worcester made vigorous appeals for more faith, and further support came from Sir Ivor Atkins. But when the question was put to the meeting, several people refused to vote. The decision to hold a Festival in Hereford was carried by about twenty-five votes to six. A new Secretary, Mr T.O.D. (Tom) Steel, was appointed and the dust blown from the programme planned for the abandoned Festival of 1939, which was used to form the basis of the revival. Detailed preparations went ahead and were well advanced when, just three months before the start of the Festival, came a major blow.

Percy Hull, who had been unwell since the beginning of 1946, now suffered a nervous breakdown. Hull's doctors, unable to predict how soon he would be well enough to resume his duties, advised him that the organizers should be prepared for his complete absence from the Festival. At an emergency committee meeting held on 7 June 1946 it was resolved to ask Sir George Dyson to accept the position of deputy conductor for the Festival. The next day he travelled to Hereford and addressed the committee:

> He stressed very strongly that it was the very essence of the tradition of the Festival that the Conductor should be the local Cathedral Organist and he felt that if, for any reason, the local organist was not able to conduct this should be undertaken by the other two. He gratefully acknowledged the compliment implied by the invitation but did not feel that it would be wise to break with tradition, particularly as this Festival was a revival after the war. He was equally emphatic that an outside professional conductor should not be engaged and pointed out that all the preliminary work would have to be undertaken by the local Cathedral organists and their assistants and that it would, in his view, be very unjust to them to engage another conductor for the final performances. In any event he thought it very unlikely that an outside conductor would be able to spare sufficient time for rehearsals

and would not get to know the chorus. He was himself ready and willing to do anything he could to help and, in particular, to do anything which had to be done in London.[2]

And so the devolution of the conductor's duties, which even before the war had begun to reduce the concentration of responsibility in the hands of the local organist, was carried still further as a result of Percy Hull's illness. Sir Ivor Atkins and Herbert Sumsion shared the work of preparing the 1946(H) Festival, greatly helped by the Hereford assistant organist, Colin Mann. Tom Steel and all concerned with the administration made Herculean efforts to ensure the smooth running of the Festival, even persuading the local MP to organize the derequisitioning of the Green Dragon and City Arms hotels. Although the incomes of those who formed the bulk of the Stewards had undoubtedly diminished since the previous Hereford Festival in 1936, fears of financial failure proved to be unfounded. Starved of live music throughout the war, greater numbers than ever applied for Stewardships; indeed it was necessary to close the subscription list when by June it had reached 612.

The success of the Festival was, reported the *Hereford Times* on 4 January 1947, 'a tale of expectations surpassed and new records achieved', and £2,450 was raised for the destitute charity.

The London Symphony Orchestra under its new Leader, George Stratton, was engaged in 1946. Among the principals were the sopranos Isobel Baillie, Mary Linde and Elsie Suddaby; the contraltos Astra Desmond and Gladys Ripley; the tenors Heddle Nash and Eric Greene; the basses George Pizzey and Tom Williams; the pianist Phyllis Sellick; the violinist Jelly d'Aranyi; and Lionel Tertis, the most famous viola-player of his time, who had played at Three Choirs frequently from 1927, had retired from the concert platform in 1936 but had re-emerged during the war. (Lionel Tertis died in 1975 in his ninety-ninth year.)

Happily, Percy Hull had recovered sufficiently to conduct *Elijah* and *Gerontius*. Sir George Dyson took charge not only of his own *Quo Vadis?* and song, 'The Wife of Bath' (with Isobel Baillie as soloist), but also a fine performance of Vaughan Williams's *Pastoral Symphony*. The conducting load was further shared by other composers directing their own works – Alexander Brent Smith, *Elegy*; Edmund Rubbra, the orchestral suite *Improvisations on Virginal Pieces* (Giles Farnaby); E.J. Moeran, *Sinfonietta in C*; Gordon Jacob, the orchestral suite *William Byrd*; Samuel Barber, *Adagio for Strings*; and Gerald Finzi, *Dies Natalis*. With this last, rapturously sung by Elsie Suddaby, it became clear that Three Choirs had returned with a work of lasting worth in its hand – 'inexpressibly rare and delightful and beautiful'.

Although war had denied Three Choirs the first performance of *Dies Natalis*, a return to peace ushered in a strong bond between Gerald Finzi (1901–56) and the Festival. Finzi, his artist wife Joy and two sons, Christopher and Nigel, were frequently to be seen among the familiar Festival faces, often in company with the magisterial figure of Vaughan Williams. When *Dies Natalis* was repeated in 1947(G) the soloist was the tenor Eric Greene who, as a relaxing preparation for the performance, joined the whole Finzi family in a game of rounders on the Gloucester King's School paddock[3] – a typical example of Three Choirs off-stage informality and fun.

During and immediately after the war the Revd Walter Hussey of St Matthew's, Northampton, brought considerable distinction to his church through the commissioning of several works of art, including a number of Festival anthems, the first of which, Britten's *Rejoice in the Lamb* in 1943, was followed by pieces from Rubbra, Berkeley and, in September 1946 to mark the fifty-third anniversary of the consecration of the church, Gerald Finzi's *Lo, the full final sacrifice*. This exquisite setting of verses by Richard Crashaw (1612–49) was conducted by Finzi at Three Choirs in both 1947(G) and 1948(W), establishing itself among the most distinguished pieces of 'sacred' music produced in England in the twentieth century.

Finzi had studied with Sir Edward Bairstow of York Minster and, as Christopher Palmer has pointed out:

> . . . doubtless what he absorbed there of the 'immemorial sound of voices' endowed him with a rare fluency and felicity in the handling of (voices). He . . . took pains in polishing and refining each of the comparatively small number of works he gave to the world. But they were vehicles for ideas and feelings rather than for beliefs. *Lo, the full final sacrifice, Dies Natalis, In Terra Pax* and *Intimations of Immortality* are all intensely 'religious' in this wider sense, even though they are the work of a confessed agnostic . . . The austerity of Finzi's harmonic language tempers and contains the ecstasy of the words; restraint controls the passion. His music is the diet of tranquillity, a glass of water drawn up from a deep cold well; the work, surely, of a man long subject to the authority and teaching of solitude.

In 1920 Finzi had heard Elsie Suddaby, accompanied by Bairstow, practising a song by another who was no stranger to solitude: 'Sleep' from Ivor Gurney's *Five Elizabethan Songs*. He felt at once that it was one of the great songs, written with such intensity of feeling that it was like an electric light bulb that burns to brilliance before it explodes.[4] This led him to discover Gurney and for the rest of his life, with the assistance of Joy Finzi and of his friend Howard Ferguson, he worked to gather Gurney's poems and songs from absolute obscurity; and Finzi paid a further compliment to Gloucester's neglected son, orchestrating four of the *Five Elizabethan Songs*: 'Under the Greenwood Tree', 'Sleep', 'Spring', and 'Orpheus with his Lute'. It was fitting, therefore, that these four songs should be included in a programme played by the Jacques String Orchestra on the final night of the 1947 Gloucester Festival – and fitting too that they were sung by Elsie Suddaby.

The year 1947 had begun well with the announcement of Percy Hull's knighthood in the New Year's Honours List. In an effort to attenuate further the post-war gloom, the Festival Ball was revived for the first time at Gloucester since 1874. Only one new work was heard at the Festival: Christopher le Fleming's *Five Psalms* for soprano solo (Elsie Suddaby), chorus and orchestra. Sir George Dyson conducted his overture *At the Tabard Inn* and *Quo Vadis?*; Edmund Rubbra, his Symphony No. 3; and Herbert Howells, his *Elegy* for Viola and Strings with Jean Stewart as soloist. The pianist Kathleen Long played the César Franck Symphonic Variations and the Fauré *Ballade* for Piano and Orchestra. Vaughan Williams conducted a broadcast performance of his Symphony No. 5 in D major which, under his baton, had been heard for the first time at a Promenade Concert in 1943, and the third movement of which, a *Romanza*, has been linked with the Larghetto of Elgar's Second Symphony as one of the highest peaks of Romantic English music. The basses Norman Walker and Gordon Clinton were heard at Three Choirs for the first time, Clinton singing in *The Apostles*, Kodály's *Budavari Te Deum* and the *St Matthew Passion*. Walker also sang in the Bach as well as *Quo Vadis?* and *Messiah*. Nine hundred Stewardships were sold, compared with four hundred in 1937. And it was in 1947 too that the Archbishop of Canterbury conferred the Lambeth degree of D. Mus. on Herbert Sumsion. A vintage Three Choirs year – but there was a single disappointment.

The name which was on everyone's lips was that of the sensational young contralto who had made her operatic début in Britten's *Rape of Lucretia* at Glyndebourne in 1946: Kathleen Ferrier. Sumsion had tried to engage Ferrier for the 1947 Gloucester Festival, only to discover that she had been booked to appear during the same week at the very first Edinburgh Festival. The Secretary of the Gloucester Committee, Anthony A. Scott, wrote to the Provost of Edinburgh, as Chairman of the Edinburgh Festival Committee, suggesting that even though no action might be possible for 1948, consideration should be given to the dates of the two festivals in future years.[5] Although his Lordship's reply expressed the hope that it would be possible to cooperate for a common purpose the two festivals have continued to coincide to the present day.

Kathleen Ferrier did sing at Three Choirs in 1948, sharing the principal contralto parts with Mary Jarred. Ferrier's contributions included *Messiah* with Isobel Baillie, Heddle Nash and Norman Walker; *Gerontius* with Heddle Nash and Harold Williams; Debussy's *The Blessed Damozel* with Isobel Baillie; and the *St Matthew Passion*, in the Elgar/Atkins edition, with Elsie Suddaby, Broadbridge White and Gordon Clinton. Mary Jarred sang in *The Kingdom*, Szymanowski's *Stabat Mater* and Kodály's *Missa Brevis*, orchestrated and, in part, rewritten for the Festival and conducted by Kodály himself.

Kathleen Ferrier returned to sing in *Gerontius* with William Herbert and Hervey Alan at Hereford in 1952. Who, listening then to that glorious voice, could possibly have guessed that so shining a spirit would be extinguished in less than a year?

One significant and, until 1955, isolated break with a long tradition occurred in 1948. Because of Promenade Concert commitments the London Symphony Orchestra was unable to play at Three Choirs; the London Philharmonic Orchestra was hired in its place.

This was Sir Ivor Atkins's last Festival as Director. He was entering his eightieth year, bore the brunt of the conducting, and was as indefatigable as ever. Sir Percy Hull too was coming to the end of a long career and conducted for the last time as Director of the Hereford Festival in 1949. When both men retired in 1950 Sir Percy had been in post for almost thirty-two years and Sir Ivor for fifty-three, exceeding even the long record of William Done at Worcester. 'P.C.' returned to Three Choirs as a guest conductor in 1952(H), 1955(H) and 1957(W) when, at the age of seventy-nine, he took up the baton to direct the City of Birmingham Symphony Orchestra in a performance of the *Enigma Variations* – a final tribute to his old friend, Edward Elgar.

Sir Ivor Atkins died on 26 November 1953. At his funeral in Worcester Cathedral the Very Revd A.W. Davies, Dean Emeritus of Worcester, paid tribute to Sir Ivor as an honoured and familiar figure in the cathedral and the city; to his strong sense of duty, attention for the truth and for accuracy in detail. 'He had sometimes been unbending in the presence of his fellow men, but in the presence of God he was a humble and devout Christian man.' Sir Ivor's ashes were interred below the Gerontius window close to the resting place of W.H. Reed.

The Gloucester Festival of 1950, remembered for the first performances of Gerald Finzi's *Intimations of Immortality* and Herbert Howells's *Hymnus Paradisi*, marked Herbert Sumsion's ascendancy from the junior member of the trio of conductors to 'the father figure, helping and advising two very much younger men'.[6] Both of these younger men, David Willcocks at Worcester and Meredith Davies at Hereford, had displayed brilliance as students, served with distinction in the war, established notable reputations and, with Sumsion, laid the foundations of the modern Three Choirs Festival before moving on to wider renown in national and international careers.

Sir David Willcocks (b. 1922) had been a chorister in Westminster Abbey, and afterwards organ scholar of King's College, Cambridge. After the war, in which he won the Military Cross while serving in the Duke of Cornwall's Light Infantry, he was successively Fellow of King's College and organist of Salisbury Cathedral before his appointment to Worcester.

Meredith Davis (b. 1922) was only eight when he entered the Royal College of Music as a junior exhibitioner. In 1941 he went up to Oxford as organ scholar of Keble College, where his studies were interrupted by war service in the Royal Artillery. He gained the Limpus and Read Prizes for the FRCO, together with the Silver Medal of the Worshipful Company of Musicians, and held the post of organist at St Alban's Cathedral for three years before his appointment to Hereford. Thereafter he spent some time studying conducting at the Accademia di Santa Cecilia in Rome.

In association with David Willcocks and Meredith Davies, Herbert Sumsion embarked upon his happiest Three Choirs years. At the 1950(G) Festival, Willcocks conducted both of the two major Elgar works in the programme: the Cello Concerto with Anthony Pini as soloist, and *Gerontius* with Gladys Ripley, Heddle Nash and Norman Walker. Davies conducted the Fauré *Requiem* with Elsie Morrison and William Parsons, and the Symphony No. 5 by Sibelius. Both men took their place in the organ-loft: Davies for morning and Willcocks for evening performances.

Another, even younger, man played the organ at the Sunday Service, the 5.00 p.m. Evensongs and for the Fauré *Requiem*: the twenty-year-old assistant organist at Gloucester, Donald Hunt.

Herbert Sumsion conducted the first performance of *Intimations of Immortality*, a setting of Wordsworth's ode, dedicated to Adeline Vaughan Williams. The work was conceived and much of it written before 1939 when, interrupted by war, Finzi laid it aside, completing it only in 1950. The first tenor soloist was Eric Greene.

One could not help thinking in this cathedral how Parry would have been pleased at this choice and setting of noble words. Finzi's melodic idiom has been nourished on English madrigals, folk-song, Bach, and Parry, but it is his own and his harmony has a modern richness not to be found in the tradition from which this noble cantata derives.[7]

Herbert Howells wrote *Hymnus Paradisi*, his masterpiece, to assuage a private grief. In 1935 he had taken his only son to cricket in Cheltenham. Only ten years old, Michael had said an extraordinary thing: 'I want to see Hammond score a century before I die.' Within a week the boy was dead, a victim of meningitis.

Hit more by this death than by anything else, Howells was frozen mentally for three years. Then one day his daughter Ursula said, 'Why don't you write some music about Mick?'[8]

> The sudden loss of an only son, a loss essentially profound and, in its very nature, beyond argument, might naturally impel a composer, after a time, to seek release and consolation in language and terms most personal to him. Music may well have power beyond any other medium to offer that release and comfort. It did so in my case, and became a personal, private document.[9]

Howells kept the work 'under his pillow' for twelve years, showing it only to his wife and daughter, and to Herbert Sumsion who suggested the title. In 1950 Ralph Vaughan Williams asked to see *Hymnus Paradisi*, and insisted that Howells release it. The first performance, conducted by the composer, was given at the 1950(G) Festival; the soloists were Isobel Baillie and William Herbert.

The Worcester Festival of 1951 was included as one of the principal musical attractions of the Festival of Britain – that great attempt to boost national morale and to celebrate the achievements of post-war recovery. From 3 May until 30 September huge crowds were drawn to the South Bank site in London, the permanent legacy of which is the Royal Festival Hall. Fears that Three Choirs might suffer as a consequence resulted in the first-ever Arts Council guarantee to the Festival against the possibility of loss – a grant of £750.

No new works were commissioned for the 1951 Worcester Festival (David Willcock's first), but *Intimations of Immortality* and *Hymnus Paradisi* were repeated, and Julius Harrison (1885–1963) was present in the county of his birth to conduct his *Worcestershire Suite* and to hear Willcocks direct his Mass in C, with Ena Mitchell, Grace Bodey, Richard Lewis and Harold Williams. Douglas Fox, who had lost his right arm in the war, played Ravel's Piano Concerto for the Left Hand, and two singers made their final appearances at Three Choirs: Elsie Suddaby in the Mass in B minor and Harold Williams in *Gerontius*. On the last evening the Boyd Neel Orchestra gave a concert in the College Hall which, in addition to works by Handel and Bach, included Stravinsky's *Apollon Musagette*, Britten's *Les Illuminations* (with Richard Lewis) and the Prelude and Scherzo by Shostakovitch.

King George VI died on 6 February 1952. In the minds of many, Britain was now about to enter on a new era of greatness matching that of the reign of the first Elizabeth, even though the Korean War continued to sap the nation's energy. In Hereford, Meredith Davies prepared for his first Festival as Director, intent on establishing confidence, trying to absorb all that he was being told about the true spirit and character of Three Choirs, but aware that the 'nascent festivals at Edinburgh and Aldburgh were setting standards and winning musical prestige which could leave the Three Choirs looking like a very old-fashioned amateur junketing – as, indeed, some critics were beginning to suggest'.[10]

Davies knew that the key to any 'reform' lay in somehow rationalizing the ludicrous rehearsal schedule. A full chorus rehearsal held in the cathedral on the afternoon of the Saturday preceding the Festival and 'Black Monday' were still the only opportunities for chorus and orchestra to rehearse together.

> Innovation in 1952 was modest, and more historical than radical: a harpsichord ousted the grand piano as a continuo instrument [in the *St Matthew Passion* and *Messiah*: Boris Ord was the player],

Alfred Deller was a soloist [in Purcell's *My Beloved Spake* and Bach's *Erfreute Zeit Im Neuen Bunde*], and a Sunday evening organ recital was programmed [Harold Darke] – even then I thought it strange to assemble the Stewards on Saturday, with no official performance until the Tuesday morning.[11]

Davies wrote to Benjamin Britten asking for a new work for the Festival but Britten, too busy to comply, suggested a performance of his *St Nicholas* instead; but this was not given at Three Choirs until 1958(H) when Britten himself came to Hereford to conduct it. Only two new works were given in 1952: Donald Bridges was the soloist in the Concerto for Oboe and String Orchestra by George Stratton, the Leader of the LSO (Stratton died in 1954), and *Cantiones Sacrae* by John Gardner who had achieved great success with the performance of his First Symphony at the Cheltenham Festival of 1951. 'It was', wrote Martin Cooper in *The Musical Times*, 'these tit-bits which lured the London critics, like so many cats, to the feast at Hereford.' But of *Cantiones Sacrae*; 'the choral writing provided the choir with considerable difficulties, some of which seemed gratuitous; but it is good that they should confront contemporary obstacles, and this work made an effective test-piece.'[12] The total combined rehearsal time available to choir and orchestra for this particular 'test-piece' had been forty minutes.

The schedule of full chorus and orchestra rehearsals on the afternoon of the Saturday and the 'Black Monday' preceding the 1953 Gloucester Festival gives a clear idea of the pressure facing all those involved:

Saturday, September 5th

2.30	National Anthem *
	Three Hymns *
	Brewer in D *
	Let their celestial concerts *Handel*
3.0	Elijah *Mendelssohn*
3.45	A Prayer *Bridge*
4.0	St John Passion *Bach*
	(4.0 to 4.15 Interval for Orchestra)
4.45	Te Deum * *Walton*
5.15	Let the bright Seraphim * *Handel*
	Slow Movement * (Symphony No 4) *Brahms*

* Music for Opening Service on Sunday, September 6th

Monday, September 7th

10.0	National Anthem *Elgar*
10.5	Israel in Egypt *Handel*
10.45	Dona Nobis *Vaughan Williams*
11.30	Magnificat *Monteverdi*
	(11.30 to 11.45 Interval for Orchestra)
12.0	Intimations *Finzi*
12.45	Job *Vaughan Williams*

1.0	Interval
2.0	These things shall be *Ireland*
2.30	Psalmus Hungaricus *Kodály*
3.10	Gerontius *Elgar*
3.50	Messiah *Handel*
	(3.50 to 4.05 Interval for Orchestra)
4.5	Coronation Mass *Haydn*
4.50	Alto Rhapsody *Brahms*

The coronation of Queen Elizabeth II had taken place on 3 June 1953, and so William Walton's *Coronation Te Deum* was a clear choice for inclusion in the Opening Service. The Wednesday evening concert in the cathedral began with Walton's stirring Coronation March, *Orb and Sceptre* and, although not programmed, the *Te Deum* was repeated. The only new work performed during the week was Anthony Scott's *Chorale Variations*. Richard Arnell made his single Three Choirs appearance conducting *Sinfonia quasi Variazioni* (Op. 13); Herbert Howells conducted his *Elegy for Strings*; and Vaughan Williams *Job* and *Dona Nobis Pacem* with Joan Alexander and Bruce Boyce as soloists. Among the distinguished instrumentalists who performed during the Festival were Campoli (the Brahms Violin Concerto), Dennis Brain (Horn Concerto No. 2, K417 by Mozart), Gervase de Peyer (Finzi's Clarinet Concerto), and the Amadeus String Quartet. A startlingly successful and imaginative innovation was a performance of Monteverdi's *Magnificat* from the Vespers of 1610:

> Dr Sumsion had absorbed the style of the music unlike any other and still in these days of infinite regression into the past, virtually unknown. With the help of Dr Redlich's edition and half a dozen soloists he revealed for modern ears the strange mixture of what in 1610 was both old and new.[13]

The six soloists were Ena Mitchell, Joan Fullerton, Nancy Evans, Eric Greene, David Galliver, and Richard Stanton substituting for Thomas Hemsley who was unable to appear.

After the 1951 and 1952 Festivals, David Willcocks and Meredith Davies had more time to think about the problems of inadequate rehearsal-time. Davies remembers talking to Willcocks late into the night, and the rehearsal schedules for the Festivals of 1954(W) and 1955(H) reveal that modern practice, achieved in two strides, probably came out of that conversation.

At Worcester in 1954 full chorus rehearsals with orchestra were held on Saturday afternoon, Monday morning *and* Wednesday morning, thus releasing Monday afternoon and evening for performances: a Public Hall recital of songs and instrumental pieces in the afternoon (Isobel Baillie, Thomas Matthews (violin), Eileen Ralf (piano), and Meredith Davies as accompanist), and a choral concert in the cathedral in the evening (Holst's *Hymn of Jesus* and the Verdi *Requiem*). New works during the week were Herbert Howells's *Missa Sabrinensis* and Vaughan Williams's Christmas cantata *This Day* (*Hodie*) dedicated to Howells.

Sir David Willcocks remembers how Vaughan Williams at the age of eighty-two was, by then, becoming very deaf, and somewhat infirm, so we had anxious moments at rehearsals. I shall never forget the difficulty that he experienced conducting the first movement of that work [*Hodie*] with its changing rhythmic patterns. At the final rehearsal there was a moment when things came apart, and in his endearing manner 'Uncle Ralph' shouted: 'I have told you 100 times – don't watch me!' The performance went without a hitch because singers and orchestra were determined to give of their best for this great, beloved musician, who had inherited the mantle of Elgar as a father-figure of the Three Choirs Festival.[14]

Herbert Sumsion's memories of V.W. at Three Choirs reflect equal warmth: 'Never happier than when sitting holding hands with a young damsel on either side of him, he was heard to remark: "These Festivals would be marvellous, if it wasn't for the music!" . . . If the conductor asked him in advance how he would like certain passages to be played, his advice was always the same: "You play it as you would like it; and I will tell you if I don't like it."'

Vaughan Williams conducted not only *Hodie* in 1954 but also on the previous day, Tuesday, his *Pastoral Symphony* (with Isobel Baillie) following a performance of *The Apostles* in which both Norma Procter and Wilfred Brown made the first of many Three Choirs appearances; the other soloists were Isobel Baillie, Gordon Clinton, Norman Walker and Roderick Jones. And on Thursday John Carol Case began a twenty-year association with Three Choirs – singing the part of Christus in the *St Matthew Passion* alongside Joan Alexander, Grace Bodey, Eric Greene, Wilfred Brown and Norman Walker. It was during rehearsals for this that, astonished by one of Boris Ord's breathtaking keyboard runs on the harpsichord, Norman Walker produced a roar of laughter when in a deep northern accent he said: 'Ee, Boris, there are too many beads on that curtain!'[15]

It was a week of many triumphs for David Willcocks, not least of which was his success in persuading the Dean and Chapter to give permission for the first time at Worcester for the audience to face the performers instead of each other across the centre aisle. Because the staging at Worcester (and Hereford) is erected at the west end of the cathedral there had formerly been strong opposition to any suggestion that the audience should turn their backs to the altar. Now at least some comfort was possible.

Meredith Davies again made ambitious plans for the 1955 Hereford Festival: Sir Thomas Beecham conducting *The Creation*; Dietrich Fischer-Dieskau singing in Brahms's *Ein Deutsches Requiem*; and Elisabeth Schwarzkopf, then at the height of her powers, as a principal soloist. These aspirations met with disappointment. Neither Beecham nor Fischer-Dieskau was able to accept, and Walter Legge, Elisabeth Schwarzkopf's husband and agent, replied to an offer of five hundred guineas with an emphatic 'five hundred times *No!*'[16]

In spite of these set-backs Davies was able to persuade the committee to accept a hugely innovative programme, the engagement of two orchestras instead of one, and a complete re-structuring of the rehearsal schedule. All this in the face of financial difficulties which had left the 1952 Festival with a deficit of £217. Hugh Ottaway, writing in *Musical Opinion*, welcomed Davies's vision:

Worcester's innovations were retained and developed this year, though hardly, it seems, in any attempt to balance the account; for some radical changes, likely to alienate the older supporters, were made in the programme, and an expected deficit of £1,000 was announced at the outset. Such a policy is inevitably described as courageous or reckless, splendid or shameful, according to one's point of view. That changes *had* to be made in the type of programme, sooner rather than later, should not need special pleading: a tradition hangs with a dead weight when its emphasis is always on the past, or when it views the present with its own chosen type of blinkers. But in these western shires there is a good deal of blind conservatism, and such innocent steps as the omission of *Messiah* (for the first time since 1875!) and the inclusion of Stravinsky's *Symphony of Psalms* (composed in 1930 but not previously performed by the Three Choirs) are likely to lead to a palace revolution or, more appropriately, a storming of the organ-loft.

Those who had always stood in the way of *Belshazzar's Feast* found themselves quietly outflanked at Hereford by Humphrey Searle's *Night Music*; they also heard Racine Fricker's Prelude, Elegy and Finale (the first considerable orchestral work by a young Englishman to be included in the cathedral programme since Walton's Viola Concerto was given at Worcester in 1932), and the first performances in England of choral works by Francis Poulenc [*Stabat Mater*] with Jennifer Vyvyan as soloist] and Paul Huber [*The Prodigal Son*]. None of this is so very 'radical' by general musical standards, but it appears to have revived the capricious question as to what is suitable for cathedral performance. To judge by the chatter at a Festival luncheon, views on this are merely a reflection of personal taste; it is hard to find anything more objective, for wholly secular works, in the shape of classics from the orchestral repertory, have long been included in the Three Choirs programmes without objection. This is usually justified on the grounds that all great music is ennobling – but only, it seems, if it is long-established or its idiom accords with one's personal taste. Perhaps the only significant side to the question is that the passing of time seems to make it irrelevant: 'Time consecrates, and what is grey with age becomes religion.' However, the dissident voices were clearly in a minority and one found support for the programme in some unexpected quarters.[17]

The 1955 Festival represents a successful attempt by Meredith Davies to open up the week as never before and to place rehearsals nearer the related performances. The orchestra for the Opening Service and the Monday concerts was the City of Birmingham Symphony Orchestra. In addition to accompanying the choir in Stravinsky's *Symphony of Psalms* on Monday afternoon, they gave the Concerto Grosso No. 1 in F by Handel, and a 'good, firm performance' of the *Eroica* Symphony. For these two works they were under their own conductor, Rudolf Schwarz. The soloists in the Verdi *Requiem* on Monday evening were Amy Shuard, Constance Shacklock, Rowland Jones, and Owen Brannigan replacing Norman Walker who was indisposed.

The London Symphony Orchestra took over on the second day for the rest of the week. The Wednesday programme included Lennox Berkeley's *Four Poems of St Teresa of Avila* (with Norma Procter) and the first performance of a Choral Suite by Geoffrey Bush, *In praise of Mary* (with Isobel Baillie).

Wednesday brought the fullest programme: a morning Chamber recital (Isobel Baillie and Julian Bream), three major orchestral works in the afternoon and, finally, a choral-orchestral concert which typified the Festival's 'new look'. The afternoon left a strong impression of Meredith Davies's grasp of the orchestra. Few cathedral organists would attempt *La Mer*; few indeed might be expected to bring it off convincingly, for it requires the utmost attention to detail and a complete mastery of orchestral values. Despite some sluggishness in the first movement, the performance was a triumph; it made a grand sound in the cathedral and was one of the highlights of the week.[18]

As the spacious grandeur of Debussy's seascape cascaded into the nave and eddied about the ancient pillars, Dr Sydney Watson, a long-time Steward of the Festival, turned to his neighbour and whispered: 'Ah, *La Cathédrale engloutie*!'[19]

The Thursday evening concert ended with a brilliant performance of Sir Arthur Bliss's *Colour Symphony*, conducted by the composer who, in 1953, had succeeded Arnold Bax as Master of the Queen's Music.

Apart from one unfortunate venture [Huber's *The Prodigal Son*], the Festival may be reckoned an important success. All in all, the choral standard was very impressive, and a new interest was kindled in the tradition's future. Now that a more bracing climate has been introduced, steps should be taken to avoid a depression next year . . . The Gloucester programme will be awaited with the keenest of interest.[20]

Both the LSO and the CBSO again played at the 1956(G) Festival, the latter in a concert in the Regal Cinema on the Wednesday afternoon, the Gloucester Shire Hall having been converted into an office-block since the previous Festival! Rudolf Schwarz conducted the CBSO in a programme which opened with the overture to *The Mastersingers*, a work which Sumsion had wanted to include in the 1950 cathedral programme but which had been vetoed by the Music Committee after Alexander Brent Smith had complained that 'the performance of such secular music was putting the Cathedral to a wrong use'.[21] The remainder of the CBSO concert comprised Dag Wiren's *Serenade for Strings*; Bliss's *Meditations on a Theme by John Blow*; Beethoven's Piano Concerto No. 3, in which Phyllis Sellick was the soloist; and *La Valse* by Ravel.

Hugh Ottaway, in his 1955 article, had suggested a number of works which came to mind as Three Choirs possibilities. Among these was Ernest Bloch's *Sacred Service*, an impulsively rhapsodic, intensely subjective setting of Jewish liturgy, and this was given by Herbert Sumsion in 1956:

The role of the Cantor, the leader of the exacting ritual, was effectively undertaken by Mr Hervey Alan . . . The lavish, vivid colours of Bloch's instrumentation, and the many Oriental inflections of his music, stood in the strongest possible contrast to the reticent rhapsody and peculiarly English atmosphere of Vaughan Williams's Romance for violin and orchestra, *The Lark Ascending*.[22]

Frederick Grinke was the soloist in *The Lark Ascending* and Vaughan Williams himself took up the baton to conduct. He was one month from his eighty-fourth birthday. As the great man took his place on the rostrum both audience and choir rose to their feet in tribute. They stood again at the end. Ursula Vaughan Williams has described that memorable Festival, the last for R.V.W:

The best week of all that summer was that of the Gloucester Festival. A large party stayed at the King's School House, just behind the cathedral; the whole Finzi family were there, the organist of Worcester, David Willcocks, and of Hereford, Meredith Davies, Howard Ferguson, and Harold Browne, the Treasurer of the South Western Arts Association. It was like an end of term week at a glorified educational school, Ralph said. We had a wonderful Sunday when the Finzi's drove us out to Chosen Hill[23] and Gerald described how he had been there as a young man on Christmas Eve at a party in the tiny house where the sexton lived and how they had all come out into the frosty midnight and heard bells ringing across Gloucestershire from beside the Severn to the hill villages of the Cotswolds. Gerald's Festival work, *In Terra Pax*, was a setting of a poem by Robert Bridges about such an experience. For us it was still summer, with roses in the tangled churchyard grass where the sexton's children were playing; blackberries in the hedges and the gold September light over the country we all knew and loved. Another expedition we four made was to see Rutland and Kathleen Boughton. After much wandering we found their house [at Kilcot] and sat and talked through the morning.
. . . One night we came out of the concert to find rainy clouds carrying shadows of the floodlit cathedral, four towers standing mighty and mysterious in the sky above the real tower.[24]

There is a sad postscript to attach to the account of that visit to Chosen Hill. While there the happy group again called at the tiny cottage in the churchyard. One of the sexton's children was suffering from chicken-pox and Finzi, already weakened by leukaemia, contracted the virus. On returning home to Ashmansworth after the Festival he became ill and the doctor sent him to hospital in Reading. He took a number of manuscripts with him but was unable to work and quickly became unconscious. Gerald Finzi died on 27 October 1956 at the age of fifty-five.

The 1956(G) Festival had included the first full orchestral version of Finzi's *In Terra Pax*, with Elsie Morrison and Bruce Boyce as soloists, Vaughan Williams's *Hodie* and Symphony No. 8 in addition to *The Lark Ascending* ('The choirs nearly fell out of their seats watching the timpani and percussion players in the last movement of *No 8*'[25] conducted by Meredith Davies), and the first performance of Howard Ferguson's *Amore Langueo*, conducted by Herbert Sumsion and with Eric Greene singing the solo tenor part. *Amore Langueo* was dedicated to Gerald Finzi and his wife Joy.

But there was *Gerontius*, and *Messiah* was back too. Hugh Ottaway was not impressed:

> When asked my opinion of the programme (*Musical Opinion*, August 1956), I had to let off steam – just one tentative puff. 'Any programme is third-rate,' I said, 'if it insists on plugging *Messiah* and *Gerontius* to the total exclusion of the Mass in D and *Belshazzar's Feast*.' That did it! 'Plugging', it seems, is a rude word, Walton's work should never be mentioned, and perhaps the Beethoven has been socially smeared by Edinburgh's stooping to folly. At all events, I was strongly suspected of sapping and mining the cathedral fabric. . . . What can you do with a supposedly responsible group of people – namely, the Stewards – who, when *Messiah* is miraculously dropped, as it was last year at Hereford, immediately demand its performance in full? I ask again, what can you do? I know what I should do, but we had better not go into that . . . So *Messiah* was given in full, 'by general request of the Stewards'. Respectability was thus restored and honour saved! And that brazen young man at Hereford is leaving anyway – stricken with remorse, no doubt, for his unpardonable sin . . . Now David Willcocks has done *Belshazzar's Feast* at Birmingham, and done it well. If he can persuade his committee to include the work next year at Worcester, I promise to march from Malvern and help defend his organ-loft; for some of those terrible Stewards would surely resort to fire and sword. And if he cannot? – well there will be other years. I shall not consign *Belshazzar's Feast* with Leamington Spa and the Baghdad Pact to the limbo of lost causes. On the contrary, I propose the formation of a Babylonian League – subject to a grant from O.U.P. – whose sole aim shall be that of securing a Cathedral performance of Walton's choral masterpiece. Once the ice has been broken, Belshazzar will probably do the hat-trick. That would indeed be occasion for feasting![26]

For almost thirty years Three Choirs had turned aside from a work which had become a standard part of the choral repertoire of leading choirs in the country. Mention of eunuchs and concubines in the text had resulted in *Belshazzar's Feast* being considered unsuitable for performance at the Festival. The ice *was* finally broken in 1975(W), and *Belshazzar* has now been given six times – twice in each city.

> Without uncertainty it is possible to congratulate David Willcocks upon his performance of *Belshazzar's Feast* . . . At last – in Worcester – it has been heard in a cathedral setting which vibrates sympathetically to the impact of its concentrated force and enhances the splendour of its scintillating clamour.[27]

Hervey Alan, the soloist, distinguished himself also during the week in a repetition of Bloch's *Sacred Service*; *Elijah*; *Messiah*; the Mass in B minor; *A Tribute of Praise* by Anthony Lewis, Barber Professor of Music at the University of Birmingham; and the first performance of the *Requiem* by Julius Harrison, in which he was joined by Heather Harper, Marjorie Thomas and William Herbert. Heather Harper was also the soloist in the first performance of Anthony Milner's *The City of Desolation*; joined Hervey Alan in *A Tribute of Praise*; Marjorie Thomas in Debussy's *The Blessed Damozel*; Marjorie Thomas, Eric Greene and speakers Patricia Pilkington and Sir Steuart Wilson in Honegger's *King David*; and Pamela Bowden, Eric Greene and John Carol Case in the Bach *Magnificat*.

Denis Matthews played with the LSO under Willcocks in a performance of Mozart's Piano Concerto in A major, K488, and also gave a piano recital in the Public Hall which included works by Alan Rawsthorne and William Alwyn.

Meredith Davies and David Willcocks made immense contributions to Three Choirs, both in conducting and shaping policy. Both brought imagination and vitality to the Festival at a crucial time; and both left within the same year.

Davies moved to Oxford in 1956 as organist and supernumerary Fellow of New College – but his future lay in conducting, a fact presumably recognized by the Hereford Dean and Chapter who had the vision to release him for two periods, each of three months, at the Accademia di Santa Cecilia in Rome in 1954 and 1956. While at Oxford, Meredith Davies became associate conductor of the CBSO, returning to Three Choirs in that capacity each year from 1957 to 1960. He was also the conductor of the City of Birmingham Choir, 1957–64. In 1959 he left New College for a career in conducting, appearing at Covent Garden and Sadler's Wells. Closely associated with the music of Benjamin Britten, Davies conducted, among much else, the first performance of *War Requiem* at the consecration of the new Coventry Cathedral in May 1962, when the soloists were Heather Harper, Peter Pears and Dietrich Fischer-Dieskau.

From 1964 to 1971 Meredith Davies conducted widely in the UK and abroad while also holding the post of conductor of the Vancouver Symphony Orchestra. In 1971 he became conductor of the Royal Choral Society and joined the staff of the Royal Academy of Music, moving to Trinity College of Music as Principal from 1979 to 1988. He was appointed CBE in 1982.

David Willcocks returned to Cambridge from Worcester in 1957 to take up the post of organist of King's College, remaining there until his appointment as Director of the Royal College of Music in 1974 following the retirement of Sir Keith Falkner. He became conductor of the Bach Choir in 1960 and was knighted in 1977.

Following the resignations of Davies and Willcocks, Melville Cook was appointed organist of Hereford Cathedral in 1956, and Douglas Guest of Worcester in 1957. Both men conducted at the 1957 Worcester Festival: Cook in *Elijah* and Guest the Symphony No. 6 of Edmund Rubbra.

Vaughan Williams was also expected to conduct in 1957 – his work, *Five Variants of 'Dives and Lazarus'*; but a day or two before the concert he had left a nursing home following an operation and was unable to be present. At the concert, given by the Three Cathedral Choirs, a message of good wishes from V.W. was read out.

Two weeks before the Hereford Festival of 1958, Ralph Vaughan Williams died quietly in his sleep.

Notes

1.   Hereford Festival Minute Book, 1936–69
2.   Ibid.
3.   Memories of the late Joy Finzi
4.   Ibid.
5.   Gloucester Festival Minute Book, 1947
6.   Memories of Sir David Willcocks, Hereford Festival programme book, 1979
7.   *The Times*, 7 September 1950
8.   Recorded memories of Herbert Howells, National Sound Archives
9.   Memories of Herbert Howells (see Christopher Palmer, *Herbert Howells, A Study* (Novello, 1978), pp. 46–7
10. Memories of Meredith Davies
11. Ibid.
12. MT 1952, pp. 513–14
13. *The Times*, 12 September 1953
14. Letter from Sir David Willcocks to the author, 27 June 1991
15. Memories of Meredith Davies
16. Memories of Rodney Bennett
17. *Musical Opinion*, November 1955, pp. 81 and 83
18. *Musical Opinion*, November 1955, p. 83
19. Memories of Meredith Davies
20. *Musical Opinion*, November 1955, p. 83
21. Gloucester Festival Minute Book, 1950
22. *Daily Telegraph*, 7 September 1956
23. Churchdown, close to Gloucester
24. Ursula Vaughan Williams, *RVW – A Biography of Ralph Vaughan Williams* (OUP, 1964), p. 374
25. Ibid.
26. *Musical Opinion*, November 1950, pp. 79 and 83
27. A.T. Shaw, *The Worcester Journal*, 6 September 1957

ASSOCIATION

Although the committees of the Gloucester, Hereford and Worcester Festivals had met together from time to time, usually to discuss financial problems, no satisfactory arrangements had been made for regular meetings and cooperation until 1946. On 14 March in that year, representatives from the three cities met at The Deanery in Hereford to discuss a proposition made by the Dean of Gloucester, Dr H. Costley-White. There was, he said, a real need for a central body to advise and assist, financially and otherwise, the diocese holding the Festival.[1] That need became particularly apparent at Hereford in 1946 when a decision had to be made on whether or not to revive the Festival. A new joint advisory body was formed and continued to meet for the next ten years – and financial problems continued to dominate the agenda.

Alarm bells began to ring following Hereford's small deficit in 1952. Then, in 1953, the London Symphony Orchestra put the Festival on notice that its charges would be increased by one fifth. Doubts were expressed about the ability of Worcester and Hereford to continue to hold the Festival unless Gloucester was able to provide a subsidy.[2] The Gloucester balance sheet showed a total surplus of £2,870 at the beginning of 1954 (collections for the charity amounted to £1,292 of this) but the total surplus was down £730 on 1950. Worcester had been obliged to make alterations in the programme of the 1954 Festival in a search for economies, and Hereford was anticipating a loss of as much as £1,000 in 1955.

Under these circumstances the Joint Standing Committee agreed that a reserve fund was essential, and at Gloucester it was recommended that a quarter of the 1953 Festival profits should be placed to a general reserve subject to the other two Festivals agreeing to do the same in their turns.[3]

On 3 December 1953, a meeting was held in Worcester between representatives of the Arts Council and the conductors and secretaries from the three cities. The Arts Council of Great Britain, formed in 1940 as the Council for the Encouragement of Music and Arts and whose charter was renewed under the new title in 1946, was asked to throw Three Choirs a safety-line. The Council representative made it clear that the Council would be anxious to help the Festival, 'but that this could only be done if some constitution linking the three cities was adopted and that under such constitution no part of the proceeds from the concerts should be used for charitable purposes'.[4] Gloucester and Worcester rejected these conditions and it was left to Hereford to raise the matter again in 1955.

Meredith Davies, faced with rising orchestral fees, doubted that he could make appreciable economies without lowering musical standards. A partial solution was found in engaging the City of Birmingham Symhony Orchestra to play for the first part of the week in place of the more expensive London Symphony Orchestra, thus setting a precedent for the next few years. Even so, an Arts Council grant was going to be necessary if ticket prices were to be held at a reasonable level and a large deficit avoided. A formal application seeking a guarantee of between £750 and £1,000 was submitted to the Arts Council – and the lower sum was approved 'with a view to keeping the Festival alive until a more permanent basis could be obtained'.[5]

In the autumn of 1955, Herbert Sumsion held discussions with the Music Director of the Arts Council on the possibility of regular assistance to the Festival. Once again the point was made that the Three Choirs Festival must be regarded as one undertaking, and any profits from concerts paid into a reserve fund, to which the Arts Council would contribute annually over a period of years until the fund was sufficiently in credit to obviate the necessity for support. The point was driven home by a warning that 'the Arts Council were prepared to support the Festival in this way now, but might not be so later on'.[6] The Joint Standing Committee reached a decision in time for the Festival year of 1956 to benefit from an Arts Council grant of £750, payable as soon as the new organization, The Three Choirs Festival Association Ltd, became formally incorporated.

The Assistant Secretary of the Gloucester Festival, Mr Roland Pepper, a local solicitor, was asked to devise the necessary legal machinery – and incorporation was achieved on 18 March 1957. From this time the Charity for the Widows and Orphans of the Clergy would benefit only from collections and the proceeds of any events expressly organized for it, which in 1956 included the first Festival Garden Party organized by the Ladies Committee.

The association was fortunate in its first three years: in addition to an Arts Council annual grant there were special donations from ABC Television Ltd, the Gulbenkian Foundation, and the Trustees of the Gloucester Shire Hall Organ Fund, and both the Gloucester and Worcester Festivals made a profit. For the next triennium the Arts Council offered no grant but gave instead a cumulative guarantee spread over three years. Thanks to the Gloucester Festival again making a profit, this proved to be adequate. Thereafter the Arts Council never again offered a guarantee against loss other than on an annual basis.

Against this backcloth Melville Cook (b. 1912) rejoined the Three Choirs family after almost twenty years. A chorister of Gloucester Cathedral from 1923 to 1928, Cook became an articled pupil under Herbert Sumsion for three years from 1929 and assistant organist of Gloucester Cathedral from 1932 to 1937. He was also the organist of All Saints' Church, Cheltenham from 1935 to 1937. In 1938 he was appointed organist of Leeds Parish Church, remaining there until December 1956 when he took over from Meredith Davies at Hereford. In 1940 Cook took the Durham degree of D. Mus. after a period of study with Sir Edward Bairstow.

While working in Yorkshire, Melville Cook met Peter Pears, visiting Halifax to sing in *Messiah*. When, a little later, the English Opera Group visited Leeds, Pears

introduced Benjamin Britten to Cook; a meeting which led to an occasional correspondence and, when installed at Hereford, a determination on Cook's part to invite Britten to
Three Choirs. Unaware that Meredith Davies had already tried unsuccessfully to tempt
Britten to Three Choirs, Colin Mason, writing in *The Spectator* following the 1957(W)
Festival, had suggested that 'the most important composer of religious music in England
since Elgar and Vaughan Williams' had never yet been represented by the Three Choirs,
and that this persistent ignoring of him seemed 'quite deliberate and rather suspect'. Of
course, this was not strictly true: the *Variations on a Theme of Frank Bridge* had been given
in 1948(W), *Les Illuminations* in 1951(W), and the *Seven Sonnets of Michelangelo* in
1953(G). But in 1958(H) Britten and Pears came to Three Choirs in person.

> At long last, Mr Benjamin Britten has 'arrived' at the Three Choirs Festival. And about time too.
>   Tonight in Hereford Cathedral . . . Mr Britten conducted his *St Nicholas* cantata and his *Sinfonia
> da Requiem*. Tomorrow afternoon, in the Shire Hall, he is to give, with Miss Norma Procter and
> Mr Peter Pears, a recital which includes his *Abraham and Isaac* canticle.
>   I am not sure that *St Nicholas* . . . was the best choice for Mr Britten's West country 'arrival'. It
> suffers somewhat from the awkward naiveties of Mr Crozier's libretto and it does not suit a Cathedral
> quite so well as it suits, say, Aldeburgh Parish Church . . .
>   The iron-tongued *Sinfonia da Requiem* suited the Cathedral unexpectedly well. Not a detail, even in
> the macabre frenzy of the *Dies Irae*, was lost. If this performance, by the London Symphony
> Orchestra, was not the best the amazing and profoundly moving work has ever had, it sounded like
> it. Mr Britten has improved beyond measure as an orchestral conductor since he conducted the
> *Sinfonia* with a visiting orchestra at Birmingham Town Hall during the war years.
>   The concert had begun with Berlioz's *Te Deum*, which made it abundantly clear that in Dr Cooke
> Hereford has again acquired an organist who is also an excellent conductor.[7]

In addition to Benjamin Britten, Cook also brought Peter Racine Fricker to Hereford
to conduct his *Litany for double string orchestra*, and *The Light Invisible* by Kenneth
Leighton and *Genesis* by Frank Reizenstein were given their first performances. From the
past, *Messe des Morts* by the seventeenth-century composer Jean Gilles and, from the
present, Poulenc's *Stabat Mater* represented French ecclesiastical music. Peter Pears
joined Jennifer Vyvyan, Ilse Wolf, John Whitworth, Nicholas Long, David Galliver,
Richard Standen and Bruce Boyce in a performance of Monteverdi's *Vespers of the Blessed
Virgin* (1610). The Sunday evening organ recital was given by the great Italian organist
of St Peter's, Rome, Fernando Germani, and popular tradition was followed in
performances of the Verdi *Requiem*, *Messiah*, *The Kingdom*, and *Gerontius* with William
Herbert singing the title role for the last time at Three Choirs.

Melville Cook took the lion's share of the conducting load upon himself, but Herbert
Sumsion directed Finzi's *Fall of the Leaf* and Vaughan Williams's *Hundredth Psalm*, and
Douglas Guest the Piano Concerto in C minor, K491 by Mozart (with Colin Horsley)
and Poulenc's *Stabat Mater*. The CBSO orchestral concert, conducted by Meredith
Davies, included Schubert's Symphony No. 3, the Brahms Violin Concerto (with
Manoug Parikian), and Hindemith's suite for orchestra, *Nobilissima Visione*.

Compared with such diversity, the programme of the 1959 Gloucester Festival
contained little to surprise: an all-Vaughan Williams concert, *Missa Solemnis*, *St Matthew
Passion*, *Messiah*, *Gerontius*, and *Intimations of Immortality*. But there were new works: the
first Three Choirs performance of the *Requiem* by Maurice Duruflé, with Helen Watts and
Richard Standen; Adrian Crufts's *A Passiontide Carol*, again with Helen Watts; and the

première of Howard Ferguson's *The Dream of the Rood* – a setting of an anonymous Anglo-Saxon poem translated for Ferguson by Dorothy de Navarro:

> Dr Ferguson, who never hesitates to speak out boldly, gives the story a powerful setting. It is impressive in its beauty and thrilling in its climaxes.
>
> The full and lovely voice of Heather Harper, who sang the solo part, gave us the first of these. There were others by the choir, though none the equal of the mighty annunciation, 'But the Lord arose by his great might to succour man' preceded by a vigorous and splendidly executed orchestral preface.
>
> (The *Dream of the Rood*) was the supreme moment of last night's music. It was intended that it should be and it was.[8]

Howard Ferguson dedicated *The Dream of the Rood* to Dame Myra Hess, and she acknowledged the honour by visiting Gloucester for the first performance, conducted by Herbert Sumsion. Two days earlier the Melos Ensemble gave a polished chamber recital in the cathedral (surely a contradiction in terms) of the Schubert *Octet* and Howard Ferguson's boldly original Octet Op. 4 of 1933, his largest chamber work.

By the early 1960s Howard Ferguson had come to a realization that he had no more to say as a composer and made up his mind to stop writing, devoting himself instead to musicology. His bond with Three Choirs has remained strong and Ferguson is, happily, still a familiar and respected figure at the Festival. In recent years there has been a renewed interest in his compositions which, although comparatively few in number, are of consistently high quality. Ferguson's *Amore Langueo* was last performed at Three Choirs in 1983(G), and *The Dream of the Rood* in 1988(H).

Douglas Guest (b. 1917), like David Willcocks, came to Worcester from Salisbury Cathedral; and both were organ scholars at King's College.

Guest was a student at the Royal College of Music from 1933 to 1935, and studied with Sir Ernest Bullock among others. From 1935 to 1939 he was organ scholar at King's College, Cambridge under Boris Ord. David Willcocks succeeded him in 1939.

From 1939 to 1945 Guest was on active service in the Royal Artillery. He commanded a battery in the D-Day assault force, on 6 June 1944, and was Mentioned in Despatches.

After the war until 1950 he was director of Music at Uppingham School. In that year he succeeded Willcocks at Salisbury and as conductor of the Salisbury Musical Society. From 1950 too he carried out frequent engagements as deputy conductor of the Bournemouth Symphony Orchestra. He also conducted other orchestras in London, including broadcast performances with the Philharmonia, as well as several provincial concerts with the London Symphony Orchestra. He was Chairman of the Governing Council of the National Youth Orchestra of Great Britain for thirty-four years.

Douglas Guest directed the Worcester Festivals of 1960 and 1963 before his appointment, in the latter year, as organist of Westminster Abbey, a post which he held until 1987. He received the honour CVO in 1975.

Writing of the 1960(W) Festival in *The Musical Times*, Ernest Bradbury described Guest's work as 'invariably distinctive, energetic, and generally appealing'.[9] He might have added that Guest had also proved himself to be a very quick thinker.

After a week of rain, sunshine gilded the flag-bedecked streets of Worcester as the civic procession walked from the Guildhall to the cathedral for the Opening Service.

Crowds of spectators watched as the Lord Mayors of Birmingham, Bristol and Coventry, ten mayors, a deputy mayor, local MPs and other civic representatives passed by. The procession reached the north door of the cathedral and waited . . . and continued to wait for more than ten minutes.

Through a misunderstanding about the time of the service, the coach carrying members of the City of Birmingham Symphony Orchestra to Worcester had set out late. Realizing that there had been an error, Douglas Guest rang the CBSO office in Birmingham, asking for a police escort. The police sent a patrol car to escort the coach – but the coach driver thought that the police were checking his speed and slowed down! Only when a police officer boarded the coach was the driver persuaded to put his foot down. The orchestra arrived at the cathedral and scrambled into their places, the civic procession made its stately way into the nave followed by the Lord Lieutenant of Worcestershire, Admiral Sir William Tennant, in naval uniform, and his deputy lieutenants, then by the procession of the clergy.

The unfortunate start was soon forgotten in the combined splendours of church music and pageantry, and the congregation of three thousand heard the Master of the Queen's Music, Sir Arthur Bliss, read the first lesson. (Bliss conducted his *Music for Strings* on the Thursday evening.)

Douglas Guest needed to think quickly too when, four months before the Festival, he learned that Anthony Milner would be unable to finish his new oratorio, *The Water and the Fire*, in time. To his great credit Guest chose not to substitute a well-tried war-horse but to give the first public performance in Britain of *In Terra Pax* by the Swiss composer Frank Martin. Described by Martin as an 'oratorio-brève', *In Terra Pax* was written in 1944 as a result of a commission from Radio-Geneva to compose a choral work to mark the armistice of the Second World War; it was completed in 1945. In Worcester the soloists were Heather Harper, Jean Allister, David Galliver, John Carol Case and Hervey Alan.

> No one will deny that Douglas Guest had tackled his first 'official' Three Choirs with resolution and enterprise. Kodály's *Budavári Te Deum*, Petrassi's *Magnificat* and Janáček's *The Eternal Gospel* were relatively unfamiliar items in a programme that also included Verdi's *Quattro Pezzi Sacri*, Bruckner's E minor Mass and Berkeley's *Stabat Mater* . . . and even the Bach Passion was changed this year, from the usual St Matthew to the St John.[10]

Kodály's *Budavári Te Deum* was given as the first item in the Monday evening programme and, unexpectedly, Kodály joined the audience to hear it. The soloists were Eileen Poulter, Marjorie Thomas, Wilfred Brown and Hervey Alan. During the performance, Eileen Poulter noticed a smell of burning. The *Worcester Evening News* takes up the tale:

> Miss Poulter . . . has an exceptionally keen sense of smell, and it seemed worse to her during an interval when she went to the artists' room below the stage.
> She mentioned it to Mr Wilfred Brown, tenor soloist, who diagnosed an electrical fault, and without further ado telephoned the Midlands Electricity Board. Their representative was promptly on the spot, a fuse box was found to be nearly red-hot, and a circuit seriously overloaded.
> The floodlighting on all but the North face of the Cathedral was turned off immediately, a circumstance which puzzled those who came out of the Cathedral later and found only one side illuminated.

Benjamin Britten and Peter Pears returned to Hereford for the 1961 Festival, appearing with Barry Tuckwell in a Shire Hall recital which included Schumann's Adagio and Allegro for Horn and Piano and *Dichterliebe*, Britten's canticle *Still falls the Rain* and songs by Ireland and Bridge. On the Wednesday evening in the Cathedral, Pears was a soloist, along with Jennifer Vyvyan, Helen Watts and Roger Stalman in Mozart's Coronation Mass in C, K317, conducted by Herbert Sumsion; in Britten's *Nocturne*, Op. 60, conducted by the composer; and in Fricker's *The Vision of Judgement*, with Jennifer Vyvyan, the Festival Chorus and the LSO conducted by Melville Cook.

John Mitchinson and Janet Baker both made their Three Choirs débuts in 1961: Mitchinson in *Messiah* and Baker in the first British performance of Paul Hindemith's *Requiem 'For Those We Love'*, a work described by Frank Howes in *The Times* as 'gray and interminable, for all its moments of redeeming lyrical beauty'.[11] Janet Baker also joined Ilse Wolf, Wilfred Brown and Donald Bell in the three *Latin Motets* by Bernard Naylor.

The year 1961 was a memorable one for Herbert Sumsion: he was awarded the CBE ('too little too late' wrote Sir Arthur Bliss in his letter of congratulation), became an Honorary Fellow of the Royal College of Music, and elected an Honorary Associate of the Royal Academy of Music, all in that year – his thirty-third as organist at Gloucester. 'I believe (and Hindemith, if I read *A Composer's World* aright would support me)' wrote Arthur Jacobs, 'that there is a moral worth in having performances conducted by men who belong to, and are loved by, the community which provides their audiences.'[12] Sumsion, known affectionately to all his friends as John, is just such a figure, and in retirement retains the genuine warmth and respect born of long, dedicated service to music.

It is a measure of Sumsion's generous spirit that in 1962 he gave opportunities to two young musicians, one on the threshold of his career and the other rapidly establishing himself in the music-making life of Gloucester, to bring their compositions to a wider audience at Three Choirs. Both men chose to present a *Te Deum*.

John Sanders, Sumsion's assistant organist from 1958, conducted his *Te Deum* at the Opening Service:

> . . . a splendid setting composed for the occasion. It owes – at any rate for purposes of description and categorization – something to Walton; it is sustained on a pervasive figure suggestive of bells and it is modern in its well-judged use of clanging dissonance; its scoring is clear and well adapted to a large church.[13]

During the organ recital which preceded the 1959(G) Opening Service John Sanders had included a piece entitled *Whitsunday Procession* by Tony Hewitt-Jones. A Londoner, Hewitt-Jones went up to Christ Church, Oxford, but his studies were interrupted by war service in the Royal Navy. Returning to Oxford, where he was a pupil of Bernard Rose, he completed his musical studies and then took a teaching appointment in Gloucestershire. He was the first conductor of the Gloucestershire Youth Orchestra, formed in 1956; studied with Herbert Sumsion; and was made an Associate of the Royal College of Organists in 1957, when he was awarded the Limpus and Read prizes. Composing from 1951, Hewitt-Jones had completed a *Sinfonietta for Strings* in 1959 and went on to write music in many forms, much of it for particular occasions. The Three Choirs Festival of 1962 was the first such occasion of major importance. Arthur Jacobs again:

The last day brought Tony Hewitt-Jones's *Te Deum* for soloists [Norma Procter, Wilfred Brown and Hervey Alan], chorus and orchestra. The composer (born 1926) was unwise enough in the programme-note to allow his music to be wrapped in numerological mumbo-jumbo: we were told in all seriousness how the figure 3 (as in Three Choirs and in the Holy Trinity, to which the cathedral is dedicated) is symbolized in the musical forces used (violins 1, 2, 3; violas 1, 2, 3,.; triple woodwind, *etc.*) and even in the musical construction, with a canon in 27 parts (3³)! For Mr Jones's sake one rejoiced that trumpets already have three valves. But three (if the composer will pardon the liberty) cheers for music with an arresting quality and a very individual approach.

A young composer might have set the traditional text with traditional church polyphony; or *à la* Britten; or with reverence to today's fashionable serialist models. Instead, Mr Hewitt-Jones has adopted a monumental, many-voiced, firmly diatonic style which one might almost call '20th-century Gabrieli'.[14]

The *Te Deum* was repeated at the 1968(G) Festival and will be heard again in 1992(G). Hewitt-Jones's association with Three Choirs extended over more than thirty years as composer, as music adviser to the county of Gloucestershire, and as a singer in the Festival Chorus whose solid bottom C was the pride of the second basses. Tony Hewitt-Jones died in 1989.

Benjamin Britten and Peter Pears were unable to accept an invitation to appear at the 1962(G) Festival but none the less the programme included Britten's *Nocturne* sung by Gerald English, and the *Missa Brevis* for Boys' Voices and Organ. Sir Arthur Bliss conducted the first performance, in an appropriate cathedral setting, of his *Beatitudes*. (The première at the Coventry Festival was given in a theatre.) Honegger's *A Christmas Cantata* was conducted by Douglas Guest, with a capable baritone in James Walkley – a Gloucester Cathedral lay clerk. The London Mozart Players gave a concert under their conductor Harry Blech. The LSO played until Thursday, and the Bournemouth Symphony Orchestra appeared at Three Choirs for the first time on Friday afternoon, coincidentally marking three other 'firsts': Sir Adrian Boult as Festival conductor; a Mahler Symphony – the fourth, with Elizabeth Harwood as the soprano soloist; and Tony Hewitt-Jones's *Te Deum*.

An even more surprising 'first' occurred on the Wednesday evening – a complete performance at Three Choirs of Vaughan Williams's *Sea Symphony*. The last movement had been given twice before, at Gloucester in 1925 and Hereford in 1936, but until 1962 the other sections had been banished from the cathedrals by Deans and Chapters set against the lack of orthodoxy in Whitman's texts.

An unbeliever may rub his ears on hearing Vaughan Williams's *Sea Symphony* – with its prophecy of a poet whom Whitman pointedly calls 'the true son of God' – in a cathedral. Presumably (to alter a dictum ascribed to Rossini) what is too blasphemous to be said may be sung.[16]

Until 1962 books of words had been sold for each Festival concert in addition to an outline programme for the week. In that year, at Sumsion's suggestion, a single combined programme book was introduced – a precedent followed at all subsequent Festivals.

Herbert Sumsion, convalescing from illness, was unable to attend the 1963 Worcester Festival. His place was taken by John Sanders, conducting Carissimi's *Jephte*; David Willcocks, back to conduct the *Passacaglia, Chorale and Fugue* by Kenneth Leighton; and Christopher Robinson, assistant organist and organist-elect of Worcester Cathedral, in the traditional concert of the Three Cathedral Choirs. The City of Birmingham Symphony Orchestra and the Royal Philharmonic Orchestra were both engaged, the latter for the first time at Three Choirs, and on the Saturday evening the National Youth Orchestra of Great Britain, conducted by Rudolf Schwarz, presented a sparkling programme, the principal work in which was Dvořák's Symphony No. 8 in G.

Sir Arthur Bliss was again present to conduct in 1963: Norma Procter, John Carol Case, the chorus and CBSO in the first performance of his cantata *Mary of Magdala*. The text, partly a reworking by Christopher Hassall of a seventeenth-century poem, deals with the mystery of the empty tomb in Gethsemane. Sadly, Hassall died soon after he finished the libretto and before hearing the completed work.

For Douglas Guest the lasting memory of the 1963 Festival, his last, is a sense of thrilling intoxication while conducting Benjamin Britten's *War Requiem*, only the third public performance anywhere. 'I never felt anything like it again,' he said. 'The Cathedral turned upside down.' Frank Howes expressed it perfectly:

> Britten's *War Requiem* was a bold undertaking for a choir and conductor with a week's festival to sustain, but Mr Guest's courage was amply justified and his own stature as a conductor made patent for all to admire. The geographical problem of placing the very large forces required was solved by putting the boys in one side aisle and the chamber orchestra in the other with the main stage between; the soloists also were at the sides with their backs to pillars, Miss Heather Harper to the left and Mr Gerald English and Mr John Shirley-Quirk to the right of the conductor.
>
> All three had entered into the spirit of the requiem – and what a spirit it is that reconciles into a single work of art the conflicting, distracted, and terrifying emotions of war as no other piece of music has ever done, but Mr English should perhaps have the recognition that he followed Mr Peter Pears in the part without at all resembling him.
>
> The chorus sang securely and Mr Guest controlled it all with a judgement that seemed hardly ever at fault even in so tricky a matter as balance. The result was that this masterpiece gripped with something like awe.[16]

Britten's *War Requiem* was again the centrepiece of the 1964 Hereford and 1965 Gloucester Festivals, conducted on both occasions by Melville Cook. In 1964 too, the long-awaited oratorio by Anthony Milner, *The Water and the Fire*, at last received its first performance by Heather Harper, Gerald English, John Shirley-Quirk, the chorus and the LSO conducted by Melville Cook.

Anthony Milner, a Roman Catholic, based his dramatic oratorio on man's emergence from the wastelands of life to a dream of perfect happiness. It was, according to Milner, inspired by pictures from the Bible. The composition contains a love-duet, religious dance movements and a *Gloria* in which choirboys ring bells. The text includes passages from the Bible, the Liturgy and the Eucharist. *The Water and the Fire* was composed with the resonances of a Gothic cathedral in mind, as was Bernard Naylor's *Stabat Mater*, the other work to recieve its first performance at Hereford in 1964.

Written for a double chorus of women's voices and orchestra the *Stabat Mater*, dedicated to Melville Cook, was finished early in 1962. A note in the score reads: 'The work is designed for performance in a spacious building in which sounds last longer, or much longer, than their written notes indicate.'

Describing *The Water and the Fire* as 'the most powerful and evocative score' which Milner had yet composed, Felix Aprahamian, in a *Guardian* review, considered 'outstanding . . . the depiction of the torrents of perdition in the first scene, of the waters of night in the second and the luminous beauty of the scene in which the Paschal Fire blazes'. Naylor, in his *Stabat Mater*, had 'succeeded in creating the kind of musical texture which floats through the spaces of Hereford Cathedral with magical effect . . . Both works should be heard in London. But where?'

Melville Cook proved himself a true revolutionary by dropping *Messiah* from the programme – and this time it remained dropped for thirteen years. In addition to the Milner and Naylor premières, modern music included Stravinsky's *Symphony of Psalms* and Poulenc's *Gloria*, as well as the *War Requiem*. 'The ancient festival may not be *avant-garde*', declared John Waterhouse, 'but it is certainly no longer a museum.'[17] The old myth that Three Choirs was firmly cemented in an outmoded tradition seemed at last to be crumbling.

There might not have been any shortage of new works at Hereford but there was a very definite shortage of new voices in the Hereford contingent of the Festival Chorus, especially men. By 1964 Hereford could muster only five tenors, against ten from Gloucester and twenty-one from Worcester. Melville Cook placed an appeal for tenors and basses in the local newspapers, but numbers continued to fall. Hereford was only able to send three tenors and five basses, other than lay clerks, to Worcester in 1966. Overall balance seems not to have suffered from this deficit, and in 1965(G) *The Times* praised the firm choral attack of the three choirs under Melville Cook in *The Hymn of Jesus*: 'Dr Cook brought dramatic understanding and an appropriate touch of flamboyance to his tempi and his timing, so as to recall something of the thrilling novelty which this music originally conveyed.'[18]

There was praise too for a performance of Anthony Milner's *Salutatio Angelica*, and especially for Janet Baker's interpretation of the contralto solos. But Herbert Sumsion was not spared the critical stripes of the London Press. He was accused of providing an unyielding accompaniment in the Verdi *Te Deum* and the Sibelius Violin Concerto (with Yfrah Neaman), of a disappointing neutrality in Bach's Cantata No. 100 (with Janet Baker and Robert Tear), and of not demanding enough from his performers in Handel's early *Dixit Dominus*. On the other hand, there was warm praise for his realizations of *Gerontius* (Marjorie Thomas, Kenneth Bowen and Roger Stalman) and *Elijah* (Rae Woodland, Maureen Lehane, John Mitchinson and John Dethick). Sir Adrian Boult, who had arrived before breakfast to help Sumsion prepare for his first Festival in 1928, arrived on the final day of Sumsion's last Gloucester Festival – to conduct the LSO in Vaughan Williams's *Norfolk Rhapsody* in E minor and Elgar's Symphony No. 1 in A flat. Between the two, Sir Arthur Bliss conducted his *Music for Strings*.

From the beginning, cathedral concerts at Three Choirs had been received in reverent silence. This long and worthy tradition almost came to an end in 1965 – but not quite. The final work on the evening of Thursday 9 September was a vivid performance of *Belshazzar's Feast* under the baton of Christopher Robinson. The soloist was John Dethick. The chorus sang as they had seldom sung before. In the highly-charged moment following the final 'Alleluia!' a stifled cheer and ripple of applause broke the silence in the South Transept. The noise, which lasted only a moment, betokened that silent thanksgiving would not survive the end of the decade.

Melville Cook resigned his post at Hereford in 1966 and went to Canada to take up an appointment as conductor of the Winnipeg Philharmonic Choir, then later as organist of All Saints' Church, Winnipeg. After a year he moved to the Metropolitan United Church, Toronto, remaining there until his retirement and return to England in 1986.

Herbert Sumsion conducted at Three Choirs for the last time in 1967(H) – Haydn's *Nelson Mass* with Elizabeth Harwood, Janet Baker, Wilfred Brown, John Barrow, the Festival Chorus and the Royal Philharmonic Orchestra. His thirty-nine years of service as organist at Gloucester Cathedral came to an end on 28 September 1967. At a presentation ceremony in the King's School the Dean of Gloucester, the Very Revd Seiriol Evans, paid tribute:

> He has the great and rare gift of being so completely in command as to inspire the utter confidence of all of us. You sometimes found this gift in the war among young commanders of destroyers and M.T.B.s – no side, no self-importance, no self-consciousness; as quiet as anything, yet able to be master of every situation. [19]

Herbert Sumsion to the letter.

Notes

1. Hereford Festival Minute Book, 1936–69
2. Gloucester Festival Minute Book, 1953
3. Ibid.
4. Hereford Festival Minute Book, 1936–69
5. Ibid.
6. Gloucester Festival Minute Book, 1955
7. The *Birmingham Post*, 9 September 1958
8. *The Citizen*, 11 September 1959
9. MT 1960, p. 697
10. MT 1960, p. 697
11. *The Times*, 6 September 1961
12. MT 1962, p. 689
13. *The Times*, 4 September 1962
14. MT 1962, p. 691
15. MT 1962, p. 689
16. *The Times*, 5 September 1963
17. The *Birmingham Post*, 9 September 1964
18. *The Times*, 9 September 1965
19. *The Citizen*, 26 September 1967

CHAPTER NINETEEN

A NEW EPOCH

Worcester 1966

When recalling impressions of the Opening Service, the one incident which looks biggest in retrospect is that Benjamin Britten's setting of the National Anthem was sung instead of the setting by Elgar which has hitherto been heard at the opening of the festival for as long as most people can remember.

After hearing that modern setting of the familiar tune, which seemed – perhaps because of key affinity – to fall into place naturally and appropriately, as if it were born of the mood of trust and hope generated by Elgar's prelude to The Kingdom, a new epoch, I felt, had dawned upon the Three Choirs Festival: Christopher Robinson had made his mark!'[1]

Christopher Robinson was born in 1936 at Peterborough and educated at St Michael's College, Tenbury; Rugby; and Christ Church, Oxford. He was assistant organist at Christ Church from 1955 to 1958. During his last year at the university he was assistant organist at New College under Meredith Davies, and was then on the music staff at Oundle School for three years before taking the post of assistant organist at Worcester Cathedral in 1962. He succeeded Douglas Guest as Master of the Choristers and Organist in 1963, when he also became conductor of the City of Birmingham Choir in succession to Meredith Davies.

In 1966 Robinson brought to Three Choirs not only the impressive and grandiose *Grande Messe des Morts* of Berlioz, but also, and long overdue, the music of Sir Michael Tippett in the year in which he was knighted: *A Child of our Time*, with Jennifer Vyvyan singing magnificently in the part of the Mother, and with Joan Allister, John Mitchinson and John Carol Case. At the Friday afternoon orchestral concert, Sir Adrian Boult conducted Tippett's Concerto for Double String Orchestra. There was also the first performance, commissioned by the National Federation of Music Societies, of *Changes* by Gordon Crosse. Described by the composer as 'A Nocturnal Cycle for Soprano, Baritone, Chorus and Orchestra', *Changes* is intended for large amateur choirs. The title refers to changes from day to night (symbolizing life and death) and changes in bell-ringing, which provide many musical motifs of the work. Christopher Robinson conducted the Festival Chorus and the Royal Philharmonic Orchestra (appearing at Three Choirs for the first time, in place of the LSO) in a spirited and assured performance, with excellent contributions in the important solo parts from Noëlle Barker and John Noble.

Changes showed the strong influence on Gordon Crosse of Benjamin Britten, whose music was represented at the Festival by *St Nicholas*, conducted by David Willcocks (stepping in to replace Melville Cook) with Gerald English as the tenor soloist; and the *Cantata Academica*, with Jennifer Vyvyan, Marjorie Thomas, John Mitchinson and Owen Brannigan under Robinson's own direction.

Sir Percy Hull was the principal visitor to the 1967 Hereford Festival: one month from his eighty-ninth birthday, accompanied by Lady Hull, carrying a walking stick which had belonged to Elgar, and which he used constantly. 'I am delighted,' he said, 'to find the festival still in a thriving condition and I do congratulate Hereford on acquiring its new young organist, Mr Richard Lloyd, a real find.'[2] Sir Percy Hull died at his home in Surrey on 31 August 1968.

Richard Hey Lloyd was born in Cheshire in 1933 and educated at Lichfield Cathedral School, at Rugby, and Jesus College, Cambridge, where he was Organ Scholar (1952–5). From 1957 to 1966 he was assistant organist at Salisbury Cathedral and moved to Hereford in succession to Melville Cook on 1 September 1966. He first appeared at Three Choirs conducting at the concert of the three cathedral choirs in the 1966 Worcester Festival and in the following year directed his first Hereford Festival.

A long-time devotee of Three Choirs, Lloyd had been attending the Festival for nearly twenty years when he was appointed to Hereford. He was keenly aware that many in the Festival Chorus had sung under the baton of Elgar and that there was, for instance, a 'Three Choirs way' of performing *Gerontius*. He was conscious, too, of the direct link to Elgar which had been maintained through Hull and Sumsion, and he had admired particularly the work which Meredith Davies had done in raising Festival conducting standards. From the outset, Lloyd set himself the task of building up the depleted Hereford Chorus – and within a year all the deficiencies had been made good. The Hereford contingent of the Festival Chorus at the 1967(H) Festival with their Chorus Superintendent, Michael Morris, numbered ninety-three apart from choristers and lay clerks, and included fourteen tenors and eighteen basses.

Lloyd included several modern English works in his first Festival programme. Of these, Alun Hoddinott's *Dives and Lazarus*, commissioned for the 1965 Farnham Festival, was the most interesting. *The Annunciation* by Bernard Naylor, written in 1949 and broadcast in 1951, was given its first public performance at Hereford in 1967; in spite of fine solo work by Noëlle Barker and Wilfred Brown it failed to please, and Norman Kay's *King Herod* fared little better.

On the other hand, Bruckner's Mass in F minor was given a stunning performance under Richard Lloyd on Thursday evening. On the last night Lloyd was blessed by that rare thing, a near-perfect group of soloists in *Gerontius*: Janet Baker, Ronald Dowd and Roger Stalman.

But this memorable *Gerontius* was close to cancellation when, just before the performance, a hoaxer phoned to say that a bomb had been planted in the cathedral. Thanks to the action of the police (who merely said a parcel had been lost) a stampede was avoided, unlike the metaphorical bombshell which had burst on the previous day, following publication of an article by William Mann in *The Times*:

It is difficult to be sure in what frame of mind one should approach the Three Choirs Festival. Is it a local jollification during which, for one week, the organists of the three cathedrals try their hands at the role of Toscanini and match their choir-master-organist talents (not necessarily those of a good conductor) against as wide a stretch of the choral and symphonic repertory as they fancy? Is it, as England's oldest musical festival . . . to be regarded *ipso facto* as an event of natural cultural importance, to be judged by the standards of, say, Glyndebourne or Edinburgh? Or as a respectable shop window for all that is most worth while in choral and orchestral music of all countries and periods?

Or do we have to admit that an existence of 240 years inevitably induces some sort of senile decay and that, in its present form, the Three Choirs Festival needs to be replaced or retired for the musical health of the country?

In recent years, I have arrived at Three Choirs Festivals suspecting that the first or last of these attitudes must be the appropriate one, and either the choice of music or the setting, more rarely the quality of performance, has induced a more respectful frame of mind. First impressions this year, after two concerts today, are less favourable.[3]

William Mann went on to review the only two concerts which he had actually attended: one in which the Naylor and Kay works had been given; the other, a performance of the Verdi *Requiem*:

The fires did not blaze, the choir sang like mice, and the four soloists [Rae Woodland, Sibyl Michelow, Ronald Dowd and Roger Stalman] prophesied everlasting doom and searing physical agony as sedately as if they were rendering Victorian ballads about platonic love or the pleasures of life on the ocean. Musical drama was missing, and I am still waiting for a sign that this festival is as lively as it is old.[4]

Mann's attack generated considerable anger among Festival supporters and it was rumoured that a petition condemning it had been organized from the Festival Club. But there was no more unanimity among the critics in 1967 than at any other time, and there were those who praised Lloyd's Verdi *Requiem* as a performance of notable excellence. The more general attack upon the abilities of the organists to assume the role of conductors contained nothing new. It had been repeated innumerable times over the years and is still heard today. It is an argument which takes no account of the impossibility, clearly identified by Sir George Dyson in 1946, for an outside conductor to be able to spare sufficient time for rehearsals and to get to know the chorus, given the distance of Three Choirs from London and the number of works to be prepared for each Festival. Nor does it give a moment's consideration to the possibility that two factors have, above all else, contributed to the long survival of the Festival. One, the continued needs of the charity; the other, the very continuity guaranteed by the sure presence of the cathedral organists.

None the less, the advantages of relinquishing control of non-choral concerts to professional conductors are self-evident and, at the first Gloucester Festival under the direction of John Sanders, the conducting load was shared by Hugo Rignold (the CBSO), Sir Adrian Boult (the RPO), and Raymond Leppard (the English Chamber Orchestra), in addition to Christopher Robinson and Richard Lloyd.

John Sanders was born in Essex in 1933. He was educated at Felsted School, Essex; the Royal College of Music; and at Gonville and Caius College, Cambridge, where he was Organ Scholar. After two years military service in the Royal Artillery he became assistant organist at Gloucester. In 1963 he was appointed organist of Chester Cathedral, returning as organist at Gloucester on the retirement of Dr Sumsion. In 1990 he received the Lambeth degree of Doctor of Music.

The year 1968 marked the centenary of the death of Rossini, whose *Stabat Mater* Sanders had chosen as the principal choral work for the Monday evening concert. And the Italian flavour continued on Tuesday afternoon with a performance of Verdi's *Four Sacred Pieces* conducted by Richard Lloyd in a concert which ended with the première of Christopher Steel's Mass in Five Movements, Op. 18, conducted by John Sanders.

The most famous foreign singer to appear at the Festival for many years was to have been the German soprano Rita Streich, celebrated for her singing of Mozart and Richard Strauss coloratura roles, and engaged to appear at Three Choirs in 1968(G). Two days before the Festival began John Sanders was told by the London agents, Ibbs and Tillett, that Rita Streich was ill and could not appear. They suggested that Richard Lewis, who was singing in Tel Aviv, might be engaged in her place. An urgent cable was sent to Tel Aviv. Lewis accepted and flew from Israel on Tuesday 27 August, sang in a broadcast recital from the Gloucester College of Education on the following Thursday morning, and left for the Edinburgh Festival the next day, where he sang the same programme: Purcell, Schubert, Beethoven, Vaughan Williams, Butterworth and Britten. In Gloucester the famous tenor was accompanied by Geoffrey Parsons.

Rita Streich had also been engaged to sing the *Four Last Songs* of Richard Strauss in the Tuesday evening concert, given by the CBSO under their principal conductor, Hugo Rignold. Her place was taken by Elizabeth Harwood who, on the previous evening, sang in Christopher Steel's Mass along with Kenneth Bowen, and on Wednesday evening in Beethoven's 'Choral' Symphony, with Norma Procter, John Mitchinson and Raimund Herincx, the Festival Chorus and RPO conducted by John Sanders.

The fiftieth anniversary of Sir Hubert Parry's death fell in 1968. As a tribute to his memory Sir Adrian Boult gave his services to the Festival to conduct the Symphonic Variations for Orchestra on Thursday evening. The last item in the same concert, Haydn's Mass in B flat (*The Teresa Mass*), conducted by Richard Lloyd, marked the last appearance at Three Choirs of the tenor Wilfred Brown.

Perfect diction, an unerring feeling for words, a faultless technique, and a golden personality: qualities which informed Wilfred Brown's superb artistry, and qualities which may still be experienced, not merely heard, in his gramophone recordings. Well known as a radio broadcaster as well as a concert artist, Brown took exactly the same care over singing hymns on BBC religious programmes as he did when performing in great masterpieces. His recording of Gerald Finzi's *Dies Natalis*, made in 1963 with the English Chamber Orchestra conducted by Christopher Finzi, is a never-to-be-bettered memorial to a great singer. Four years after making it, while on a cycling holiday with his wife on the Isle of Wight, Brown suddenly found that he couldn't pull on the brakes with one hand: the first ominous sign of a brain tumour. He died on 5 March 1971.

The National Youth Orchestra again visited Worcester in 1969 and – in response to youthful exuberance – the tradition of centuries was finally broken. On Sunday evening applause broke out spontaneously after the NYO and one of their young trumpeters had given the Trumpet Concerto in E flat by Hummel, conducted by Rudolf Schwarz – and sustained applause greeted each work for the rest of the concert. The audience were silent on Monday evening following Beethoven's *Missa Solemnis*, but on Tuesday afternoon a single outburst of clapping was heard after Richard Lloyd had conducted Peter Maxwell Davies's *Five Carols for Boy's Voices*. More consistent applause was heard on Tuesday evening, though on Wednesday the audience were strangely silent following Rossini's effervescent *Petite Messe Solennelle*. Both of Thursday's concerts were applauded – but then Sir Adrian Boult asked for no applause for Friday afternoon's concert by the RPO, much to the disappointment of the local press: 'The audience were getting used to the idea of clapping . . . and applause at a concert to be broadcast . . . would have ditched the outworn tradition once and for all.'[5] Not everyone agreed that applause in the cathedrals was a welcome precedent, and a lively correspondence was carried on in the Worcester and Hereford newspapers in 1969 and 1970. But the momentum of change was too great for effective protest; the silence had been broken for ever.

Four composers whose music was performed during the week were present at the 1969(W) Festival. Luigi Dallapiccola's *Due Liriche di Anacreonte* and *Quadro Liriche di Antonio Machade* were given in a Monday afternoon recital at Hartlebury Castle by the Vesuvius Ensemble of London; the soprano soloist in both works was Jane Manning. Dallapiccola was also present in the cathedral on Thursday afternoon to hear Christopher Robinson conduct the RPO and Festival Chorus in his *Canti di Prigionia*, a work described by John Waterhouse as 'among the most powerful gestures of "protest through music" ever made: the work may be regarded as the supreme musical symbol of all the anguish, suffering and frustrated idealism of the Italian people during the tragic last phase of the Fascist regime and the catastrophic events which followed.'[6]

Elizabeth Maconchy was in Worcester for the first performance by the three cathedral choirs and the Birmingham Brass Consort of her *And Death Shall Have No Dominion*; and a setting of Psalm 150 by William Mathias was heard for the first time in the Opening Service.

Heralded by A.T. Shaw in the *Worcester Evening News* as the first performance of a new work to make such a profound impression upon a vast audience in nearly fifty years, Jonathan Harvey's dramatic cantata *Ludus Amoris* was performed by Janet Price, Gerald English, Tony Church (speaker), the Festival Chorus and RPO conducted by Christopher Robinson on Tuesday evening. Importantly, it was the first work ever to be commissioned by Three Choirs with funds provided by the Arts Council. Free to applaud, the Festival audience gave *Ludus Amoris* a near-frenzied reception. The RPO manager even asked Christopher Robinson if he would bring the Festival Chorus to take part in a performance of the work at the Royal Festival Hall in the following June, and Kenneth Loveland writing in *The Times* praised: '. . . Not only the fact of Mr Harvey's work but the care and pride of presentation it received in Christopher Robinson's hands [which] suggested that the festival is rediscovering its relevance to the contemporary British musical scene.'[7]

The performance of *Ludus Amoris* went ahead at the Festival Hall on 16 June 1970 and was well received as the work of a composer equally aware of the conservative English choral tradition and of post-serial techniques, which Harvey had reconciled with remarkable success. Even so, it failed to take root and has not yet been repeated at Three Choirs.

Among distinguished visitors to the 1969 Worcester Festival was Edward Heath, then Leader of the Opposition, accompanied by Worcester MP Peter Walker. Within a year Mr Heath was the Prime Minister, and Peter Walker his Secretary of State for the Environment.

The pattern of contemporary and new works woven together with the established, the familiar and the popular continued to provide the basis for Festival programme planning throughout the 1970s.

At Hereford in 1970 Richard Lloyd enveloped much new music in an Elgarian sandwich. The week began with *The Kingdom*, given by Sheila Armstrong, Norma Procter, Alexander Young, John Carol Case, the Festival Chorus, and the RPO conducted by Sir Adrian Boult. On Friday, Lloyd conducted *Gerontius* with Marjorie Thomas, Alexander Young, Roger Stalman, the chorus and CBSO. In between, among other things there were Sir Lennox Berkeley's *Magnificat* and Benjamin Britten's *Spring Symphony*, both given for the first time at Three Choirs; *In the Beginning* by Aaron Copland; the first British performance of *Psalm 150*, Op. 5 by the Argentinian composer, Alberto Ginastera; and the premières of three British works: Christopher Brown's cantata *David*; Bryan Kelly's *Stabat Mater*, conducted by the composer; and *Notturni ed Alba* by John McCabe.

Notturni ed Alba, commissioned by the Festival, is a setting of four medieval Latin poems presenting different aspects of night, though in most cases approached from a subjective viewpoint. It was composed in response to a request made by Richard Lloyd while he and John McCabe were enjoying a pint of beer in Salisbury: 'What I want,' Lloyd had said, 'is a *Dies Natalis* of the 70s.' *Notturni ed Alba* was the result. The first performance, given by the soprano Sheila Armstrong with the CBSO conducted by Louis Frémaux, remains in Richard Lloyd's memory as the single most important new work to be given at Hereford during his years there. It was repeated at the 1985 Festival.

A fourth new work promised for the 1970(H) Festival: a motet, *Out of the Deep Have I Called* by Alun Hoddinott, had to be cancelled when the score failed to arrive in time. But the largest new work of the 1971 Gloucester Festival was also commissioned from Hoddinott: *The Tree of Life*, for soprano and tenor soloists, chorus, organ and orchestra. As Desmond Shawe-Taylor wrote in the *Sunday Times*:

> It was essentially a throw-back to our oratorio past, with little in the way of fresh impulse or idea to enliven the stale tradition; it even drew, amid loyal cathedral applause, a few hisses – the first I can recall in such surroundings, and surely among the first to complain of music as being not vanguard, but rearguard.[8]

The soloists in *The Tree of Life* were Margaret Price and Gerald English, with the Festival Chorus and RPO conducted by John Sanders.

Following a major rebuild which cost £35,000 and took a year to complete, the Gloucester Cathedral organ was re-dedicated at the Opening Service of the 1971 Festival. It was appropriate, therefore, that the programme should include the first performance of a substantial organ work: a specially-commissioned concerto by Peter Dickinson. On Thursday evening the Prime Minister, Mr Edward Heath, and Mr and Mrs Peter Walker visited the Festival to hear a concert in which Richard Lloyd conducted the RPO and Festival Chorus in Haydn's *Harmoniemesse*, with Margaret Price, Alfreda Hodgson, William McAlpine and Benjamin Luxon; and Christopher Robinson conducted Samuel Barber's *Adagio for Strings* and Rachmaninoff's *The Bells*, again with Price, McAlpine and Luxon.

At the end of the concert, and when the intrigued audience had finally been persuaded to leave, Mr Heath climbed to the organ-loft and spent a few minutes playing the refurbished instrument – presumably a welcome break from the rigours of Industrial Relations legislation then at the forefront of British politics!

Two soloists engaged for the 1971(G) Festival withdrew at short notice: the contralto Helen Watts was released from her contract in order to take up an offer to sing at the Salzburg Festival; and Robert Tear, who should have joined Alfreda Hodgson and Benjamin Luxon in *Gerontius* on the last night, fell ill. He was replaced by Gerald English.

The guests of honour at the Festival Garden Party on Monday were Sir Arthur and Lady Bliss. The Chairman of the Festival, Mr Anthony Scott, presented Sir Arthur with a framed print of Gloucester Cathedral on behalf of the committee. Having admitted to being rather embarrassed, Sir Arthur thanked the committee not only for the gift, but also for his invitation to perform at Three Choirs in 1922. 'There is an atmosphere here unlike any other festival,' he said. 'It is like being one member of a great big family.'[9]

In a not very successful attempt to boost the numbers of young people attending the Festival, Wednesday, 25 August 1971 was advertised as Youth Day. The idea was that for just £3 a student could purchase a 'package-deal' ticket to all the events for that day, winding up with a late-evening Folk Music Party (Steel Eye Span, Pigsty Hill and The Song Wainers!) at nearby Highnam Court. This all-night pop concert was styled a 'Fringe Event' in the local press[10] and, while not advertised or organized as a Festival Fringe, it seems to have been the first occasion upon which Three Choirs ventured into the sphere of modern light entertainment in an event outside the main programme. And a personality from the world of light entertainment ventured into the Festival too: Eartha Kitt, in Gloucester to open a Samaritans Centre, caused heads to turn when she popped in to one of the Mayor's Festival Luncheons at the Guildhall, stopping long enough to chat with the Bishop of Gloucester, the Rt Revd Basil Guy, and to sign autographs before leaving.

The centenary of the birth of Vaughan Williams was commemorated at Worcester in 1972 by a Sunday evening concert in which Sir Adrian Boult conducted the CBSO and soloists Jennifer Vyvyan and John Shirley-Quirk in the *Five Mystical Songs*, *Tallis Fantasia*, and *A Sea Symphony*. Ursula Vaughan Williams and Hugh Ottaway contributed essays on R.V.W. to the programme book. 'The depths in Vaughan Williams's music are visionary and intuitive,' wrote Ottaway, going on to praise his vitality, freshness and the force of his personality. 'Vaughan Williams will always appeal most keenly to listeners with an ear for the Englishness of English music; but those who only hear the Englishness, whether admirers or detractors, have failed to get to grips with the substance of his work.' During the week, Vaughan Williams's Mass in G minor and *Serenade to Music* were also given.

There was something akin to that peculiarly English institution, the 'Prom', at the Monday evening concert given by the RPO conducted by Meredith Davies and with the cellist Thomas Igloi. This was actually advertised as a 'Promenade Concert' and tickets for the promenade area in the side aisles were sold for a nominal 40p. The experiment was a partial success – but so many people wanted to sit that there was very little space for those who chose to stand. No matter, standing or sitting, the cathedral was crowded to capacity. In his programme book article, Michael Kennedy described the four works given as 'Passionate Pilgrimages': Mendelssohn's overture *Fingal's Cave*, the *Walk to the Paradise Garden* by Delius, Walton's Cello Concerto, and a luminous and eloquent account of the Symphony No. 2 in E flat by Elgar. 'In the mastery and certainty of its orchestration,' wrote Kennedy, 'in the emotional range of its expressive content, Elgar's Second Symphony remains one of the most searching musical experiences, incomparably described by its creator as "the passionate pilgrimage of the soul".'

Two new works were given their first performance on Tuesday: in the afternoon recital by the three cathedral choirs, John Joubert's *Three Office Hymns of St Oswald* conducted by John Sanders; and in the evening, *Voyage* by John McCabe, with Jane Manning, Meriel Dickinson, Charles Brett, Brian Rayner Cook, the chorus and RPO conducted by Christopher Robinson. 'It was natural,' wrote Kenneth Loveland in *The Times*, 'that the festival should return to McCabe after *Notturni ed Alba* (Hereford 1970), the best new work heard at the Three Choirs in recent years':

> This time a large-scale choral work has resulted. *Voyage* is about the legendary search of St Brendan for the promised land, a seven-year journey which makes him a kind of coracle-born flying Irishman.
> Monica Smith's libretto reduces the story to manageable lengths, but retains the Celtic romanticism, twilight fancies and rather endearing belief in the unbelievable. There are quotations from the song of Taliesin, Marcus Aurelius and Shakespeare. McCabe translates all this into a similarly evocative score, generously endowed with glittering percussion sounds (maracas, marimbas, vibrophones) appropriately permeated with the touch of the visionary . . . and generally matching the picturesque with the picturesque . . . One hopes that he has a return ticket; there is much in *Voyage* that is exciting and deserving of an early repeat performance.[11]

Brian Rayner Cook, taking the part of St Brendan, was making the first of his many Three Choirs appearances. The work received a prolonged ovation punctuated by shouts of 'Bravo!' – the urgent spirit of applause had finally escaped completely from its dusty bottle. Even so, and surprisingly, *Voyage*, still awaits its second Three Choirs sailing.

Kenneth Loveland, who pointed out that the choral writing in *Voyage*, richly varied with some moments of hysterical whispering and speech, was in the manner of Penderecki, had previously drawn attention to the position of Jonathan Harvey's *Ludus Amoris* in a continuing tradition extending from Bach through to Penderecki in that the crowd is a strong vocal participant in the evolution of Harvey's narrative. The involvement of 'spoken whisperings rising to a hysterical crescendo and the fragmentary string writing and percussion textures' in *Ludus Amoris* seemed similarly reminiscent of Penderecki's *St Luke Passion*.

The first opportunity for Three Choirs audiences actually to hear the music of Krysztof Penderecki came at the 1972(W) Festival: an excellent performance of the *Stabat Mater*, written in 1962. 'Had it been heard a few years earlier,' wrote Loveland, 'the line of descent of more than one new work heard {at Three Choirs} might have been apparent . . . In its immediacy and clarity the performance spoke volumes for the preparation with which Christopher Robinson had invested it.'[12]

To celebrate the seventieth birthday of Lennox Berkeley, Three Choirs commissioned from him a short orchestral work, *Voices of the Night*, which was played by the CBSO under the composer's direction at the Hereford Festival in 1973 at the start of an orchestral concert which also included the Schumann Cello Concerto in A minor (with

Christopher Van Kampen) and Elgar's First Symphony, both conducted by Andrew Davis.

Other new works in 1973(H) included the first Festival commission from Geoffrey Burgon, *The Fire of Heaven*, given by the three cathedral choirs conducted by Richard Lloyd; and *Let there be Light*! by Bryan Kelly, a setting of the first chapter of the Book of Genesis:

> Such is the pace of technological progress that Mr Kelly manages to despatch the whole of creation in 25 minutes, as against Haydn's two hours.
>   That he is able to do this is due partly to the employment of a narrator [Gabriel Woolf] in addition to chorus, orchestra and soprano soloist [Jennifer Vyvyan] and partly to the lack of expansion of the musical ideas.[13]

Let there be Light! was accompanied by the RPO, again conducted by Richard Lloyd.

Two tenors for long associated with Three Choirs made their first appearances in 1973: Neil Jenkins and David Johnston.

Jennifer Vyvyan sang at Three Choirs for the last time on the evening of Thursday, 23 August 1973, with Richard Lewis and the RPO, in the first performance in England of the *Te Deum* by Bizet, conducted by John Sanders, and also, appropriately, in *Hymnus Paradisi*, again with Richard Lewis and conducted by Richard Lloyd. Music was robbed of that lovely voice only seven months later by her untimely death at the age of forty-nine.

Richard Lloyd had begun the 1973 Festival with *Elijah*, not given in Three Choirs at Hereford since 1914; he ended the week with *The Apostles*, unheard there for a decade longer. Wendy Eathorne and Marjorie Thomas sang in both works, joined by David Johnston with Raimund Herincx in *Elijah*, and Alexander Young, John Carol Case, David Thomas and Roger Stalman in *The Apostles*.

In 1974 Richard Lloyd was appointed organist of Durham Cathedral, and in 1985 became deputy headmaster of Salisbury Cathedral School, remaining there until 1988 when ill health forced his retirement. In 1974, too, Christopher Robinson left Worcester to go to Windsor as Organist and Master of the Choristers of St George's Chapel. In 1986 he received the honour LVO, and in 1991 was appointed organist of St John's College, Cambridge.

Throughout the 1960s and '70s a notable feature of the Festival was the steadily increasing number and variety of events held in venues outside the cathedrals: song and chamber music recitals, exhibitions and displays, poetry readings, lectures and discussion groups – too numerous and diverse to describe in detail. This has remained the pattern for the modern Festival. Typically, in 1974(G) audience choices included a chamber concert at the Gloucestershire College of Education in which Ralph Holmes (violin) and Gillian Weir (harpsichord) performed works by Bach; another chamber concert two days later given by the Georgian String Quartet at Prinknash Abbey and devoted to Haydn's *The Seven Last Words of Our Saviour on the Cross*, Op. 51; and an afternoon concert in Tewkesbury Abbey given by the Academy of the BBC conducted by Meredith Davies including, among works by Mozart, Elgar, Weber and Beethoven, the Symphonies for Chamber Orchestra, Op. 11 by Gordon Crosse, written in 1964 for the Orchestra da Camera.

To celebrate the centenary of the birth of Gustav Holst in 1974 his daughter Imogen gave a lecture entitled 'Holst in Gloucestershire' in the Gloucestershire College of Education. Her father, she said, had been grateful to the Three Choirs for giving first performances of some of his works. Not all his visits to the Festival were happy occasions, sometimes standards had been disappointing, but there had also been some very good performances. An example was Holst's motet *Evening Watch*, first performed at Gloucester in 1925. There was, too, his great *Choral Fantasia*, composed at the request of Herbert Sumsion and hated by most people when first unveiled at Gloucester in 1931. This, *The Planets Suite* and the *Hymn of Jesus* were given at the 1974(G) Festival. Of the *Choral Fantasia* Imogen Holst said: 'It is my father's best "thank you" to Gloucestershire for having given him his life. It is also the nearest he came to his own ideal of a tender austerity.'[14]

New works at the 1974 Gloucester Festival included two Festival commissions: Wilfred Josephs' overture, *The Four Horsemen of the Apocalypse*, Op. 86 and *The Temple*, an unaccompanied triptych by Philip Cannon. There was also the first public performance of Christopher Steel's *Paradise Lost*.

Wilfred Josephs had predicted that *The Four Horsemen of the Apocalypse* might be his noisiest work – and so it proved: 'At the end there were decibel-battered eardrums and protesting echoes to prove the point.'[15] It was the first item in a concert given by the CBSO under Louis Frémaux which also included Saint-Saëns' Symphony No. 3 in C minor (with Ralph Downes at the organ) and Holst's suite, *The Planets*.

'With *The Temple*,' wrote Robert Henderson, 'Philip Cannon confirmed his reputation as one of the most accomplished of our choral composers':

> The text by the 17th-century poet George Herbert had the advantage of combining simplicity of language with precise, yet evocative imagery, making them particularly amenable to musical setting. And Cannon seized upon every inflection of this imagery with an admirable blend of discretion and imaginative tact.[16]

Although *The Temple* was well received by critics and public alike, it was the unwitting cause of John Sanders' closest brush with 'industrial action' by the Gloucester contingent of the Festival Chorus. Anxious to lighten the load on his singers, Sanders decided that the choral concert in the afternoon preceding the première of *The Temple*, a performance of the Monteverdi Vespers of 1610, would be given by a semi-chorus from Worcester and Hereford only. The evening concert, which included Bononcini's *Stabat Mater* and Holst's *Choral Fantasia* in addition to *The Temple*, was allotted to a semi-chorus from Gloucester only. Far from being delighted about his equitable distribution of the workload, angry voices were raised among the Gloucester contingent that they were being prevented from singing in the Monteverdi – and John Sanders was the unhappy recipient of a petition of protest against the imagined injustice!

The Guest of Honour at the 1974(G) Festival was Herbert Howells. Presenting him – at the Festival Garden Party – with a wine glass especially engraved by Mr Geoffrey Frith, John Sanders described Dr Howells as 'one of England's greatest living musicians, and one of the best loved. We thank him', he said, 'for all he has done to enrich this Festival.' At a Gloucester Literary Luncheon Club meeting on the next day, Howells said that he was tempted to accuse Gloucester of showing insensibility to one of his greatest friends, Ivor Gurney:

It would be most ungracious of me if I accused Gloucester of this, because I know the city has its deep interests, and has lived up to most of them throughout its long history.

But some day this city and all its music lovers, and lovers of culture of any kind, have got to remember that remarkable man. I do hope – and I hope to see it before I die – that Gloucester really turns its face to Ivor Gurney.[17]

Happily, Herbert Howells lived just long enough to see a re-awakening of interest in Ivor Gurney as both composer and major poet; an interest which has spread far beyond the City of Gloucester and which shows no sign of waning.

In January 1975 Donald Hunt succeeded Christopher Robinson as Organist and Master of the Choristers at Worcester Cathedral. Born at Gloucester, Hunt was a cathedral chorister there and was educated at the King's School. Articled to Herbert Sumsion, he became assistant organist at the cathedral in 1947 at the age of seventeen, remaining there until 1954 when he went to Torquay as organist at St John's Church. In 1957 he was appointed Director of Music at Leeds Parish Church – a post he held for seventeen years. In Yorkshire, Hunt was soon involved with the great West Riding choral tradition, becoming conductor of the Halifax Choral Society; the Leeds Philharmonic Society (following Sir Malcolm Sargent); and Associate Conductor and Chorus Master of the Leeds Festival. In 1971 he founded the Yorkshire Sinfonia Orchestra and in 1972 was appointed Leeds City Organist – the post having lapsed for over fifty years. In his years at Leeds he taught harmony and counterpoint at the Leeds College of Music and became well known as an adjudicator and recitalist. In May 1975 he received the degree of Doctor of Music, *honoris causa*, from the University of Leeds, for services to music in Leeds and Yorkshire. Three months later he directed his first Worcester Festival.

From the beginning, Donald Hunt has imprinted his own authority upon the Festival, along with a determined blend of vigorous energy, ambitious dynamism, and stubbornness in the pursuit of self-imposed standards. From the beginning, too, his affinity with the music of Elgar, gained at one-remove by Herbert Sumsion's side, was manifest in an instinctive feel for an authentic Elgarian style, and it was with the march composed by Elgar for the coronation of King George V that Hunt began the Opening Service of the 1975(W) Festival.

When the civic and ecclesiastical dignitaries had taken their places the traditional act of worship began with the playing of the Meditation from Elgar's *The Light of Life*. 'It was', said A.T. Shaw, 'impossible to escape the feeling that the Order of the Service had been planned to take our minds off the "Pomp and Circumstance" inseparable from civic participation in the event, and to fix our thoughts upon love as a principle of life.'[18] The *Te Deum* of Verdi; selected readings from Coleridge, Hadow and Ruskin; and Vaughan Williams's *Serenade to Music* confirmed the mood.

Almost inevitably, it seemed, Hunt chose *The Dream of Gerontius* for his first concert of the Festival – a rapturous performance in which he conducted the Festival Chorus, the Worcester Cathedral Choir and the CBSO, with Alfreda Hodgson, David Galliver and Michael Rippon.

On the morning of the second day a brass band was heard for the first time in Worcester Cathedral: the Great Universal Stores Footwear Band under their conductor Stanley Boddington, and Ifor James (horn) gave a recital which included the first complete performance of McCabe's *Goddess Trilogy*. In the evening the cathedral was again crowded for Beethoven's *Missa Solemnis* given by the RPO and the Festival Chorus conducted by Donald Hunt, with soloists Anne Conoley, Janet Hughes, John Mitchinson and Raimund Herincx.

On Tuesday afternoon in Perrins Hall at the Worcester Royal Grammar School, the Music Group of London and Ian Partridge (surely the natural successor to Wilfred Brown) gave a recital which included the première of *Severnside*, a song-cycle in four seasons for tenor voice and string quartet – settings of four poems by Mary Dawson which were published for the first time in the programme book.

Settings for soprano, choir and orchestra by Richard Rodney Bennett of six poems by Kathleen Raine, under the title *Spells*, received their first performance by Jane Manning, to whom the work is dedicated, on Thursday evening. 'Unmistakably a major addition to the English choral repertory,' wrote Martin Cooper. 'The choral and orchestral writing is precisely conceived to make a maximum impact and the RPO and Festival Chorus under Donald Hunt achieved an admirably disciplined and strongly characterised performance.'[19]

Richard Rodney Bennett's strong representation in the programme earned him the appellation Festival Composer 1975. His Piano Concerto, dedicated to Stephen Bishop-Kovacevich, was played by Malcolm Binns at the Wednesday evening orchestral concert given by the CBSO under Louis Frémaux, and this was followed by a late-night entertainment in the Swan Theatre featuring Richard Rodney Bennett and Marion Montgomery. The next afternoon in his organ recital at Pershore Abbey, Christopher Robinson played Bennett's *Alba* (1973) in a programme which also included works by Messiaen, *L'Ascension*, and Frank Martin, *Passecaille*. Messiaen was again represented in the Friday morning recital given by the three cathedral choirs:

> Donald Hunt gave us a memorable performance of Messiaen's *Trois Petites Liturgies de la Présence Divine*. The choristers of the three cathedrals and the strings of the R.P.O. with piano played by Keith Swallow, Ondes Martinot operated by John Morton, and percussion, obtained effects of the utmost loveliness in a performance which is in my opinion the highlight of the festival.
>
> Over and again as the music revealed fresh aspects of the composer's sensibility and as the choristers astonished us by the brilliance of their singing I found myself wishing that a performance of such outstanding quality could have been recorded.[20]

Frank Martin's *Requiem* was written a year before his death in 1974 and received its first performance in this country under John Sanders at the 1975 Worcester Festival in the presence of Madame Maria Martin, the composer's widow. The soloists with the RPO and Festival Chorus were Jane Manning, Jean Allister, Neil Jenkins and Michael Rippon. 'It is,' wrote Martin Cooper, 'anything but a work of consolation and remains, from its uncomfortable opening almost to the end, full of the mediaeval fear of death and the final reckoning.'[21]

Earlier in this same concert Neil Jenkins and Michael Rippon had sung in a good, strong performance of Vaughan Williams's *Sancta Civitas* under the baton of the new man at Hereford – Roy Massey.

Born in Birmingham in 1934, Roy Massey was educated at Moseley Grammar School in that city, and received his musical education at the University of Birmingham and under David Willcocks at Worcester. While still a student he became accompanist and organist to the City of Birmingham Choir, and worked closely with David Willcocks, Meredith Davies and Christopher Robinson. He was organist of St Alban-the-Martyr, Bordesley, Birmingham, 1953–60, and of St Augustine's, Edgbaston, Birmingham, 1960–5. He then became Warden of the Royal School of Church Music at Addington Palace, Croydon, a post held concurrently with that of organist of Croydon Parish Church. He returned to Birmingham as organist of the cathedral in 1968, and in 1974 took up his present appointment at Hereford. In 1991 he received the Lambeth degree of Doctor of Music.

The 1976 Hereford Festival marked not only Roy Massey's Three Choirs début as Director, but also the first Festival appearances of three outstanding soloists: Felicity Lott, Anthony Rolfe Johnson and Stephen Roberts, two of whom took part in Massey's first concert on Sunday evening – a confident reaching-back to Handel's epic oratorio of 1738, *Israel in Egypt*, receiving only its second Three Choirs performance since the beginning of the century. The soloists were Honor Sheppard, Felicity Lott, Margaret Cable, Neil Jenkins, David Thomas and Stephen Roberts, with Donald Hunt (organ), Roger Judd (harpsichord), the Festival Chorus and CBSO.

On Tuesday there was an evening of all-French music. Donald Hunt conducted Poulenc's *Stabat Mater* (with Wendy Eathorne) and Saint-Saëns's Symphonic Poem, *La Jeunesse d'Hercule*; and Massey conducted the *Requiem* of Maurice Duruflé, with Wendy Eathorne, Alfreda Hodgson and Michael Rippon. The orchestra was the RPO. Among a number of Festival commissions and new works, by far the most important was the first performance on Thursday evening of the *Requiem* by Geoffrey Burgon, with Janet Price (a late substitute for Felicity Palmer), Kevin Smith and Anthony Rolfe Johnson, the Festival Chorus and RPO conducted by Roy Massey.

At about the time of writing *The Fire of Heaven* for the 1973(H) Festival, in which he used the serenely mystical poetry of Thomas Traherne, Geoffrey Burgon had discovered the poetry of the sixteenth-century Carmelite friar, St John of the Cross, and his first setting was the 1974 Cheltenham Festival commission, *Noche oscura*. With the *Requiem* of 1976 Burgon reached the culmination of his interest in St John of the Cross's poetry, combining it with the standard liturgical text of the requiem to create his largest-scale work to date.

'It is not a mass in any sense,' said Burgon, who has expressed a horror of organized religion, 'but sets out to convey the concept of requiem by the dual idea of eternity "experienced" during life and after death.' As in several of Burgon's works, dreams played a part in the inspiration for the turbulent *Dies Irae*, omitted from his original conception.

In contrast to the *Requiem* of Frank Martin, full of tortured fear and lacking any trace of serenity, that of Geoffrey Burgon is entirely consolatory. 'The heart of the work', wrote Hugo Cole, 'lies in the serene and contemplative setting of the poems by St John of the Cross, in which the sense of timelessness and unity are matched by music that is often transparent, quiet, slow almost to the point of stasis.'[22]

> I entered in, I know not where,
> And I remained, though knowing naught,
> Transcending knowledge with my thought.

The 1976 Hereford Festival ended with *The Dream of Gerontius*:

David Johnston brought to the name-part a sense of urgency and passion that was not dispersed or lost in the high-vaulted spaces of the great cathedral. Roy Massey took the music as freely and expansively as even Elgar himself could have wished.

The Hereford semi-chorus sounded truly angelic. Clear, well-tuned, steady singing was needed, and was provided, and the Cathedral did the rest.[23]

Notes

1. A.T. Shaw, *Hereford Evening News*, 6 September 1966
2. *Hereford Evening News*, 7 September 1967
3. *The Times*, 7 September 1967
4. Ibid.
5. *Hereford Times*, 30 August 1969
6. Worcester Festival programme book, 1969, p. 60
7. *The Times*, 28 August 1969
8. *Sunday Times*, 29 August 1971
9. *The Citizen*, 24 August 1971
10. *The Citizen*, 19 August 1971
11. *The Times*, 31 August 1972
12. *The Times*, 2 September 1972
13. *Daily Telegraph*, 21 August 1973
14. *The Citizen*, 20 August 1974
15. *The Times*, 19 August 1974
16. *Daily Telegraph*, 24 August 1974
17. *The Citizen*, 21 August 1974
18. *Worcester Journal*, 28 August 1975
19. *Daily Telegraph*, 30 August 1975
20. A.T. Shaw, *Worcester Evening News*, 30 August 1975
21. *Daily Telegraph*, 28 August 1975
22. *Country Life*, 16 September 1976, p. 730
23. Ibid.

CHAPTER TWENTY

JUBILEE

It was a double celebration: the silver jubilee of Her Majesty the Queen and, accepting Sir Ivor Atkins's dating of Three Choirs from 1715, the commemoration of two hundred and fifty years of music-making in Gloucester, Hereford and Worcester. In that same year Edinburgh was mounting only its thirty-first Festival and Cheltenham its thirty-third. Six orchestras, more than thirty soloists, seven conductors, instrumental and choral groups, and a Festival extending over eight days from 20 to 28 August; a strong Commonwealth flavour with performers from Australia, New Zealand and Canada; documentaries of Three Choirs broadcast on radio and television; new works from Harrison Birtwistle, Peter Maxwell Davies, Rory Boyle, Ronald Tremain and Tony Hewitt-Jones; and the centrepiece – a large choral composition from Malcolm Williamson, Master of the Queen's Musick, *Mass of Christ the King*, dedicated to the queen for her jubilee: an ambitious musical feast for the 1977 Gloucester Festival.

The programme had been planned to feature the music of composers who have had a major influence on the Festival during its long history: Bach's Mass in B minor; the Verdi *Requiem*; Kodály's *Jesus and the Traders*; *Messiah*; *The Hymn of Jesus*; Vaughan Williams's *Tallis Fantasia*; Beethoven's Choral Fantasia; Britten's *Cantata Academica* and *Missa Brevis*; Penderecki's *Stabat Mater*; and, of course, Elgar – the Cello Concerto, *Caractacus* and *Gerontius*. Herbert Howells was present to hear *Hymnus Paradisi* and had been commissioned to write a *Festival Fanfare* for the Opening Service, during which the first performance of Tony Hewitt-Jones's anthem *Let us now praise famous men* was also given. A wide sweep of musical history was embraced, from French medieval ballads, secular and sacred music of the English Renaissance and anthems by Victoria, Schütz and Gabrieli, to sounds with the freshness of paint: Peter Maxwell Davies's *A Mirror of Whitening Light* and Harrison Birtwistle's *Silbury Air*, both played in a Contemporary Music Network concert by the London Sinfonietta.

An early disappointment had been the necessity to exclude from the programme the first performance of Richard Rodney Bennett's suite, *The Christians*, based upon his music for the television series of the same name, due to Bennett's inability to complete the composition in time for the Festival. But there were early hints that there might also be problems with Malcolm Williamson's Mass.

Australian-born Malcolm Williamson has lived in England since 1953. A pupil of Sir Eugene Goossens at the Sydney Conservatorium, he studied piano there under Alexander Sverjensky, as well as french horn and violin. In London, struggling to make ends meet, he worked as a nightclub pianist and organist at a Limehouse church. He studied composition with Erwin Stern and Elisabeth Lutyens, and Benjamin Britten helped him to get his first piano sonata published. Sir Adrian Boult introduced his music to Three Choirs in 1969(W): the overture, *Santiago d'Espada*, composed in 1957 and dedicated to Boult.

In 1965 Williamson was one of four young composers commissioned to write an opera for Sadlers Wells and the result, his fifth opera, *The Violins of Saint-Jacques*, was produced with great success in 1966; but a success tinged with the pain of personal tragedy: the death some months earlier of a baby daughter.

Williamson's considerable output includes not only operas, symphonies, concertos, orchestral works, chamber music, piano and organ pieces but also, believing passionately as he does that music should be for everybody, church music in a pop-song style and little mini-operas, which he calls 'cassations', for performance by handicapped children. A remarkable man whose brilliance is framed by compassion, Williamson is master of six languages, has doctorates in medicine and psychology, and has held a university fellowship researching the problems of handicapped children.

Sir Arthur Bliss died in March 1975 and Williamson was appointed Master of the Queen's Musick in his place. Pressures both personal and professional began to increase.

When the writer Paul Jennings visited him for a *Radio Times* interview prior to a BBC2 broadcast of *The Violins of Saint-Jacques* (6 November 1976), he found that Williamson had been up all night working on the *Mass of Christ the King*:

> Malcolm Williamson is a man utterly without the mask that most men (let alone creative artists) present to the world. His thoughts flash and subside, with sparks of allusion, tailings-off, recurrent grand central themes, darting side-flashes of wit, like a turning bird's wing in his own music, particularly in its Messiaen moods.

Williamson is a Roman Catholic.

> 'Messiaen said "Je suis musicien surtout catholique", and that's what I am: I became a Catholic when I was 20 – it was terrible, I can't imagine any other idea of life . . .
> 'Come and look at this: I was struggling with it last night.' On the piano was the Kyrie of a Mass of Christ the King . . .
> 'The Feast of Christ the King was only created in modern times. I'm very interested in it: what we need is this gentle authority of God. See: the soprano calls out, higher each time, above the choir, *Kyrie Eleison*, have mercy on us – come on, you're in a choir: let's have a go. . . .'[1]

At the beginning of March 1977 a Press Conference was called at the offices of the Arts Council in Piccadilly to give details of the Gloucester Festival; Williamson had been invited to speak. He arrived late and, to the astonishment of the organizers and the relish of the Press, launched into a bitter attack against the Arts Council which had 'totally rejected' his application for a £5,000 commissioning fee for *Mass of Christ the King*. Major articles appeared in all the leading papers the next day.

> 'My feelings towards the Arts Council in regard to this are of total disgust because of their lack of support. I asked for £5,000 and got nothing . . . It is simply one more humiliation in a long list of

humiliations I have suffered from the Arts Council over a great many years . . . A lot of the humiliation has been of the verbal kind, and it would certainly be denied by the people who luxuriate in this form of insult to composers. I think this is felt by many composers.'

It was, he claimed, an unhappy fact that both the BBC and the Arts Council instituted 'reprisals' against people who spoke out against them.

'The lack of financial support for me to write this composition has impeded work on it very much. I hope somehow the difficulties will be solved and that it will be possible for the work to be presented. At the moment I have serious doubts about it . . . Given the concentration that goes into it, one is receiving less than a bus conductor gets pro rata.

'But what sustains me is the distinction of the occasion and the fact that one has the honour of having Her Majesty the Queen graciously accepting the dedication.'

He had only been able to undertake the work because the Johnson Wax company had promised £2,000, to be paid after completion. The firm's ultimate contribution would be £3,500, including printing costs. The Royal Philharmonic Orchestra had lent him £1,000 to enable him to proceed.

Mr Williamson said he had been speaking 'very much for the senior composers, many of whom who had knighthoods and other distinctions and had to behave like English gentlemen when applying for financial help.

'There is, of course, this vexed Anglo-Saxon habit of glossing over matters concerning money.'[2]

Here, of course, was all the stuff of a good gossip story: the Master of the Queen's Musick denouncing the Arts Council and the BBC for their lack of artistic support for his work and insisting that both organizations had taken reprisals against composers who had displeased them – points pursued by the *Evening Standard* in the 'Londoner's Diary' column later in the day of the Arts Council Press Conference:

'I have certainly encountered this in the past,' [Williamson] told me today. 'At the BBC there was the case of some lost tapes of mine. Afterwards when I complained, I was told my performance was below standard and my criticism was deplorable. In fact the work has never been broadcast.

'People who I have spoken to today who have been on the receiving end of reprisals have pleaded with me not to be named. Nevertheless I cannot retract the statement. Composers, orchestral bodies, Festivals are conditioned to dumb acceptance of the Arts Council verdicts.'

John Cruft, Music Director of the Arts Council, says: 'I am sorry Malcolm Williamson did not discuss with me the things troubling him rather than astonishing a gathering in this building who had come to hear about plans for the 250th Three Choirs Festival.'

Williamson again: 'Mr Cruft's assumption that I will starve and behave like a good little boy to protect the Arts Council's anonymity and at the same time write an enormous work is very unhelpful.'[3]

If Williamson had wished to make the maximum impact he could not have chosen a more telling time and place to make his protest. Under the title 'Just how much is a composer worth?' a lengthy article by Peta Levi appeared in the next edition of the *Sunday Times*. Triggered by Williamson's attack on the Arts Council, it contained an investigation into the hazards and rewards of composers, exposing the pitiful level of commission fees in this country. The article also revealed that in the following July, Williamson would be doing a tour in America – 'time he can ill afford since he has three years of composition to do in one'.[4] Inevitably, lack of funds forced him to accept too many commitments.

Malcolm Williamson was able to keep his bowl upright in 1977, subsidizing himself by taking on the music for the film of Richard Adams's *Watership Down*. This on top of a twenty-minute jubilee mini-opera to be performed by thousands of schoolchildren in the queen's presence in the Liverpool streets on 21 June; an LPO commission for a symphony to be performed at a Royal Jubilee concert on 8 December; the *Mass of Christ the King* in Gloucester on 28 August; *and* the American tour in July.

By the end of July 1977 John Sanders knew that the *Mass* would not be finished in time. There was no problem with the vocal score – prepared in three parts and separately colour-coded: red, white and blue – the last portion of which was received two weeks before the Festival. The orchestration was another matter.

One week before the Festival, John Sanders was in London for an orchestral rehearsal of the Mass with the RPO; the parts had still not arrived and he was obliged to fill in with *Gerontius*. Half-way through the rehearsal a taxi pulled up and Simon Campion, Williamson's assistant, rushed in with orchestral parts for about two-thirds of the work. Back in Gloucester, more of the orchestral score continued to arrive piecemeal, by train, day by day.

Even more hair-raising, on the very day of the performance Malcolm Williamson himself arrived in Gloucester with additional missing parts and went into retreat in a feverish attempt to complete the orchestration. An eleventh-hour rehearsal was called, during which the drip-feed of manuscript continued apace until, out of time, Sanders at last called a halt. The performance went ahead minus the *Gloria* and *Credo*; the responsorial psalm for solo tenor and orchestra, although fully scored, also had to be omitted, a casualty of Sanders' deadline. One other movement, the *Agnus Dei*, dedicated with the queen's permission to Benjamin Britten who had died the previous December, was performed with organ accompaniment. To compensate for the missing sections of the *Mass*, Sanders revised the programme of the concert to include a repeat of Howells's *Festival Fanfare*; Elgar's arrangement of the National Anthem; and two anthems composed by Handel for the coronation of King George II in 1727: *Zadok the Priest* and *The King shall Rejoice*.

In spite of such an inauspicious genesis, the incomplete *Mass of Christ the King* was received with considerable critical acclaim as a work containing some of the composer's most remarkable music. Ronald Crichton in the *Financial Times* was 'impatient to hear the whole work as soon as possible'[5]; and in a thoughtful review for *The Times*, William Mann said that 'It would be idle to assess *Mass of Christ the King* until it is performed complete. I can only assure those readers who spurn Williamson's simplistic music (its invention all the stronger because it has to be instantly performable) that the new Mass is an elaborate composition, grand and often surprising, for all that the choral music draws on ecclesiastical traditions, especially on plainsong. It makes a jubilant and variegated noise, approachable yet demanding concentration . . . The solo vocal music, such as we heard of it, gave uplifting scope to April Cantelo's easy, pure high tones and Philip Langridge's fluent melifluous tenor. Loris Synan . . . displayed an impressive high mezzo register.'[6] The bass part was ably taken by Geoffrey Chard.

John Sanders, in spite of all the heart-stopping tensions of the previous weeks, had steered Williamson's work to success and shown it to be worthy of the effort. 'Sometimes it could be sensed', wrote William Mann:

that balance was imperfect, the chorus slow to blaze, the orchestra battling bravely but tentatively, the conductor determined of spirit if he could not obtain at short notice real accuracy. It would be a pity if these forces were deprived of the glory of the work's first integral performance.[7]

On the next evening Sanders, the Festival Chorus and RPO were on *terra firma* once more and granted their reward in a sublime performance of *Gerontius*: Maureen Guy a radiant, warm-voiced Angel; Ian Comboy a superbly dark-toned bass-baritone; and Robert Tear at the peak of his powers, and filling the cathedral with thrilling sound at 'Take me away . . .' – magnificent.

On Saturday afternoon Donald Hunt conducted the three cathedral choirs and the Orchestra of St John's, Smith Square, in an exemplary performance of *Messiah*, with Felicity Lott, Paul Esswood, Anthony Rolfe Johnson and Stephen Roberts. And there was more glorious singing on Saturday evening: Dame Janet Baker and John Mitchinson, accompanied by the CBSO under Louis Frémaux, in Mahler's *Das Lied von der Erde*.

The extended Festival continued into Sunday 28 August: in the afternoon, a concert by the Orchestra of St John's, Smith Square, conducted by John Lubbock at the Pittville Pump Room, Cheltenham. The final concert was given in the cathedral by the CBSO and the Festival Chorus. John Sanders conducted a repeat performance of Tony Hewitt-Jones's Festival anthem, and Beethoven's Fantasia in C, in which Anthony Peebles was the pianist. Donald Hunt took charge of performances of Britten's *Cantata Academica* (with Felicity Lott, Jean Allister, Anthony Rolfe Johnson and Brian Rayner Cook) and Poulenc's Organ Concerto (with Roy Massey). And John Sanders brought the Festival to a close with Dvořák's *Te Deum*, first introduced to Three Choirs at Worcester in 1899. But before the vast audience dispersed everyone joined in the singing of Vaughan Williams's setting of the Old Hundredth – a stirring climax to a memorable week.

After every Festival, memories of performances and works jostle each other for favoured status in the mind. But some concerts are not simply remembered – they are impossible to forget, and one feels a sense of privilege at having been present. For this writer two memories of the 1977(G) Festival have this indelible quality. Firstly, and in spite of the wholly inappropriate setting (the Gloucester Leisure Centre), Brian Rayner Cook's inspired singing in *Caractacus*. The other, a recital of English music at Prinknash Abbey: songs by Vaughan Williams, C.W. Orr, Ivor Gurney, and Herbert Howells – who sat in a monk's stall, head up, eyes closed in concentration and perhaps thanksgiving as Gloucestershire paid tribute to its own. Angela Malsbury played the Clarinet Sonata by Bax and Finzi's Five Bagatelles; and then at the end the tenor soloist, David Johnston, was joined by his young son, Nicholas, and the pianist David Pettit in Benjamin Britten's canticle *Abraham and Isaac*. Here was perfect balance: music and place; innocence and experience.

Donald Hunt's obvious enthusiasm for French music was given full rein at the 1978 Worcester Festival: the overture *Le Carnival Romain* by Berlioz; Debussy's *Nocturnes*; and *Chant des Captifs* by Jean Martinon were all heard on Monday evening in a RPO and Festival Chorus concert conducted by Hunt, with Meryl Drower, Neil Jenkins and Michael Rippon, ending with a sizzling performance of Walton's *Belshazzar's Feast* – linked to the Martinon piece by the common use in part of the same text: Psalm 136. Messiaen was represented on Tuesday by *Trois Petites Liturgies de la Présence Divine*, and on Wednesday by *L'Ascension*. Simon Preston's organ recital on Thursday was given over to Messiaen's *La Nativité du Seigneur*, and earlier in the afternoon, a century after its composition, the first complete British performance of the *Requiem Mass*, Op. 54 by Saint-Saëns.

Compared with Malcolm Williamson's financial struggles in 1977, Saint-Saëns one hundred years earlier seems to have been provided for by a providential hand. Whit Sunday 1877 brought the death of the French Postmaster-General, Saint-Saëns' friend Albert Libon. In his will Libon left Saint-Saëns a legacy of 100,000 francs 'intended to take him away from the servitude of the organ at La Madeleine to allow him to devote himself entirely to composition'. In return Libon asked only that Saint-Saëns compose a requiem to his memory, though a codicil, dictated only hours before his death, removed this condition which, he suggested, 'revealed a sentiment of vanity'. Even so, Saint-Saëns felt an obligation to complete the work and in the spring of 1878 left Paris for Berne in search of quietness – again, a commodity apparently denied to Williamson. In his Swiss hotel room Saint-Saëns conceived, wrote and orchestrated the entire Requiem within eight days. The first performance was given at Saint-Sulpice on 20 May 1878. Widor was at the organ and Saint-Saëns conducted. In Worcester the soloists were Jane Manning, Margaret Cable, Kenneth Bowen and David Thomas, with the Worcester Festival Chorus and the BBC Northern Symphony Orchestra (now the BBC Philharmonic) under Donald Hunt. A beautifully written and orchestrated work, the Requiem deserves to be heard more often.

Earlier, Sir Lennox Berkeley's *Magnificat* and *Voices of the Night* were heard. Berkeley, who was designated 'The Festival Composer', celebrated his seventy-fifth year in 1978. In recognition of this, performances of several of his works were featured at the Festival, including the première of the motet *Judica Me*, specially commissioned for the occasion.

Two guest conductors appeared at the Festival: Sir Charles Groves, who not only directed *Gerontius* on Sunday evening but also preached at the Opening Service earlier in the day, the first layman to do so; and the late Bryden Thomson, who conducted the BBC Northern Symphony Orchestra in music by Wagner, Messiaen and Elgar on Wednesday evening.

The concert on Tuesday evening, given by the three cathedral choirs and the BBC Northern Symphony Orchestra under Donald Hunt, began with Schubert's neglected Mass No. 3 in B flat, edited and published by Hunt in a new edition from the original manuscript in the British Museum. The programme also included Sir Lennox Berkeley's *Antiphon for String Orchestra*, conducted by the composer from memory – he had forgotten to bring his spectacles – and the première of Anthony Payne's *Ascensiontide* and *Whitsuntide* cantatas, Festival commissions funded by the Arts Council: two relatively brief pieces which served to complete a process, begun with the *Passiontide* cantata of 1974, whereby Payne had celebrated key festivals in the Christian year.

On Friday evening there was an all-Czech programme: Dvořák's setting of Psalm 149 and the *New World* Symphony, and Janáček's *Glagolitic Mass*, with Jane Manning, Maureen Guy, John Mitchinson and David Thomas, the CBSO, Worcester Cathedral Choir and Festival Chorus conducted by John Sanders.

Saturday was a day of startling contrast. In the afternoon, the British première of David Fanshawe's *African Sanctus*: the Worcester Chorus, cathedral choristers and the soprano Meryl Drower joined by an instrumental ensemble of piano, bass guitar, percussion and pre-recorded tape of frogs, war drums, death laments, marriage songs and the Islamic call for prayer. The Festival ended on Saturday evening with Mahler's

Symphony No. 8 in E flat, 'The Symphony of a Thousand', performed for the first time at Three Choirs.

In a Thursday morning lecture at the Swan Theatre, David Fanshawe had explained how he had dreamt of hearing his work in an English cathedral as he had watched tribal natives lamenting the death of a fisherman in a small mud hut on Lake Victoria. For five years he had hitch-hiked around Africa, collecting tapes of tribal music – a journey fraught with disasters, delays in jail and battles with wildlife. On one occasion he was recording a love song from a canoe when his paddle hit a hippopotamus on the head. The angry beast tossed him into the river along with his tape machine and twenty tapes, and he was chased to the river bank.

In the Sudan, Fanshawe heard of mountains that were thought to be like Paradise. After many weeks on a camel, fruitlessly searching for music, he heard a remarkable chanting on a mountain-top, and on hearing the music had lain down and wept. Four men were swaying from side to side on a prayer mat in a deep trance and Fanshawe managed to record them without their knowing that he had been there.

Africa came to Worcester in 'a blaze of sound and colour', wrote A.T. Shaw. 'The order of the day for the chorus was informal, wear as garish as possible.' Donald Hunt conducted in a red bush-shirt. 'Such was the enthusiasm aroused at the end of the work that applause continued until the conductor took the unprecedented step of repeating the setting of The Lord's Prayer.' And of the Mahler:

> In its long history the Three Choirs Festival has produced a fine crop of memorable performances, but nothing quite so astonishing, so thrilling, and so ultimately satisfying as the performance of Gustav Mahler's eighth symphony given under the direction of Donald Hunt on Saturday night . . .
>
> The soloists in this gigantic work were: Elizabeth Harwood, Jane Manning, Meryl Drower, Anne Collins, Maureen Guy, John Mitchinson, Norman Welsby and John Tomlinson. The important organ part was played by Paul Trepte . . .
>
> The soul-shattering sound generated by this immense ensemble made it possible to understand what Mahler meant when he said: 'Imagine the whole universe beginning to sing and resound . . .'
>
> The last day of this the best festival of the century was a heady affair. The stupendous Mahler, the ebullient David Fanshawe throwing carnations to the chorus, and even an encore were things to remember and striking enough. But it was for Donald Hunt that the cheers went up. It was unquestionably his day.[9]

That was not the end of music-making for the Three Choirs in 1978. Malcolm Williamson's *Mass of Christ the King* was performed for the first time in its entirety on Friday, 3 November 1978 in Westminster Cathedral. Sir Charles Groves conducted the RPO, the Three Choirs, together with Goldsmiths Choral Union, Elizabeth Connell, Philip Langridge and Brian Rayner Cook. Queen Elizabeth the Queen Mother attended the performance, welcomed by Cardinal Hume and Malcolm Williamson – an historic moment as a British queen set foot in an English Roman Catholic cathedral for the first time in four hundred years, and at the end she walked forward to thank Sir Charles and all who took part. 'The Music,' wrote William Mann, 'is characteristically eclectic in manner, its terms of reference ranging from plainsong to the neo-classic Stravinsky, via succulent Poulenc and austere Holstian harmony, with some piquant side-glances at Prokofiev's scoring. As a good Australian, Williamson selects at will, and then contrives that the finished product has his own personality to dominate the ingredients.'[10]

John Sanders included Williamson's *Mass* again in the 1986(G) Festival programme thanks to generous funding from Central Independent Television plc. From early in the 1960s Three Choirs had become increasingly dependent upon commercial sponsorship. Without the support of Johnson Wax Ltd, *Mass of Christ the King* is unlikely to have been completed or the first London performance to have taken place. As the *Daily Telegraph's* 'Mandrake' put it: 'Sponsorship of the arts by industry takes on a special glow with the news that Johnson Wax Ltd are subsidising the first full performance in Westminster Cathedral . . . of Malcolm Williamson's *Mass of Christ the King* . . . Long may it continue to shine.'

Notes

1. *Radio Times*, 31 October 1976
2. *Daily Telegraph*, 3 March 1977
3. *Evening Standard*, 3 March 1977
4. *Sunday Times*, 6 March 1977
5. *Financial Times*, 30 August 1977
6. *The Times*, 27 August 1977
7. Ibid.
8. *Worcestershire Evening News*, 4 September 1978
9. Ibid.
10. *The Times*, 6 November 1978

Chapter Twenty-One

THEME WITH VARIATIONS

F ollowing the extended Festival of 1977, Three Choirs at Gloucester and Worcester settled to an established eight-day pattern: a reception and a preliminary recital or concert on the first Saturday; the Opening Service on Sunday afternoon and a concert in the evening; and the last night on the following Saturday. At Hereford, where both the city and the cathedral are smaller than their sisters, the previously established six-day programme has been retained: the first concert is given on Sunday evening and the last on the following Friday. Not only is this a more modest programme in economic terms but there is much to be said, in the interests of maintaining the highest standards in fewer works, for freeing the chorus and organizers from the possibility of overstretching themselves.

At Worcester the Opening Service has, since 1984, been replaced by a Festival Dedication immediately preceding the Sunday evening concert: a change not universally welcomed.

The Monday evening concert at Hereford in 1979 began with a powerful performance of John Ireland's choral cantata *These Things Shall Be*, and Ireland's song cycle *The Land of Lost Content* was the central work in a recital by Ian and Jennifer Partridge on Tuesday afternoon, both marking the centenary of the composer's birth. In *These Things Shall Be* the soloist was Stephen Roberts, accompanied by the CBSO under Donald Hunt, taking over from John Sanders who had been prevented by illness from appearing at the Festival.

Also on Monday evening, Roy Massey conducted the cantata *This Worlde's Joie* by William Mathias, with Janet Price, Kenneth Bowen, Stephen Roberts, Robert Green (organ), the choristers of the three cathedrals, the Festival Chorus and the CBSO. Contemporary British music was again well represented in the Tuesday morning recital by the three cathedral choirs: an *Easter Sequence* by Kenneth Leighton, *Two Carols* by Richard Rodney Bennett, and Geoffrey Burgon's *At the Round Earth's Imagin'd Corners*.

Donald Hunt beckoned the Festival to France on Monday evening, conducting Poulenc's last major work, *Sept Répons des Ténèbres*. The soloist was Honor Sheppard, who also sang in the symphonic poem *King David* by the French-born Swiss composer Arthur Honegger, joining Margaret Cable and David Johnston, the Festival Chorus and CBSO under Roy Massey. The part of the Witch of Endor was taken by Elizabeth Evans, and the performance was further distinguished by the familiar voice of the popular broadcaster Richard Baker as the Narrator.

Of greater rarity was *Hymnus Amoris* by Carl Nielsen, given on Thursday evening by Julie Kennard, admirable in her first Three Choirs appearance, Brian Burrows, Stephen Roberts and David Thomas, the Festival Chorus and RPO conducted by Roy Massey. This was followed by the première of John Joubert's *Herefordshire Canticles*, a Festival commission repeated at Hereford in 1991 with the same soloists – Julie Kennard and Stephen Roberts, and again conducted by Massey.

A plea for peace and a condemnation of man's inhumanity to man are themes of Peter Maxwell Davies's opera *The Martyrdom of St Magnus*, commissioned by the BBC for the jubilee year of 1977 and included in the 1979 Hereford Festival – the first complete opera to be staged at Three Choirs. The production in the Nell Gwynne Theatre on Monday afternoon was given by The Fires of London conducted by John Latham-Koenig, with a cast which included Mary Thomas, Neil Mackie, Michael Rippon, Brian Rayner Cook and Ian Comboy. The novel *Magnus* by George Mackay Brown upon which the opera is based has Magnus, a Viking pacifist, martyred in a (Nazi) concentration camp.

Although not the result of a deliberate design, choral works based on anti-war themes have been a feature of Roy Massey's Festival programmes, and four of these have left an especially profound and lasting impression upon him personally. Becomingly modest, Massey reflects that if, as he puts it, he 'had achieved nothing more at Three Choirs, then at least I have conducted those four works'. They are:

1985	– Sir Michael Tippett, *A Child of our Time*, with Julie Kennard, Margaret Cable, Neil Jenkins, Michael George, the Festival Chorus and the CBSO.
	– Michael Berkeley, *Or Shall We Die?*, with Wendy Eathorne, Stephen Roberts, the Festival Chorus and the RPO. This was only the second performance of the work, the première of which had been given at the Royal Festival Hall on 6 February 1983.
1988	– Benjamin Britten, *War Requiem*, with Julie Kennard, Maldwyn Davies, Michael George, choristers of the three cathedrals, the Festival Chorus and the CBSO.
1991	– Sir Arthur Bliss, *Morning Heroes*, with Brian Kay as the Narrator, the Festival Chorus and the Royal Liverpool Philharmonic Orchestra.

There had been near disaster in 1985. Janet Price, the soloist engaged for Berkeley's *Or Shall We Die?* developed tonsillitis. 'In less than a day, Wendy Eathorne studied and sang the immensely difficult soprano role with deservedly triumphant personal success',[1] unforgettable as the desperate mother searching for her daughter among the rubble of a devastated Hiroshima:

> All night I searched for my daughter.
> At dawn a neighbour told me
> she had seen her by the river,
> among the dead and dying . . .

Although Roy Massey concedes that his programming might have been more conservative on the whole than that of his Gloucester and Worcester colleagues, it is surely clear that many rare, innovative or new things have been presented at his Hereford Festivals. For example, the first performance of William Mathias's *Veni Sancte Spiritus*, sung by the three cathedral choirs in 1985 – a Festival commission scored for four-part choir, organ, two trumpets and tuned percussion. 'This concise, immediately attractive piece,' wrote Barrie Grayson in the *Birmingham Post*,

> a setting of the sequence for Whit Sunday, had all the hallmarks of the composer's style . . . The words are a prayer requesting immortal light and Mathias with his singular imaginative skills, produced cathedral choir music that blowed and flashed with pictorial sound.
> It was an uplifting performance, directed convincingly by Roy Massey and sung with English cathedral choir panache . . .
> I have not forgotten the first time I heard Mathias's *This Worlde's Joie* [it was repeated in 1985]. Now I am convinced the work has made a major contribution to the contemporary repertoire.[2]

In 1988 there was Paul Spicer's *The Darling of the World*, a setting of Robert Herrick's poem *What Sweeter Music can we bring than a Carol*. Commissioned by the Birmingham Bach Society, it is dedicated to Richard Butt and was written as a companion piece to Britten's *St Nicholas*, being scored for tenor, choir, strings, piano, organ and light percussion. At Hereford the soloist in both works was Adrian Thompson. Roy Massey conducted *The Darling of the World*, and John Sanders *St Nicholas*, with the Girls' Choir of Hereford Cathedral School and the English String Orchestra.

Two notable birthdays occurred in 1988: the eightieth of Howard Ferguson and the ninetieth of Herbert Sumsion; and both were present at the Hereford Festival. On Tuesday evening John Sanders conducted a performance of Ferguson's *The Dream of the Rood*, with Wendy Eathorne, the Festival Chorus and the CBSO, and at the annual Finzi Trust Friends luncheon Andrew Burn gave a lecture on Ferguson's music. Sumsion's anthem *They that go down to the sea* was sung by the three cathedral choirs at choral evensong on Monday evening, when the canticles were to Paul Patterson's 'Norwich' service. And the Thursday evening concert ended with the first performance of Patterson's *Te Deum*. As Andrew Burn explained in his programme book note:

> With the *Te Deum*, Patterson has completed the last of three large-scale choral works which he likes to refer to as a 'Three Choirs Trilogy'. The *Mass of the Sea* was commissioned for Gloucester in 1983; such was its success that Roy Massey immediately requested a work for this year's festival [1988] and Patterson was also commissioned by the Huddersfield Choral Society to compose a work for their centenary in 1986 – the *Stabat Mater*. However, before Patterson had even put pen to paper, John Sanders decided to include this work in the 1986 Gloucester Festival, thus giving its second performance.

John Sanders, a serious, contemplative man whose professionalism inspires respect and loyalty, had been aware from his early days as assistant organist at Gloucester that the Festival was in danger of becoming a 'cosy club'. With the baton in his grasp he set about the task of widening its horizons, maintaining a staunch championship of English music but, at the same time, steadily introducing a more international flavour into his programming. Equally, his commitment to the improvement of choral standards became increasingly evident as the 1980s progressed.

E.J. Moeran, Peers Coetmore, Herbert Sumsion, Jelly d'Aranyi, Alice Sumsion, Joy and Gerald Finzi – Hereford, 1946 (photograph courtesy of Alice Sumsion)

David Willcocks, Herbert Sumsion, Ralph Vaughan Williams, Gerald Finzi and Meredith Davies – Gloucester, 1950 (photograph: *The Citizen*, courtesy of Maurice Hunt)

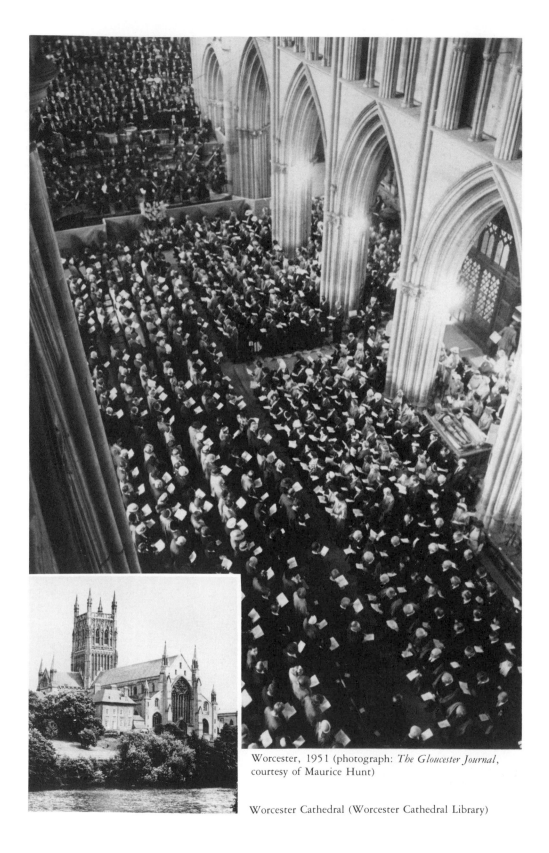

Worcester, 1951 (photograph: *The Gloucester Journal*, courtesy of Maurice Hunt)

Worcester Cathedral (Worcester Cathedral Library)

Worcester, 1954 (*top left, clockwise*): Ralph and Ursula Vaughan Williams; Herbert Howells; Gladys Ripley; Gordon Clinton; William Herbert; Norman Walker (*left*), Wilfred Brown (*second right*) and Roderick Jones (*right*); Edmund Rubbra (*left*) and Julius Harrison (*right*) (all photographs by Brendan Kerney, courtesy of R.S. Thompson)

Benjamin Britten and Peter Pears with the Ross High School Girls' Choir, following a rehearsal of *St Nicholas* – Hereford, 1958 (photograph: *The Hereford Times*, courtesy of Basil Butcher)

Melville Cook conducting the Verdi *Requiem* – Hereford, 1958 (photograph: Derek Evans, courtesy of Melville Cook)

Left to right: Hugh McGuire (Leader of the LSO), Douglas Guest, Sir Arthur Bliss, Melville Cook and Herbert Sumsion – Worcester, 1960 (photograph: Berrow's Newspapers, courtesy of Melville Cook)

Gerald English and John Shirley-Quirk rehearsing Britten's *Cantata Misericordium* – Hereford, 1964 (photograph: Derek Evans, courtesy of Melville Cook)

Raimund Herincx – Gloucester, 1968 (photograph: *The Citizen*)

Gloucester, 1968. Festival soloists (*left to right*): *top* – Rae Woodland, Barbara Robotham and Roger Stalman; *centre* – Norma Procter, John Mitchinson and Raimund Herincx; *bottom* – Elizabeth Harwood and Kenneth Bowen (photographs: *The Citizen*)

Gloucester, 1968 – garden party in the Cloister Garth (photograph: *The Citizen*)

The Prime Minister, Rt Hon. Edward Heath, and John Sanders – Gloucester Cathedral organ, 26 August 1971 (photograph: *The Citizen*)

Gloucester, 1971. Sir Arthur Bliss and Mrs Eleanor Budge, Chairman of the Ladies Committee, with a presentation print of Gloucester Cathedral (photograph: *The Citizen*)

Gloucester, 1974 (*left to right*): Christopher Robinson, John Sanders and Richard Lloyd (photograph: *The Citizen*)

Gloucester, 1974: *top* – John Sanders and the Gloucester Festival Chorus; *centre* – Richard Lloyd and the Hereford Festival Chorus; *above* – Christopher Robinson and the Worcester Festival Chorus (all photographs: *The Citizen*)

Her Majesty Queen Elizabeth the Queen Mother, John Sanders, Roy Massey and Donald Hunt –
Malcolm Williamson's *Mass of Christ the King*, Westminster Cathedral, 3 November 1978 (photograph:
Artricia)

Worcester, 1981. The three Head Choristers (*left
to right*): John Padley, Hereford; Jonathan
Garstang, Gloucester; and Rupert Harvey,
Worcester (photograph: *Worcester Evening News*)

Sir Charles Groves and Donald Hunt – Worcester,
1978 (photograph: *Worcester Evening News*)

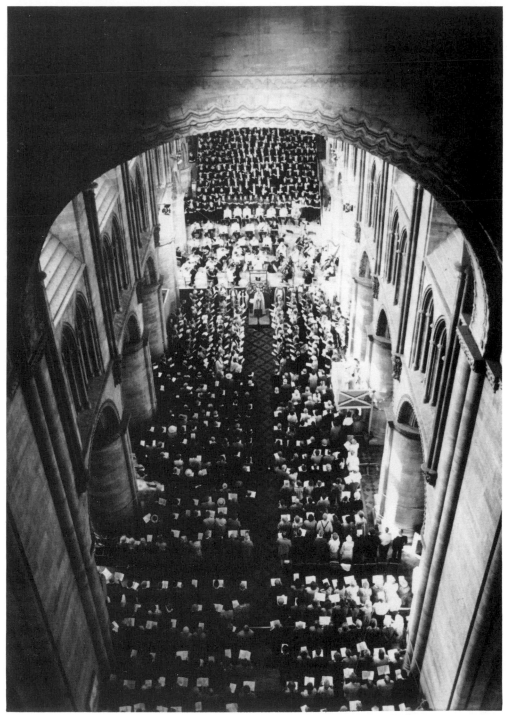

Hereford, 1991 – the Opening Service (photograph: Gareth Rees Roberts)

Hereford, 1991: *left, top to bottom*: Roy Massey acknowledging the Festival Chorus; Festival Chorus; Vernon Handley rehearses with Steven Isserlis and RLPO – Howard Blake's Diversions for Cello and Orchestra (photographs: Gareth Rees Roberts); *top right*: Roy Massey, Wulstan Atkins and Winston, following the unveiling of the memorial to Dan and *Enigma* Variation XI

In 1980(G) expected homage was paid to Elgar: *The Kingdom*, and the Cello Concerto with Amaryllis Fleming as soloist. There was music by Handel, Parry and Vaughan Williams; Tippett's first String Quartet (played by the Chilingirian String Quartet), and Walton's great Symphony No 1 in B flat minor (the RPO conducted by Walter Weller); Richard Strauss's *Tod und Verklärung* in an otherwise all-Russian programme (the CBSO under Norman del Mar); the Wagner *Wesendonck Lieder* (Sarah Walker); music of the thirteenth, fourteenth and fifteenth centuries and a concert of baroque choral and orchestral music.

Then, too, there was a repeat of David Fanshawe's *African Sanctus*; Janáček's *Glagolitic Mass* and, in honour of Sir Peter Pears's seventieth birthday, a moving account of Britten's *War Requiem* under Donald Hunt's direction, with Galina Vishnevskaya, Pears himself and Thomas Hemsley. There were the world premières of *Lord of Light* by Philip Cannon, Gerard Schurmann's *Piers Plowman*, commissioned by Netherlands Radio, *Buccinate Tuba* by Elis Pehkonen, together with the first English performances of Nicholas Maw's *Serenade*, Anthony Payne's *Footfalls echo in the memory*, and Peter Maxwell Davies's *Solstice of Light*.

Following the première of *The Temple* in 1974(G), Philip Cannon had received high praise for his orchestral treatment of the five-part unaccompanied choir, for seeking a sound which would match the emotional content of George Herbert's text, and for taking into account precisely the acoustic characteristics of Gloucester Cathedral. No such praise followed *Lord of Light*, subtitled 'A Gloucester Requiem' since at the end the text passes into the medieval plainsong hymn *Christe Redemptor Omnium*, one of the Gloucester Chimes restored in 1979. Set for soprano, tenor, baritone, boys' voices, chorus, orchestra (including organ) and, in its apotheosis, a recording of the Gloucester Chimes, the work 'proved a vast, wild, musical fresco', wrote Felix Aprahamian: 'full of sound and fury, its impasto thickly laid on with a trowel, the plainsong *Christe Redemptor Omnium* its only really solid ingredient. Mr Cannon's extravagant vocal and instrumental demands were met to almost painfully stunning effect under John Sanders.'[3] The soloists in *Lord of Light* were Iris Dell'Acqua, Kenneth Bowen and Graham Titus.

Anthony Payne's *Footfalls echo in the memory* (deliciously misprinted in a *South Wales Argus* review as 'Footballs echo in the memory'!) takes its title from the first of T.S. Eliot's *Four Quartets*, 'Burnt Norton'. It is a short violin and piano piece in which the composer reworks some of the materials in his 1971 piano work *Paean*.

Footfalls echo in the memory was given in Prinknash Abbey at a Friday morning recital by Erich Gruenberg and John McCabe. On Saturday afternoon in the Pittville Pump Room, Cheltenham, the Orchestra of St John's, Smith Square, under John Lubbock gave Nicholas Maw's revised *Serenade*. Deliberately lightweight and entertaining, there is, thought Andrew Clements writing in the *Financial Times*, 'the danger that the *Serenade* will fall between two audiences: not melodic enough for those who find contemporary music "difficult", while making too many concessions for Maw's admirers'.[4]

Peter Maxwell Davies's *Solstice of Light* was first performed at the 1979 St Magnus Festival, Orkney and, as in *The Martyrdom of St Magnus*, the composer used a text by the Orcadian poet George Mackay Brown. The first English performance was given at Three Choirs in 1980 by Michael Power (tenor), the three cathedral choirs and the organist Andrew Millington under the direction of Roy Massey during a Tuesday morning recital in Gloucester Cathedral. 'It was', wrote Kenneth Loveland, 'a model of how to achieve concentration and contrasts within a pattern of restrained but subtly varied textures . . . it is wonderfully shaded, carefully shaped towards a growing climax.'[5]

The outstanding success of the 1980(G) Festival was the première of Gerard Schurmann's *Piers Plowman*. Born in Java of Dutch parents, Shurmann lived in England from childhood until 1981, when he settled in the United States. He studied composition with Alan Rawsthorne and piano with Kathleen Long, and his works include a Piano Concerto (commissioned by the late John Ogden), a Violin Concerto (premièred by Ruggiero Ricci), the orchestral song-cycle *Chuenchi'i* on poems from the Chinese, the purely orchestral *Six Studies on Francis Bacon* and *Variants*, a work for unaccompanied chorus *The Double Heart* on poems by Andrew Marvell, a wide variety of solo instrumental and chamber music, incidental music for the theatre, and for many feature films.

The text of *Piers Plowman* is based on incidents in William Langland's great fourteenth-century allegory, *The Vision of Piers the Plowman*, historically covering the latter part of the reign of Edward III and the succession of ten-year-old Richard II under the regency of the Duke of Lancaster, John of Gaunt. Langland, however, was more concerned with the prevailing moral issues than with political history, and it is the parallels between these and those of our own time which fired Schurmann's imagination.

The première of *Piers Plowman* was given during the Friday evening cathedral concert at the 1980(G) Festival by Felicity Lott, Sarah Walker, Anthony Rolfe Johnson and Norman Welsby, the Festival Chorus and RPO under the assured hand of John Sanders. A better performance is hard to imagine.

> In a direct modern tonal idiom, steeped in Britten, Walton and Gerhard, clean orchestration supported gloriously rich chorales, associated dramatic outbursts and soaring lyrical lines to which the four soloists . . . generally responded sensitively. The Royal Philharmonic Orchestra . . . excelled themselves.[6]

Piers Plowman was repeated at the 1989 Gloucester Festival, when the composer travelled from his home in California to be present.

In its variety and balance, stretching from the comforting familiarity of Mozart and Schubert to the startling *avant-garde* freshness of Globokar, Ichiyanagi and Wiegold,[7] the 1980(G) programme typifies John Sanders's continuing search to widen the horizons of the Festival.

One work programmed in 1983(G) promised to be interesting but failed to live up to expectations. Handel's *Occasional Oratorio*, apparently not performed in full in England since 1763 and never sung at Three Choirs, was given in a new edition prepared by Merlin Channon. Douglas Drane wrote:

> Personally, after hearing the almost two hour abridged performance in Gloucester Cathedral, I would not regret it if that was my last occasion to hear it.
> It proved to be insipid and uninspiring. Unlike some of the other fine performances this week the [Gloucester] Festival Chorus could find no lustre to add and the principals: Wendy Eathorne, Angela Beale, Neil Jenkins and John Shirley-Quirk seemed unable to get it together.[8]

The *Occasional Oratorio* was accompanied by the Orchestra da Camera under John Sanders. The orchestra and its Leader Kenneth Page have been popular visitors to Three

Choirs for many years. In 1983 the *Occasional Oratorio* was the last engagement of their silver jubilee celebrations. As Douglas Drane put it: 'Alas! It had to be this work to conclude them.'

The first performance of Paul Patterson's *Mass of the Sea* (*Missa Maris*), on the other hand, scored a very considerable success at the 1983(G) Festival.

Andrew Burn has explained that:

> the music of the Polish *avant-garde*, and in particular Penderecki, was a major formative influence on Paul Patterson, apparent in works like *Time-Piece* (1972) and *Kyrie* (1971), which established his reputation in the 1970s as a composer of a vivid, colourful imagination . . . During the eighties he increasingly moved away from the textural configurations of his earlier works to a language that may be broadly summed up as a rapprochement between neo-classical sensibility and the 20th century English tradition of composers like Britten.[9]

Nigel Edwards, writing in the *Hereford Times*, expressed perfectly the enthusiasm felt by the great majority of those present at the première. Here was a new work for which further performances could hardly be in doubt:

> The 36-year-old composer . . . was called to the platform again and again to the cheers of delighted music lovers both from the packed audience and from the 250-strong chorus whch had just performed it.
>
> Lasting 40 minutes exactly, it proved to be one of the most striking, exciting and immediately likeable choral works to have been written for some years – a very fine piece indeed!
>
> . . . The Kyrie is treated as a cry for help from the first chaos before creation when 'there was only sea and darkness was upon the face of the deep'.
>
> The Gloria becomes a rhythmic and vigorously structured dance of joy as the waters are divided and the glory of creation takes place. Christ the Saviour, walking upon the water, becomes the subject of an etherial, loftily conceived Sanctus, while the Agnus Dei prepares us for that promised vision in the Book of Revelations of a time when there will be no more sea.
>
> Simple in concept, and yet a stroke of genius, it works extremely well. The Royal Philharmonic Orchestra and the Festival Chorus conducted by John Sanders responded magnificently. Only the soloists, Janet Price, Mary King, Kenneth Bowen and Christopher Keyte, failed to reach the highest demands of this work and were at times disappointing. But it must be added that their parts contained some of the most complex writing.[10]

In 1983 the city of Gloucester celebrated the 500th anniversary of the granting of the Charter of Incorporation by Richard III on 2 September 1483, elevating the town to the dignity of a borough. To commemorate this event the city commissioned Gloucester-born composer, Richard Shephard, to write a celebratory piece, and the result, *Let us now praise famous men*, an extensive choral piece with organ and obbligato trumpet, was given its first performance by the St Cecilia Singers under Andrew Millington in their Friday morning cathedral recital. The trumpet was played by Crispian Steele-Perkins.

Another distinguished son of Gloucester, the composer and writer Michael Hurd (whose *Missa Brevis* was performed at the 1968(G) Festival), presented the first of two talks on Ivor Gurney included in the 1983 programme of fringe events. Hurd, Gurney's biographer, spoke on 'Ivor Gurney – the Man and his Music'. Later in the week the poet, Andrew Motion, spoke on 'Ivor Gurney's Poetry' at the annual meeting of the Finzi Trust Friends, and John Shirley-Quirk included three songs by Gurney – *Severn Meadows*, *Black Stitchel* and *Sleep* – in his Friday afternoon song recital at Painswick Parish Church.

The first complete performance of Elis Pehkonen's Symphony for orchestra and soprano was given by April Cantelo and the Gloucestershire Youth Orchestra, conducted by Mark Foster, on the opening Saturday, and in an RPO orchestral concert conducted by Sir Charles Groves the next evening, John Scott was the soloist in the première of the Concerto for Organ, Strings and Percussion by Charles Camilleri.

Among the highlights of the 1983(G) Festival which linger in the memory is a luminous performance of Mahler's Symphony No. 10, given in the late Deryck Cooke's completed edition, by the CBSO under Simon Rattle. He had, wrote Helen Reid in the *Western Daily Press*:

> coaxed his string section into playing with a wonderful richness and the important woodwind and brass passages could not have been better played.
>
> The whole work rang with concentrated commitment and after the last movement, which is one of pure serene beauty, the audience paid the magical tribute of perfect silence before they applauded.[11]

Certainly the finest singing of the week was heard on the previous evening, Wednesday, when Jill Gomez was the soloist in the *Four Last Songs* by Richard Strauss, singing them 'with radiant purity, producing some notes of astonishing beauty'.[12] Perhaps the inspiration of this performance flowed into the Festival Chorus for the next work: Brahms's *Ein Deutsches Requiem*, sung in German, with Jill Gomez and Brian Rayner Cook splendid in the solo parts.

No doubt the inclusion of Carl Orff's *Carmina Burana* in the last night programme was bound to excite comment – and it did. Monastic drunkenness, gambling and lust are not everyone's idea of appropriate topics for cathedral performance, no matter how exciting the music!

As we have seen, Malcolm Williamson's *Mass of Christ the King* finally achieved a complete performance at Three Choirs in 1986(G), when it was conducted by Donald Hunt. But the outstanding success of that Festival was yet another new work by Paul Patterson: his *Stabat Mater*, commissioned by the Huddersfield Choral Society for their 150th anniversary and first performed by them earlier in 1986. At Gloucester, John Sanders secured a fine performance. As Kenneth Loveland wrote:

> Mr Patterson writes music that strikes home. He has an imaginative fund of ideas, but is never out of reach of his audience, and always well within the physical capacity of the singers. In a phrase, he writes the sort of new music which the choral tradition needs if it is to survive. It is very much of its time and looks forward, but it is all done with discipline and an eye to practicality.[13]

Hugely successful commercially, the first Three Choirs performance of Andrew Lloyd Webber's *Requiem* divided critical opinion far more sharply than did Patterson's *Stabat Mater*. Does it belong in a cathedral festival? 'For my money', wrote Kenneth Loveland after the convincing performance secured by John Sanders,

> it certainly does. The background of showbiz publicity and ballyhoo hardly prepares one for its high seriousness and more than competent writing.
>
> The elements of jazz and pop which are integrated are not out of place. Mr Lloyd Webber is writing in the idiom in which he best expresses himself, and it is never superficial music. He knows about originality of orchestral colour and detail, and like Mr Patterson, gives his choir something which is a challenge, but a practicable one.[14]

Barrie Grayson took an entirely opposite point of view:

> John Sanders, Miriam Bowen, Arthur Davies, Master Douglas Mason, Chorus and Orchestra [the RLPO] gave their all to a work which owes more to the popularity of the composer than in this instance, the quality of the music.
>
> This easily forgotten work with its borrowings and gimmicky pastiche sounds as though it was conceived bar by bar at the piano and passed on to a synthesizer expert for up-market sound colour.
>
> Unfortunately, there is little of uplifting spiritual quality in the music, and even less artistic cohesion.[15]

Of a quite different order was a concert given in Prinknash Abbey by the Amaryllis Consort: Jennifer Smith, Gillian Fisher, Charles Brett, Ian Partridge, Stephen Roberts and Michael George. Their programme was drawn from the court of Elizabeth I, a golden spring in the history of English music, and among others included pieces by Gibbons, Morley, Wilbye and Tomkins, reaching a central climax with Byrd's settings of two funeral songs for Sir Philip Sydney: *Come to me, grief, for ever* and *O that most rare breast*.

The 1986(G) Festival ended with a revival after thirteen years of Mendelssohn's *Elijah*, in an abridged version and without an interval. The cuts, seen by some as judicious, were thought by others to be butchery of a masterpiece:

> Two hours flat, no interval and some of the loveliest items cast aside – 'Cast thy burden', 'He that shall endure', the 'Holy, Holy, Holy' quartet and chorus. Poor old Elijah was not even allowed to 'go on his way in the strength of the Lord!' lamented Douglas Drane. We realise that Liverpool is a long way away and the Band [the RLPO] wanted to get back to their hearth and home before midnight, but to do this is a travesty.[16]

Of the performance itself there were few grumbles: Brian Rayner Cook dramatically authoritative in the title-role; Helen Walker, Penelope Walker and Maldwyn Davies all excellent; and the young treble Andrew Wooldridge singing with bright-toned confidence.

As always, one particular Festival memory is cemented into the mind – one lovely voice hovering above a spellbound cathedral audience – Sarah Walker, sublime in the song-cycle *Les nuits d'été* by Berlioz, and sensitively accompanied by the RPO under Sanders on Monday evening.

The 1989 Gloucester Festival began on Friday 18 August: a day early to allow the children of the Downs School, Colwall, Malvern to perform in the 'world première' of the concert version of a children's musical play – *Simpkin and the Tailor of Gloucester* by Douglas Young – and this was repeated on Saturday afternoon. Originally expected to be of sufficient length to stand alone as a single-item entertainment mainly for children, it became clear at a very late stage that *Simpkin* would, after all, be quite a short piece. The headmaster of the Downs School (and conductor of *Simpkin*), Andrew Auster, was obliged to provide additional items to supplement the programme. Unfortunately, the result was a mismatch which reduced a kindly-meant opportunity for children to contribute to the Festival into an embarrassing hybrid, unsuitable in combination for either young or old.

'There are moments when the Three Choirs' planning can seem surprisingly amateur.

It would be hard to imagine a more unwieldy programme than Saturday afternoon's concert in St Catharine's Church,' wrote Simon Mundy in *The Independent*. '*Simpkin and the Tailor of Gloucester* finally emerged in an abbreviated form. Why, one wonders, was that allowed to be so? Is it acceptable that Europe's oldest music festival should mount a bit of narration and a few pleasant choruses and call the result a world première? . . . Douglas Young has written more interesting scores than this, even for youth forces, and a proper staging of the whole children's opera, without the hour of irrelevant music that had to be endured first, would have been a more worthwhile undertaking.'[17]

Elizabeth Harwood generously agreed to assist in bridging the gap between *Simpkin* and an assortment of other, amateur, contributions. She sang Britten's *Cabaret Songs* and Strauss *Lieder* – tough fare for toddlers. And what a pity that this, her last recital at Three Choirs after so many years, should not have been set in a kinder acoustic.

1989(G) will be remembered for Parry, Pehkonen and pipistrelles.

What Elgar is to Worcester Sir Hubert Parry is, or should be, to Gloucester, and a genuine attempt was made in 1989 to reverse a long neglect. Music by Parry was featured on seven days of the Festival:

Saturday	–	Symphony No. 5 in B minor. The Gloucestershire Youth Orchestra conducted by Mark Foster.
Sunday	–	The Great Service in D major setting of the evening canticles and the hymn *Laudate Dominum* at the Opening Service.
Monday	–	Symphonic Variations. The RPO conducted by Roy Massey.
Tuesday	–	Lecture by Michael Kennedy, 'Parry, man of his time'.
Wednesday	–	Sonata for Cello and Piano in A major. Rachel Howgego (cello) and Stephen Lea (piano) in a fringe recital.
Thursday	–	*Ode on the Nativity*. Festival Chorus and RLPO conducted by Donald Hunt.
Friday	–	*Lady Radnor's Suite*. English String Orchestra conducted by William Boughton.

And, with some of the finest choral singing heard during the week,

Saturday	–	*Songs of Farewell*. The Rodolfus Youth Choir conducted by Ralph Allwood.

On Thursday morning Parry's biographer, Dr Jeremy Dibble, gave an enthralling lecture on the composer –'Hubert Parry – a personal sketch' – with musical illustrations by the Renaissance Singers of Ontario and most moving readings by Parry's descendant, Laura Ponsonby. The talk, given in the church at Highnam founded by Parry's father, Thomas Gambier Parry, was introduced by another descendant of the composer and present Squire of Highnam, Tom Fenton.

The music of Elis Pehkonen was first heard at Three Choirs in 1980(G): *Buccinate Tuba*, scored for soprano solo, boys' voices, chorus, brass, timpani and organ, and ideally suited to the forces which John Sanders employed at the Opening Service throughout the 1980s: a brass ensemble, an effective and economical alternative to a full symphony orchestra. Pehkonen's Symphony was performed by the Gloucestershire Youth Orchestra under Mark Foster in 1983. His *Russian Requiem*, commissioned by the Birmingham Festival Choral Society, received its first performance in that city in November 1986 when it was described by the *Birmingham Post* critic, Barrie Grayson, as a 'momentous and memorable occasion . . . a profoundly moving experience'. The work was repeated on the Thursday afternoon of the 1989 Gloucester Festival.

Of Finnish extraction, Elis Pehkonen was born in Norfolk, studied at the Royal Academy of Music with Peter Racine Fricker, and at various times with Benjamin Britten, Richard Rodney Bennett and Anthony Payne.

Russian Requiem, directly influenced by documented events following the Russian Revolution of 1917, is dedicated to 'the stubborn child of Gorodietsky'. The work is a plea for the peace of reconciliation through the unifying love of Christ. Pehkonen does not set the entire *Missa Pro Defunctis* (there is no *Sanctus*, *Libera me* or *In Paradisum*). Instead, he highlights selected passages with quotations from The Revelations of St John the Divine, Canto 3 in *Hell* of Dante's *Divine Comedy*, Boris Pasternak's *Zhivago* poems – *Gethsemane* and *Winter Night*, as well as comments from Collected Works of Lenin. The work is scored for soprano and contralto soloists (Christine Bunning and Susan Mason), chorus, oboe, cor anglais, two trumpets, timpani, percussion, organ and strings. The Gloucester performance was conducted by John Sanders.

> On paper [wrote Kenneth Loveland] the appearance of two requiems in one day looked heavy going. It did not turn out that way. Elis Pehkonen's *Russian Requiem* is the latest to blend liturgy and literature, including Dante and Pasternak, and is a work of convincing statement, dramatic pulse and accessibility. The music, though often heavy with grief, suggests the glowing richness of the Russian Orthodox Church, and is at its best in the shimmering final quotations from *Winter Night* (an unexpected visitor in Fauré seems to hover) where Sanders blended Pehkonen's gentle repetitions into a beautiful mosaic. Pehkonen's sincerity is a winning factor, and so, in a different way, is that of John Rutter, who conducted his *Requiem* later the same day. And he is a genial and pleasant hand at a tune. But one wonders whether the genial and the pleasant are really what one looks for in a requiem.[18]

And the pipistrelles? From the first note of the first concert an erratic squadron of tiny bats appeared from the cathedral tower to patrol the air-space above the audience. Kodály's *Budavári Te Deum* on Monday evening seemed to interest one musical *Fledermaus* in particular, swooping down towards the conductor and causing Roy Massey to duck and weave. *Piers Plowman* followed – more bats 'scrambled' but were satisfied to limit themselves to high-level reconnaissance. The *Birmingham Post* went so far as to interview Hilary Ward, a spokesman for the Nature Conservancy Trust, who said that the unusually high number of pipistrelles in the cathedral was probably due to the mild weather: most of the young had survived.

The Festival closed with a performance of Elgar's *Caractacus*, blessed with a perfect quartet of soloists: Julie Kennard, Robert Tear, Michael George and, in the title-role, Brian Rayner Cook, with the Festival Chorus and RLPO under John Sanders. Brian Rayner Cook, who on Friday morning had woven magic spells of his own in a song-recital with Clifford Benson at Painswick Parish Church, put the thoughts of many into words after *Caractacus*: 'That was John Sanders at his very best.'

Caractacus finished, the audience joined chorus and soloists in Parry's *Jerusalem* to the accompaniment of Elgar's 1922 orchestration. A fitting and proud ending to what was, above all, Parry's week.

Donald Hunt had drawn together two predominant themes in devising his programme for the 1981 Worcester Festival – looking north to Scandinavia and, yet again, south to France. But this time the French connection was further strengthened by invitations to internationally-famous French performers and composers to make contributions to the Festival.

The Scandinavian theme, prompted by the fiftieth anniversary of the death of Carl Nielsen, was established not only by several of that ˙ most eminent of Danish composer's works, but also by the first British concert performance of the *Te Deum Danicum* by his fellow-countryman Knud Jeppeson whose two motets, *Herre hvar* and *Jeg sletted som tåge*, together with works by other Danish composers, were sung by the Copenhagen Boys Choir on Monday afternoon. The music of Finland was also featured: a magnificent performance of Sibelius's Second Symphony by the RPO under Sir Charles Groves on Wednesday evening, and on Thursday *Finlandia* to open a concert given by the Festival Chorus and the BBC NSO conducted by Donald Hunt, which included the first British performances of Aulis Sallinen's *Dies Irae* and, surprisingly, the *Missa Solemnis* by Liszt.

The Sallinen piece is a setting of the poem *It was Christmas Day* by the Finnish poet Arvo Turtianainen: an apocalyptic vision of the world's nuclear destruction one Christmas Day. Sallinen hammers home the stark message of *Dies Irae* by stone-hard orchestration, percussive clamour and the austerity of an all-male choir. It is a journey from light to darkness, relieved only at the end by a single spark of hope born of a visit to destroyed Earth by a space-traveller, a representative of nobler and saner humanity elsewhere in the universe.

The inspiration for Edwin Roxburgh's *The Rock*, on the other hand, is the spiritual journey from darkness to light. Aware that his subject has inspired many of the world's greatest works of art, Roxburgh chose the Revelations of St John the Divine as the main text for *The Rock*, drawing also on a wide range of sources, from the Koran to T.S. Eliot.

In structure the work is woven around fragments from the medieval Worcester school: isolated manuscripts of fourteenth century music recovered from book bindings and wrappers to bundles of accounts. *The Rock* was given at the Tuesday evening concert in 1981(W) with soloists Jane Manning, Mary King, Kenneth Bowen and John Noble, the Festival Chorus, cathedral choristers and the RPO under Donald Hunt. Critical opinion was sharply divided along the margins of decibel tolerance. For Nigel Edwards the work was a superb unfolding of the spiritual journey:

> . . . we tasted the bitter depths of the dark and eventually rejoiced in the spiritual bliss of the heavenly realms with 'Alleluia Tympanum', quoted from the Worcester fragments with telling effect . . . the overall effect was magnificently convincing.[19]

Kenneth Loveland remained unconvinced by *The Rock* but found pleasure in the first performance of Herbert Sumsion's *In Exile: By the waters of Babylon*, heard in the cathedral on Tuesday morning:

> . . . What can be said of Edwin Roxburgh's *The Rock* . . . the work's message is submerged in waves of indisciplined sound, and not all the advocacy of Donald Hunt, the chorus, the valiantly battling soloists, and the R.P.O. could bring it to the surface. Herbert Sumsion's *In Exile*, a setting for double choir of Psalm 137, was a happy event . . . a much loved figure at the festival, he had the maximum goodwill going for him, and a devoted account by the Donald Hunt Singers showed the new motet to be a skilled piece of professionalism . . . Of the new music, Jonathan Harvey's *Resurrection* made the strongest impression [given by the three cathedral choirs under Donald Hunt on the Friday morning]. Using mirror techniques, ascending chords for the resurrection text, descending ones for death, and allusive organ textures (Paul Trepte coped superbly) with muttered bass comments and treble insinuations, Harvey produced a sense of the inexorable by insistent repetitions.[20]

Friday, 28 August 1981 was rather a special day for the Harvey family. Singing in Jonathan Harvey's commissioned work *Resurrection* were Worcester head chorister Rupert Harvey and his father, Dr Brian Harvey, the composer's brother and a voluntary cathedral bass lay clerk. Later in the day, father and son were singing Jonathan Harvey's anthem *I love the Lord* at Choral Evensong, and the organ voluntary that concluded the service, *Laus Deo*, was also by him.

Another Worcester Cathedral lay clerk to play a significant and versatile role at Three Choirs over many years was Trevor Owen. Apart from his valuable presence among the tenors of the three cathedral choirs and the Festival Chorus, Owen sang with the male voice quintet Opus 5 (John Vickers, Trevor Owen, John Wilman, Roger Hemingway and Alan Fairs) at the 1977(G), 1979(H) and 1984(W) Festivals. At Worcester, as conductor of the Festival Junior Chorus, he directed several delightful performances of choral works and opera for young people, which included in 1981 Purcell's *Dido and Aeneas* and Peter Maxwell Davies's *The Two Fiddlers* at the Worcester Technical College. And who should have been in the Junior Chorus and taking part in *Dido and Aeneas* but yet another member of the Harvey family: Rupert's young sister, Amanda! In 1991 Trevor Owen moved from Worcester to Chichester.

The 1981(W) Festival week had begun on Saturday evening with a recital of French organ music given by Jean Langlais, the celebrated blind organist of the Basilique Sainte-Clothilde. In addition to works of his own, Langlais played pieces by Couperin and two of his predecessors at Sainte-Clothilde – César Franck and Charles Tournemire. At the Festival Eucharist on the following morning Langlais's Mass, *Grant us thy peace*, commissioned by the Worcester Cathedral Choir Association for the Festival, was given its first performance, along with two motets by Pierre Villette: *O sacrum convivium* and *O salutaris hostia*.

In 1976 Donald Hunt had approached M. Villette to write a new work for Three Choirs. The composer had already begun a Mass to mark the sixth centenary of the foundation of Saint Evode Choir School, Rouen Cathedral, and had completed the *Agnus Dei*. Originally commissioned to make a setting of the vernacular text with an accompaniment of two organs, Villette was now presented with the opportunity to complete the work on a larger scale. The terms of the original commission were amended, and Villette received a special grant for the composition from the French Minister of Culture. The first performance of Villette's *Messe en Français* was given at the 1981(W) Wednesday afternoon concert by Wendy Eathorne, Margaret Cable, Alastair

Thompson and David Wilson Johnson, the Worcester Festival Chorus and the BBC NSO conducted by Donald Hunt, whose championship of the composer was entirely vindicated. The orchestral concert given by the RPO under Sir Charles Groves on Wednesday evening also began with a work by Villette – his beautiful *Trois Préludes pour cordes*, described by the composer as 'full of mystery and reverie'.

Jean-Claude Malgoire's interpretation of Handel's *Messiah* on the last Saturday afternoon was something of a disappointment. Conducting his chamber orchestra, La Grande Ecurie et la Chambre du Roy, the Worcester Cathedral choristers and lay clerks of the three cathedral choirs, Malgoire had the opportunity to break free from the nineteenth-century *Messiah* tradition. Instead, he attempted to produce a monumental idea of the work, unsupported by large-scale sound, leaving his audience in no man's land. Theresa Lister, Charles Brett, Alastair Thompson and Nicklaus Tüller gave wholly admirable accounts of their solos.

The 1981 Festival ended with a blazing performance of the *Grand Messe des Morts* by Berlioz, played by the CBSO under Donald Hunt, and with the Festival Chorus rising magnificently to the challenge of the massive composition.

And a single, lasting memory of the Festival? The truly inspired singing of Rosalind Plowright and Alfreda Hodgson in Mahler's Second Symphony (*The Resurrection*) on Friday evening. Originally to have been conducted by Günther Herbig, and later advertised as under the direction of Bernhard Klee, finally it was Sir Charles Groves who took charge of the BBC NSO and Festival Chorus, conveying superbly Mahler's dazzling vision of eternal certainty.

The centenary of Dvořák's visit to the Festival and the fiftieth anniversaries of the deaths of Delius, Holst and also that of Elgar, all fell in 1984. In that year, too, the Festival became an integral part of the Worcester Cathedral 900th anniversary celebrations.

Where better than Worcester to celebrate so important an Elgar anniversary? Certainly the BBC seized the opportunity, mounting an invitation-only television production with the Festival Chorus of *The Dream of Gerontius* on the opening Saturday evening, 18 August. Only the second occasion since 1977(G) that a part of the Festival had been televised, this well-intentioned tribute did not quite come off:

> It would have been proper recognition of all he [Dr Hunt] has done to strengthen music at Worcester if he had been given the opening performance of *The Dream of Gerontius* [wrote Kenneth Loveland], but this had all the appearance of a starry package designed by the B.B.C. for its viewers rather than something intended by the festival for its own public. There was the tiring necessity of sitting through the ritual service dedication. To the stifling oppression of one of the hottest nights of the summer was added the almost unbearable heat and glare of television lights. In front of my seat a television camera repeatedly soared heavenwards as though trying to catch the soul of Gerontius in flight. It all worked against the atmosphere in which *The Dream* best conveys its message, and although Janet Baker, Stuart Burrows and Benjamin Luxon each did notable things, the chorus gave of their best, and Andrew Davis secured conscientious playing from the B.B.C. Welsh S.O. (the introduction to Part 2 was particularly beautiful), concentration was not possible.[21]

(Donald Hunt, having no part to play in these proceedings, changed into casual wear and took himself off to the Perdiswell Sports Centre to listen to Acker Bilk and his Paramount Jazz Band – only to be thrown out by the bouncer for failing to have a ticket!)

Rehearsals for this sweltering and mediocre *Gerontius* left no available time for the century-old traditional Opening Service. Hence the 'ritual service of dedication' which took its place and which has been retained at Worcester up to the time of writing (1991): a thirty-minute service immediately preceding the first concert. In compensation, and taking an appropriate place on Sunday morning, a Festival Eucharist which incorporates the Festival Sermon has been introduced. In 1984 this included the motets, *A Spiritual Temple* by John C. Phillips and the first performance of *Most glorious Lord of Life* by Donald Hunt, commissioned by the Worcester Cathedral Choir Association. Since then, the Festival Eucharist, sung by the Worcester Cathedral choir under Donald Hunt, has provided further opportunities for new commissions: Festival Masses by Howard Blake in 1987 and by Jonathan Willcocks in 1990.

The television cameras remained in place for the 1984(W) Sunday evening concert – a programme of music taking America as its theme: Copland's *Fanfare for the Common Man* and *Appalachian Spring*; Bernstein's *Chichester Psalms*, with Worcester Cathedral chorister James Davis a clear and confident treble soloist; and two pieces composed by Delius on American visits, 'Sunset' and 'Daybreak' from the *Florida Suite*, and *Sea Drift* in which Stephen Roberts was the baritone soloist with the Festival Chorus and the CBSO under Donald Hunt – altogether more enjoyable than the previous evening's *Gerontius* in spite of equally torrid television lighting.

The American theme continued on Monday morning with a disappointing organ recital by Carlo Curley, struggling with an organ badly affected by heat changes in the cathedral over the previous days. And on Monday afternoon the American John T. Hamilton Chorale gave a recital of American choral music in All Saints Church, including pieces by Howard Hanson, Jerome Kern, Norman Luboff and Horatio Parker.

Almost inevitably, Dvořák's visit to Worcester in 1884 was linked coincidentally to the Festival's American theme. His String Quartet No. 12 in F, Op. 96 (*The American*) was included in a recital by the Delmé String Quartet at Hartlebury Castle on Tuesday afternoon, in addition to the Elgar String Quartet in E minor and *Meditation on an old Czech Hymn: Saint Wenceslaus* by Dvořák's favourite pupil, Josef Suk.

On Monday evening Donald Hunt conducted the CBSO in a vigorous performance of Dvořák's Symphony No. 6 in D, one of the works conducted by the composer himself during his Worcester visit (the 27-year-old Elgar then among the first violins), and on Tuesday evening Dvořák's Requiem Mass was given an assured performance under John Sanders's direction, with Mimfred Sand, Fiona Kimm, Kenneth Bowen and John Noble, the Festival Chorus and the CBSO.

Three very different sound-worlds were brought together on Friday evening in a concert given by the ladies voices of the Donald Hunt Singers and the BBC Philharmonic Orchestra conducted by Edward Downes: Elgar's *Froissart*; the Nocturne, *Paris (The Song of a Great City)* by Delius; and Holst's masterpiece, *The Planets*. All three composers had been represented on Thursday morning in a programme of English choral music given in the cathedral by the Donald Hunt Singers and Osian Ellis (harp): *Unaccompanied Part-Songs*, Op. 53 and *Go, song of mine* by Elgar; *On Craig Ddu* and *The splendour falls on castle walls* by Delius; and Holst's *Choral Hymns from the Rig Veda (Third Set)* Op. 26 No. 3. This fascinatingly varied programme also included William Mathias's Three Improvisations for Harp, Op. 10, Britten's Suite for Harp, Op. 83, and the first performance of Richard Rodney Bennett's *Sea Change*, an *a cappella* choral suite dedicated to Donald Hunt and commissioned by the Festival with funds provided by West Midlands Arts. The texts for *Sea Change* are taken from Shakespeare's *The Tempest*, from Andrew Marvell, and from Spenser's *Faerie Queene*.

> *Sea Change* was [wrote Hugo Cole] resourceful and imaginative, fairly lightweight music with a delightful setting of Marvell's *Remote Bermudas* (the prologue and epilogue most beautifully sung by an un-named tenor from the choir) [Trevor Owen].
>
> The evocation of sea monsters by means of *sprechgesang* was also effective, though Bennett's own individual voice was less apparent here, while in the setting of *Full Fathom Five*, the technical ingenuity of reflecting four upper voices with four lower voices muddied the harmonic waters without any great expressive gain.[22]

Monteverdi's *Vespers of the Blessed Virgin* had been performed four times at Three Choirs between 1958 and 1979. In 1984 Donald Hunt programmed the work again – but this time for performances by the three cathedral choirs without augmentation by any element of the Festival Chorus. The performance, directed by Roger Norrington, was outstanding. Hugo Cole again:

> . . . eight perfectly matched soloists, the three cathedral choirs and a familiar team of baroque specialists the London Baroque Players, showed how few performers are needed to produce spectacular and brilliant effects in this kindly environment. In spite of Roger Norrington's fervour, the three choirs stuck to their normal serene and unimpassioned mode of singing; the contrast with the highly expressive singing of the soloists Gillian Fisher, Theresa Lister, Paul Esswood, Andrew Arthur, Martyn Hill, Joseph Cornwell, Michael George and Stephen Varcoe was in its way very effective.
>
> Norrington's plain realization is consistent and unobtrusive. With performers of this calibre there is no danger in a high degree of exposure, and clarity of sounds brings us even closer to Monteverdi.[23]

In 1984 another important source of funding for new commissions became available to the Worcester Festival. Ken Pott's statue of Elgar which gazes out at the cathedral from the southern end of High Street had been unveiled by HRH The Prince of Wales on the composer's birthday, 2 June 1981. Such had been the response to the Elgar Statue Appeal that the project was realized with considerable funds to spare. Mindful of the spirit in which donations to the statue fund had been made, the Appeal Committee decided that surplus monies should be used to commission triennially a major work for the Worcester Festival. In 1987 the Elgar commission was Richard Rodney Bennett's Third Symphony, and in 1990 the song-cycle *A Song for Birds* by Paul Spicer, but the first Elgar commission was Peter Racine Fricker's *Whispers at these curtains*, Op. 88, given by Stephen Roberts, the Festival Chorus and the BBC Philharmonic Orchestra conducted by Donald Hunt at the 1984(W) Thursday evening concert.

The text of *Whispers at these curtains* is chosen from the Devotions, Sermons and Prayers of John Donne. Fricker selected them from many different sources to illustrate three main lines of Donne's thinking: the obsession with bells and death, the voice of God and the whispers of the dead and of Christ's voice, and Donne's triumphant assumption of glory.

Whispers at these curtains was followed by Elgar's Cello Concerto, with Robert Cohen an inspired soloist. His performance, wrote Kenneth Loveland, was remarkable as an example of the complete identification of player and music. With an accompaniment which spoke of instinctive rapport (B.B.C. P.O., Hunt) Cohen, filling the cathedral with a rich tone, explored eloquently the music's self-communing inner tragedy, and the despairing backward glance can rarely have been more poignant.[24]

The concert ended with the *Hymn of Jesus*, reminding us yet again of how very much was lost to English music by Holst's untimely death at only fifty-nine. As Donald Hunt pointed out in a programme note,

much of Holst's musical language stems not only from the French-influenced fashions of his day, but also from his predilection for the music of Byrd, Palestrina and Bach. Indeed, it was following a performance of Bach's Mass in B minor in Worcester Cathedral that Holst said he found himself clutching the arm of his chair during the Sanctus. He felt he was floating on air, and he feared lest he should find his head bumping against the groined roof!.[25]

The 1984(W) Festival had begun with *Gerontius* and the spirit of Elgar was never far away. On Wednesday, Donald Hunt conducted Elgar's rare symphonic cantata *The Black Knight* and, even rarer, *Sursum Corda* for strings, brass and organ. On Friday morning Michael Kennedy gave a fascinating talk on Elgar's oratorios in St George's Roman Catholic Church, where the composer had been organist in the 1880s. But the triumph of the week was reserved for Saturday, when Donald Hunt directed *The Apostles* in the afternoon and *The Kingdom* in the evening. The experience of hearing the two works in sequence invited re-assessment, wrote Kenneth Loveland:

The consistency of their creative urgency became more apparent; the motifs they share, and Elgar's transformation of them, were shown to have stronger relevance to changing situations; the almost operatic significance was heightened. The performances were devoted, with the choir providing eager response, tiring only a little at one point in *The Kingdom*, the R.L.P.O. immediately supportive of Dr Hunt's search for those subtleties of instrumental colour that are among the most interesting aspects of these works, and a totally committed team of soloists in Elizabeth Harwood, Alfreda Hodgson, Robert Tear and Michael Rippon plus, in *The Apostles*, Brian Rayner Cook a profoundly moving Jesus, and John Noble so powerfully involved as Judas. Dr Hunt's courage was completely justified, and late on the last night a packed cathedral audience rose to cheer him.[26]

As if to balance the American theme of the 1984(W) Festival, Donald Hunt's musical compass swung to the east in 1987, pointing up distinctive Eastern European and Russian flavours: Szymanowski, Enescu, Borodin, Rachmaninov, Tchaikovsky and Penderecki.

The beautifully restored Countess of Huntingdon's Hall was used as a Three Choirs concert venue for the first time at the 1987(W) Festival, providing over five hundred seats in a building of both local and national importance within a short walking distance of the cathedral. The hall, a converted chapel, was built in 1773 by Selina, Countess of Huntingdon, to accommodate early followers of the Huntingdon Connexion (related to Calvinistic Methodism) who were regarded – according to discriminatory legislation still active – as dissenters. The chapel was twice extended in the nineteenth century to house a growing congregation. The last service was held in 1976, and in 1977 the City of Worcester Building Preservation Trust was set up to save the fine Georgian chapel and to restore and adapt it as a concert hall, arts centre and music school to serve Worcester and the Severn region.

The inaugural concert in the Countess of Huntingdon's Hall was held on the afternoon of Sunday, 23 August; an all-English programme, beginning appropriately with William Boyce's *Worcester Overture* (Symphony No. 8 in D) played by the Worcester-based English String Orchestra, conducted for this special occasion by Sir David Willcocks.

Several other recitals were given in the hall during the week, three of them by the Medici String Quartet. On Monday afternoon their programme included Borodin's String Quartet No. 1 in A and Richard Rodney Bennett's *Lamento d'Arianna*; and on Friday afternoon three equally contrasted quartets – Beethoven's Op. 130, Borodin's second, and Penderecki's first. On Wednesday morning the Medici Quartet were joined by Richard Pascoe, Barbara Leigh Hunt and the pianist John Bingham in a wholly delightful presentation of the life and music of Sir Edward Elgar written by Michael Kennedy: *Wood Magic*, an account, told as far as possible in Elgar's own words or in those of his friends and contemporaries, of how Elgar came to write the four masterpieces with which his composing life virtually closed in 1918–19: a violin sonata, string quartet, piano quintet, and the autumnal Cello Concerto.

On Thursday morning the Countess of Huntingdon's Hall was shown to be an ideal song recital venue when John Shirley-Quirk, sensitively accompanied by Christopher Robinson, presented an all-English programme: Purcell, Vaughan Williams, Warlock, Gurney and Howells. Enveloped in all this was Donald Hunt's cycle, *Strings in the earth and air*, settings of poems taken from the collection *Chamber Music* by James Joyce, and composed by Hunt as a wedding gift for his son Thomas and daughter-in-law Joanna.

The 1987 Elgar commission, Richard Rodney Bennett's Third Symphony, was performed for the first time at the Monday evening concert given by the BBC PO, conducted by Edward Downes to whom it is dedicated.

Bennett had intended to fulfill the commission with a short orchestral piece called *Tapestry* but subsequently extended the work to become his Third Symphony. In a programme note he explained that it

> . . . was written in New York City and London between April and July 1987. My first two symphonies, commissioned respectively for the London Symphony and New York Philharmonic orchestras, were composed in the late 1960s and are primarily extrovert, display pieces in which I was exploiting the resources of the modern orchestra, creating show pieces for the virtuosity of the players.
>
> The new symphony, composed twenty years after the second, is a very different proposition. The orchestra is moderate . . . only nine wind players and modest percussion in addition to the usual strings, plus piano and harp.
>
> The music is mostly thoughtful and lyrical in nature, more or less monothematic, and has a strong feeling of tonality, particularly at the opening and closing of the score.

Among other major works performed in the cathedral during the 1987(W) Festival, Howard Blake's oratorio *Benedictus* and the *Te Deum* of Krysztof Penderecki were, in their very different ways, memorable and important.

Howard Blake grew up in Brighton and at eighteen won a scholarship to the Royal Academy of Music, studying piano and composition. In the following decade or so he worked as a free-lance session pianist, composer, conductor and orchestrator. In 1971 he went to live in a water-mill in Sussex where he began to forge a personal style of composition which is rhythmic, contrapuntal and, most importantly, melodic. *Benedictus*, started in 1978, was the 'culmination of this period of creativity and developed the idiom to the full, at the same time presenting in dramatic form Blake's other preoccupation of those years – a search for spiritual meaning'.[27] Orchestral works, choral works, songs, ballets, chamber and instrumental works have all followed, including the highly successful piece for narrator and orchestra, *The Snowman*, a perennial best-seller on disc and video.

Benedictus was inspired by the teachings of St Benedict as laid down in his book, *The Rule*, so called because 'it guides straight the life of those who obey'. Blake's work is a dramatic oratorio for tenor, speaker, large choir and orchestra; a solo viola is also employed to haunting effect in his absorbing score. At Worcester, the impressively operatic tenor soloist was Arthur Davies, with Jeffrey Fenwick (speaker), Christopher Balmer (viola), the Festival Chorus and RLPO in thrilling form under Donald Hunt.

Krysztof Penderecki was born at Debrica, Poland in 1933. He studied composition with Malawski and Wiehowicz at the Krakow Music Academy, graduating in 1958. A year later, his *Threnody to the Victims of Hiroshima* won international acclaim for its intensely expressive use of new string sonorities, achieved through a thorough exploration of the instruments and playing techniques. The much larger *St Luke Passion* (1963–5), still unheard at Three Choirs, made an equally deep impression.

Penderecki's *Te Deum* received a first gripping Three Choirs performance on the Tuesday evening of the 1987(W) Festival when it was conducted by the composer. As well as the *Te Deum* and the String Quartet No. 1, Penderecki's *Capriccio* for Oboe and Strings was also included in the Festival programme, performed at the Countess of Huntingdon's Hall on Saturday afternoon by Nicholas Daniel in an English String Orchestra concert conducted by William Boughton.

The Hungarian-born conductor, Antal Dorati, had been engaged to direct the Festival Chorus and RPO in Beethoven's cantata *Calm Sea and Prosperous Voyage* and the Symphony No. 9 in D (*Choral*) on Friday evening, with Alison Hargan, Alfreda Hodgson, Robert Tear and Gwynne Howell. Ill health prevented Dorati from appearing and his place was taken at short notice by the Swiss, Karl Anton Rickenbacher. Soloists and choir responded magnificently to Rickenbacher's clear, incisive command, but the orchestra maintained a strange and wayward detachment.

Alfreda Hodgson, Robert Tear and Gwynne Howell again joined the Festival Chorus and RPO on the last night of the 1987(W) Festival in a superb performance of *Gerontius* under the sure hand of Donald Hunt.

Between the lines of the Latin text of the central Sanctus section of his *Te Deum*, Penderecki interpolated lines from an old national hymn, its plea both ancient and modern, sung in Polish and translated as follows:

> God of Poland, before all time, wrapped in great light,
>   power and glory,
> Before Thine altar we bear our petition:
> Father, restore to us our rightful land.

As the 1980s came to an end the cries for freedom in Eastern Europe appeared to have been answered. Political change flowed at breath-taking speed behind the 1989 tearing down of the Berlin Wall, and by 1990 a new optimism had replaced the pertrified gloom of more than four decades of cold war. Certainly the mood of the Worcester Festival in that year seemed to reflect spontaneously a lighter-hearted internationalism: in the cathedral, Italian, Russian and English evenings; a French afternoon; Bach, Haydn, Beethoven and Mahler aplenty; Berg side-by-side with Elgar; and at outside events the music of Latin America and northern India, a brass band, jazz and much more – the whole a tribute to imaginative programming and planning.

One of the most keenly anticipated events of the Festival was the first UK performance of George Lloyd's Twelfth Symphony, given on Friday evening by the BBC PO under the composer's own direction. And how good it was to see a living British composer with a wide popular following on both sides of the Atlantic mounting the rostrum at Three Choirs to conduct a new, large-scale work.

George Lloyd was born at St Ives, Cornwall in 1913. Illness precluded his attending school until the age of twelve, but after two years he left to pursue a full-time musical education, studying violin with Albert Sammons and composition with Harry Farjeon, then briefly attending Trinity College of Music in London. Lloyd began composing at the age of ten, and prior to the Second World War three symphonies and two operas, *Iernin* and *The Serf* (with libretti by his father) were performed – the former at Penzance in 1934 and the latter at Covent Garden in 1938. These early successes were brought to an end by the war. In 1942, while on an Arctic convoy in a cruiser, he was badly shell-shocked. After partially recovering his health, he was commissioned to write his third opera, *John Socman*, for the Festival of Britain, 1951. His health again deteriorated and he and his wife settled in Dorset where they operated a market garden, growing carnations and mushrooms, and only composing intermittently.

By 1973 Lloyd had written six more symphonies and several concertos, and his health had recovered sufficiently for him to return to full-time composing. A broadcast of his Eighth Symphony in 1977 marked a renewal of public interest in his music. Numerous performances with the BBC PO followed, and in 1988 he was appointed Principal Guest Conductor with the Albany Symphony Orchestra of New York State, who commissioned his Eleventh Symphony and for whom he wrote the Twelfth.

George Lloyd's music has aroused the considerable enthusiasm of those thirsting for lyrical beauty, melody and exuberance from a modern composer, and the disdain of others who hear no more than skilful scoring in a nineteenth-century manner, derivative and banal to the point of being anodyne. 'But what music is not derivative in some sense and to some degree?' wrote David J. Brown in *The Musical Times*. 'Are some sources of derivation acceptable and some not? And was the same charge of banality not levelled at Mahler until fairly recently, before the discovery that it was really irony; *ergo* acceptable; *ergo* great?'[28]

In any event, the Worcester audience welcomed Lloyd's approachable clarity, even though the single-movement Twelfth is far from his best symphony, the over-long *fugato* of its final section outstaying its welcome. 'No-one now living, though, can make an orchestra *sing* as he does, and our musical life has plenty of room for, and would be poorer without, his unique contribution.'[29]

The single 'world première' of the Festival was Mussorgsky's *Saint Nicholas Mass*, 'an unashamed hybrid' as Philip Lane, who realized and edited the work, described it in his programme note. Mussorgsky, of course, wrote no such Mass. What Lane has done is to intersperse three choruses from *Salammbo* with the cantatas *Joshua* and *The Destruction of Sennacherib*, and substituted the Ordinary of the Mass for the original texts – an ingenious if not entirely convincing device for making little-known music accessible. Donald Hunt conducted the RLPO and Festival Chorus, with Alison Pearce and Matthew Best the ideal soloists.

This Monday evening concert continued with the Tchaikovsky B flat minor concerto, played on an inadequate piano by Boris Beresovsky, and ended with a thrilling account of Prokofiev's *Alexander Nevsky*:

> Roy Massey conducted both works, the latter being particularly distinguished by Linda Strachan's haunting obsequy for the dead of the Battle on the Ice (which itself made one fear premature collapse of Worcester Cathedral's structurally endangered central tower).
>
> The evening before was all-Italian, opened by Petrassi's half-hour *Magnificat*, arguably the most musically substantial and syntactically original of the Festival's unfamiliar big works, and one whose date of 1940 added further accusatory point. Though it was obviously a major challenge for the Festival Chorus, John Sanders's dedicated direction carried the day. Wisely, he allowed the R.L.P.O. (in splendid form for all five of their concerts) their head, and they duly relished Petrassi's pungently juxtaposed and often vividly exciting orchestral textures. Why is this composer, now 86, not heard far more often? One could ask the same about Respighi (leaving aside the Roman trilogy), but the ensuing not-ideally-paced performance of *Church Windows* under Donald Hunt will not, I fear, have made many converts.[30]

Wednesday evening brought the *St John Passion*, played on original instruments and at baroque pitch by the Hanover Band directed by Simon Preston, with the three cathedral choirs and a team of soloists of rare quality: Ian Partridge (Evangelist), Michael George (Christus), Luise Horrocks, Charles Brett, William Kendall and Peter Savidge.

Less satisfactory was the cathedral concert which on Saturday evening began the whole Festival. Again a first-rate team of soloists: Helen Field, Alison Pearce, Luise Horrocks, Sally Burgess, Linda Strachan, Neil Jenkins (stepping in for the indisposed Anthony Roden), Alan Opie and Stafford Dean; the RLPO in cracking form and, if not quite 'of a Thousand', a combined choir well capable of raising the roof – the Festival Chorus, choristers of Worcester Cathedral and the Worcester Junior Festival Chorus – in Mahler's vast Eighth Symphony under Libor Pesek. But somehow the performance never added up to the sum of its parts, and an essential sense of unity between conductor and choir was noticeably lacking.

From such immensity it was refreshing to turn to the intimacy of the Countess of Huntingdon's Hall, where on Tuesday and Wednesday morning the Alberni String Quartet captured a magical mood. In both of their recitals the central work was a model of word-setting for singer and instrumental ensemble. On Tuesday, Samuel Barber's setting of Matthew Arnold's *Dover Beach* for baritone and string quartet, in which Thomas Hunt was the sensitive soloist. And on Wednesday the quartet was joined by Philip Dennis and Donald Hunt in Ivor Gurney's song-cycle for tenor, string quartet and piano to poems by A.E. Housman, *Ludlow and Teme*; surely seven of the most beautiful of English songs.

Gurney was in·the company of seven other composers, all with strong Three Choirs links, in an exquisite recital given by Ian and Jennifer Partridge at the Countess of Huntingdon's Hall on Friday morning: Stanford, Atkins, Brewer, Parry, Howells, Britten and Paul Spicer whose song-cycle *A Song for Birds*, settings of medieval Latin poems translated into English by Fleur Adcock, and poems by Laurie Lee, was given its first performance.

Gerontius was again the climax to a dazzling week:

> . . . an unequal assumption of the title role [William Cochran] was fortunately compensated by Sally Burgess, substituting at the last minute for Alfreda Hodgson . . . detracts in no way from the overwhelming emotional and spiritual impact of this of all works in this of all venues. [Alan Opie was powerfully impressive as the Priest and the Angel of the Agony.] The B.B.C. P.O., the Festival Chorus and Donald Hunt proved, as anticipated, worthy keepers of the Seal.
>
> The single finest performance, though, was of arguably the greatest work. On the Tuesday evening the Chorus and R.L.P.O., and (yet again), an exceptional solo team [Alison Pearce, Sally Burgess, Neil Jenkins and Matthew Best] were driven by Donald Hunt through an unfaltering (and uninterrupted) *Missa Solemnis* which more than any other live performance I have heard positively relished the stratospheric choral difficulties and constant challenges of balance in a superbly coherent projection of Beethoven's mighty and eternally unsettling vision. Malcolm Stewart's violin solo in the Benedictus touched perfection.[31]

Notes

1. *Birmingham Post*, 22 August 1985
2. *Birmingham Post*, 20 August 1985
3. *Sunday Times*, 24 August 1980
4. *Financial Times*, 30 August 1980
5. *South Wales Argus*, 29 August 1980
6. *Daily Telegraph*, 25 August 1980
7. In a morning concert at the Gloucester College of Education by Fresh Air Concerts: a programme of avant-garde music with an element of theatricality.
8. *The Citizen*, 26 August 1983
9. Hereford Festival 1988 programme book, p. 156
10. *Hereford Times*, 26 August 1983
11. *Western Daily Press*, 26 August 1983
12. *Western Daily Press*, 25 August 1983
13. *South Wales Argus*, 29 August 1986
14. Ibid.
15. *Birmingham Post*, 25 August 1986
16. *The Citizen*, 25 August 1986
17. *The Independent*, 22 August 1989
18. MT 1989, p. 700
19. *Worcester Evening News*, 26 August 1981
20. MT 1981, p. 690
21. MT 1984, p. 660
22. *Guardian*, 24 August 1984
23. Ibid.
24. MT 1984, p. 660
25. Worcester Festival 1984 programme book, p. 152
26. MT 1984, p. 659–60
27. Worcester Festival 1987 programme book, p. 19
28. MT 1990, p. 616
29. Ibid.
30. Ibid.
31. MT 1990, p. 617

CHAPTER TWENTY-TWO

HOUSES OF THE MIND

Reputations die hard. If you've never been to the Three Choirs Festival, perhaps you feel you can imagine the scene all too clearly: tea and warm sandwiches in marquees, lots of old ladies of the kind who wear woolly stockings in midsummer, an atmosphere of somnolent soulfulness reflecting the English Choral Tradition at its heaviest, and unremarkable musical standards to match.

Well, the Three Choirs may have been like that once. But it isn't now, as I discovered in the course of a pair of memorable visits to Gloucester in 1986 and to Hereford in 1988.[1]

Thus Malcolm Hayes, writing in the *Daily Telegraph* at the beginning of the 1990 Worcester Festival, puts his finger on the most frequently-heard criticism of Three Choirs from those whose experience is based on the long-ago, an old photograph or a mother's tale. But upholders of the modern Festival have no cause to sneer at its past reputation.

If for more than two centuries Three Choirs was, in the main, the province of nobility, gentry and the affluent, then those were the very people who, year after year, were prepared to sustain the continuance of its tradition from their own pockets, effectively subsidizing the pleasure of the less-well-to-do who always made up a fair proportion of the audience. Such patronage was essential throughout the long years when English music was at its nadir, marking time until the so-called 'land without music' could once more boast composers of genius; of Parry, Elgar, Vaughan Williams and all that host. When the time at last came the Festivals were waiting; an established platform for the renaissance.

Once a mainly local, albeit large-scale, event Three Choirs now attracts a considerable number of visitors from all parts of Britain and from overseas; a larger number in fact than from Gloucestershire, Herefordshire and Worcestershire. At a time when many music festivals have fallen into the danger of outgrowing their artistic strength, Three Choirs retains a sense of scale linked to its lack of full-time paid staff. Indeed, it comes as a surprise to find that an international festival can still succeed when so dependent upon efforts given *con amore*. 'But this is a festival whose special atmosphere now co-exists with performance standards that are impressively high,' wrote Malcolm Hayes, 'and a festival which also . . . spreads its musical wings as wide as any other, and indeed wider than most.'[2]

The 'special atmosphere' of Three Choirs is almost impossible to put into words. There is that sense of fellowship among performers, composers, critics and audience who mingle freely in the Festival Club, at the Garden Party, or Civic Luncheon. Old friends meet year after year, and new friendships are formed. There is an awareness of being part of a long tradition; of feeling the closeness of the Spirits of Greatness-Past. And love of music is the cement which binds all together. But there is something else which, in an increasingly secular age, is even more difficult to define and which is not restricted to membership of sect or creed: a literal communion.

John T. Hamilton, an American visitor of many years' standing who brought the chorale which bears his name to sing at the 1984 Worcester Festival, found expression for yet another element intrinsic to Three Choirs:

> Several years ago at Worcester I had taken my nave seat somewhat earlier than usual and was sitting contemplating the scene. My seatmate interrupted my reverie by inquiring rather impatiently, 'When do you think the performance will start?' I replied, 'It has already started,' and began conspicuously to look about, up and around. 'Oh yes, I see what you mean,' she said quietly. The nine centuries were putting on a spectacular pre-concert show if one only took the trouble to look . . .[3]

This is close to something which Sir Arthur Bliss once said to Douglas Guest: 'They can never replace Three Choirs – it goes to the eye as well as to the ear.'

But festivals, no less than cathedrals, do not survive on veneration and idle hope; without money and constant effort they collapse – and the age of the wealthy aristocrat patron is long past. For many years Three Choirs has produced a heavy deficit, covered only by donations from local authorities, the fund-raising activities of the Festival Ladies Committee, friends and well-wishers, Arts Council grants (currently roughly sufficient to cover the cost of one major concert per Festival), and commercial and private sponsorship. (Large-scale commercial sponsorship of specific concerts was first secured at Worcester in 1975.) An Endowment Fund was opened by the Three Choirs Festival Association in 1989 in the hope that the Festival could enter the twenty-first century with a secure financial foundation, but to date this has achieved only moderate success.

None the less, Three Choirs continues to expand musically, to commission new work and to engage musicians of the highest international reputation. Through the activities of the fringe, again a Worcester initiative in 1975, the Festival is reaching out to a wider cross-section of the local communities in the three cities than ever before.[4]

Sam Driver White, Chairman of the Three Choirs Festival Association and of the Worcester Festival Committee, has often been asked to explain the secret of the success of Three Choirs. 'It is not', he says, 'as secret as the legendary recipe for Worcestershire Sauce, but the ingredients may be as many, and the skill lies in ensuring the right mix: the music of the English choral tradition performed in the inspiring surroundings of a great cathedral; the individual flavour of the programmes selected by the three cathedral organists; the opportunity for audiences to experience the best in chamber music, song recitals, poetry reading, lectures, jazz, and music and dance from many different parts of the world – all giving balance to the week's main concerts in the cathedral.

'A major part of the magic', he says, 'is in the warmth and friendship that pervades all parts of the Festival, from a smile and friendly banter with a lady serving salads in the

Festival Club, to the care and concern of the accommodation secretary, to the interesting chat with a Texas choirmaster you may have met at the last Festival.

'Over the generations, the Festival has used unashamedly the freely and happily given talents of some of the most able professional and business men and women in its area to manage, administer and arrange the finances of its undertaking. Such energy and talent could not be gathered more than once every three years, but that talent with its innovative ideas and wealth of experience will continue to be the bulwark upon which the quiet and efficient management of all aspects of the Festival will rely and without which such a large and complicated undertaking would fall into chaos.'[5]

One tradition, the oldest of the Festival and more than once the mainstay in preventing its abolition, has been modified in recent years. The Charity for the Benefit of Widows and Orphans of the Clergy in the three dioceses remained the largely unaltered *raison d'être* of the Festival from 1724 until 1986. In that year important changes were made. As a result of responsible funding by the Church and more adequate provision by the State, Gloucester and Worcester had been finding it increasingly unnecessary to look to the proceeds of Festival collections to assist their care of clergy widows and orphans, although it was accepted that a similar position had yet to be reached in Hereford Diocese. There remained a feeling that, in a Festival centred on three great Christian churches, some charitable emphasis should remain and, while future policy was still under discussion, Gloucester broke with tradition and divided the 1986 collection equally between the continuing needs of Hereford Diocese for help with its clergy widows and orphans, and the Friends of Cathedral Music, a charity concerned to safeguard the unique tradition of cathedral and collegiate chapel music throughout the land.

In 1987 the Dean and Chapter of each of the three cathedrals agreed that the purposes of the Festival collections should be widened to embrace the relief and support of clergy families in special need, and that collections should be taken only at the Opening Service (or after the first evening concert), at Choral Evensong during Festival week and after the last evening concert. And so at Hereford in 1991 collections were divided equally among the three dioceses and allocated by them to such charitable work related to the needs of the families of the clergy as they determined.[6]

The 1991 Hereford Festival began on Sunday, 18 August. Roy Massey, resplendent in the robes of his Lambeth doctorate, conducted the Festival Chorus and Royal Liverpool Philharmonic Orchestra in a most impressive Opening Service, marred hardly at all by the lady who, during the prayer 'that through music we may raise man from the sorrows of this world to the joy of your divine presence' called out loudly: 'and women!' A sign of the times?

Hereford is the only one of the three cities to retain an Opening Service accompanied by full orchestra, a luxury made possible in 1991 by the generosity of Hereford City Council; and Roy Massey's determination to continue this tradition was well justified by the dignity and grandeur of the occasion.

On Monday a tremor of apprehension disturbed the festive calm as news came through that in the USSR Mikhail Gorbachev had been toppled in a leadership coup. Were 'the sorrows of this world' again to overwhelm our nascent optimism in a new order? Against this background the performance of *Morning Heroes* on Monday evening was particularly piercing. The largest of the works by Sir Arthur Bliss included in the Festival to mark his centenary year, *Morning Heroes* was for Roy Massey and many in his audience an overwhelming emotional experience. Written by a composer who had seen the brutality of war at first hand through soldier's eyes, its impact in performance is greater than can be anticipated from the printed score – especially so when the narration of *Hector's Farewell to Andromache* and Wilfred Owen's *Spring Offensive* are entrusted to a narrator of Brian Kay's ability.

> Halted against the shade of the last hill,
> They fed, and, lying easy, were at ease,
> And, finding comfortable chests and knees
> Carelessly slept. But many there stood still
> To face the stark, blank sky beyond the ridge,
> Knowing their feet had come to the end of the world.

Earlier in the evening a small ceremony took place on the riverbank of the Wye opposite the cathedral – one of those slightly dotty and wholly delightful occasions which serve to make an English summer memorable. Organized by the City of Hereford's Environment Department, a suitably inscribed stone had been set into place to mark the approximate spot where G.R. Sinclair's bulldog Dan had so famously splashed into the river and the *Enigma Variations*. The site had been identified by Elgar's godson, Wulstan Atkins, and an unveiling ceremony was performed by Roy Massey, together with his dog, Winston, at 5 p.m. on 19 August. Winston dragged his master towards the small gathering and, once off the leash, pulled aside the artificial grass covering the plaque, paused while Massey spoke a few well-chosen words, and then, like Dan before him, sped down the riverbank into the waters of the Wye!

The bicentenary of the death of Mozart, an anniversary which at times in 1991 threatened almost to overwhelm national musical life, was not forgotten at Hereford. Kenneth Page conducted the Orchestra da Camera at Leominster Priory on Tuesday afternoon in lively performances of the Symphonies No. 40 and 41, and Stephen Coombs and Ian Munro played the Concerto in E flat, K365 for two pianos and orchestra. The first afternoon in the cathedral the same orchestra was conducted by Roy Massey in the Sinfonia Concertante in E flat, K297b, for oboe, clarinet, bassoon, horn and orchestra; the youthful and brilliant soloists were Nicholas Daniel, Joy Farrall, Julie Andrews and Stephen Bell. The concert, which had begun with Denys Darlow's *Te Deum*, Op. 12, ended with the Mass in C minor, K427 by Mozart, a beautifully balanced performance, the Hereford Festival Chorus and soloists Jennifer Smith, Margaret Field, Andrew Tusa and George Banks Martin floating silver sound to the vault, and Roy Massey in seeming-reverie at the end, leaving almost too late his acknowledgement of Leader Kenneth Page and the orchestra.

Wednesday and Thursday evenings contained the two high spots of the week:

Vernon Handley brought from the Royal Liverpool P.O. playing of richness and character in Bliss's *Introduction and Allegro*. So he did in Gordon Jacob's arrangement of the Elgar Organ Sonata [Wednesday]. The chorus responded sympathetically to the many pleasantries of Howard Blake's *Song of St Francis*. It sounded grateful music to sing, something which could not be said of Joubert's *Herefordshire Canticles* [Thursday]. The chorus had a tough week, and it was no mean achievement that on the last day they should sing so jubilantly in the Poulenc *Gloria*, and so vigorously in the Berlioz *Te Deum*.[7]

By the last day, news bulletins had shown Boris Yeltsin defying the Moscow old guard from atop a tank and the restoration of the Soviet *status quo*. Worst fears again subsided and full-throated Berlioz affirmed our thankfulness.

But ironically [wrote Kenneth Loveland] the best remembered events had nothing to do with choralism. They were cellist Steven Isserlis's brilliant playing of Howard Blake's *Diversions* [Wednesday, with RLPO and Handley], with its skilful commentary on traditional forms, Emma Johnson's winning musicality in Stanford's Clarinet Concerto [Thursday, with RPO and Sanders], and most of all, Vernon Handley's total authority and control in a profoundly felt *Enigma Variations* [Wednesday].[8]

The year 1992 has begun: a Gloucester year and one in which Three Choirs will celebrate Britain's full entry into the European Community, and full and overdue honour will be given to Herbert Howells to mark the centenary of his birth.

Among the many works by Howells to be included in the 1992(G) Festival programme, both sacred and secular, his *Rhapsodic Quintet* for clarinet, two violins, viola and cello, Op. 31 (1919) will be played by the doyenne of English clarinettists, Thea King, with the Britten String Quartet.

By happy chance, the same team recorded the piece for the Hyperion label in 1991; part of a compact disc which was selected by Roderick Swanston as a 'record of the year' for the BBC's *Record Review* programme. 'It was', said Swanston, 'an example of 20th-century English clarinet music which I would have dismissed with contempt as a student.' Having listened to Howells's *Rhapsodic Quintet* he was 'bowled over' by the piece, describing it as most sumptuous, and Howells as a vibrant and disgracefully neglected composer. Equal enthusiasm was expressed by the other members of the BBC review team. It was 'an elaborate stunner' said the not-easily-pleased Rodney Milnes; it contained 'a sense of regret at lost innocence'; there was in it 'the peace of ages'; and the ending contained 'one of the loveliest moments in music'[9] – a timely discovery that there is more to Howells than Evensong. How he would have loved it!

And how he would have valued the widening horizons of the Festival, the increasing interest shown in it by a growing audience, and the prospects for even greater vigour to come. Writing in 1977, Howells said:

In my Gloucester-Worcester-Hereford wanderings during the past sixty years I have encountered half-truths (and sometimes their authors) often.

One such experience still lingers with me. A tightly-packed audience was slowly moving out of Hereford Cathedral after an evening performance. It suddenly heard – and was, doubtless, *meant* to hear – a man's pontifical voice, declaring that 'the trouble with these festivals is that they're so parochial.' (A half-truth, innocuous – except for the ill-chosen moment. For the crowd round the 'loudspeaker' fellow had just been deeply moved, listening to beloved Kathleen Ferrier singing almost certainly for her last time at the Three Choirs Festival. And it was the 'Angel's Farewell'. The date: September, 1952).

The 'parochial' observation has a far-away historical truth. It implies, of course, a parish. That was no real concern for the near-cynic emerging with the rest of us from the Cathedral. But it might well be ours. And thinking constructively about the Parish could be a compelling and appropriate exercise for all devoted 'parishioners'.

As one of that company I have, for long years, tried to feel, define and express what is meant, to a potential musician, to have been nurtured in a countryside of companionable hills, two lovely but very diverse rivers, and three magical cathedrals: so that it has seemed that the Severn and the Wye could be flowing in one's veins, and that the three great churches of Worcester and Hereford and Gloucester had become the Houses of the Mind. Further: in one's youth, there might have been undisciplined music flaring in one's mind; but with it (providentially) the exciting certainty that for a whole week in early September there would be, in one or other of the three cities, the presence and spell of the reigning Festival giants – Hubert Parry, Edward Elgar, and the younger Ralph Vaughan Williams; and more than a glimpse of some other dedicated 'parishioners', their successors. All this. And a crowning certainty – that for *all* 'parishioners' (predestined leaders or not) *place* and *frame of mind* would be an unbroken unit. [10]

In radio talks and conversations[11] Howells spoke of his first efforts in music, rousing the house at 4 a.m. in his Forest of Dean childhood with things like *Bluebells of Scotland*; of being taken to Herbert Brewer when he was fourteen and seeing him every Saturday for about three years before Brewer took him from Lydney Grammar School to be articled at Gloucester Cathedral. He first saw Elgar in Brewer's drawing-room. The great man took a pencil out of Howells's hand: 'You shouldn't do it that way – let me change it.'

Herbert Howells never wanted to write a symphony or an opera. He said that he 'composed out of the sheer love of trying to make nice sounds' and that he loved music 'as a man can love a woman'. He loved the act of composing. And he never turned his back on the 'trinity of supreme English Cathedrals made indivisible by providential grace' in which that love was nurtured. 'We may,' he said, 'be nostalgic'; may perhaps wish Elgar among us once more or to hear again the artistry of Kreisler. Howells could never forget Ralph Vaughan Williams in 1910 – 'that strange, incomprehensible fantasia for strings' which kept the audience waiting impatiently for *Gerontius* for twenty-five minutes.

'All has passed', he said, 'but the Three Choirs Festival is now concerned with what is to come. In other words, with history in the making.'

Notes

1. *Daily Telegraph*, 18 August 1990
2. Ibid.
3. Worcester Festival 1984 programme book, p. 74
4. Detailed listing of fringe entertainments provided during the Festival lies beyond the scope of this history.
5. Letters from Mr S. Driver White to the author
6. See Rodney Bennett, *The Three Choirs Festival Charity*, Hereford Festival 1991 programme book, p. 36
7. MT 1991, p. 522
8. Ibid.
9. *Record Review*, BBC Radio 3, Saturday 28 December 1991
10. Herbert Howells, 'Memories from the Twentieth Century', an essay published in *Two Hundred and Fifty Years of the Three Choirs Festival* (Three Choirs Festival Association, 1977)
11. National Sound Archives (M751W, M2070R, M5927R and M5084)

ANNALS OF THE THREE CHOIRS

by
Christian Wilson

Appendix I

List of works, other than Services, anthems, etc., performed in the cathedrals and other principal venues, 1890–1991 and, up to 1953, at the Secular and Chamber Concerts

Key:

FP – First Performance
* – conducted by the composer
s – performed at the Secular Concerts
c – performed at the Chamber Concerts

G – Gloucester
H – Hereford
W – Worcester

NB   This list ignores separate songs and comparable items; and it does not deal with music performed at the Opening Services. It follows the format adopted by Watkins Shaw in *The Three Choirs Festival* (Worcester, 1954), but deals only with the Festivals of the last 101 years, i.e. from the first performance of Elgar's *Froissart* at Worcester. The list published in Dr Shaw's book begins at 1870, the date from which an unbroken series of programmes is available.

Albinoni, T. (1671–1751)
  Concerto Op. 7, No. 5 (arr. Roberts for brass): 1986G

Andrews, Herbert K. (1904–65)
  Ah, see the fair chivalry: 1964H

Anon.
  Sing we now merrily (arr. Roberts for brass): 1986G

Arensky, Anton (1861–1906)
  Variations on a Theme of Tchaikowsky: 1947G^c

Arne, Thomas (1710–78)
Libera me: 1978W

Arnell, Richard (b. 1917)
Sinfonia, Op. 13: 1953G*

Arnold, Malcolm (b. 1921)
Serenade for Guitar and Strings: 1986G
Sinfonietta No. 1, Op. 48: 1988H

Atkins, Sir Ivor (1869–1953)
Hymn of Faith: 1905W–FP*, 1908W*, 1920W, 1990W

Bach, C.P.E. (1714–88)
Magnificat in D: 1971G

Bach, J.C. (1735–82)
Concerto for Harpsichord in B flat: 1935W
Concerto for Oboe in F: 1971G

Bach, J.S. (1685–1750)
Passion according to St Matthew: 1911W, 1912H, 1913G, 1920W, 1938W, 1947G, 1948W, 1950G, 1952H, 1954W, 1959G, 1978W, 1985H
Passion according to St John: 1929W, 1953G, 1960W, 1976H, 1990W
Mass in B minor: 1893W, 1906H, 1923W, 1924H, 1927H, 1930H, 1931G, 1932W, 1933H, 1934G, 1936H, 1937G, 1946H, 1949H, 1951W, 1955H, 1957W, 1961H, 1966W, 1977G, 1982H
Mass in G: 1983G
Cantatas:
No. 11 ('Ascension Oratorio'): 1935W, 1970H, 1985H
A stronghold sure: 1890W, 1897H, 1956G
Christ lag in Todesbanden: 1980G
Come, Redeemer of our race: 1905W, 1921H
Erfreute Zeit im neuen Bunde: 1952H
Give the hungry man thy bread: 1925G
God goeth up: 1900H
Herz und Mund: 1983G
Ich will den Kreustab: 1958H
Jauchzet Gott: 1955H, 1972W
Jesu, der meine Seele: 1963W
Jesus sleeps: 1903H
My spirit was in heaviness: 1892G
O light everlasting: 1928G
Ready be my soul: 1926W
Sleepers, wake: 1901G, 1931G
The Lord God is a sun: 1902W
Was Gott thut: 1965G
Motets:
Be not afraid: 1909H
Now shall the grace: 1907G, 1922G
Jesu, meine Freude: 1976H

Der Geist hilft: 1985H, 1991H
Singet dem Herrn: 1974G, 1983G
Christmas Oratorio: 1894H, 1896W, 1898G, 1962G
Magnificat in D: 1908W, 1934G, 1956G, 1957W, 1971G
Concertos:
Brandenburg Concerto No. 1: 1928G^s, 1979H; No. 2: 1926W^c, 1969W; No. 3: 1921H^s, 1934G, 1947G^c, 1956G, 1977G; No. 4: 1968G, 1983G; No. 5: 1985H; No. 6: 1954W
Concerto for two Violins in D minor: 1935W, 1964H, 1974G
Violin Concerto No. 2 in E: 1910G, 1967H, 1983G
Harpsichord Concertos: in F minor: 1929W^c, 1970H; in D minor: 1976H; in A: 1983G
Italian Concerto: 1934G
Concerto for Flute, Violin and Harpsichord in A minor: 1935W
Chaconne for Violin in D minor: 1897H^c
Fantasia and Fugue in C minor (arr. Elgar): 1922G, 1990W
Fugue à la Gigue (arr. Holst): 1931G^s
Chromatic Fantasia and Fugue: 1952H^c
Suites:
No. 1 in C: 1983G; No. 3 in D: 1972W, 1973H
Sinfonia, Cantata No. 29: 1985H
Organ:
Ricarcare a 6: 1955H
Trio Sonata: 1959G
Partita, O Gott, du Frommer Gott: 1961H
Passacaglia and Fugue in C minor: 1962G, 1971G
Prelude and Fugue in B minor: 1964H
Prelude and Fugue in G minor: 1970H
Prelude and Fugue in E flat: 1965G
Prelude and Fugue in E minor (Wedge): 1978W, 1985H

Bainton, Edgar (1880–1956)
Hymn to God the Father: 1926W–FP*, 1927H*
The Tower: 1924H–FP*
Epithalamion for Orchestra: 1929W–FP*^{s}
Three pieces for Orchestra: 1921H*^{s}
And I saw a new Heaven: 1962G

Bairstow, Edward (1874–1946)
Introit: Let all mortal flesh: 1957W, 1965G
Blessed City, heavenly Salem: 1962G

Bantock, Granville (1868–1946)
The Burden of Babylon: 1928G–FP
Christ in the Wilderness: 1907G–FP*
Gethsemane: 1910G–FP*

Song of Songs (Prelude and First Day): 1922G–FP*
The Time Spirit: 1904G*
Hebridean Symphony: 1925G*
Orchestral Poem, Witch of Atlas: 1902W–FP*
The Wilderness (Interlude from *Christus*):
    1903H–FP*
Overture to a Greek Tragedy: 1911W–FP*ˢ
The Pierrot of the Minute: 1908W–FP*ˢ 1924Hˢ
Incidental music to Macbeth: 1927H*
Serenade for String Orchestra: 1912Hˢ
Old English Suite (arr. for small orchestra):
    1909H–FP*ˢ
Sappho Songs: 1921H*ˢ
Three Celtic Songs: 1930H–FP*ˢ

Barber, Samuel (1910–81)
    Adagio for Strings: 1946H, 1971G
    Capricorn Concerto: 1973H
    Variations on a Sharp-note Hymn (Wondrous
        Love): 1990W

Bartók, Béla (1881–1945)
    Piano Concerto No. 3: 1961H
    Divertimento for String Orchestra: 1970H
    A Little Suite from 'For Children', Vol. 1:
        1976H

Bassett, Peter
    Two Pieces for Wind Orchestra: 1980G

Batten, Adrian (*c*. 1585–1637)
    Hear my prayer, O Lord: 1960W, 1966W

Battishill, Jonathan (1739–1801)
    O Lord look down (arr. Elgar): 1923W, 1970H

Bax, Arnold (1883–1963)
    St Patrick's Breastplate: 1934G
    The Morning Watch: 1935W–FP
    To the Name above every Name: 1923W–FP
    Summer Music: 1934G
    Quintet for Oboe and Strings in G minor: 1931Gᶜ
    Tintagel: 1983G

Beckerath, Rudolf (1907–76)
    Towermusik (for Brass): 1967H

Beethoven, Ludwig van (1770–1827)
    Mass in C: 1895G, 1970H, 1984W
    Mass in D (*Missa Solemnis*): 1897H, 1909H,
        1926W, 1959G, 1969W, 1975W, 1986G,
        1990W, 1991H
    Mount of Olives (*Engedi*): 1890W, 1971G
    Symphonies:
    No. 2: 1934G, 1949H, 1990W
    No. 3: 1891H, 1898G, 1901G, 1910G, 1922G,
        1955H
    No. 4: 1905W

No. 5: 1890W, 1892G, 1897H, 1902W,
    1912H, 1938W
No. 6: 1896W, 1953G
No. 7: 1893W, 1899W, 1966W
No. 8: 1904G, 1967H, 1974G, 1976H
No. 9: 1900H, 1911W, 1927H, 1933H,
    1968G, 1987W
Calm Sea and Prosperous Voyage: 1987W
Piano Concertos:
No. 3: 1937Gˢ, 1956G; No. 4: 1929W, 1949H,
    1954W, 1960W, 1973H
Violin Concerto in D: 1907G, 1908W, 1947G,
    1949H, 1952W, 1956G, 1963W, 1979H,
    1986G
Overtures:
Leonora No. 3: 1950G, 1962G, 1973H
Coriolanus: 1894Hˢ, 1923Wˢ, 1964H
Egmont: 1966W, 1970H, 1977G
Prometheus: 1903Hˢ, 1986G
Equali: 1920W, 1924H, 1954W
Romance No. 1 in G, Op. 40: 1990W
Romance No. 2 in F, Op. 36: 1990W

Bell, William H. (1873–1946)
    Symphonic Prelude, A Song in the Morning:
        1901G–FP*ˢ

Benjamin, Arthur (1893–1960)
    Overture to an Italian Comedy: 1937Gˢ

Bennett, Richard Rodney (b. 1936)
    Spells: 1975W–FP
    Two Carols: 1979H
    Piano Concerto: 1975W
    Symphony No. 3: 1987W

Berg, Alban (1825–1935)
    Violin Concerto: 1990W

Berger
    Canzona, Eighth Tone: 1969W

Berkeley, Lennox (1903–90)
    Domini est terra: 1938W*
    Four Poems of St Teresa of Avila: 1955H
    Stabat Mater: 1960W
    Magnificat: 1970H, 1978W
    Voices of the Night: 1973H–FP, 1978W
    Judica me: 1978W
    Serenade for Strings: 1966W
    Divertimento: 1967H
    Antiphon for Strings: 1978W*
    Fantasia: 1978W

Berkeley, Michael (b. 1948)
    Or shall we die?: 1985H

Berlioz, Hector (1803–69)
    Grande Messe des Morts: 1966W, 1981W

L'Enfance du Christ: 1952H, 1963W
Te Deum: 1906H, 1926W, 1958H, 1967H, 1974G, 1987W, 1991H
Les Nuits d'été, Op. 7: 1986G
Overtures:
Carnival Romain: 1920W, 1978W, 1988H
Beatrice and Benedict: 1969W
Benvenuto Cellini: 1983G
Symphonie Fantastique: 1975W
Dance of the Sylphs and Hungarian March: 1897H

Berners, Lord Gerald (1883–1950)
Fugue for Orchestra: 1929W

Bernstein, Leonard (1918–90)
Chichester Psalms: 1975W, 1984W
Missa Brevis: 1990W

Bizet, Georges (1838–75)
Te Deum: 1973H–FP in England, 1980G
Symphony in C: 1966W

Blair, Hugh
Blessed are they who watch: 1896W–FP*
Song of Deborah and Barak: 1902W–FP*

Blake, Howard (b. 1938)
Benedictus: 1987W
Diversions for violoncello and orchestra: 1991H
Song of Saint Francis: 1991H

Bliss, Arthur (1891–1975)
Meditations on a Theme by John Blow: 1956G
The Beatitudes: 1962G*
Mary of Magdala: 1963W–FP*
The World is charged: 1971G, 1983G
Colour Symphony: 1922G–FP*, 1955H*, 1989G
Morning Heroes: 1933H, 1991H
Music for Strings: 1947G, 1960W, 1965G*
Introduction and Allegro: 1991H

Blitheman, John (c. 1525–91)
In pace: 1968G

Bloch, Ernest (1880–1959)
Sacred Service: 1956G, 1957W, 1988H

Blow, John (1649–1708)
The Lord is my Shepherd: 1957W
My God, my God: 1960W
Salvator mundi: 1964H
Overture and Ground in D minor: 1957W
Prelude and Canzona: 1960W, 1966W

Boccherini, Luigi (1743–1805)
Cello Sonata No. 6 in A minor: 1906H^c

Body, Jack (b. 1944)
Carol to St Stephen: 1977G

Bononcini, Antonio (1677–1726)
Stabat Mater: 1974G

Borodin, Alexander (1833–87)
Nocturne and Scherzo for String Quartet: 1930H^c
Overture, *Prince Igor*: 1977G, 1987W

Bowers-Broadbent, Christopher (b. 1945)
Deo Gratias: 1978W–FP

Boyce, William (1710–79)
Lord, Thou hast been our refuge: 1960W
O where shall wisdom be found: 1961H
Turn thee unto me: 1970H
Symphonies:
No. 4 in F: 1979H
No. 5 in D: 1960W, 1969W, 1974G
No. 8 in D minor ('Worcester'): 1957W

Boyle, Rory (b. 1951)
Toccata for Organ: 1977G–FP

Brahms, Johannes (1833–97)
German Requiem: 1893W, 1899W, 1904G, 1912H, 1924H, 1931G, 1933H, 1948W, 1952H, 1960W, 1971G, 1983G
Alto Rhapsody: 1910G, 1912H, 1921H, 1937G, 1953G, 1967H, 1985H
A Song of Destiny: 1895G
Four Serious Songs: 1959G
Three Festival Motets: 1983G
Symphonies:
No. 1: 1901G, 1903H, 1908W, 1926W, 1936H
No. 2: 1900H, 1913G, 1922G, 1930H, 1970H, 1977G, 1985H
No. 3: 1902W, 1906H, 1923W, 1933H, 1949H, 1955H
No. 4: 1905W, 1924H, 1929W, 1962G
Piano Concertos:
No. 1: 1932W; No. 2: 1950G
Violin Concerto in D: 1934G, 1953G, 1958H
Overture, Academic Festival: 1947G, 1969W, 1971G, 1979H
Variations on a Theme of Haydn (*St Antoni*): 1898G, 1907G, 1921H, 1925G, 1946H, 1951W, 1956G, 1961H, 1968G, 1973H, 1988H
Variations on a Theme of Paganini: 1952H^c
Piano Quintet in F minor: 1894H^c
String Quartet Op. 5, No. 2 in A minor: 1909H^c
Trio for piano, violin and horn, Op. 40: 1938W^c
Trio in C minor for piano, violin and cello: 1936H^c

Brent Smith, Alexander (1889–1950)
Choral Concerto: 1929W–FP*

Elegy: 1946H–FP*
Hymn on the Nativity: 1927H–FP*
In glorious freedom: 1923W–FP*
Cotswold Concerto: 1935W*ˢ
Introduction and Rondo: 1924H–FP*ˢ
Suite, 'In the Cotswolds': 1926W–FP*ˢ
Overture, 'Barton Fair': 1929Wˢ
Worcestershire Rhapsody for Orchestra: 1920W–
    FP*ˢ

Brewer, Herbert (1865–1928)
Magnificat and Nunc Dimittis in D: 1959H,
    1965G
Emmaus: 1901G–FP*, 1907G*
God within: 1928G
The Holy Innocents: 1904G–FP*, 1922G*
Sir Patrick Spens: 1913G*ˢ
Summer Sports: 1910G–FP*ˢ, 1925G*ˢ
Elizabethan Pastorals: 1906H–FP*ˢ, 1907G*ˢ,
    1909H*ˢ, 1911W*ˢ, 1921H*ˢ, 1923W*ˢ,
    1930Hˢ
Song Cycle, 'A Sprig of Shamrock': 1925G–FP*ˢ,
    1933Hᶜ
Suite, 'Miller's Green': 1924H–FP*ˢ
Gloucestershire Song Cycle, 'For your Delight':
    1927H–FP*ˢ, 1928Gˢ

Bridge, Frank (1879–1941)
A Prayer: 1953G
Londonderry Air (String Quartet): 1921Hˢ

Bridge, John Frederick (1844–1924)
The Cradle of Christ: 1894H–FP*
The Forging of the Anchor: 1901G–FP*ˢ
The Lord's Prayer: 1892G–FP*
The Repentance of Ninevah: 1890W–FP*

Britten, Benjamin (1913–76)
Missa Brevis (boys' voices): 1962G, 1977G,
    1987W
War Requiem: 1963W, 1964H, 1965G, 1973H,
    1980G, 1988H
Cantatas:
Cantata Misericordium: 1964H, 1968G, 1978W
St Nicholas, Op. 42: 1958H*, 1966W,
    1988H
Cantata Academica, Op. 62: 1966W, 1977G
Rejoice in the Lamb, Op. 30: 1971G, 1979H
Praise we great men (op. post.): 1986G
Les Illuminations: 1951W
Variations on a Theme of Frank Bridge: 1948W
Seven Sonnets of Michelangelo: 1953G
A Hymn to the Virgin: 1961H
A Ceremony of Carols: 1965G
Serenade: 1967H
Fanfare for St Edmundsbury: 1976H

Spring Symphony: 1970H, 1972W, 1982H,
    1987W
Hymn to St Cecilia, Op. 27: 1974G, 1987W
Hymn to St Peter: 1987W
Choral Variations, A Boy was born, Op. 3:
    1987W
Sinfonia da Requiem, Op. 20: 1958H, 1983G
Nocturne, Op. 60: 1961H*, 1962G, 1989G
Four Sea Interludes: 1967H
Six Metamorphoses after Ovid, Op. 49: 1987W
Serenade for Tenor, Horn and Strings, Op. 31:
    1988H

Brown, Christopher (b. 1943)
David, a Cantata, Op. 21: 1970H–FP

Bruch, Max (1838–1920)
Violin Concerto No. 1 in G minor, Op. 26:
    1976H

Bruckner, Anton (1824–96)
Mass in E minor: 1960W 1989G
Mass in F minor: 1967H
Te Deum: 1966W
Three Motets: 1971G

Bull, John (*c.* 1562–1628)
In the Departure of the Lord: 1961H

Burgon, Geoffrey (b. 1941)
The Fire of Heaven: 1973H–FP, 1983G
Requiem: 1976H–FP
Hymn to St Thomas: 1982H–FP
At the round earth's: 1979H

Bush, Alan (b. 1900)
For a Festal Occasion: 1961H–FP

Bush, Geoffrey (b. 1920)
In praise of Mary: 1955H–FP

Butterworth, George (1885–1916)
Rhapsody, A Shropshire Lad: 1960W
The Banks of Green Willow: 1989G

Buxtehude, Diderik (1637–1707)
Prelude and Fugue in F sharp minor (organ):
    1971G
Prelude and Fugue in G minor (organ): 1981W

Byrd, William (1543–1623)
An earthly tree: 1923W
Laetentur Coeli: 1929W, 1966W
Justorum Animae: 1923W, 1962G
Sing joyfully: 1922G, 1923W, 1964H
Haec Dies: 1960W, 1963W, 1965G
Laudibus in sanctis: 1961H, 1969W
Ave verum corpus: 1958W, 1962G
Exsurge, Domine: 1963W, 1967H
Victimae paschali: 1969W

O quam suavis: 1969W
Fantasia for Strings: 1923W

Camilleri, Charles (b. 1931)
Organ Concerto: 1983G

Campra, André (1660–1744)
Suite de Tancrede: 1981W

Cannon, Philip (b. 1929)
The Temple: 1974G–FP
Lord of Light, A Gloucester Requiem: 1980G–
FP

Carissimi, Giacomo (1605–74)
Jephte: 1963W

Cavalli, Pietro Francesco (1602–76)
Laudate Dominum: 1971G
Salve Regina: 1976H

Chadwick, George W. (1854–1931)
Overture, Melpomene: 1902W

Chandler, Mary
Concerto for Oboe d'amore and Strings: 1986G

Charpentier, Marc-Antoine (c. 1645–1704)
Te Deum: 1973H
Concerts à quatre parties: 1981W

Cherubini, Luigi (1760–1842)
Mass in D minor: 1901G

Chopin, Frédéric (1810–49)
Funeral March: 1901G

Coleridge-Taylor, Samuel (1875–1912)
The Atonement: 1903W–FP*
The Soul's expression (Contralto and Orchestra):
1900H*
Ballade in A minor: 1898G–FP*s
Idyll for Orchestra: 1901G–FP*
Solemn Prelude for Orchestra: 1899W–FP*

Copland, Aaron (1900–90)
In the Beginning: 1970H, 1990W
Appalachian Spring: 1984W, 1990W
Quiet City: 1975W
Fanfare for the Common Man: 1984W
Three Dance Episodes from Rodeo: 1980G
Passacaglia (organ): 1990W
Sextet: 1990W

Cornelius, Peter (1824–74)
Surrender of the Soul: 1905W
Die Vätergruft: 1899W

Cowen, Frederick (1852–1935)
The Transfiguration: 1895G–FP*
Overture, The Butterfly's Ball: 1908Ws

A Phantasy of Life and Love: 1901G–FP*s,
1907Gs
Indian Rhapsody: 1903H–FP*s

Crosse, Gordon (b. 1937)
Changes, Op. 17: 1966W–FP

Crossley-Holland, Peter (b. 1916)
The Sacred Dance: 1954W*

Cruft, Adrian (1921–87)
Interlude for String Orchestra (1951): 1957W
Passiontide Carol: 1959G

Dag Wiren (see Wiren)

Dale, Benjamin J. (1885–1943)
Before the paling of the Stars: 1921H*
Romance in D flat for Viola and Orchestra:
1946Hs

Dallapiccola, Luigi (1904–75)
Canti di Prigionia: 1969W
Piccola Musica Notturna: 1971G

Darke, Harold (1888–1976)
An Hymn of heavenly beauty: 1938W*
Psalm 122, I was glad: 1957W

Darlow, Denys (b. 1921)
Te Deum: 1991H

Davidson, Malcolm G.
These are thy glorious works: 1923W–
FP

Davies, Peter Maxwell (b. 1934)
Five Carols for Boys' voices: 1969W
A Mirror of Whitening Light: 1977G–FP
Solstice of Light: 1980G–FP in England,
1991H

Davies, Sir Walford (1869–1941)
Christ in the Universe: 1929W–FP
Everyman: 1908W
Fantasy for Tenor, Chorus and Orchestra:
1920W–FP*
Heaven's Gate: 1921H*
High Heaven's King: 1926W–FP*
Lift up your hearts: 1906H–FP*
Men and Angels: 1925G–FP*
Noble Numbers: 1909H–FP*
The Sayings of Jesus: 1911W–FP*
The Temple: 1902W–FP*
Six Pastorals: 1906Hc
A Children's Symphony: 1927H–FP*s
'Peter Pan' Suite for String Quartet: 1924Hc
Piano Quintet in C: 1927H–FPc (with the
composer at the piano)

Day, Edgar
   Magnificat and Nunc Dimittis in B flat: 1954W,
      1957W

Debussy, Claude (1862–1918)
   The Blessed Damozel: 1938W, 1948W, 1957W,
      1962G
   Nocturnes: 1928G^s, 1978W
   L'après-midi d'un faune: 1908W^s, 1923W^s
   Petit Suite: 1924H^s
   Cortège and *Air de Danse* from same: 1932W^s
   String Quartet in G minor: 1934G^c
   Danse Sacrée and *Danse Profane*: 1922G^s, 1923W^c
   La Mer: 1955H

Deering, Richard (*c*. 1580–1630)
   Quem vidistis pastores: 1962G
   Cantate Domino: 1977G

Delden, Lex van (b. 1919)
   Notturno for Harp: 1965G

Delius, Frederick (1862–1934)
   Songs of Farewell: 1975W, 1990W
   Cello Concerto: 1927H^s
   Violin Sonata, No. 3: 1938W^c
   Dance Rhapsody: 1909H–FP^{*s}
   On hearing the first cuckoo: 1925G^c
   Song before sunrise: 1930H^s
   Walk to the Paradise Garden: 1932W^s, 1972W
   Air and Dance: 1950G^c
   Summer Night on the River: 1963W
   Sea Drift: 1968G, 1984W
   In a Summer Garden: 1982H
   Florida Suite: 1984W
   Nocturne, Paris: 1984W

Dickinson, Peter (b. 1934)
   Organ Concerto: 1971G–FP

Downes, Andrew
   Overture, In the Cotswolds: 1986G

Drakeford, Richard
   Psalm 22: 1966W–FP
   Suite for Brass: 1967H–FP

Drayton, Paul
   Canticle of Bells: 1976H–FP

Dupré, Marcel (1886–1971)
   Prelude and Fugue in G minor (organ): 1971G

Duruflé, Maurice (1902–86)
   Requiem: 1959G, 1976H
   Four Motets on Gregorian melodies: 1965G

Dvořák, Antonin (1841–1904)
   Requiem Mass: 1894H, 1984W

Stabat Mater: 1898G, 1902W, 1912H, 1921H,
      1956G
Te Deum: 1899W, 1923W, 1948W, 1969W,
      1977G, 1985H
Psalm 149: 1978W
Symphonies: No. 6 in D: 1984W; No. 8 in G:
      1959G, 1963W; No. 9 in E minor: 1978W
Carnival Overture: 1913G, 1991H
Serenade for Strings in E, Op. 22: 1948W,
      1977G
Slavonic Dances: 1893W
String Quartet in F, Op. 96: 1931G^c
String Quartet in E flat, Op. 51: 1903H^c
Piano Quintet: 1897H^c, 1930H^c
Nocturne in B, Op. 40: 1986G
Violin Concerto in A minor: 1982H

Dyson, George (1883–1964)
   St Paul's Voyage to Melita: 1933H–FP*,
      1934G*, 1937G*, 1952H*
   Nebuchadnezzar: 1935W–FP*, 1936H*,
      1948W*
   Quo vadis? Part 1: 1946H–FP*, 1947G*
   Quo vadis? Parts 1 and 2: 1949H–FP*
   Overture, At the Tabard Inn: 1947G*
   Prelude, Fantasy and Chaconne for Cello and
      Orchestra: 1936H–FP*
   Symphony in G: 1938W*
   Suite for Orchestra: 1934G^s, 1948W* (revised)
   Magnificat and *Nunc Dimittis* in D: 1961H,
      1962G, 1967H

Eccard, Johann (1553–1611)
   Presentation of Christ in the Temple: 1903H

Edwards, Henry John (1854–1933)
   Praise to the Holiest: 1891H–FP*

Elgar, Edward (1857–1934)
   The Dream of Gerontius: 1902W*, 1903H,
      1905W, 1906H, 1908W, 1910G*, 1912H*,
      1913G*, 1920W, 1921H*, 1923W*,
      1924H*, 1927H*, and at every Festival
      1928* to 1938 and 1946 to 1971; then
      1975W, 1976H, 1978W, 1979H, 1984W,
      1985H, 1987W, 1990W
   The Apostles: 1904G*, 1905W*, 1906H,
      1907G*, 1909H, 1921H*, 1922G*, 1925G*,
      1926W*, 1930H*, 1935W, 1936H, 1947G,
      1954W, 1973H, 1981W, 1984W
   The Kingdom: 1907G*, 1908W*, 1922G*,
      1923W*, 1924H*, 1926W*, 1928G*,
      1929W*, 1933H*, 1934G, 1946H, 1948W,
      1949H, 1951W, 1958W, 1964H, 1970H,
      1980G, 1984W, 1989G
   Caractacus: 1977G, 1989G
   Caractacus, Scene 3: 1900H^s

For the Fallen: 1920W*, 1922G*, 1923W*, 1925G*, 1926W*, 1932W*

Go, song of mine: 1909H–FP*, 1911W, 1924H

The Music Makers: 1920W*, 1927H*, 1932W*, 1938W, 1975W, 1983G, 1988H

The Spirit of the Lord: 1957W, 1963W

Sursum Corda, Op. 11: 1963W, 1984W, 1985H

Give unto the Lord: 1967H, 1973H, 1982H

The Light of Life: 1896W–FP*, 1899W*, 1975W

Snow and Singing Bird: 1982H

Sea Pictures: (2 songs – 1911W^s) 1983G, 1991H

Te Deum: 1985H

Suite from Starlight Express: 1978W

Black Knight: 1984W

A Christmas Greeting: 1982H

Falstaff: 1989G

Coronation Ode: 1990W

Symphonies:

No. 1 in A flat: 1909H*, 1910G*, 1925G*, 1930H*, 1932W*, 1956G, 1965G, 1973H, 1979H, 1987W

No. 2 in E flat: 1911W*, 1913G*, 1927H*, 1929W*, 1934G, 1951W^s, 1957W, 1972W, 1978W, 1986G, 1990W

Violin Concerto: 1911W*, 1927H*, 1931G*, 1936H, 1938W, 1951W, 1961H, 1969W, 1977G, 1981W, 1988H

Cello Concerto: 1921H*^{s}, 1923W*^{s}, 1924H*, 1928G*^{s}, 1935W^s, 1937G, 1950G, 1959G, 1966W, 1976H, 1980G, 1984W, 1988H

Ditto arr. for Viola: 1933H*^{s}

Overtures:

Cockaigne: 1901G*^{s}, 1902W*^{s}, 1909H*^{s}, 1927H^s, 1936H^s, 1963W, 1985H

Froissart: 1890W–FP*^{s}, 1984W, 1990W

In the South: 1904G*^{s}, 1930H*^{s}, 1948W^s, 1987W

Prelude – The Kingdom: 1960W, 1966W

Introduction and Allegro for Strings: 1905W*^{s}, 1906H*^{s}, 1920W*^{s}, 1924H*^{s}, 1929W*^{s}, 1935W, 1937G, 1946H, 1953G, 1957W, 1971G, 1975W, 1979H, 1986G

Enigma Variations: 1899W*^{s}, 1903H*^{s}, 1926W*^{s}, 1938W^s, 1946H^s, 1949H, 1952H, 1957W, 1976H, 1987W, 1991H

Elegy for Strings: 1960W, 1963W

Serenade for Strings: 1950G^c, 1970H, 1977G, 1978W, 1986G

Dream Children: 1926W^c, 1978W

Marches:

Coronation: 1911W*^{s}

Orb and Sceptre: 1973H, 1975W

Imperial, Op. 32: 1963W, 1971G, 1975W, 1977G, 1979H, 1985H

Triumphal March (from Caractacus): 1972W, 1979H

Homage: 1976H

Pomp and Circumstance, No. 1: 1981W; No. 5: 1969W, 1973H, 1985H

Nursery Suite: 1931G*^{s}

Severn Suite: 1932W*^{s}–FP of orchestral version

Wand of Youth Suite, No. 2: 1908W–FP*

Crown of India Suite: 1912H–FP*^{s}

Piano Quintet: 1921H^c, 1932W^c

Fanfare: 1967H, 1973H

Chanson de Nuit: 1978W

Chanson de Matin: 1978W

Organ Sonata, Op. 28: 1972W, 1982H, 1991H (orchestrated by Gordon Jacob)

Ellicott, Rosalind Frances (1857–1924)
The birth of Song: 1892G^s
Henry of Navarre: 1898G^s
Fantasie in A minor for Piano and Orchestra: 1895G–FP^s

Ellis, David (b. 1933)
Sequentia 5, Genesis: 1975W–FP

Fanshawe, David (b. 1942)
African Sanctus: 1978W, 1980G

Fauré, Gabriel (1845–1924)
Requiem: 1938W, 1947G, 1950G, 1963W, 1973H, 1987W
Ballade for Piano and Orchestra: 1947G^s
Pavane: 1925G^s, 1929W^s
Piano Quartet No. 2, Op. 45: 1935W^c
Suite, Pelléas et Mélisande: 1956G

Ferguson, Howard (b. 1908)
Two Ballads for Baritone and Orchestra: 1934G^s
Amore Langueo: 1956G–FP, 1983G
Octet: 1959G
The Dream of the Rood: 1959G–FP, 1988H

Finzi, Gerald (1901–56)
Intimations of Immortality: 1950G–FP*, 1951W, 1953G, 1959G, 1982H
Lo, the full, final sacrifice: 1947G, 1948W, 1979H
In terra pax: 1956G
Dies Natalis: 1946H*, 1947G*, 1955H, 1978W
Fall of the Leaf: 1958H
Farewell to Arms (Introduction and Aria): 1951W*^{s}
God is gone up: 1961H
For St Cecilia: 1981W
Magnificat: 1983G
Love's Labours Lost: 1989G
Concertos:

Clarinet Concerto: 1949H–FP*, 1953G, 1968G*, 1979H, 1983G
Cello Concerto: 1957W, 1986G

Fischer, Johann C.F. (*c*. 1670–1746)
Overture in the French style and Gavotte: 1980G

Françaix, Jean (b. 1912)
Marche Triomphale: 1983G
L'Horloge de Flore: 1985H

Franck, César (1822–90)
The Beatitudes (selection): 1905W
Symphony in D minor: 1920W, 1927H
Variations Symphoniques: 1930H[s], 1933H[s], 1947G[s], 1948W[s]
Piano Quintet: 1912H[c]
Organ Cantabile: 1974G
Choral No. 1 in E (Organ): 1983G

Fricker, Peter Racine (b. 1920)
The Vision of Judgement, Op. 29: 1961H
Prelude, Elegy and Finale: 1955H
Litany (for double String Orchestra): 1958H*
Whispers at these curtains: 1957W, 1984W

Gabrieli, Giovanni (*c*. 1557–1612)
Magnificat: 1957W
Jubilate: 1966W, 1977G, 1978W
O magnum mysterium: 1967H
In ecclesiis: 1969W
Canzona, Seventh Tone: 1969W
Canzona, *La Spiritata*: 1978W
Sonata pian e' forte (brass): 1982H, 1983G
Canzoni per sonara 4: 1976H

Gardiner, H. Balfour (1877–1950)
Overture, Comedy: 1936H[s]
Shepherd Fennel's Dance: 1927H[s]

Gardner, John (b. 1917)
Cantiones Sacrae: 1952H–FP
God is our hope and strength: 1961H
Sonata da Chiesa: 1979H

Geminiani, Francesco (*c*. 1680–1762)
Concerto Grosso in C minor, Op. 2, No. 2: 1964H

German, Edward (1862–1936)
Theme and Six Diversions: 1925G*[s], 1933H[s]
Suite for Orchestra: 1895G*[s]
The Willow Song (from 'Othello'): 1922G[s]
Harvest Dance (from 'The Seasons'): 1922G[s]
Valse gracieuse: 1928G[s]

Gershwin, George (1898–1937)
Piano Concerto in F: 1987W

Gibbons, Orlando (1583–1625)
God is gone up: 1925G

Hosanna to the Son of David: 1925G, 1958H
O clap your hands: 1925G, 1959G, 1967H

Gibbs, C. Armstrong (1889–1960)
The Birth of Christ: 1930H–FP*
The Love Talker: 1933H–FP*[s]
Song Cycle, Old wine in new bottles: 1933H–FP[c]
The Enchanted Wood: 1929W*[c]
String Quartet in A, Op. 73 (Scherzo): 1933H[c]

Giles, Jean (1668–1705)
Messe des Morts: 1958H–FP in Britain

Ginestra, Alberto (1916–83)
Psalm 150, Op. 5: 1970H–FP in Britain

Glazunov, Alexander (1865–1936)
Symphony No. 6: 1907G

Glinka, Mikhail (1804–57)
Komarinskaja: 1904G[s], 1925G[s], 1928G[s]

Goetz, Hermann (1840–76)
By the waters of Babylon: 1896W, 1910G

Goossens, Eugene (1893–1962)
Silence Poem: 1922G–FP*

Gounod, Charles François (1818–93)
Redemption: 1892G, 1897H

Grainger, Percy (1882–1961)
Molly on the Shore: 1921H[c], 1950G[c], 1986G

Greene, Maurice (*c*. 1694–1755)
O clap your hands: 1961H

Grieg, Edvard (1843–1907)
Piano Concerto: 1897H[s], 1936H[s]
Peer Gynt Suite: 1890W[s], 1892G[s]
Two Elegiac Melodies, Op. 34: 1986G
Holberg Suite, Op. 40: 1986G
Unfinished String Quartet in F: 1909H[c]

Grigny, Nicholas de (1672–1703)
Tierceen Taille: 1971G

Guilain-Freinsberg, Jean (*fl.* 1702–39)
Pièces d'orgue pour le Magnificat: 1974G

Guillou, Jean (b. 1930)
Eighteen Variations: 1974G

Handel, George Frideric (1685–1759)
Messiah: every year, in whole or in part, since 1876 (and before) to 1954W; then 1956G, 1957W, 1958H, 1959G, 1960W, 1961H, 1962G, 1963W, 1977G, 1981W
Israel in Egypt: 1893W, 1953G, 1976H
Ditto (selections): 1903H, 1904G, 1913G
Solomon: 1972W

Occasional Oratorio: 1983G
Ditto (selections): 1904G
Judas Maccabaeus (selections): 1898G, 1904G, 1922G, 1936H
Joshua: 1892G
Samson (selections): 1896W
Saul (Part III): 1938W
Theodora (selections): 1904G
The King shall rejoice: 1902W, 1959G
Zadok the Priest: 1897H, 1954H, 1966W
Dettingen Te Deum: 1935W
Utrecht Te Deum: 1969W
Hallelujah Chorus: 1955H
Ode on St Cecilia's Day: 1955H, 1975W
Dixit Dominus: 1963W, 1965G, 1980G, 1989G
Let the Bright Seraphim and Let their Celestial Concerts: 1965G
Psalm 42: 1968G
A Canticle of Praise: 1980G
O praise the Lord: 1985H
Overtures:
D minor (arr. Elgar): 1954W, 1965G, 1979H
Samson: 1959G
Royal Fireworks Music (arr. for Brass by Roberts): 1986G
Concerti Grossi:
No. 2 in F: 1970H; No. 4 in F: 1977G; No. 9 in F: 1951W, 1955H
Organ Concerti:
No. 4: 1892G; No. 7 in B flat: 1901G, 1928G, 1971G; in F: 1934G, 1950G
Violin Sonata in A: 1946H[c]
Violin Sonata in D: 1946H[c]
Royal Fireworks Music: 1974G
Water Music, Suite No. 1: 1976H, 1981W
Silete Venti: 1973H

Handl, Jacob (1550–91)
Two Motets: 1971G

Harris, William H. (1883–1973)
Michael Angelo's Confession of Faith: 1935W–FP*
Flourish for an Occasion: 1955H
Fair is the Heaven: 1958H

Harrison, Julius (1885–1963)
Mass in C: 1951W
Canterbury Pilgrims (Introduction and Love Duet): 1923W–FP*[s]
Worcestershire Suite: 1920W*[s], 1936H[s], 1951W*[s]
Cavalier Songs: 1930H–FP*[s]
Rhapsody for Contralto and Orchestra: 1933H*[s]
Psalm 100: 1954W, 1960W
Requiem Mass: 1957W–FP

Bredon Hill, Rhapsody for Violin and Orchestra: 1985H

Harvey, Jonathan (b. 1939)
Ludus Amoris: 1969W–FP
Resurrection: 1981W–FP

Harwood, Basil (1859–1949)
Inclina Domine: 1898G*
Love Incarnate: 1925G–FP
Ye choirs of new Jerusalem: 1928G–FP
Organ Concerto in D: 1910G–FP
Sonata in C sharp minor (organ): 1959G

Hathaway, J.W.G.
The call of the woods: 1928G–FP[s]

Hawes, Jack
Psalm 98: 1989G

Hay, N.
Paean: 1932W

Haydn, Franz Joseph (1732–1809)
Imperial (Coronation) Mass in D minor: 1953G, 1954W
St Cecilia Mass: 1958H
Nelson Mass: 1967H, 1982H
St Theresa Mass: 1968G, 1981W
St Nicholas Mass: 1980G
Missa Solemnis: 1971G
The Creation Part I: 1897H, 1898G, 1900H, 1909H, 1921H, 1932W, 1949H
The Creation, Parts I and II: 1890W, 1894H, 1899W
The Creation (complete): 1921H, 1950G, 1952H, 1964H, 1974G, 1979H, 1981W, 1987W
Te Deum: 1932W, 1934G, 1946H, 1969W, 1982H
Symphonies:
No. 47 in G: 1977G
No. 64 in A: 1988H
No. 83 in G minor: 1968G, 1990W
No. 85 in B flat: 1962G
No. 87 in A: 1973H, 1976H
No. 88 in G: 1929W[c], 1964H
No. 90 in C: 1924H[s], 1970H
No. 91 in E flat: 1986G
No. 93 in D: 1932W[s]
No. 95 in C minor: 1961H
No. 96 in C: 1924H[s]
No. 98 in B flat: 1923W[c]
No. 103 (Drum Roll): 1930H, 1937G
Sinfonia Concertante in B flat: 1948W, 1972W
String Quartets:
Op. 74 No. 1 in C: 1953G[c]
Op. 64 in D: 1930H[c]; in E flat: 1927H[c]

Op. 77 No. 1 in G: 1903H^c, 1932W^c
Trumpet Concerto: 1982H
Oboe Concerto in C: 1963W
Piano Trio in G: 1937G^c

Hervey, Arthur (1855–1922)
   The Gates of Night, for Baritone and Orchestra:
   1901G–FP^s

Hewitt–Jones, Tony (1926–89)
   Te Deum: 1962G–FP*, 1968G
   Let us now praise famous men: 1977G–FP
   Festival Benedicite: 1986G–FP
   Fanfare and Processional: 1985H

Hindemith, Paul (1895–1963)
   A Requiem: 1961H–FP in England
   Nobilissima Visione: 1958H
   Symphony, *Mathis der Maler*: 1960W

Hoddinott, Alun (b. 1929)
   Dives and Lazarus: 1967H
   Out of the Deep: 1970H
   The Tree of Life: 1971G–FP

Holbrooke, Joseph (1878-1958)
   Dreamland, Orchestral Suite No. 2: 1906H–FP^s

Holst, Gustav (1874–1934)
   The Hymn of Jesus: 1921H*, 1924H, 1927H,
   1931G*, 1932W**, 1935W, 1949H, 1950G,
   1954W, 1965G, 1974G, 1977G, 1984W,
   1988H
   The Evening Watch: 1925G–FP
   Choral Fantasia: 1931G–FP*, 1974G
   Short Festival *Te Deum*: 1926W
   Two Psalms: 1922G, 1923W, 1928G
   Ballet Music, 'The Perfect Fool': 1932W^s,
   1947G^s
   Oriental Suite, 'Beni Mora': 1929W^s
   St Paul's Suite: 1947G^c
   Marching Song (from 'Two Songs without
   words'): 1925G^c
   Four Songs for Voice and Violin: 1924H^c
   Psalm 148: 1974G
   Egdon Heath: 1967H
   Suite, 'The Planets': 1934G, 1969W, 1974G,
   1984W ('Jupiter' 1934G^s)
   Fugal Concerto: 1977G

Honegger, Arthur (1892–1955)
   King David: 1928G, 1957W, 1967H, 1979H
   Une Cantate de Noël: 1962G
   Pastorale d'été: 1973H

Howells, Herbert (1892–1983)
   Hymnus Paradisi: 1950G–FP*,   1951W*,
   1952H*, 1956G, 1965G, 1973H, 1977G
   Paradise Rondel: 1925G–FP*

Puck's Minuet: 1925G*^{s}
Elegy for Strings: 1934G^s, 1937G*, 1947G*,
   1953G*
Procession: 1934G
Sine Nomine, 1922G–FP
In   Green   Ways   (song   group):   1928G–FP*^{s},
   1931G*^{s}, 1951W*^{s}
Missa Sabrinensis: 1954W–FP*
Requiem: 1982H
Like as the Hart: 1959G
Let God arise: 1959G
Here is the little door: 1962G
A spotless Rose: 1962G
Three Motets: 1978W
Te Deum (Collegium Regale) 1986G
Festival Fanfare: 1977G–FP
Paean (for Organ): 1976H
Merry Eye: 1982H

Huber, Paul
   The Prodigal Son: 1955H–FP in Britain

Hull, Molly
   Three Songs with String Quartet: 1932W^c

Hummel, Johann (1778–1837)
   Trumpet Concerto in E flat: 1969W

Humperdinck, Engelbert (1854–1921)
   Overture, Hansel and Gretel: 1928G^s

Hunt, Donald
   God be gracious unto us: 1987W

Hurd, Michael (b. 1928)
   Missa Brevis: 1968G

Ireland, John (1879–1962)
   These things shall be: 1953G, 1979H
   Concertino Pastorale: 1950G^c
   Vexilla Regis: 1978W
   A London Overture: 1959G

Ives, Charles (1874–1954)
   Three Psalms: 1975W
   Psalms 67 and 90: 1990W

Jackson, Francis (b. 1917)
   Homage to Vaughan Williams: 1962G*

Jacob, Gordon (1895–1984)
   Symphony in C (slow movement): 1934G*
   Suite, William Byrd: 1946H*
   Fantasia on the Alleluiah Hymn: 1968G

Janáček, Leoš (1854–1928)
   The Eternal Gospel: 1960W
   Glagolitic Mass: 1969W, 1978W, 1980G

Jeppeson, Knud (1892–1974)
   Te Deum Danicum: 1981W–FP in Britain

Jongen, Joseph (1872–1958)
Sonata Eroica: 1962G

Josephs, Wilfred (b. 1927)
Overture, Four Horsemen of the Apocalypse:
1974G–FP

Joubert, John (b. 1927)
Three Office Hymns of St Oswald: 1972W–FP
Herefordshire Canticles: 1979H–FP, 1991H

Kaminski, Heinrich (1886–1946)
Magnificat: 1929W

Karg-Elert, Sigfrid (1877–1933)
Legend (from Triptych, Op. 141, No. 2): 1976H

Kay, Norman
King Herod: 1967H

Kee, Piet (b. 1927)
Choral, *Austiefer* (organ): 1983
Fantasia, *Wachet auf* (organ): 1983G

Kelly, Bryan (b. 1934)
Stabat Mater: 1970H–FP*
Let there be Light: 1973H–FP*

Kirbye, George (?–1634)
Vox in Rama audita est: 1959G

Kodály, Zoltán (1882–1967)
Jesus and the Traders: 1937G*, 1977G
Psalmus Hungaricus: 1928G*, 1929W, 1930H,
1934G, 1949H, 1953G, 1967H, 1982H
Budavari Te Deum: 1937G*, 1938W, 1947G,
1960W, 1989G
Missa Brevis: 1948W*, 1950G, 1978W
Symphony in C: 1962G
Dances of Galanta: 1937G*ˢ, 1948Wˢ

Lalo, Edouard (1823–92)
Two Aubades: 1925Gᶜ

Lambert, Constant (1905–51)
Aubade héroique: 1952H

Lang, C.S.
Passacaglia for Organ: 1953G

Lasso, Orlando di (c. 1530–94)
Tristis est anima mea: 1964H

Le Fleming, Christopher (1908–85)
Five Psalms: 1947G–FP

Leigh, Walter (1905–42)
Concertino for Harpsichord and Strings: 1970H,
1976H

Leighton, Kenneth (1929–88)
The Light Invisible: 1958H–FP
A Hymn of the Nativity: 1961H

Drop, drop slow tears: 1964H, 1965G
An Easter sequence: 1979H
Crucifixus pro nobis: 1989G
Pasacaglia, Chorale and Fugue (organ): 1963W

Lewis, Sir Anthony (1915–83)
A Tribute of Praise: 1954W, 1957W

Liszt, Franz (1811–86)
Missa Solemnis: 1981W–FP in Britain
Hungarian Rhapsodies: No. 1: 1902Wˢ,
1911Wˢ, 1923Wˢ; No. 2: 1900Hˢ; No. 5:
1896Wˢ

Locke, Matthew (c. 1621–77)
Music for His Majesty's Sackbuts and Cornetts:
1955H, 1960W, 1968G

Lloyd, Charles Harford (1849–1919)
Hymn of Thanksgiving: 1897–FP*
Sir Ogie and the Ladie Elsie: 1894H–FP*
A Song of Judgement: 1891H–FP*
To Morning: 1890Wˢ
The righteous live for evermore: 1901G–FP*
Organ Concerto in F minor: 1895G–FP*,
1904G*

Lloyd, George (b. 1913)
Symphony No. 12: 1990W*

Lully, Jean-Baptiste (1632–87)
Te Deum: 1959G

Lyon, J. (1735–94)
The Legend Beautiful: 1930H–FPˢ

Mackenzie, Alexander Campbell (1847–1938)
Bethlehem: 1894H
The Rose of Sharon (Scene II): 1901G*
Overtures:
Britannia: 1899Wˢ, 1904Gˢ, 1921Hˢ
The Cricket on the Hearth: 1907Gˢ
The Little Minister: 1908Wˢ
Benedictus, for Orchestra: 1891H

Maconchy, Elizabeth (b. 1907)
And Death shall have no dominion: 1969W–FP

Mahler, Gustav (1860–1911)
Symphonies:
No. 2 (Resurrection): 1981W
No. 4 in G: 1962G
No. 8 (Symphony of a Thousand): 1978W,
1986G, 1990W
No. 10: 1983G
Song Cycle, *Das Lied von der Erde*: 1977G

Marcello, Benedetto (1686–1739)
Oboe Concerto: 1955H, 1966W

Martin, Frank (1890–1974)
In Terra Pax: 1960W–FP in Britain
Requiem Mass: 1975W–FP in Britain

Martinon, Jean (1910–76)
Psalm 136, *Chant des Captifs*: 1978W

Mathias, William (b. 1934)
O sing unto the Lord: 1968G
Praise ye the Lord: 1969W–FP
This Worlde's Joie: 1979H, 1985H
Veni Sanctus Spiritus: 1985H–FP
Lux aeterna: 1982H–FP
Let us now praise famous men: 1984W
Divertimento for String Orchestra: 1963W
Organ Concerto: 1989G

Maw, Nicholas (b. 1935)
Serenade: 1980G–FP in Britain

McCabe, John (b. 1939)
Notturni ed Alba: 1970H–FP, 1985H
Voyage: 1972W–FP
Rounds for Brass Quintet: 1976H

McEwen, John B. (1868–1948)
Prelude for Orchestra: 1925G[s]
Border Ballad for Orchestra: 1927H[s]

Mendelssohn, Felix (1809–47)
Elijah: every Festival from 1890 (and some prior) until 1929W; then 1931G, 1932W, 1933H, 1935W, 1937G, 1938W, 1946H, 1953G, 1957W, 1965G, 1973H, 1986G
Hymn of Praise: every Festival from 1891 (and some prior) until 1908W, 1910G, 1920W, 1936H
St Paul: 1890W, 1891H, 1896W
Psalm 42: 1894H
Four Motets: 1977G, 1991H
Symphonies:
No. 2 in B flat: 1975W
No. 4 in A: 1967H, 1972W, 1979H
Symphony for Strings, No. 9 in C: 1970H
Symphony for Strings in G minor: 1972W
Violin Concerto in E minor: 1934G[s], 1955H, 1971G, 1975W
Overture, Fingal's Cave: 1925G[s], 1933H[s], 1972W, 1991H
Incidental Music to A Midsummer Night's Dream: Scherzo: 1923W[c]; Nocturne: 1983G
Octet in E flat, Op. 20: 1929W[c], 1966W
Organ Sonatas: No. 3 in A: 1972W; No. 4 in B flat: 1972W

Messiaen, Oliver (1908–92)
O sacrum convivium: 1968G
Trois Petites Liturgies: 1975W, 1978W, 1990W
Transports de Joie: 1971G

Miles, Philip Napier (1865–1935)
Fantasia for Orchestra on two Elizabethan themes: 1927H[s]

Milford, Robin (1903–59)
A Prophet in the Land: 1931G–FP

Milner, Anthony (b. 1925)
The City of Desolation: 1957W* (first public performance)
The Water and the Fire: 1964H–FP
Salutatio Angelica: 1965G

Moeran, Ernest John (1894–1950)
Sinfonietta in C: 1946H*

Monteverdi, Claudio (1567–1643)
Magnificat: 1953G
Vespers: 1958H, 1961H, 1974G, 1979H, 1984W
Beatus Vir: 1971G, 1982H
Symphonies de l'Orfeo: 1981W

Moore, John W. (1807–89)
Kentucky, for String Quartet: 1946H[c]

Morley, Thomas (1557–1602)
De profundis: 1968G

Morris, Reginald Owen (1886–1948)
Sinfonia in C: 1931G[s]
Suite for Cello and Orchestra: 1934G[s]

Mortari, Virgilio (b. 1902)
Sonata Prodigio: 1965G

Mozart, Wolfgang A. (1756–91)
Masses:
Requiem Mass, K626: 1890W, 1891H, 1895G, 1905W, 1911W, 1934G, 1962G, 1988H
Mass in C minor, K427: 1956G, 1982H, 1991H
Coronation Mass, K317: 1961H
Missa Brevis, K192: 1972W, 1975W
Vesperae solennes de Confessore, K339: 1966W, 1988H
Litanie de Venerabili, K243: 1973H
Te Deum in C, K141: 1973H
Overtures:
The Marriage of Figaro: 1893W[s], 1901G[s], 1928G[s], 1929W[c]
The Magic Flute: 1897H[s], 1900H[s], 1902W[s], 1961H
Symphonies:
in C (Jupiter), K551: 1892G[s], 1901G, 1926W[c], 1969W, 1977G
in E flat, K543: 1909H[s]
in G minor, K550: 1894H, 1898G, 1903H, 1921H, 1923W, 1946H, 1951W, 1964H, 1980G, 1981W, 1986G

in A, K134: 1979H
in G, K318: 1971G
in D, K385: 1967H
in C, K425: 1960W
in C, K551: 1969W, 1977G
Piano Concertos:
in G, K453: 1962G
in B flat, K456: 1913G^s
in F, K459: 1933H
in D minor: K466: 1949H
in A, K488: 1930H, 1980G
in C minor, K491: 1958H
Violin Concertos:
in E flat, K268: 1906H^s
in G, K216: 1968G
in D, K218: 1954W
in A, K219: 1980G
Oboe Concerto, K314: 1980G
Clarinet Concerto in A, K622: 1960W, 1964H, 1970H
Ditto, arr. for Viola: 1946H
Horn Concerto, K417: 1953G
Horn Concerto No. 4 in E flat, K495: 1968G, 1977G, 1988H
Sinfonia Concertante, K364: 1936H, 1947G, 1971G, 1974G, 1977G
Sinfonia Concertante, K297b: 1991H
Clarinet Quintet, K581: 1894H^c, 1952H^c
Oboe Quartet, K370: 1931G^c
String Quartets: in C: 1897H^c; in D minor: 1927H^c
Piano Trio in E, K542: 1937G^c
Divertimento in B flat, K137: 1950G^c
Divertimento in D, K316: 1975W, 1986G
Violin Sonata in B flat: 1936H^c
Fantasia in F minor (organ), K608: 1964H, 1991H

Mundy, William (*fl.* late sixteenth century)
O Lord, the Maker: 1958H, 1961H

Mussorgsky, Modest (1839–81)
Coronation Scene, Boris Godounov: 1980G
St Nicholas Mass (arr. Philip Lane): 1990W

Naylor, Bernard (1907–86)
Three Motets: 1961H
O Lord, Almighty God: 1964H
Stabat Mater: 1964H–FP*
Annunciation according to St Luke: 1967H–FP

Naylor, Edward W. (1867–1934)
Vox dicentis clama: 1967H

Neilson, Carl (1865–1931)
Tre Motetter, Op. 55: 1975W, 1981W
Hymnus Amoris: 1979H

Søvnen No. 2: 1981W
Symphony No. 2: 1981W
Commotio (organ): 1981W

Nicholson, Sydney (1875–1947)
O Salutaris Hostia: 1977G

Nickson, John (b. 1949)
Festival Jubilate: 1977G

Orff, Carl (1895–1982)
Carmina Burana: 1983G

Pachelbel, Johann (1653–1706)
Canon (arr. Roberts for brass): 1986G

Palestrina, Giovanni (*c.* 1525–94)
O Bone Jesu: 1926W, 1947G, 1954W
Stabat Mater: 1899W, 1911W, 1951W, 1965G, 1989G
Surge, illuminare: 1912H
Dum complerentur dies Pentecostes: 1959G
Tu es Petrus: 1962G, 1976H
Missa Brevis: 1970H
Exultate Deo: 1976H

Parker, Horatio W. (1863–1919)
Hora novissima: 1899W*
St Christopher (Part III): 1902W*
A Wanderer's Psalm: 1900H–FP*
Organ Concerto: 1907G

Parry, Hubert (1848–1918)
Beyond these voices: 1908W–FP*, 1910G*
Blest Pair of Sirens: 1899W*, 1920W, 1922G, 1924H, 1934G, 1946H, 1949H, 1955H, 1962G, 1970H, 1977G, 1985H
De profundis: 1891H–FP*, 1905W*
Jerusalem (orch. Elgar): 1923W, 1989G
Job: 1892G*, 1893W*, 1894H*, 1901G*, 1909H*, 1925G
Judith (Scenes from): 1937G*
King Saul: 1895G
Magnificat: 1897H–FP*
Peace (from War and Peace): 1926W
Ode to Music: 1910G*^s, 1922G
Ode on the Nativity: 1912H–FP*, 1989G
Ode on St Cecilia's Day: 1890W*^s
Song of Darkness and Light: 1898G–FP*
Songs of Farewell (complete or in part): 1920W, 1921H, 1922G, 1923W, 1927H, 1950G, 1959G, 1967H, 1980G, 1989G
The glories of our blood and state: 1929W, 1947G
The love that casteth out fear: 1904G–FP*, 1907G*
The soul's ransom: 1906H–FP*
Te Deum (Coronation): 1911W*, 1948W

Te Deum (Thanksgiving): 1900H–FP*, 1913G
Voces clamantium: 1903H–FP*, 1928G
I was glad: 1954W, 1961H, 1968G, 1973H, 1979H
The Soldier's Tent (song with orchestra): 1901G*s, 1902W*s
The 'Great' Service, *Magnificat* and *Nunc Dimittis*: 1989G
Prelude on Rockingham (arr. Finzi): 1950G
Symphonic Variations: 1922Gs, 1968G, 1989G
Overture to an Unwritten Tragedy: 1893W–FP*s, 1967H
Symphony No. 5 in B minor: 1989G
Chorale Prelude, *Jesu dulcis* (organ): 1968G
Fantasia and Fugue in G (organ): 1968G, 1969W

Patterson, Paul (b. 1947)
Mass of the Sea: 1983G–FP
Stabat Mater: 1986G
Te Deum, Op. 65: 1988H

Payne, Anthony (b. 1936)
Cantatas, Ascensiontide and Whitsuntide: 1978W–FP

Peeters, Flor (1903–86)
Entrata Festiva: 1983G

Pehkonen, Elis (b. 1942)
Anthem, *Buccinate Tuba*: 1980G–FP
Symphony: 1983G (first complete performance)
Russian Requiem: 1989G

Penderecki, Krzysztof (b. 1933)
Stabat Mater: 1972W, 1977G
Te Deum: 1987W*

Pergolesi, Giovanni (1710–36)
Magnificat a Quattro Voci, in B flat: 1988H

Petrassi, Goffredo (b. 1904)
Magnificat: 1960W, 1990W

Pezel, Johann Christoph (1639–94)
Suite for Brass: 1969W
Three Sonatinas (Brass, arr. Roberts): 1986G

Philips, Peter (*c.* 1560–1628)
Ascendit Deus: 1961H
Tibi Laus: 1964H
Two Motets: 1971G
Cantibus organis: 1965G

Pitt, Percy (1870–1932)
Coronation March: 1902W

Poulenc, Francis (1899–1963)
Stabat Mater: 1955H–FP in Britain, 1958H, 1976H

Gloria: 1963W, 1964H, 1972W, 1983G, 1991H
Quem vedistis: 1970H
Hodie: 1970H
Sept Répons des Ténèbres: 1979H
Litanies à la Vierge de Rocamadour: 1990W
Concerto in G minor (organ, strings and timpani): 1965G, 1977G, 1990W

Preston, Simon (b. 1938)
Psalm 100: 1966W

Prokofiev, Sergei (1891–1953)
Alexander Nevsky, Op. 78: 1990W
Violin Concerto No. 2 in G minor: 1989G

Prout, Ebenezer (1835–1909)
Organ Concerto in E minor: 1898G

Puccini, Giacomo (1858–1924)
Messa de Gloria: 1974G

Purcell, Henry (1659–95)
Jehovah, quam multi: 1929W, 1959G, 1964H
An Evening Hymn: 1932W
My beloved spake: 1952H
Te Deum in D: 1879H, 1895G, 1930H
The Blessed Virgin's Expostulation: 1923W
O sing unto the Lord: 1957W
Hear my prayer: 1958H
Benedicite: 1959G
Remember not, Lord, our offences: 1960W
Rejoice in the Lord alway: 1960W
Man that is born of a woman: 1961H
Thou knowest, Lord: 1964H
Praise the Lord, O my soul: 1966W
My heart is inditing: 1980G
Elegy upon the death of Queen Mary: 1968G, 1976H
Chaconne in G minor: 1946H, 1951H, 1964H, 1969W

Rachmaninov, Sergei (1873–1943)
The Bells, Op. 35: 1971G, 1987W
Piano Concerto No. 2: 1938Ws

Rainier, Priaulx (1903–86)
Cycle for Declamation: 1973H

Rameau, Jean-Philippe (1683–1764)
Suite, *Les Indes Galantes*: 1926Wc, 1970H

Ravel, Maurice (1875–1937)
Introduction and Allegro: 1952Hc
La Valse: 1956G
Pavane pour une Infante défunte: 1926Wc, 1961H
Piano Concerto for the left hand: 1951Ws

Rawsthorne, Alan (1905–71)
Piano Concerto No. 1: 1955H

Elegaic Rhapsody: 1968G
Divertimento for Chamber Orchestra: 1962G

Reed, W.H. (1876–1942)
Aesop's Fables: 1924H–FP*, 1925G*
Caprice, Will o' the Wisp: 1913G–FP*, 1923W*, 1932W*
Miniature Suite: 1929W–FP*
Overture, Merry Andrew: 1946H–FP*
Orchestral Fantasia, Scenes from the Ballet: 1904G*
Scherzo Fantastique, Caliban: 1907G–FP*
Somerset Idylls: 1926W–FP*, 1928G*, 1935W*
Symphony for Strings (first movement): 1933H–FP*
Ditto (complete): 1934G*
Rhapsody for Viola and Orchestra: 1927H*, 1928G*
The Lincoln Imp: 1921H–FP*, 1922G*, 1930H*
Variations for Strings: 1911W–FP*

Reizenstein, Franz (1911–68)
Genesis: 1958H–FP

Respighi, Ottorino (1879–1936)
Vetrata di Chiesa (Church Windows): 1990W
Gli Uccelli (The Birds): 1990W

Rimsky-Korsakov, Nicolai (1844–1908)
Aria from the Tsar's Bride: 1980G
Capriccio Espagnol: 1922G[s], 1963W
Introduction and Cortège (from The Golden Cockerel): 1928G[s]
Scheherazade: 1920W[s]
The Bumble Bee: 1928G[s]

Ritter, Alexander (1833–96)
O amantissime sponse Jesu: 1912H, 1930H, 1931G, 1946H

Rootham, Cyril Bradley (1875–1938)
Ode on the Morning of Christ's Nativity: 1934G*

Ropek, Jiri (b. 1922)
Variations on Victimae Paschali Laudes: 1970H

Rorem, Ned (b. 1923)
Te Deum: 1990W

Rossini, Giocchino (1792–1868)
Stabat Mater: 1924H, 1968G
Petite Messe Solennelle: 1969W, 1986G
Overture, William Tell: 1935W[s]
Sonata in G (strings): 1969W; in C: 1970H

Roussel, Albert (1869–1937)
Psalm 80, Op. 37: 1964H
Sinfonietta for Strings, Op. 52: 1963W

Roxburgh, Edwin (b. 1937)
The Rock: 1981W
Suite Antiphonale: 1978W

Rubbra, Edmund (1901–86)
The Morning Watch: 1948W*
Song of the Soul, Op. 78: 1957W
Symphony No. 3: 1947G*[s]; No. 6: 1957W
Sinfonia Concertante for piano and orchestra: 1948W*[s]
Improvisations on virginals pieces by Farnaby: 1946H*[s]
Inscape: 1978W

Rubinstein, Anton (1829–94)
Ballet Music, Feramors: 1896W[s]

Rutter, John (b. 1945)
Gloria: 1989G
Requiem: 1989G*

Saint-Saëns, Camille (1835–1921)
The Promised Land: 1913G–FP*
The heavens declare: 1897H
Requiem: 1978W
Symphony No. 3 in C minor, Op. 78: 1974G
Symphonic Poem, Op. 50: 1976H

Sallinen, Aulis (b. 1935)
Dies Irae: 1981W–FP in Britain

Sanders, John (b. 1933)
Psalm 100: 1968G*
Te Deum: 1962–FP*, 1983G*

Saunders, Neil
Fantasia for Brass: 1968G

Scarlatti, Alessandro (1660–1725)
Christmas Cantata: 1961H
Stabat Mater: 1977G, 1985H

Schubert, Franz (1797–1828)
Masses:
in G: 1973H
in B flat: 1978W
Great is Jehovah: 1896W
Lazarus (selection): 1909H
Symphonies:
No. 2 in B flat: 1952H
No. 3 in D: 1958H, 1969W
No. 5 in B flat: 1962G, 1968G, 1980G, 1990W
No. 7 in C: 1928G, 1969W
No. 8 in B minor ('Unfinished'): 1893W[s], 1912H, 1923W, 1947G, 1956G, 1974G, 1976H
Overture, Rosamunde: 1905W[s], 1958H
Entr'acte and Ballet Music, Rosamunde: 1928G[c]
Quartet-satz: 1930H[c], 1935W[c], 1946H[c]
Quartet in A minor, Op. 29: 1953G[c]
Octet in F, Op. 166: 1959G

Schumann, Robert (1810–56)
Symphonies:
in B flat, Op. 38: 1891H^s, 1969W
in E flat ('Rhenish'), Op. 97: 1896W^s
in D minor, Op. 120: 1895G
Piano Concerto in A minor: 1912H^s, 1955H
Cello Concerto in A minor, Op. 129: 1973H
Piano Quintet in E flat: 1891H^c, 1900H^c, 1934G^c, 1946H^c
Overture, Manfred: 1980G

Schurmann, Gerard (b. 1928)
Piers Plowman: 1980G, 1989G

Schütz, Heinrich (1585–1672)
Lamentatio Davidi: 1895G
Magnificat: 1964H, 1972W, 1985H
Deutsches Magnificat: 1981W
Motet, Sumite psalmum: 1966W

Scott, Anthony
Chorale Variations: 1953G–FP
Hymn-Anthem, Almighty Word, Immortal Love: 1956G, 1965G

Scriabin, Alexander (1872–1915)
Le pòeme de l'extase, for orchestra: 1922G

Searle, Humphrey (1915–82)
Night Music: 1955H

Seiber, Matyas (1905–60)
Four Greek Folk-Songs (string orchestra): 1948W^c

Shaw, Martin (1875–1958)
Sursum Corda: 1933H–FP*
Water Folk (song sequence): 1932W^c

Shephard, Richard (b. 1949)
Let us now praise famous men: 1983G–FP
Mass: 1989G

Shostakovich, Dmitri (1906–75)
Prelude and Scherzo: 1951W^c
Symphony No. 5, Op. 47; 1968G

Sibelius, Jean (1865–1957)
Symphonies:
No. 1 in E minor, Op. 39: 1937G, 1986G
No. 2 in D, Op. 43: 1931G, 1948W, 1977G, 1981W
No. 3 in C, Op. 52: 1956G
No. 5 in E flat, Op. 82: 1935W, 1950G
No. 7 in C (in one movement), Op. 105: 1952H, 1972W
Violin Concerto in D minor, Op. 47: 1948W, 1965G, 1989G
Tone Poems:
Finlandia: 1925G, 1981W

Luonnotar: 1913G^s
Return of Lemminkainen: 1937G^s
Swan of Tuonela: 1937G^s
Valse Triste: 1925G^s
Karelia Suite: 1980G
Romance in C, Op. 42: 1986G
Intrada (organ): 1983G

Smetana, Bedřich (1824–84)
Overture, The Bartered Bride: 1906H^s, 1910G^s, 1921H^s, 1931G^s

Smyth, Ethel (1858–1944)
Mass in D (extracts): 1925G*
Ditto (complete): 1928G
Canticle of Spring: 1926W*
Overtures:
The Boatswain's Mate: 1926W*^{s}
The Wreckers: 1925G*^{s}
Two interlinked French Melodies for orchestra: 1928G*^{s}
String Quartet in E minor: 1921H^c

Spicer, Paul (b. 1952)
The Darling of the World: 1988H

Spohr, Ludwig (1784–1859)
Calvary: 1891H
The Fall of Babylon: 1892G
God, thou art great: 1890W, 1896W
The Last Judgement: 1893W, 1894H, 1897H, 1899W, 1901G
Quartet in G minor: 1891H^c

Stainer, John (1840–1901)
St Mary Magdalen: 1891H*

Stanford, Charles V. (1852–1924)
The Battle of the Baltic: 1891H^s
The Last Post: 1900H–FP*, 1901G^s, 1922G
Songs of the Sea: 1907G^s
Ditto (selections): 1925G^s
Stabat Mater: 1908W*, 1925G, 1936H, 1952H
Te Deum: 1904G*
Ye Holy Angels bright: 1913G–FP
Magnificat: 1956G
Three Latin Motets, Op. 38: 1957W, 1964H
Jubilate in B flat: 1958H
Magnificat and *Nunc Dimittis* in B flat: 1960W
Ditto in A: 1964H, 1966W, 1976H
Psalm 150: 1965G
Gloria: 1970H
Magnificat for 8-part Chorus (unaccompanied), Op. 164: 1977G
Symphony No. 5 in D (Adagio and Finale): 1898G*
Clarinet Concerto in A minor: 1991H
Overture, Shamus O'Brien: 1924H^s

O come, ye servants: 1958H
Praise ye the Lord: 1968G

Valls, Francisco (1665–1747)
Missa Scala Aretina: 1980G

Vaughan Williams, Ralph (1872–1958)
Benedicite: 1932W*, 1946H, 1959G, 1981W
Dona Nobis Pacem: 1937G*, 1938W*, 1953G*, 1959G, 1986G
Fantasia on Christmas Carols: 1912H–FP*
Fantasia on The Old 104th: 1950G–FP*
Five Mystical Songs: 1911W–FP*, 1952H*, 1960W, 1964H, 1967H, 1972W, 1976H
Psalm 100: 1950G*, 1958H, 1963W, 1974G
Lord, thou hast been our refuge: 1923W*, 1958H, 1965G, 1980G
Magnificat: 1932W–FP*, 1934G, 1947G
Six Choral Songs (selection): 1933H*
Sancta Civitas: 1929W*, 1930H*, 1935W*, 1951W, 1952H, 1961H, 1975W, 1985H
Shepherds of the delectable mountains: 1927H, 1933H*
Hodie: 1954W–FP*, 1956G, 1960W, 1976H
Mass in G minor: 1972W
Te Deum in G: 1961H
O clap your hands: 1967H
Toward the unknown region: 1980G
On Wenlock Edge: 1989G
Flos Campi: 1954W, 1963W
Symphonies:
No. 1 (Sea Symphony): 1925G*, 1936H* ('The Explorers' only); 1962G, 1967H, 1972W, 1983G, 1991H
No. 2 (London Symphony): 1967H
No. 3 (Pastoral Symphony): 1926W*, 1927H, 1934G, 1946H, 1949H*, 1954W*
No. 4 in F minor: 1961H
No. 5 in D: 1947G*, 1951W, 1959G, 1971G, 1982H
No. 6 in E minor: 1950G*
Overtures:
The Wasps: 1926W*ˢ, 1929W*ˢ, 1938W*ˢ, 1951W*ˢ, 1985H
The Poisoned Kiss (and songs): 1937G*ˢ
Fantasias:
on Greensleeves: 1935Wˢ*
on a Theme of Thomas Tallis: 1910G–FP*, 1921H*, 1938W*, 1948W*, 1955H, 1960W, 1965G, 1972W, 1977G, 1981W
on Sussex Folk Tunes: 1983G
Suites:
Job: 1931G*ˢ, 1935W*, 1948W*, 1953G*, 1957H, 1964H, 1983G
Charterhouse: 1928G*ˢ
Suite for viola and orchestra: 1936H*ˢ

Concertos:
Concerto Grosso (string orchestra): 1973H
Oboe Concerto: 1978W
The Lark Ascending: 1928G*ˢ, 1931G*, 1956G*, 1966W, 1977G, 1982H
Five Variants of Dives and Lazarus: 1957W
Serenade to Music: 1959G, 1972W, 1975W
A Norfolk Rhapsody: 1934Gˢ, 1965G
An Oxford Elegy: 1957W
The Running Set: 1935W*ˢ
Two Hymn Preludes for orchestra: 1936H–FP*
Prelude and Fugue in C minor for orchestra: 1930H–FP*
Song Cycles:
On Wenlock Edge: 1924Hᶜ, 1931Gᶜ, 1989G
Songs of Travel (selections): 1933Hᶜ
Four Hymns for tenor and strings: 1920W–FP*

Verdi, Guiseppe (1813–1901)
Requiem: 1896W, 1900H, 1901G, 1907G, 1910G, 1913G, 1920W, 1922G, 1925G, 1928G, 1937G, 1949H, 1954W, 1955H, 1958H, 1967H, 1972W, 1977G, 1982H, 1989G
Stabat Mater: 1898G–FP in England, 1929W
Te Deum: 1898G–FP in England, 1929W, 1965G, 1975W, 1983G
Quattro pezzi sacri: 1960W, 1968G, 1990W
Overture, La Forza del Destino: 1988H

Victoria, Tomas (c. 1548–1611)
Missa O quam gloriosum: 1969W
O magnum mysterium: 1964H
Gaudent in coelis: 1965G
Ave Maria: 1977G
Requiem (1605): 1986G

Villette, Pierre (b. 1926)
Messe en Français: 1981W
Three Preludes for strings: 1981W, 1990W

Vivaldi, Antonio (1676–1741)
Guitar Concerto in D: 1986G

Wagner, Richard (1813–83)
Wesendonck Lieder: 1980G
Die Götterdämmerung (closing scene): 1899Wˢ, 1920Wˢ
Lohengrin, Introduction to Act III: 1890Wˢ
Ditto, Lohengrin's Farewell: 1908Wˢ
Die Meistersinger, Incidental Music Act III: 1899Wˢ
Preludes:
Parsifal: 1891H, 1894H, 1902W, 1904G, 1906H, 1913G, 1926W, 1949H, 1983G
Tristan (and *Liebestod*): 1911Wˢ, 1932Wˢ, 1974G
Lohengrin: 1978W

Appendix II

Cathedral organ recitals and programmes of events, other than fringe events, performed in alternative venues, 1954–91

1954 WORCESTER

Organ Recital   *Sir William McKie*

Toccata in A minor	Sweelink
Variations on Puer nobis nascitur	Sweelink
Capriccio in A minor	Sweelink
Toccata, Adagio and Fugue in C	J.S. Bach
Three Chorale Preludes	Brahms
Prelude, Fugue and Variations	Franck
Saraband	Howells
Introduction, Passacaglia and Fugue	Willan

Recital   *Isobel Baillie (sop.) Eileen Ralf (piano), Thomas Matthews (vln.), Meredith Davies (accomp.)*

Where shall the Lover rest?	Parry
Crabbed age and youth	Parry
Absence	Berlioz
The unknown land	Berlioz
Sonata for Violin and Piano in C, K296	Mozart
The Nightingale	Delius
Twilight Fancies	Delius
Love's Philosophy	Delius
I heard a piper piping	Bax
Spring	Gurney
Sonata for Violin and Piano in D minor, Op. 108	Brahms

Piano Recital   *Phyllis Sellick*

Le Bavolet Flottant	Couperin
Le Carillon de Cythère	Couperin
Sonata in G	Scarlatti
Sonata in E flat, Op. 31, No. 3	Beethoven
Country Tune	Bax
The Hobby Horse	Leo Livens
The Lake in the Mountain	Vaughan Williams
Two Bagatelles	Howard Ferguson
Toccata	Holst
Etudes Symphoniques, Op. 13	Schumann

Recital   *Nancy Evans (contralto), Herbert Sumsion (piano), Leon Goossens (oboe)*

Suite for Oboe and Piano	Scarlatti
An die Nachtigal	Brahms
Immer leiser wird mein Schlummen	Brahms
Vergebliches Ständchen	Brahms
Der Schmied	Brahms
Sonata for Oboe and Piano	York Bowen
L'invitation au Voyage	Duparc
Exstase	Duparc
Clair de lune	Fauré

Ici-bas	Fauré
Après un rêve	Fauré
Sonatina for Oboe and Piano	Malcolm Arnold

1955 HEREFORD

Organ Recital *Michael Illman*
Opening Service

Passacaglia and Fugue in C minor	J.S. Bach
Prelude on Psalm 34, v. 6	Howells
Pastorale	Herbert Sumsion

Organ Recital *Francis Jackson*

Prelude and Fugue in E flat	J.S. Bach
Fantasia in F minor, K 594	Mozart
Voluntary in E	Samuel Wesley
Toccata in C (1953)	Gordon Philips
Rhapsody on a Ground	Heathcote Statham
Variations on a Noël	Dupré

Recital *Isobel Baillie (sop.), Julian Bream (guitar), Herbert Sumsion (piano)*

Five Songs	Brahms
Wie Melodien zieht es mir	
Immer leiser wird mein Schlümmer	
Minnelied	
Schwesterlein	
Vergebliches Ständchen	
Lute Solos	
Pavan	Bulman
Carman's Whistle	Johnson
Forlorne Hope	Dowland
Galliard	Dowland
My Ladye Hunsdon's Puffe	Dowland
Songs	
Sylvelin	Christian Sinding
With a water lily	Grieg
The first primrose	Grieg
Before my window	Rachmaninov
The Lilacs	Rachmaninov
Spring Waters	Rachmaninov
Solos for Guitar	
Three Preludes	H. Villa Lobes
Hommage à Tarrega	J. Turina

Recital *Bruce Boyce (bar.), Ralph Holmes (violin), David Willcocks (piano)*

Verklärung	Schubert
Totengräbers Heimweh	Schubert
Dem Unendlichen	Schubert
Drei Harfenspieler Lieder	Hugo Wolf
La Folia, Variations sérieuses	Corelli–Leonard
Sonata No. 1 in G minor	J.S. Bach
Wondrous Machine (Ode to St Cecilia)	Purcell
A Divine Song	Purcell
King David	Howells

The Fox	Peter Warlock
I hear an Army	Samuel Barber
Sonata No. 2, Op. 94	Prokofiev

1956 GLOUCESTER

Organ Recital *Wallace Ross*
Opening Service – Music by Gloucestershire Composers

Rhapsody, Op. 17, No. 3	Howells
Larghetto in F sharp minor	S.S. Wesley
1st Movement from Sonata, Op. 5	Harwood
Finale in F	William Hine

Organ Recital *Dr George Thalben-Ball*

Suite in G	John Stanley
À la venue de Noël	Balbâtre
Chorale Prelude: Schmücke dich	J.S. Bach
Prelude and Fugue in E flat	J.S. Bach
Sonata Eroica	Joseph Jongen
Le moulin	A. Cellier
Fête	Langlais
Andante, Symphony No. 4	Widor
Lied to the Sun	Flor Peeters

1957 WORCESTER

Organ Recital *Douglas Fox*
Opening Service

Trumpet Sonata	Purcell
Partita	J.S. Bach
Adagio in E	Frank Bridge
3rd Movement of Sonata in D	Galuppi
Fugue in E minor (Wanderer)	Parry

Organ Recital *Harold Darke*

Sonata in G	Elgar
Fantasie-Chorale No. 2	Whitlock
Prière	Jongen
Introduction, Passacaglia and Fugue	Healey Willan

Piano Recital *Denis Matthews*

Four Preludes and Fugues	J.S. Bach
Rondo in A minor, K551	Mozart
Sonata in D minor, Op. 31, No. 2	Beethoven
Sonata alla Toccata	William Alwyn
Bagatelles for Piano (1938)	Alan Rawsthorne
Sonata in A, Op. 120	Schubert

1958 HEREFORD

Organ Recital *Michael Burton*
Opening Service

Trumpet Tune in D	Purcell–Dupré
Toccata in F	J.S. Bach
Voluntary in C minor	Maurice Greene

| Postlude in D minor | C.V. Stanford |
| Choral Song and Fugue | S.S. Wesley |

Organ Recital *Fernando Germani*
Toccata VIII, Bk. 2	Gerolamo Frescobaldi
Toccata, No. 3 Bk. 2	Gerolamo Frescobaldi
Canzona in F, No. 4	Gerolamo Frescobaldi
Variations, Mein junges Leben	Jan Sweelinck
Toccata, Adagio and Fugue in C	J.S. Bach
Variations sur un vieux Noël	Marcel Dupré
Toccata	Fernando Germani
Choral Fantasie, Op. 40, No. 2	Max Reger

Recital *Norma Procter (cont.), Peter Pears (tenor), Benjamin Britten (piano)*
Morning Hymn	Purcell
Mad Bess	Purcell
Two Canzonets	Purcell
Dialogue: Corydon and Mopsa	Purcell
Duet: Nun wer die Sehnsucht kennt	Schubert
Die Stradt	Schubert
Der Taubenpost	Schubert
Lachen und Weinen	Schubert
Wenn ich Früh	Schumann
Duet: Vor dem Fenster	Schumann
Canticle, Abraham and Isaac	Britten
Folk Songs	arr. Britten

1959 GLOUCESTER

Organ Recital *John Sanders*
Opening Service
Flourish for an Occasion	W.H. Harris
Folk Tune	Percy Whitlock
Introduction and Passacaglia	W.G. Alcock
A Fantasy	Harold Darke
Whitsunday Procession	Tony Hewitt-Jones

Organ Recital *Francis Jackson with James Walkley (bass)*
Voluntary in D	Boyce-Campbell
Concerto in G minor	Matthew Camidge
Fantasia, K594	Mozart
Solo Cantata No. 82: It is enough	J.S. Bach
(James Walkley and John Sanders – Organ)	
Variations on an Original Theme, Op. 58	Flor Peeters
Toccata, Chorale and Fugue	Francis Jackson

1960 WORCESTER

Organ Recital *John Birch*
Opening Service
Paean	Herbert Howells
Choral Song	S.S. Wesley
Fugue No. 1 on BACH	Schumann
Fugue in D minor (The Fiddle)	J.S. Bach
Flourish for an Occasion	W.H. Harris

Organ Recital   *Ralph Downes*
Three Pieces	Thomas Tomkins
Fantasia and Fugue in C minor	J.S. Bach
Pastorale	Roger-Ducasse
Sonata in G, Op. 28	Elgar

Recital   *Allegri String Quartet with Gervase de Peyer (clarinet)*
Quartet in D, Op. 64, No. 5	Haydn
Clarinet Quintet in A, K581	Mozart
Quartet in D minor (Op. Post.)	Schubert
(Death and the Maiden)	

Piano Recital   *Denis Matthews*
Three Preludes and Fugues	J.S. Bach
Fantasy in C minor, K475	Mozart
Sonata in C minor, K457	Mozart
Four Preludes	Debussy
Sonata in B flat	Schubert

1961 HEREFORD

Organ Recital   *Michael Burton*
Opening Service
Fantasia in G	J.S. Bach
Saraband Processional	W.H. Harris
Paean	Peter Hurford

Organ Recital   *Peter Hurford*
Prelude and Fugue in C	J.S. Bach
Suite, Laudate Dominum	Peter Hurford
Cortège et Litanie	Dupré
Introduction and Allegro	Arthur Wills
Choral Dorien	Jehan Alain
Paraphrase on 'O filii et filiae'	Ralph Downes
Prelude and Fugue in B minor	J.S. Bach

Recital   *Peter Pears (ten.), Barry Tuckwell (horn), Benjamin Britten (piano)*
Dichterliebe, Op. 48	Schumann
Adagio and Allegro for Horn and Piano, Op. 70	Schumann
Canticle III, Still falls the rain, Op. 55	Britten
Songs:	
The Soldier	John Ireland
The Trellis	John Ireland
Go not, happy day	Frank Bridge
When you are old and gray	Frank Bridge
Love went a-riding	Frank Bridge

1962 GLOUCESTER

Organ Recital   *John Sanders*
Opening Service
Prelude in C	Vaughan Williams
Toccata, Chorale & Fugue	Francis Jackson
Fanfare	Percy Whitlock

Recital   *John Birch (organ) with Gervase de Peyer (clarinet) and Melville Cook (piano)*

Prelude and Fugue in C BWV545	J.S. Bach
Two Chorale Preludes	J.S. Bach
Voluntary in D	John James
Choral No. 1 in E	Franck
Sonata in E flat, Op. 120, No. 2 for Clarinet and Piano	Brahms
Rhapsody, Op. 17, No. 1	Howells
Prelude, Toccata and Chaconne	Brian Brockless
Andante in E flat	S.S. Wesley
Berceuse	Vierne
Prelude and Fugue, Christ lag in Todesbanden	Hermann Schroeder

Concert   *London String Quartet*

Quartet in A minor, Op. 51, No. 2	Brahms
Quintet in C, Op. 163	Schubert

Piano Recital   *Denis Matthews*

Suite in G minor	Purcell
Sonata in F minor	Brahms
Four Romantic Pieces	Alan Rawsthorne
Sonata No. 30 in E, Op. 109	Beethoven

1963 WORCESTER

Organ Recital   *Christopher Robinson*
Opening Service

Prelude in E flat	J.S. Bach
Kyrie, Gott Vater in Ewigkeit	J.S. Bach
Christe, aller Welt Trost	J.S. Bach
Kyrie, Gott heiliger Geist	J.S. Bach
Fugue in E flat	J.S. Bach

Concert   *The Jubilate Players*

Sonata in F for Recorder, 2 Violins and Continuo	J.F. Fasch
Three Fantasias	Gibbons
Three Sonatas for Harpsichord	Scarlatti
Troisième Concert	Rameau
Trio Sonata No. 5 in E minor	Avison
Quartetto for Recorder, 2 Violins and Continuo	Scarlatti
Sonata No. 1 in A for Cello and Continuo	Boccherini
Trio Sonata in G, S1027	J.S. Bach

Concert   *Amadeus String Quartet*

String Quartet in G, Op. 77, No. 1	Haydn
String Quartet in D, K499	Mozart
String Quartet in C minor, Op. 51, No. 1	Brahms

1964 HEREFORD

Organ Recital   *Roger Fisher*
Opening Service

Toccata, Adagio and Fugue in C	J.S. Bach
Scherzo, from Sonata in E flat	Edward Bairstow
Carillon	Herbert Murrill

Crown Imperial	William Walton
Toccata in F	J.S. Bach

Organ Recital   *Marilyn Mason*
Toccata, Adagio and Fugue in C	J.S. Bach
Four Pieces	John Bull
Fantasia	John Bull
Variations, John come kisse me now	Byrd
The Queene's Command	Gibbons
Fantasy and Fugue on BACH	Liszt
Fantasy	Ross Lee Finney
Carol-Prelude on Greensleeves	Searle Wright
Suite for Organ	Edmund Haines
Carillon de Westminster	Vierne

Concert   *Allegri String Quartet*
String Quartet No. 14 in G, K387	Mozart
String Quartet in D, No. 4, Op. 83	Shostakovich
String Quartet in F minor, Op. 95	Beethoven

Piano Recital   *Sergio Varella-Cid*
Sonata in C minor, Op. 13 (Pathétique)	Beethoven
Sonata in B minor, Op. 58	Chopin
Sonata (1924)	Stravinsky
Sonata	Francisco Mignone
Sonata No. 3	Prokofiev

1965 GLOUCESTER

Organ Recital   *Richard Latham*
Opening Service
Canzona	Buxtehude
Prelude and Fugue in C minor	J.S. Bach
Praeludium	Micheelson
Toccata and Fugue	Reger

Organ Recital   *Noel Rawsthorne*
Grand Jeu	Pierre du Mage
Two Schübler Preludes	J.S. Bach
Toccata in F	J.S. Bach
Variations on Est-ce Mars	Sweelinck
Incantation pour un Jour Saint	Jean Langlais
Master Tallis's Testament	Herbert Howells
Joie et clarté des corps glorieux	Olivier Messiaen
Les Anges	Olivier Messiaen
Toccata	Maurice Duruflé

Recital   *John Shirley-Quirk (bar.), Alastair Graham (piano), Betty Mulcahy and Leonard Clark*
Songs and Poems of Gloucester, Hereford and Worcester under the title: Coloured Counties

Concert   *Aeolian String Quartet*
Quartet in C, Op. 33 No. 3 (Bird)	Haydn
String Quartet No. 5	Bartók
Quartet in E flat, Op. 127	Beethoven

1966 WORCESTER

Organ Recital *Harry Bramma*
Opening Service
    Fantasia in G   J.S. Bach
    Two Chorale Preludes   J.S. Bach
    Toccata, Adagio and Fugue in C   J.S. Bach

Organ Recital *Peter Hurford*
    Dialogue sur les Grands Jeux   Nicholas de Grigny
    Noel, Josephe est bien marie   Jean-François Dandricu
    Sonata III   Hindemith
    Chorale No. 1 in E   Franck
    Two Chorale Preludes   J.S. Bach
    Prelude and Fugue in E flat   J.S. Bach

Concert *The Purcell Consort of Voices*
English music of the sixteenth- and twentieth-centuries, Italian Madrigals,
French Chansons — 22 Items listed

Piano Recital *David Wilde*
    Serenade in A   Stravinsky
    Nocturne and Jig   Holst
    Sonata in A flat, Op. 26   Beethoven

Recital *Alberni String Quartet*
    Two 4-part Fantasias   Purcell
    String Quartet in B flat (1941)   Arthur Bliss
    String Quartet in E flat   Dvořák

Concert *The Philip Jones Brass Ensemble and The Pro Arte Trio*
Brass
    Toccata from L'Orfeo   Monteverdi
    Canzona a 4   Gabrieli
    Canzona a 5   Gabrieli
Strings
    Trio in E flat   Beethoven
Brass
    Suite for Brass Septet   Stephen Dodgson
Strings
    Trio   Lennox Berkeley
Brass
    Canzon Cornetto   Scheidt
    Contrapunctus IX, Art of Fugue   J.S. Bach

1967 HEREFORD

Organ Recital *Roger Fisher*
Opening Service
    Dialogue sur les Grands Jeux   Nicolas de Grigny
    Prelude and Fugue in D   J.S. Bach
    Tu es Petra   Henri Mulet
    Finale, Symphony No. 1   Vierne

Organ Recital   *Francis Jackson*
Introduction and Fugue in A .... James Nares
Toccata and Fugue in F, BWV540 .... J.S. Bach
Introduction, Passacaglia and Coda (1966) .. Brian Brockless
Fantaisie in A .... Franck
Scherzo .... Eugène Gigout
Fantasia and Fugue on BACH .... Liszt

Recital   *Amici String Quartet*
String Quartet in F, Op. 77, No. 2 .... Haydn
String Quartet in F (1902) .... Ravel
String Quartet in D minor, No. 14, D810 .. Schubert
   (Death and the Maiden)

Lecture Recital   *Dennis Matthews (piano)*
Beethoven's Diabelli Variations

Recital   *Wilfred Brown (ten.), David Pettit (piano), Betty Mulcahy and Leonard Clark*
'. . . the idea of man on the Earth . . .' 28 readings and 16 songs listed (British composers)

1968 GLOUCESTER

Organ Recital   *Richard Latham*
Opening Service
Prelude and Fugue in C minor .... Mendelssohn
Paean .... Howells
Exultate .... Bryan Kelly
Chorale Prelude on The Old 100th .... Hubert Parry
Organ Concerto No. 4 in F .... Handel

Organ Recital   *Gillian Weir*
Fantasia in G .... J.S. Bach
Sonata No. 1 .... Hindemith
Prelude and Fugue in C minor .... Samuel Wesley
Les Eaux de Grâce .... Messiaen
Combat de la Mort et de la Vie .... Messiaen
Impromptu .... Vierne
Fantasia and Fugue on BACH .... Liszt

Recital   *The Robles Trio*
Trio for Flute, Viola and Harp .... Leclair
Variations and Rondo Pastorale (Harp) ...... Mozart
Sonata for Flute, Viola and Harp .... Debussy
Elegiac Trio .... Bax

Song Recital   *Richard Lewis (ten.), Geoffrey Parsons (piano)*
Songs by Purcell, Schubert, Beethoven, Vaughan Williams, Butterworth and Britten

1969 WORCESTER

Recital   *The Vesuvius Ensemble of London*
Trio in E flat, K498 .... Mozart
Three Pieces .... Stravinsky

Due Liriche di Anacreonte	Dallapiccola
Quadro Liriche di Antonio Machade	Dallapiccola
Marchenersahlungen	Schumann
Concert Piece	Mendelssohn

Organ Recital   *Brian Runnett*
Praeludium in D minor	Pachelbel
Movements from Messe pour les Paroisses	Couperin
Prelude and Fugue in A major	J.S. Bach
Christmas Meditations	Arthur Wills

Recital   *John Shirley-Quirk (bar.), Martin Isepp (piano)*
| *Winterreise* | Schubert |

Lecture-Recital   *James Blades (percussion), Joan Goossens (piano)*
An 'entertainment' with no detailed programme supplied '. . . followed by Buffet Luncheon for the under-twenties at the King's School'

1970 HEREFORD

Organ Recital   *Robert Green*
Opening Service
Prelude and Fugue in F minor, BWV534	J.S. Bach
Carillon	Herbert Murrill
Paean	Howells
Prelude and Fugue in A minor, BWV 543	J.S. Bach

Lecture   *Ivor Keys*
'The Music of the Festival'

Chamber Concert   *The Venturi Ensemble*
Divertimento	Malcolm Arnold
Sonatina	Rawsthorne
Sonatina	Lennox Berkeley
Prelude, Recit. and Variations	Maurice Duruflé
Trio in E flat, K498	Mozart

Composers' Forum   *With Lennox Berkeley, Alun Hoddinott, Bryan Kelly, John McCabe, Christopher Brown*

Recital   *Rosalind Shanks, Leonard Clark, John Barrow (bar.), David Williamson (piano)*
43 items of Poetry and Songs under the general title: 'From Dust I rise'

1971 GLOUCESTER

Lecture   *Watkins Shaw*
The Three Choirs Festival

Concert   *The LaSalle String Quartet*
Three 4-part Fantasias	Purcell
Six Bagatelles	Webern
Grosse Fugue in B flat, Op. 133	Beethoven
String Quartet in F	Ravel

Concert *The Purcell Consort of Voices and The London Gabrieli Brass Ensemble*
Music for the Two Elizabeths	Various
Lament for Brass	John Dowland
In praise of Oriana	Various
In praise of Elizabeth II	Various
Lauds (Festival commission)	Christopher Brown

Concert *The Music Group of London*
Trio in F, Op. 24	Franz Danzi
Trio in E minor, Op. 90	Dvořák
Trio in E flat, Op. 40	Brahms

1972 WORCESTER

Lecture-Demonstration

'Meet the Wind Section, Birmingham Wind Players': No programme but indicates '. . . followed by Young People's Luncheon at the [Swan] Theatre'

Recital *The Purcell Consort of Voices*

The Continental Renaissance – 12 Items
400th Anniversary of the Death of Thomas Tomkins – 7 Items
The first half of the Twentieth Century – 7 Items

Recital *'Composers in Person' John McCabe, John Joubert, David Carhart, Gordon Crosse, Peter W.F. Lawson with Meriel Dickinson (M-Sop.) and Peter Dickinson (piano)*
Aubade (Study No. 4, 1970)	McCabe
Piano Sonata No. 1	Joubert
Chinese Songs (First performance)	Carhart
Momenta 94	Lawson
The New World, Op. 25 (First performance)	Crosse

Recital *Aeolian String Quartet with Terence Weil (cello)*
String Quartet in A minor (1947)	Walton
String Quartet in C, Op. 163	Schubert

An Entertainment *Cleo Laine and John Dankworth with The Recital Quartet*

An Entertainment *The Barrow Poets*

Organ Recital *Nicholas Kynaston*
Fantaisie in A	Franck
Toccata on the Chorale Jerusalem, Op. 65	Karg-Elert
Phantasie in F minor, KV608	Mozart
Fantasia and Fugue on the Chorale, Ad nos	Liszt

1973 HEREFORD

Play *A Sleep of Prisoners – Christopher Fry*

Chamber Concert *New London Wind Ensemble*
Concerto in A minor	Vivaldi
Divertimento in F, K213	Mozart
Divertimento in B flat	Haydn
The Earl of Oxford's March	Byrd

La Cheminée du Roi René   Darius Milhaud
Divertimento   Malcolm Arnold
Quintet   Reicha

Chamber Concert   *English Consort of Viols with Voices* – 16 items listed

Wine and Cheese Party   *The King's Singers*

Illustrated Lecture   *James Blades*
'The History of Percussion Instruments'

Recital   *The Lindsay String Quartet*
Quartet in C minor, Op. 18, No. 4   Beethoven
Quartet No. 5   Bartók
Quartet in D, Op. 76, No. 5   Haydn

1974 GLOUCESTER

Lecture   *Imogen Holst*
'Holst in Gloucestershire'

Orchestral Concert   *Academy of the BBC conducted by Meredith Davies with Jack Brymer (clarinet)*
Overture, Don Giovanni   Mozart
Elegy for Strings   Elgar
Clarinet Concert No. 2   Weber
Symphonies for Chamber Orchestra   Crosse
Symphony No. 8   Beethoven

Chamber Concert   *Ralph Holmes (violin), Gillian Weir (harpsichord)*
Sonata in B minor   J.S. Bach
Partita in D minor   J.S. Bach
Partita in E minor (Klavier Ubungen)   J.S. Bach
Sonata in A   J.S. Bach

Recital   *Georgian String Quartet*
The Musician (Poem)   R.S. Thomas
Seven Last Words of Our Saviour, Op. 51   Haydn

Organ Recital
Prelude and Fugue in F sharp minor   Buxtehude
Tanz-Toccata   Anton Heiller
Récit de tierce en taille   de Grigny
Dialogue sur les Grands Jeux   de Grigny
Verset pour la Fête de la Dédicace   Messiaen
Les Anges   Messiaen
Dieu parmi nous   Messiaen
Sonata for Organ   Tony Hewitt-Jones
Deuxième Fantasie   Jehan Alain
Fugue in E flat (St Anne)   J.S. Bach

1975 WORCESTER

Concert   *GUS Footwear Band (in the cathedral)*
Overture, Magic Flute   * Mozart

Solemn Melody	* Walford Davies
Euphonium Concerto	Horovitz
Fantasy for Brass	Malcolm Arnold
English Folk Song Suite	* Vaughan Williams
Severn Suite	Elgar
Yeomen of the Guard	* Sullivan
The Lost Chord	* Sullivan
Prometheus Unbound	Bantock
Nimrod, from Enigma Variations	* Elgar
Recit. and Romance	Reginald Heath
Entertainments	Gilbert Vinter
	* *arrangement*

Recital   *Ifor James (horn), John McCabe (piano)*

Horn Sonata in F, Op. 17	Beethoven
Chaconne for Piano, Op. 32	Nielsen
The Goddess Trilogy I	McCabe
The Goddess Trilogy II	McCabe
Piano Sonata in E flat	Haydn
The Goddess Trilogy III	McCabe

Recital   *The Dolmetsch Ensemble*
17 items listed 'followed by Young People's Luncheon in the Swan Theatre'

Recital   *Music Group of London with Ian Partridge (tenor)*

Trio No. 25 in G	Haydn
On Wenlock Edge	Vaughan Williams
Severnside (First performance)	Richard Benger
Piano Quintet in A, Op. 81	Dvořák

An Entertainment   *Marian Montgomery and Richard Rodney Bennett*

Organ Recital   *Christopher Robinson*

Passacaglia and Fugue in C minor	J.S. Bach
Elegy (1965)	McCabe
Alba (1973)	Richard Rodney Bennett
L'Ascension	Messiaen
Passecaille	Frank Martin
Sonata No. 1 in F minor	Mendelssohn

Recital   *Maureen Smith (cello), Keith Swallow (piano)*

Sonata in A, Op. 47	Beethoven
Theme and Variations	Messiaen
Sonata in E minor, Op. 82	Elgar

1976 HEREFORD

Organ Recital   *Robert Green*
Opening Service

Toccata and Fugue in D minor (Dorian)	J.S. Bach
Finale, Sonata No. 1 in D minor	Guilmant
Passacaglia and Fugue in C minor	J.S. Bach

Chamber Concert *The English Consort of Viols* – 14 items listed

Concert *Michael and Doreen Muskett*
Recorders, Crumhorn, Clarinet, Bagpipes, Psaltery, Snake
Charmer, Spinet, *et al.*

Recital *Jeffrey Harris (Moór two-manual piano)*

Organ Prelude and Fugue in D	J.S. Bach
Toccata, Adagio and Fugue in C	J.S. Bach
Chaconne in G	Handel
Fantasie fur eine Orgelwalze, K608	Mozart
Fantasie in C, Op. 17	Schumann
Six Bagatelles for double keyboard	Timothy Baxter
Hungarian Rhapsody No. 12	Liszt
La Campanella	Liszt

Organ Recital *John Bishop*

Partita on Auf, auf, mein Herz	Flor Peeters
Prelude and Fugue in B minor	J.S. Bach
Variations, Weinen, Klagen	Liszt
Allegro in D	Carvalho
Scherzo in E	Gigout
Apparition de l'église éternelle	Messiaen
Transports de joie (L'Ascension)	Messiaen

Wine and Cheese Party *The Scholars*
17-plus items listed: music of fifteenth, sixteenth and seventeenth centuries

Chamber Concert *The Schiller Trio*

Trio No. 1 in C	Frederic Duvernoy
Impromptus in A flat and E flat	Schubert
Trio for Violin, Horn and Piano (First performance)	Graham Whettam
Trio in E flat, Op. 4	Brahms

1977 GLOUCESTER – 250th FESTIVAL

Concert *The King's Singers (in the cathedral)* 'Secular and Sacred Music of the English Renaissance'
Madrigals

All at once well me	Weelkes
On a fair morning	Morley
Come again	Dowland
This sweet and merry month	Byrd
Gaudeamus omnes	Byrd
Ave Verum Corpus	Byrd
Five Songs from a Greek Anthology	Elgar
The House of Sleepe (1972)	R. Rodney Bennett
A Group of Spirituals	

An Entertainment *Opus 5 Male Voice Quartet*
20 items including first performance of
Five Songs   Roger Hemingway

Lecture   *Wulstan Atkins*
'Personal Reminiscences of Elgar'

Chamber Concert   *Camerata of Canada*

Contrasts	Bartók
The Musical Offering	J.S. Bach

Organ Recital   *Jane Parker-Smith*

Fantasia and Fugue in G minor	J.S. Bach
Allein Gott	J.S. Bach
Valet will ich der Geben	J.S. Bach
Scherzo, Op. 2	Duruflé
Toccata, Op. 12	Germani
Clair de Lune, Op. 53, No. 5	Vierne
Impromptu, Op. 54, No. 2	Vierne
Ad nos	Liszt

Concert   *Contemporary Music Network (London Sinfonietta and The Medieval Ensemble of London)*

S'aincy estoit (ballade)	Solage
Hoquetus David	Machaut
Le sault perilleux	Galiot
Sumite Karissimi	Zacharias
Le greygnour bien	de Perusio
A Mirror of Whitening Light	P. Maxwell Davies
Se doit il plus	Haucourt
Angelorum psallat	Rodericus
Puisque je suis	Hasprois
Tout par compas	Cordier
Jusqu'aujourd'hui	Velut
Silbury Air	Harrison Birtwistle

Recital   *Nicholas Johnston (treble), David Johnston (tenor), Angela Malsbury (clarinet), David Pettit (piano)*
Music of Vaughan Williams, Gurney, Bax, Orr, Howells, Finzi, Britten

Orchestral Concert   *The Orchestra of St John's, Smith Square*

Serenade for Strings in E minor	Elgar
Trumpet Concerto in D major	Capel Bond
Brandenburg Concerto No. 3 in G major	Bach
Serenade for Strings in E major	Dvořák

Chamber Concert   *Camerata of Canada*
A Beethoven Anniversary Programme
Variations on Mozart's 'La ci darem la mano'
Trio in B flat for clarinet, cellow and piano, Op. II
Six Variations in D major on Ich Denke Dein
Duet for flute and clarinet in G major
Piano Trio, Op. 121a
Ten Variations on 'Ich bin der Schneider Kakadu'

1978 WORCESTER

Organ Recital   *Paul Trepte*
Opening Service

Sonata No. 2 in D minor	Reger
Trois Danses	Alain

Concert *Black Dyke Mills Band (in the cathedral)* – 13 items listed

Late Night Jazz *Landscape*

Young Musicians Concert *12 players listed*
Divertimento in B flat, K317	Mozart
Sonata in A, D664	Schubert
Romance	Elgar
Masques (First performance)	Paul Hughes
Songs	Vaughan Williams
Flute Sonata	Poulenc
Septet, Op. 65	Saint-Saëns

Song Recital *Margaret Cable (cont.), Kenneth Bowen (ten.), Christopher Robinson (piano)*
Songs	Schubert
Songs	Elgar
Diary of a Young Man who disappeared	Janáček

Youth Opera
All the King's Men	R. Rodney Bennett
The Happy Prince	Malcolm Williamson

Chamber Recital *Felix Kok (violin), Ann Steel (piano)*
Sonatina in G minor, Op. 137, No. 3	Schubert
Violin Sonatina, Op. 17	Lennox Berkeley
Violin Sonata in A minor	Beethoven
Violin Sonata, Op. 21	Dohnányi

Recital *The Arioso Ensemble*
Clarinet Quartet in E flat	Hummel
Prelude and Fugue	Finzi
Octet in F, Op. 166	Schubert

Illustrated Lecture *David Fanshawe*
'A musical Journey of the Nile'

Organ Recital *Simon Preston*
La Nativité du Seigneur	Messiaen

Recital *Medici String Quartet*
Quartet in A minor, Op. 39	Schubert
Quartet No. 2	Janáček
Quartet in E minor	Elgar

Ballet Workshop *Cambridge Ballet Workshop*
'Homage to Britten'

1979 HEREFORD

Organ Recital *Robert Green*
Opening Service
Sonata No. 1 in F minor	Mendelssohn

Fugue on 'Ad nos, ad salutarem undam'   Liszt
Dancing Toccata (First performance)   Christopher Steel
Passacaglia and Fugue in C minor   J.S. Bach

Composers' Forum   *John Joubert, William Mathias and Christopher Steel*

Chamber Opera   *The Fires of London*
The Martyrdom of St Magnus   Peter Maxwell Davies

Song Recital   *Ian and Jennifer Partridge*
Song Cycles by Grieg, Trevor Hold, John Ireland
Six Songs by Bush, Quilter, C.W. Orr, Gurney

Recital   *Osian Ellis (harp)* Listed as 'A late night Show'

Chamber Concert   *Malsbury-Wallfisch-Pettit Trio*
Trio, Op. 11   Beethoven
Sonata for Clarinet and Cello   Phyllis Tate
Trio   Brahms

Autobiographical Talk   *Dame Isobel Baillie, John Grierson (accompanist)*

Recital   *Trevor Williams (violin), Christopher Green (cello), Simon Lindley (organ)*
Six Pieces for Violin and Organ, Op. 150   Rheinberger
Suite Gothique   Boëllmann
Third Symphonic Chorale for Organ, Violin and Soprano Karg-Elert
Elégie   Fauré
Suite Brève   Langlais
Suite, Op. 149   Rheinberger

Organ Recital   *Melville Cook*
Praeludium   Sweelinck
Carol, Een Kindeken   John Bull
Trio Sonata No. 6 in G   J.S. Bach
Fantasia in F minor   Mozart
Invocations, Op. 35   Mathias
Psalm Prelude, Op. 32   Howells
Fantasia on 'Wachet auf'   Reger

1980 GLOUCESTER

Organ Recital   *Andrew Millington*
Opening Service
Entrata Festiva   Flor Peeters
March Héroique   Herbert Brewer
Allegro Marziale   Frank Bridge
Finale, Symphony No. 5   Vierne

Recital   *Chilingirian String Quartet*
Quartet in E flat, Op. 64, No. 6   Haydn
Adagio, String Quartet Op. 11   Barber

| Quartet Movement in C minor | Schubert |
| String Quartet No. 1 | Tippett |

Concert *Fresh Ear Concerts — tenor, trombone, percussion and electronics* — 8 items listed

Recital *New London Consort*
31 Items under: Troubadours and Trouvères
Ars nova in Florence
Music in Medieval England
The Minnesingers
Music in Medieval Spain

Recital *Erich Gruenberg (violin), John McCabe (piano)*

Sonata for Violin and Piano in F, K377	Mozart
Footfalls echo in the memory (first performance)	Anthony Payne
Sonata for Violin and Piano	Debussy
Sonata for Violin and Piano, No. 10 in G	Beethoven

Organ Recital *Keith John*

Toccata	Guillou
Adagio and Rondo, K617	* Mozart
Concerto in D	* Vivaldi
Scènes d'Enfant, Part 1 (first British performance)	Guillou
Orpheus	* Liszt
Toccata, Op. 11	* Prokofiev
	* arranged Guillou

The Recital was 'a tribute to Jean Guillou in his 50th birthday year'

1981 WORCESTER

Organ Recital *Jean Langlais*

Offertoire sur les Grands Jeux	Couperin
Voix Humaine	Couperin
Elevation	Couperin
Prelude, Fugue and Variation	Franck
Final	Franck
Consummatum est	Tournemire
La cinquième trompette	Langlais
Arabesque sur les Flutes	Langlais
Thèmes	Langlais
*Double Fantasie pour deux organistes	Langlais
Improvisation sur un thème donné	Langlais
* with Marie-Louise Langlais	

Organ Recital *Paul Trepte*
Opening Service
No details given

Lecture *Michael Kennedy*
'Elgar of Worcester'

Piano Recital *Keith Swallow*

| Dream Children | Elgar |

Skizze; In Smyrna	Elgar
Danse, Tarantelle Styrienne	Debussy
Espanana	Satie
Saudades do Brazil No. 9	Milhaud
Suite, Napoli	Poulenc

Recital *Copenhagen Boys' Choir, with Niels Nielsen (organ)* – 17 items listed

Opera *Worcester Junior Festival Chorus*
  'The Two Fiddlers'   Peter Maxwell Davies

Recital *Ioan Davies (cello), Colin Parr (clarinet), Keith Swallow (piano), The Donald Hunt Singers*
Part-Songs, Cello and Clarinet solos; Music of Finzi, Vaughan Williams, Rubbra, Howells; first performance of Sumsion's In Exile

Baroque Concert *Scottish Baroque Ensemble*
Fantasia in G	J.S. Bach
Sonata in B minor for Flute and Harpsichord	J.S. Bach
The Musical Offering	J.S. Bach

Lecture *Ernest Bradbury*
  The English Choral Tradition

Opera *Worcester Junior Festival Chorus*
| Dido and Aeneas | Purcell |

Lecture *Kenneth Loveland*
  'Off the Cuff' – Reminiscences of a Music Critic

Cello Recital *Rohan de Saram, Druvie de Saram (accompanist)*
Suite No. 3 in C	J.S. Bach
Sonata in G minor	Rubbra
Sonata in D minor	Debussy
Metamorfora	Aulis Sallinen
Sonata in G minor	Rachmaninov

Recital *Worcester Junior Festival Chorus*
Five Part-Songs	Holst
Song around a Song, Op. 50 (first British performance)	Aulis Sallinen
The Snow	Elgar
Fly Singing Bird	Elgar

Music Workshop *Margaret Cotton, Anne Collis*
  'Re-Percussions'

Chamber Concert *Athena Wind Ensemble*
Quintet in B flat, Op. 56, No. 1	Danzi
Album	Jonathan Harvey
Summer Music, Op. 31	Barber
Wind Quintet, Op. 43	Nielsen

Concert   *City of Birmingham Symphony Orchestra*
'Viennese Serenade'
Music by Mozart, Schubert, Johann Strauss I, Johann Strauss II, Josef Strauss, Eduard Strauss

Chamber Concert   *The Nash Ensemble*

Flute Quartet in D, K285	Mozart
Clarinet Quintet	Bliss
Commedia II	R. Rodney Bennett
Piano Quintet in A minor	Elgar

1982 HEREFORD

Organ Recital   *Robert Green*
Opening Service

Prelude and Fugue in E flat (St Anne)	J.S. Bach
Transports de joie (L'Ascension)	Messiaen
Rhapsody in C sharp minor	Howells
Symphony No. 6, 1st movement	Widor

Composers Forum   *William Mathias, Geoffrey Burgon*

Recital by Blind Musicians   *Michael Campbell, John James, William Martin*

Sonata in F	Handel
Sonatina for Clarinet and Piano	William Martin
Syrinx	Debussy
Danse de la Chèvre	Honneger
Arabesque for Piano	Schumann
Petite Suite for Clarinet and Piano	John James
Concertino for Flute and Piano	Chaminade
Five Pieces for Solo Clarinet	Gordon Jacob
Four Waltzes	Shostakovich

Concert   *The Sheba Sound*
French and English Baroque and Contemporary music by Couperin, Marcland, Rameau, Harvey, Arne, Purcell, Maconchy, Ozi, Damase

Late Night Show   *Kenneth Loveland*
'An informal programme of a critic's reminiscences . . .'

Children's Concert   *The Sheba Sound*
Music by Bull, Henry VIII, Telemann, Daquin, The Beatles, Senaille, Stephen Oliver

Exhibition   'Treasures from the Music Library of St Michael's College, Tenbury'
With two programmes of Music; French/English

Concert   *The Academy of Ancient Music*
'An afternoon with Dr Haydn'
Trio in D, Two Songs, String Quartet in B flat, Scottish Songs, Symphony No. 100 in G

Organ Recital   *Frederick Swann*

Fantasia and Fugue in G minor	J.S. Bach

Deuxième Fantasie	Alain
Choral No. 1 in E	Franck
Scherzo, Op. 2	Duruflé
Prelude and Fugue on Union Seminary (First performance)	Gerre Hancock
Even Song	J. La Montaine
Moto Ostinato (Sunday Music)	Petr Eben
Introduction, Passacaglia and Fugue	Searle Wright

Recital   *Ex Cathedra*

Five Negro Spirituals	Tippett
Laudibus in Sanctis	Byrd
When David heard	Tomkins
Hosanna to the Son of David	Weelkes
Hymn to St Cecilia	Britten
Trois Chansons de Charles d'Orléans	Debussy
Four Part Songs	Elgar
Trois Chansons	Ravel
The Lover's Ghost	Vaughan Williams
The Turtle Dove	Vaughan Williams
Dance to your Daddy	Ian Humphries

1983 GLOUCESTER

Lecture   *Diana McVeagh*
'Gerald Finzi'

Chamber Concert   *Medici String Quartet*

String Quartet in D minor, K421	Mozart
String Quartet in F	Ravel
String Quartet No. 3, Op. 94	Britten

Chamber Recital   *The Landini Consort*
'Fair Angel of England – Music from the Golden Age of Tudor England'
22 items listed

Song Recital   *John Shirley-Quirk (bar.), Martin Isepp (accompanist)*
Songs and Cycles by Purcell, Rachmaninov, Gurney, Warlock, Finzi, Ravel

Serenade Concert   *Three Counties Radio Orchestra*
Music by Haydn, Percy Grainger, Grieg, Elgar, Dvořák, Lehár, Johann and Joseph Strauss, Mozart, Bach, Tchaikovsky, Sondheim, Debussy

1984 WORCESTER

Organ Recital   *Carlo Curley*

Fantasy in F minor	Mozart
Concerto Movement No. 4 in C	Bach
Suite du Premier Ton	Clérambault
Fantasia, Op. 10, No. 1	Reger
Elves	Bonnet
Prelude and Fugue in B minor	Bach
Grande Pièce Symphonique, Op. 17	Franck

Recital   *John T. Hamilton Chorale*
'American Choral Music'
19 items listed

Chamber Recital   *Delmé String Quartet*

Meditation on Saint Wenceslaus	Suk
String Quartet in E minor	Elgar
String Quartet No. 12 in F	Dvořák

Light Entertainment   *Opus 5*
'Sweet and Low'

Drama   *'Here's a Health unto His Majesty'*
The private life of King Charles II in readings, songs and lute music

Recital   *Westminster Piano Trio*

Second Violin Sonata	Ferguson
Elegy	Finzi
Piano Trio	Sumsion

Recital   *Donald Hunt Singers*
'English Choral Music'
Elgar, Mathias, Delius, Holst, Britten, Bennett

Young People's Opera   *Worcester Junior Festival Chorus*

The Golden Vanity	Britten
The Rhyme of the Ancient Mariner	David Bedford

Illustrated Talk   *Michael Kennedy*
'Elgar's Oratorios'

Baroque Concert   *Orchestra da Camera (directed by Kenneth Page); Paul Esswood (counter-tenor), Takashi Shimuzu (violin)*

Concertino No. 5 in B flat	Pergolesi
Stabat Mater	Vivaldi
The Four Seasons	Vivaldi

Organ Recital   *Rodney Baldwyn*

Messe pour les Paroises	Couperin

Chamber Concert   *Worcester Music Group*

Carnival of the Animals	Saint-Saëns
The Soldier's Tale	Stravinsky

Late Night Concert   *Academy of Worcester Cathedral*
'An English Serenade'
Music of Britten, Delius, Elgar, Holst, Sullivan

Concert   *Desford Colliery Dowty Band (in the cathedral)*
Festal Brass with Blues	Tippett
Men marching	Robin Holloway
Moorside Suite	Holst
Little Suite No. 1	Arnold
Enigma Variations	Elgar

1985 HEREFORD

Organ Recital   *David Briggs*
Opening Service
Ricercare a 6 (Musical Offering)	J.S. Bach
Marche Pontificale, Symphony No. 1	Widor
Suite Brève	Langlais
Symphony No. 2, Last Movement	Vierne

Finzi Trust Friends   *Howard Ferguson, Diana McVeagh*
Talk on Thomas Hardy Songs

Composers' Forum   *Michael Berkeley, William Mathias and Adrian Williams*

Song Recital   *Brian Rayner Cook (bar.), Adrian Williams (accompanist)*
Three Songs (from 'Maud')	Somervell
Three Hardy Settings	Finzi
The Morning waits	Adrian Williams
Songs of Travel	Vaughan Williams
Three Songs	Armstrong Gibbs

Concert   *English String Orchestra*
Introduction and Allegro for Strings	Elgar
Fantasia Concertante on a Theme of Corelli	Michael Tippett
Four Seasons	Vivaldi

Lecture Recital   *Robert Gower, Malcolm Riley*
'The Life and Music of Percy Whitlock'

Lecture   *Dr Percy Young*
'Edward Elgar – The Hereford Years'

Concert   *The Fine Arts Brass Ensemble*
Music by Mouret, Vivaldi, Joubert, Lutoslawski, Bozza, J.S. Bach, Thomas Waller

Concert   *The Aldwyn Consort of Voices*
Sixteenth- and seventeenth-century music – 34 Items

Organ Recital   *Thomas Trotter*
Allegro Maestoso, Sonata in G, Op. 28	Elgar
Prelude and Fugue in G	J.S. Bach
Concerto in D minor	Vivaldi/Bach
Three Schübler Preludes	J.S. Bach

Fantasia and Fugue on Ad Nos   Liszt
Scherzo, A Midsummer Night's Dream   Mendelssohn/Warren
Final, Symphony No. 6   Vierne

Recital   *Adrian Jones (flute), John James (piano)*
Works by Handel, Gluck, Moscheles, John James, Fauré, Roussel — 6 Items

Children's Concert   *The Ebony Quartet*
Works by Jacobs, Byrd, Johnson, Mozart, Carter, Horowitz, Goodman

Recital   *The Strongbow Quartet*
Songs and Madrigals by Lassus, Josquin des Pres etc.

1986 GLOUCESTER

Lecture   *Kenneth Loveland*
'The Night they got the Bird'

Chamber Concert   *The Deakin Trio*
Phantasie Trio in A minor   John Ireland
Trio for Violin, Cello and Piano   Sumsion
Piano Trio in B flat, Op. 99   Schubert

Chamber Concert   *The Amaryllis Consort of Voices*
'The Lady Oriana: Music from the Court of Elizabeth I'
Works by Farmer, Gibbons, Morley, Wilbye, Greaves, Byrd, Tomkins, Weelkes, Bennet, Cavendish
18 Items listed

Master Class   *Timothy Hugh (cello) with Kathron Sturrock (piano)*
'Finzi's Cello Concerto'

Lecture Recital   *Michael George (bass-bar.), Christopher Mahley (accompanist)*
Songs by Peter Warlock

Concert   *The David Munrow Anniversary Ensemble*
Songs for two counter-tenors and harpsichord   Purcell
Sonata, In Imitation of Birds   William Williams
A-Wake-Again, for two counter-tenors, two recorders and   Gordon Crosse
harpsichord
To Musick, for two counter-tenors, two recorders, cello   Michael Ball
and harpsichord
Songs for counter-tenor and continuo   Purcell
Ode on the Death of Mr Henry Purcell, for two counter-   John Blow
tenors, two recorders and continuo

Concert   *The Desford Colliery Dowty Band (in the cathedral) with Roy Massey (organ)*
Cloudcatcher Fells   John McCabe
Symphonic Suite, The Fenlands   Arthur Wills
Aubade Joyeuse   Philip Lane
La Cathédrale Engloutie   Debussy, arr. Snell
Severn Suite   Elgar

Concert *London Bach Orchestra, Tess Miller (oboe), Mark Wildman (bass)*

Concerto a Quattro No. 2 in G	Galuppi
Cantata No. 82, Ich habe genug	J.S. Bach
Violin Concerto, Op. 3 No. 12	Vivaldi
Concerto for Oboe and Strings in G minor	Handel
Suite in G, Don Quixote	Telemann
Violin Concerto, La Tempesta di Mare	Vivaldi

1987 WORCESTER

Concert *English String Orchestra*
(Inaugural Concert for the Countess of Huntingdon's Hall)

Symphony No. 8 in D (Worcester overture)	Boyce
Serenade in E, Op. 20	Elgar
Let us Garlands bring	Finzi
Music for Strings	R. Rodney Bennett
Variations on a Theme of Frank Bridge Op. 10	Britten

Concert Recital *Christopher Robinson*

Sonata No. 1 in D	Guilmant
Trois Pièces, Op. 29	Pierné
Passacaglia and Fugue in C minor	Bach
Troisième Suite de Pièces de Fantaisie, Op. 54	Vierne

Recital *Worcester Junior Festival Chorus*
Works by Fauré, Richard Rodney Bennett

Chamber Recital *Medici String Quartet*

String Quartet in C, Op. 76, No. 3	Haydn
Lamento d'Arianna	R. Rodney Bennett
String Quartet No. 1 in A	Borodin

Talk *Michael Kennedy*
'Music and Cricket'

An Entertainment *Sweet and Low*

Piano Recital *Peter Donohoe*

Sonata in C minor (*Pathétique*) Op. 13	Beethoven
Four Impromptus	Schubert
Thirteen Preludes, Op. 32	Rachmaninov

Poetry Reading *Gabriel Woolf as Alfred, Lord Tennyson*

Opera *Worcester Junior Festival Chorus*
The Girl and the Unicorn

Dance *Chitraleka Bolar*
Classical Indian Dance

Recital *Eugene Sarbu (violin), Carmina Sarbu (accompanist)*

Scherzo in C	Brahms
Sonata No. 2 in F, Op. 6	Enescu
Valse-Scherzo, Op. 34	Tchaikovsky
Sonata	Ravel
Sonata in E, Op. 82	Elgar

An Entertainment *Richard Rodney Bennett*
'Fascinating Rhythm' featuring music of George Gershwin

Recital *Medici String Quartet and others*
'Wood Magic.' A presentation of the life and music of Sir Edward Elgar, written by Michael Kennedy

Recital *Dharanbir Singh*
Sitar Music

Song Recital *John Shirley-Quirk (bar.), Christopher Robinson (accompanist)*

Two Hymns by Bishop William Fuller	Purcell
Songs of Travel	Vaughan Williams
Strings in the earth and air	Donald Hunt
Mr Belloc's Fancy	Peter Warlock
Sleep	Ivor Gurney
King David	Herbert Howells
Sleep	Peter Warlock
Captain Stratton's Fancy	Peter Warlock

Illustrated Talk *Michael Hurd*
'Ivor Gurney'

Recital *The London Early Music Group*
English and Italian Music – 23 Items listed

Recital *Caliche*
'Latin American Music.' Music of the Andes played by Caliche, a 5–piece band of Chilean musicians

Chamber Recital *Medici String Quartet*

String Quartet No. 13 in B flat, Op. 130	Beethoven
String Quartet No. 1	Penderecki
String Quartet No. 2 in D	Borodin

Military Band Concert *Band of the Grenadier Guards (in the cathedral)*

Fanfare, Nova Centenary	Kimberley
March, La Ronde	Gounod
Arrival of the Queen of Sheba	Handel
Overture, Cockaigne	Elgar
Three Bavarian Dances	Elgar
Variations on a Theme from Verdi's La Traviata	Lorreglio
English Dances	Arnold
Variations for Oboe and Wind Band	Rimsky Korsakov
Suite, Vivat Regina	Johnson

Concert   *English String Orchestra conducted by William Boughton; Nicholas Daniel (oboe)*
Symphony No. 6 in E flat	Mendelssohn
Nocturne	Borodin arr. Sargent
Grosse Fugue, Op. 133	Beethoven arr. Weingartner
Capriccio for Oboe and Strings	Penderecki
Little Suite for Strings, Op. 1	Nielsen
Toy Symphony	Leopold Mozart

1988 HEREFORD

Organ Recital   *David Briggs*
Opening Service
Suite from 'La Danserye'	Susato (arr. Briggs)
Two Fugues on B-A-C-H	Schumann
Grand Choeur Dialogué	Gigout

Organ Recital   *David Sanger*
Praeludium in E minor, Op. 59 No. 1	Max Reger
Benedictus	Max Reger
Prelude and Fugue in C, BWV547	J.S. Bach
Divertimento	Percy Whitlock
Introduction, Passacaglia and Fugue in E flat minor	Healey Willan
Valse Mignonne, Op. 142, No. 2	Karg-Elert
Riff-raff	Giles Swayne
Prelude and Fugue on BACH	Liszt

Recital   *The Age of Gold*
Pastoral Pleasures'
Sixteenth- to eighteenth-century vocal, harpsichord and recorder music

Illustrated Talk   *Paul Patterson*
'Composer in Person'

Concert   *Orchestra da Camera*
Sinfonietta No. 1, Op. 48	Malcolm Arnold
Horn Concerto No. 4 in E flat, K495	Mozart
Serenade for Tenor, Horn and Strings, Op. 31	Britten
Symphony No. 64 in A	Haydn

Concert   *English Wind Ensemble*
Arrival of the Queen of Sheba	Handel
Octet-Partita in F, Op. 57	Franz Krommer
Prelude and Fugue in E minor	Nicolaus Bruhns
Passacaglia in D minor BuxWV161	Buxtehude
Serenade No. 12 in C minor, K388	Mozart
Choral IV	Andriessen
Divertimento in E flat	Gordon Jacob

Talk   *Andrew Burn*
'The Music of Howard Ferguson'

Concert   *English Wind Ensemble Quartet*
'Woodwind Matinee'; 10 items listed

Recital   *I Fagiolini*
Vocal music of the sixteenth, seventeenth and twentieth centuries

Recital   *John James (piano), Michael Campbell (flute)*
Works by Handel, Chopin, Bach, Poulenc, John James

Lecture Recital   *Anup Kumar Biswas (cello), Aloke Biswas (tabla), Nigel Clayton (piano)*
'Indian Classical Music'
Included Sonata for Cello and Piano in G minor, Op. 19   Rachmaninov

Concert   *The Camerata of London and The Companie of Dansers {sic}*
'Music for the Spanish Armada'

Lecture   *Dr Percy Young*
'Great was the Company of the Preachers'

Recital   *Jennifer Smith (soprano), Nicholas Sears and Richard Jackson (baritones), Graham Johnson (piano)*
'The Songmakers Almanac'
Works by Schumann and Brahms specified but not listed

1989 GLOUCESTER

Musical Play   *The Downs School*
Simpkin and the Tailor of Gloucester   Douglas Young
Concert version, with Song Recital by Elizabeth Harwood

Concert   *London Gabrieli Brass Ensemble*
Works by Soler, Bach/Vivaldi, Philip Lane (Festival commission), Scheidt, Stanley, Bozza, Gabrieli,
Montsalvatage, etc. with demonstrations of ancient instruments

Lecture   *Michael Kennedy*
'Parry, man of his time'

Concert   *The Hilliard Ensemble*
'Pastimes to delight the mind'

Lecture   *Andrew Burn*
'The background to the Bliss Colour Symphony'

Concert   *The Renaissance Singers of Ontario, conductor Ray Daniels*
Madrigals and Victorian songs

Chamber Concert   *Endellion String Quartet*
Quartet in E flat, Op. 64 No. 6   Haydn
Quartet No. 3   Bridge
Quartet in E minor, Op. 44, No. 2   Mendelssohn

Song Recital   *Brian Rayner Cook (bar.), Clifford Benson (piano)*
Songs by Somervell, Butterworth, Schubert, C.W. Orr and Adrian Cruft

Concert   *English String Orchestra conducted by William Boughton, with Jerry Hadley (tenor)*
Music by Butterworth, Vaughan Williams, Britten, Parry and Finzi

1990 WORCESTER

Opera   *Worcester Junior Festival Chorus*
Joseph and his amazing technicolor dreamcoat   Lloyd-Webber

Organ Recital   *Simon Preston*
Imperial March Op. 32   Elgar
Symphonie-Passion   Dupré
Vesper Voluntaries Op. 14   Elgar
Toccata Op. 5   Duruflé

Recital   *Kiran Pal Singh (santoor), Davinder Kaur Deeora (tanpura), Sanjay Jhalla (tabla)*
North Indian classical music

Song Recital   *Pro Cantione Antiqua directed by Mark Brown*
'The English in Love'
Charles Brett, Timothy Penrose, James Griffett, Ian Partridge, Gordon Jones, Christopher Keyte

Recital   *Alberni String Quartet with Thomas Hunt (baritone)*
String Quartet No. 1   Ives
String Quartet No. 1 Op. 11   Barber
Dover Beach Op. 3   Barber
String Quartet Op. 74   Beethoven

Lecture   *Robert Ponsonby*
'The mysterious art of the conductor'

Dance Recital   *Chitraleka*
Classical Indian Dance

Recital   *Claire Briggs (horn), Martin Roscoe (piano)*
Works by Dukas, Beethoven, Chopin, Poulenc, Saint-Saëns, Liszt, Schumann

Recital   *Jonathan Milton (counter-tenor), David Barry (tenor), Mark Shepherd (piano)*
Songs by Purcell, Britten's Abraham and Isaac and piano music by Bridge and Ireland

Recital   *Alberni String Quartet with Philip Dennis (tenor) and Donald Hunt (piano)*
String Quartet in E minor, Op. 83   Elgar
Song Cycle: Ludlow and Teme   Gurney
String Quartet in F minor, Op. 95   Beethoven

Recital   *The Donald Hunt Singers with Adrian Partington (organ), Jonathan Milton (counter-tenor), Thomas Blunt (treble)*
Works by Ned Rorem, Copland, Searle Wright, Ives, Barber, Bernstein

Talk   *Anthony Boden*
'A personal view of Ivor Gurney'

Poetry and Prose Reading   *Gabriel Woolf*

Concert   *The Prometheus Ensemble*
Chamber music by Beethoven, Mendelssohn, Copland

Recital   *Caliche*
Music of the Andes played by Chilean musicians

Recital   *Ian Partridge (tenor), Jennifer Partridge (piano)*
A recital of English Song, including music of Stanford, Atkins, Brewer, Parry, Howells,   Gurney, Britten, and the first performance of the song cycle 'A Song for Birds' by Paul Spicer, with Five Western Watercolours (for piano) by Ivor Gurney

Lecture   *Dr Percy Young*
'Newman, Elgar, and The Dream of Gerontius'

Concert   *Besses o' th' Barn Band with Nelson Arion Male Voice Choir (in the cathedral)*
Music of the sixteenth to twentieth centuries

Reading   *Zena Millar and John Crocker*
'My Friends pictured within'

1991 HEREFORD

Organ Recital   *Geraint Bowen*
Opening Service

Toccata and Fugue in D minor	Bach
Sonata in B flat	Mendelssohn
Allegro Marziale	Bridge

Talk   *Andrew Burn*
'Sir Arthur Bliss'

Concert   *Tuba Magna*
Works for trumpet and organ by Purcell, Rossini, Whitlock, Barbra Streisand, Vierne, Haydn

Concert   *Jeux*
Works for flute, cello and harp by Haydn, Villa-Lobos, Ravel, Dussek, Fauré, Jongen

Organ Recital   *Ian Tracey*
Works by Pierre du Mage, Bach, Mozart, Enrico Bossi, Roger-Ducasse, Bridge, Whitlock, Dupré

Concert   *Orchestra da Camera with Stephen Coombs and Ian Munro (piano)*

Symphony No. 40 in G minor, K550	Mozart
Concerto in E flat, K365 for two pianos and orchestra	Mozart
Symphony No. 41 in C, K551	Mozart

Piano Recital   *Margaret Fingerhut*
Works by Ireland, Bliss, Spicer, Elgar, Ferguson, Ireland

Talk *Dr Percy Young*
'Gerald Finzi and the Metaphysical Idea'

Concert *Music on Offa*
Works by Madeleine Dring, Simon Proctor, Ethel Smyth, Alan Richardson, Khachaturian, Franz Doppler

Recital *Evelyn Glennie*
'Percussion with a difference'
Works by James Basta, Askell Masson, George Hamilton Green, John McLeod, Paul Ruders, Paul Smadbeck, Jeno Hubay, Ney Rosauro

Concert *The Arden Duo*
Music for lute and guitar (not listed)

Recital *Raimund Gilvan (tenor), Andrew Beaizley (keyboard)*
Works by Handel, Schubert, Elgar, Britten (not listed)

Concert *Domus*
Piano Quartet No. 1 in D, Op. 23	Dvořák
String Trio (1934)	Bohuslav Martinu
Distance and Enchantment	Judith Weir
Piano Quartet in G minor, K478	Mozart

Lecture *Dr Percy Young*
'The Rev Mr Picart (Hereford) and Seb. B'
A debt to the Wesleys

Concert *The Amaryllis Consort*
Music of Thomas Weelkes and his contemporaries

INDEX